# Frequently Consulted Adv

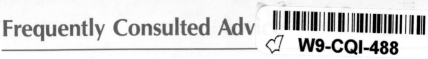

W9-CQI-488

| 7b, p. 165 | Meaning aligned with grammatically important words |
| 7f, p. 172 | Action conveyed through verbs rather than nouns |
| 7g, p. 172 | Active voice preferred |
| 7k, p. 180 | Clarity through free subordination |
| 9c, p. 244 | Sentence fragment |
| 9e, p. 249 | Run-on sentence |
| 10b, p. 258 | Subject-verb agreement |
| 10f, p. 272 | No comma between subject and verb |
| 11c, p. 277 | Dangling modifier |
| 11j, p. 286 | Restrictive versus nonrestrictive modifier |
| 11m, p. 290 | Commas on both sides of an interrupting element |
| 13b, p. 308 | Pronoun antecedent included |
| 13c, p. 308 | Clear pronoun antecedent |
| 17a, p. 351 | Independent clauses joined by comma and coordinating conjunction |
| 18b, p. 361 | No fragment following a semicolon |

# The Random House House

# Handbook

FIFTH EDITION

# The Random House

# Handbook

**FIFTH EDITION**

## Frederick Crews

University of California, Berkeley

RANDOM HOUSE   NEW YORK

Fifth Edition
9876543
Copyright © 1987 by Random House, Inc.

Library of Congress Cataloging in Publication Data

Crews, Frederick C.
  The Random House handbook.

  Includes bibliographical references and index.
    1. English language—Rhetoric.    2. English language—
Grammar—1950-    .    I. Title.
PE1408.C715    1987          808'.042          87-23316
ISBN  0-394-33944-4

Manufactured in the United States of America

FOR BETTY
again and always

# Preface

*The Random House Handbook* has been around for quite a while, but instead of aging gracefully, it is only getting friskier. Of five editions, this latest one marks the boldest departure from its predecessor. To be sure, the *Handbook* retains its distinctive outlook and tone. It still treats the student writer as a colleague, sharing a common struggle for clarity and eloquence, and it still offers some laughs along with sober tips about composition. But much is radically new—so much that only a list can do justice to it:

1. In a smaller trim size, the fifth edition is now more literally a *hand*book, easier to carry and consult.

2. In this edition, everything of importance is graphically prominent and clearly stated. Instead of having to excavate points of advice from my prose, students will find alphanumerically ordered directives, along with a thumb index that makes short work of tracking down the ample cross references.

3. Obeying my own injunction to be concise, I have shortened some too-chatty discussions, thus making room for much fuller treatment of such classic problems as the run-on sentence, the fragment, subject-verb agreement, and faulty parallelism.

4. Where there used to be just three chapters attempting to amalgamate all "Problems of Usage," "Punctuation," and "Spelling and Other Conventions," there are now nineteen, allowing chapter-length concentration on pronoun reference, capitalization, the handling of quotations, and so forth.

5. One chapter appearing in previous editions has been scrapped: "A Review of Grammar." Though certain grammatical concepts are essential to effective revision, I now feel that they should be raised as necessary within the contexts where they apply. The trouble with the chapter-length grammar review was that for many students it *wasn't* a review but a baffling, intimidating new challenge. Partly through the Glossary of Terms (p. 581) and partly through expanded discussions of usage problems, this edition provides as much grammatical information as ever—but it does

so without putting a barrier between the student writer and the task of composing.

6. A student no longer has to consult separate parts of the book in order to learn how certain constructions are properly *formed* and properly *punctuated.* Chapter 11, for example, moves straight from the choice and placement of modifiers to rules for punctuating them. Surely that is the most natural and useful order. At the same time, the *Handbook* accommodates readers who want to track down a punctuation rule by its usual mark (the comma, the semicolon) instead of by the type of construction being punctuated. With cross referencing, anyone who needs to consult the fuller of two discussions is led directly to it.

7. Rather than begin with full essay modes, the *Handbook* now introduces students to paragraph-sized *strategies* of description, narration, analysis, and argument. How many full descriptive essays, after all, will be required in college work? My aim is not to isolate the modes artificially but to sharpen an array of skills that belong in the student's repertoire. Someone who conscientiously does the exercises in Chapters 1-4 will learn to move between strategies as the occasion requires.

8. The exercises just mentioned, along with most others in this edition, immediately follow the discussions pertaining to them. Thus the *Handbook* not only offers more exercises than ever before— 142 sets—but places them where they logically belong. This reform gives the book a dimension of self-paced learning; by trying the exercises after a given discussion, students will discover whether they ought to proceed or review.

9. I have restored a popular early feature of the *Handbook:* the Index of Usage (p. 562), which covers points of typical uncertainty in student prose (*disinterested* versus *uninterested,* etc.).

10. Chapter 29 now offers full coverage of both "new MLA" and APA styles of documentation, yet it also explains the "alternative MLA" footnote/endnote style preferred by some instructors. Chapter 30 shows how the same list of references changes its form between MLA and APA styles.

11. For the first time, the *Handbook* addresses the task of writing about literature (pp. 48-55). Two complete student essays on literary topics have been included. And finally:

12. Wherever the use of a word processor offers a unique advantage, this edition includes a specially marked discussion, "With a Word Processor," explaining how to proceed.

Every change I have made renders this book more accessible to a wide audience, including students who would have found earlier editions mystifying. But there is no "talking down" here—just a better logic of organization, a greater clarity of statement, and a more pointed emphasis on common problems.

What has prompted so much fundamental revision? The answer is that between the fourth and fifth editions, Sandra Schor and I were busy devising a related text, *The Borzoi Handbook for Writers.* Using the fourth edition as a point of departure, we created a no-nonsense reference handbook containing almost all of the features named above. Now it is time for *The Random House Handbook* to catch up with *Borzoi,* incorporating the strong innovations while keeping its own purpose and tone. The two books are alike in many ways, but *Random House* contains more examples (including some droll ones), offers exercises, and gives central focus to the college essay. In contrast, *Borzoi* is an all-purpose reference tool.

Since this text comes shrink-wrapped with Michael Hennessy's superb *Random House Practice Book for Writers,* instructors who want to go beyond the exercises in the *Handbook* can do so without causing their students extra cost or inconvenience. I have prepared a new *Instructor's Manual* explaining alternative ways to use the book and providing answers to the exercises found in both the *Handbook* and the *Practice Book.* For students with access to IBM-compatible word processors, Random House offers a free diskette, *The Practice Program for Writers,* containing still further exercises and answers. The software is keyed specifically to this text, as is Hennessy's *Practice Book.*

I remain sincerely grateful to everyone who has been mentioned in previous acknowledgments. Space permits me to single out only those generous people who have enriched this edition in distinctive and indispensable ways: Jeannine Ciliotta, Marion Corkett, Michael Hennessy, Steve Pensinger, Sandra Schor, and Jennifer Sutherland.

Frederick Crews

# Contents

Introduction     1

## PART I     EXPLORING PROSE STRATEGIES     7

**1 Strategies of Description and Narration**     **9**
Description     9
Narration     19

**2 Strategies of Analysis and Argument**     **28**

## PART II     COMPOSING WHOLE ESSAYS     57

**3 Developing a Topic and a Thesis**     **59**
Topic     63
Thesis     72

**4 Toward a Complete First Draft**     **84**

**5 Revising**     **99**

## PART III     EFFECTIVE EXPRESSION     137

**6 Paragraphs**     **139**
Paragraph Unity     140
Paragraph Continuity     144
Paragraph Development     152

**7 Sentences**     **163**
Distinct Expression     164
Subordination     178

Emphasis    186
Variety    193

8  **Words**                                                   **201**
Appropriate Meaning    202
Liveliness    217


# PART IV    USAGE                                              235


9  **Complete Sentences**                                      **237**

10  **Subject-Verb Relations**                                 **256**

11  **Modifiers**                                               **274**
Choosing and Placing Modifiers    275
Punctuating Modifiers    284

12  **Cases of Nouns and Pronouns**                            **295**

13  **Pronoun Reference**                                       **306**

14  **Parallelism**                                             **314**

15  **Relations between Tenses**                                **329**


# PART V    PUNCTUATION                                        343


16  **Period, Question Mark, Exclamation Point    345**
Period    345
Question Mark    347
Exclamation Point    349

17  **Comma**                                                   **351**

18  **Semicolon and Colon**                                     **360**
Semicolon    360
Colon    362

**19   Dash and Parentheses**                                366
Dash      367
Parentheses      370

**20   Quoting**                                             374
Setting Off a Quotation      376
Introducing a Quotation      382
Omitting Material from a Quotation      384
Inserting Material into a Quotation      387

# PART VI    CONVENTIONS                                     389

**21   Verb Forms**                                          391

**22   Plurals and Possessives**                             403
Plurals      403
Possessives      408

**23   Comparing Adjectives and Adverbs**                    416

**24   Spelling**                                            419
Troublesome Words      419
Spelling Rules      429
Hyphenation Rules      433

**25   Capitals**                                            441

**26   Italics, Abbreviations, Numbers**                     450
Italics      450
Abbreviations      454
Numbers and Figures      459

**27   Forming and Spacing Punctuation Marks**               465

# PART VII    THE RESEARCH ESSAY                             471

**28   Finding and Mastering Sources**                       473

**29  Documenting Sources**                                    **501**

**30  A Sample Research Essay**                                 **531**

## PART VIII    APPLIED WRITING                                543

**31  Examination Answers and In-Class Essays**                **545**

**32  Business Letters**                                       **550**

**33  Résumés**                                                **559**

**An Index of Usage**                                          **562**

**Glossary of Terms**                                          **581**

**Index**                                                      **607**

# The Random House House

# Handbook

FIFTH EDITION

# Introduction

## Looking Ahead

If you are like most students entering a composition course, you arrive with a mixture of hope and worry. The hope is that the course will help you to put your thoughts into written words with greater precision and effect. The worry is that nothing of the sort will happen and that you will have to go through a painful, humiliating ordeal. Essays, you know, will be required of you on short notice. Will you be able to write them at all? Looking ahead, perhaps you experience a feeling that assails every writer from time to time—the suspicion that words may fail you. (And if words fail you, the instructor may fail you, too.)

It may seem odd at first that putting your thoughts into words should be so challenging. Since childhood, after all, you have been speaking intelligible English. When you talk about things that matter to you, the right words often come to your lips without forethought. Again, in writing letters to friends you scribble away with confidence that you will be understood. But in writing essays you find yourself at a disadvantage. You know that your prose is expected to carry your reader along with a developing idea, but you don't have a clear notion of who that reader is. Instead of exchanging views with someone who can see your face, interpret your gestures, and tell you when a certain point needs explanation or support, you have to assume a nonexistent relationship and keep on writing. It is almost like composing love letters "to whom it may concern" and mailing them off to "Occupant" or "Boxholder."

Faced with this real but manageable challenge, some students make matters worse by conceiving of "good writing" as a brass ring to be seized or, more probably, missed on their first and only try. Condemning themselves in advance as people who lack a writer's mysterious gifts, they imagine that their function in the months ahead will be merely to produce errors of expression so that their instructor can continue to believe that the language is going downhill. For them, the game is over before its rules have been explained.

To stave off such defeatism you need only realize that effective prose is not like a brass ring at all; it is more like the destination of a journey, approachable by steps that anyone can follow. People who turn out dazzling work without blotting a line are so rarely found that you can put them out of your mind. Everyone who writes for a living knows what you too should remember: by and large, *writing is rewriting*. Even the most accomplished authors start with drafts that would be woefully inadequate except *as* drafts—that is, as means of getting going in an exploratory process that will usually include a good many setbacks and shifts of direction. To feel dissatisfied with a sample of your prose, then, is not a sign of anything about your talent. The "good writer" is the one who can turn such dissatisfaction to a positive end by pressing ahead with the labor of revision, knowing that niceties of style will come more easily once an adequate structure of ideas has been developed.

Thus it is also a mistake to think of yourself as either having or not having "something to say," as if your head were a package that could be opened and inspected for inclusion of the necessary contents. We do not *have* things to say; we acquire them in the process of working on definite problems that catch our attention. If you grasp that crucial fact, you can stop worrying about writing in general and prepare yourself for writing *within a context*—that is, inside a situation that calls for certain ways of treating a typical range of questions.

Everything you encounter in a college course provides elements of context, helping to make your writing projects less like all-or-nothing tests of your inventiveness and more like exercises in the use of tested procedures. Before long, in any course that calls for written work, you will have picked up important clues about characteristic subject matter and issues, conventions of form and tone, and means of gathering and presenting evidence. And as you do so, you will find yourself not only writing but also thinking somewhat like a historian, an economist, or whatever. That practice in operating within the idiom, or accepted code, of various disciplines is a good part of what a successful college experience is about.

In a composition course, most of your contextual clues will be gleaned not from readings or lectures but from your instructor's way of explaining assignments, discussing common problems, and commenting on your submitted work. It is essential, therefore, that you get over any lingering image of the composition teacher as a mere fussbudget, hungry to pounce on comma faults and dangling modifiers. If you arrive with that stereotype in mind, you may start out by writing papers that are technically careful but windy and devoid of feeling. In other words, you may think that the game is to be won through negative means, by producing the lowest possible number of mistakes. You should realize instead that your instructor's standards, like your own when you pick up a magazine, are chiefly positive. It is perfectly true that English teachers prefer correctly formed sentences to faulty ones; so do you. But you also expect an article to engage you in a lively and well-conceived topic, to support a consistent central idea, and to convey information clearly and efficiently, without needless pomp. Your instructor will hope for nothing less—and nothing fancier—from your own essays.

Nevertheless, like many another freshman student, you may feel ill at ease addressing this still unknown and potentially troublesome person. Very well: don't even try. You can get the desired results if, while you compose, you think of your classmates, not the instructor, as your audience. This is not to say that you should write in dormitory slang. The point is that if you think of trying to convince people of your own age and background, you will get a reliable sense of what needs proving, what can be taken for granted, and what tone to adopt. If the student sitting next to you would probably choke on some contrived generalization, leave it out. If you suspect that the class as a whole would say *Make that clearer* or *Get to the point,* do so. Your instructor will be delighted by any paper that would impress most of your classmates.

## Writing to Achieve Different Effects

Many college-bound students have been taught to aim at a prissy, rule-conscious, rigidly formal notion of "good English." The outcome is prose that sounds as if it were meant to pass a parade inspection rather than to win a reader's sympathy or agreement. In college and beyond you will find that no single formula can suit the variety of writing contexts you will meet. The rules you may have memorized in high school—*avoid the passive voice, never use* I *and* me, *do not begin a sentence with a conjunction or end it with a preposition* — must now be reconsidered in the light of shifting audiences and purposes.

You will always want to adjust your **rhetoric** to the specific audience and purpose you have in mind. That advice may leave you uneasy if you think of rhetoric in its casual meaning of insincere, windy language, as in *Oh, that's just a lot of rhetoric.* But in its primary meaning rhetoric is simply *the strategic placement of ideas and choice of language* — the means of making an intended effect on a reader or listener. Rhetoric need never call for deceptive prose; it calls, rather, for making a strong case by satisfying your audience's legitimate expectations.

## Confronting the Essay

By the end of your composition course you will almost certainly be better able to write papers for any other course, regardless of its subject matter. But your composition instructor will not be assigning such "disciplinary" papers. You will be asked instead to create *essays* conveying a characteristic blend of opinion and evidence, of intimacy and objectivity.

An **essay** can be defined as *a fairly brief piece of nonfiction that tries to make a point in an interesting way*:

1. *It is fairly brief.* Some classic essays occupy only a few paragraphs, but essays generally fall between three and twenty typed pages. Under that minimum, the development of thought that typifies an essay would be difficult to manage. Above that maximum, people might be tempted to read the essay in installments, like a book. A good essay makes an unbroken experience.

2. *It is nonfiction.* Essayists try to tell the truth; if they describe a scene or tell a story, we presume that the details have not been made up for effect.

3. *It tries to make a point . . .* An essay characteristically tells or explains something, or expresses an attitude toward something, or supports or criticizes something — an opinion, a person, an institution, a movement. A poem or a novel may also do these things, but it does them incidentally. An essay is directly *about* something called its **topic**, and its usual aim is to win sympathy or agreement to the point or **thesis** it is maintaining.

4. *. . . in an interesting way.* When you write an answer to a question on an exam, you do not pause to wonder if the reader actually *wants* to pursue your answer to the end; you know you will succeed if you concisely

and coherently satisfy the terms of the question. But a full-fledged essay tends to be read in another way. Its reader could agree with every sentence and still be displeased. What that reader wants is not just true statements, but a feeling that those statements support an idea worth bothering about.

As an essayist, then, you should aim to harmonize reason and rhetoric, trying to be at once lively, fair, and convincing. You must

| | | |
|---|---|---|
| tell the truth | ⟶ | but first make people interested in hearing it; |
| write with conviction | ⟶ | but consider whether the ideas will stand up under criticism; |
| supply evidence | ⟶ | but not become a bore about it; |
| be purposeful | ⟶ | but not follow such a predictable pattern that the reader's attention slackens. |

But why, you may ask, should you have to write essays at all? No doubt they provide good training for students who want to become professional essayists, but what about future nurses or computer programmers or social workers? I think there are four reasons for the persistence of the essay in freshman English:

1. In a population of freshmen who have varying career plans (including, in some cases, no plan at all), it is impossible to have all students write the kinds of specialized papers or reports they will be producing in their majors.

2. Writing that draws chiefly on opinion and personal experience can spare you the inconvenience of having to do outside reading for every writing assignment.

3. All college writing tasks place a premium on certain common points that are highlighted by the essay: coherence, clarity, persuasive order of presentation, and correctness of usage, punctuation, and other conventions.

4. More generally, practice in supporting opinions is also practice in forming them—in thinking clearly, weighing objections, and preferring solid evidence to prejudice.

Still, there is that anxiety triggered by the blank page in your typewriter. How can you master it? Beyond reminding you that such a feeling is normal, this book proposes a two-step remedy. First, we begin with specific writing tasks that will sharpen the skills you need in creating whole essays; you can develop a knack for essay prose in a piecemeal fashion. And second, when you do arrive at the total work of composing, we will break that process into manageable parts, showing how you can get started purposefully and, in the drafting stage, exit from an occasional blind alley. Nothing can spare a writer from meeting obstacles; but with your instructor's participation and your own effort, the advice and exercises that follow ought to convince you that strong, consecutive, even graceful prose lies within your reach.

# I

# EXPLORING PROSE STRATEGIES

1. Strategies of Description and Narration

2. Strategies of Analysis and Argument

## EXPLORING PROSE STRATEGIES

This section covers the most common techniques that skillful writers use to gain a reader's involvement, trust, and agreement. Whole essays always combine such strategies, typically setting a descriptive scene, comparing one thing to another, showing how a narrated incident lends support to an opinion, conceding one objection to that opinion but then refuting another. If you get to feel comfortable with a full array of strategies, you will be able to make shrewd and varied choices at the appropriate time.

Prose strategies fall into two natural categories according to their relation to physical experience. The "immediate" strategies, **description** and **narration**, are alike in that they appeal directly to the senses, calling scenes or episodes to the reader's mind. Chapter 1 covers principles for imparting an air of reality and drama to the objects and events you will want your reader to picture. Chapter 2, by contrast, introduces two strategies that belong together because they appeal primarily to the reader's understanding and judgment: **analysis** and **argument**. To analyze is not to present the physical actuality of an experience but to explain something so that the reader will appreciate its function, its importance, or its relation to something else. And to argue is to justify a position on an issue so that the reader will come to share that position instead of a rival one.

None of these aims is inherently superior to the others. We begin with description and narration not because there is anything rudimentary about them, but because they require a sharpness of language that can serve to keep your prose lively even when you are dealing with abstract and complex issues.

# 1

# Strategies
# of Description
# and Narration

## DESCRIPTION

### 1a  Aim for Vividness in Describing.

When you write a passage of **description**, you want to *make vivid* a place, an object, an animal, a character, or a group. That is, instead of trying simply to convey facts about the thing described, you want to give your readers a direct impression of it, as if they were standing in its presence. Your task is one of translation: you are looking for words to capture the way your senses have registered the thing, so that a reader will have a comparable experience.

Early in a composition course you may be asked to write a descriptive sketch of one provocatively simple thing, such as a pencil or an apple. If so, your first move should be to open your senses to its physical characteristics. As soon as you do, you will be surprised by the object's endless particularity: the lopsidedness of the apple, its creases and scars and speckles, the fuzziness of its stem, and so forth. And you will begin to appreciate the real lesson your instructor has in mind: the value of language that conveys vividness by being both concrete and specific.

## Concrete versus Abstract Language

A **concrete** word or phrase denotes an actual, observable thing or quality such as *skin* or *crunchy*. Words of the opposite sort, like *nutrition* or *impossible assignment,* are called **abstract**; they address the mind without calling the senses into play. To familiarize yourself with this distinction, study 8k, p. 225. You will see that concrete (also called *sensuous*) terms are essential to most description because they are the only ones that can bring the perceived thing to life in your reader's imagination.

## Specific versus General Language

Among the possible concrete terms you might use, the relatively *specific* ones will call up sharper images than the relatively *general* ones. Specific language gets down to particulars: not *red* but *greenish-red*, not *too soft* but *dented by my thumbprint*. Note, incidentally, that although we can distinguish clearly between concrete and abstract language by the test of "appeal to the senses," a word is specific only by contrast with a more general one. Thus, *hound* is specific by contrast with *dog* but general by contrast with *bloodhound*.

## Creating a Picture

Detail alone, however, does not make for vividness, as you can tell from these opening sentences of a book about baseball:

> It weighs just over five ounces and measures between 2.86 and 2.94 inches in diameter. It is made of a composition-cork nucleus encased in two thin layers of rubber, one black and one red, surrounded by 121 yards of tightly wrapped blue-gray wool yarn, 45 yards of white wool yarn, 53 more yards of blue-gray wool yarn, 150 yards of fine cotton yarn, a coat of rubber cement, and a cowhide (formerly horsehide) exterior, which is held together with 216 slightly raised red cotton stitches.[1]

Here we have an abundance of concreteness and specificity. The baseball is not just *made of different materials inside* but *made of a composition-cork nucleus encased in two thin layers of rubber . . .* ; it is not merely *stitched* but *held together with 216 slightly raised red cotton stitches*; etc. Yet the effect created is not descriptive but remote. Why?

descr
1a

The answer is that the writer has made no effort as yet to *show* us the baseball. Rather, he is analyzing its components in the spirit of a statistical review. Note, for example, how little appeal to our senses is made by the difference between 2.86 and 2.94 inches or by the idea of 150 yards of wound yarn or of 216 stitches. Even though the stitches are on the surface of the ball, we could never see more than a fraction of them at a time. The implied point of view, then, is not that of someone who is looking at a baseball, but of someone who knows the manufacturer's secrets.

This writer, who knows how to be as vivid as anyone, is here deliberately adopting a dry analytic stance, holding in check his enthusiasm for baseballs and baseball so that we will be struck by the release of that enthusiasm a few sentences later:

> Pick it up and it instantly suggests its purpose; it is meant to be thrown a considerable distance—thrown hard and with precision. Its feel and heft are the beginning of the sport's critical dimensions; if it were a fraction of an inch larger or smaller, a few centigrams heavier or lighter, the game of baseball would be utterly different. Hold a baseball in your hand. As it happens, this one is not brand-new. Here, just to one side of the curved surgical welt of stitches, there is a pale-green grass smudge, darkening on one edge almost to black—the mark of an old infield play, a tough grounder now lost in memory. Feel the ball, turn it over in your hand; hold it across the seam or the other way, with the seam just to the side of your middle finger. Speculation stirs. You want to get outdoors and throw this spare and sensual object to somebody or, at the very least, watch somebody else throw it. The game has begun.[2]

Once again we find highly concrete and specific diction: *just to one side of the curved surgical welt of stitches, there is a pale-green grass smudge, darkening on one edge almost to black.* . . . But now the definite language presents something we can take in, moment by moment, with our senses; the writer *is* being vivid. Even though quite a bit of his language is abstract ( *purpose, precision, the sport's critical dimensions, memory, speculation,* etc.), our attention is occupied not by analytic findings but by the ball itself as we would see and feel it.

The key to vividness, then, lies less in a certain range of language than in a certain relationship with one's reader. The idea is to invite the reader into the scene and make it believable as immediate experience.

One way to stimulate vivid description is to pretend that you have no prior idea about the nature and function of the object in view. Thus a student writer begins a descriptive essay in this way:

The object stands as high as one's knee, a foot and a half wide, a cylinder of deep gray metal. It is topped by a somewhat transparent plastic dome, of a dark tint, which looks uniformly dirty, as though it had been left in a smoky room for a few months. The object may look at first like a wastecan. On further inspection it might be mistaken for a bomb.

On the side of the cylinder, at ankle height, white squares of plastic as big as one's palm bulge from a strip of blue metal in a row around the entire girth. There are eight of them, protruding half an inch and spaced two inches apart, as if they were somehow protecting the cylinder. Choosing one, I kick it. It springs back, a sort of huge button. But the object itself remains still.

As the essay continues beyond this point, we gradually infer that the object is a robot. By delaying that identification, the writer has usefully obliged himself to rely on precise details and points of comparison to better-known things.

---

**EXERCISES**

1. Write a descriptive paragraph about an object you can see as you sit at your desk. Begin the paragraph with a sentence supplying an idea to cover the details that follow.

2. Choose any convenient outdoor location, and go there as early in the morning as you can manage, taking notes on what you observe. Return to the same spot at night and repeat the process. Then write and submit two descriptive paragraphs corresponding to the two scenes. Try to make your reader feel how daylight and darkness (or artificial light) change the way objects are perceived.

3. Like the writer of the "robot" passage above, choose an object that your reader will not immediately recognize. Take two or three paragraphs to describe it, as if you yourself were trying to identify it by noting its features and relating them to more familiar things.

---

## 1b    Establish a Descriptive Point of View.

The term **point of view** can have two meanings, both of which are relevant to effective description within an essay. First, a point of view is literally a place of observation, a stationary or moving vantage from which the reader is invited to look. Instead of presenting a scene as if it stood apart from any perceiver, you can heighten involvement by setting up such a vantage. Note, for instance, how Joan Didion enlists her reader to be the driver of a car—a role that is deeply appropriate to a tour of southern Californian subdivisions:

> Imagine Banyan Street first, because Banyan is where it happened. The way to Banyan is to drive west from San Bernardino out Foothill Boulevard, Route 66: past the Santa Fe switching yards, the Forty Winks Motel. Past the motel that is nineteen stucco tepees: "SLEEP IN A WIGWAM—GET MORE FOR YOUR WAMPUM." Past Fontana Drag City and the Fontana Church of the Nazarene and the Pit Stop A Go-Go; past Kaiser Steel, through Cucamonga, out to the Kapu Kai Restaurant-Bar and Coffee Shop, at the corner of Route 66 and Carnelian Avenue. Up Carnelian Avenue from the Kapu Kai, which means "Forbidden Seas," the subdivision flags whip in the harsh wind. "HALF-ACRE RANCHES! SNACK BARS! TRAVERTINE ENTRIES! $95 DOWN." It is the trail of an intention gone haywire, the flotsam of the new California. But after a while the signs thin out on Carnelian Avenue, and the houses are no longer the bright pastels of the Springtime Home owners but the faded bungalows of the people who grow a few grapes and keep a few chickens out here, and then the hill gets steeper and the road climbs and even the bungalows are rare, and here—desolate, roughly surfaced, lined with eucalyptus and lemon groves—is Banyan Street.[3]

Similarly, these sentences by Mark Twain invite you not just to contemplate a sunset but to scan the Mississippi River and its banks as if you, too, were a cub pilot on the bridge of a steamboat:

> Now when I had mastered the language of this water, and had come to know every trifling feature that bordered the great river as familiarly as I knew the letters of the alphabet, I had made a valuable acquisition. But I had lost something, too. I had lost something which could never be restored to me while I lived. All the grace, the beauty, the poetry, had gone out of the majestic river! I still kept in mind a certain wonderful sunset which I witnessed when steamboating was new to me. A broad expanse of the river was turned to blood; in the middle distance the red hue brightened into gold, through which a solitary log came floating, black and conspicuous; in one place a long, slanting mark lay sparkling upon the water; in another the surface was broken by boiling, tumbling rings, that were as many-tinted as an opal; where the ruddy flush was faintest, was a smooth spot that was covered with graceful circles and radiating lines, ever so delicately traced; the shore on our left was densely wooded and the somber shadow that fell from this forest was broken in one place by a long, ruffled trail that shone like silver; and high above the forest wall a clean-stemmed dead tree waved a single leafy bough that glowed like a flame in the unobstructed splendor that was flowing from the sun. There were graceful curves, reflected images, woody heights, soft distances, and over the whole

descr
1b

scene, far and near, the dissolving lights drifted steadily, enriching it every passing moment with new marvels of coloring.[4]

The other meaning of *point of view* is an attitude or mental perspective, a way of "seeing things" more judgmentally. To be psychologically compelling, your essayistic descriptions should reflect a consistent point of view in this sense. Sometimes you can state your judgment directly, in Didion's manner: *It is the trail of an intention gone haywire, the flotsam of the new California.* Or, like Mark Twain, you can let the overtones of your language do the work of creating an attitude. The vagueness and abstractness of Twain's final sentence, for example, are deliberate; they convey a rapt inattentiveness to those particulars that the river pilot must learn to read not as a sublime whole but as specific perils to navigation.

Again, consider how another writer, N. Scott Momaday, establishes a strong point of view in both meanings of the term:

A single knoll rises out of the plain in Oklahoma, north and west of the Wichita Range. For my people, the Kiowas, it is an old landmark, and they gave it the name Rainy Mountain. The hardest weather in the world is there. Winter brings blizzards, hot tornadic winds arise in the spring, and in summer the prairie is an anvil's edge. The grass turns brittle and brown, and *it cracks beneath your feet.* There are green belts along the rivers and creeks, linear groves of hickory and pecan, willow and witch hazel. *At a distance in July or August the steaming foliage seems almost to writhe in fire.* Great green and yellow grasshoppers are everywhere in the tall grass, popping up like corn *to sting the flesh,* and tortoises crawl about on the red earth, going nowhere in the plenty of time. *Loneliness is an aspect of the land.* All things in the plain are isolate; *there is no confusion of objects in the eye, but* one *hill or* one *tree or* one *man. To look upon that landscape in the early morning, with the sun at your back, is to lose the sense of proportion. Your imagination comes to life, and this, you think, is where Creation was begun.*[5]

Everything we have changed to italics here enlists the reader's participation in a mood, beginning with a sense of physical hardship and ending with a general awe at a landscape that frustrates every wish for comfort, moderate weather, gentle scenery, sociability, and human scale. The writer's point of view has become our own.

---

EXERCISES

4. Choose an activity with which you are very familiar, and write a paragraph describing it in a way that gives your reader a sense of being present as

the activity is performed. You can make the reader either a performer or an observer.

5. Think of a place you are fond of; it could be as small as your bedroom or as large as your home town. Write two descriptive paragraphs about that place. In the first one, try simply to "give the facts" in a neutral, precise way, without any special emphasis. Then convey the same information in a vivid, engaging paragraph in which your point of view (attitude) is strongly apparent. Try to convey your point of view through descriptive commentary rather than through direct statements of opinion.

6. Choose any scene and think how it would look from the vantage of a certain moving vehicle (a truck, a plane, a boat, etc.). Making your reader into a passenger, write and submit a paragraph or two registering the reader's experience of that passing scene. Remember that you can make use of any sense impressions, not just visual ones.

7. In *Life on the Mississippi*, Mark Twain's romantic description of the river (pp. 13–14) is followed by a hard-boiled paragraph which reviews the same scene with the mentality of an experienced pilot: *that slanting mark on the water refers to a bluff reef which is going to kill somebody's steamboat one of these nights*, etc. Think of a scene that would look very different from two points of view—a hermit's, say, and a weekend backpacker's. (Choose a different contrast from that one.) Submit two paragraphs describing the scene from those two psychological outlooks. Remember that your two observers are actively making judgments, not just taking in the scenery.

## 1c    Describe through a Revealing Action.

When the thing to be described is a person or animal, you should try to include a characteristic action—either a revealing incident or a habit. Note, for example, how a student writer characterizes her stepfather by telling a little story which puts his best-remembered quirk into a form that the reader, too, will be likely to remember:

> Poor Harvey meant well by all of us, but the truth is that we made him uncomfortable—especially as we grew into gangly adolescence and began changing shapes and voices. Youthful bosoms and peach-fuzz mustaches across the dinner table were too much for his suspicious, uptight nature to bear. He could hardly criticize us for getting older, but he *could* take his nervousness out on Blacky the dog, who was forever scratching wherever he pleased in a carefree, immodest way, as dogs will do even while grace is being said at Thanksgiving.

Harvey would sit at the head of the table, not knowing how to control the squirming and giggling teenagers he had acquired as relatives, but then he would spot Blacky off in the corner scratching away most indecently, and he couldn't contain himself. "Blacky, Blacky!" he would yell, *"Stop it! Stop that right now!"* Blacky would stop scratching for just a moment—long enough to stare back at Harvey as you would too if a lunatic were trying to interrupt your normal life for no reason—but when he started up again, he had a large and appreciative audience.

---

### EXERCISE

8.  Write a descriptive paragraph or two about someone you know well, using an act of characteristic behavior to show your reader what impression that person usually makes on others. Before submitting your paragraph, revise it to make it as lively as possible, short of silliness.

---

## 1d    Describe through Figurative Language.

**Figurative**, or *metaphorical,* language is a means of making something imaginatively striking by presenting it in terms of something that is very different in kind but appropriate in at least one limited respect. In essay prose, an effective description may well contain some sharply figurative language. Consider examples in passages already studied:

> It is . . . the flotsam of the new California (Didion).

> A broad expanse of the river was turned to blood (Twain).

> the surface was broken by boiling, tumbling rings, that were as many-tinted as an opal (Twain).

> a single leafy bough that glowed like a flame (Twain).

> in summer the prairie is an anvil's edge (Momaday).

> the steaming foliage seems almost to writhe in fire (Momaday).

As readers, we instinctively ignore the literal absurdity of such statements and take them in the intended spirit. River water, we know, is not blood, but we ourselves have probably seen a river turn blood-red at sunset, and so the implied comparison brings the scene to life. That is what is remarkable about strong figurative language: by taking us momentarily away from the literal scene, it makes our participation in that scene more intense.

To see how figurative language can enliven a description, note the emphasized expressions in this passage:

> The sun is up and the pens are empty. As the deck is hosed down and the trash fish pitchforked overboard, the noise from the birds rises *hysterically—barnyard sounds,* shrieks, whistles, *klaxon horns.*
>
> Now the birds can be seen flying in a circle around the boat. Each can hold position for only a few moments beside the point where the remains of fish are washing over. Then it falls astern and has to come up to windward on the other side of the boat, cross ahead and fall backward to the critical point. The birds pumping up the windward side *look like six-day bicycle riders, earnest and slightly ridiculous,* but when they reach the critical point there is a miraculous moment of aerobatics as the birds brake, wheel and drop in the broken air.
>
> Gulls snatch, gannets plunge, but the little kittiwakes balance delicately, their tails spread *like carved ivory fans.* There is *a column* of descending, shrieking birds, *a scintillating feathered mass.* The birds revolving about the boat *have made themselves not only guests at the feast but have formed the wreath as well.* [6]

The elements we have put in italics here, by proposing how an imaginative observer would relate the sea birds to more familiar, landlocked experience, turn the reader into that observer. If the images of the six-day bicycle racers and the wreath of birds are somewhat daring, the accuracy of literal description elsewhere in the passage encourages us to trust their appropriateness.

Similarly, another writer combines precise literal details with figurative effects in order to rivet our attention on the object described—in this case, a performer who dives from a forty-foot ladder into a play pool of twelve-inch-deep water:

> LaMothe dives, however—doesn't jump—into water that scarcely reaches his calves as he stands up, his hands in a Hallelujah gesture. His sailor hat never leaves his head, his back stays dry unless the wash wets him, and yet so bizarre is the sight of a person emerging from water so shallow that one's eye sees him standing there as if with his drawers fallen around his feet. As he plummets, his form is as ugly and poignant as the flop of a frog—nothing less ungainly would enable him to survive—and, watching, one feels witness to something more interesting than a stunt—a leap for life into a fire net, perhaps. [7]

This writer combines sharply rendered particulars with a continual appeal to our imagination. First LaMothe is said to assume *a Hallelujah gesture,* as if he were in a revival meeting. Then we see him *as if with his drawers fallen around his feet*; nothing of the sort has actually occurred. Then LaMothe's fall is likened to *the flop of a frog*, and finally we regard the whole jump as if it were *a leap for life into a fire net*. The writer has gained effect not just from close observation, but also from freely relating what he perceives to other forms of experience.

---

## EXERCISES

9. Photocopy and submit any passage (for example, one taken from the assigned readings in this course) that describes by means of effective figurative language. Underline the relevant parts and submit a brief discussion of the effects achieved. Be specific in treating the author's particular choice of image in each instance.

10. Resubmit any passage you have written for a previous exercise in this chapter. Along with it, submit a second version in which you have tried to appeal to your reader's imagination through figurative language. Underline the sentences that aim at that effect.

---

## 1e   Try Different Ways of Ordering a Description.

Note these principles for arranging the elements of a description:

1. If you give the observer a means of locomotion, as in Joan Didion's drive to Banyan Street (p. 13), arrange the details in their "trip sequence."

2. If you are describing a landscape or an object, ask yourself what is most impressive about it, and try to save that feature for last. If it is a small detail, begin with larger ones; if it lies in the foreground, begin in the distance; and so on.

3. Similarly, if one fact about a described person stands out as more imposing than the others, look for a way of leading up to it.

4. If you are recounting a characteristic action, follow that action to its climax or conclusion. If it is a single incident, give it an introductory context so that your reader will understand why it is typical (Harvey's yelling at the dog, pp. 15–16). Alternatively, you can plunge your reader into the incident and then supply the context, as in a "baited opener" (5d, p. 107).

5. If you want to convey a certain mood or idea, look for an order that will gradually develop and intensify the desired response (the mysterious effect of Rainy Mountain, p. 14).

**EXERCISE**

11. Choose any two of the five listed principles for ordering a description, and submit two descriptive passages, each following one of those principles. Indicate which principle you are illustrating in each instance. If you wish, you may use some of the same descriptive material in both passages.

## NARRATION

Much that bears saying about description in essay prose applies equally to **narration** or storytelling, for both modes aim at reproducing experience. Indeed, we have already seen that the recounting of characteristic actions is a common means of describing. Since all the virtues of a good description apply to narration as well, begin your mastery of narrative strategies by reviewing points 1a–e above.

### 1f    Choose an Appropriate Tense for Your Narration.

Your choice of either the customary narrative past tense (*went, did*) or the less usual present tense (*goes, does*) should rest on whether or not you are after a special effect. Since narrated actions are always "over," the past tense is generally appropriate and expected. (To see how such a past-tense framework governs the use of related tenses, look at 15b, p. 331.)

For past actions that were typical or recurrent, employ the **auxiliaries** *would* and *could*: *I would cry every Saturday night,* etc. The following student paragraph shows the auxiliaries in typical use:

When I was a child I could always tell what the next day's weather would be. If, for example, rain was on the way, I would know it many hours in advance, without having to listen to weather forecasts. Sometimes I would notice a small change in the sky, such as the arrival of the first wisps of cirrus clouds that come before a front. Or again, I would realize that the flies around our apartment were acting sluggish in a way that usually spelled rain to me. Most often, though, I would simply feel "rainy inside," as I called it; the drop in barometric pressure would take down my mood and my energy level before there were any visible signs of a storm.

Choosing the present tense, by contrast, creates a more immediate effect, giving readers a sense of participating directly in the scene:

It is high noon. The sand burns the feet of the little children, who leave their palm leaf balls and their pin-wheels of frangipani blossoms to wither in the sun, as they creep into the shade of the houses. The women who must go abroad carry great banana leaves as sun-shades or wind wet cloths about their heads. Lowering a few blinds against the slanting sun, all who are left in the village wrap their heads in sheets and go to sleep. Only a few adventurous children may slip away for a swim in the shadow of a high rock, some industrious woman continues with her weaving, or a close little group of women bend anxiously over a woman in labor. The village is dazzling and dead; any sound seems oddly loud and out of place. Words have to cut through the solid heat slowly. And then the sun gradually sinks over the sea.[8]

Sometimes, too, a narrator will choose the present tense to suggest that the events being told are still fresh in memory and that they are accompanied by strong feelings. Thus a student writes:

I turn on the public television station, expecting to hear a thoughtful program on Africa scheduled for this hour. But tonight there is a fund-raising "special" instead. I am annoyed, but I try to be understanding; after all, the station needs extra contributions to survive. But before long I am completely fed up with the whole undertaking. It seems that the station manager has asked every unemployable comedian and punk band in town to put in an appearance. They are "special," yes—in just the way that marked-down loaves of yesterday's bread are "special" in the supermarket.

Notice how the writer's impatience is made more convincing by his telling the story as if it were occurring as he writes.

---

### EXERCISES

12. Think of a significant incident in your life and narrate it in one or two paragraphs, using a straightforward time sequence and the past tense.

13. Choose a person to write about—either someone you know or someone in public life—and write a narrative paragraph that (a) shows the person in action, and (b) uses the present tense.

---

## 1g    Choose between Direct and Indirect Discourse.

One frequently used feature of narration is the reporting of speech or thought. When the language is quoted, the result is **direct discourse**. Direct discourse involving two or more people constitutes **dialogue**:

"Mayday! Mayday! We're going down!" Those were the captain's last recorded words.
   "Try to make it to the runway," pleaded the flight controller. "We've got the fire trucks on line for you." But there was no reply; the plane had already begun its fatal plunge.

The obvious advantage of such quotation is that you give your reader the impression of being right on the scene.
   Note that a paragraph of dialogue can be as brief as one speaker's remark. You should begin a new paragraph with every change of speaker.
   If your purpose is merely to convey *what* was said, without reproducing speech patterns and tone, you can use **indirect discourse** instead of dialogue:

In his last recorded words the captain declared that the plane was going down. There was no reply to the flight controller's plea that he try to reach the runway; the plane had already begun its fatal plunge.

Compared with the dialogue version, this is colorless. But no writer needs to be colorful at every moment — and no reader could stand it. In many situations you will find that indirect discourse suits your purpose well. You may also want to keep relatively incidental remarks in indirect discourse, shifting into dialogue when you feel that the speaker's exact words are dramatic or important.
   Since a person's unspoken thoughts are less precise than statements, it is generally best to render them without quotation marks. Note, however, that you can do so in direct discourse:

I can't keep up this pretense much longer, thought Kate. In another week or so, anyone will be able to read my face like a billboard.

Alternatively, you can put a character's thoughts into the past tense and thus render them indirectly:

Friedland felt a wave of sadness, a sense of loss made sharper by the fact that he had been away; he could have contributed *something,* he thought, if he had stayed. But you couldn't be on call 24 hours a day, 365 days a year, and death, he mused, has never waited on the convenience of doctors. He found some comfort in having arranged the end of Maria's life as she had wanted it and having prepared her family adequately—or, anyway, extensively—for it. He felt that there was—he chose the word carefully—an *appropriate* time to die, and that that time had come for Maria. It ran cross grain with his training and his heart to say so; it was like asking a soldier on a battlefield to lay down his arms and admit defeat, even when it made no sense to fight on. He knew what had lain ahead for Maria and her family had she lingered. The spectacle of her death, he thought, would have distorted her in memory for her survivors. She would have become, in her deepening dementia, a nonperson. She would have ceased being Maria.[9]

For the problem of mixing direct and indirect discourse within a single sentence, see 15d, p. 337. For punctuation rules governing the presentation of dialogue, see 20b–20e, pp. 376–378.

---

**EXERCISES**

14. Write three paragraphs of narration in which two speakers are represented. Make use of both direct and indirect discourse, saving the former for utterances that deserve to be highlighted.

15. Write a paragraph in which you represent someone's thoughts and feelings about any subject. Put some of those reflections into direct discourse and others into indirect discourse, as in the "Friedland" paragraph above *(The spectacle of her death, he thought, would have distorted her in memory for her survivors)*.

---

## 1h   Practice Anticipatory Narration.

Because every story occurs in a time sequence, the most natural order of telling is a chronological (straightforward) one, from the first incident to the last. That order, which characterizes all the examples of narration we have thus far reviewed, is the easiest one to master.

Once you feel at home with straightforward narrating, you can experiment with an order that requires more planning but also offers greater possibilities for inspiring your reader's curiosity. Instead of starting at the earliest moment, choose a more dramatic scene and reveal just enough about it to provoke interest. After that act of **anticipation**, you can skip back to the earliest relevant moment, filling in the circumstances that led to the climactic dramatic scene, and then carry the story through to its end. Here, for instance, are the opening paragraphs of an essay about the way a championship boxer and his manager came together:

narr
1h

> In a dressing room in Bakersfield, California, last April, Al Stankie was work-ing Paul Gonzales into a fighting mood.
> Gonzales won the gold medal in the 106-pound weight class at the 1984 Olympics in Los Angeles. Last February, in only his third professional fight— he had missed almost a year with an injured hand—Gonzales met Alonso Strongbow, the North American Boxing Federation flyweight champion. And although Gonzales had fought only a six-round and an eight-round bout as a pro, he went twelve rounds against the determined Strongbow and beat him decisively for the title.
> Now, in Bakersfield, it was moments before the champion's fourth profes-sional fight, a nontitle 10-round match against Javier Barajas.
> "Fight time," said Stankie in his raspy, urgent voice. "Think of where you are. And where you're going. I see it all. I see it all. Nothing is going to stop you. It's time for you, son. Time to shine. Up, up and away. Whoooo."
> Soon, Stankie and the fighter were walking out into the arena on their way to their next victory.
> It was another night in the long and turbulent relationship between a 45-year-old half-Italian, half-Polish policeman (formerly Stankiewicz) from Erie, Pennsylvania, and the 22-year-old Mexican-American he dragged off the streets of Los Angeles about a dozen years before. The cop and the kid, two people whose lives came together in the most curious of ways.[10]

Note how the final sentence of this passage prepares us for the filling-in of the two men's early histories.

---

### EXERCISE

16. Look through some newspapers and magazines for a story that tells the outcome of previous events. (For example, a murder trial obviously fol-lows a murder; the banning of a dangerous drug follows the harm it has been causing; the resumption of fishing in a once-polluted lake follows a crackdown on polluters.) Photocopy and hand in the story. Using your own words, write and submit several paragraphs of narration in which you begin by anticipating the most recent development in that story and then fill in relevant events from the more distant past. Feel free to invent details if necessary.

## 1i    Give Your Story an Implied Point.

In any engaging narration you will necessarily be expressing an attitude or position: admiration or anger, compassion or detachment, a sense of urgency or of helplessness. Sometimes a narrator will put such editorializing directly into words, but too many statements of opinion can slow a story down and break the reader's concentration. The trick, then, is to color the narrated events within the very telling of them.

Look, for instance, at this opening paragraph of an essay:

A muskrat, also called musquash, or technically, *Ondatra zibethica zibethica* Linn. 1766 – the creature didn't give a hoot about nomenclature – fell into our swimming pool, which was empty except for a puddle of winter water. It huddled in a corner, wild frightened eyes, golden brown fur, hairless muddied tail. Before I could find instruments suitable for catching and removing muskrats, a passing neighbor (unfamiliar with rodents per se, or even with rodents living in Czechoslovakia since 1905), deciding he'd come across a giant rat as bloodthirsty as a tiger and as full of infections as a plague hospital, ran home, got his shotgun, and fired at the muskrat until all that was left was a shapeless soggy ball of fur with webbed hind feet and bared teeth. There was blood all over the sides and bottom of the pool, all over the ball of fur, and the puddle of water was a little red sea. The hunting episode was over, and I was left to cope with the consequences. Humankind can generally be divided into hunters and people who cope with consequences.[11]

Without directly condemning his neighbor, this writer distances himself from the rodent-hating mentality. He does so not only in his icy final sentence but also at the outset in his droll show of respect for muskrats as fellow creatures.

For a more extended example of an implied narrative point, consider the following complete essay by a freshman student:

"You should fix everyone's coffee or tea. You know, add the sugar, etc., and pour it. If the meat is hard to handle, you should cut it for the patient," instructed my predecessor. "After you've passed out the trays, you feed Irene and Molly."

"That's Granny Post in there. She's 106. Even though she's not particularly senile, she's lost her teeth and must be fed with a giant eyedropper." I discovered just how clear Granny Post's mind was when I tried to feed her. The dear old lady wasn't hungry and spat it back at me.

After that first day at the convalescent hospital, I was on my own. Irene was eager to please and partially fed herself, but I dreaded feeding Molly. She was blind and pitifully thin. "I'm sick. I'm sick," she'd cry. "Don't make me eat any more. Please, I'm sick."

"But Molly, you've got to eat so you can get well. Come on, one more bite. Here, hold my hand. It's not so bad." And I'd coax one more bite down her before gathering the sixty trays onto their racks and wheeling them back to the safety of the kitchen. The rest of the evening I cleaned the coffee pot, set up the breakfast trays, scoured sinks, and mopped the floors. I didn't mind sitting on the floor scrubbing at the oven or making the juices and sandwiches for the evening nourishment. It was when I confronted the elderly people on the other side of that kitchen door that I became nervous and awkward.

In a few weeks I mastered the hospital routine, the names of most of the patients, and their idiosyncrasies.

Opposite the kitchen was what was fondly called "the ward." Dora, a small, white-haired woman who was continually nearly slipping out of the bottom of the wheelchair to which she was tied, was the ringleader of this group. She cussed up a storm at anyone who came near her and perpetually monotoned, "What can I do? Tell me, what can I do?" May accompanied her with "Put me to bed. I want to go to bed." One evening as I entered with dinner, the woman across from Dora was gaily slinging her waste matter about the room, especially at anyone who threatened to come near her. A nurse and some aides calmed her down.

As far as the two sisters in room twelve were concerned, they were traveling on a huge ocean liner. When I brought their trays, they always asked, "How long till we get to port?" or "I'm sorry. We can't eat today because we're seasick."

John mumbled perpetually about the batty ladies in the TV room. He liked his smokes and his sports magazine.

Mr. Harrison fed a stray cat that stayed outside his sliding-glass door. He loved his cat and I gave him leftovers to feed it. One day a car rushed down the hill and struck his cat. Mr. Harrison told me his cat ran away, but it would come back as always. He stood at his door watching for it.

There were two Ethels. Dora advanced to feeding herself so I began feeding Ethel Irene. Ethel Irene was small, roly-poly, and had gray-black hair cut short like a little boy's. She liked to joke and use large words. Sometimes when she grasped for a word, it just wouldn't come and great big tears would form in her eyes. She liked sunshiny days and the sound of birds singing. She liked me to sing to her, too. Always clamped tightly in her hand was the buzzer to call the nurse. It was Ethel Irene's lifeline. Occasionally it fell out of her hand and she became so frantic she couldn't speak, only pointing and crying.

I tried to regard the other Ethel as just one of the many patients to whom I delivered food. When I brought dinner, I fixed Ethel's tea, cut her meat, and tucked in her napkin. Then I'd clearly shout, "Enjoy your dinner." But instead of letting me leave, she'd pull me down to her and in a low, halting voice struggle out, "I like you. Can I kiss you?"

It became increasingly difficult to leave Ethel. She'd refuse to release my arm, purposely eat slowly so I was forced to return just to retrieve her tray, and cry when I succeeded in making my exit. To avoid upsetting her, I began sneaking into the room to take her tray or sending someone else. If she realized the deception, she'd let out an anguished cry and begin sobbing. I couldn't bear to pass Ethel's room and see her arms reaching out for me.

Many of the patients were lonely like Ethel and starved for attention. Some were on welfare and had few or no relatives. Most were just forgotten. Ethel's son visited one day. Roaring drunk, he first tried to get fresh with me and then stomped into the kitchen demanding food.

Molly had visitors once, too. When I reached work and dropped by to see Molly, two or three of her relatives were standing about her. Molly was breathing laboriously, her nose and mouth were attached to an oxygen tank. She was dying now. The relatives left shortly. Molly's bed was empty when I returned the next day.

I worked in the convalescent hospital only sixteen hours a week for eight months. The old people remained there twenty-four hours a day for months or years, depending on how "lucky" they were. They were fed, diapered at night, and sponge-bathed in the morning. But what they needed most . . .

The age is gone when three generations occupy the same house. Young people want a life of their own.

My parents are nearly fifty now.

This essay has some minor flaws, but they are outweighed by its compassion and control. The memorable description of Ethel Irene with her "lifeline" buzzer and the understated recounting of Molly's death seem like reality itself. And the apparent disorganization covers a subtle and effective movement engaging the reader in the writer's own ordeal of first learning her chores, then coping with the patients' oddities, then facing the ultimate fact of death, and finally turning her thoughts to her own parents, who "are nearly fifty now" and may someday be like Molly and Mr. Harrison. Will she look after them in their senility? The abrupt ending leaves us troubled, not only by grotesque and tender images from the convalescent hospital, but also by conflicting feelings toward parents who deserve our care but who threaten to invade "a life of [our] own."

---

## EXERCISES

17. From your assigned readings or any other source, photocopy a passage that strikes you as effectively conveying an implied point. Submit the passage along with a paragraph of your own analyzing how the writer has achieved that effect. Be specific about the writer's choice of language.

18. Think of a real or imaginary story that would lead to some perception or generalization. Put that point into a sentence at the top of a page.

Then skip some lines and write the story in several paragraphs (or more, if you use dialogue) so that the story implies your point without completely stating it.

## NOTES

[1] Roger Angell, *Five Seasons: A Baseball Companion* (New York: Simon, 1977) 11.

[2] Angell 12.

[3] Joan Didion, *Slouching Towards Bethlehem* (1968; New York: Washington Square, 1981) 20–21.

[4] Mark Twain, *Life on the Mississippi* (1883; New York: Signet, 1961) 67–69.

[5] N. Scott Momaday, *The Way to Rainy Mountain* (Albuquerque: New Mexico UP, 1969) 5.

[6] William G. Wing, "Christmas Comes First on the Banks," *New York Times* 24 Dec. 1966: 18.

[7] Edward Hoagland, *Red Wolves and Black Bears* (New York: Random, 1972) 19–20.

[8] Margaret Mead, *Coming of Age in Samoa* (New York: Blue Ribbon, 1928) 16–17.

[9] Peter Goldman and Lucille Beachy, "One Against the Plague," *Newsweek* 21 July 1986: 50.

[10] Phil Berger, "Two Long Roads That Led to the Title," *New York Times* 17 July 1986, national ed.: 20.

[11] Miroslav Holub, "Shedding Life," trans. Dana Hábová and Patricia Debney, *Science 86* Apr. 1986: 51–52.

# 2

## Strategies of Analysis and Argument

Narrowly construed, **analysis** is a means of explanation whereby something is separated into its parts. But in common use, the word covers a number of ways to grapple with a problem. When one instructor asks you to "analyze the effects of the *Challenger* explosion on the American space program," while another wants an "analysis of the differences between problems of school discipline in 1988 and those in 1948," and still another says, "analyze the last scene of *Macbeth*," you can gather that *analysis* has become a roomy term. Here we will take it to include every customary means of explanation.

**Argument**, or the use of persuasive reasoning to convince others that a certain position on an issue is justified, has traditionally been recognized as an essay mode in its own right. And with good reason: since argument always involves opposing someone else's position, an argumentative essayist must be unusually alert to objections. Actually, though, all the merits of a sound argument can be found in many analytic essays as well. And conversely, every strategy of analysis is serviceable in argumentation.

Rather than insist on fine distinctions before we have arrived at the full essay, then, we can think of analysis and argument together here. As opposed to the *physical immediacy* of description and narration (Chapter 1), analysis and argument make up the strategies of *mental operation* — those designed to show that the writer's understanding of a given problem is a reasonable one.

## 2a Make Purposeful Use of a Definition.

In defining, a writer specifies exactly what a certain thing or idea is, so that it cannot be mistaken for anything else. **Definition** of things or ideas usually involves two basic steps:

1. *classification,* showing what kind of thing *x* belongs to:

- A snail is a mollusk of the class *Gastropoda,* . . .

2. *differentiation,* showing how *x* differs from all other members of its class:

- . . . having a spirally coiled shell of a single valve and a ventral muscular foot on which it slowly glides about.

These two steps are fundamental because they encompass the mind's most common procedure for making sense of the world. To decide what any unfamiliar object is, we must first align it with already familiar things having the same general nature or purpose: all snails are mollusks, and among the mollusks all snails fall within a smaller grouping, the gastropods. But precisely because there are other gastropods, we must spell out features of the snail which, taken together, apply to *no other* gastropods. When that has been done, the definition is adequate.

Again, if we want to say just what a hammock is, we cannot avoid beginning by classifying it as a type of bed. Then we will want to locate the smallest possible subclass of beds to which every hammock belongs: *it is a hanging bed.* Yes, but an upper bunk in a ship or prison may also be a hanging bed. Since the subclass contains members which are not hammocks, we must specify features that show hammocks to be a unique kind of hanging bed: *A hammock is a hanging bed* (classification) *made of canvas, netted cord, or the like* (differentiation).

Formal definition of this kind, however, is rarely found in good essay prose. Indeed, nothing puts a reader to sleep faster than the hapless "dictionary definition opener" (5d, p. 105)—a telltale sign that the writer is casting about for something, anything, to say. You should define only those terms that are both crucial to your point and seriously in need of clarification. And you should do so in a vivid, helpful way, avoiding the tone that says in effect, "We interrupt this graceful essay to bring you the following bulletin from *Webster's Unabridged*."

### Defining by Example

Often the best way to define a tricky term is to use a concrete example, as in this preliminary attempt to fix the meaning of "complexity":

So, what is a complex thing? How should we recognize it? In what sense is it true to say that a watch or an airliner or an earwig or a person is complex, but the moon is simple? The first point that might occur to us, as a necessary attribute of a complex thing, is that it has a heterogeneous structure. A pink milk pudding or blancmange is simple in the sense that, if we slice it in two, the two portions will have the same internal constitution: a blancmange is homogeneous. A car is heterogeneous: unlike a blancmange, almost any portion of the car is different from other portions. Two times half a car does not make a car. This will often amount to saying that a complex object, as opposed to a simple one, has many parts, these parts being of more than one kind.[1]

---

#### EXERCISES

1. Submit dictionary definitions for any five familiar terms (e.g., *opera, cancer, handbag*), indicating in each case which part of the definition is *classification (C)* and which part is *differentiation (D)*.

2. Ask yourself which, if any, of the following activities ought to be regarded as *sports:* hiking, chess, bowling, bodybuilding. Then write a paragraph or two in which you resolve that issue by carefully defining what you mean by the term *sports.* (Must a sport be physical, competitive, etc.?)

3. Choose a term, such as *freedom* or *democracy* or *patriotism,* that you find to be interpreted *positively but very differently* by different individuals or groups. (For example, leaders of nations with entirely opposed political systems regard those nations as *democracies.*) Using your dictionary, your memory, and any other handy sources, gather as many different senses of your chosen term as you can. Then submit several paragraphs in which you define the term as *you* think it should be construed, showing why you prefer that definition to other possibilities.

---

## 2b    Divide an Object or Idea into Its Parts.

In **division** the work of analysis consists of spelling out the parts or stages that make up some whole. Since the parts of one thing will always differ in some way from those of anything else, division can be close in function to definition; naming all the parts is a means of grasping what is unique about the object or idea. Thus the writer who specified all the ingredients of a baseball (p. 10) was using division to indicate what the ball *must* contain to be properly considered a baseball and not, for example, a softball.

Especially when used near the beginning of an essay, division can perform the simple but useful function of indicating the scope of a subject:

> The predators—insects that kill and consume other insects—are of many kinds. Some are quick and with the speed of swallows snatch their prey from the air. Others plod methodically along a stem, plucking off and devouring sedentary insects like the aphids. The yellowjackets capture soft-bodied insects and feed the juices to their young. Mud-dauber wasps build columned nests of mud under the eaves of houses and stock them with insects on which their young will feed. The horse-guard wasp hovers above herds of grazing cattle, destroying the bloodsucking flies that torment them. The loudly buzzing syrphid fly, often mistaken for a bee, lays its eggs on leaves of aphid-infested plants; the hatching larvae then consume immense numbers of aphids. Ladybugs or lady beetles are among the most effective destroyers of aphids, scale insects, and other plant-eating insects. Literally hundreds of aphids are consumed by a single ladybug to stoke the little fires of energy which she requires to produce even a single batch of eggs.[2]

Observe how the writer has first defined predator insects and then divided them into various kinds. Yet instead of making a dry, listlike effect, she has sustained interest by descriptively capturing each species' most typical action. More important, she has demonstrated her wide knowledge and laid a foundation for her main point, disclosed in a later paragraph: that indiscriminate spraying of pesticides kills a great many insects that would otherwise help to control agricultural pests.

By dividing a subject into its parts, you can also bring order out of apparent confusion. Look, for example, at how a student writer leads into a discussion of buying a ten-speed bicycle:

> What should you look for when shopping for a ten-speed bike? It is easy to get confused by glossy advertisements saying that you can't do without the latest molybdenum frame and cantilever brakes. But you can bring some sense into

the matter if you keep in mind that all ten-speed bikes are designed primarily either for *touring* or for *racing*. Which activity do you prefer? The answer will tell you whether to go for a stiff frame or a more comfortable one; whether you want tight steering or a capacity for no-hands cruising on the highway; whether you should be more interested in quickness of shifting or in having a low enough bottom gear for hauling luggage up a mountain road.

Here the act of division—separating all ten-speed bikes into touring and racing cycles—leads to a series of further distinctions, each of which can be developed in a subsequent paragraph.

## EXERCISES

4. Submit several paragraphs in which you divide college or high-school teachers into a number of main types. (If you want to be humorous, go ahead.) Try to include at least one characteristic action to illustrate each of your types.

5. Take a public problem or issue, such as air pollution or gene transplants or the arms race, and break that problem or issue into what you consider to be its component parts—namely, the narrower issues that go to make it up. (If the issue were abortion, for example, the subissues might be the rights of the unborn, how to determine when human life begins, parents' right to control family size, religious prohibitions, health risks to mothers, and the effects of making abortion legal or illegal. But now that this example has been supplied, you should choose a different issue.) Underline the items on your list that strike you as deserving the most concern, and then write the introductory paragraph to an essay about the issue, emphasizing the important subissues. Hand in your underlined list along with the paragraph.

## 2c  Illustrate a Point.

Illustration is the providing of examples to flesh out an idea and to show that the idea really does rest on demonstrable cases:

Foreigners are buying America. It's no longer just the smart money or the tax-evasion money. It's the savings of a Bavarian innkeeper who can earn only 3.5 per cent a year at his bank at home; it's the British Airways pension fund, which owns a shopping center in Houston. It's the oil money of Iranians, among them a sister of the Shah, who have bought so many of the million-dollar homes in the Trousdale Estates section of Beverly Hills that the natives call it "the Persian Gulf." And it's the Eurodollars in the coffers of polyglot multinationals in Stockholm and Stuttgart, using the profits from their exports to the U.S. to build and buy factories here. The Germans make Volkswagen Rabbits in a Pennsylvania factory that Chrysler had to abandon. The Japanese bottle Coca-Cola in New Hampshire, raise cattle in Utah and make soy sauce in rural Wisconsin.[3]

The opening sentence of this paragraph, stating its point, is meant to be a shocker. But by the end, having been subjected to a battery of instances, we realize that the writer has a real phenomenon in mind.

A humorous or whimsical thesis stands in just as much need of illustration as a serious one:

"I eat bread sparingly," writes Tom Osler. "In the summer, I consume large quantities of fruit juices. . . . I do not use salt at the table or at the stove. I do not use sugar, because it seems to make my skin break out in acne." In an article titled "Running Through Pregnancy" in *Runner's World*, we learn that runners "have little trouble with irregularity. Some even experience a frequency increase in bowel movements." In the pages of the same magazine Joe Henderson reports that he thinks of a running high "as the way we're supposed to feel when not constipated." If one did not know what was being talked about—running—one might feel like an eavesdropper listening in on conversations in a nursing home for the elderly.[4]

---

**EXERCISES**

6. Scan the readings for this or any other course until you find an analysis that uses substantial illustration of a point. (If your example comes from outside this course, submit a photocopy of it.) Hand in a paragraph of your own in which you state the writer's point and back it up with several of the illustrative examples cited. Be careful to use your own language.

7. Think of some general statement you would feel comfortable justifying (e.g., *Students on this campus are more interested in parties than in books*), and jot down as many illustrative instances as you can think of. Then write and submit a paragraph in which you set forth and illustrate your idea.

---

## 2d    Establish Causes and Effects.

Most writing about cause and effect proceeds from known effects—that is, from accomplished facts such as a burst dam or an economic recession or a change in climate—to supposed causes, which are usually multiple. The following student paragraph shows a common pattern of beginning with the effect, disposing of relatively minor causal factors, and then treating the factors that seem weightiest:

| | |
|---|---|
| the effect to be explained<br>cause #1 | In recent decades the reported death rate from cancer has been rising dramatically. How alarmed should we be by this statistical change? One cause of the mounting curve is probably the simple fact that we are more conscious of cancer now than we used to be, and less ashamed to mention the feared disease. |
| cause #2<br><br>the more serious causes:<br><br>#3, #4, #5 | Another cause may be the fact that more and more people are dying in hospitals and undergoing autopsies: in earlier times the comparable deaths at home from cancer might have been attributed to "old age." But factors like these take us only so far. Eventually we have to admit that cancer has been gaining on us in an absolute sense. If so, the real causes must be environmental: the continued increase in smoking, the use of dangerous pesticides and food additives, and increased pollution from automobiles and industry. Some of those sources must be more responsible than others, but until we know more than we do, we had better give urgent attention to all of them. |

After this strong introduction, which showed a proper caution about making one-to-one connections between causes and effects, the writer devoted the rest of her essay to the three causes she had identified as most significant.

## Correlation

Much treatment of causes and effects wisely steers away from flat assertions that *x* is *the* cause of *y*. Instead, the writer significantly associates, or *correlates,* *x* with *y,* leaving open the possibility that factors *a, b,* and *c* may also have played a part in bringing about *y.*

Consider the following student passage, which correlates a popular dance style with various characteristics of the 1970s:

The clearest example of all is provided by disco dancing, which became a national craze in 1978. In several respects disco was the perfect expression of the decade that produced it. For one thing, the seventies combined a rediscovery of "roots" with an easing of the racial tensions that were so explosive in the sixties. Black and Latin in its origins, disco remained somewhat ethnic in flavor, yet it was accepted by the whole society. Second, disco was a high-technology form; its amplified sounds and its dazzling lights suggested the network of electronics that many people had come to regard as their real environment. Third, disco expressed "the me decade" both in its demand for physical fitness and in its emphasis on display. And finally, disco was more disciplined than the do-your-own-thing dances of the sixties. Disco swept the country at a time when nearly everyone who had once joined "the counter-culture" was ready to give the sense of order a second chance.

an/
arg
2e

Observe that in this passage, cause-and-effect reasoning merely *associates* a complex of factors with a certain result. The writer wisely refrains from risking everything on only one of four possible sources of the 1970s' disco craze – the emphasis on race, technology, self, and discipline.

## EXERCISES

8. Think about something you have done that now strikes you as wrong; it can be either a specific act or the adoption of a habit or prejudice. What were the probable causes, or determining factors, leading to your act or habit? Submit a paragraph in which you proceed from *what* you did to *why* you think you did it.

9. To explore relations between intended causes and effects, find an adver-tisement that implies a strong but farfetched connection between an advertised product and an appealing image, personality, or style of liv-ing. Submit the advertisement or a photocopy of it along with two or three paragraphs analyzing what you take to be the intended effect of the ad. (Of course, the ultimate intended effect is that people buy the product. You should concentrate on the immediate intended effect – for example, to link the product with a certain pleasurable feeling.)

10. Find a news story about an event that probably had at least three separate causes, and submit two or three paragraphs summarizing the event and explaining what you take to have been its main causes.

## 2e Develop Comparisons and Contrasts.

In a sense, we could say that all thinking comes down to comparing (matching things that are alike) and contrasting (pointing out differences). We cannot have an idea about anything without setting that object of thought beside similar things and then asking ourselves how it differs from them. Not surprisingly, then, **comparison** and **contrast** can be found at all levels of writing, from the structure of sentences and para-graphs through the central purpose of an essay or book. Definition, as we saw (2a, p. 29), works by comparison and contrast, and so does many a passage of description and narration (Chapter 1).

Note, for example, how a student writer sets the story of one tornado against that of an earlier one, thus making the more recent calamity stand out more dramatically:

resemblances {

The tornado that struck our farm in 1978 looked at first just like the one I had seen four years before. The nearby clouds had the same dark and jumbled look, and the thin, twisting, black funnel appeared much the same, like some kind of putty-like upside-down vacuum cleaner sucking things out of the sky on the horizon. But that time, the funnel *stayed* on the horizon

differences {

until it veered out of sight, and I never knew what it was doing on the ground until I saw the television reports of the damage. This time the tornado came right at us, quietly at first and then with a sickening roar. We all ran for the shelter, of course, and we made it with time to spare; the funnel couldn't have been moving faster than about thirty miles an hour. Even so, leaves and straw were already flying about wildly as we pulled down the hatch. And when we peeked out ten minutes later, we saw that our truck had been overturned; two walls of the barn had collapsed; and half the roof of our house was lying in the field a quarter of a mile away.

Again, a student writer who wanted to show how different Hamlet and Laertes are devoted a richly detailed early paragraph to showing that the two characters deserve to be considered together:

We need only abstract Laertes' five brief appearances in order to see that he and Hamlet are meant to be taken as parallel figures. In Act I, scene 2, Laertes asks the King for permission to return to France; in the same scene we learn that Hamlet has asked the King for permission to return to Wittenburg. In Laertes' second appearance he reproaches his sister for her receptivity to Hamlet; Hamlet later gives a comparable lecture to Gertrude. Hamlet's loss of a father through murder is mirrored by Laertes' loss of Polonius to Hamlet's own sword, and in Act IV, scene 1, Laertes reappears with the Hamlet-like idea of killing his father's murderer. Again, Laertes' cries of grief at Ophelia's funeral are travestied by Hamlet, who leaps after him into the grave. And in Laertes' fifth appearance, in Act V, he and Hamlet square off for a duel of offended sons — and the result of the scene is that both of them die and both are avenged. Laertes, we might say, scarcely exists apart from Hamlet. Super-ficially, at least, they harbor the same desires and grievances, love the same woman, behave alike, and are drawn into a single fate at the end.

Having established these strong parallels, the writer went on to show how the reckless passion of Laertes stands out against Hamlet's doubts and hesitations.

Whichever element comes first—resemblances or differences—we can be fairly sure that the *second* element will receive major emphasis. This rule applies, for example, to paragraphs that include both elements. Thus, seeking to dwell on the differences between the American Bill of Rights and the *Communist Manifesto,* a student writer wisely began her paragraph with comparisons, not contrasts:

**resemblances** { The authors of our Bill of Rights and of the *Communist Manifesto* shared an idea that previous forms of government had protected injustice and inequality. Both were determined to write a charter for a new kind of society in which ordinary people would be free from tyranny.

**differences** { The two documents, however, are absolutely opposed in their conceptions of human liberty. The Bill of Rights seeks to limit the powers of government by specifying the rights of individuals, whereas Marx's *Manifesto* seeks—chiefly by denying the rights of inheritance and private property—to protect the masses from powerful individuals. We will see that this difference of philosophy runs straight through the two documents, making one of them, the *Manifesto,* a list of what *must* be done and the other, the Bill of Rights, a list of what *must not* be done to interfere with the will of citizens.

The pivotal word *however* doesn't simply divide this writer's paragraph in two; it correctly predicts that in her essay the differences between the *Communist Manifesto* and the Bill of Rights will outweigh the characteristics they share.

It is especially important to keep to an orderly structure if your comparison-and-contrast is going to be complex. In the following passage, for example, the writer wants to contrast both soccer and basketball on the one hand with both football and baseball on the other. But since the latter pair show important differences from each other, he begins by addressing those differences:

Both football and baseball lend themselves to quantification—to statistically based strategies—but for different reasons. Football rewards top-down coordination. The sport is made to order for machine-like teamwork scripted by the head coach because it permits teams to pause and regroup after each play. For its part, baseball is so individualistic that only situational teamwork is required; the crux of the game is the pitcher/batter confrontation. Coordination

an/
arg
2f

is achieved through the design of the sport. The manager can concentrate on filling out and revising the lineup card, player by player, based on historical performances and match-ups.

In effect, football and baseball are contrasting models of vertical decision-making: football exemplifies centralization; baseball, decentralization. What soccer and basketball have in common—and what sets them apart from football and baseball—is an emphasis on the horizontal dimension, on shared decision-making. Soccer and basketball place a premium on the capacity of players to coordinate themselves as a unit while play is in progress. The coach serves as a facilitator.

Soccer and basketball are truly international games; both are androgynous, readily understandable, and intimate in the sense that each depends on the ability and resolve of players to work together spontaneously. Coincidentally, the first ball ever used in basketball—by the game's inventor, James Naismith—was a soccer ball. [5]

For a complete essay of comparison and contrast, see page 53.

### EXERCISES

11. Looking through magazines and newspapers, find two editorials or columns expressing opinions about the same public issue. Submit copies along with two or three paragraphs of your own in which you compare and contrast the two pieces, emphasizing the points of opinion or style or tone that you find most significant.

12. Write two paragraphs about two movies that seem to you alike in certain ways and different in others. Use your two paragraphs to establish the most important resemblances and differences. You can deal with themes, leading characters, techniques, or effects.

13. Think of two individuals or groups that are often considered to be extremely different (e.g., two famous public figures, men and women, babies and old people, Texans and New Yorkers). Jot down all the ways in which you could show that the seeming opposites are really alike. Then submit a paragraph in which, beginning with the obvious points of difference, you emphasize the little-noted similarities.

## 2f    Cover the Steps of a Process.

Sometimes the stages to be covered in an analysis are actions or steps which, performed correctly and in a certain fixed order, make up a routine for accomplishing some end. The strategy of laying out such steps is called **process analysis**.

A process analysis can serve its purpose only if all of the essential steps appear in their necessary order. If, for instance, you were teaching your reader how to drive a stick-shift car, you might decide that the essential parts of the process are (1) familiarizing oneself with ignition, clutch, brake pedal, accelerator, and emergency brake; (2) starting and stopping; (3) steering while remaining within one gear; (4) shifting gears; (5) making turns; and (6) backing up. If item 1 appeared farther down the list, or if item 4 were missing, or if a triviality like *reading the odometer* were thrown in, the analysis would be flawed.

an/
arg
2f

Process analyses occur frequently in technical writing—for example, in reports of experimental procedures or in operating instructions for new equipment. When essayists use the same strategy, they usually have some further idea in mind. Thus one writer analyzes a motorcycle mechanic's diagnostic steps, not in order to teach motorcycle repair, but to show that the mechanic uses exactly the same principles of reasoning as a scientist:

Skill at this point consists of using experiments that test only the hypothesis in question, nothing less, nothing more. If the horn honks, and the mechanic concludes that the whole electrical system is working, he is in deep trouble. He has reached an illogical conclusion. The honking horn only tells him that the battery and horn are working. To design an experiment properly he has to think very rigidly in terms of what directly causes what. This you know from the hierarchy. The horn doesn't make the cycle go. Neither does the battery, except in a very indirect way. The point at which the electrical system *directly* causes the engine to fire is at the spark plugs, and if you don't test here, at the output of the electrical system, you will never really know whether the failure is electrical or not.

To test properly the mechanic removes the plug and lays it against the engine so that the base around the plug is electrically grounded, kicks the starter lever and watches the spark-plug gap for a blue spark. If there isn't any he can conclude one of two things: (a) there is an electrical failure or (b) his experiment is sloppy. If he is experienced he will try it a few more times, checking connections, trying every way he can think of to get that plug to fire. Then, if he can't get it to fire, he finally concludes that *a* is correct, there's an electrical failure, and the experiment is over. He has proved that his hypothesis is correct.[6]

What distinguishes such a paragraph from sheer narrative is its reference, not to something that happened once, but to a procedure that must be followed every time a certain problem arises.

Sometimes, however, you can include elements of process analysis within prose that *is* primarily narrative, saying in effect *This is how I used to do* x. Notice, for example, how one writer zeroes in on a process while recalling his boyhood days as a yo-yo champion:

> The greatest pleasure in yo-yoing was an abstract pleasure—watching the dramatization of simple physical laws, and realizing they would never fail if a trick was done correctly. The geometric purity of it! The string wasn't just a string, it was a tool in the enactment of theorems. It was a line, an idea. And the top was an entirely different sort of idea, a gyroscope, capable of storing energy and of interacting with the line. I remember the first time I did a particularly lovely trick, one in which the sleeping yo-yo is swung from right to left while the string is interrupted by an extended index finger. Momentum carries the yo-yo in a circular path around the finger, but instead of completing the arc the yo-yo falls on the taut string between the performer's hands, where it continues to spin in an upright position. My pleasure at that moment was as much from the beauty of the experiment as from pride. Snapping apart my hands, I sent the yo-yo into the air above my head, bouncing it off nothing, back into my palm.[7]

### EXERCISES

14. Think of some result that is usually arrived at by stages (e.g., developing a conscience, losing one's innocence, understanding computers, becoming an alcoholic). Write a paragraph of process analysis in which you set forth those stages in their usual order.

15. Think of some process that you have mastered or are trying to master (e.g., juggling, cooking an omelet, writing computer programs), and jot down the stages of that process—either the stages of learning it, or, if you prefer, the stages of executing it. Then write a paragraph or two in which you analyze the process by describing those stages as accurately as possible.

16. Think of a general point that could be supported by one of the analyses you wrote for Exercises 14 and 15 (e.g., *There are no shortcuts to learning how to program computers* or *Anyone can become a juggler, but only by mastering the relevant skills in their necessary order*). Submit a paragraph in which you make that point, including as much process analysis as you find necessary for illustration.

## 2g    Present Evidence for a Claim.

The more controversial your idea, the greater your need to back it with **evidence**, or supporting facts, reasons, or authoritative testimony. To supply evidence is not simply to illustrate something by providing instances of it (2c, p. 32), but rather to bring in considerations from any source that will show why your reader ought to reach the same conclusion that you have.

### "Facts and Figures"

When most people think of evidence, they call to mind "facts and figures" —statements and numerical data that are regarded as well established. Though useful evidence goes well beyond such items, they can have a compelling effect on a reader. Suppose, for example, you were intuitively convinced that American blacks are economically much worse off than the usual income figures show. Personal testimony could be affecting, but what you would really need is statistics to support your point. You could discover them in a U.S. Census Bureau report of 1986 which calculated relative *wealth* rather than income. To be sure, the average income of blacks is more than half that of whites. But the *wealth* of blacks— measured as home equity, savings, and personal property—is ten times lower than the wealth of whites. Armed with that finding, you would be able to make your case with confidence.[8]

To see how an array of facts and figures can add weight to a claim, study the following paragraph from an essay advocating that warning labels be placed on alcoholic beverage containers:

> Alcoholism and alcohol abuse are recognized as two of our nation's most serious problems. According to estimates, 18.3 million American adults are "heavy drinkers," which is defined as consuming more than 14 drinks per week. In 1985, over 12 million American adults had one or more symptoms of alcoholism, an increase of 8.2 percent from 1980. In addition, an estimated 3.3 million teen-agers show signs that they may develop serious alcohol-related problems. These statistics are all the more alarming when considered against the staggering human cost involved with drunken driving. In 1984 there were 44,241 traffic fatalities nationwide, 53 percent of which were deemed to be alcohol-related.[9]

This paragraph does not in itself clinch the writer's case for warning labels. Indeed, an opponent might question some of the alleged facts and assumptions and point out that the writer has at most sketched a problem, not proven that warning labels would be the solution to it. Yet his paragraph of statistics does make a strong impression; *something,* we feel, should be done. Moreover, the writer gains standing as a person who has done his homework on the subject.

## Reasoning

an/
arg
2g

When you put forward a challengeable claim, you naturally want to show that "logic is on your side." This does not mean that you have to move stiffly from premises to conclusions, as if you were conducting a formal proof. That way lies tedium for your reader. Simply, you should be ready to appeal to the reader's commonsense grasp of sound reasoning.

Study the following student paragraph, written before Congress repealed the 55-miles-per-hour speed limit:

> Most people believe that the lower speed limit has saved many thousands of lives—but can we be sure? Highway fatalities certainly dropped after the 55-mph limit was imposed in 1974. Yet they have continued to drop in subsequent years, as drivers' speeds have been creeping steadily *upward* toward the old 65-mph norm. This can only mean that other factors—safer cars and roads, less reckless driving habits, mandatory seat belt laws, harsher penalties for drunken driving—have been influencing the statistics. Thus, strictly speaking, we have no way of knowing how much the lower speed limit has actually contributed to safety.

We could restate this writer's reasoning more formally using **syllogisms**, or chains of deduction from premises to conclusions:

Opponents believe:

Premise:      If highway deaths decline, the lower speed limit deserves the credit.

Premise:      Highway deaths have declined.

Conclusion:   Therefore the lower speed limit deserves the credit.

*But:* The lower speed limit has been gradually disregarded by drivers, while deaths have continued to decline. So:

Premise:      If actual speeds have been increasing while deaths have been declining, we cannot say for sure that the lower speed limit is responsible for the savings in lives.

Premise:      Speeds *have* increased, and deaths *have* declined.

Conclusion:   We cannot say for sure that the lower speed limit is responsible for the savings in lives.

Principles of sound reasoning are violated by **fallacies**, or illegitimate shortcuts to a favored conclusion. For the most important fallacies, see 3i–3n, pages 73–79. Learning to detect fallacious reasoning will help you not only to strengthen the evidence for your own conclusions but also to fend off fallaciously based objections.

an/
arg
2g

## Citation of Authority

In theory, the least impressive evidence ought to be the citing of authority; after all, authorities are often proved to have been wrong. In practice, however, we all wisely respect the judgment of people who are better placed than we are for understanding a given issue or technical field. Thus, if a committee of distinguished scientists declares that a proposed weapons system lies beyond the reach of existing technology, we have to be impressed—even if we may harbor some doubts about their unstated political motives. Again, an opponent of placing warning labels on alcoholic beverages (p. 41) could score a telling point by mentioning that the prestigious American Council on Alcoholism *disapproves* of such labeling. Such citation of authority does not by itself win an argument, but it can leave your reader favorably disposed toward your more substantial evidence.

Not all authorities need be prominent figures or councils. For corroboration of your own judgment, you can enlist the opinion of any well-situated and nonpartisan observer. Consider, for example, this writer's quotation of an expert who shares his dismay over the involuntary subjection of mental patients to heavy drug dosages:

> In late 1973, Richard Cole, then a third-year law student at Boston University, arrived with permission to open a legal-services office on the hospital grounds. Soon appointed head of the institute's civil-rights committee, he found no lack of patient interest in his services. According to Mr. Cole, one of the patients' most frequent and disturbing complaints concerned the involuntary administration of antipsychotics. "When patients were treated against their will," says Mr. Cole, now a lawyer at Greater Boston Legal Services in the city's Roxbury section, "they felt their humanity being offended. I have met many former patients who tell me that because of their experience with involuntary treatment and the loss of self-respect and feelings of powerlessness it engendered, they never want to see a psychiatrist again. I think that's sad, because many of them really need some help."[10]

Faced with such a judgment from an informed source, readers who believed that psychiatric patients *should* be treated against their will would probably feel obliged to come up with equally knowledgeable contrary testimony. Thus the writer has used citation of authority to put the ball in his adversaries' court.

EXERCISES

17. Find an article or a chapter that contains an abundance of "facts and figures," and submit a paragraph in which you use some of that factual
information as evidence to support a claim. Use your own language,
not the author's. Hand in a photocopy of the passage or passages you
have drawn upon.

18. Find an article or a chapter that supplies at least three items of evidence
to support a claim. Submit an analysis of the author's reasoning. If you
like, use the syllogism format, as on page 42. Do you find the author's
logic satisfactory? If not, why not? (Consult 3i–3n, pp. 73–79, for logical
fallacies.) Accompany your analysis with a photocopy of the passage or
passages you have assessed.

19. Reread the article(s) or chapter(s) you drew upon for Exercises 17 and
18. Find a statement, written (not quoted) by the author of one piece,
that strikes you as especially convincing and important. Then submit
a paragraph of your own in which you provide evidence for a claim,
including among that evidence a citation of the author's authoritative
statement. (If the previously used sources look unsuitable, find a different one and submit a photocopy of the relevant page.)

## 2h  Handle Objections through Concession and Refutation.

If you think of likely objections to your central claim, you should pause
over them attentively. A writer who simply ignores an opposing reason is
gambling that it won't occur to the reader. But the gamble is risky. A
wiser course would be to grant, or make a **concession** of, minor points
that count against your case and to disprove, or make a **refutation** of,
points that lack merit. The more persuasive-looking and damaging the
objection, the more care you should devote to it.

When you do decide to concede an objection, you must go on to
restore your own positive point of view. Observe the two essential steps in
this passage advocating population control:

> He who says "The earth can support still more people" is always right; for,
> until we reach absolute rock bottom, we can always lower the standard of liv-
> ing another notch and support a larger population. The question is, which do
> we want: the maximum number of people at the minimum standard of living—
> or a smaller number at a comfortable, or even gracious, standard of living?[11]

Always take care to state objections fairly instead of sneering at them. Leave your reader with the impression that you are compelled by fair-mindedness, not by prejudice, to adhere to the judgment you have chosen. Notice, for example, how a student writer calmly summarizes the case against her view and then addresses it with an effective refutation:

**an/
arg
2h**

**objections
are summa-
rized . . .**

Opponents of antismoking laws greet such proposals with several answers, some of which look very impressive at first glance. The new laws would be unenforceable, they say; smoking is an irrational addiction, and millions of smokers would simply defy the law. The government, we are told, should direct its efforts not to hiring Smoke Police but to developing harmless cigarettes. Furthermore, we are reminded that regulation of smoking would cause economic hardship for tobacco growers, advertisers, and people connected with bars and arenas – places where smoking is so customary that a ban on smoking would affect patronage. Above all, the defenders of smoking point out that no studies have yet demonstrated a connection between lung cancer and *accidentally* inhaled smoke. Perhaps, then, we who favor new laws have failed to distinguish between a mere annoyance and a health hazard.

**. . . and then
refuted**

Let us review these arguments in turn. Is it obvious, first of all, that antismoking laws couldn't be enforced? People said the same thing about "pooper scooper" ordinances directed at dog owners, but those ordinances are actually working in New York City and elsewhere. It is not a question of hiring more police, but of using the law to raise consciousness, make violators feel criticized, and bring about voluntary compliance. To say that the government should try to develop safe cigarettes is true but beside the point; we must decide what to do *until* such cigarettes are on the market.

Again, the "hardship" argument has some merit but is not decisive. If smoking did decrease, farmers could be compensated and aided in switching crops; advertisers would surely continue to get cigarette accounts; and bars and arenas could be exempted from the law on the grounds that most of their patrons *voluntarily* expose themselves to smoke. As for the lack of proven connection between second-hand smoke and lung cancer, we should remember that lung cancer is by no means the only disease associated with cigarette smoke. It *has* been proven that people who suffer from heart and respiratory diseases can be seriously affected by a smoke-filled environment. It is these people – not the rest of us who just find smoking distasteful – whose rights are at issue.

**EXERCISES**

20. Reread the paragraph offering "facts and figures" in support of warning labels on alcoholic beverages (p. 41). Regardless of your actual views, think of everything you could say *against* the position taken there. Treating that passage as an objection to your own opinion that the warning labels are a bad idea, submit a paragraph or two answering that objection. You may use both concession and refutation if both seem appropriate.

21. Choose a topic of controversy about which you feel strongly. (It should be unrelated to Exercise 20.) In one sentence, write down your position on that issue. Then list below it as many objections as you can, and place check marks beside the points that you would feel obliged to raise if you were defending your position in an essay. Submit this page of work, and be prepared to explain why you checked certain points instead of others.

22. Write and submit a paragraph or two in which you deal with one of the checked objections (Exercise 21) by means of *concession*. Show your reader that this negative point, though true enough, is less important than another, positive, consideration.

23. Take any of the checked objections (Exercise 21) and submit a paragraph or two in which you *refute* that objection.

## 2i Develop an Analogy.

Think for a moment of the nuclear arms race. A writer who likened that competition to a struggle for trade supremacy would be *comparing* two things that are similar enough to be considered together (2e, p. 35). But suppose, instead, the writer said this: *In their nuclear arms race, the U.S. and the U.S.S.R. are like two people sitting in a pool of gasoline. One of them has seven matches and the other has only five.* [12] That would be an **analogy**—an extended likeness purporting to show that the rule or principle behind one thing also holds for the quite different thing being discussed.

Why bother with analogies when more direct forms of explanation are available? The "arms race" example shows why: a good analogy makes a point vivid, memorable, and easy to comprehend. We immediately see what is foolish about stockpiling matches while sitting in a pool of gasoline, and our minds readily apply that lesson to the arms race. If a nuclear war will engulf both nations in destruction, both should stop "playing with matches."

But this same example also shows the limited force of even the best analogies. An analogy can be persuasive on an emotional or imaginative plane, but it can never prove the intended point. An opponent is always free to brush the analogy aside and talk about factors that the analogizer has left out of account. An advocate of nuclear "parity," for example, could maintain that the theory of deterrence has prevented another world war for over forty years now, whereas the theory of nuclear disarmament faces many untested difficulties. For every analogy urging one side of the case, a contrary analogy could be devised: *The U.S. and the U.S.S.R. are like two people who hate each other but have to act cautiously because they live together in a room full of TNT. The advocates of nuclear disarmament would take away the explosive and leave the adversaries alone with their guns and knives.* Which of the two analogies is "right"? Neither. Both of them are simply means of dramatizing beliefs that rest on other grounds.

Analogies can be used not only to argue but also to make an explanation clearer by putting it in simpler and more pictorial terms. Wherever you are worried that things may be getting too complicated for your reader to follow, you can consider resorting to this device. Here, for example, a writer who is seeking to explain a disastrous conjunction of weather fronts uses the more readily apprehended image of an automobile crashing into a wall:

> The real problem with forecasting the generation of a storm such as this is gauging its severity. It is not like following a fully developed storm for several days as it moves across the ocean, watching it weaken or strengthen with some sort of regularity. It is more like watching a car about to crash into a brick wall; you know there is going to be a crash, there is an 80 percent chance the gas tank will explode, but you don't know how much gas is in the tank! Just as with the car, the measure of a storm's severity is gauged by its ingredients; the existence of a front (the brick wall), the amount of cold air coming down behind the front (speed of the car), and the degree of circulation in the upper air approaching the front (amount of gas in the tank).[13]

Note how carefully this writer has developed the elements of his analogy, drawing out its lesson without pursuing it to the point of tedium or pedantry.

Analogies are much like elaborated figures of speech (ld, p. 16). In analogizing, however, you do not merely liken one thing to something quite different; you extract a rule from that second thing and declare it applicable to the first. Thus analogizing is truly a form of reasoning—though, as we have seen, it works best as a secondary, backup means of making a point.

**EXERCISES**

24. Examine and, in a paragraph or two, evaluate the use of analogy in the following paragraph by a writer who wants the oil industry to be subject to fewer regulations:

> To return to our analogous world of the entertainment industry, we may ask why it is fair that someone earn a fortune because he is born with flexible hips and durable vocal cords. To my knowledge, most people do not chastise entertainers for making a fortune rocking in the jailhouse in blue suede shoes. We accept that market outcome and fuss very little about its equity. Why is it that we place emphasis on political justice in petroleum but not in amusement? When we have answered that question, if we can, and when we have decided to allow petroleum companies and consumers the same rights we grant rock musicians and their audiences, I strongly suspect we will find the public better served.[14]

25. Think of an activity, hobby, sport, or business that you might want to explain to someone who knew nothing about it. Jot down as many analogies as you can think of, and write a paragraph in which you use the most promising-looking of those analogies to make the topic clear to an outsider.

## 2j    Reveal a Pattern in a Text.

What should you do when asked to "analyze" a poem, a short story, a scene from a play, or a passage from a novel? First, you should realize what kind of task is involved: **interpretation**. Interpretation is the making of judgments about the meaning or coherence of a piece of writing, a work of art, or an event or a movement. By its nature, interpretation can never be definitive. Thus, though you will be looking for a way in which the work "hangs together," you must understand that different observers will see other patterns that may be as legitimate as yours. And second, precisely because interpretation is so open-ended, you should gather every clue as to what kind of interpretive analysis is expected. Find out if you are to concentrate on meaning (thematic emphasis) alone or on formal qualities (features of expression such as poetic meter or significant images) as well. Be sure you know whether your instructor wants you to treat the text by itself or to relate it to other texts you have been reading lately.

All good literary interpretations do have one important thing in common: they get down to specifics about the author's language. A work of verbal art is not a direct message — even when it is phrased like one — but a structure of words which arouses a certain range of thoughts and feelings through its manner of expression. The most fundamental advice about interpretation, therefore, is this: *stay close to the text* instead of skipping quickly to your own ideas. If a poem, for example, deals with the sorrow of parting, don't use up space telling about your own sorrows; show your reader how this particular artistic structure makes (or fails to make) its intended effect.

In looking for meaning, read and reread the text in search of its underlying idea. If a certain theme catches your notice, check to see if it recurs. When you find a deliberate insistence, go over the text again in the light of your half-formed interpretation, taking notes on further details that fit the pattern—or that conspicuously don't. (As one example of the kind of evidence you may come across, look again at the "Laertes" paragraph on page 36.)

Another hint: always discuss formal features *in relation to meaning,* not for their own sake. Your reader will have little interest, for example, in a mechanical run-through of a poem's stanza length, rhyme scheme, and meter, yet any one of those qualities could be usefully brought into a wider interpretation. Keep in mind that you are trying to show what is unique, not what is commonplace, about the text.

To get a more concrete idea of how interpreters work, study the two following complete student essays. The first deals with what the writer takes to be the central theme of a famous story.

### MAN'S MORAL BANKRUPTCY

In Joseph Conrad's story "Heart of Darkness," the darkness is apparent in the hearts of men as well as in the unknown and mysterious jungle where nature runs riot. But the evil that is associated with the darkness is entirely man-made; it exists not only in the jungle but outside in the Belgian city and, indeed, on the Thames. Yet in the darkness of the jungle, "moral" man's immorality is made more explicit. This is why Marlow, the story's chief narrator, declares that the darkness, paradoxically, illuminates.

The story begins with the narrator conjuring up images of the glorious past, which break through the foreboding gloom of the sunset. Instead of viewing the scene as Marlow does—as a place of darkness—the narrator speaks of the "unceasing service" of the "tidal current" (p. 252, *Norton Anthology of Short Fiction*). The waters become a fountain of memories, overflowing with majesty—jewels, gold, kings, knights, memories of men and ships, the pride of a nation. But there is another side, the dark side of conquests past, which is all but forgotten, except perhaps by those like Marlow who have been initiated into the degradation accompanying "progress." The gloom of the setting sun reminds Marlow that the site was also once a place of darkness. The

**an/
arg
2j**

town where the threatening darkness lingers overhead was at one time an unknown landmass, a wilderness, with all the savagery of the Dark Continent. The waters of the Thames that saw the likes of Drake and Sir John Franklin were also the waters that carried the invasion of the Romans. Marlow envisions the difficulty the Romans would have had in meeting with the demands of an uncivilized land—the hostile climate, unfriendly natives, the unnavigable terrain, and death. He paints a picture of all the evil lurking in the darkness of the unknown. Thus, a reverse is made in the narrative from the brilliance of history to the dark, gloomy atmosphere of a pre-Drake era.

Marlow has prepared his audience for his own modern-day descent into darkness. He explains that his experience with darkness has somehow illuminated his thoughts. Hence, not only does the darkness become an instrument whereby one learns, but also Marlow implicitly suggests that the darkness exists in the mind. To learn, one must shed light on the mind by seeking truths, or absolutes, via conflicts with evil. Charmed by the memories of childhood and a seemingly self-imposed heavenly mission, Marlow seeks the ideals that remain immutable in a lawless land. As he transports his audience from their "sleepless" port through the nightmares of his voyage, the darkness —and evil—become more and more pronounced. The darkness he so vividly described as an occasion in the past—the Roman invasion—is reenacted in the narrative of his expedition into the Congo.

As he foreshadowed his tale with the example of the Roman conquest of Britain, he foreshadows his own experience with the tale of his predecessor Fresleven. In it there exist all the elements of evil seen previously in the Roman example. Out there, in the center of the jungle, Fresleven is slain by a stab through the heart. The brute savagery, the "robbery and violence" (p. 255) that made the Romans "men enough to face the darkness" (p. 254), is supplemented in the conquest by Fresleven and his company with the introduction of an alleged "noble cause" (p. 257). Thus, the symbolic death: something is wrong at the heart of things here. The gentle, quiet creature Fresleven beats an old man "mercilessly" (p. 257). The darkness that dwells in the interior of Africa is augmented by imported elements. The close conditions of survival and the apparent failure of ideals transform the gentle man Fresleven into a beastly creature, wild to recapture "his self-respect in some way" (p. 257), behaving in the same wanton manner as a Roman two thousand years before.

The first indications that the darkness is in the heart appropriately adumbrate Marlow's next step: his visit to the company headquarters. He describes the city as a "whited sepulchre," an image which suggests evil disguised by falsehoods. And guarding the door of hell are the two knitters of black— dispassionate, heartless creatures who knowingly introduce men into a perdition from whence they are never expected to return. There, Marlow signs a contract—the archetypal contract—with the faceless man, who in retrospect appears more clearly as the devil's disciple. The doors to the devil's house stand invitingly ajar for men like Marlow to slip through the cracks. There is no need for the angel of death to *guard* such structures. The contract is a seemingly meaningless document, since dead men tell no tales, nor do they give away company secrets. The conflicting ceremonies raise the issue of the corruption and evil, the meaninglessness and uselessness, the heartlessness and moral insensibility of the men who constitute the bureaucratic regime. The company doctor exemplifies the same paradox. The man who by the very nature of his profession should exhibit a concern for the physical well-being of his patients examines Marlow while contemplating other things. The "other things" that take precedence over the health of his charges are his enigmatic scientific experiments, which will never reach maturity since the participants all vanish. Like the contract, there is no substance to them; they are as hollow as the men who conduct such ceremonies.

From the heart of darkness – this bureaucratic network of moral dissolution – flows the agent of its conspiracy. All along the coast of Africa, Marlow witnesses inexplicable destruction and waste. The baffling scenes of tax collectors and soldiers disembarking only to drown or to be swallowed up by an unfathomable wilderness, or of the man-of-war stoically shelling the bush while its crew is dying, show the relentless force behind heartless bureaucracy. Priorities seem to be all mixed up, for at every nightmare the people encounter, they simply glide on by as though nothing out of the ordinary had occurred. The facade of moral ideology is gone by the time Marlow reaches the company's station. There, in the middle of the jungle, a white bureaucrat sits in white starched collar and cuffs ruminating over his figures, while outside the ill-clad shadows of natives pass out of existence from starvation and exhaustion. The absolute horror of such a scene no words can possibly paint, and yet they move on with their "objectless blasting" and tireless unconcern (p. 263).

Marlow's only hope for salvation is the work for which he was hired, and as he passes through the jungle toward his steamship at the central station, he encounters the same wanton waste he has seen with growing intensity since he passed through the doors of hell: paths lead nowhere, and men keep up roads that don't exist. Finally, he reaches the central station, the apotheosis of degradation. Faithless pilgrims with long staves wander about praying for ivory. There exists an air of sterility, with men absorbed in the production of nothing. Like the contract and the scientific experiments, everything lacks substance. Even the men appear to Marlow as hollow devils, things without substance. The darkness, now, inhabits the hollowness of men. As Marlow sits in useless occupation, waiting for rivets to repair the steamer, he envisions the elusive Kurtz as being the redeeming man of moral rectitude in the mire of bureaucracy. In the interim, before the arrival of the repair materials, he contemplates how the man of moral ideals – Kurtz – might work once *he* reaches the top of the administration. Will he backslide into the darkness of bureaucracy, or will he resurrect the ideologies of "civilized" man?

The white man went to Africa expecting to find immorality – darkness – in the natives, from which in his ignorance he expected to reclaim them; but what he brought them was worse. The evil side of darkness existed not only in the minds and the hollowness of the white man but in his ideologies as well. The whole moral justification for the white man's actions lay in his conviction that the black man needed improvement, and his moral bankruptcy was exhibited when instead of improving the natives he degraded them. Throughout the story the image of the jungle is one of teeming, burgeoning, riotous, brutal life, which asserts itself implacably against all contrary forces and embodies the power of nature which knows no rules beyond self-preservation and boundless growth. The life of the jungle even invades man's preserves before he is quite done with them; grass grows up through the city streets in Belgium. In the extremity of their suffering, the workers hide in the grove of death; and after the killing of Fresleven the grass grows up through his bones; the irony is that the jungle has reclaimed the white man.[15]

Second, here is an essay written in response to the assignment "Write a comparative analysis of Alfred, Lord Tennyson's 'Crossing the Bar' and Wallace Stevens's 'The Death of a Soldier.' " First, though, the two poems:

**CROSSING THE BAR**

Sunset and evening star,
    And one clear call for me!
And may there be no moaning of the bar,
    When I put out to sea,

But such a tide as moving seems asleep,
    Too full for sound and foam,
When that which drew from out the boundless deep
    Turns again home.

Twilight and evening bell,
    And after that the dark!
And may there be no sadness of farewell,
    When I embark;

For tho' from out our bourne of Time and Place
    The flood may bear me far,
I hope to see my Pilot face to face
    When I have crost the bar.
                                    —Alfred, Lord Tennyson

**THE DEATH OF A SOLDIER**

Life contracts and death is expected,
    As in a season of autumn.
The soldier falls.

He does not become a three-days personage,
Imposing his separation,
Calling for pomp.

Death is absolute and without memorial,
As in a season of autumn,
When the wind stops,

When the wind stops and, over the heavens,
The clouds go, nevertheless,
In their direction.

— Wallace Stevens

## DEATH, WITH AND WITHOUT THE TRIMMINGS

In juxtaposing Tennyson's "Crossing the Bar" and Stevens's "The Death of a Soldier," we get some sense of the chasm separating the late-Victorian era from modern times. The common subject matter—dying and its aftermath, if any—only sharpens the contrast. Tennyson, writing in 1889, makes of death something downright attractive, a peaceful and passive transition to eternal reward. Stevens, writing in the ominous year 1918, has said goodbye to all that. Death, for his soldier, is just itself, the Big Stop that will be followed by nonexistence.

We are told in history courses that World War I struck a heavy blow against Christian faith. These two poems could provide some indirect evidence for that thesis. In 1889 Tennyson can still "hope," at least, that his "Pilot" will welcome him into heaven. But when Stevens says that the soldier "does not become a three-days personage" (is not resurrected like Christ), he is ironically understating the case. An anonymous victim of the so-called Great War will presumably not be in line for any kind of salvation, much less for being made divine. Stevens's indifferent clouds pass, significantly, "over the heavens."

Tennyson's poem has proved far more popular than Stevens's, but sometimes mass appeal can be a sign that a poet has made things too easy for himself. Considered in the light of "The Death of a Soldier," "Crossing the Bar" strikes me as rather sentimental and self-indulgent. The poet says, in effect, *Hold back your tears, everybody; my passing will be nothing more painful or final than floating out through the harbor on an ebb tide.* It sounds humble at first, but on rereading, it comes to seem quite self-centered: "And one clear call for me!" A century's-worth of lulled readers have gladly entertained the daydream that they, too, may be granted such a tasteful exit from this world.

"Lulled" does appear to be the appropriate word. "Crossing the Bar" begins like an incantation, with two strong beats introducing a free-standing phrase that puts us into a dim half-light, and then the incantation is renewed in the exact middle of the poem:

Súnsét añd éveniñg stár,
. . . . . . . . . . . .
Twilíght añd éveniñg béll, . . .

Meanwhile, the very tide "seems asleep," and all the usual agony of real dying is smothered under a drowsy ease, pleasantly "full" and "boundless." This atmosphere really is enchanting—so much so that we aren't bothered by the absurdity of the old poet's asking a sand bar to kindly refrain from "moaning" on his behalf, or by the apparent confusion of his floating out to sea and *then* perhaps coming across the ship's pilot. "Crossing the Bar" is a great emotional success, though of a kind that a conscientious modern poet wouldn't dare to strive for.

"The Death of a Soldier" illustrates the modern reticence and tough-mindedness to an exceptional degree. Victorian self-dramatization is ruled out from the start by Stevens's choice of the third person instead of the first; the poet's own eventual death isn't even remotely contemplated. Until the closing lines, the poem remains pointedly abstract and cold: "Life contracts and death is expected"; "Death is absolute and without memorial." Instead of Tennyson's full boundlessness, we get the barest of reports ("The soldier falls") followed by negation: "He does not become. . . ." All is prosaic here, in contrast to Tennyson's delicately hushed language, predictable rhymes, and mostly regular meter, flowing like the benevolent tide. And though both poets finish every stanza with a very short line, the effects achieved are opposite. Tennyson's stanzas end succinctly because, with the comfort of salvation in view, little more need be said. In "The Death of a Soldier," each stanza seems to "run out of poetry" in the presence of a final nothingness.

But this is not to say that "The Death of a Soldier" lacks artfulness. On the contrary, the poem hinges on a brilliant surprise. The simile "As in a season of autumn" sets up a trite anticipation: the soldier falls, we assume, as do autumn leaves. In the third stanza, with the strange repetition of line 2, we begin to see that something more unusual is brewing: death is somehow like the stopping of autumn *wind*. Only in the final stanza do we grasp why. What matters about death, for Stevens, is not that a life ceases but that everything else proceeds as before: "The clouds go, nevertheless, / In their direction." Thus even the absoluteness of death is, we might say, nothing to write home about.

Why does Stevens repeat the clause "When the wind stops"? I think he is playing a subtle game with us. At the end of stanza 3 we still suppose that everything ends with the hapless soldier's death. Dying, then, is like the sudden stopping of a breeze. But by immediately repeating "When the wind stops" and then *continuing,* the poem catches its breath, as it were, passing right by the soldier's meaningless corpse. Thus "The Death of a Soldier" mirrors its own message by keeping going, nevertheless, in its direction.

Although "The Death of a Soldier" suits my taste better than "Crossing the Bar," it would be unfair to say that Stevens has written the better poem. Each work is well suited to the spirit of its age, and even today many readers must find Tennyson's outlook on death to be not only more reassuring but also more plausible than Stevens's. Each poet offers us a curiously complete experience. Instead of choosing between them, we might do better to grant both poets their initial assumptions—and let the poetry do its expert work on our feelings.

an/
arg
2j

## EXERCISE

26. In several paragraphs, interpret a text chosen by your instructor. First, try to establish what you take to be its meaning or theme, and then show how that meaning is conveyed through particular uses of language.

## NOTES

[1] Richard Dawkins, *The Blind Watchmaker* (New York: Norton, 1986) 6.

[2] Rachel Carson, *Silent Spring* (Boston: Houghton, 1962) 249–50.

[3] "The Buying of America," *Newsweek* 27 Nov. 1978: 78.

[4] Joseph Epstein, *Familiar Territory: Observations on American Life* (New York: Oxford UP, 1979) 159–60.

[5] Robert W. Keidel, letter, *New York Times* 17 July 1986, national ed.: 22.

[6] Robert M. Pirsig, *Zen and the Art of Motorcycle Maintenance: An Inquiry into Values* (New York: Morrow, 1974) 110.

[7] Frank Conroy, *Stop-time* (New York: Viking, 1967) 114–15.

[8] See Peter T. Kilborn, "U.S. Whites Ten Times Wealthier Than Blacks, Census Study Finds," *New York Times* 19 July 1986, national ed.: 1+.

[9] Sen. Strom Thurmond, "Should Congress Pass Legislation to Require Warning Labels on Alcoholic Beverages?" *New York Times* 9 July 1986, national ed.: 8.

[10] Paul S. Appelbaum, "Can Mental Patients Say No to Drugs?" *New York Times Magazine* 21 Mar. 1982: 51.

[11] Garrett Hardin, *The Limits of Altruism: An Ecologist's View of Survival* (Bloomington: Indiana UP, 1977) 58–59.

[12] Adapted from a quotation of Barbara Boxer by Herb Caen, daily column, *San Francisco Chronicle* 27 May 1982: 37.

[13] Rob Mairs, "How the Storm Developed," *Yachting* Nov. 1979: 120.

[14] Edward J. Mitchell, "Oil, Films, and Folklore," *Chevron World* Fall 1978: 25.

[15] Laura A. Morgan, "Man's Moral Bankruptcy," *Student Writers at Work: The Bedford Prizes*, ed. Nancy Sommers and Donald McQuade (New York: St. Martin's, 1984) 106–9.

# II

# COMPOSING WHOLE ESSAYS

3. Developing a Topic and a Thesis

4. Toward a Complete First Draft

5. Revising

## COMPOSING WHOLE ESSAYS

*Having surveyed the main paragraph-by-paragraph strategies that essayists employ to generate the four modes of nonfiction prose, we turn now to the conceiving, drafting, and revising of full essays. In college writing, such essays are rarely descriptive or narrative in purpose. Though we have already seen (Chapter 1) that description and narration can be put to excellent use in any kind of writing, the dominant college strategies are **analysis** and **argument** (Chapter 2). Accordingly, we will focus on them here.*

*In analysis and argument the **thesis**, or central point, is of paramount importance. We will highlight the process of searching for a thesis and refining it (Chapter 3), of using it as a guide in drafting (Chapter 4), and of revising it whenever it begins to unravel (Chapter 5). Nonetheless, these chapters are not meant to dictate just how you must proceed in composing. Think of them rather as putting into an ideal order the problems that good writers typically overcome, sometimes through sudden intuition, sometimes through following an order like the one suggested here, and sometimes through painful reassessment after a draft has gone awry. What finally matters is not that you take a prescribed route toward a viable thesis and organization, but that you persist until you get there.*

# 3

# Developing a Topic and a Thesis

## 3a Recognize the Differences between a Subject Area, a Topic, and a Thesis.

The key to writing a successful college essay is a strong and clear *thesis* — that is, a central idea to which everything else in your essay will contribute. You cannot get by with only a *topic* or, worse, a *subject area*.

### Subject Area

A **subject area** is a large category within which you hope to find your actual topic — the specific question you will address. Thus, if you are asked to "recount a personal experience" or "discuss open admission to college" or "write an essay about *Catch-22*," you have been given not topics but subject areas: a personal experience, open admission to college, *Catch-22*.

### Topic

The **topic** of an essay is the particular, focused issue or phenomenon being addressed. Thus, within the subject area "Open Admission to College," some workable topics might be:

The effect of open admission on "high potential" students

My debt to the policy of open admission

Why did open admission become popular in the late 1960s?

The success (or failure) of open admission

Is open admission a means to social equality?

Notice that these topics take up considerably more words than "Open Admission to College." Potential "topics" that are expressed in few words may be subject areas in disguise.

### Thesis

Your **thesis** is the one ruling idea you are going to propose *about* your topic. Thus a thesis is never material to be investigated. It is always an *assertion*—an idea you will support in the body of your essay. And because it always makes a claim, a thesis lends itself to expression in one clear sentence.

Here is a chart that illustrates the contrast between a subject area, a topic, and a thesis. Notice that two possible theses are given for each topic.

| SUBJECT AREA | TOPIC | THESIS |
|---|---|---|
| Open admission to college | The success of open admission | 1. The success of open admission in my large urban college can be measured by the effectiveness of our basic instruction in reading and writing. |
| | | 2. Unconventional students admitted under a policy of open admission have had a positive influence on the education of traditional students. |
| A personal experience | My night in jail | 1. After my night in jail I will have more respect for prisoners' rights. |
| | | 2. My night in jail helped to make me a safer driver. |

| SUBJECT AREA | TOPIC | THESIS |
|---|---|---|
| Agricultural production | The effect of mechanization on farm employment | 1. The typical farm employee has changed from a migrant laborer to a sophisticated regular with the skills to operate large machines.<br><br>2. Many migrant farm laborers have become the unskilled unemployables of the cities. |
| Civil liberties | Phone tapping as an issue of civil liberties | 1. When government officials place innocent citizens under observation and routinely tap one another's phones, everyone's civil liberties are threatened.<br><br>2. Despite its infringement of civil liberties, phone tapping is the most effective device the government has for procuring evidence in criminal cases. |

topic
3a

**EXERCISE**

1. Each of the following is either a *subject area,* a *topic,* or a *thesis*:

    A. Mass urban transportation
    B. The space shuttle should not be used primarily for military research.
    C. Protection of rape victims from harmful publicity
    D. Network news programs
    E. The return of the convertible car

Submit a whole sheet of paper that you have first marked as follows, leaving ample space between the horizontal lines:

| | Subject Area | Topic | Thesis |
|---|---|---|---|
| A. | | | |
| B. | | | |
| C. | | | |
| D. | | | |
| E. | | | |

For each letter matching the items listed, (a) put a check in the appropriate column, and (b) fill in examples for the two remaining columns. Thus, if you think that item A is a topic, check the "Topic" column and add a related subject area and thesis.

## 3b    Recognize the Flexibility of the Composing Process.

Many students believe that good writing is a matter of sheer inspiration or luck; they furrow their brows and hope that a light bulb will flash over their heads. When it does not, they lose heart. But experienced writers know that good ideas, instead of dropping (or not dropping) from the sky, must be generated by activities that place one thought into relation with another. And one of those activities is writing itself. In the labor of writing you will be forced to zero in on connections, comparisons, contrasts, illustrations, contradictions, and objections, any of which may point you toward a central idea or alter the one you began with.

Thus the finding of that idea, or *thesis,* is not a fixed early stage of the composing process, but a concern that is urgent at first and will probably become urgent again when you run into trouble or realize that a better idea has come into view. The sooner you arrive at a thesis—by any means, including random writing—the better; but your choice will be continually tested until you are ready to type up the final copy of your essay. At any moment you may find yourself having to take more notes, to argue against a point you favored in an early draft, or to throw away whole pages that have been made irrelevant by your improved thesis. Do not imagine that such annoyances set you apart from other writers; they put you in the company of the masters.

So, too, the other "stages of composing" normally leak into one another. Although you cannot complete your organizing, for example, until you have arrived at a thesis, unexpected problems of organization may point the way to a better thesis. Even a simplified diagram of your options at such a moment would look complex:

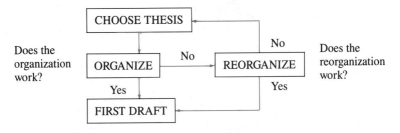

And even the revising of paragraphs for internal unity may prompt a more fundamental change of direction. Writing is almost never a linear process; it typically doubles back on one phase because a later one has opened new perspectives.

Thus, though we will discuss composing as a logical sequence of steps, its actual order in any one instance defies summary. At nearly every point you are free either to move ahead or to reconsider a previous decision. A reasonably ample flow chart for composing, then, would look like this:

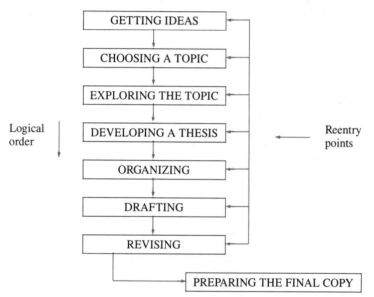

The lesson here is that, wherever your composing hits a snag, it is normal and useful to double back. Such rethinking is nothing to be alarmed about; it is the usual means by which weak ideas and structures give way to stronger ones.

## TOPIC

### 3c    Narrow Your Subject Area.

Once you recognize that you have been given a subject area rather than a topic, you can work toward possible topics by dividing and subdividing the subject area. That maneuver will not in itself present you with a topic.

"Chicago," for instance, is narrower than "Illinois," and "Lakeshore Drive" is narrower still, but all three lack a suitable focus; they remain subject areas because no question has yet been asked about them. Yet the process of breaking a large subject area into several smaller ones may bring such questions into mind.

**topic 3c**

If all you have to go on is the vast subject area "Education," for example, you can start by noting as many *categories* of education as you can. It may help to think of the categories as sets of opposites:

Education:

> private/public
>
> religious/secular
>
> vocational/academic
>
> lower/higher

Which of these categories do you feel most comfortable with? Write it down and run through the categorizing operation again:

Higher education:

> undergraduate/graduate
>
> science/humanities/engineering
>
> privately supported/state-supported/federally supported

Now study each item in your second list and ask what *issues or questions* it raises in your mind. One of them should prove to be an acceptable topic. Thus, if you are looking at *federally supported higher education,* you might ask these questions:

1. How much influence does the government exercise on admission policies?

2. Do professors in a federally supported institution enjoy greater academic freedom than those in a privately supported institution?

3. Has the program of federal loans to students been cut back too far?

4. To what extent can the government insist that men's and women's athletic programs be equally funded?

5. What is the effect of tying federal aid to student responsibilities, such as registering for the draft?

**EXERCISE**

2. Take any subject area other than "education" and subdivide it twice, in the manner of the example above. In your second list, check the item that looks most promising to you, and add three questions about it, each of which might prove to be a good topic. Submit this page of work.

## 3d    Use Notes to Develop Your Thoughts.

You should take notes throughout the composing process, raising previously unforeseen questions, commenting on earlier notes, jotting down changes of plan, and reminding yourself of the next two or three points you ought to cover. Even if you are working from an outline (4e, p. 93), your notes can overrule any segment of it.

When your essay is supposed to deal with an assigned text, your note taking should begin during your reading of the text. Do you own the book? If so, mark it up. Underline passages that look significant and write comments and questions in the margins. Wherever one part of the text helps you to understand another part, make a marginal cross reference such as "see p. 134." And as soon as you have finished reading or, preferably, rereading, get your miscellaneous impressions onto paper so that you can begin dealing with *them* instead of with the whole text. Of course you will need to keep returning to the text, but now you can do so with specific, pointed questions in mind.

Some writers use uniform-sized index cards for all their notes, restricting themselves to one idea per card, but you may prefer full pages of scratch paper. In either case, you can use your notes to quote passages from your reading, record or summarize facts, make comparisons, launch a trial thesis as it occurs to you, express doubts or warnings, or comment on your comments, developing a dialogue of pros and cons.

## 3e    Get Ideas from Your Experience.

Instructors sometimes assign essays of a certain structural type (for example, comparison and contrast) without specifying a subject area or a topic. When you find yourself thus free to choose a topic, think at once about your own interests and areas of special knowledge—activities, skills, attitudes, problems, and unique or typical experiences. The reason is simple:

what doesn't interest you is not likely to engage a reader, whereas it is easy to be convincing when you can draw on firsthand information.

### Reviewing Course Work and Recent Reading

One source of interest may be your course work in composition or any other discipline. Have you come across a significant problem in the assigned reading? If you have been taking notes during class, do the notes contain questions or observations that could lead to a thesis? Wherever you have recorded doubts or strong agreement or connections with ideas of your own, you may have in hand the beginnings of an essay.

So, too, you can search for topics in the books and magazines that happen to be within easy reach. The goal, of course, is not to copy someone else's words or ideas (see 29a, p. 501), but to find an issue that meets up with experience or knowledge or an opinion of your own.

### Keeping a Journal

Your search for ideas will be easier if you keep a *journal*. Unlike a diary, which has no restriction of focus, a journal is a daily record of your experience and thoughts within a certain area. A typical journal, for example, might trace your progress in understanding musical theory or mastering computer skills. Alternatively, it could store your reflections about life in general, your plans and ambitions, your ideas for short stories you hope to write, and so forth. You may even be asked to keep a journal about your efforts and problems in this very course. Whatever material it deals with, a journal can point you toward a topic by reminding you of already developed interests and opinions.

---

### EXERCISES

3. Take some notes reflecting on any recent experience of yours that you think you could make interesting to readers. Submit the notes along with a paragraph developing one idea you have selected from those notes.

4. Writing once a day for a week, keep a journal of your thoughts about any one subject that interests you—a world crisis, for example, or your own work habits, or the problems you face as a student writer. Submit your entries along with a paragraph or two about the experience of journal keeping. Did you find that one day's entry responded to the previous one? Did your ideas become more definite as you went along? Did the

existence of the journal affect the rest of your life in any way? Have you found the possible makings of an essay?

5. Using either cards or pages, take notes on anything you find significant in a piece of writing assigned by your instructor. Submit your notes along with a paragraph that develops one idea you have selected from those notes.

## 3f    Try Freewriting or Brainstorming.

If you have ever told yourself or others, *I don't know what I want to say until I've written it out,* consider yourself normal. Writing *is* a primary way of arriving at ideas, and teachers have increasingly been recognizing that fact. By forcing yourself to hook up nouns and verbs, subjects and predicates, you can draw forth insights that you didn't know you possessed.

You can even begin writing before having any idea of what your topic will be. When you feel stymied, assign yourself a ten- or fifteen-minute stint of **freewriting**. The trick is to put pen to paper at "Go" and to keep writing until "Stop" without pausing between your sentences or fragments of sentences. If you get stuck, just repeat a key word in the last sentence you have written and build a further statement around it. And even if one freewriting session appears to take you nowhere, a second one, started a few minutes later, may pick up on thoughts that were not quite ready for expression in a first effort.

Here, for example, are two passages of freewriting that a student produced in quick succession:

FIRST FREEWRITING:

Well, what do I have to say? Not much it appears! Sitting here "free" writing, so they tell me. How free is freewriting on demand, with the stopwatch ticking? Freedom in general—it always confuses me. I never know whether it's supposed to be freedom to go out and do something you'd like to, or freedom to keep somebody else from doing something mean to you. Anyway, would sure like to be free from freewriting! What is so sacred about exactly ten minutes worth of this stuff? How about nine or eleven? Stuck for ideas—ugh! Well, just keep pushing this pencil until time's up. . . .

SECOND FREEWRITING:

OK, maybe something here after all. Idea of freedom. *Total* freedom is empty, unattractive, boring—we always have something in mind to be free *for*—i.e. something that won't leave us so free any more. E.g., religious freedom usually means spending that freedom on some belief and/or practice – some "service." Or does it? What about unbelievers? I guess they have a right to a freedom that stays negative: no, thanks. . . . But historically, the fighters for freedom have always been people with strong beliefs of their own. Luther, Jefferson, Lincoln, King . . . Maybe an essay here? "Freedom For or Freedom From"?

**topic 3f**

Although neither of these passages has the grammatical completeness and the logical continuity of finished essay prose, and although the writer is clearly uncomfortable with an imposed task, his struggle to keep writing finally yields a likely-looking idea.

---

*With a Word Processor:* To keep yourself from pausing to edit, turn down the brightness control knob for your monitor. Turn it back up again when the time has expired. You may also want to use your computer's alarm function as a stopwatch.

---

Whereas freewriting teases forth ideas by means of our urge to link one sentence with the previous one, **brainstorming** works by the opposite principle, discontinuity. To brainstorm is to toss out suggestions without regard for their connections with one another. Since no development is called for, nothing stands in the way of your leaping from one notion to a completely unrelated one.

You can brainstorm by yourself, listing random words and phrases as they occur to you, scribbling across a notepad, or talking into a tape recorder. Or you can work in a group, either among friends or in the classroom, where the "notepad" is a shared chalkboard. In discussion or reflection, certain ideas will begin to look more fruitful than others – and you are on your way toward a topic.

When brainstorming works, it sometimes evolves naturally into freewriting as one hastily mentioned idea starts to look more interesting than the others:

Freedom / freedom fighters / free-for-alls / freed slaves / "free gifts" / I.e., come-ons for renting (or buying) a car, going to grand opening, etc. What's really free – nothing! Who pays? The customers, of course; extra costs added back into prices. Notice that "free gifts" come only when the customers aren't buying. . . .

By this point the writer already has a clear topic in view: the hidden costs and motives behind "free" merchandise.

## EXERCISE

6. Write freely for ten minutes without planning or pausing. After a brief rest, read what you have written and then write for ten more minutes, this time taking off from any promising-looking idea in the first passage. Submit both passages along with a carefully revised paragraph that turns the second passage into typical essay prose, with consecutive development of a central idea.

topic
3g

## 3g  Test Your Trial Topic.

Once you are sure you have arrived at a topic rather than a subject area, you may feel so relieved that you yearn to start the actual writing of your essay. But that would be a mistake. In the first place, your writing will quickly bog down if you still lack a thesis—a main point that answers the question implied or stated in your topic. And second, how do you know that the first topic to come to mind is the best one for your purpose? Your **trial topic** should stay on probation until you are sure it can pass six tests:

1. Is this trial topic narrow enough?
2. Is it likely to sustain my interest?
3. Is it appropriate to my intended audience?
4. Can it lead to a reasonable thesis?
5. Does it involve enough complexity—enough "parts"—for development at essay length?
6. Do I have enough supporting material to work with?

If, without further thought, you can answer all of these questions positively, consider yourself lucky. More probably, you will need to explore your trial topic by one or more of the following means.

### Focused Freewriting or Brainstorming

If freewriting and brainstorming can lead to preliminary ideas for an essay, they can also help you to explore a trial topic. The same rules apply (see pp. 67–68). The only difference is that now you begin with a definite focus and try to keep it—developing, not miscellaneous thoughts about anything, but specific features of the trial topic. As before, the idea is to set aside worries about correctness of organization and expression and to see what happens.

### Asking Reporters' Questions

**topic 3g**

Another simple yet surprisingly helpful way to expand your view of the trial topic is to run through the standard list of questions reporters are supposed to answer in covering a story: *who? what? when? where? how? why?* Unlike a reporter, of course, you are not trying to make sense of a single event, yet the procedure can work because it keeps returning you to the same material from fresh perspectives.

Suppose your trial topic were the merits of a proposed law that encouraged recycling of glass by requiring a five-cent returnable deposit on all bottles. Asking the six standard reporters' questions, you might come up with answers like these:

*Who?* The elected official of your community or state.

*What?* Pass a law requiring a five-cent deposit on every returnable bottle.

*When?* At the next session of the city council or legislature; law to take effect at start of next calendar year.

*Where?* Only within the boundaries of this community or state.

*How?* Fix penalties for noncompliance by sellers of bottles, give the law wide publicity, warn first offenders, then begin applying penalties.

*Why?* Reduce waste and pollution; raise public consciousness about conservation; cut prices through use of recycled glass.

Any of these brief notes could carry you beyond your first thoughts and lead to an adequately focused thesis. For example, will a five-cent deposit be large enough to ensure returns? Will there be special problems associated with putting the law into effect so soon? If the law applies only within a small geographic area, will consumers take their business elsewhere? Are the penalties for noncompliance too strict? Not strict enough?

### Applying Analytic Strategies

Whether or not you intend to write a whole essay of analysis, you can explore your trial topic by considering it in the light of the classic analytic strategies (Chapter 2), which can hardly fail to stimulate new trains of thought.

*Definition:* How does a law differ from a regulation? A misdemeanor from a felony? What kinds of containers would be included or excluded?

*Division:* What are the separate provisions of the bill? What types of stores would be affected?

topic
3g

*Illustration:* Which communities and states have already established deposit laws? What reports of success or failure are available? Do we have case histories of bottling companies and grocery chains that have accommodated themselves to the law, of individuals who were prosecuted, of others who have made a subsistence living by collecting other people's empty bottles for refund?

*Cause and effect:* What events and trends have made passage of the law likely or unlikely? What differences in consumers' behavior would the law bring about? Would littering be significantly curtailed? In the long run, would prices of bottled products go up or down?

*Comparison and contrast:* In what ways does this law resemble others that have been enacted elsewhere? How does it differ from them? Are the conditions (commercial, political, environmental) in this community or state like those elsewhere, or must special factors be taken into account? Do young and older people hold different views of the law?

*Process analysis:* How will violations of the law come to public notice, arrive at a prosecutor's desk, and be subsequently handled? Does the law allow unknowing violations to be treated differently from outright defiance? If so, at what point would such a difference be recognized? And what flow of payments and reimbursements is expected between the consumer, the grocer, and the distributor?

---

**EXERCISES**

7. Return to Exercise 2, p. 65, and choose one of your "subdivisions" as a trial topic. Submit a paragraph of focused freewriting about that idea.

8. Take another of your "subdivisions" from Exercise 2 and apply the six "reporters' questions" to it. Submit this page of work.

9. Choosing any of your "subdivisions" from Exercise 2, submit a page of notes in which you apply any *three* analytic strategies (definition, division, etc.) to that trial topic, posing questions like those supplied above for the bottle bill.

---

# THESIS

## 3h    Write Out a One-Sentence Trial Thesis.

When you have arrived at a **trial thesis**, or preliminary idea for an essay, put it into one clear sentence that you can then consider from several angles. That sentence may or may not eventually find its way into the body of your essay. Its function for now is to let you make sure that you have *one* central idea—not zero, not two—and that it looks sufficiently challenging and defensible. To these ends it is important that you keep to the one-statement limitation. Though your trial thesis can contain several considerations, one point should control all the others.

Typical trial theses for an essay about instituting a bottle law (p. 70) might be these:

### EXPLANATORY TRIAL THESES:

Increased fear that the environment is becoming polluted and that raw materials are growing scarce has provided broad-based support for laws requiring deposits on returnable bottles.

The passage or failure of bottle-deposit legislation in any given state or community can be directly correlated with the proportion of voters under age thirty.

### ARGUMENTATIVE TRIAL THESES:

The minor inconvenience of paying a deposit and having to return empty bottles to a store is far outweighed by the benefits that all citizens would receive from a well-drafted law requiring the deposits.

A deposit law would not only hurt small business people by adding to their expenses and reducing their sales but also result in more, not less, pollution because of the increased trucking it would require.

None of these four examples is good or bad in itself; everything would depend on whether the writer had appropriate material on hand to make a convincing case. But all four trial theses meet the requirement of presenting just one main idea.

---

### EXERCISE

10. Return to Exercise 9 on page 71. Using the work you did there, submit three trial theses, each making a single statement. Add a paragraph

explaining why one of those trial theses looks more promising to you than the others.

## 3i   Limit the Scope of Your Thesis.

A thesis that quickly proves unworkable may suffer from too broad a scope. Remember that you have only a short essay in which to develop your idea successfully. Instead of discarding a thesis that seems to lead nowhere, try recasting it in narrower terms, replacing vague general concepts with more definite ones.

thesis<br>3i

| TOPIC | THESIS TOO BROAD | THESIS IMPROVED |
|---|---|---|
| The popularity of garage sales | Garage sales reflect the times we live in. | Garage sales circulate goods during periods of high inflation and high unemployment. ["The times" are carefully defined.] |
| A "Star Wars" missile defense system | We need to invest in a "Star Wars" missile defense system. | Although extremely costly, a "Star Wars" missile defense system may be our only safeguard against nuclear war. [Considerations of cost and safeguarding our future are both expressed in the thesis.] |
| Late marriages and the changing American family | Late marriages are creating a different kind of American family life. | Because marriage is often postponed to accommodate careers, Americans are creating a new kind of family in which parents are old enough to be their children's grandparents. [Reason for late marriage and a detailed explanation of "different" belong in the thesis.] |

### Faulty Generalization

When you write out a trial thesis, examine it for telltale danger words like *all, none, no, any, always, never, only,* and *everyone.* Such all-inclusive terms usually signal the presence of **faulty generalization**, the illegitimate extension of *some* instances to cover *all* instances of something. Suppose, for example, you want to argue that *There is no reason to delay immediate adoption of a national health insurance program.* Ask yourself: no reason at all? Will I be anticipating *all* possible reasons in my essay? Perhaps I can avoid unnecessary trouble by making my thesis more modest: *Adoption of a national health insurance program would answer needs urgently felt by the poor, minorities, and the chronically ill.*

You should be especially wary of faulty generalization if you find that you have written a thesis that covers centuries of history or makes sweeping judgments of right and wrong.

DON'T:

x  The decay of our culture has been accelerating every year.

x  The West is guided by Christian morals.

x  The purpose of evolution is to create a higher form of human being.

Encyclopedias of support could not establish the plausibility of such theses. Consider: (1) What universally recognized indicators of "cultural decay" do we have, and how could anyone show that cultural decay has been "accelerating every year"? (2) Can something as vague and various as "the West" be said to be "guided" by certain "morals"? How will the writer explain away all the brutalities of the past twenty centuries? (3) How has the writer been able to discover a purpose hidden from all professional students of evolution?

## Keeping Personal Experience in Perspective

We have said that personal experience can be an important source of ideas for a college essay (3e, p. 65). Yet you should also recognize the risks of generalizing from such experience. If the question, for instance, is whether the human species has an innate aggressive instinct, you may feel inclined to look in your heart and say either yes or no. To do this, however, would be to rely on guesswork and an inadequate sample of just one case. The same lapse occurs when a foreign-born writer asserts, x *The idea that immigrants want to become "Americanized" is contradicted by all experience,* meaning *I, for one, do not want to be "Americanized."* Someone else writes, x *Professors actually enjoy making students suffer,* meaning *I had an ugly experience in History 10.* Personal experience can usefully illustrate a thesis, but the thesis itself should rest on more public grounds.

**EXERCISE**

11. Invent and submit three deliberately defective trial theses that suffer from faulty generalization, including at least one example of overgeneralizing from personal experience. For each defective statement, add a brief explanation of its weakness. Then supply three versions that remedy the problem.

## 3j   Avoid a Weaseling or a Circular Thesis.

A **weaseling thesis** asserts so little that it expresses nothing more than the writer's wish to stay out of trouble.

DON'T:

x  A deposit law is very controversial.

x  Although some people approve of a deposit law, others do not.

To secure interest in your topic you must propose an idea that will require support and illustration to be made convincing. Turn back to 3h, page 72, for "deposit law" theses that do take the necessary degree of risk.

A **circular thesis** doubles back on itself, saying only what is already implied by some of its language.

DON'T:

x  The growing popularity of sports shows that people are more interested in athletics than ever before.

x  Contact sports should be banned because they involve the violent impact of one body on another.

If the popularity shows the popularity, or if contact is bad because it involves contact, the trial thesis is biting its own tail.

DO:

• The growing popularity of sports expresses nostalgia for a more physically challenging existence.

• Contact sports should be banned because they whet an unhealthy appetite for violence and harm.

Whether or not you agree with these revised trial theses, at least they escape circularity.

---

**EXERCISE**

12. Invent and submit two examples each of a weaseling thesis and a circular thesis, and briefly explain what is wrong with each of the four statements. Then supply four satisfactory versions.

---

## 3k   Do Not Beg the Question.

Beware of settling an issue in advance by posing it in "loaded" language. Such **begging the question** (prejudging the issue) is apparent in each of the following argumentative theses.

DON'T:

x A.  It is inadvisable to let hardened criminals out of prison prematurely so that they can renew their war on society.

x B.  Society has no right to lock up the victims of poverty and inequality for indefinite periods, brutalizing them in the name of "rehabilitation."

Writers A and B are addressing the same issue, but each of them has settled it in advance. The word *prematurely* already contains the idea that many convicts are released too soon, and other terms—*hardened criminals, renew their war*—reinforce the point. For writer B there is no such thing as a criminal in the first place. Prisoners have already been defined as *victims,* and imprisonment is equated with *brutalizing.* Similarly, the quotation marks around *rehabilitation* dismiss the possibility that a criminal might be taught to reform. The trouble here is that both writers A and B, in their eagerness to sweep away objections, are portraying themselves as closed-minded. No one will want to read an essay whose very thesis forbids all disagreement.

Of course your thesis should convey an attitude, but it should do so in fair language.

DO:

• A.  The policy of releasing prisoners on probation has not justified the social risks it involves.

• B.  If the goal of prisons is to rehabilitate, the prison system must be considered on balance to be a failure.

Note that these two versions are just as hard-hitting as the ones they replace; the difference is that their language does not beg the question.

---

EXERCISE

13. Invent and submit three defective trial theses that beg the question, and briefly explain what is wrong with each. Add three versions that remedy the problem.

thesis
3m

---

## 3l   Avoid Either-Or Reasoning.

Make sure your thesis does not pull the alarmist trick of **either-or reasoning** – that is, pretending that the only alternative is something awful. Thus a writer favoring legal abortion might claim, x *We must legalize abortion or the world will become disastrously overpopulated,* and a writer on the opposite side might reply, x *We must prevent legal abortion or the family will cease to exist.* Both writers would be delivering an ultimatum. *Which do you choose, overpopulation or legal abortion? What will it be, legal abortion or the survival of the family?* The choice is supposed to be automatic. All a reader must do, however, to escape the bind is to think of one other possibility. Is there no means to control population except through abortion? Might legal abortion have some lesser consequence than the destruction of family life? Your wisest course would be to admit that people favoring an opposite stand from yours have good reasons for their view – reasons that you do not find decisive. If the issue *were* one of total right versus total wrong, you would probably be wasting your time debating it.

---

EXERCISE

14. Invent and submit three defective trial theses that illustrate either-or reasoning, and briefly explain what is wrong with each. Add three versions that remedy the problem.

---

## 3m   Avoid *Post Hoc* Explanation.

Bear in mind that two events or conditions can be associated in time without being related as cause and effect. Perhaps this seems obvious, but most of us become superstitious when partisan feelings or pet beliefs are involved. Democrats claim that Republican administrations "cause" economic recessions; Republicans call their rival "the war party" because most wars have erupted when Democrats were in power; and some people support their beliefs by arguing that their dreams were fulfilled or that a certain result followed their witnessing an unusual phenomenon: "I saw a black cat and then lost control of the car"; "I landed my job after I saw a rainbow." This fallacy goes by its Latin name, *post hoc, ergo propter hoc*: "after this, therefore because of it." It was most memorably exemplified by the Canadian humorist Stephen Leacock: "When I state that my lectures were followed almost immediately by the union of South Africa, the banana riots in Trinidad, and the Turco-Italian war, I think the reader can form some opinion of their importance."

**thesis**
**3n**

POST HOC THESIS:
x Aspirin cures colds, as can be seen from the fact that a cold will disappear just a few days after you begin taking regular doses of aspirin.

REVISED THESIS:
• Though aspirin relieves some cold symptoms, the idea that any currently available medicine "cures" a cold is not supported by evidence.

---

EXERCISE

15. Submit three defective trial theses that illustrate *post hoc* explanation, and briefly explain what is wrong with each. Add three versions that remedy the problem.

---

## 3n  Be Fair to an Opposing Position.

### Misstating the Opposing Case: The Straw Man

In formulating your thesis, be careful not to distort a position contrary to your own. Such distortion creates a so-called **straw man** – that is, an imaginary opponent that can be all too easily knocked over. Thus, if the question is whether students should be allowed to serve on faculty committees, a writer would be creating a straw man with this thesis: *Faculty efforts to keep the student body in a state of perpetual childhood must be resisted.* Here the specific issue – the pros and cons of student participation – has conveniently disappeared behind the straw man of wicked faculty intentions. A fairer thesis would be *If faculty members really want to make informed judgments about conditions on campus, they ought to welcome student voices on their committees.*

## Attacking Personalities: *Ad Hominem* Reasoning

Still another fallacious shortcut is to attack the people who favor a certain position rather than the position itself. This is known as ***ad hominem*** (Latin, "to the man") reasoning. Sometimes such an argument tells us real or invented things about somebody's character or behavior. The implication is that if we disapprove of certain people, we had better reject the idea that has become linked with them. More often the writer simply mentions that a despised faction such as "Communism" or "big business" supports the other side.

DON'T:

x  By now we should all recognize the dangers of national health insurance, a scheme for which subversives have long been agitating.

x  The benefits of home videotaping are obvious to everyone except the money-crazed Hollywood moguls who stand to lose by it.

DO:

• To judge from the British example, national health insurance might impose an intolerable burden on our economy.

• Although movie executives are understandably worried about competition from home videotaping, they would do better to adapt to the new technology instead of trying to have it banned.

As politicians realize, *ad hominem* attacks do often have their desired effect. Because none of us has time to think through the pros and cons of every public issue, we sometimes rely on surface clues; if certain "bad guys" are revealed to be on one side, we automatically favor the other. As citizens, though, we ought to recognize that the *ad hominem* appeal is a form of bullying. And as writers, we ought to get along without the cheap advantage it affords. If you *can* win an argument on its merits, do so; if you cannot, you should change your position or even your whole topic.

---

EXERCISE

16. Invent and submit four unfair trial theses, two creating a straw man and two indulging in *ad hominem* argument. Briefly explain what is wrong with each and add four satisfactory versions.

---

thesis
3o

## 3o   Develop a Full Thesis Statement That Mentions the Most Important Elements in Your Case.

Let us suppose that your thesis is no longer on trial: it has passed the tests of definiteness and reasonable scope, and you are ready to go with it. At this point you would do well to take an extra step that may look unnecessary at first. Cast your thesis into a **full thesis statement** — a sentence that not only names your main point but also includes its most important parts, supplies reasons why that point deserves to be believed, and/or meets objections to it. This statement will probably be long and cumbersome. Never mind: it will *not* appear anywhere in the body of your essay. It is simply a private guide which will help you (a) be completely sure that you are in control of your material and (b) choose a sound organization for your essay's parts (4d, p. 90).

Sometimes your unexpanded thesis will possess the complexity that can carry you into the work of organizing. We have already met one such thesis/thesis statement: *A deposit law would not only hurt small business people by adding to their expenses and reducing their sales but also result in more, not less, pollution because of the increased trucking it would require.* Here we see three crucial factors begging to be made structurally prominent: added expense, reduced sales, increased pollution. The writer is ready to decide on an effective order for these main supporting points.

More often than not, though, a thesis will be too simple in form to serve as a thesis statement. The remedy is to spell out some of the large considerations that made you adopt the thesis in the first place. You can add *main details, reasons,* and/or *objections,* all of which will become prominent units of your organization.

### Including Main Details

Suppose your tested and approved thesis is a sentence as plain as this: *Chinese farming methods differ strikingly from American ones.* Fine — but are you sure you know exactly which differences you will be emphasizing in your essay? Now is the time to clear up any lingering doubt by working those differences into a full thesis statement.

Since you will eventually have to choose an order of presentation for your main details, why not decide right now, as you are drawing up your thesis statement? The final position is generally the most emphatic one, whether the unit be a sentence, a paragraph, or a whole essay. Think, then, about the relative importance of your points and arrange them accordingly within your thesis statement:

**thesis**
**30**

DO:
- Chinese farming differs strikingly from American farming in its greater concern for using all available space, its handling of crop rotation, its higher proportion of natural to manufactured fertilizers, and, above all, its emphasis on mass labor as opposed to advanced machinery.

Here you already have a complete blueprint for a brief essay, which you could begin writing without delay.

### Supplying Reasons

In some theses the main statement does not lend itself to the kind of expansion we have just considered. Yet you can always find more "parts" for your essay—and thus for your full thesis statement—by listing the reasons why you think the thesis deserves to be believed. Suppose, for example, you intend to maintain that *The first year of college often proves to be a depressing one.* That is a fair beginning, but it tells you only that *x proves to be y.* How is a whole paper going to result from such a simple declaration? Ask yourself, then, why or in what ways you find that year typically depressing.

If you tell why in one or more *because* clauses, your thesis statement becomes an organizational blueprint:

- The first year of college often proves to be a depressing one, because many students have moved away from their parents' homes for the first time, because it is painful to be separated from established friends, and because homework and grading are usually more demanding than they were in high school.

Now you have laid out the nature of your analysis: you are reasoning from an effect (depression) to its causes, which you will discuss one by one in your essay.

## Meeting Objections

If your thesis is controversial—and all argumentative theses and many analytic theses are—you should expect to deal with at least one major objection to it. Typically, you will want to handle that point either through **refutation** or through **concession**—that is, either by showing that the objection is wrong or by granting its truth while showing that it does not overrule your thesis (2h, p. 44).

If the objection will be discussed in your essay, it should also appear in your full thesis statement. Include that objection in an *although* clause:

- Although some students find their freshman year exciting and rewarding, many others find it depressing, because they have moved away. . . .

Again, suppose you intend to maintain that the government should not insist on equal expenditures for men's and women's athletic programs in college. You know that to be convincing you will have to blunt the force of at least one strong point on the opposing side. Get that point into your full thesis statement, add your positive reasons, and you are ready to go:

- Although men and women in college should certainly have equal opportunities to participate in sports, the government should not insist on equal expenditures for men's and women's athletic programs, because in colleges where a football program exists it requires disproportionately high expenditures, and because such a program can produce income to support the entire spectrum of men's and women's athletics.

A mouthful! But, again, a thesis statement is only a roadmap, not an excerpt from your essay. You need not try to make it concise. It will succeed in its purpose if it allows you to move confidently to the next phase of planning.

---

### EXERCISES

17. In the left column of a sheet of paper, write out any three of the revised trial theses you prepared for Exercises 11–16. In the right column, write three corresponding *full thesis statements* possessing enough complexity to serve as organizational guides for the writing of brief essays.

thesis
30

18. Submit a full thesis statement whose main details, like those in the expanded "Chinese farming" statement on page 81, give the statement an adequate degree of complexity.

19. Jot down an analytic trial thesis that, like *The first year of college often proves to be a depressing one,* lacks the complexity of a full thesis statement. Then expand that core thesis by surrounding it with an *although* clause and one or more *because* clauses. Hand in your complete thesis statement.

thesis
30

# 4

# Toward a Complete First Draft

Let us suppose that you now have in hand a full thesis statement (3o, p. 80) that has earned your confidence. If you feel quite sure how your essay should develop, you may want to begin your first draft immediately. Some further planning, however, can save you a lot of grief. Even if you think you won't need an outline (4e below), you should pause to think about your expected relation to your audience (pp. 3–4). How will you want to sound—dry and objective, or personally engaged and spontaneous? And will you prefer to make your points straightforwardly or with a measure of ironic detachment? These are questions of voice and stance, with which we begin.

## 4a  Choose between a Personal and an Impersonal Voice.

**Voice** refers to the "self" projected by a given piece of writing. The relevant question to ask is not "what am I really like?" but "what is the nature of this occasion?" For certain occasions you will want to maintain a formal, impersonal air, while for others you will want readers to feel much closer to you as an individual.

Consider the following deliberately impersonal paragraph:

## IMPERSONAL VOICE:

Asked to compare benefits of academic jobs with jobs in government or business, over 90% of humanities graduate students cited greater flexibility in the use of time. Two-thirds or more mentioned freedom to do as one wished, opportunities to experiment with differing life-styles, and ability to flout social conventions. On the down side, one-quarter to two-fifths expressed suspicion that a teaching job would carry less social prestige and less job security. They were divided almost evenly on whether teaching would involve less leisure or more. The chief drawback to the academic career identified by the majority was relatively lower earning power.[1]

draft
4a

The authors of this passage want to show a serious, well-informed audience that they are reliable transmitters of information. They do not refer even distantly to their own experiences, opinions, or feelings; nor do they ask their readers for anything beyond attention to the reported results. In this deliberately neutral prose, "the facts speak for themselves." The absence of intimacy is a deliberate stylistic effect, well suited to the businesslike work of conveying information. Whenever that is your chief purpose — as, for example, in a report of facts you have uncovered or of laboratory results you have obtained — you will want to adopt such an **impersonal voice**.

The following student paragraph illustrates an opposite effect.

## PERSONAL VOICE:

Eating the catered meals they serve on airplanes is always a memorable experience. In the first place, you have to admit it is exciting to open that little carton of salad oil and find a stream of Thousand Islands dressing rocketing onto your blouse. Then, too, where else would you be able to dig into a *perfectly* rectangular chicken? And let's not forget the soggy, lukewarm mushrooms which are accused by the menu of having "smothered" the geometrical bird. They look and taste exactly like the ear jacks that are forever falling off your rented headset. Come to think of it, what *do* they do with those jacks when the flight is over?

This writer, using a **personal voice**, everywhere implies that she is drawing on her private experience, and she insists on an involved response by addressing her reader as an individual: *you have to admit; your blouse; where else would you be able; your rented headset.* Since the "facts" in this passage are not facts at all but witty exaggerations of widely shared inconveniences, the writer wants us to gather that she is saying at least as much about her own wry, mildly cynical attitude toward life as she is about airline food.

By choosing an appropriate voice, you also help to establish the **tone**, or quality of feeling, of your essay, paper, or report. An impersonal voice necessarily carries a dry, factual tone, but a personal voice can be intense, respectful, supportive, fanciful, mocking, worldly, or authoritative, depending on your purpose. Compare the wry tone of the "airline food" passage, for example, with that of the following lines by Martin Luther King, Jr., addressing a "letter" to eight Alabama clergymen who had urged him to proceed cautiously in seeking racial justice. Both voices are personal, but King's tone is noble and angry:

draft
**4a**

> We know through painful experience that freedom is never voluntarily given by the oppressor; it must be demanded by the oppressed. Frankly, I have yet to engage in a direct-action campaign that was "well timed" in the view of those who have not suffered unduly from the disease of segregation. For years now I have heard the word "Wait!" It rings in the ear of every Negro with piercing familiarity. This "Wait" has almost always meant "Never." We must come to see, with one of our distinguished jurists, that "justice too long delayed is justice denied."[2]

Here is the rhetoric of a writer who knows that he cannot bank on much agreement from his immediate readers; after all, they had just written *him* a highly critical letter. Instead of swallowing his feelings, King defiantly stands on his own authority: *I have yet to engage in a direct-action campaign that was "well timed"* and *For years now I have heard the word "Wait!"* He and other black activists *know through painful experience* what the eight timid clergymen will never know about how freedom is won.

## Choice of Governing Pronoun

Notice that the **governing pronoun** you choose for your essay helps to establish a consistent voice. If you call yourself *I*, you are guaranteeing at least a degree of personal emphasis. Even greater intimacy is implied if, like the "airline food" writer, you presume to call your reader *you*. That pronoun can quickly wear out its welcome, however; a reader resents being told exactly what to think and feel. If, like King, you occasionally shift from the personal *I* to the community *we*, you can imply a sense of shared values between yourself and all fair-minded readers. And if you want a strictly formal, impersonal effect, you should refer to yourself rarely, if at all—and then only as a member of the indefinite "editorial" *we*, as in *We shall see below. . . .*

---

**EXERCISE**

1. Using any handy source—for example, a science textbook—locate some facts or ideas that might bear on a controversial topic (creation, evolution, energy development, environmental protection, abortion, foreign aid, etc.). Submit two connected paragraphs dealing with some of that material. In the first, make use of an *impersonal voice*. In the second, continue to develop a position, now using a *personal* voice to indicate your involvement or conviction. Use a change in governing pronoun to help convey the shift in voice.

draft
**4b**

---

## 4b    Generally Prefer a Forthright Stance.

Most essays and nearly all college papers, like the prose of this present book, are meant to be taken "straight." Readers sense that the writer is taking a **forthright stance**—a straightforward, trustworthy rhetorical posture. Thus they assume that the writer is being sincere in making assertions and in endorsing certain attitudes while disapproving of others.

The following paragraph from a freshman essay shows the usual features of the forthright stance:

> When this University switched from quarters to semesters, my first reaction was dismay over my shortened summer. The last spring quarter ended in mid-June; the first fall semester began in August. Was this what the new order would be like—a general speedup? It took me a while to realize that my lost vacation was not a permanent feature of the semester system but a one-time inconvenience. Now that I have survived nearly two whole semesters, I am ready to admit that there is much to be said for the changed calendar. As for vacations, those five weeks of freedom around Christmas have turned my vanished summer into a trivial, faded memory.

Note how this writer, using readily understandable language and maintaining an earnest manner, carefully lays out the reasons why she had first one reaction and then another to the semester system. She gives us no cause to doubt any of her statements.

2. Submit any paragraph of your own prose that uses a forthright stance. You may write a new paragraph or make use of previous work. (Note, however, that you may be asked to modify this same paragraph in Exercise 3, page 90; plan accordingly.)

## 4c   Note the Special Effect of an Ironic Stance.

Once in a while, instead of taking the usual forthright stance (4b), a writer may strike an *ironic stance,* saying one thing in such a way as to express a different or even opposite meaning. **Irony** is delicious when it works and disastrous when it does not. Before practicing it, you should understand what kinds of opportunities and difficulties it typically presents.

Irony can be either subtle or broad and either local or sustained. Local and subtle irony, lasting only for a sentence or two and scarcely striking the reader's attention, can enter into any essay possessing a personal voice (4a). Take, for example, the sentence *Recovery from an all-out nuclear attack would not be quite the routine project that some officials want us to believe.* The irony here, barely noticeable at first, is concentrated on the word *quite.* Taken at face value, the sentence claims that recovery from an all-out nuclear attack would be *almost* routine. But of course the writer means just the reverse—that there would be nothing routine about it. The word *quite* serves two ironic functions, twitting the business-as-usual mentality of the bureaucrats and hinting, through *understatement,* at the unspeakable horror of an actual nuclear attack. After such a sentence, the writer would want to shift to a straightforward stance and paint the gruesome details.

Broad irony, in contrast to the subtle kind, is deliberately outrageous in turning the world upside down to make fun of some disapproved policy or position. We can hardly escape the ironic point, for example, when an opponent of the "Star Wars" program writes:

> To do this we will need a vast array of radars, infrared sensors, and technologies that do not exist. All of this will be controlled by large computers, like the ones used by the telephone company to generate wrong numbers.[3]

In a whole essay of broad irony, the idea is to pretend to take seriously a ridiculous extension of some dubious policy or position and to run through its consequences with seeming enthusiasm. Thus, in the most famous example of broad irony, Jonathan Swift's "A Modest Proposal" suggested that the Irish children who were being starved by English absentee landlords could be profitably butchered and sold as meat for their persecutors' tables. Swift was not of course putting forward any such plan; he was ironically exposing the landlords' inhumanity.

For a modern sample of broad irony, consider the following excerpts from an essay mocking the bewildering options faced by consumers after the breakup of the national telephone monopoly in 1984. The writer pretends that gas and electricity, too, are about to be deregulated:

**draft**
**4c**

> With the proposed breakup of PG&E, many subscribers have been thrown into confusion over exactly *how* it will work once gas and electricity are distributed according to age, sex and zip code. . . .
>
> Using guidelines established in the recent AT&T breakup, the new PG&E will become Gasco and ElectroCorp, with customers billed for each, either by the month or triannually, depending. Those over sixty-five will be billed weekly. . . .
>
> Subscribers to Gasco will have their choice of gas and, in some cases, meter readers. Those with gas ranges and gas heaters can choose between gas piped in from Alaska (more expensive but hotter) and gas that comes directly from local gas lines (more toxic but cheaper). People who use a lot of gas and not much electricity—or vice versa—will be able to decide which of several smaller gas and electric companies they prefer.
>
> Major gas users may find it more economical to forgo Gasco and subscribe to either Big Boy Gas or FumeCo, "no-frills" companies able to supply low-cost gas on a prorated, per-annum, prix-fixe basis. Those with a greater demand for electricity may decide to go with Specific Gas & Electric, which has a twenty-four-hour service that provides energy to customers "by the appliance." Here is how it works. Say you have a washing machine, a gas stove, a TV set, two radios and a canary. When your bill arrives, there will be a separate page for each appliance under 540 milliwicks. . . .
>
> It is, of course, still possible to rent a utility pole or gas main by the month, but it's probably cheaper to buy your own, if you're a regular user of either gas or electricity. The average utility pole costs anywhere from $175 to $250, and comes in various sizes and decorator colors; the most popular is the Evergreen, which clamps onto any standard back-fence jack.
>
> "But I never *bought* a gas main before," you may say. You are not alone. Many people have not, so it's going to mean a period of adjustment for many. Tough.
>
> Most neighborhoods have utility pole and gas main boutiques, where one may drop in and ask to look at the various models available. Or you might want to attend a natural gas show at the Civic Auditorium. No one but you can be the ultimate judge of the *kind* of gas main that will best fit your daily needs. . . .[4]

If you have a fruitful premise to work with—one like "Let's pretend that Irish children can be sold as table meat" or "Let's pretend that energy is going to be deregulated as the phone business was"—you can build a whole essay upon broad irony, working out the various implications of the absurd situation you have created. But if you are just poking fun at others or yourself, you would do well to keep your irony relatively low-keyed. A whole essay taking the stance of the "airplane food" passage (p. 85), for example, would become tiresome.

draft
4d

If you plan to submit an essay of broad irony, check with your instructor first. Many writing assignments have important purposes that cannot be met once you have adopted the broad-ironical stance. Beware of reaching for irony simply because you would rather not fulfill the terms of the assignment.

---

**EXERCISE**

3. Submit a new version of the paragraph you wrote for Exercise 2, now making use of an ironic stance. If you decide to try local ironic touches rather than broad irony throughout, indicate with marginal checks which sentences you expect your reader to take ironically.

---

## 4d    Find the Most Effective Organization for Your Ideas.

The key to arriving at a sound essay structure is to put yourself in your reader's place. Beginning in ignorance, your reader wants to know certain things that fall into a natural order:

1. what is being discussed;

2. what the writer's point is;

3. why objections, if any, to that point are not decisive;

4. on what positive grounds the point should be believed.

As a diagram, then, the most reliable essay structure would look like this:

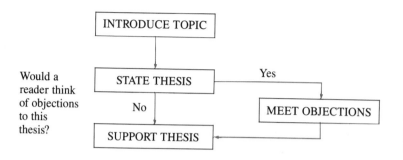

If you try to rearrange this common order, you will find it difficult. How, for example, could a reader want to know the writer's thesis before knowing the issue at stake? Why ask for supporting evidence before knowing what it is evidence *for*? Even the optional part of the sequence, the handling of objections, falls into a logical place. When (as in any argument) it does become important to address objections, the handiest place to do so is right after the thesis has been revealed—for that is where the objections are most likely to occur to the reader and hence to threaten the writer's credibility.

## Using the Full Thesis Statement as a Guide

By following the simplified model just discussed you can derive the structure of a brief essay directly from your full thesis statement.

1. The *topic,* the first element of the model, is known from the thesis statement because it is the question answered by the thesis.

2. The *thesis* is directly named in the thesis statement.

3. If the thesis contains an *although* clause, at least one important *objection* has been isolated.

4. *Because* clauses in the thesis statement specify the final element of structure, the main points of support for the thesis.

## Moving beyond a Fixed Pattern

The principles of organization mentioned above will serve you best if you take them as a starting point rather than as an inflexible guide. There are things the model cannot do—choices you must settle either through a detailed outline (4e) or through problem solving as you struggle with your draft. Specifically, the model

> —does not tell you how to catch a reader's interest;

> —does not say how many objections, if any, you should deal with, or whether they should be met by concession or by refutation (2h, p. 44);

> —does not indicate which analytic strategies you should rely on (Chapter 2);

> —does not say how much space you should devote to any single point; and

> —does not indicate whether you will need a formal concluding paragraph.

Thus your developing sense of problems, opportunities, and paragraph-by-paragraph tactics should be your final guide.

Suppose, for instance, you notice that the best positive evidence for your thesis consists of points that also answer main objections. In that case it would be wasteful to treat objections and supporting evidence separately. Or, again, the decision to include or skip a summary paragraph at the end is a matter of weighing available alternatives. If your essay is long and complex, a conclusion is probably called for. But if you have saved a decisive point of evidence, a revealing incident, or a striking sentence, you may be well advised to end dramatically with that clincher and omit a concluding paragraph.

---

### EXERCISE

4. Suppose you wanted to write essays based on the following five theses. In which instances would you include a discussion of *objections* to the thesis? Briefly justify each of your answers.

   A. Recurrent images of rottenness and disease help to convey Shakespeare's thematic emphasis in *Hamlet.*

   B. In the interest of public safety, Congress should pass a law requiring the installation of restraining air bags in all new automobiles.

   C. Although soccer has grown enormously in popularity, it is still largely boycotted by the major television networks.

   D. The decline of the Roman Empire, so often attributed to loose living and military errors, was in reality caused chiefly by lead poisoning from toxic earthenware.

E.  Airlines should not be held financially liable for problems of hearing loss experienced by people who live close to major airports.

## 4e  Suit an Outline to Your Purpose.

An outline can be an important aid to your composing, but to make good use of it you must first appreciate what it *cannot* do. Briefly, it cannot replace a sound thesis.

Some writers, equating an outline with "good organization," are tempted to go directly from a subject area or topic (3a, p. 59) to an outline:

DON'T:

x Topic: Commercial Airlines
    I.  Relation to Military
    II.  The Jet Age
    III.  Fare Wars in the 1980s
    IV.  Future of the Industry

An analytic or argumentative essay, you recall, must pursue a point from beginning to end. In contrast, the outline above merely identifies assorted subtopics that the writer hopes to cover. It is actually doing the writer a disservice by giving a false appearance of order and purpose. Be sure, then, that any outline of your own is preceded by and derived from a thesis statement. Even if some parts of your outline look like subtopics, you will know that they represent necessary steps in the case you will be making for your thesis.

Competent writers differ greatly in their fondness for an outline. If, like some of them, you find that you simply cannot work from an outline in writing your first draft, you should nevertheless make an outline of that draft when you have finished it. There is no better way of spotting redundancies and inconsistencies that need fixing.

### Scratch Outline

If your essay is going to be brief and you simply need to decide on an order for several paragraphs, you will be adequately served by a **scratch outline**—that is, one showing no subordination of some points to others.

Suppose, for instance, you had hit upon the following thesis statement for an analytic 600-word essay: *Although television and radio both cover*

*news developments and sports events, their styles are necessarily differ-*
*ent, TV leaning toward "editorial" and radio toward "reportorial" coverage.*
A serviceable scratch outline of your paragraphs might look like this:

1. TV and radio cover many of the same happenings, e.g., news developments and sports events.

2. Thesis: But the two styles differ. Because TV can show what radio
   has to describe, TV has more air time to comment on events.

3. News developments (film clips of speeches, interviews, battles,
   election returns, etc.): only on TV are the events partly allowed to
   speak for themselves, with occasional or follow-up commentary by
   news analysts.

4. Sports events: TV, relatively free from reporting what is happening,
   includes more commentary than radio does.

5. In summary: TV coverage doesn't abolish the spoken word, but
   because we can *see,* the balance tips toward "editorial" as opposed
   to radio's "reportorial" coverage.

## Subordinated Outline

For longer and more complex essays you may want to use a **subordinated
outline**—one that shows, through indention and more than one set of
numbers, that some points are more important than others.

Suppose, for instance, you had decided to write a thousand-word argument opposing rent control of off-campus housing, and you were satisfied
with the following thesis statement: *Although off-campus rent control is
aimed at securing reasonable rents for students, it would actually produce
four undesirable effects: establishment of an expensive, permanent rent-
control bureaucracy; landlord neglect of rental property; a shortage of
available units; and a freezing of currently excessive rents.* Knowing that
your argument would be fairly complex, you might want to draw up a
full outline:

I. The Problem Is That Students Now Face Hardships in Securing Adequate
   Housing.
   A. Students are currently subject to rent gouging.
   B. High rents force many students to live far from campus.

II. The Promise Is That Rent Control Will Guarantee Reasonable Rents near
    Campus.

III. The Reality Is That the Actual Effects of Rent Control Would Be Undesirable.
  A. An expensive, permanent rent-control bureaucracy would be established.
  B. Landlords would neglect rent-controlled property.
  C. The shortage of units would *worsen,* because:
     1. Owners would have no incentive to increase the number of rental units.
     2. Competition for rent-frozen units would be more intense.
  D. Currently excessive rents would be frozen, thus ruling out any possible reduction.

draft
4e

Notice that this outline establishes three degrees of importance among your ideas. The Roman numerals running down the left margin point to the underlying structure of the essay, a movement from problem to promise to reality. These main categories come straight from the thesis statement. The *problem* is the topic itself; the *promise* is the "although" consideration, which is taken care of early; and the *reality,* the thesis itself, consists of the "four undesirable effects" of off-campus rent control.

At the next level of subordination, the indented capital letters introduce ideas that contribute to these larger units. The problem, says Part I of the outline, has two aspects: rent gouging and the forcing of students to seek lower rents far from campus. By listing those aspects as *A* and *B,* you assign them parallel or roughly equivalent status in your argument.

Points A through D in Part III are also parallel, but one of them, C, is supported in turn by two narrower points. By assigning those two points Arabic numerals and by a further indention from the left margin, you indicate to yourself that these considerations go to prove the larger idea just above them. Thus the three sets of numbering/lettering and the three degrees of indention display the whole logic of your essay.

## Sentence versus Topic Outline

The example just given is a **sentence outline**, using complete sentences to state every planned idea. A sentence outline is the safest kind, because its complete statements ensure that you will be making assertions, not just touching on subjects, in every part of your essay.

But if you are confident of keeping your full points in mind, you can use the simpler **topic outline**, replacing sentences with concise phrases:

I. The Problem
  A. Rent Gouging
  B. Students Forced to Live Far from Campus (etc.)

The form you choose for an outline is hardly an earthshaking matter; just be sure the outline gives you enough direction, and do not waste time making it more intricate and hairsplitting than your essay itself will be.

## Keeping Outline Categories in Logical Relation

**draft
4e**

If you do use subordination in an outline, observe that one heading or subheading should always have at least one mate—no *I* without *II*, no *A* without *B*. The reason is that headings and subheadings represent divisions of a larger unit, either a more general point or the thesis of the whole essay. It is of course impossible to divide something into just one part. If you have a lonesome *A* in a draft outline, work it into the larger category:

ILLOGICAL:

x  I. Problems
     A.  Excessive Noise

  II. Cost Factors
     A.  Overruns

BETTER:

•  I. Problems of Excessive Noise

  II. Cost Overruns

In addition, you should always check a draft outline to make sure that all the subheadings under a given heading logically contribute to it. Do not try to tuck in irrelevant items just because you find no other place for them; that would defeat the whole purpose of outlining, which is to keep your essay coherent and logical in moving from one idea to the next.

*With a Word Processor:* If your word-processing program allows you to place "windows" on the screen beside your developing draft, fill one window with your outline. Consult the outline as you proceed from paragraph to paragraph. When you see that your essay must deviate from the outline (4f), stop to revise the entire rest of the outline, double-checking it for coherence.

---

5. For any of the theses appearing in Exercise 4 (pp. 92–93), submit a full thesis statement (3o, p. 80) and a scratch outline for an essay.

6. Submit a subordinated sentence outline and a subordinated topic outline that would constitute two fuller alternatives to the scratch outline you prepared for Exercise 5.

draft
**4f**

7. Suppose you have been taking notes for an essay defending the private automobile against those who regard it as a social menace. Your notes include the following miscellaneous statements:

We could find new fuels and impose limits on horsepower.

Cars waste precious energy.

We don't have to make all-or-nothing choices between private cars and mass transit.

Congestion and smog are real problems.

Cars give people initiative and individualism.

Thousands of people are killed every year in traffic accidents.

Without cars, no one could live outside major population centers.

The government can require stricter safety standards.

Abolish the dangers and inconveniences, not the cars themselves.

Using some or all of these statements—and a few more, if you like—write a full thesis statement for your essay, and submit that thesis statement along with a subordinated outline of the type (sentence or topic) preferred by your instructor.

---

## 4f    Mix Improvising with Planning in Writing Your First Draft.

Even after much preparation, you may feel some resistance to committing your first draft to paper. If the opening paragraph looms as an especially big obstacle, try skipping it and starting with a later one. If you seem to be losing momentum in the middle of a sentence, shift into a private short-hand that will keep you from worrying about the fine points of expression; you can return to them later. And instead of writing, you may find it easier to talk into a tape recorder and then transcribe the better parts. Whether you write or dictate, do not be afraid to include too much, to leave blank spaces, or to commit errors of usage and punctuation. What matters is that you move ahead, understanding that you will have a substantial job of revision to do (Chapter 5).

Do not be alarmed if you find new possibilities coming into view as you finish one sentence and struggle to begin the next one. Some of your best ideas—perhaps even a radically improved thesis—can be generated by that friction between the written sentence and the not-yet-written one. So long as you anticipate the need to reconsider and reorganize after your first draft is complete, the tug of war between plans and inspirations should result in a subtler, more engaging paper than you originally expected to submit.

**draft
4f**

---

### NOTES

[1] Ernest R. May and Dorothy G. Blaney, *Careers for Humanists* (New York: Academic, 1981) 71.

[2] Martin Luther King, Jr., *Why We Can't Wait* (New York: Harper, 1964) 82–81.

[3] Fred Reed, "The Star Wars Swindle: Hawking Nuclear Snake Oil," *Harper's* May 1986: 39.

[4] Gerald Nachman, "Your Home Guide to Energy Divestiture," *San Francisco Chronicle* 25 Mar. 1984, Sunday Punch: 2.

# 5

# Revising

## 5a Anticipating the Need to Revise.

Many students are willing enough to revise their work but are held back by two misconceptions. First, they suppose that revision begins only when an essay is nearly ready to be turned in; and second, they think that revision involves only a tidying up of word choice, spelling, punctuation, and usage. But experienced writers revise their prose even while they are first producing it—adding, deleting, replacing, and rearranging material at every opportunity (3b, p. 62). They never assume that any given draft will be the last one. And they stand ready to make conceptual and organizational changes as well as editorial ones.

### Seeking Responses to a Draft

If you could put a draft aside for a week or two, you would see flaws in it that a quick reading cannot uncover. Unfortunately, student writers rarely have that luxury. But perhaps a classmate, a roommate, a writing lab tutor, or your instructor may be willing to advise you about needed revisions. You, of course, must be the final judge of which advice to take and which to disregard as unreliable. Yet by posing key questions, you can actually oblige people to give you their best judgment. Ask them:

1. Can you accurately state my thesis?

2. What is the main impression (positive or negative) my essay has made on you?

3. Have I left you with any unanswered questions? If so, what are they?

4. What points need further – or less – development?

5. Are my opening and closing paragraphs effective?

6. Which words strike you as "off" in meaning, tone, correctness of usage, or spelling?

rev
5b

These questions form only a fraction of the checklist you should apply to your own work (5i, p. 120), but anyone who addresses all of them will be doing you a considerable favor.

---

### EXERCISE

1. Show one of your drafts to a classmate, friend, or roommate, and ask for an evaluation of strong and weak points. Return to the draft, and see where you agree and disagree with your helper. Then submit two or three paragraphs explaining what, if anything, you have learned from this seeking out of criticism. Were the criticisms always justified? Did friendship interfere with frankness? Do you expect to make use of such "peer judgment" in the future?

---

## 5b   Attend to Conceptual and Organizational Revision.

Because sentence-by-sentence composing often leads to new ideas (4f, p. 97), you must read through your completed draft to be sure it makes a consistent impression. Do not hesitate to alter your thesis or even reverse it if you become more swayed by objections than by supporting points. Such a shift can be painful and time-consuming, but in the long run it will spare you many hours of trying to show interest in ideas that you now consider fatally weak.

You should be prepared to make less sweeping conceptual changes as well. Have you exaggerated your claims? Are your explanations clear? Do you need to supply more evidence? Give your conceptual revisions top priority; there is no reason to tinker with phraseology if the whole direction of your essay has to be changed.

After you have made necessary changes in your ideas, check your draft to see if your points appear in a logical and persuasive order. Have you placed your thesis prominently? Have you waited to unveil it until you have attracted the reader's interest and clearly identified the topic? Have you avoided digressions, or passages that stray from the issue at hand? Have you avoided redundancy, or needless repetition of assertions? Are all of your quotations succinct and necessary? And have you included all necessary information—for example, the setting for your discussion of an event, the rules of a little-known game, or the plot of an unassigned novel? Here as elsewhere the key to successful revision is to "play reader" and probe for sources of puzzlement or dissatisfaction.

rev
5c

## 5c    Revise to Ensure a Reasonable Tone.

The **tone**, or quality of feeling, conveyed by an essay can be somber or playful, formal or informal, earnest or droll, excited or deliberate, angry or appreciative. But whatever tone you are aiming for, you must check your draft to see that you have sustained it throughout.

Tone is not something to fuss about in the early stages of writing an essay. Once you have finished a draft, however, try to reread it as if you didn't know the writer, and ask yourself, "What is this person's mood?" Frequent underlinings, dashes, and exclamation points, for example, are signs of excitement. Is that the effect you want to create in the final version? In revising, you may decide you would rather show composure and control. On the other hand, if your draft sounds like the work of a bored and listless writer, you can look for ways of showing more engagement.

### Avoiding Emotionalism

Strong emotions have their place in essay rhetoric. Sometimes, for example, righteous sarcasm works better than a studiously neutral weighing of pros and cons—provided the writer can count on the reader's sympathy. Hence the abrupt and cutting tone in much commentary found in magazines whose audience consists of a single political faction. But in college writing there is rarely a good reason for sounding as if you couldn't possibly be wrong.

The chief threat to an adequately controlled tone comes not from strong emotions but from **emotionalism**, the condition of someone who is too upset to think clearly. Compare, for instance, the following passages:

x  A. The slaughter of whales is butchery pure and simple! Can you imagine
    anything more grotesque than the hideous, tortured death of a whale, shot

with a grenade-tipped harpoon that *explodes* deep inside its body? *And for what?* Why the sadistic murder? Because certain profiteers want to turn the gentlest creature on this planet into *crayons, lipstick, shoe polish, fertilizer, margarine,* and *pet food,* for God's sake! If this doesn't make you sick—well, all I can say is that you must be ripping off some of those obscene profits yourself.

rev
5c

The second passage shows at least as much conviction—probably more—but the emotionalism of passage A is nowhere to be seen:

- B. The killing of a whale at sea isn't pleasant to witness or even to contemplate. Hunted down through sonar and other highly specialized equipment, the whale has no more chance of escape than a steer in a slaughterhouse. The manner of his death, however, is very different. A grenade-tipped harpoon explodes deep within his body, often causing prolonged suffering before the gentle giant, whose intelligence may be second only to our own, is reduced to a carcass ready for processing into crayons, lipstick, shoe polish, fertilizer, margarine, and pet food.

    The inhumane manner of death, however, is the least part of the scandal known as the whaling industry. Much more important is the fact that the killing is quite unnecessary. Adequate substitutes exist for every single use to which whale carcasses are currently put, and although some 32,000 whales are killed every year, the sum of commodities they provide is insignificant in the world's economy. Indeed, two already wealthy nations, Russia and Japan, account for eighty percent of all the whales "harvested" annually. Though the Japanese claim that whale meat is a vital source of protein for them, less than one percent of the Japanese protein diet actually comes from that source. Yet the slaughter goes on unchecked. The alarming truth is that one of the noblest species on earth is being pressed toward extinction for no justifiable reason.

If you already agree with the author of passage A, you may find yourself aroused by his overemphatic prose. In that case nothing has been gained or lost. If you disagree, you find yourself insulted as a profiteer. And if you are neutral, wondering which side possesses the strongest argument, you may notice how little relevant information is being offered. Should whaling be stopped because of the mere fact that whales are slaughtered and turned into commodities? So are many other animals. In his outrage the writer has neglected to supply a reasoned analysis that would keep him from being regarded as a sentimentalist.

The measured language of passage B is much more effective than the exclamations and italics of passage A. Take the description of a whale's death: we see, not the writer emoting over the fact, but the fact itself, which becomes more impressive without the signs of agitation. Similarly, by not calling special attention to the list of commodities from *crayons* through *pet food,* passage B achieves a powerful quality of **understatement**, whereby the mere reality appears more expressive than any editorializing about it would be. And above all, note that writer B provides detailed evidence for the belief that whale slaughter, whether or not it revolts us, is economically unnecessary. In reading passage A, our only options are to share or reject a fit of temper. But even if we lean at first toward a pro-whaling stance, we find it hard to dismiss writer B's objectively reported facts. Here and elsewhere, reasons prove to be not just fairer but also more persuasive than fits of sentiment.

The problem of maintaining a fair tone will probably be most acute when you are coping with objections to your thesis. See 3n, p. 78.

rev
5c

---

## EXERCISES

2. Here are three passages illustrating very different tones:

   A. Yes, you CAN stop drinking! I tell you it's really possible! The fact that you're reading these words means that you have the MOTIVATION, the WILL POWER, to make the change now—*today!*—and to STAY ON THE WAGON FOREVER!! Think and believe, *I am just as good as everybody else! I don't NEED that bottle!* It's really true. You have more potential than the HYDROGEN BOMB! Just take yourself in hand *today,* and by tomorrow you'll start feeling like a NEW PERSON—the person that you really are inside!

   B. While it has seemed probable that addiction to alcohol is at least in part due to the development of physiological tolerance to the drug, there have been to date no clear demonstrations that alterations in the blood level of alcohol alone (without concomitant experiential factors of taste and ingestion) were sufficient to produce a lasting enhancement of alcohol preference subsequent to treatment. Here we report a method capable of producing a lasting enhancement of alcohol preference without concomitant oral stimulation. . . .

   This enhancement of preference has been achieved by prolonged passive infusion of alcohol into the stomach of rats. After recovery from surgical preparation, the rats were placed in a Bowman restrainer cage to adapt for 24 hours. After this initial period each rat was connected to a pump. . . .[1]

   C. A man who once developed printed circuits for computers begs on street corners for enough coins to buy another bottle of cheap port. A woman whose husband walked out when she couldn't stop drinking at home sits stupefied on a park bench, nodding senselessly at passers-by. An anxious teenager raids her parents' liquor closet at every opportunity. These people, though they have never met, suffer from the same misfortune. If they were placed together in a room, each of them might recognize the others as alcoholics. Yet what they have most in common is their inability to see *themselves* as alcoholics—and this is the very worst symptom of their disease. For until the alcoholic's self-deception can be broken down, not even the most drastic cure has a chance of success.

Study passages A, B, and C, and then submit an essay in which you discuss their differences of tone, pointing to specific uses of language in each case. Include an assessment of each writer's probable audience and purpose.

3. The following passage may serve as an extreme example of emotionalism in prose:

Supermarket prices are a damn ripoff! The middlemen and store managers take us customers for a bunch of suckers! Hamburger "extended" with soybeans but labeled as pure meat costs more than steak did a few years ago! Hey, man, don't try to tell me it's just inflation! The filthy con artists shake you down for all you're worth! "Specials" in bins turn out to cost more per item than the cans on the shelves, for God's sake! I've *had* it with those dudes! Have you seen the way they put candy right by the checkout counter, where your kid will grab it and throw a tantrum if you don't buy it?

Write a paragraph of your own in which you express some or all of this writer's grievances, but in a tone suitable for a typical college essay.

## 5d    Revise to Arouse Your Reader's Curiosity.

Once you have finished a draft, you will want to polish the opening sentences and paragraphs of your essay to make them enticing. A good introductory paragraph customarily accomplishes three things. It catches your reader's interest; it establishes your voice and stance (4a–4c, pp. 84–90); and—usually but not always—it reveals the one central matter you are going to address. Only in a very brief essay would a shrewd writer begin by blurting out the thesis and immediately defending it. The standard function of an introduction is to *move toward* disclosure of the thesis in a way that makes your reader want to come along.

### Avoiding the Deadly Opener

An experienced reader can usually tell after two or three sentences whether the writer commands the topic and will be able to make it attractive. Whatever else you do, never slip your reader one of the following classic sleeping pills:

1. *The solemn platitude:*

x Conservation is a very important topic now that everyone is so interested in ecology.

Ask yourself if *you* would continue reading an essay that began with such a colorless sentence.

2. *The unneeded dictionary definition:*

x The poem I have been asked to analyze is about lying. What is lying? According to *Webster's Eighth New College Dictionary,* to lie is "1: to make an untrue statement with intent to deceive; 2: to create a false or misleading impression."

Ask yourself if your reader is actually in the dark about the meaning of the word you are tempted to define. *Lie* obviously fails that test.

3. *Restatement of the assignment, usually with an unenthusiastic declaration of enthusiasm:*

x It is interesting to study editorials in order to see whether they contain "loaded" language.

If you are actually interested, you would do well to *show* interest by beginning with a thoughtful observation.

4. *The bald statement of the thesis:*

x In this essay I will prove that fast-food restaurants are taking the pleasure out of eating.

But you are also taking the pleasure out of reading. You want to *approach* your thesis, not drop it on the reader's foot like a bowling ball that has slipped out of your grasp.

5. *The "little me" apology:*

x After just eighteen years on this earth, I doubt that I have acquired enough experience to say very much about the purpose of a college education.

Is this going to whet your reader's appetite for the points that follow?

### Using a Funnel Opener

One common device for introducing a topic or thesis is the so-called **funnel opener**. This paragraph begins with an assertion that covers a broader area than your topic will; it is an "umbrella sentence," giving your reader a wide perspective and a context for understanding the actual topic when it is stated. Then in subsequent sentences the funnel opener narrows to the topic or thesis, which is usually revealed at or near the end of the paragraph.

The following example shows the pattern:

> Only a few politicians have taken a craftsman's pride in self-expression, and fewer still—Caesar, Lord Clarendon, Winston Churchill, De Gaulle—have been equally successful in politics and authorship. Of these, Churchill may be the most interesting, for he was not only among the most voluminous of writers, but also commented freely on the art of writing. He was, in fact, a writer before becoming a politician.[2]

By the end of this paragraph we know that the topic will be Churchill's writing, but we arrive at that knowledge by sliding down the funnel:

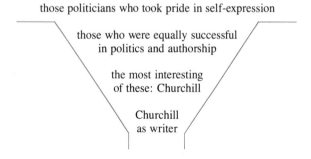

those politicians who took pride in self-expression

those who were equally successful
in politics and authorship

the most interesting
of these: Churchill

Churchill
as writer

You can also get a "modified funnel" effect without such steady narrowing. Just place your topic or thesis last in a sequence of items that establish your voice and tone (4a–4c, pp. 84–90):

> One can find many ways to have fun in west Texas. Some people sit on their front porches and count the number of cars with only one headlight that go by. Others see how far they can throw bottle caps. It is considered a lot of fun to go to a church bake sale to discover who bought a pie from the grocery store instead of baking one. Despite continual warnings from the area's religious and moral leaders, a small minority of west Texans embrace darker pursuits. Of such pursuits, none is darker or more dangerous than dancing in honky-tonks.[3]

The examples of "fun" preceding the main one, honky-tonk dancing, show that an ironic effect (4c, p. 88) is intended.

## Using a Baited Opener

A **baited opener** is an introduction that teases the reader by withholding a clear sense of the essay's topic. We are drawn ahead in the hope of getting our bearings:

rev
5d

> Natasha Crowe, a close acquaintance of mine, recently received an unsolicited invitation from Joanne Black, senior vice president of the American Express Co.'s Card Division. "Quite frankly," the letter began, "the American Express Card is not for everyone. And not everyone who applies for Card membership is approved." Tasha (as she is affectionately called) ignored the letter. A few weeks later she received a follow-up offer from a different vice president, Scott P. Marks Jr. "Quite frankly," Mr. Marks reminded her, "not everyone is invited to apply for the American Express Card. And rarer still are those who receive a personal invitation the second time."
>
> Despite the honor, Tasha has continued to disregard this and similar invitations she has lately been receiving. For one thing, she has no job. Her savings are minimal. Her credit history is essentially a vacuum and therefore her credit rating, I'd imagine, is lousy. She doesn't even speak English. She's my cat, and I love her.[4]

## Sharpening the Opening Sentence

If your first paragraph is the most important one, its first sentence is your most important sentence as well. When that sentence betrays boredom or confusion, you reduce your chances of gaining the reader's sympathy. If it is crisp and tight and energetic, its momentum can carry you through the next few sentences at least. This is why some people take pains to make that first sentence *epigrammatic* – pointed and memorable. Thus one writer begins a review of a book about Jewish immigrants by declaring:

> The first generation tries to retain as much as possible, the second to forget, the third to remember.[5]

Another wittily begins an essay on divorce:

> There was a time when a woman customarily had a baby after one year of marriage; now she has a book after one year of divorce.[6]

And a student writer advocating gun control begins:

> Thousands of people in this country could make an overwhelming case for the banning of handguns, except for one inconvenient fact: they aren't so much *in* the country as *under* it, abruptly sent to their graves with no chance to protest or dissuade. Arguing with a gun nut may be futile, but have you ever tried arguing with a gun?

rev
5e

### EXERCISES

4. Look through the essays you have already written for this or any other course, and find a first paragraph that you would now regard as a "deadly opener" (pp. 104–105). If you cannot find one, choose the weakest opening paragraph you have handy. Copy and submit it along with a revised version that leads engagingly toward your thesis. Briefly explain what was wrong with the first version and why the second is better.

5. Suppose you have been asked to write an essay about any topic of your choice. Pick a topic that you know quite well, and take notes on the way that topic relates to larger ones. (For example, if the topic is a meltdown of a nuclear reactor, think of such an event as one particular kind of disaster among all the possible other ones.) Using your sense of these broader relations, write and submit a funnel opener for your essay, beginning on the broadest level and narrowing to your actual topic. Give your reader a sense of what is special and important about your topic.

6. Taking any topic you find congenial (including the one used in Exercise 5), submit a baited opener for an essay.

## 5e    Revise for Clear Linkage between Your Paragraphs.

When you have a draft essay in hand, look through it with special attention to the last sentence of each paragraph and the first sentence of the following one. As a reader, do you find a smooth and prominent connection between the two? Of course your paragraphs as total structures must actually *be* logically consecutive; that is a matter of organizational revision (5b, p. 100). But if the connections are hidden, you can bring them to the surface by means of appropriate signals.

Look ahead to points 6b and 6c, pages 144–148. There you will find some classic ways of hooking one sentence into the previous one. Exactly the same devices, used near the outset of a new paragraph, can bring out its tie with the preceding one.

Note, for instance, how the sample essay on pages 130–134 frequently "answers" the end of one paragraph with the beginning of the next one:

> We pass by, disappointed and vaguely bothered.
>      And perhaps vaguely envious as well. . . .

> Why, then, is there something unsettling about watching her electronic trance?
>      I can only answer for myself. . . .

rev
5e

> In particular, I am worried about three implications of the headset vogue: a growing dependency on artificial means of staying calm, decreased contact with reality, and a corresponding shrinkage of concern for other people.
>      First, the matter of dependency. . . .

> For Sally, in contrast, the music *is* the action; reality will get through to her only when it is compatible with her mental Muzak.
>      But what worries me most about the headphone wearers is their social — and therefore political — indifference. . . .

> One can always raise the volume if the world's troubles approach too near.
>      Of course I am overdramatizing here; we are not yet a nation of callous zombies. . . .

### Enumeration

One rather formal but occasionally helpful way of linking paragraphs is to enumerate points that have been forecast at the end of the earlier paragraph. If you assert, for example, that there are three reasons for favoring a certain proposal or four factors that must be borne in mind, you can begin the paragraphs that follow with *First, . . . , Second, . . . ,* and so on.

### The Paragraph Block

A relatively long essay typically develops in groups of paragraphs that address major points. Within each of these **paragraph blocks**, one paragraph will usually state the dominant idea and the others will develop it. A writer working, for example, from the "rent control" outline on pages 94–95 might decide to introduce Part III, the heart of the argument, with a "thesis" paragraph marking a major shift in emphasis:

> Such is the promise that advocates of rent control offer to students who are weary of expensive housing and long trips to campus. If the promise could

be even partially realized, it might be worth giving rent control another try. Unfortunately, there is no reason to think that another experiment would work better than all previous ones. However bad the present housing crisis is, you can be sure that rent control would make it worse.

Then four paragraphs, covering points A through D in the outline, would follow, making a single paragraph block about the disappointing results of rent control.

**rev**
**5e**

### Conciseness in Making Transitions

Try not to devote a substantial paragraph to explaining how much of your outline has been covered so far:

DON'T:

x We have now seen that the question of human rights posed at the beginning of this essay cannot be easily answered, and that, specifically, two serious considerations stand in our way. The first of those considerations has now been dealt with, though not perhaps as fully as some readers might prefer. It is time now to go on to the second point, after which we can return to our original question with a better sense of our true options.

Such a paragraph merely tells your reader that you are having trouble making things fit together smoothly.

From time to time, however, you may want to devote a *brief* paragraph to announcing a major shift of direction. Do so with a minimum of distraction from the sequence of ideas.

DO:

• But how can such violations of human rights be swept under the rug? Unfortunately, as we will see, the method is simple and practically foolproof.

*With a Word Processor:* If you have an editing program that can highlight the first and last sentences of every paragraph, make use of it. (If you don't, you can still "select" those sentences and make a document out of them.) Check to see that the connections between last and next (paragraph-opening) sentences are clear, and revise if necessary to make effective use of these naturally strong positions.

**EXERCISES**

7. Look through a completed essay, either for your present course or for another, and check the relation between the last sentence of each paragraph and the first sentence of the next one. Did you always make that relation apparent with your language? Revise where necessary. When you are satisfied that all your sets of last-and-first sentences make for easy and logical transitions, copy those sentences, numbering each set of two, and hand them in.

rev
5f

8. Think of a point you would like to make about any topic. Write out that point in one sentence, and then ask yourself how you could best support it. Write at least two sentences that would help establish your main idea. You need not submit any of these sentences. Using them as a starting point, however, do submit a three-paragraph block (p. 109) in which the first paragraph *states* your idea and the other two *support* it.

## 5f   Revise to End Your Essay Strongly.

Readers want to feel, at the end of a piece of writing, that it has truly finished and not just stopped like some toy soldier that needs rewinding. Further, they like to anticipate the end through a revealing change in tone or intensity or generality of reference.

### Avoiding the Deadly Conclusion

Though you may not always come up with a punchy conclusion, you can avoid certain lame devices that would threaten your good relations with your reader. Check your draft endings against the following cautions:

1. Do not merely repeat your thesis.

2. Do not embark on a completely new topic.

3. Do not pretend to have proven more than you have.

4. Do not apologize or bring your thesis into doubt. If you find anything that requires an apology, fix it!

Remember that readers come away from an essay with the last paragraph ringing in their ears. If you end by sounding bored or distracted or untrustworthy or hesitant, you are encouraging your readers to discount everything you have worked so hard to establish.

## Looking beyond the Thesis

Just as you can lead to your thesis by beginning on a more general plane (5d, p. 106), so you can end by looking beyond that thesis, which has now been firmly established. Thus, in a paper claiming that unilateral disarmament is a dangerous and unwise policy, a student writer concluded as follows:

rev
5f

> There is no reason to expect, then, that the world would be safer if we laid down our arms. On the contrary, we could do nothing more foolhardy. *We must look to other means of ensuring our security and that of the nations we have agreed to protect.*

The sentence we have emphasized "escapes" the thesis, posing a relevant goal for some future investigation. But note that it does so without embarking on a new topic; it provokes thought by looking further in the direction already taken.

## Saving a Clinching Statement or Incident

The final position within any structure—sentence, paragraph, or whole essay—is naturally emphatic. Look especially for a striking quotation or story or phrase that might drive your point home. Here are two examples.

> In many ways the task of stopping AIDS is simple in the United States compared to other places, such as Africa and Haiti, where the disease is widespread. We have a literate population, and there is an excellent chance education can be effective. Dr. Mann of the World Health Organization is also optimistic about the chances in other parts of the world. "Cultures," he said, "know how to survive. And when faced with a threat to their young and previously healthy men and women, cultures will find ways to adapt." We can only hope that such optimism is justified.[7]

> The higher standard of living enjoyed by the industrial nations is not the result of greater productive efficiency, but of an enormously expanded increase in the amount of energy available per person. In 1970 the United States used up the energy equivalent of twelve tons of coal per inhabitant, while the corresponding figure for India was one-fifth ton per inhabitant. The way this energy was expended involved far more energy being wasted per person in the United States than in India. Automobiles and airplanes are faster than oxcarts, but they do not use energy more efficiently. In fact, more calories go up in useless heat and smoke during a single day of traffic jams in the United States than is wasted by all the cows of India during an entire year. The comparison is even

less favorable when we consider the fact that the stalled vehicles are burning up irreplaceable reserves of petroleum that it took the earth tens of millions of years to accumulate. If you want to see a real sacred cow, go out and look at the family car.[8]

Another way to end strongly, if you have already touched your reader's feelings, is to highlight a seemingly minor detail that "says it all":

> I know the dog is dead. I have his hair to prove it. I have the bill from the vet. The canceled check from the crematorium. Conversations about him are in the past tense. Yet tucked away in our hearts is a refusal to believe that he's gone—really gone. And tucked into corners of the refrigerator are table scraps—a steak bone and some chicken soup growing mold.[9]

### Recalling the Opening Paragraph

Look for ways of making your concluding paragraph show some evident, preferably dramatic, relation to your introductory one. If you already have a sound first paragraph and are groping for a last one, reread that opener and see if it contains some hint that you can now develop more amply. Here, for instance, is the concluding paragraph of a student essay that began by asking whether Mahatma Gandhi was nothing more than a religious fanatic:

> Gandhi's arguments reveal an underlying shrewdness. Far from betraying the dogmas of a fanatic, they are at once moral and cunningly practical. His genius, it seems, consisted in an unparalleled knack for doing right—and, what isn't quite the same, for doing the right thing. It is hard to come up with another figure in history who so brilliantly combined an instinct for politics with the marks of what we call, for lack of a better name, holiness.

Note how the writer has put his opening question into storage until it can be answered decisively, with a pleasing finality, in his closing lines.

### Omitting a Formal Conclusion

A short essay may make its point thoroughly within five hundred words; your readers will be insulted or bored by a heavy-handed reminder of the points they have just finished reading. Sometimes a brief concluding paragraph—consisting of no more than one or two sentences—can effectively end a short essay. But you can also save one of your strong supporting points for the last paragraph, counting on an emphatic final sentence to give a feeling of completion.

**rev**
**5g**

9. Photocopy and submit *any two* effective conclusions to articles or chapters that you can find in any source. For each conclusion, supply a paragraph of analysis explaining why the conclusion succeeds as rhetoric. In each case, be specific about the writer's language and the relation between the conclusion and the rest of the piece.

10. Repeat the procedure of Exercise 4 (p. 108), this time using a *concluding* paragraph that strikes you as relatively ineffective. Use your revised paragraph to *expand upon*—not to repeat—the thesis of your essay, and try to make your language vivid and pointed.

## 5g    Attend to Editorial Revision.

Though editorial revision—improvement of wording and conventions—is rarely the most important kind, it does cover the greatest number of problems. In every case, effective editorial revision means putting the reader's convenience ahead of your own.

| FEATURE | REVISE FOR | HELPS READER TO |
|---|---|---|
| paragraphs | unity, continuity, development | see relations between major and minor points |
| sentences | distinctness, subordination, emphasis, variety | follow ideas, avoid tedium |
| words | appropriateness, liveliness | get clear information, avoid jarring effects |
| usage, punctuation, spelling, other conventions | conformity with standard written practice | concentrate on substance of essay |
| citation form | fullness, exactness, consistency | have access to secondary information |

For an idea of how instructors typically draw attention to editorial problems and how students then revise, consider the following made-up paragraph and the **symbols for comment and revision** (see the inside back cover) that have been added to it:

Once people[have gone to the trouble of acquir-
ing the capacity to treat everyone as equals,] *wdy*
they can work with others for the common good.

*exag* [A great example is how the Los Angeles area *pred*
handled it's pollution problem. Everyone was *sp*
*chop* aware of the stifling smog. But the majority
of these people were willing only to complain. *ref*
One group of citizens, however came up with a *p*
creative plan for carpooling. Providing an *dm*
incentive, one lane of freeway was set aside
for cars carrying three or more people. [But
*wdy* after a short period of time,] the committment *sp*
was abandoned. [Because of the godawful traffic *coll/g*
*frag* jams in the other lanes.] It was a promising *ref*
*pass* idea, but most people are made[less upset by *comp*
smog so that] they actually prefer it to traffic
*red* jams in freeway lanes.

*¶ un*     **rev
5g**

The most important of these markings is **¶ un**, since it calls for
a substantial rewriting that would automatically eliminate some of the
smaller problems. But if the student were to address those problems as
they stand, the diagnoses and the most likely remedies would be these.

| SYMBOL | PROBLEM AND SOLUTION | UNREVISED VERSION | REVISION |
|--------|----------------------|-------------------|----------|
| **wdy** | the expression is wordy; make it more concise | Once people have gone to the trouble of acquiring the capacity to treat everyone as equals | Once people can recognize others equals |
| | | after a short period of time | soon |

rev
5g

| SYMBOL | PROBLEM AND SOLUTION | UNREVISED VERSION | REVISION |
|---|---|---|---|
| **exag** | the expression is overstated; tone it down | A great example | One example |
| **pred** | faulty predication; do away with the mismatch between subject and predicate | A great example is how . . . | One example is the handling . . . ; *or* Consider, for example, how Los Angeles handled . . . |
| **sp** | spelling error; look the word up and spell it correctly | it's<br><br>committment | its<br><br>commitment |
| **chop** | choppy sentences: several plain, brief sentences in a row; introduce variety of structure | A great example is how Los Angeles . . . willing only to complain. | Consider, for example, how Los Angeles handled its pollution problem. Even though everyone was aware of the stifling smog, few people were willing at first to do anything more than complain. |
| **ref** | pronouns or demonstratives lack clear, explicitly stated antecedents; make the reference clear | these people<br><br>It was a promising idea | residents<br><br>The carpooling plan was a promising idea |
| **p** | punctuation error; correct it | One group of citizens, however came up with | One group of citizens, however, came up with |
| **dm** | dangling modifier; supply an agent to perform the action | Providing an incentive, one lane of freeway was set aside | Providing an incentive, county officials set aside |

| SYMBOL | PROBLEM AND SOLUTION | UNREVISED VERSION | REVISION |
|--------|----------------------|-------------------|----------|
| **colloq** | the expression falls beneath the level of diction appropriate to this paper; find a middle-level substitute | godawful | serious |
| **frag** | sentence fragment; rewrite or combine to form a grammatically complete sentence | Because of the godawful traffic jams in the other lanes. | But because of serious traffic jams in the other lanes, the commitment was soon abandoned. |
| **pass** | unnecessary use of passive voice; shift to active voice | most people are made less upset | most people would rather |
| **comp** | faulty comparison; match the compared terms or completely recast the expression | most people are made less upset by smog so that | most people prefer smog to traffic jams; *or* most people find smog less offensive than traffic jams |
| **red** | this expression repeats an earlier one; rephrase it | traffic jams in the other lanes . . . traffic jams in freeway lanes | . . . most people prefer lung congestion to traffic congestion |

As for ♯ *un*, notice that the writer began by asserting that *people can work for the common good* but then went on to illustrate a nearly opposite point, that *most people cannot put the public interest before their immediate convenience.* Until that contradiction is resolved, no amount of tinkering can make the paragraph effective.

To weigh the writer's options, ask yourself which idea shows more regard for real experience, the initial one or the one that surfaced in the drafting process. It is really no contest. *Working with others for the common good* is a limp "motherhood" concept, wishful and bland. The conflict between selfish private habits and the common good is a more balanced, less simplistic notion—one that indicates an ability to face facts.

Thus the writer would do well to skip the moralizing and rethink the whole thesis. An eventual, radically improved version of the paragraph might look like this:

> When selfish private habits and the common good come into con-
> flict, the outcome is likely to be all too predictable. Take
> a recent example from Los Angeles, where everyone's health
> would be safeguarded by a significant reduction in automobile
> exhausts. Acting on the suggestion of a citizens' group,
> county officials tried to promote carpooling by setting aside
> one lane of each freeway for cars carrying three or more peo-
> ple. If it had worked, this plan would have enabled everyone
> to breathe more easily. The plan had to be dropped, however,
> when so few people cooperated that motorists refusing to share
> rides were hopelessly clogging the remaining lanes. Forced to
> choose between lung congestion and traffic congestion, Los
> Angelenos will take lung congestion every time.

---

### EXERCISE

11. Using your instructor's comments on previously submitted work, decide *which three* kinds of editorial problems you have least under control. List them and then, in two columns, provide several of the marked examples of each weakness, with improved versions in the right column. Submit this work.

---

## 5h    Make Your Title Definite.

Do not bother thinking of a title until you have finished at least one draft, and be ready to change titles as your later drafts change emphasis. If you begin with a title, it will probably indicate little more than the subject matter treated in your essay. Replace it later with a title expressing your *view of* that subject matter, or at least posing the question answered by your thesis. Thus, asked to write about revision, do not remain satisfied with "Revision" or "Revising College Essays"; such toneless titles suggest that you have no thesis at all. Instead, try something like "The Agony of Revision," "Revision as Discovery," or "Is an Essay Ever Really Finished?" Each of those versions tells the reader that you have found something definite to say.

That impression will be especially strong if you can make your title surprising and vivid. Look for a striking figure of speech (8l, p. 227) that could suggest your thesis with pointed wit. One common device is to combine such a phrase with a more straightforwardly informative subtitle:

**rev
5h**

- Downhill All the Way: My Melting Career as a Ski Racer

- Going High for the Rebound: Drugs as a Menace to Athletes' Careers

If your essay contains especially significant phrases (original or quoted), see if any of them could be borrowed for your title. One freshman student, for example, began a prizewinning essay about *Hamlet* with the following paragraph:

```
While showing Guildenstern how to play the recorder, Hamlet
remarks that it is "as easy as lying" (III.ii.343).  In a
sense, much of the play's meaning is expressed in this line.
Almost every character in Hamlet is to some extent living a
lie: hiding thoughts, playing a role, trying to deceive
another character.  Claudius conceals his crime; Hamlet feigns
madness; private schemes prevail.  In the end, Hamlet may even
be deceiving himself, forcing himself into a role of avenger
when he may not actually fit.
```

For a title, the writer chose "As Easy as Lying"—a phrase that stirred curiosity and gave promise of a well-considered, original thesis.

---

### EXERCISES

12. Look through available magazines and newspapers for titles of articles that are both definite and inviting. Submit three such titles along with brief analyses of why they work.

13. Look through your own previously submitted papers for this or any other course until you find a title that could be significantly improved. Submit a brief discussion of the problem and include one or more new titles that now seem more satisfactory.

## 5i   Test Your Draft against a Checklist for Revision.

Since you cannot always count on having a friendly critic available, you will need to test your drafts yourself against standards that readers commonly hold. The following questions form a checklist that you can consult as soon as you have finished a draft or two. Running through the questions, you may be able to pinpoint any remaining problems and locate the relevant discussions of them in this book.

---

**A CHECKLIST FOR REVISION**

1. Do I have a clear, properly limited, and interesting thesis? (3h–3o, pp. 72–82)

2. Have I adequately supported my thesis? (2g, p. 40; 3o, p. 80)

3. Have I dealt with probable objections to my thesis? (2h, p. 44; 3o, p. 80)

4. Is my thesis conspicuously stated? (5b, p. 100)

5. Are my voice and stance appropriate to my audience and purpose? (4a–4c, pp. 84–90)

6. Are my paragraphs unified and fully developed? (6, pp. 139–162)

7. Does my first paragraph attract the reader's interest? (5d, p. 104)

8. Have I made clear and helpful transitions between paragraphs? (5e, p. 108)

9. Does my last paragraph give enough sense of completion? (5f, p. 111)

10. Does my title indicate that I have a definite point to make? (5h, p. 118)

11. Are my sentences distinct, with effective subordination of minor elements? (7a–7m, pp. 163–186)

12. Do my sentences show enough emphasis and variety of structure? (7n–7w, pp. 186–199)

13. Do all of my words mean what I think they mean? (8a–8c, pp. 202–208)

14. Is my language appropriate to the occasion? (8d–8h, pp. 209–218)

15. Is my language as lively as the occasion allows? (8h–8m, pp. 217–233)

16. Have I looked up the spelling of doubtful words? (24, pp. 419–440)

17. Have I kept to standard written usage? (9–15, pp. 237–342)

18. Does my punctuation bring out my meaning? (16–19, pp. 345–373)

19. Have I followed correct form for quoting other people's words? (20, pp. 374–388)

20. Have I followed correct form for capitals, italics, abbreviations, and numbers? (25–26, pp. 441–464)

21. Have I supplied all necessary documentation and followed a standard form for doing so? (29, pp. 501–530)

**EXERCISE**

14. In preparing an assigned essay, pause after completing a draft and run through the Checklist for Revision, using the page references to look up any unclear points. Evaluate and revise your draft accordingly, keeping notes on the changes you are making at this stage. Then submit a paragraph or two explaining what weak features of your draft became apparent to you in light of the checklist.

## 5j    Follow Standard Typescript Form in Your Final Copy.

No matter how many changes you make between drafts, the essay you eventually submit should look unscarred, or nearly so. It should also meet certain technical requirements of form. The following advice reflects general practice and should be followed whenever your instructor does not specify something different.

1. Type your essay if possible, using standard-sized (8½″ × 11″) unlined white paper of ordinary weight, not onionskin. If you must write longhand, choose paper with widely spaced lines or write on every other line. Type with an unfaded black ribbon or write in dark ink. Use only one side of the paper.

2. Put your name, the course number, your instructor's name, and the date of submission on four double-spaced lines at the upper right corner of your first page, above your title. Skip four lines between your title and the beginning of your text.

3. If you are asked to supply a thesis statement and/or an outline, put them on a separate page along with your name, the course number, your instructor's name, the date of submission, and the title of your essay. Repeat the title on your first page of text.

4. Allow at least one-inch margins on all four sides of each page of your main text. Your right margins need not be even. In a handwritten essay, be sure to leave as much space as in a typewritten one.

5. Leave the first page of text (and notes and bibliography, if any) unnumbered, but put unpunctuated Arabic numerals (2, 3, 4) in the upper right corners of subsequent pages.

6. Double-space your whole essay, including any reference list (29b–29c, pp. 505–518), endnotes (29e, p. 523), or bibliography (29e, p. 528). Follow your instructor's specifications for the spacing of extracted quotations (20h, p. 380).

7. Indent the first line of each paragraph by five type-spaces, or, in a handwritten essay, about an inch. Do not skip extra lines between paragraphs. Indent extracted quotations (20h, p. 380) by ten spaces.

8. Retype any pages on which you had to make more than a few last-minute changes. Otherwise, type those changes or write them clearly in ink, using the following conventions:

   a) Remove unwanted letters with a diagonal slash:
      indigestio/n

   b) Remove unwanted words by running a line through them:
      ~~nasty~~

   c) Replace a letter by putting the new letter above your slash:
      s
      compo/ition

d) Replace words by putting the new word above your canceled one:

                   writer
    please every ~~reader~~

e) Add words or letters by putting a caret (∧) at the point of insertion and placing the extra words or letters above it:

          notable
    Another∧feature of this device

f) Separate words or letters by placing a vertical line between them:

    steel and⎮iron

g) Close up separated letters with a curved line connecting them from above:

    hic⌢cup

h) Transpose (reverse) letters or words with a curved enclosing line:

    Al⁀ice, Carroll Lewis

i) Indicate a paragraph break by inserting the paragraph symbol before the first word of the new paragraph:

    depends on development.¶Transitions, too, have a
    certain importance.

j) Run two paragraphs together by connecting them with an arrow and writing **no¶** in the margin:

    She has found a way of turning "nothing" time into
    <u>pleasure or learning.</u>⤸
**no¶** ⤶Isn't that better than having some trivial chit-
    chat on the sidewalk?

9. Carefully proofread your final copy, looking especially for typing errors. Check all quotations against your notes or, better, against the printed passages.

10. Make sure you have assembled your pages in order. Fasten them with a paper clip or, second best, with a staple.

11. Make a carbon copy of your essay or photocopy it, and retain the copy until you get the original back. Keep the graded original at least until the course is over. These steps will protect you if your instructor should mislay an essay or misrecord a grade.

---

For the forming and spacing of punctuation marks, see Chapter 27, pages 465–469. For citation form, see Chapter 29.

## 5k    Observe the Composition of One Essay from Start to Finish.

A freshman student found herself with a week and a half in which to write a thousand-word essay on any topic within the subject area "Technology and the Quality of Life." She knew that her topic would have to be narrower than that. In her earliest notes she mulled over several possibilities:

> Computers . . . too broad. Subject doesn't seem to fascinate me anyway.
>
> Cordless phones: nothing here? So you can take the phone into the kitchen without tripping over the cord. That's nice, but so what?
>
> VCR's: Betamax etc. OK in theory—no real ideas yet.
>
> Portable headsets—maybe something here? The world is getting divided into people who do and don't live inside those things.
>
> Robots in factories?

Already Janet was beginning to crystallize her attitude toward portable headsets. She felt it was time to draw out further thoughts through a session of freewriting (3f, p. 67):

> People looking like space creatures; bugs; glazed eyes. Turtles inside their shells? But be fair: they're getting technically great sound quality. Run longer without boredom, blot out ugly street sounds—well, why not? Sights too; life goes by like a movie. Except here the music *is* the movie, i.e., the main thing, instead of being background. Maybe it's not so good in less obvious ways, too. Shrinking into yourself: trend of the 80s? These people look peaceful, but what have they got (besides some money for toys)? Another fix that they may not be able to do without. (But this is getting a bit too moralistic, maybe?) Anyway, general problem: technological marvels bring new fun but make us less able to be *really* calm when *really* alone. Also, no improvement in the stuff people want to hear.

Having gone this far, Janet was reasonably sure she would keep her tentative topic, but now she had to decide what *kind* of essay to write:

> Argument or Analysis? What would an argument be—that headsets should be banned? I distrust them, but *that's* too strong. So—no policy issue here. OK, Analysis, but what kind? Maybe cause & effect: show where the fad came from and what it may do to us.

Her next step was therefore to make lists of causes and effects:

Causes:

    technological advances

    outgrowth of stereo boxes

    general conditioning to an electronic environment

    retreat from public world—cult of privacy?

Effects:

    physical danger? (maybe too trivial)

    restlessness *without* sets—no real peace

    more shrinking into oneself

    less tolerance for disturbance, diversity—just play *your* already known
      program

    loss of sympathy with others? political indifference?

    Looking over these lists, Janet realized two things: that she was much more interested in the effects of stereo headsets than in their causes and that all the effects she had named were negative. Her essay, then, was beginning to take shape as *an analysis of the negative social effects of the headsets*. But now she had to consider her reader, who might regard her as a spoilsport and a fanatic if she took a doomsday approach to a harmless-looking appliance. Thus, as a last exercise before attempting a thesis statement, Janet tried to moderate her stance by listing as many "pluses" as she could find:

Pluses:

    great quality

    soothing

    convenient

    no noise for others—not a nuisance

    tool for learning—e.g., a language

    run farther, skate to rhythm, ski without fear?

She was determined to work at least some of those positive qualities into her essay, preferably at a point early enough to stave off doubts about her open-mindedness.

In her first stab at a thesis statement, Janet came up with this:

**TRIAL THESIS STATEMENT:**

Although we can at least be thankful that portable headphone sets are quiet, they are a perfect symbol of a society that has become dependent on artificial sources of calm, out of touch with reality, and indifferent to other people's problems.

That statement had the degree of complexity Janet needed for a 1000-word paper, but it left her uneasy. The "although" clause seemed like a throw-away remark rather than a real concession; the sweeping condemnation of all American society looked excessive; and there was something awkward about accusing a *society* of being indifferent to *other people's* problems. In a second version Janet scaled down her claims and tried to sound fairer:

**REVISED THESIS STATEMENT:**

Although portable headphone sets are undoubtedly convenient and pleasurable, they raise disturbing questions about many Americans' dependency on artificial sources of calm, decreased contact with reality, and shrinkage of concern for others.

Since the point about "shrinkage of concern" was the one that mattered most to Janet, she kept it in the last (most emphatic) position.

Because her essay was to be only a few pages long, Janet thought she could make do with a casual scratch outline (4e, p. 93):

1. Introduce headsets as topic.

2. Admit appeal.

3. No immediate threat to anybody.

4. But (thesis here) three disturbing implications (name them).

5. #1: Dependency for calm.

6. #2: Loss of reality.

7. #3: Shrinkage of concern for others.

8. Conclusion: Though more a symptom than a cause of isolation, sets fit all too well with trend of the times.

As things turned out, Janet found no need to revise this plan. But because she was worried about making her case too one-sided, she devoted two paragraphs instead of one to the positive appeal of the headsets.

At last it was time to draft the essay itself. In its earliest version, this was her opening paragraph (already somewhat revised for conciseness):

rev
5k

```
When I stop to think about technology and the quality of life,

several interesting possibilities come to mind.  Personal com-

puters, of course, are revolutionizing the world in many ways.

Robots in industry are giving us more reliable products at the

same time that they are throwing many potential consumers out

of work.  In the field of entertainment, we are deluged with

video games and special-effects extravaganzas from Hollywood.

But if I had to choose one piece of technology to sum up the

quality of our times--a none too flattering symbol for the

eighties--I think I would take those portable headsets that

one sees everywhere in the street today.
```

Shown this paragraph, Janet's roommate commented that it would do in a pinch but that she didn't feel particularly motivated to keep reading. Janet had created a classic "funnel opener" (p. 106), but she had also come close to a "deadly opener" (p. 104) as well—the kind that lamely calls an assignment "interesting" instead of showing interest in it. Her revised introduction, Janet decided, would be a "baited opener" (p. 107)— a vivid image of somebody cruising down the sidewalk under earphones. (See p. 130 for the final version.)

As for editorial revisions, Janet worked chiefly on problems her instructor had spotted in earlier papers. For example:

| PROBLEM | ORIGINAL | REVISED |
|---|---|---|
| exaggerated language, sarcasm | No doubt it is glorious to be surrounded by one's favorite music (however awful) all day. . . . | No doubt it is pleasant to be surrounded by one's favorite music all day. . . . |

| PROBLEM | ORIGINAL | REVISED |
|---------|----------|---------|
| comma faults | The quality of sound, as I discovered when I once borrowed a set for thirty seconds is extraordinary. | [add comma after *seconds*; remove comma after *know*] |
| faulty parallelism | People who should know, claim that the reproduction is as faithful as an expensive home stereo. | . . . as faithful as that of an expensive home stereo. |

And since she knew that her main liability was wordiness, Janet worked to tighten her phrasing throughout the essay. For example:

**FIRST DRAFT:**

But what worries me the most about the people who wear head-
phones is their indifference to other people--an indifference
that probably has some political effects, too.  Even when he
or she is doing something as active as running or skiing, the
person who is wearing the speakers has retreated within a cozy
space that is shut off from the real-life situations and needs
of other people.  The same holds true if the headset is being
worn on a city street.  Perhaps the street is full of old people, or sick people, or crazy people.  It wouldn't matter who
they are--workers, people out on strike, immigrants, or whoever.  It would be as if they weren't there at all.  For all
that the headset wearer knows or cares, World War III could be
starting!

**REVISED:**

What worries me most about the headphone wearers is their
social--and therefore also political--indifference.  Even when

```
running or skiing, the person sandwiched between the speakers
has retreated within a cozy space, insulated from the claims
of other people and their problems.  That space remains just
as private on a city street, where no one--not the old or the
sick or the crazy, not workers or strikers or immigrants or
beggars--can interrupt the programmed mood.  If the city is
decaying, if depression or race war is just around the corner,
what does it matter?  One can always raise the volume if the
world's troubles approach too near.
```

For a title, Janet had expected to use either "Personal Convenience versus Social Concern" or "Stereo Headsets: Symbol of the Indifferent Eighties." The second seemed better because it was more definite, but neither of them sounded especially lively. Reading through a draft, Janet ran across something more promising, the phrase "head tripper." What about "The New Head Trippers" for a title? It might whet the reader's interest, set an informal tone, hint at Janet's disapproval of the stereo fad, and refer both to headgear and to portability.

Here is Janet's essay as submitted:

Janet Stein

English 1A, sec. 2

Mr. Peterson

### THE NEW HEAD TRIPPERS

Most of us by now have had the experience of coming across a friend or acquaintance dreamily tuned in
to a stereo headset as she weaves through a crowd of
pedestrians.  We are glad to recognize Sally, as I
will call her; we slow down, smile, and prepare a
greeting.  But Sally, though she is looking our way,
sees nothing at all.  She is on automatic pilot,
avoiding the other walkers by a kind of radar that
never requires her eyes to focus.  And suddenly we
change our mind about saying hello to her.  To take
Sally away from her tapes--assuming we could get her
attention at all--would be as intrusive as waking her
with a midnight phone call or dropping in to share her
dinner.  We pass by, disappointed and vaguely bothered.

And perhaps vaguely envious as well.  For, unless
we happen to have a headset of our own, we can only
imagine how agreeable it must be for Sally to occupy a
movable cocoon of rock music or Beethoven or language
lessons.  Sally has missed out on a small personal
encounter, but so what?  She has found a way of turning "nothing" time into pleasure or learning.  Isn't

2

that better than having some trivial chitchat on the
sidewalk?

Let us admit it: those little tape players are a
marvel. The quality of sound, as I discovered when I
once borrowed a set for thirty seconds, is extraordinary. People who should know claim that the reproduc-
tion is as faithful as that of an expensive home
stereo. In fact, if you want sheer music without distraction or irrelevant noise, you might do better to
play tapes on your headset than to attend the finest
live concert.

Though Sally may risk being run over in the
intersection, she is not threatening or endangering
anyone else. Indeed, she makes a favorable contrast
with the brash kid who climbs aboard a bus with his
giant hand-held stereo box turned all the way up. He
may be looking for trouble; at the very least he is
trying to impose his music on a captive audience. But
Sally is the very picture of somebody minding her own
business. Why, then, is there something unsettling
about watching her electronic trance?

I can only answer for myself. For all I know, I
may be the only person in the world to find this
latest wonder of technology a little scary. But even
very enjoyable novelties can have negative consequences for the society as a whole. Many informed

rev
5k

rev
5k

experts now consider television, for all its obvious benefits, to be such a mixed blessing, and video games may offer a less debatable example. Surely there is something a little flabby and weird about a mass passion for shooting down little figures of spaceships that appear on idiotically beeping screens. To me, the tiny stereos look like a similar development. In particular, I am worried about three implications of the headset vogue: a growing dependency on artificial means of staying calm, decreased contact with reality, and a corresponding shrinkage of concern for other people.

First, the matter of dependency. No doubt it is pleasant to be surrounded by one's favorite music all day, but I wonder if the experience isn't addictive. To be constantly under the earphones in the midst of other activities seems rather like having to pop "happy pills" to keep one's sanity or good temper. What becomes of the headset junkies when they are stranded without their fix? I suspect that they are left more fidgety than they were before Sony or Sanyo came to their aid. The possibility is worth looking into, anyway.

Second, as you could tell from seeing her glazed expression, Sally is not exactly alert to new experience. In a literal sense she has become a head trip-

4

per, tuning out whatever may be fresh or unpredictable in her environment while she strolls to the beat of tapes that are totally, soothingly familiar. She is turning life into a movie with background music--but there is a revealing difference. In the movies, the music builds appropriate excitement or emotion for a significant action. For Sally, in contrast, the music is the action; reality will get through to her only when it is compatible with her mental Muzak.

But what worries me most about the headphone wearers is their social--and therefore political-- indifference. Even when running or skiing, the person sandwiched between the speakers has retreated within a cozy space, insulated from the claims of other people and their problems. That space remains just as pri- vate on a city street, where no one--not the old or the sick or the crazy, not workers or strikers or immigrants or beggars--can interrupt the programmed mood. If the city is decaying, if depression or race war is just around the corner, what does it matter? One can always raise the volume if the world's trou- bles approach too near.

Of course I am overdramatizing here; we are not yet a nation of callous zombies. Furthermore, for all I know, the movable cocoon may be more a symptom than a cause of isolation. Let me admit the point but

rev
5k

5

still insist that even as symbolism, the image of the musically tranquilized citizen, aloof from everything except that steady tapping on the cranium, tells us something unsettling about the times we live in. Not long ago, the latest toy was CB radio--a means of communicating, even when there was nothing much to say. If the Eighties are to be the self-absorbed era of the head tripper, those who wear the sets are not the only ones who will want to put the whole decade out of mind as soon as it is over.

rev
5k

## NOTES

[1] J. A. Deutsch and H. S. Koopmans, "Preference Enhancement for Alcohol by Passive Exposure," *Science* 179 (1973): 1242.

[2] Manfred Weidhorn, "Blood, Toil, Tears, and 8,000,000 Words: Churchill Writing," *Columbia Forum* Spring 1975: 19.

[3] William C. Gruben, "Dangers of Honky-tonk Dancing," *Atlantic* Aug. 1986: 32.

[4] Steven J. Marcus, "How to Court a Cat," *Newsweek* 22 Mar. 1982: 13.

[5] Theodore Solotaroff, rev. of *World of Our Fathers,* by Irving Howe, *New York Times Book Review* 1 Feb. 1976: 1.

[6] Sonya O'Sullivan, "Single Life in a Double Bed," *Harper's* Nov. 1975: 45.

[7] Robert Bazell, "Surviving AIDS," *The New Republic* 24 Nov. 1986: 23.

[8] Marvin Harris, *Cows, Pigs, Wars, and Witches: The Riddles of Culture* (New York: Vintage, 1974) 26–27.

[9] Barbara Lazear Ascher, "Hers," *New York Times* 30 Oct. 1986, national ed.: 20.

# III

# EFFECTIVE
# EXPRESSION

6. Paragraphs

7. Sentences

8. Words

## EFFECTIVE EXPRESSION

*The chapters in Part III presuppose that you can already write
complete sentences that make a grammatically coherent statement
(Chapter 9). If you feel uncertain about fundamentals of usage, it
would be wise to pause and look ahead to the whole of Part IV.
But on the assumption that the best way to remedy any continuing
weaknesses is to keep writing and learning new devices from the
accomplished essayist's repertoire, we turn here to more positive
stylistic opportunities. The following chapters pursue Chapter 5's
emphasis on revision, now with special focus on the ways you can
sharpen the effectiveness of your paragraphs (Chapter 6), sentences
(Chapter 7), and choice of words (Chapter 8).*

# 6
## Paragraphs

Once you have mastered paragraph form, you have an invaluable means of keeping your reader's interest and approval. Although each sentence conveys meaning, an essay or paper or report is not a sequence of sentences but a development of one leading point through certain steps of presentation. Those steps are, or ought to be, paragraphs.

The sentences within an effective paragraph support and extend one another in the service of a single unfolding idea, just as the paragraphs themselves work together to make the thesis persuasive. In key respects, then, you can think of the paragraph as a mini-essay. Like the full essay, a typical paragraph

1. presents one main idea;
2. conveys thoughts that are connected both by logical association and by word signals;
3. often reveals its main idea in a prominent statement, usually but not always toward the start;
4. usually supports or illustrates that idea;
5. may also deal with objections or limitations to that idea, but without allowing the objections to assume greater importance than the idea itself; and
6. may begin or end more generally, taking an expanded view of the addressed topic.

In one sense nothing could be easier than to form paragraphs; you simply indent the first word of a sentence by five spaces. But those indentions must match real divisions in your developing thought if you are to keep your reader's respectful attention. All readers sense that a new paragraph signals a shift: a new subject, a new idea, a change in emphasis, a new speaker, a different time or place, or a change in the level of generality. By observing such natural breaks and by signaling in one paragraph how it logically follows from the preceding one, you can turn the paragraph into a powerful means of communication.

## PARAGRAPH UNITY

¶ un
6a

### 6a   Highlight Your Leading Idea.

As a rule, every effective paragraph has a leading idea to which all other ideas in the paragraph are logically related. A reader of your essays or papers should be able to tell, in any paragraph, which is the **main sentence** (often called *topic sentence*)—the sentence containing that one central point to be supported or otherwise developed in the rest of the paragraph.

It is true that in some prose—descriptions, narratives, and the parts of a report that present data or run through the steps of an experimental procedure—many paragraphs contain no single sentence that stands out as the main, controlling one. Such a paragraph can be said to have an implied main sentence: "This is the way it was," or "These are the procedures that were followed." But in college essays and term papers, which call chiefly for analysis and argument (Chapter 2), you should try to see that each paragraph contains not only a leading idea but an easily identified main sentence as well.

We will see (6f–6h, pp. 152–158) that a main sentence can occur anywhere in a paragraph if the other sentences are properly subordinate to it. More often than not, however, the main sentence comes at or near the beginning, as in this student example:

> Walt Whitman's "A Noiseless Patient Spider" is built on a comparison of the poet's soul to a spider. Both of them, he says, stand isolated, sending something from inside themselves into the surrounding empty space; in their obviously different ways they are both reaching for *connection*. Whitman does not say what the spiritual connection may be, except that his soul hopes to find "the spheres to connect" the "measureless oceans of space" out there. He is vague—but so is the unknown realm toward which he yearns.

The heart of this paragraph is its opening sentence, which reveals the leading idea: Whitman's poem is built on a comparison of the poet's soul to a spider. Reread the other three sentences and you will see that each of them contributes to that leading idea, remaining within its organizing control.

## Avoiding Self-Contradiction

A paragraph can include negative as well as positive considerations, but it should never "change its mind," canceling one point with a flatly contrary one.

DO:

- A.   The seepage of dioxin into a community's water supply always terrifies everyone once it has been discovered. Citizens naturally expect the Environmental Protection Agency and the guilty industry to remove the source of risk as soon as possible. Unfortunately, however, this chemical is so incredibly toxic in small doses that decades may pass before the threat to public health is truly over.

DON'T:

x B.   The seepage of dioxin into a community's water supply always terrifies everyone once it has been discovered. Citizens naturally expect the Environmental Protection Agency and the guilty industry to remove the source of risk as soon as possible. Yet many people react to the crisis quite calmly, refusing to worry about cancer, birth defects, and other proven results of contact with dioxin.

¶ un
6a

Each of these paragraphs ends with a sentence that "goes against" the preceding two sentences. In paragraph A, however, there is no contradiction; the writer simply turns from one aspect of the dioxin problem (citizens' demand for a speedy solution) to a more serious aspect (long-term toxicity). But in paragraph B the writer says two *incompatible* things: that everyone is alarmed and that some people are not alarmed. The writer of paragraph B could eliminate the contradiction by rewriting the opening sentence.

DO:

- The seepage of dioxin into a community's water supply provokes mixed reactions once it has been discovered. Citizens naturally expect the Environmental Protection Agency and the guilty industry to remove the source of risk as soon as possible. Yet many people react to the crisis quite calmly, refusing to worry about cancer, birth defects, and other proven results of contact with dioxin.

## Keeping to the Point

A paragraph that shows strong internal continuity (6b–6e, pp. 144–151), hooking each new sentence into the one before it, can cover a good deal of ground without appearing disunified. Every sentence, however, should bear some relation to the leading idea — either introducing it, stating it, elaborating it, asking a question about it, supporting it, raising a doubt about it, or otherwise reflecting on it. A sentence that does none of those things is a **digression** — an irrelevancy. Just one digression within a paragraph may be enough to sabotage its effectiveness.

Suppose, for example, paragraph A on dioxin contained this sentence: *The Environmental Protection Agency, like the Federal Communications Commission, is an independent body.* Even though that statement deals with the EPA, which does figure in the paragraph, it has no bearing on the paragraph's leading idea: that dioxin can remain hazardous for decades. Thus the statement amounts to a digression. Unless the writer decided to switch leading ideas, the digression would have to be eliminated in a later draft.

¶ un
6a

## Giving Your Leading Idea the Last Word

Although it is sometimes useful to include statements that limit the scope of a paragraph's leading idea or that raise objections to it (6g, p. 154), you should try never to *end* a paragraph with such a statement. Final positions are naturally emphatic. If your last sentence takes away from the main idea, you will sound indecisive or uncomfortable, and the paragraph will lack emphasis.

INDECISIVE:

x A. One reason for the recent popularity of Hollywood autobiographies must surely be the decline of serious fiction about important, glamorous people. We know that readers crave intimacy with the great, and we also know that modern novelists have ignored that craving. What people no longer get from fiction, they now seek in true confessions from Tinseltown. Of course, other factors must be at work as well; literary fads are never produced by single causes.

FIRM:

• B. One reason for the recent popularity of Hollywood autobiographies must surely be the decline of serious fiction about important, glamorous people. Of course, other factors must be at work as well; literary fads are never produced by single causes. But we do know that readers crave intimacy with the great, and we also know that modern novelists have ignored that craving. What people no longer get from fiction, they now seek in true confessions from Tinseltown.

Notice that these paragraphs say the same thing but leave the reader with different impressions. Paragraph A trails off, as if the writer were having second thoughts about the leading idea. Paragraph B gets its "negative" sentence about *other factors* into a safely unemphatic position and then ends strongly, reinforcing the idea that was stated in the opening sentence. The confident treatment of an objection makes the paragraph supple rather than self-defeating.

¶ un
6a

### EXERCISES

1. Write out a main sentence for a paragraph on any topic. (That is, state a leading idea.) Follow it with three sentences that develop, explain, or illustrate your leading idea. Number all four sentences and, beneath your paragraph, briefly explain each sentence's function. (E.g., "Sentence 4 gives an example of the idea proposed in sentence 3.")

2. Find the digressive sentence that has been inserted into the following paragraph. Submit an explanation of why that sentence interferes with paragraph unity.

   In 1886 Grinnell suggested in the pages of *Forest and Stream* that concerned men and women create an organization for the protection of wild birds and their eggs, its administration to be undertaken by the magazine's staff. Grinnell did not have to grope to name this organization. He had grown up near the home that the great bird painter, John James Audubon, had left to his wife and children at his death. As a boy Grinnell had played in an old loft cluttered with stacks of the red muslin-bound copies of the *Ornithological Biography* and boxes of bird skins brought back by Audubon from his expeditions. He had attended a school for small boys conducted by Lucy Audubon nearby. All his life he would remain an avid reader. Grinnell quite naturally called the new organization the Audubon Society.[1]

3. Choosing any topic not already used in Exercise 1, write three paragraphs that suffer, respectively, from contradiction, digression, and failure to give the leading idea the last word. Label and submit the three faulty paragraphs along with a fourth, adequately unified, paragraph on the same topic.

4. Since a paragraph can be regarded as a mini-essay (p. 139), you ought to be able to boil down an essay to paragraph size. Try that experiment with

an essay you have already read for this course. Your paragraph should have as its sentence a statement of the essay's thesis, and your other sentences should cover the author's most important supporting points.

5. Suppose you have been writing an essay about the difficulties people face when they try to write essays. You have just ended a paragraph with this sentence: *Writing provides rich confirmation of Murphy's Law: "If anything can go wrong, it will."* Your next paragraph will supply an example from your own experience as a student writer. Submit that paragraph, including (a) a main sentence stating what your experience taught you, and (b) several supporting sentences describing that experience. (If you have no relevant story to tell, make one up.)

¶ con
6b

## PARAGRAPH CONTINUITY

### 6b    Respond to the Previous Sentence.

To maintain **continuity**, or linkage between sentences or whole paragraphs, you need to write each new sentence with the previous one in mind. You want your reader to feel that one statement has grown naturally out of its predecessor—an effect that comes from picking up some element in that earlier sentence and taking it further.

If, for example, the most recent sentence in your draft reads *The economic heart of America has been shifting toward the Sunbelt,* you could maintain continuity in any of the following ways, depending on the point you wish to make:

- The economic heart of America has been shifting toward the Sunbelt. But how much longer will this trend continue? [Ask a question.]

- The economic heart of America has been shifting toward the Sunbelt. The recent history of Buffalo, New York, is a case in point. [Illustrate your point.]

- The economic heart of America has been shifting toward the Sunbelt. It may be, however, that the country also has a quite different kind of heart—one that is not so easily moved. [Limit your point.]

- The economic heart of America has been shifting toward the Sunbelt. Without forgetting that trend, let us turn now to less obvious but possibly more important developments. [Provide a transition to the next idea.]

- The economic heart of America has been shifting toward the Sunbelt. If so, it can only be a matter of time before the moral or spiritual heart of the country is similarly displaced. [Reflect on your point; speculate.]

In short, reread the sentence you have just written and ask yourself, "All right, what follows from this?" What follows may be

1. a question (or further question);

2. an answer (if the sentence above is a question);

3. support or illustration of the point just made;

4. a limitation or objection to the point just made;

5. further support or illustration of an earlier point, or further limitation or objection to an earlier point;

6. a transition; or

7. a conclusion or reflection appropriate either to the sentence above or to the whole idea of the paragraph.

¶ con
6c

---

**EXERCISE**

6. Write out a sentence stating an idea about any topic. Then, on separate lines, write five numbered sentences, *each* of which could be the next sentence following that one in a paragraph. (Your numbered sentences are not meant to form a sequence; they are five alternative ways of maintaining continuity with the first sentence.) Give your five numbered sentences the form of (1) a question, (2) a supporting point or illustration, (3) a limitation or objection, (4) a transition, and (5) a conclusion or reflection.

---

## 6c    Include Signal Words and Phrases.

Though you may sometimes want to delay stating your paragraph's leading idea (6g–6h, pp. 154–158), you should never put your reader to the trouble of puzzling out hidden connections. By using unmistakable **signals of relation** from sentence to sentence, you can let the reader see at a glance that a certain train of thought is being started, developed, challenged, or completed.

Those signals are chiefly words or phrases indicating exactly how a statement in one sentence relates to the statement it follows. The possible types of relation, along with examples of each type, are these:

CONSEQUENCE:

- therefore, then, thus, hence, accordingly, as a result

LIKENESS:

- likewise, similarly

CONTRAST:

- but, however, nevertheless, on the contrary, on the other hand, yet

AMPLIFICATION:

- and, again, in addition, further, furthermore, moreover, also, too

EXAMPLE:

- for instance, for example

CONCESSION:

- to be sure, granted, of course, it is true

INSISTENCE:

- indeed, in fact, yes, no

SEQUENCE:

- first, second, finally

RESTATEMENT:

- that is, in other words, in simpler terms, to put it differently

RECAPITULATION:

- in conclusion, all in all, to summarize, altogether

TIME OR PLACE:

- afterward, later, earlier, formerly, elsewhere, here, there, hitherto, subsequently, at the same time, simultaneously, above, below, farther on, this time, so far, until now

Notice how a careful use of relational signals (italicized) brings out the logical connectedness of sentences in the following paragraph:

In the winter of 1973–74 drivers lined up all over America to fill their gas tanks. *But* it was not merely a question of a fifteen-minute wait and back on the road again. *On the contrary,* cars often began to congregate at dawn. *Similarly,* walkers appeared early on frigid mornings with an empty five-gallon can in one hand and a pint of steaming coffee in the other, determined to wait out the chill and avoid disappointment. Everybody had to wait. *As a result,* high-school kids took Saturday morning jobs as gas line sitters; spouses drove their mates to work and spent the rest of the day in line; and libraries had a surge of activity as people decided to catch up on their reading while waiting. *All in all,* Americans were at their best during that bizarre season, abiding by the new rules as if a place in the gas line had been guaranteed to everyone by the Bill of Rights.

¶ con
6c

In addition to signal words that show logical connections, you can gain continuity through words indicating that something already treated is still under discussion. Such signal words make sense only in relation to the sentence before.

### PRONOUNS:

- Ordinary people know little about the causes of inflation. What *they* do know is that *they* must earn more every year to buy the same goods and services.

### DEMONSTRATIVE ADJECTIVES:

- Mark Twain died in 1910. Since *that* date American literature has never been so dominated by one writer's voice.

### REPEATED WORDS AND PHRASES:

- We should conserve fossil fuels on behalf of our descendants as well as ourselves. Those *descendants* will curse us if we leave them without abundant sources of light and heat.

### IMPLIED REPETITIONS:

- Some fifty Americans were trapped in the embassy when the revolution broke out. *Six more* managed to scramble onto the last helicopter that was permitted to land on the roof.

One key word, repeated several times, can do much to knit a paragraph together. Thus in the following paragraph the name *Ottawa* (italicized here for emphasis) is artfully plucked out from other names:

> Perhaps a visitor cannot truly understand the country until he has traveled from the genteel poverty of the Atlantic coast with its picturesque fishing villages and stiff towns through the Frenchness of sophisticated Quebec cities and rural landscapes, past the vigorous bustling Ontario municipalities and industrial vistas, over mile after mile of wheat fields between prairie settlements into the lush and spacious beauty of British Columbia; but he must also visit *Ottawa* and the House of Commons. *Ottawa* the stuffy, with its dull-looking houses, its blistering summer heat, its gray rainy afternoons; *Ottawa* the beautiful, on a snowy day when the government buildings stand tall and protective, warmly solid above the white landscape; on a sunny spring afternoon with the cool river winding below, and people moving easily through the clean streets, purposeful but not pushed. Even during the morning and evening traffic rushes, *Ottawa* seems to remain sane.[2]

¶ con
6c

In the first sentence *Ottawa* belatedly emerges as the key name among several; it gains importance by being weighted singly against all the "travelogue" references before the semicolon. In the second sentence (or intentional sentence fragment) the name is used insistently and fondly. And the author exploits this effect in her final sentence, using the name yet again to reinforce her idea that Ottawa stands apart from the rest of Canada.

---

**EXERCISES**

7. Take (or write) a paragraph of your own on any topic and revise it until you are satisfied that it shows adequate continuity from sentence to sentence. Number the sentences. Submit your paragraph along with a sentence-by-sentence explanation of its elements of continuity. (E.g., "Sentence 3: *furthermore* shows that another supporting statement will be added to the one in sentence 2.")

8. Revise the following paragraph for continuity, adding signal words to show relations between sentences:

> Most people hesitate to enter photo contests because they are sure that professionals will take all the prizes. Professional photographers are barred from most photo contests. When professional photographers are permitted to enter photo contests, they hardly ever win the top prizes. There is no reason for a competent amateur photographer to feel handicapped in competing against professionals.

9. Choosing any topic, submit a paragraph which, like the "Ottawa" paragraph, gains continuity from the repetition of a key word or phrase.

## 6d   Keep Related Sentences Together.

You can serve continuity by keeping together sentences that all bear the same relation to the paragraph's leading idea. To simplify, let us reduce all such relations to *support* and *limitation* (qualification). Sentences that support the leading idea by restating it, illustrating it, offering evidence for its truth, or expanding upon it belong in an uninterrupted sequence. So do all sentences that limit the leading idea by showing what it does *not* cover or by casting doubt on it.

¶ con
6d

Continuity is especially threatened when a paragraph contains two isolated sets of limiting sentences. To see why, examine the following draft paragraph:

**limitation** { x Not many people would want to endure the lonely hours, the aches and pains, and the probable injuries awaiting anyone who trains seriously for a marathon. The pride,

**main sentence** { however, that comes from finishing one's first marathon makes all the struggle seem worthwhile. But is it really

**limitation** { worthwhile? What does running twenty-six miles in glorified underwear have to do with real life? But for veteran

**support** { marathoners, long-distance racing *is* real life, while all other claims on their time are distractions or nuisances.

Here the direction established by the main sentence is pro-marathon. But that direction is opposed twice in the course of the paragraph; the main sentence is hemmed in by qualifications, and the reader is bounced back and forth between "pro" and "con" points. Compare:

**limitation** { Not many people would want to endure the lonely hours, the aches and pains, and the probable injuries awaiting anyone who trains seriously for a marathon. Is all the effort worthwhile? More than once, no doubt, exhausted beginners must ask themselves what running twenty-six miles in glorified

**main sentence** { underwear has to do with real life. Yet the pride that comes from finishing one's first marathon makes all the struggle seem

**support** { worthwhile. And for veteran marathoners, long-distance running *is* real life, while all other claims on their time are distractions or nuisances.

Now the paragraph's shuffling between pros and cons has been replaced by *one* definitive pivot on the signal word *Yet.* One such turn per paragraph is the maximum you should allow yourself. To observe that principle, make sure that your limiting and supporting sentences remain within their own portion of the paragraph—with the limiting sentences first to keep them from "having the last word."

For further discussion of the kind of paragraph that pivots to its leading idea, see 6g, p. 154.

---

**EXERCISE**

¶ con
6e

10. Write a brief analysis of the effectiveness or ineffectiveness of the order of sentences in the following paragraph. If you believe the order could be made more effective, rewrite the paragraph, keeping nearly all the same language but changing words as needed to bring out relations between supporting and limiting remarks.

> 1. Some of the most haunting music of our century was composed by the eccentric Parisian Erik Satie. 2. Once you have acquired a taste for his fanciful and melancholy works, you will find it hard to keep them out of your head. 3. But not everyone can take Satie seriously; his modesty makes him appear trivial compared, say, to the bold and colorful Stravinsky.

---

## 6e    Link Sentences through Varied and Repeated Structure.

A further means of making the sentences of a paragraph flow together is to give them some variety of structure. In particular, avoid an unbroken string of choppy sentences, each consisting of one statement unmarked by pauses (see 7r, p. 193).

Within certain limits, however, you can show continuity by *repeating* a sentence pattern. Those limits are that (a) only parts of paragraphs, not whole paragraphs, lend themselves comfortably to such effects, and (b) the sentences so linked must be parallel in meaning. When you want to make their association emphatic, you can give them the same form.

The following paragraph relates American history textbooks to a transformed society. Notice how the writer makes use of identical structures (here italicized) in two sentences to underscore the changes in America that have made history books less predictable than they used to be:

> But now the texts have changed, and with them the country that American children are growing up into. *The society that was once uniform is now a*

patchwork of rich and poor, old and young, men and women, blacks, whites, Hispanics, and Indians. *The system that ran so smoothly* by means of the Constitution under the guidance of benevolent conductor Presidents *is now* a rattletrap affair. The past is no highway to the present; it is a collection of issues and events that do not fit together and that lead in no single direction.[3]

And observe how a critic of urban planning gains emphatic continuity through two sets of identical structures:

> But look what we have built with the first several billions: Low-income projects that become worse centers of delinquency, vandalism and general social hopelessness than the slums they were supposed to replace. Middle-income housing projects which are truly marvels of dullness and regimentation, sealed against any buoyancy or vitality of city life. Luxury housing projects that mitigate their inanity, or try to, with a vapid vulgarity. Cultural centers that are unable to support a good bookstore. Civic centers that are avoided by everyone but bums, who have fewer choices of loitering place than others. Commercial centers that are lackluster imitations of standardized suburban chain-store shopping. Promenades that go from no place to nowhere and have no promenaders. Expressways that eviscerate great cities. This is not the rebuilding of cities. This is the sacking of cities.[4]

¶ con
6e

The body of this paragraph consists of intentional sentence fragments (9d, p. 247), each of which takes its sense from the writer's opening words: *But look what we have built.* . . . An entirely different parallelism of structure brings the paragraph to its emphatic end: *This is not the rebuilding of cities. This is the sacking of cities.* The writer has risked annoying us with relentless hammer blows, but her shifting to a second variety of patterning prevents monotony.

---

## EXERCISES

11. Choosing any topic, submit a paragraph which, like the "urban renewal" paragraph above, gains continuity from reuse of the same structure in sentences or intentional sentence fragments.

12. Beginning with the writer's handling of sentence structure, submit a discussion of the elements of continuity in the following paragraph:

> 1. Royalty and riots; riots and royalty. 2. There seems almost a symbiotic correlation between pomp and desperation in Britain these days. 3. In the space of twenty-four of the most memorable hours in recent British history, for example, the grindingly poor Toxteth district of Liverpool was seared by

violence yet again. 4. Dozens of people were injured and an innocent by-stander named David Moore was killed by the British police. 5. The next morning the British government—in the midst of the worst economic crisis the country has known since the Depression—dispensed some $2 million on the nuptials of the Prince and Princess of Wales. 6. The photographs of Moore's mangled body made the newspapers in London, but the day was dominated by the captivating smile of Lady Diana Spencer.[5]

## PARAGRAPH DEVELOPMENT

¶ dev
6f

Most of the advice you may have seen about constructing paragraphs deals with just one kind of development, which we will call *direct.* Direct paragraphs are indeed the most common type. Capable writers, however, also feel at home with other ways of putting a paragraph together. For simplicity's sake we will recognize three patterns—the *direct,* the *pivoting,* and the *suspended* paragraph. They illustrate classic ways of combining the types of sentences most frequently found in paragraphs:

1. a **main sentence**, which carries the paragraph's leading idea;

2. a **supporting sentence**, which backs or illustrates the leading idea; and

3. a **limiting sentence**, which "goes against" the leading idea by raising a negative consideration either before or after that idea has been stated.

### 6f    Master the Direct Pattern.

In a **direct paragraph**, the most usual pattern, you place the main sentence at or near the beginning, before you have mentioned any limiting (negative or qualifying) considerations. The second "Hollywood" paragraph (pp. 142–143), the "gas shortage" paragraph (p. 147), the "Ottawa" paragraph (p. 148), the "urban planning" paragraph (p. 151), and this present paragraph all exhibit the direct pattern.

The following example is typical:

There is a paradox about the South Seas that every visitor immediately discovers. Tropical shores symbolize man's harmony with a kind and bountiful nature. Natives escape the common vexations of modern life by simply relaxing. They reach into palms for coconuts, into the sea for fish, and into calabashes for poi. But when the tranquilized tourist reaches Hawaii, the paradise of the Pacific, he finds the most expensive resort in the world and a tourist industry that will relieve him of his traveler's checks with a speed and ease that would bring a smile to the lips of King Kamehameha.[6]

Here the main sentence announces a *paradox* — that is, a seeming contradiction — and the rest of the paragraph consists of supporting or explanatory sentences that develop the two halves of that paradox, harmonious nature and commercial exploitation. The result is extreme clarity: the structure of the paragraph fulfills the promise given in the main sentence, and the reader feels guided by that structure at each moment.

A direct paragraph can also include limiting sentences (p. 152), provided that they *follow* the main sentence and *are answered by* at least one supporting sentence. In the following student paragraph, for example, the writer can afford to offer a "con" remark, which is placed strategically between the main sentence and two final sentences of support for that statement:

¶ dev
6f

<table>
<tr><td>main<br>sentence</td><td>The "greenhouse effect," whereby the temperature of the atmosphere rises with the increased burning of hydrocarbons, may have devastating consequences for our planet within a genera-</td></tr>
<tr><td>limiting<br>sentence</td><td>tion or two. Similar scares, it is true, have come and gone without leaving any lasting mark. Yet there is an important</td></tr>
<tr><td>supporting<br>sentences</td><td>difference this time. We know a good deal more about the greenhouse effect and its likely results than we knew, say, about invasions from outer space or mutations from atomic bomb tests. The greenhouse effect is already under way, and there are very slender grounds for thinking it will be reversed or even slowed without a more sudden cataclysm such as all-out nuclear war.</td></tr>
</table>

Direct paragraphs, then, can follow two models, one including and one omitting limiting sentences:

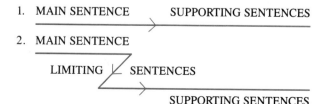

1. MAIN SENTENCE          SUPPORTING SENTENCES

2. MAIN SENTENCE

   LIMITING   SENTENCES

          SUPPORTING SENTENCES

### Main Sentence Delayed

The main sentence in a direct paragraph need not be the first one; it must simply precede any limiting sentences. Note, for example, how the following student paragraph puts the main sentence second, after an introductory sentence that prepares for a shift of emphasis:

introductory
sentence { But the statistics do not tell the whole story. If we set aside the

main { government reports and take the trouble to interview farm
sentence { workers one by one, we find an astounding degree of confi-

supporting { dence in the future. The workers are already thinking a gener-
sentences { ation ahead. Even if they have little expectation of improving
their own lives, most of them are convinced that their children
will begin to participate meaningfully in the American dream.

¶ dev
6g

---

EXERCISE

13. Submit a direct paragraph on any topic you have not treated in a previous exercise. Your paragraph should consist of an opening main sentence followed by two or three sentences of support. Below it, provide a version of the same paragraph that includes (a) an introductory sentence preceding the main sentence, and (b) one or two limiting sentences. You need not make changes in the other sentences, but do make sure that your new version is still a direct paragraph and that it "gives its leading idea the last word" (6a, p. 142).

---

## 6g  Master the Pivoting Pattern.

In a **pivoting paragraph** the writer not only delays the main sentence but also begins by "going against it" with one or more limiting sentences. Characteristically, the pivoting paragraph then turns sharply ("pivots") toward the main sentence, usually announcing that shift of emphasis with a conspicuous signal word such as *but* or *however*. The main sentence either ends the paragraph or, more commonly, is followed by one or more supporting sentences:

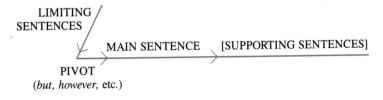

LIMITING
SENTENCES

MAIN SENTENCE    [SUPPORTING SENTENCES]

PIVOT
(*but, however,* etc.)

Our own introduction to paragraph development on page 152 typifies the pivoting pattern. The third sentence of that paragraph, containing the pivoting word *however,* points in a new direction while stating the leading idea, which is then illustrated in the two supporting sentences that follow. The same structure characterizes the improved "marathon training" paragraph (p. 149). By contrast, the first "dioxin" paragraph (p. 141) ends with its main sentence.

Notice how the following paragraph from a student essay already quoted (p. 113) pivots neatly on the word *But* and then develops its leading idea:

limiting sentence — When we think of Gandhi fasting, plastering mud poultices on his belly, and testing his vow of continence by sharing a bed with his grand-niece, we can easily regard him as an eccentric

pivot to the main sentence — who happened to be politically lucky. *But* the links between his private fads and his political methods turn out to be quite logical.

supporting sentences — Gandhi's pursuit of personal rigors helped him to achieve a rare degree of discipline, and that discipline allowed him to approach political crises with extraordinary courage. The example of his self-control, furthermore, was contagious; it is doubtful that a more worldly man could have led millions of his countrymen to adopt the tactic of nonviolent resistance.

¶ dev
6g

Similarly, the classic pivoting signal *however* shows us that the third sentence of this next paragraph is making a reversal of emphasis:

Health experts always seem to be telling Americans what *not* to eat. Cholesterol, salt and sugar are but a few of the dietary no-no's that threaten to make dinnertime about as pleasurable as an hour of push-ups. In a report last week on the role of nutrition in cancer, *however,* a blue-ribbon committee of the National Academy of Sciences offered a carrot—as well as oranges, tomatoes and cantaloupes—along with the usual admonitory stick. While some foods appear to promote cancer and should be avoided, said the panel, other comestibles may actually help ward off the disease.[7]

The further you venture from the direct pattern, the more important it is to guide your reader with signal words such as *but* or *however.* You can also make your pivot, if you prefer, by means of a whole sentence such as *That is no longer the case.* The next sentence can then state your leading idea.

The pivoting pattern is especially common in paragraphs of comparison and contrast (2e, p. 35). As we have observed, the first part of such a paragraph usually dwells on resemblances, and then a somewhat more emphatic part dwells on differences. The following student paragraph is typical:

**resemblances** { Tillie Olsen's short stories, "Hey Sailor, What Ship?" and "O Yes," both chronicle the disintegration of a close relationship. In both stories, a friendship falls apart when one or both parties find it more trying to sustain the friendship than

**main sentence** { to let it go. The underlying causes of strain, *however,* are quite different in the two cases. In "Hey Sailor . . ." a change

**differences** { in Whitey's character leads to his falling out with his family, but in "O Yes" external forces — social pressures — tear Carol and Parry apart.

¶ dev
6h

Note once again how a key signal word, *however,* alerts us to the pivoting movement.

---

**EXERCISES**

14. Reusing as many sentences as you please from Exercise 13, page 154, submit a pivoting paragraph that proposes the same leading idea. Use a pivoting word or phrase to indicate where your paragraph is turning toward the leading idea, and underline the expression.

15. Think of resemblances and differences between two of your recent teachers. Then write a pivoting paragraph of about six sentences comparing and contrasting those teachers.

---

## 6h    Master the Suspended Pattern.

Once you have a feeling for the direct and pivoting patterns, you can turn to the more taxing **suspended paragraph** — that is, a paragraph that builds to a climax or conclusion by some means other than a sharp reversal of direction. In a suspended paragraph the main sentence always comes at or near the end. Instead of taking a sharp turn, like the pivoting paragraph, it moves from discussion or exemplification to leading idea, maintaining the reader's sentence-by-sentence interest until it arrives at a statement that brings things together at last:

DISCUSSION                    MAIN SENTENCE

Thus:

|  |  |
|---|---|
| discussion { | In the early fourteenth century, northern Europe was subjected to a terrible famine. Meanwhile, economic instability caused whole kingdoms to go bankrupt. Then in 1348–50 the worst plague in history ravaged the Continent, killing perhaps half |
| main sentence { | the population. It is little wonder, therefore, that this was a period of profound social and political unrest; the supposedly stable order of feudalism had proved helpless to cope with various forms of disaster. |

Similarly:

¶ dev
6h

|  |  |
|---|---|
| discussion { | Shortly after dawn, at the Saint-Antoine produce market in the ancient French city of Lyons, a white pickup truck screeches around a corner, double-parks impatiently and disgorges a rugged man wearing a rumpled windbreaker. As if by pre-arranged signal, prize raspberries, dewy spinach and pristine baby carrots suddenly emerge from hiding places below the trestle tables where they've been saved for inspection by this very special customer. *"Viens ici, Paul,"* shouts a fruit vendor. "I've got some melons you won't believe." Slicing a sample in half, the man in the windbreaker rejects the melons and some string beans as well ("too fat"). But thirty-five minutes later, he has sniffed, nibbled, pinched, prodded, and fondled his way through the choicest fruits and vegetables, loaded fifteen crates of produce into his van and hummed off toward his next quarry: plump chickens from Bresse, Charolais beef and fresh |
| main sentence { | red mullet. Paul Bocuse, the most visible, the most influential —and possibly the best—chef in the world, has begun another working day.[8] |

Looking back on the "discussion" sentences in these paragraphs, we could regard them as providing support for the leading idea. But we cannot perceive a sentence as "supporting" if we have not yet been told what it supports. By withholding that information until the end, the suspended paragraph establishes itself as the most dramatic pattern as well as the hardest to manage.

Once you feel at ease with the suspended paragraph, you will find it especially useful as a means of introducing or concluding an essay (5d, p. 104; 5f, p. 111). An opening paragraph that ends with its main sentence—a sentence revealing either your topic or your thesis—can gradually awaken the reader's interest and eagerness to move ahead. And a suspended final paragraph allows you to finish your essay with a "punch line" — an excellent tactic if you have saved a strong point for the end.

## EXERCISES

16. Write a two- or three-paragraph analysis of the following paragraph, showing what effects the writer has gained from use of a suspended pattern:

> Knowing that it is possible to see too much, most doormen in New York have developed an extraordinary sense of selective vision: they know what to see and what to ignore, when to be curious and when to be indolent; they are most often standing indoors, unaware, when there are accidents or arguments in front of their buildings; and they are usually in the street seeking taxicabs when burglars are escaping through the lobby. Although a doorman may disapprove of bribery and adultery, his back is invariably turned when the superintendent is handing money to the fire inspector or when a tenant whose wife is away escorts a young woman into the elevator—which is not to accuse the doorman of hypocrisy or cowardice but merely to suggest that his instinct for uninvolvement is very strong, and to speculate that doormen have perhaps learned through experience that nothing is to be gained by serving as a material witness to life's unseemly sights or to the madness of the city. This being so, it was not surprising that on the night when the Mafia chief, Joseph Bonanno, was grabbed by two gunmen in front of a luxury apartment house on Park Avenue near Thirty-sixth Street, shortly after midnight on a rainy Tuesday in October, the doorman was standing in the lobby talking to the elevator man and saw nothing.[9]

17. Submit a suspended paragraph which, like the "fourteenth century" paragraph on page 157, offers sentences of discussion that lead to a logical conclusion stated by the main sentence.

18. Think of someone you know or would like to know. Then write a suspended paragraph which, like the "Paul Bocuse" example on page 157, reveals that person's identity at the end. In the preceding sentences, take your reader through an action or sequence of actions that are characteristic of that person. Make your account as vivid as you can (1a, p. 9).

## 6i   Keep to a Manageable Paragraph Length.

There is no single "right" size for all paragraphs. In newspaper reporting, where the purpose is to communicate information with a minimum of analysis, paragraphs consist of one, two, or three sentences at the most.

Paragraphs of dialogue also tend to be short; most writers indent for every change of speaker. So, too, scientific and technical journals favor relatively brief paragraphs that present facts and figures with little rhetorical development. And essayists vary considerably among themselves, both in their preference for short or long typical paragraphs and in the paragraph sizes they use within a given essay.

Even so, it is possible to tell at a glance whether your essay paragraphs fall within an acceptable range. If you hardly ever write paragraphs of more than three brief sentences, you are erring on the side of choppiness. Readers will suspect that you have no great interest in exploring your ideas. And if your typical paragraph occupies nearly all of a typewritten, double-spaced page, you are being long-winded, making your reader work too hard to retain the connection between one leading idea and the next. The goal is to show careful sentence-by-sentence thought within a paragraph without allowing the main idea to lose its prominence.

¶ dev
6i

### Avoiding the Choppy Paragraph

If you have a tendency to write brief, stark paragraphs in which the main sentence is accompanied by just one or two other short sentences, reread one of your main sentences and ask yourself what else a reader might want to know about its implications. Do any of its terms need explaining? Where does it lead? What questions or objections does it call to mind? The new statements thus generated can become supporting or limiting sentences (p. 152) that will flesh out the skeleton of your draft paragraph.

Suppose, for example, your draft paragraph looks like this.

**CHOPPY DRAFT PARAGRAPH:**

Acid rain has been destroying the forests of Canada. Although it blows northward from the United States, no one is sure that American factories are the only guilty ones. The damage is extensive, and it may take a court case to find out who is liable.

To gather material for a more developed paragraph, ask yourself what else your reader might profit from knowing:

—*What questions might be asked about acid rain?* What is it? Is the damage irreversible? Can it be prevented?

*—What objections might be raised to the charge that American factories are responsible for destroying the forests of Canada?* Are there other causes? Are American factory emissions mixed with those from Canada itself?

*—Where does the issue of acid rain lead?* For example, to questions of legal liability for "pollution at a distance."

Your revised, adequately developed paragraph might look like this:

**ADEQUATELY DEVELOPED PARAGRAPH:**

¶ dev
6i

American factories, we are told, have been discharging atmospheric wastes that drift northward and fall on Canada as acid rain, destroying valuable forests. We cannot yet tell for certain how extensive the damage is, whether it is irreversible, and whether the pollution could be effectively stopped at its source. Indeed, we cannot be sure that American factories are the only guilty ones. Yet there is little reason to doubt that those factories are the primary source of acid rain and that the damage being caused is very considerable. If so, a landmark case of liability for "pollution at a distance" would seem to be in the offing.

### Avoiding the Bloated Paragraph

If you see that your draft essay or paper contains a bloated paragraph—one that goes on and on without a strong sense of purpose—seek out its main sentence. If you cannot find it, decide what you want your leading idea to be. As soon as you are sure you have a leading idea, check to see that every sentence has some bearing on it. In some cases your long paragraph will split neatly into two new ones, but you should never indent for a fresh paragraph without verifying that both units are internally complete.

Many draft paragraphs begin purposefully but bloat as the writer gets absorbed in details.

**BLOATED DRAFT PARAGRAPH:**

limiting
sentence {
 X  1. If a person feels guilty about something, the obvious thing to do is to get that guilt out in the open. 2. But many people

main
sentence {
 take a different approach, one that only makes matters worse: they try to stifle their bad feelings by means of depressants or stimulants such as alcohol, methedrine, or marijuana. 3. A

friend of mine felt guilty about getting low grades. 4. Her solution was to stay high nearly all the time. 5. But of course that made her get even lower grades and it thus redoubled her

supporting
sentences

guilt, so she had even more bad feelings to hide in smoke. 6. I tried to talk to her about her problems, but she was already too depressed to allow anyone to get through to her. 7. Finally, she left school. 8. I lost touch with her, and I never did learn whether she straightened herself out. 9. I think that people like her deserve a lot of pity, because if she hadn't been so sensitive in the first place, she wouldn't have had the guilt feelings that sent her into a tailspin. 10. People who just don't care are sometimes better off.

This begins as a competent pivoting paragraph (6g, p. 154) contrasting two approaches to the problem of handling guilty feelings and providing an example of the second, self-defeating, approach. The momentum, however, begins to drag as the writer shifts attention to herself in sentence 6, and the paragraph falls apart completely at sentence 9, which escapes the control of the main sentence, number 2. Revising for economy and relevance, the writer decided to do without the sentences about herself and her compassionate attitude.

¶ dev
6i

**ADEQUATELY FOCUSED PARAGRAPH:**

limiting
sentence

main
sentence

supporting
sentences

If a person feels guilty about something, the obvious thing to do is to get that guilt out in the open. But many people take a different approach—one that only makes matters worse. They try to stifle their bad feelings with stimulants or depressants such as alcohol, methedrine, or marijuana. A friend of mine, for example, feeling guilty about her low grades, tried to stay high nearly all the time. The result was that she got even worse grades, felt guiltier still, smoked even more dope, and eventually dropped out of school. Her supposed remedy had become a major part of her problem.

After establishing a middle-sized paragraph as your norm, you can depart from the norm with good effect. A reader who comes across a somewhat longer paragraph will know that a particularly complex point is being developed. Occasionally you can insert a very short paragraph—a sentence or two, or even an intentional sentence fragment (9d, p. 247)—to make a major transition, a challenge, an emphatic statement, or a summary. The emphasis comes precisely from the contrast between the short paragraph and the more developed ones surrounding it.

## EXERCISES

19. Write out a main sentence for a paragraph on any topic you have not treated in a previous exercise. Beneath that sentence, write out answers to the three questions that can usually lead to a remedy for choppy paragraph structure: (a) Where does the main sentence lead? (b) What questions might be asked about the terms it contains? (c) What objections might be raised? Then, using some of the material you have developed, write an adequately full paragraph about your leading idea, using either a direct, a pivoting, or a suspended pattern (6f–6h, pp. 152–158).

20. Look through the readings assigned for this course, or any other prose you may have handy, until you find a paragraph that, in your opinion, goes on too long to be readily grasped by a reader. Rewrite the paragraph to make it more compact and comprehensible, and submit your version with the original—or with a page reference if you found the original in an assigned text. Be sure that the material you omit is not essential support for the main sentence.

¶ dev
6i

## NOTES

¹ Adapted from Carl W. Buchheister and Frank Graham, Jr., "From the Swamps and Back: A Concise and Candid History of the Audubon Movement," *Audubon* Jan. 1973: 7.

² Edith Iglauer, "The Strangers Next Door," *Atlantic* July 1973: 90.

³ Frances Fitzgerald, *America Revised: History Schoolbooks in the Twentieth Century* (Boston: Little, 1979) 10–11.

⁴ Jane Jacobs, *The Death and Life of Great American Cities* (New York: Vintage, 1961) 4.

⁵ T. D. Allman, "Pomp and Desperation," *Harper's* Nov. 1981: 14.

⁶ Timothy E. Head, *Going Native in Hawaii: A Poor Man's Guide to Paradise* (Rutland, Vt.: Tuttle, 1965) 7.

⁷ Matt Clark and Mary Hager, "A Green Pepper a Day," *Newsweek* 28 June 1982: 83.

⁸ "Food: The New Wave," *Newsweek* 11 Aug. 1975: 50.

⁹ Gay Talese, *Honor Thy Father* (1971; Greenwich, Ct.: Fawcett, 1972) 16.

# 7

# Sentences

Strong sentences have much in common with strong paragraphs and whole essays, including a clear idea, emphatic placement of that idea, and subordination of other elements. You can think of the fully developed sentence as a skeletal paragraph containing major and minor components that ought to be easy for a reader to spot:

| | ESSAY | PARAGRAPH | SENTENCE |
|---|---|---|---|
| **MAJOR** | Thesis | Leading Idea | Core Element |
| **MINOR** | Supporting Paragraphs | Supporting Sentences | Free Elements |

$$\text{MAJOR} \quad \frac{\text{Thesis}}{\text{Supporting Paragraphs}} = \frac{\text{Leading Idea}}{\text{Supporting Sentences}} = \frac{\text{Core Element}}{\text{Free Elements}}$$

On each level—essay, paragraph, sentence—your chief purpose in redrafting should be to highlight the major element and to see that it is adequately backed by minor elements that are clearly subordinate to it.

Our keynote in treating sentences will be revision in the direction of *readability,* or the ease with which a reader can grasp your intended meaning. As we will see, the kinds of revision that can make a sentence more readable are also those that can make it memorable. Specifically, we will cover four kinds of sentence improvement that can help you

1. form distinct, readily graspable statements or questions;

2. distinguish between main and subordinate elements;

3. match related elements for emphasis; and

4. vary your patterns of development.

## DISTINCT EXPRESSION

### 7a    Recognize the Core Element of Your Sentence.

**vague 7a**

Since your chief concern in writing any sentence is to communicate an idea, the logical starting point for revision is to locate the **core element** containing that idea and see if you have conveyed it as clearly as possible. Some sentences—those with two or more independent clauses (9b, p. 242) joined by words like *and* or *but*—will prove to have more than one core element, but every full sentence that makes a statement or asks a question will contain at least one. The act of isolating it can often show you where a problem of unclear expression lies.

The following sentences illustrate core elements with and without relation to other elements. The core elements are italicized:

1. *The professional basketball season now runs from September through the middle of June.*

   The whole sentence is a core element.

2. *The players are always tired,* and *they find it hard to take every game seriously.*

   The sentence makes two statements that receive equal emphasis. Both are core elements.

3. *So many teams make the playoffs,* furthermore, *that first-place finishes within a division are scarcely important.*

   One word, *furthermore,* stands apart from the interrupted core element, relating it to a previous statement. Note that the first italicized group of words requires the second one to complete its meaning; together they make one core element.

4. *Would the players,* one wonders, *have longer careers if they were given more rest?*

Note that a core element can be a question (or an exclamation) as well as a statement.

5. Although basketball may have replaced baseball as the national pastime, *we might do better to pass a little more time between seasons.*

The core element—the one that could stand by itself—does not begin until after the word *pastime.* Note that it makes full sense without the *Although* clause.

Note that in a grammatically complete sentence a core element (a) is always an independent clause, and (b) may contain a subordinate clause, as in sentence 3 above (*that first-place finishes . . . are scarcely important*). You find a core element by asking which parts of the sentence *cannot be omitted* if the statement, question, or exclamation is to make sense.

vague<br>7b

---

**EXERCISES**

1. Locate and submit the core element(s) of each of the following sentences:
   A. All over the world, airline safety has become a major issue.
   B. People are wondering whether jumbo jets are as safe as their defenders claim.
   C. Crashes caused by pilot error are just as tragic, but those resulting from defects in design and maintenance are even more unsettling to the public.
   D. Whoever is to blame, however, confidence in air travel has been shaken, at least for a while.
   E. One recent passenger at a ticket counter, asked if he would be smoking, replied, "That depends on the way you land."

2. Type out or photocopy any paragraph of your own prose, written for this or any other course. Underline the core elements, and submit the paragraph.

---

## 7b  Align Your Meaning with Grammatically Important Words.

Your reader wants above all to get the point of your sentence—to take in your main idea without difficulty. Even if that idea is a clear one, you must be sure to make it **distinct** – that is, readily understandable on a first reading of the sentence. When you go back to revise a draft sentence, mentally isolate that set of words and study it with fresh, doubting eyes, as if you didn't know what the writer had in mind. Does the idea make immediate sense? If not, the reason is probably that you have not yet put the essential parts of your idea into the grammatically strongest elements.

The strongest elements in a sentence are generally a *subject* and a *verb,* possibly linked to either a *direct object* or a *complement* (9a, p. 237).

vague<br>7b

- The *committee* S *exists* V .

- The *committee* S *meets* V on Tuesdays.

- The *committee* S *is drafting* V a *report* D OBJ .

- The *committee* S *is* V an official *body* COMPL .

- The *committee* S *seems* V *prepared* COMPL .

Consider this "correct" but unimpressive sentence:

x The *departure* S of the fleet *is thought* V to be necessarily conditional on the weather.

Here the essential grammatical elements are a subject and a verb, *The departure . . . is thought.* This is scanty information; we must root around elsewhere in the sentence to learn what is being said *about* the departure. The idea is that bad weather – here tucked into a prepositional phrase, *on the weather* – may delay the fleet's departure. Once we recognize that point, we can get *weather* into the subject position and replace the wishy-washy construction *is thought to be conditional on* with a verb that transmits action to an object.

DO:

- *Bad weather* S *may keep* V the *fleet* D OBJ at anchor.

Notice that we now have three grammatically strong elements – a subject, a verb, and a direct object – that do carry significant meaning.

DON'T:

          S                               V

x The *thing* the novelist seems to say *is* that the human race is lacking what is needed to keep from being deceived.

This whole sentence is a core element whose subject and verb convey no information: *the thing is.* To find the writer's meaning we must disentangle various embedded infinitives, subordinate clauses, and prepositional phrases, each of which adds a little more strain to our memory.

DO:

       S                                         V

• *Human beings*, the novelist seems to say, necessarily *deceive*
    DOBJ
  *themselves.*

vague
**7b**

Now the subject and verb do convey information. The key grammatical elements, subject–verb–direct object, bear the chief burden of meaning: *Human beings deceive themselves.* And as a result of this realignment, the core element now takes up just five words instead of twenty-three. Notice how the commas make it easy for a reader to tell where that core element is being interrupted.

---

**EXERCISES**

3. Type out or photocopy the following student paragraph, whose core elements are printed in italics. Above the grammatically essential parts of those core elements, write letters indicating the subject *(S)*, the verb *(V)*, and any direct object *(DO)* or complement *(C)*.

> *Our society has always prided itself on having an impersonal, unemotional system of justice.* Supposedly, *we imprison criminals* not to take revenge on them but to "rehabilitate" them under safe conditions. *Prisons,* however, *do not rehabilitate;* if anything, *they are training schools* for further crime. If, knowing this, we leave people in prisons anyway, *we evidently do care* about revenge. *Perhaps the state as a collective body has no vengeful feelings,* but *its individual members demand punishment,* not rehabilitation.

4. The passage used in Exercise 3 shows a good alignment of meaning and grammatically strong elements. To get a better feeling for the difference

between distinct and indistinct expression, rewrite that passage to make it *less* distinct. Submit your deliberately weakened paragraph.

5. Go over your own papers or drafts written for this or any other course, looking for insufficiently distinct expressions that show a weak alignment of grammar and meaning. Revise five sentences to make them more distinct, and submit both the original sentences and the revisions.

## 7c   Watch for Impossible Predication.

**Predication** — saying something about a grammatical subject — is the essence of all statement. In first-draft prose, however, writers sometimes yoke subjects and predicates that fail to make sense together. The most extreme such breakdown is *mixed construction* (10a, p. 256), whereby a reader cannot even locate the subject: x *What they promised on the phone it was very different.* But predication can also go awry if the writer asks a subject to perform something it could not possibly do.

DON'T:

x  The *capabilities* of freshmen in high school *function* on an adult level.

Can capabilities function? No; they are abstractions (8k, p. 225), not agents. People or things function, and they do so because they possess certain capabilities. Thus the revised sentence must reflect that fact.

DO:

- *Freshmen* in high school *are* capable of functioning like adults.

or

- *Freshmen* in high school *have* the capabilities of adults.

or

- The *capabilities* of freshmen in high school *match* those of adults.

You can see that the problem in impossible predication often lies in treating an abstraction as if it were a performer of action. Once you have hit upon a subject like *capabilities* (or *inventiveness, symmetry, rationality, reluctance,* and so forth), your predicate must reflect the fact that you are not writing about an agent.

Again:

DON'T:

S                           V

x  The most fundamental *interests* of the two superpowers *wish* to avoid

                                       PRED

  an all-out war.

Can interests wish? Compare:

DO:

- Both superpowers have a fundamental interest in avoiding an all-out war.

---

EXERCISE

6. Write five sentences that suffer from impossible predication. In each example, match an abstract subject with a verb that would require an agent as a proper subject. Add five adequately revised versions, and submit both sets of sentences.

---

## 7d  Avoid an Overstuffed Statement.

Check your drafts for formless sentences that do not distinguish primary from subordinate elements.

DON'T:

S V

x  *It is* what she recalled from childhood about the begonia gardens that were cultivated in Capitola that drew her to return to that part of the coastline one summer after another.

Since such a sentence demands that all of its elements be kept in mind until the point eventually becomes clear, the sentence often will require two readings. The solution, as we will see more fully below (7j–7m), lies in shortening the core element and setting the minor elements apart.

DO:

- Summer after summer, drawn by her childhood recollections of the Capitola begonia gardens, *she returned* to that portion of the coastline.

> Note how, through a separating out of a key assertion, the sentence becomes more dramatic and easier to grasp. Its core element, instead of being thirty-one words jostling together in a mass, is a readily understood eight-word statement: *she returned to that portion of the coastline.*

**vague**
**7e**

Again:

DON'T:

x  To think that an answer that would be satisfactory had taken so long to arrive was something that put him into a state of deep resentment.

DO:

- He deeply resented the long wait for a satisfactory answer.

Note that every overstuffed statement will also show a misalignment of meaning and grammatically strong sentence elements (7b, p. 165).

---

**EXERCISE**

7. Look through any handy sources, including your own writing, until you have located five overstuffed statements. Watch especially for long strings of words with little or no punctuation, especially if they contain *what* or *that* clauses. (If your search fails, make up new overstuffed statements.) Submit the five examples along with adequately revised versions.

---

## 7e   Do Not Overuse the Verb *to Be.*

You can make your drafts more expressive by cutting down on uses of the colorless, actionless verb *to be* (*is, are, were, had been,* and so forth).

"CORRECT" BUT COLORLESS:

x It *was* clear that the soprano *was* no longer in control of the high notes that *had been* a source of worry to her for years.

STRONGER:

- Clearly, the soprano *had lost* control of the high notes that *had been worrying* her for years.

  The action-bearing verbs in the revised version trim away needless words—notably the plodding prepositional phrases *in control*, *of worry*, and *to her*—and convey the key activities of losing and worrying.

Again:

**vague
7e**

"CORRECT" BUT COLORLESS:

x The knuckleball is a pitch that is hard to handle if a catcher is inexperienced.

STRONGER:

x Knuckleballs give inexperienced catchers fits.

You need not worry about eliminating every last instance of *to be*; that would be pointless and impossible. Forms of *to be* are often justified, as in this very sentence and the previous one. But you can combat weakness and woodenness in your drafts by circling each use of that verb and seeing where you could replace it with a more vivid expression.

 *With a Word Processor:* Instruct your word processor to highlight every example of *to be* in your draft: *am, is, have been, would be,* and so forth. If you cover all forms in all tenses, you can be sure that you won't miss any relevant instances.

**EXERCISE**

8. Find or invent five sentences that would show more distinct expression if they avoided forms of *to be*. Submit those sentences along with adequately revised versions.

## 7f   Convey Action through a Verb, Not a Noun.

As the examples in 7b–7e show, a sentence with an indistinct main idea typically uses nouns instead of verbs to express action. That in itself is no crime, but you can do your prose a favor by habitually moving the action into verbs: not *was no longer in control* but *had lost control*; not *is a source of worry to her* but *worries her*. You gain a little energy with each such shift. Notice the relative vitality of the "stronger" examples below:

"CORRECT" BUT COLORLESS:

x   Some young single people are in a financial arrangement that enables them to have joint ownership of a house.

STRONGER:

• Some young single people have been pooling their resources and buying houses together.

"CORRECT" BUT COLORLESS:

x   A single parent stands in need of occasional relief from the endless responsibilities of workplace and household.

STRONGER:

• Sometimes a single parent must get away from the endless responsibilities of workplace and household.

**vague 7g**

---

EXERCISE

9. Find or invent five sentences which would show more distinct expression if their action were conveyed through verbs rather than nouns. Submit those sentences along with adequately revised versions.

---

## 7g   In Most Contexts, Prefer the Active Voice.

In addition to choosing verbs that show action (7f), you can keep your sentences distinct by generally preferring the active to the passive voice in your verbs: not *was done* but *did*, not *is carried* but *carries*. There are two problems with passive verbs: they can never take direct objects, and they oblige the performer to go unnamed or to be named only in a postponed and minor sentence element.

DON'T:

x *It is believed* by the candidate that a ceiling *must be placed* on the budget by Congress.

x Their motives *were applauded* by us, but their wisdom *was doubted.*

Note how you can save words and impart vividness by substituting active forms.

DO:

• The candidate *believes* that Congress *must place* a ceiling on the budget.

• We *applauded* their motives but *doubted* their wisdom.

**vague**
**7g**

In scientific writing, which often stresses impersonal, repeatable procedures rather than the individuals who carried them out, passive verbs are common. You can also use them in essay prose whenever you want your emphasis to remain on the person or thing acted upon. Suppose, for example, you are narrating the aftermath of an accident. Both of the following sentences would be correct, but you might have good reason to prefer the second, passive, one:

ACTIVE VERB:

• Then three hospital attendants and the ambulance driver *rushed* Leonard into the operating room.

PASSIVE VERB:

• Then Leonard *was rushed* into the operating room.

Although the second sentence is less vivid, it keeps the focus where you may want it to be, on the injured man.

Passive verbs, then, are not automatically "wrong." As you revise your prose, look at each passive form and ask yourself whether you have a good justification for keeping it.

---

EXERCISE

10. Study the passive verbs in each of the following sentences. Indicate with an "OK" which sentences use the passive voice justifiably, and rewrite the others to cast the verbs in the active voice.

A. The defendant was brought to trial after a delay of eleven months.
B. The ball was kicked out of bounds by Biff on his own four yard line.
C. Novosibirsk has been called the most important city in Siberia.
D. Pollution of lakes and rivers is deeply resented by the typical Minnesotan.
E. The Declaration of Independence was called by Thomas Jefferson "the holy bond of our union."

## 7h   Use Delaying Formulas Sparingly and Only for Special Emphasis.

vague
7h

If one of your sentences begins with a subject-deferring expression such as *it is* or *there were,* take a close look at the subject (it is the *weather*; there was a *princess*). That "announced" word stands out emphatically in its unusual position. If you have a special reason for highlighting it, your delaying formula may be justified:

* It is the weather that causes her arthritis to act up.

* There was a princess whose hair reached the ground.

In the first of these sentences, *weather* is isolated as the cause of the arthritis; in the second, the writer succeeds in getting an intended "fairy tale" effect.

More often than not, however, delaying formulas show up in first-draft prose simply because the writer is postponing commitment to a clearly stated assertion. The price of delay is that, without any gain in emphasis, the writer is pushing essential information further back into subordinate parts of the sentence (7b, p. 165). Frequently the result is an awkward and indistinct statement.

DON'T:
x *There is* no reason to suspect that *there is* much difference between what she wrote in her last years and what she felt when *it was* not so easy for her to be candid in her thirties.

DO:
* Her statements in her last years probably express ideas she already held, but was censoring, in her thirties.

Note how much more easily you can take in the revised sentence; you do not have to hold your breath until you can discover what the statement is about. The complete grammatical subject, *Her statements in her last years*, immediately gives us our bearings.

---

**EXERCISE**

11. Indicate which of the following sentences use delaying formulas to good effect, and be prepared to explain what has been gained in each case. Revise the other sentences to achieve more direct expression.

    A. It was exactly at two A.M. that the killer would always strike.

    B. In 1985, there was just 4.6 percent of Americans' after-tax income that they put into savings.

    C. There can be little doubt that immigration has been enormously beneficial to our economy.

    D. There is something that helps to make the literature of the South distinctive, and that is the attempt to represent the exact cadence of local speech.

    E. It was the hard truth, not some syrupy evasion, that she now required of her ashen-faced doctor.

*vague*
**7i**

---

## 7i  Avoid an Unnecessary *That* or *What* Clause.

Look at the DON'T example on page 174 *(There is no reason to suspect that . . .)*. Part of the indistinctness of that sentence comes from its *that* and *what* clauses, which further tax the reader's patience. Such clauses can, it is true, serve a good purpose—for example, arousing a curiosity that can then be emphatically answered:

- *What he needed* above all, after eight hours of steady questioning, was simply a chance to close his eyes.

In much first-draft prose, however, *that* and *what* clauses serve only to nudge the intended statement along in little jerks.

DON'T:

x At the present time, the realities of nuclear terror are such *that* countries *that* possess equal power find, when they oppose each other, *that* the weapons *that* carry the most force are precisely the weapons *that* they cannot use.

DO:

- In this age of nuclear terror, equal adversaries are equally power-less to use their strongest weapons.

Here thirty-nine words have been compressed into sixteen, and a slack, cud-chewing sentence has become tight and balanced (*equal adversaries are equally powerless*). And notice how the grammatical core of the sentence (7b, p. 165) has been given something definite to convey: not *realities are such* but *adversaries are powerless*. Strong, message-bearing elements of thought have been moved into the positions where they normally belong.

vague
7i

EXERCISES (7a–7i)

12. The following paragraph, adapted from a competent student paper, has been doctored to *prevent* a vivid alignment of subjects, verbs, and direct objects with performers of action, actions, and receivers of action. Submit a revised version in which every core element is as distinct as you can make it.

> It is within the graveyard that Hamlet's final revelations about mortality are made. The function of the graveyard setting is operative in several ways. First, Hamlet's continuing confrontation with death receives highly dramatic emphasis here. Second, the digging up of buried motives, which has been a concern of Hamlet's from the beginning, is related to the literal digging of a grave. The buried skulls which are unearthed by the gravedigger are like the secrets toward which Hamlet's investigative efforts have been directed. Finally, Hamlet's final realization of his earthly limits is appropriate to a setting in which an abundance of anonymous bones is evident.

13. Here is a draft paragraph containing ideas that could be made more distinct. Submit a revised version, numbering your sentences to correspond with those below.

> 1. It is generally recognized that most colleges were subjected to a backlash of academic intensity after the political turmoil of the late sixties. 2. There was a desire for restoration of academic standards on the part of faculty members, students showed a concern for the acquisition of preprofessional training, and cost effectiveness was uppermost in the minds of administrators. 3. Now, however, a period of second thoughts appears to have arrived. 4. Whether or not the era of activism can be said to be over, there is a general realization that college life should make provision for something more than a professional union card. 5. What has happened is that the courses required by many colleges have actually been reduced in number in the interest of

allowing time for attendance at public lectures and concerts, good conversation, and even physical and spiritual recuperation from the daily grind of classes.

14. Each of the following sentences needs improvement on grounds of insufficiently distinct expression. To see the problem in each case, find the grammatically essential elements and ask how well they fit together. In addition, decide whether each core element is concise enough. When you are sure you see what the problem is, rewrite the sentence to align main features of meaning with main grammatical units. In most instances you will have to use fewer words to convey the main idea, demoting some parts of the original statement to secondary positions. As a sample, suppose this were the original sentence:

x Instructions are contained in this book for the identification of specific dialect features that teachers should know about if they want to understand their students' problems with the writing of standard English.

**vague**
**7i**

A sound revision might be:

• By showing how to identify specific dialect features, this book can help teachers to understand their students' problems in writing standard English.

Note that the core element of the new sentence takes up fewer words, from *this book* to the end.

A. The rise in the price of oil drilled in conventional wells is a major inspiration for a renewed consideration of the development of new techniques for the extraction of what is known as tar sand crude oil.

B. High hopes for the future of this technology are causing a hopeful mood among petroleum engineers.

C. The tar sand oil is so heavy that it cannot be pumped and instead must be strip-mined with the sand and then subjected to a process of treatment whereby the oil and sand are separated by hot water, steam, and air.

D. There are reasons to believe that the objections of environmentalists rather than technical difficulties will postpone development of this resource.

E. A choice must be made between goals of oil production to be maintained if the world is not to run out of vital energy supplies and the understandable reluctance felt by many people to permit the devastating if perhaps temporary damage caused by strip mining.

## SUBORDINATION

The first thing to do with any draft sentence is to see if you can make its core element more distinct (7a–7i). In doing so, you will usually find yourself using **subordination** – that is, giving secondary emphasis to certain parts of the sentence. As you make those parts clearly minor, you indicate to your reader that another part, the shortened core element, is primary.

## 7j    Subordinate to Highlight Your Main Idea.

When one of your thoughts in a sentence is less important than another, you should put it into a subordinate structure. Thus, if your draft sentence says *The government collects billions of dollars in taxes, and it must meet many obligations,* you should recognize that by using *and* you have given equal weight to two independent remarks. Are they of equal importance in your own mind? If you decide that you really meant to stress the meeting of obligations, you should subordinate the remark about collecting money:

> SUBORD EL
- *By collecting billions of dollars in taxes,* the government manages to meet its obligations.

But if you want to stress the collecting of money, you should turn the meeting of obligations into a subordinate element:

> SUBORD EL
- *Because it has many obligations to meet,* the government must collect billions of dollars in taxes.

When you make an element subordinate, it will usually fit into one of the following (left-hand column) categories. Note how such subordinating words as *because, where,* and *although* (9b, p. 242) not only spare us the trouble of locating the main idea but specify the relation between that idea and the subordinate element.

|  | **WITHOUT SUBORDINATION** | **WITH SUBORDINATION** |
|---|---|---|
| **Time** | The earthquake struck, and then everyone panicked. | Everyone panicked *when* the earthquake struck. |

| | WITHOUT SUBORDINATION | WITH SUBORDINATION |
|---|---|---|
| **Place** | William Penn founded a city of brotherly love. He chose the juncture of the Delaware and Schuylkill rivers. | *Where* the Schuylkill River joins the Delaware, William Penn founded a city of brotherly love. |
| **Cause** | She was terrified of large groups, and debating was not for her. | *Because* she was terrified of large groups, she decided against being a debater. |
| **Concession** | He claimed to despise Vermont. He went there every summer. | *Although* he claimed to despise Vermont, he went there every summer. |
| **Condition** | She probably won't be able to afford a waterbed. The marked retail prices are just too high. | *Unless* she can get a discount, she probably won't be able to afford a waterbed. |
| **Exception** | The grass is dangerously dry this year. Of course I am not referring to watered lawns. | *Except for* watered lawns, the grass is dangerously dry this year. |
| **Purpose** | The Raiders moved to Los Angeles. They hoped to find bigger profits there. | The Raiders moved to Los Angeles *in search of* bigger profits. |
| **Description** | The late Edward Steichen showed his reverence for life in arranging the famous exhibit "The Family of Man," and he was a pioneer photographer himself. | The late Edward Steichen, *himself a pioneer photographer,* showed his reverence for life in arranging the famous exhibit "The Family of Man." |

**sub 7j**

**EXERCISE**

15. Combine each pair of sentences below to form two new sentences using subordination. First subordinate element 1 to element 2 and then vice versa. Be prepared to explain the difference in emphasis between your sentences in each new pair.

   A. 1. Unemployment is beginning to look like a permanent problem in America.

2. Every student wants assurance that a job will be waiting after graduation.
B. 1. Postage rates are discouragingly high.
   2. There are few real alternatives to using the mails.
C. 1. Hang gliding is growing in popularity.
   2. It will never catch on in Kansas.
D. 1. I am an avid sports fan.
   2. I do not intend to watch next Sunday's underwater tug of war between the Miami Dolphins and a team of alligators.
E. 1. The alligators will do all they can to win the prize.
   2. It is hard to imagine what the alligators would do with $500,000.

## 7k   Gain Clarity through Free Subordination.

In the right-hand column of the chart on pages 178–179, note that all but two of the italicized subordinate elements are set apart from the core elements by commas. They are **free elements**—free in the sense of standing alone. By contrast, the sentences *Everyone panicked when the earthquake struck* and *The Raiders moved to Los Angeles in search of bigger profits* contain **bound elements**—that is, they are part of the core elements. Here are some further contrasts:

| BOUND | FREE |
|---|---|
| The Germany *that he remembered with horror* had greatly changed. | Germany, *which he remembered with horror,* had greatly changed. |
| Germany was now inclined toward neutralism *instead of being fiercely militaristic.* | *Instead of being fiercely militaristic,* Germany was now inclined toward neutralism. |
| Hitler had vanished from the scene *along with everything he stood for.* | *Along with everything he stood for,* Hitler had vanished from the scene. |

In general, bound elements are **restrictive**, or defining, and thus they should not be set off by commas (see 11j, p. 288). Free elements, being **nonrestrictive**, or nondefining, should be set apart. But since any phrase or subordinate clause at the beginning of a sentence can be followed by a comma (11h–11i, pp. 284–285), a restrictive element that comes first can be free—that is, followed by a comma:

RESTR AND FREE
- *In September or October,* heating bills begin to rise.

The distinction between free and bound elements is a valuable one for mastering an efficient style. When one of your draft sentences is clumsily phrased, you can often attack the problem by looking for bound elements and then setting them free.

**WITH BOUND SUBORDINATION:**

x The censorship *that is not directly exercised by a sponsor when a program is being produced* may be exercised in many instances by the producers themselves.

sub
7k

**WITH FREE SUBORDINATION:**

- *Even when a sponsor does not directly censor a program,* the producers often censor it themselves.

    Note the importance of the comma after *program,* leaving the reader in no doubt about where the shortened core element begins. Observe, too, that the revised sentence shifts from passive to active verbs (7g, p. 172). Use of the passive voice almost always results in the addition of bound prepositional phrases (*by a sponsor, by the producers*).

**WITH BOUND SUBORDINATION:**

x Nuclear power is an energy source *whose enormous risks to health and safety are out of scale in importance with the fact that it accounts for less than 5 percent of energy production in the United States.*

    Here a main idea has been glued tight to eight subordinate elements: two subordinate clauses (*whose enormous risks . . . , that it accounts for . . .* ) and six prepositional phrases (*to health and safety, of scale, in importance, with the fact, of energy production, in the United States*). The result is an unnecessarily heavy demand on the reader's patience; the sentence offers no resting place and no clear sign of its logical structure.

**WITH FREE SUBORDINATION:**

- Although nuclear power accounts for less than 5 percent of our energy production, it poses enormous risks to health and safety.

Subordination does lead to clarity in this revision, for the comma sets the subordinate element apart from the concise core element. We thus get two crucial advantages: the main idea now takes up only eight words, and the *Although* construction plainly tells us what the sentence's logic will be (*although x, nevertheless y*).

When you find a lengthy, labored core element in a draft, then, look for ways of shortening it by turning bound modifiers into free ones.

---

sub
7k

## EXERCISES

16. Each of the following sentences uses the coordinating conjunction *and* inappropriately, allowing a subordinate meaning to be lost. Rewrite the sentences, using a free element that stands clearly apart from the single main idea in each case.

   A. He is going to apply for the job, and he doesn't have a chance.
   B. She hopes to quit work early today, and she wants to get to the mountains ahead of the weekend traffic.
   C. Farmers want the price of corn to rise this year, and otherwise many of them will be driven out of business.
   D. There has been very little snow this year, and most of the ski resorts are closed.
   E. Most species of American animals have recently been declining in population, and the sea otter is one exception to the rule.

17. Each of the following sentences is clogged with bound subordinate elements that make the main idea indistinct. Without trying to cover every last bit of information in the original sentences, submit revised versions using free subordination to convey the main ideas more distinctly.
   For example:

   **ORIGINAL:**

   x Any time that an accident that involves a spill of toxic substances occurs is a time that could reasonably cause alarm to everyone who lives in the area that surrounds the scene where the accident occurred.

   **REVISION:**

   • Whenever a spill of toxic substances occurs, everyone in the surrounding area has cause for alarm.

A. It is an interesting fact that in America the statistics show that for every adult member of the population there is approximately one automobile.

B. The use of these 130 million vehicles results every day in the consumption of 5.5 million barrels of gasoline coming partly from domestic sources while the rest is made up from foreign ones.

C. Standards for the fuel economy of new cars that the government put into effect for domestic auto makers beginning in 1978 brought about a steady rise in the number of miles per gallon of new cars in each year until the return of the "muscle car" in the mid-eighties.

D. The total consumption of oil in the United States is now less by 3.5 million barrels of oil a day than it was at the time that the new fuel economy standards were passed.

E. Yet it is unfortunately true that the advantage in terms of reduction of dependence on foreign sources of oil has been largely offset by the fact that the domestic production of oil has been declining at about the same rate as the decline in the demand for gasoline.

sub
71

## 71  Place a Free Element Emphatically.

One important feature of free subordinate elements is that they can be moved without a radical loss of meaning. How can you tell where a free element would make the best effect? If you do not trust your ear, you can apply one of the following three principles:

1. *Explain or place conditions on an idea.* If your free element explains your main idea or puts a condition on it, you should consider placing the free element *first.* In that position it will allow your reader to follow your logic from the start:

- *Unless scientists come up with a better explanation,* we will have to lend our belief to this one.

- *Although he finished the test in time,* he missed many of the answers.

- *Because he becomes nervous whenever he isn't listening to music,* he wears earphones while he works.

In first-draft prose, main ideas tend to come first, with limiting or explanatory elements dragging behind. Get those elements into early positions; they will show that you have the entire logic of the sentence under control. And since last positions tend to be naturally emphatic, you can generally make a stronger effect by putting your core element after your free element.

2. *Add to an idea.* If your free element, instead of explaining the main idea or placing a condition on it, merely adds a further thought about it, you should place that free element *after* the core element:

- Her smile disguised her fierce competitiveness, *a trait revealed to very few of her early teammates.*

- His life revolved around his older brother, *who never ceased making unreasonable demands.*

3. *Modify one part of an idea.* If your free element modifies a particular word or phrase, consider placing it *right after* that word or phrase:

- Cézanne's colors, *earthy as his native Provence,* are not adequately conveyed by reproductions.

- They gave me, *a complete newcomer,* more attention than I deserved.

A less usual but sometimes effective position is *right before* the modified element:

- *Earthy as his native Provence,* Cézanne's colors are not adequately conveyed by reproductions.

sub<br>7m

---

**EXERCISE**

18. Submit three original sentences illustrating, in turn, the three principles explained above.

---

## 7m  Avoid Vague Subordination.

We have already noted that subordination in itself is not automatically a good thing. Sometimes you can make a sentence more distinct not by adding subordination but by sharpening a vague subordinate element or eliminating it altogether.

In rereading your drafts, watch especially for tags like *in terms of, with regard to,* and *being as.* Such routine expressions fail to specify how the subordinated element relates to the main idea.

DON'T:

x *In terms of swimming,* she was unbeatable.

> Here a rather pompous subordinate element hints at a cloudy connection between swimming and being unbeatable. The connection can be stated more straightforwardly.

DO:

• *As a swimmer* she was unbeatable.

or

• She was an unbeatable swimmer.

DON'T:

x He felt sympathetic *with regard to their position.*

DO:

• He sympathized with their position.

DON'T:

x *Being as it was noon,* everyone took a lunch break.

DO:

• Everyone took a lunch break at noon.

Other potentially vague subordinators include *with, as, as to, in the area of, in connection with, in the framework of, along the lines of, pertaining to,* and *as far as.*

DON'T:

x *With all that he says about the English,* I believe he has misrepresented them.

DO:

• I believe he has altogether misrepresented the English.

DON'T:

x *As far as finals,* I hope to take all of them in the first two days of exam week.

> To be correct in usage the writer would have to say *As far as finals are concerned,* . . . But unless there is some special reason for singling out finals, a more concise statement would be preferable.

sub
7m

DO:

• I hope to take all of my finals in the first two days of exam week.

---

19. Each of the following sentences shows vague subordination. Submit revised versions that eliminate the problem.

    A. In the framework of chocolate consumption, the British probably take first place.

    B. Regarding the weather, it has been unusually mild in recent weeks.

    C. She left nothing to be desired in terms of her eagerness to learn.

    D. As far as ethics, that is a subject of very little interest to them.

    E. With reference to the obligations facing him this semester, volunteer work would seem to be out of the question.

20. The following passage lacks adequate subordination. Rewrite it, combining sentences and making ample use of free elements.

> Hippocrates used garlic as a pharmaceutical. He used it to treat different diseases, and so did other early doctors. They believed that a plant or herb had a very penetrating odor so it must have a lot of therapeutic value. Tuberculosis and leprosy are not at all alike but garlic was used to treat both of them. There was a Roman naturalist named Pliny. He listed sixty-one diseases; garlic was supposed to cure them all. And he added the information that garlic has very powerful properties and you can tell this because serpents and scorpions are driven away by the very smell of it.[1]

21. In earlier papers or in a draft you have been preparing, find three sentences that now strike you as lacking adequate subordination or as using subordination awkwardly. Submit those sentences along with three revised versions that clear up the problem.

---

**emp
7n**

# EMPHASIS

## 7n  Match Two Elements That Belong Together.

You can achieve emphatic prose not only by making your main ideas stand out against subordinate elements but also by giving the same grammatical structure to elements that are closely related in meaning. Such **matching**, or bringing into **parallelism** (Chapter 14), is emphatic because it makes logical relations immediately apparent to your reader. The idea is to have your grammar reinforce your meaning, not only through the choice of a main subject and verb but also through the structural aligning of key words, phrases, and clauses.

To appreciate this advantage, compare two passages that convey the same information:

A. Animals think *of* things. They also think *at* things. Men think primarily *about* things. Words are symbols that may be combined in a thousand ways. They can also be varied in the same number of ways. This can be said of pictures as well. The same holds true for memory images.

B. Animals think, but they think *of* and *at* things; men think primarily *about* things. Words, pictures, and memory images are symbols that may be combined and varied in a thousand ways.[2]

Passage A, a classically choppy paragraph, takes seven sentences and fifty-one words to say what passage B says in two sentences and thirty-one words. In passage B, seven core elements are reduced to four, with a corresponding gain in understanding. And the key to this concentration is matching—of paired clauses (*Animals think, but they think . . .* ), of conspicuously equal halves of a sentence marked by a semicolon, of nouns in a series (*Words, pictures, and memory images*), and of verb forms (*combined and varied*). Passage B inspires confidence in the writer's control; we feel that she could not have packed her sentences with so much matching structure if she had not known exactly what she wanted to say.

Most instances of matching involve two items that are conspicuously equivalent in emphasis. The following table shows how such items can be matched, with or without **conjunctions** ( joining words such as *and* and *or*).

| PATTERN | EXAMPLE |
|---------|---------|
| $x$ and $y$ | She was tired of *waiting* and *worrying*. |
| $x$ or $y$ | If he had continued that life, he would have faced death *in the electric chair* or *at the hands of the mob.* |
| $x, y$ | He strode away, *the money in his hand, a grin on his face.* |
| $x:y$ | He had *what he wanted: enough cash to buy a new life.* |
| $x; y$ | *He wanted security; she wanted good times.* |

As you can see from these few examples, matching can involve units as small as single words (*waiting* and *worrying*) or as large as whole statements (*he wanted security* and *she wanted good times*).

For problems of usage and punctuation that can arise with parallelism, see Chapter 14.

---

**EXERCISE**

22. Looking through earlier papers or a draft that you have been working on, find a paragraph of your own prose that now strikes you as lacking in the conciseness that matching structures can provide. Type out or photocopy that paragraph, and submit it along with a revised version that is concise and rich in matching. In the revised version, underline the words that constitute the matched items.

**emp
7o**

---

## 7o    Use Anticipatory Patterns.

In the boxed sentences on page 187, each *y* element comes as a mild surprise; we discover that a matching structure is in process only when we reach the second item. But other matching formulas, known as **anticipatory patterns**, announce the pairing of items by beginning with a "tip-off" word.

| PATTERN | EXAMPLE |
|---|---|
| both *x* and *y* | *Both* guerrillas *and* loyalists post a threat to the safety of reporters covering foreign revolutions. |
| either *x* or *y* | *Either* reporters should be recognized as neutrals *or* they should not be sent into combat zones. |
| neither *x* nor *y* | *Neither* the competition of networks *nor* the ambition of reporters justifies this recklessness. |
| whether *x* or *y* | Reporters must wonder, when they wake up each morning in a foreign city, *whether* they will be gunned down by the loyalists *or* kidnapped by the guerrillas. |

| more (less)<br>x than y | It is *more* important, after all, to spare the lives of [x]<br><br>journalists *than* to get one more interview with the typical [y]<br><br>freedom fighter. |
| --- | --- |
| not x but y | It is *not* the greed of the networks, however, *but* the [x]<br><br>changed nature of warfare that most endangers the lives [y]<br>of reporters. |
| not only x<br>but also y | Now reporters covering a guerrilla war find it hard *not*<br><br>*only* to distinguish "friendly" from "unfriendly" elements [x]<br><br>*but also* to convince each side that they are not working [y]<br><br>for the other one. |
| so x that y | Such reporting has become *so* risky *that* few knowledge- [x]<br><br>able journalists volunteer to undertake it. [y] |

Note how the first word of the anticipatory formula prepares us for the rest. As soon as we read *both* or *either* or *so,* we know what kind of logical pattern has begun; we are ready to grasp complex paired elements without losing our way. Anticipatory matching always means improved readability—provided, of course, that the grammar and punctuation of your sentence make the intended structure clear.

To see how anticipatory patterns can aid a reader, compare an imagined first-draft passage with the actual finished version:

A. He swore a lot. He would swear at absolutely anybody. For him it was just the natural thing to do. The people who worked for him probably thought he was angry at them all the time, but it wasn't necessarily true. A man like that could have been just making conversation without being angry at all, for all they knew.

B. He swore so often and so indiscriminately that his employees were sometimes not sure whether he was angry at them or merely making conversation.[3]

Passage A uses more words to make more assertions, yet it never lets us see where it is headed. Nora Ephron's more economical passage B uses two anticipatory structures—*so x and so y that z* and *whether he was x or y*—to pull elements of thought into alignment without squandering whole sentences on them.

---

**EXERCISE**

23. Using any paper or draft, find three of your own sentences that you can make more readable through the use of anticipatory patterns. Submit the original sentences along with the improved versions.

emp
7p

## 7p   Use Balance for Special Emphasis.

When a sentence uses emphatic repetition to achieve matching (7n), it shows **balance**. A balanced sentence usually does two things: (1) it *repeats a grammatical pattern*, and (2) it *repeats certain words so as to highlight key differences*. Thus the two halves of *He wanted security; she wanted good times* use the same subject-verb-object pattern and the same verb, *wanted*, in order to contrast *he* with *she* and *security* with *good times*.

You can see the ingredients of balance in the following **aphorisms**, or memorable sentences expressing very general assertions:

- What is *written without effort* is in general *read without pleasure.* (Samuel Johnson)

- We must indeed *all hang together,* or, most assuredly, we will *all hang separately.* (Benjamin Franklin)

- Democracy substitutes *election by the incompetent many* for *appointment by the corrupt few.* (George Bernard Shaw)

Notice in each instance how the writer has used identical sentence functions to make us confront essential differences: *written/read, effort/pleasure, together/separately, election/appointment, incompetent/corrupt, many/few.*

The art of creating balance consists in noticing elements of sameness and contrast in a draft sentence and then rearranging your grammar so that those elements play identical grammatical roles.

DRAFT SENTENCE:

- Love of the country you live in is a virtue, but I think that it is really more important to love the human species as a whole.

BALANCED VERSION:

- Love of country is a virtue, love of the human species a necessity.

    The first sentence is adequately formed, but it still reads like an idea-in-the-making, the transcript of a thought process. The second, radically concise, sentence uses balance to convey authority and finality.

emp
7q

EXERCISES

24. Study the following passage and then submit a paragraph or two analyzing the writer's use of matching structures to gain emphasis:

    Over the past twenty-five years each new victim who has been gunned down by East German guards, who has bled to death in the barbed wire, or who, wounded by gunfire, has drowned in the Spree River, further confirms both West German impotence and East German resolve regarding the Wall. The effect has been traumatic for Germans of both East and West. The word *Mauer*, "Wall," haunts the German language as does the word *Nazi*. Like the savagery of the Third Reich, the construction of the Berlin Wall not only represents a tragic moment in the history of the German people but also suggests a grievous flaw in the German character. The Germans must wonder at their capacity for such ironic violence: Germans killing Germans trying to flee from Germany to Germany.[4]

25. Using any paper or draft, find three of your own sentences that you can revise to achieve the effect of balance. Submit both the original and the revised versions.

## 7q    Make Your Series Consistent and Climactic.

One indispensable form of matching (7n) is the **series** of coordinated items, three or more elements in parallel sequence. A series tells your reader that the items it contains each bear the same logical relation to some other part of the sentence.

- $\overbrace{Declining\ enrollments}^{x}$, $\overbrace{obsolete\ audio\ equipment}^{y}$, and $\overbrace{hostility\ from}$ $\overbrace{the\ administration}^{z}$ have hurt the language departments.

This says that *x*, *y*, and *z* are comparable factors, each making its contribution to the effect named. Such a condensed, immediately clear statement could replace as many as three rambling sentences in a draft paragraph.

Although the parts of a series must be alike in form, they may have different degrees of importance or impact. Since the final position is by far the most emphatic one, that is where the climactic item should go:

**emp**
**7q**

- He was prepared to risk everything—*his comfort, his livelihood, even his life.*

  If you try to put *his life* into either of the other positions in the series, you will see how vital a climactic order is.

Again:

- For a week and a half, it has been so hot across the South that $\overbrace{chickens\ in\ their\ sheds}^{w}$, $\overbrace{fish\ in\ their\ ponds}^{x}$, $\overbrace{ancient\ oaks\ in\ their}^{y}$ $\overbrace{woods}$, and $\overbrace{people\ in\ their\ homes}^{z}$ have died of the heat.[5]

  The writer would have looked monstrously insensitive if he had placed the *z* element, *people in their homes,* any earlier.

As you can see from the first of these two examples above, you do not always have to put *and* or *or* before the last member of a series. Omitting the conjunction can give the series an air of urgency or importance:

- A moment's *distraction, hesitation, impatience* can spell doom for an aerialist.

Again, if you want to make a crowded or overwhelmed effect, you can omit the commas and put coordinating conjunctions between all members of the series:

- No sooner does one international crisis fade from the headlines than a new one arrives, *an Angola or Nicaragua or Lebanon or South Africa.*

For problems of usage and punctuation that can arise with series, see 14j–14l, pages 325–328.

---

EXERCISES

26. For each item, compose a sentence that places the three terms in a series. Be sure to choose the most emphatic, climactic order of arrangement for those terms:

    A. courage    cheerfulness    patience
    B. the neighborhood    the county    the city
    C. grade school    college    high school
    D. terrors    worries    fears
    E. an inconvenience    an outrage    a disturbance

27. Submit three sentences containing series. In the first, omit a conjunction before the final item in the series. In the second, join all items in the series with conjunctions, not commas. And in the third, include two series, using *both* of the devices practiced in the first two sentences. Beneath each of your three sentences, briefly explain why the optional form or forms you are illustrating suit the idea or mood of this particular statement.

---

## VARIETY

### 7r Include Significant Pauses to Combat Choppiness.

Bear in mind that your prose will be read not in isolated sentences but in whole paragraphs. You, too, should read your drafts that way, checking to see that the sentences within each paragraph sound comfortable in one another's company. If they seem abrupt and awkward, the problem may be a discontinuity of thought. Yet your sentences can be related in thought and still feel unrelated because they are too alike in structure. Watch especially for **choppiness** – a monotonous string of brief, plain statements containing few if any internal pauses. What you want instead is movement between relatively plain sentences and sentences that do contain pauses.

Not all pauses, however, are equally useful in providing variety for a reader. The commas between items in a series (14j, p. 325) have little effect, for those items are all "heading the same way." But even the smallest free element (7k, p. 180), properly set off by punctuation, makes for a

var
7r

**significant pause**, for it calls attention to the relation of one part of the sentence to another.

To appreciate the importance of significant pauses, look first at the following, extremely monotonous, passage:

x  The high snow in the Wasatch Mountains is light and dry. You can't make a snowball out of it. This is Utah powder. It makes for some of the West's greatest skiing. The numerous slopes are regularly groomed. The snow crunches under your skis. It forgives your rusty technique. It gives gently under your fall. There is deep, new powder in the back bowls. You float up and over the ground. Plumes of white mist curl around your waist like smoke.

> var
> 7r

Here every sentence consists entirely of a brief core element. The passage goes almost nowhere in little jerks, like a stalled snowmobile being nudged by its starter motor. Now compare the actual published text:

•  The snow that falls high in the Wasatch Mountains is so light and dry that you can't make a snowball out of it. This is Utah powder, and it makes for some of the West's greatest skiing. On the numerous slopes that are regularly groomed, the snow crunches under your skis, forgiving if your technique is rusty, giving gently if you fall. On the deep new powder of the back bowls, you float up and over the ground, plumes of white mist curling around your waist like smoke.[6]

These four sentences contain more words than the eleven above—their average length is twenty-two words instead of seven—yet their message is more comprehensible, and certainly more pleasant to take in, than exactly the same message delivered in Dick-and-Jane sentences. Why? Since the words used are almost identical, the difference in effect must be entirely due to sentence variety. Three features are especially noteworthy:

1. The second passage requires us to deal with only five core elements, not eleven.

2. The second passage, therefore, spares us the bothersome work of deciding which among the eleven assertions are the important ones.

3. Because the five core elements are not bunched together, we enjoy some "breathing space" between emphatic statements and a sense of increasing freedom as we progress.

When you find choppy passages in your drafts, look for ways of combining sentences, turning the less important ones into free subordinate elements.

CHOPPY:

x The bill passed the Senate. It was defeated in the House.

IMPROVED:

FREE EL
• *Although the bill passed the Senate,* it was defeated in the House.

CHOPPY:

x Our coach talked about next week's game. He said it will be crucial.

IMPROVED:

FREE EL
• *According to our coach,* next week's game will be crucial.

CHOPPY:

x The chairman of the board decided to resign. He was mindful of the plunge in earnings.

IMPROVED:

FREE EL
• *Because of the plunge in earnings,* the chairman of the board decided to resign.

CHOPPY:

x Such a woman can be helpful to us. She can be our advocate.

IMPROVED:

FREE EL
• Such a woman, *furthermore,* can help us by becoming our advocate.

In addition, a pause marked by the comma separating two independent clauses works against choppiness:

• The bill passed the Senate, but it was defeated in the House.

• Earnings plunged, and the chairman of the board decided to resign.

See Chapter 11 for the relevant comma rules.

**EXERCISE**

28. Here are several choppy sentences in a row. Using much of the same language but adding and subtracting where necessary, write a revised version that eliminates the problem of choppiness. You need not keep the same number of sentences.

Atari was the pioneer in video games. The company ran into serious problems in the early 1980s. The trouble was that the real profits lay in software. Atari had invented the hardware. Any rival company could market programs that could run on Atari's console. Activision, Imagic, and Mattel's Intellivision quickly exploited that advantage. This happened as soon as they realized the opportunity before them. Atari's managers were so used to leading the field that they failed to realize they were being overtaken.

## 7s   Use an Occasional Question or Exclamation.

**var**
**7s**

Usually an idea-in-progress appears as a succession of statements, or **declarative sentences**. But to show strong feeling, to pinpoint an issue, to challenge your reader, or simply to enliven a string of sentences, you can make use of a strategically placed question or exclamation:

- *What are we to make of the decline of our automobile industry?* Let us begin with the inescapable fact of foreign competition.

- And this is all the information released so far. *Does anyone doubt that the Congressman has something to hide?*

- *A million tons of TNT!* The power of this bomb was beyond anyone's imagination.

- Once the grizzlies were deprived of garbage, their population declined steeply. *So much for the "back to nature" school of bear management!*

Note, in the second of these examples, that the writer asks the question without expecting an answer, for the question "answers itself." Such a **rhetorical question** can work well for you in driving home an emphatic point. Since rhetorical questions have a coercive air, however, you should use them sparingly.

### EXERCISE

29. Submit five numbered sets of two sentences each. In each pair, include one question or exclamation that is closely related to the point of the other sentence.

## 7t    Practice the Emphatic Interruption.

To give special emphasis to one statement or piece of information, try turning it into an interruption of your sentence:

- The street Jerry lived on—*it was more like an alley than a street*— was so neighborly that he scarcely ever felt alone.

- The hot, moist summer air of Florida—*people call it an instant steambath*—makes an air conditioner a necessity in every home and office.

- A woman of strong opinions—*her last movie grossed $50 million, and she calls it a turkey*—she is not exactly a press agent's dream come true.

var<br>7u

As you can gather, dashes are the normal means of punctuating an emphatic interruption.

In a variation on the interruptive pattern, you can begin your sentence with a lengthy element—for example, a series (7q, p. 191)—and follow it with a dash announcing that the core element of the sentence is about to begin:

- *Going to hairdresser school, marrying the steady boyfriend, having the baby, getting the divorce*—everything in her life seemed to follow some dreary script.

Such a sentence takes the reader off guard by making a **false start**. We assume at first that the opening element will be the grammatical subject, but we readjust our focus when we see that the true subject will come after the dash. (The first element is actually in apposition to the subject; see 11k, p. 288.)

---

**EXERCISE**

30. Submit five original sentences in which you practice the emphatic interruption.

---

## 7u    Practice Inverted Syntax.

Readers normally expect subjects to come before verbs, but for that very reason you can gain emphasis by occasionally reversing that order. The subject becomes more prominent as a result of such **inverted syntax**:

- In the beginning was the *Word.*

- Most important of all, for the would-be tourist, is a *passport* that has not expired.

Similarly, any sentence element that has been wrenched out of its normal position and placed first gets extra attention:

- *Not until then* had he understood how miserable he was.

- *Never again* will she overlook the threat of an avalanche.

Again:

var
7v

- *About such a glaring scandal* nothing need be said.

    The subject and verb, *nothing* and *need,* are in the usual sequence, but the writer begins with a prepositional phrase that would normally come last.

---

**EXERCISE**

31. Submit five sentences illustrating the principle of inversion. In each case underline the word or words that you have made more emphatic by means of the inverted structure.

---

## 7v    Practice the Cumulative Sentence.

A **cumulative sentence** is one whose main idea is followed by one or more free subordinate elements (7k, p. 180). It is called cumulative because it "accumulates" or collects modifying words, phrases, or clauses after the heart of the statement is complete. The following sentences, encountered earlier, are typical:

- Her smile disguised her fierce competitiveness, *a trait revealed to very few of her early teammates.*

- He was prepared to risk everything—*his comfort, his livelihood, even his life.*

- No sooner does one international crisis fade from the headlines than a new one arrives, *an Angola or Nicaragua or Lebanon or South Africa.*

The beauty of the cumulative pattern is that it offers refinement without much risk of confusing the reader. Since the basic structure of the sentence is complete before the end-modifiers (italicized above) begin, your reader has a secure grasp of your idea, which you can then elaborate, illustrate, explain, or reflect on. And since much of our speech follows the cumulative model of statement-plus-adjustment, a cumulative sentence on the page can make a pleasantly conversational effect, as if one afterthought had brought the next one into mind.

**EXERCISE**

32. Find five relatively plain sentences in your own writing, and submit them along with five expanded versions that have been made cumulative.

var
7w

## 7w    Practice the Suspended Sentence.

If you substantially delay completing your main idea, forcing your reader to wait for the other shoe to drop, you have written a **suspended sentence** (often called a *periodic sentence*). Through its use of delaying elements (italicized in the following examples), a suspended sentence can be an effective means of leading to a climax:

• It appears that their success was due more to the influence of their father, *so dominant in the worlds of business and politics that every door would open at his bidding,* than to any merits of their own.

• The states argued that they had indeed complied, *if compliance can mean making a good-faith effort and collecting all the required data,* with the federal guidelines.

• If you are still unused to the idea of gasohol, you will certainly not be ready to hear that some diesel engines will soon be running on *that most humble and ordinary of products, taken for granted by homemakers and never noticed by auto buffs,* vegetable oil.

**EXERCISES (7r–7w)**

33. Starting from any five sentences, perhaps including some already used in recent exercises, add the subordinate elements necessary to create five suspended sentences. Submit only the revised versions.

34. Study the use of sentence variety in the following paragraph, and then submit a three-sentence paragraph of your own, on any topic, making use of the same patterns you perceive here:

> Men wear their belts low here, there being so many outstanding bellies, some big enough to have names of their own and be formally introduced. Those men don't suck them in or hide them in loose shirts; they let them hang free, they pat them, they stroke them as they stand around and talk. How could a man be so vain as to ignore this old friend who's been with him at the great moments of his life?[7]

35. Taking the numbered sentences one by one, analyze all the elements of sentence variety that you find in the following paragraph:

> 1. In desperate fantasy one thinks, at times, of escaping. 2. From childhood there remains a faint memory, nearly lost, of a stream in a Northern forest: a stone dam, a trickling sluice, a hut of some sort where the dam-keeper lives. 3. The loon cries over a lake, the pines stretch endlessly, black against the sky. 4. And then one thinks of *The New York Times* on Sunday, five pounds of newsprint, a million-and-a-half copies a week. 5. How many miles of forest, birds flung from their nests, the work of honey bees wasted, does our Sunday paper, thrown aside between breakfast and lunch, consume?[8]

var
7w

---

## NOTES

[1] Adapted from Michael Field, *All Manner of Food* (New York: Knopf, 1970) 4–5.

[2] Susanne K. Langer, "The Lord of Creation," *Fortune* Jan. 1944: 140.

[3] Nora Ephron, "Seagrams with Moxie," *New York Times Book Review* 11 Mar. 1979: 13.

[4] Timothy W. Ryback, "Why the Wall Still Stands," *Atlantic* Aug. 1986: 23.

[5] Dudley Clendinen, "Even the Fish Die in Streams As the Dust-Dry South Bakes," *New York Times* 17 July 1986, national ed.: 1.

[6] "Skiing Utah Powder," *Sunset* Jan. 1976: 39.

[7] Garrison Keillor, *Lake Wobegon Days* (New York: Penguin, 1986) 5.

[8] Jason Epstein, "Living in New York," *New York Review of Books* 6 Jan. 1966: 15.

# 8
## Words

To convey your ideas successfully, you need to know words well and to respect their often subtle differences from one another. Specifically, when revising your drafts you should make sure that your words

1. mean what you think they mean;

2. are appropriate to the occasion;

3. are concise;

4. are neither stale, roundabout, nor needlessly abstract;

5. show control over figurative, or nonliteral, implications; and

6. use "sound effects" to the advantage of your meaning.

This chapter explains and illustrates all six requirements. In addition, beginning on page 563 you will find an alphabetically ordered Index of Usage which identifies and resolves common misunderstandings. You should consider the Index of Usage an extension of this chapter as well as a permanent reference tool.

# APPROPRIATE MEANING

## 8a    Use Your College Dictionary.

To make progress in your control of **denotation**, or the dictionary meaning of words, it is essential that you own a college dictionary such as *The Random House College Dictionary, Funk and Wagnalls Standard College Dictionary, Webster's New World Dictionary of the American Language, Webster's New Collegiate Dictionary, The American Heritage Dictionary of the English Language,* or *The Gage Canadian Dictionary.* These volumes are large enough to meet your daily needs without being too cumbersome to carry around. Once you learn from the prefatory guide to your dictionary how to interpret its abbreviations, symbols, and order of placing entries, you can find in it most—perhaps all—of the following kinds of information:

| | | |
|---|---|---|
| spelling | capitalization | symbols |
| parts of speech | origins | biographical and given names |
| definitions | usage levels | places and population figures |
| synonyms | syllable division | weights and measures |
| alternate forms | principles of usage | names and locations of |
| pronunciation | abbreviations | colleges |

To see what a college dictionary can and cannot do, look at *Random House's* entry under *fabulous*:

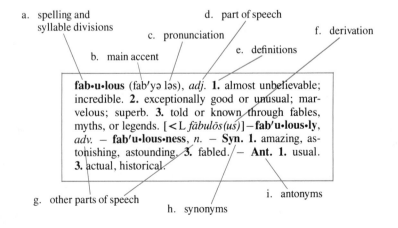

a.  spelling and
syllable divisions

b.  main accent

c.  pronunciation

d.  part of speech

e.  definitions

f.  derivation

**fab·u·lous** (fab'yə ləs), *adj.* **1.** almost unbelievable; incredible. **2.** exceptionally good or unusual; marvelous; superb. **3.** told or known through fables, myths, or legends. [ < L *fābulōs(us)* ] — **fab'u·lous·ly,** *adv.* — **fab'u·lous·ness,** *n.* — **Syn. 1.** amazing, astonishing, astounding. **3.** fabled. / — **Ant. 1.** usual. **3.** actual, historical.

g.  other parts of speech

h.  synonyms

i.  antonyms

The entry shows, in the following order:

a. how the word is spelled and the points where syllable divisions occur (*fab-u-lous*);

*Comment:* The lower-case *f* shows that *fabulous* is not normally capitalized.

If this word could be spelled correctly in different ways, the less common form would appear in a separate entry with a cross reference to the more common form; thus the entry for *reenforce* merely sends you to *reinforce.* In your writing, use the spelling under which a full definition has been given.

Syllable division is not completely uniform from one dictionary to another, but you cannot go wrong by following your dictionary's practice in every case. (You can also spare yourself trouble by not breaking up words at all; a little unevenness in right-hand margins is normal.)

mean
8a

b. where the main accent falls (*fab'*);

*Comment:* If the word had another strongly stressed syllable, like *hand* in *beforehand,* you would find it marked with a secondary accent: *bi • for'* hand'.

c. how the word is pronounced;

*Comment:* The pronunciation key at the bottom of every pair of pages reveals, among other things, that ə = *a* as in *alone.* (One dictionary's key will differ from another's.) College dictionaries make no attempt to capture regional or nonstandard pronunciations, like x *n$\overline{oo}$' kul • ər* for *n$\overline{oo}$' klē ər (nuclear).*

d. the part of speech (*adj.* for *adjective*);

*Comment:* Some words, like *can* and *wait,* occupy more than one part of speech, depending on the context. Definitions are grouped according to those parts of speech. Transitive verbs (those that take an object—9a, p. 237) are usually listed separately from intransitive verbs (those that take no object). Thus *Random House* gives all the intransitive senses of *wait* (*v.i.*), as in *Wait for me,* before the transitive senses (*v.t.*), as in *Wait your turn!*

e. three definitions of *fabulous*;

*Comment:* No dictionary lists definitions in the order of their acceptability. The dictionary illustrated here begins with the most common part of speech occupied by a given word and, within each part of speech, offers the most frequently encountered meaning first. Some other dictionaries begin with the earliest meaning and proceed toward the present. The system used in your dictionary is clearly set forth in the prefatory material, which you should read through at least once.

f.  the word's derivation from the first three syllables of the Latin word *fabulosus*;

*Comment:* The derivation or *etymology* of a word is given only if its component parts are not obviously familiar—as they are, for example, in *freeze-dry* and *nearsighted.* Many symbols are used in stating etymologies; look for their explanation in the prefatory material of your dictionary.

g.  an adverb and a noun stemming from the main word;

*Comment: Fabulously* and *fabulousness* are "run-on entries," words formed by adding a suffix (24f, p. 429) to the main entry.

h.  synonyms of definitions 1 and 3;

*Comment:* In most dictionaries a word with many apparent synonyms—words having the same or nearly the same meaning—is accompanied by a "synonym study" explaining fine differences. Thus, this dictionary's entry for *strength* concludes:

> —**Syn.  4.** STRENGTH, POWER, FORCE, MIGHT suggest capacity to do something. STRENGTH is inherent capacity to manifest energy, to endure, and to resist. POWER is capacity to do work and to act. FORCE is the exercise of power: *One has the power to do something. He exerts force when he does it. He has sufficient strength to complete it.* MIGHT is power or strength in a great degree: *the might of an army.*

This would be useful information if you were wondering which of the four similar words to use in a sentence. If you looked up *power, force,* or *might,* you would find a cross reference to the synonym study under *strength.*

i.  antonyms (words with the opposite meaning) of definitions 1 and 3.

*Comment:* If you are searching for a word to convey the opposite of a certain term, check its listed antonyms. But if you still are not

mean
8a

satisfied, look up the entries for the most promising antonyms and check their synonyms. This will greatly expand your range of choice.

So much for *fabulous*. But other sample entries would reveal still further kinds of information:

1. *inflected forms.* Some entries show unusual inflected forms—that is, changes in spelling expressing different syntactic functions. You will find unusual plurals (*louse, lice*); unusual principal parts of verbs (*run, ran, run*—see 21b, p. 394); pronoun forms (*I, my, mine,* etc.); comparative and superlative degrees of adjectives (*good, better, best*—see 23a, p. 416).

2. *restrictive labels.* The entry will show how a word's use may be limited to a particular region (*Southern U.S., Austral., Chiefly Brit.*); to an earlier time or a particular occasion (*Archaic, Obs., Poetic*); to a particular subject (*Bot., Anat., Law*); and, most important for the writer, to a level of usage for words not clearly within standard American English (*Nonstandard, Informal, Slang*).

3. *usage study.* Beyond its usage labels, your dictionary may offer especially valuable discussions of usage problems surrounding certain controversial words or meanings, such as *ain't, different from/ than,* or *hardly* with negative forms:

> **—Usage.**  HARDLY, BARELY, and SCARCELY all have a negative connotation, and the use of any of them with a supplementary negative is considered nonstandard, as in *I can't hardly wait* for *I can hardly wait.*

mean
**8a**

---

## EXERCISES

1. After consulting your dictionary, use your own words to write brief definitions of both terms in each of the following pairs:

   A. accent, accentuate *(verbs)*
   B. accused, suspected *(adjectives)*
   C. adverse, averse
   D. alternate, alternative *(adjectives)*
   E. barbaric, barbarous
   F. childish, childlike

G. elemental, elementary
H. healthful, healthy
I. infect, infest
J. possible, feasible

2. Using your dictionary as necessary, explain the chief differences of denotation, or dictionary meaning, between the following paired words:

A. ample, excessive
B. avenue, road
C. cunning, politic
D. overhear, spy
E. ecstatic, happy
F. bold, brash
G. erotic, lustful
H. impartial, indifferent
I. simulate, fake
J. opponent, enemy

mean
8b

## 8b    Keep a Vocabulary List.

The only way to be certain that you have broadened your written vocabulary is to try out new words in your papers, risking an occasional inaccuracy while gradually building your store of useful words. But how are you to acquire those words in the first place?

Many student writers rely heavily on a *thesaurus,* or dictionary of synonyms and antonyms. Synonyms, however, are rarely exact, and the thesaurus will not indicate fine differences of meaning. If you consult a thesaurus, do so to jog your memory of words already known, not to get fancy new language into your prose. The best way to build vocabulary is to notice how unfamiliar words are used by published authors and to keep a record of your discoveries.

By taking the following steps, you can systematically increase the number of words whose meanings you have mastered:

1. Whenever someone criticizes your use of a word or you come across an unfamiliar word in your reading, look it up or make a note of it until you can get back to your dictionary.

2. After you have looked it up, write the word and its definition on a notebook page.

3. Every time you add an entry, quickly scan the previous entries to see if you have mastered them yet. Cross out entries that you now consider to be part of your normal working vocabulary.

To supplement your vocabulary list, go over the Index of Usage (pp. 563–580). Make an entry for each word whose indicated meaning is new to you. Note especially those terms that get easily confused (*affect* versus *effect, imply* versus *infer,* etc.). If you tend to use either term in the pair incorrectly, add both of them to your list.

*With a Word Processor:* Put your draft papers through a "SEARCH ALL" command for the words that you have previously tended to misuse. With each questionable instance highlighted, you can check to see if you now have the problem under control.

**mean
8c**

---

**EXERCISE**

3. Once your vocabulary list has begun to grow, copy and submit any five entries, including a definition for each word.

---

## 8c    Use Words in Established Senses.

English is probably the fastest-changing of all languages, and yesterday's error often becomes today's standard usage. As a writer, however, you should be concerned not with anticipating shifts in taste but with communicating your ideas effectively. Many readers are upset by diction that is being used in some capricious or momentarily popular way. By being conservative in your choice of words, you can avoid arousing automatically negative responses to the content of your work.

Many fad words have a common feature: they usually belong to one part of speech but are being used as another. Sometimes a suffix (24f, p. 429) such as *-wise* or *-type* has been added to turn a noun into an adjective or adverb.

DON'T:

x *Gaswise,* the car is economical.

x *Preferencewise,* she is looking for a *commuter-type* car.

DO:

- The car gets good mileage.

- She wants a car suitable for commuting.

More often, one part of speech simply takes over another.

DON'T:

x  It was a *fun* party.

x  She *authored* the book in 1987.

x  We *gifted* the newlyweds with a toaster.

x  Mark is a *together* person.

x  I would give anything for an *invite* to the party.

DO:

- The party was *fun*.

- She *wrote* the book in 1987.

- We *gave* the newlyweds a toaster.

- Mark is a *confident, competent* person.

- I would give anything for an *invitation* to the party.

## Attributive Nouns

The use of nouns as adjectives deserves special mention in an age of spreading bureaucracy. Standard English allows many such **attributive nouns**, as they are called, as in *mountain time, night vision, cheese omelet,* and *recreation director.* But officials have a way of jamming them together in a confusing heap. A frugal governor, for example, once proposed what he called a *community work experience program demonstration project.* This row of nouns was meant to describe, or perhaps to conceal, a policy of getting welfare mothers to pick up highway litter without receiving any wages. As a student writer, you would be wise to avoid changing the customary part of speech of a word or piling up attributive nouns.

---

EXERCISE

4. Study the following entries in the Index of Usage (pp. 563–580): *enormity, enthuse, fortuitous, fulsome, hopefully, imply/infer, literally, mad, militate/mitigate, otherwise, part/portion, phenomena, plus, possible,*

*rebut/refute, reticent,* and *usage.* Choose the five expressions that you yourself tend to use most often in the criticized ways. If you have to stop before five items, fill out the quota with those expressions that you think are most commonly misused by other writers. For each of the five terms, submit a pair of original sentences, first showing a typical misuse and then a correct one.

## 8d    Control Connotations.

The prime requirement for controlling meaning is to know the *denotations,* or dictionary definitions, of the words you are using. (See 8a–8c.) But words also have important **connotations** – further suggestions or associations derived from the contexts in which the words have been habitually used. By and large, you will not find connotations in your dictionary; you have to pick them up from meeting the same words repeatedly in reading and conversation. Of course you cannot expect to learn all the overtones of every English word. But as a writer you can ask yourself whether the words you have allowed into your first drafts are appropriate to the occasion. When you are unsure, think of related words until you find one that conveys the right associations.

mean
8d

Take, for example, the words *store, shop,* and *boutique.* Because of the contexts in which the words most often appear, they *connote* different things. When we think of a *store,* we picture an establishment where merchandise is sold. A *shop* suggests a smaller establishment selling a specific type of goods, or a department in a larger store, such as the *card shop* at Field's. A *boutique* is a small shop that specializes in fashionable items, often clothing or accessories for women. If you were writing about the corner grocery that keeps your neighborhood in bread, milk, and other staples seven days a week, you would want to call it a *store.* To call it a *shop* or a *boutique* would undercut your purpose in pointing out the establishment's diverse and ordinary stock.

Consider two further examples, *complex* versus *complicated* and *workers* versus *employees.* Although the members of each pair are close in denotation, their connotations differ. Suppose you wanted to characterize an overelaborate instruction manual. Would you call it *complex* or *complicated*? We hope you would choose *complicated,* which can imply not just intricacy but more intricacy than is called for. And if you were criticizing harsh factory conditions, you would want to write about mistreated *workers,* not mistreated *employees.* These words denote the same people, yet *employees* characterizes them from a corporate point of view, whereas *workers* calls to mind laborers whose interests and loyalties may be quite different from those of the company.

Note that there is such a thing as getting connotations too lopsidedly in favor of your own position on an issue. Suppose, for example, you were writing an essay about discourtesy among adolescents. If you chose the term *young thugs* to characterize teenagers, you would certainly be making your feelings clear, but you would also be *begging the question* (3k, p. 76), forcing your reader to respond emotionally with you or against you. In revising your essays, tone down any inflammatory language that seems to convey ready-made conclusions.

---

**mean**
**8e**

**EXERCISES**

5. Explain whatever differences of connotation you find between the following paired words:

    A. stout, fat
    B. express, communicate
    C. hasten, scurry
    D. talented, gifted
    E. investigate, inquire

6. Submit a paragraph of your own prose written for this or any other course. Circle three words whose connotations strike you as appropriate to your precise intention. Then, beneath the paragraph, briefly discuss the connotations of all three words, contrasting them with the connotations of three other words that would have proved less appropriate. (Your rival choices should be "near misses," not wildly implausible terms.)

---

## 8e  Avoid Racist and Sexist Language.

Since you are writing to convince, not to insult, nothing can be gained from using offensive terms. Racial slurs like *nigger, honky,* and *wop,* demeaning stereotypes like *pushy Jew* and *dumb Swede,* and sexually biased phrases such as *lady driver, female logic,* and *typical male brutality* make any fair-minded reader turn against the writer.

The problem of sexism in language deserves special discussion because it goes beyond any conscious wish to show prejudice. In recent decades people have been increasingly realizing that long-accepted conventions of word choice imply that women are inferior or are destined for restricted roles. To keep sexist language out of your prose, then, it is not enough to avoid grossly insulting terms like *tomato* and *broad*; you must be watchful for subtler signs of condescension as well.

If, for example, you call William Shakespeare *Shakespeare,* why should you call Emily Dickinson *Miss Dickinson* or, worse, *Emily*? Such names imply that a woman who writes poems is not really a poet but a "poetess," a "lady poet," or even a "spinster poet." Write about *Dickinson's poetry,* thus giving it the same standing you would the work of any other author. Similarly, use *sculptor* and *lawyer* for both sexes, avoiding such designations as *sculptress* and *lady lawyer.* And do without *coed,* which suggests that the higher education of women is an afterthought to the real (male) thing. Make your language reflect the fact that, in North America at any rate, men and women are now considered equally eligible for nearly every role.

mean
8e

Tact is necessary, however, in deciding how far to go in changing traditional expressions. The ideal is to avoid sexism without sacrificing clarity and ease of expression. If you wrote *actor* for *actress* and *waiter* for *waitress,* for example, your readers would be confused; rightly or wrongly, common usage still recognizes separate terms for male and female performers of those functions. But when in doubt, choose a sex-neutral term: not *mankind* but *humanity,* not *man-made* but *artificial.*

### *-Person*

Try to find nonsexist alternatives to awkward *-person* suffixes, which sound ugly to many readers of both sexes.

| SEXIST | NONSEXIST BUT AWKWARD | PREFERABLE |
|---|---|---|
| chairman | chairperson | chair, head |
| Congressman | Congressperson | Representative |
| mailman | mailperson | letter carrier |
| policeman | policeperson | police officer |
| weatherman | weatherperson | meteorologist |

### The Pronoun Dilemma

Perhaps the sorest of all issues in contemporary usage is that of the so-called **common gender**. Which pronouns should you use when discussing an indefinite person, a "one"? Traditionally, that indefinite person has been "male": *he, his, him,* as in *A taxpayer must check his return carefully.* For the centuries in which this practice went unchallenged, the masculine pronouns in such sentences were understood to designate not actual men but people of either sex. Today, however, many readers find those words an offensive reminder of second-class citizenship for women. Remedies that have been proposed include using the phrase *he or she* (or *she or he*) for the common gender, treating singular common words as plural (*A taxpayer must check their return*), combining masculine and feminine pronouns in forms like *s/he,* and using *she* in one sentence and *he* in the next.

Unfortunately, all of these solutions carry serious drawbacks. Continual repetition of *he or she* is cumbersome and monotonous; many readers would regard *A taxpayer must check their return* as a blunder, not a blow for liberation; pronunciation of *s/he* is uncertain; and the use of *she* and *he* in alternation, though increasingly common, risks confusing the reader by implying that two indefinite persons, a female and a male, are involved.

mean
8e

To avoid such awkwardness, follow these five guidelines:

1. Use *she* whenever you are sure the indefinite person would be female (a student in a women's college, for example):

* Someone who enters a nunnery must sacrifice everything from *her* former life.

2. Do not use *she* for roles that have been "traditionally female" but are actually mixed: secretary, school teacher, laundry worker, and so forth. Female pronouns in such contexts imply an offensive prejudgment about "women's place." Use plural forms to show a sex-neutral attitude.

DON'T:
x  A kindergarten teacher has *her* hands full every day.

DO:
* Kindergarten teachers have *their* hands full every day.

3. Use an occasional *he or she* or *she or he* to indicate an indefinite person:

* When a driver is stopped for a traffic violation, *he or she* would do well to remain polite.

But be sparing with this formula; it can quickly become annoying.

4. Avoid the singular whenever your meaning is not affected.

DON'T:

x  A taxpayer must check *his* return.

DO:

• Taxpayers must check *their* returns.

5. Omit the pronoun altogether whenever you can do so without awkwardness.

ACCEPTABLE:

• Everyone needs *his or her* vacation.

BETTER:

• Everyone needs *a* vacation.

mean
8f

---

EXERCISE

7. Rewrite each of the following sentences, removing sexist implications without creating an awkward effect:

    A. A nurse's heavy responsibilities can eventually cause her to experience what is known as "nurse's burnout."

    B. You had better take those soiled sheets to the nearest laundress.

    C. Someone who drives too slowly on the freeway is a menace to his fellow drivers.

    D. A policeman in that neighborhood had better be prepared to defend himself against muggers.

    E. All mankind is eager for peace.

---

## 8f  Avoid Jargon.

**Jargon** is specialized language that appears in a nonspecialized context, thus giving a technical flavor to statements that would be better expressed in everyday words. When you are writing a paper in, say, economics, anthropology, or psychology, you can and should use terms that are meaningful within the field: *liquidity, kinship structure, paranoid,* and so forth. But those same terms become jargon when used out of context.

DON'T:

x  My liquidity profile has been weak lately.

DO:

• I have been short of cash lately.

DON'T:

x Her kinship structure extends from coast to coast.

DO:

• Her family is scattered from coast to coast.

DON'T:

x Roland was really paranoid about the boss's intentions.

DO:

• Roland was suspicious of the boss's intentions.

mean
8f

Most jargon today comes from popular academic disciplines such as sociology and psychology, from government bureaucracy, and from the world of computers. Here is some of the more commonly seen jargon, accompanied by everyday equivalents that would usually be preferable.

| JARGON | ORDINARY TERM |
| --- | --- |
| access (v.) | enter, make use of |
| behaviors | acts, deeds, conduct |
| correlation | resemblance, association |
| cost-effective | economical |
| counterproductive | harmful, obstructive |
| ego | vanity, pride |
| facilitate | help, make possible |
| feedback | response |
| finalize | complete |
| input | response, contribution |
| interface (v.) | meet, share information with |
| maximize | make the most of |
| obsession | strong interest |
| parameters | borders |
| prioritize | prefer, rank |
| reinforcement schedule | inducements |

| JARGON | ORDINARY TERM |
|--------|---------------|
| sociological | social |
| syndrome | pattern |
| trauma | shock |
| user-friendly | uncomplicated |

You can put jargon to good comic or ironic use, but when you find it appearing uninvited in your drafts, revise.

---

mean
8f

**EXERCISE**

8.  Here is a fictitious letter making fun of a certain "official" style. Pick out several examples of jargon and submit comments on the way they convey or disguise meaning:

Dear Miss Dodds:

Thank you for your letter deploring the 14,000 fish deaths apparently related to thermal outflow into Long Island Sound from our nuclear power facility at Squaw Point. While the blame for this regrettable incident might most properly be ascribed to the fish, which swam closer to the Connecticut shore than is their normal habit, we believe that the ultimate solution must be found in terms of "the human element." Specifically, it is a task of public education in this era when customer demand for power markedly exceeds the deliverability capability of the electrical segment of the energy usage industry.

Do you ever stop to think, Miss Dodds, where the power comes from when you flick on your air-conditioner, your hair dryer, your cake mixer, your vacuum cleaner, and the myriad other appliances that enable you to live in "the lap of luxury" vs. the meager subsistence standard enjoyed by most of the peoples of the world? Until the American housewife is willing to go back to the egg beater and the broom, the utilities industry cannot be made the scapegoat for occasional episodes of ecological incompatibility.

Many consumers today advocate "zero growth" and a turning back of the clock to a simpler agrarian past. Quite frankly, if the rural American of 1900 had been as counter-oriented to the ongoing thrust of technology as certain romantic elements are in 1973, the outhouse would never have been supplanted by the flush toilet.

Very truly yours,
NORMAN R. HOWELL
Vice President for Consumer Relations
AFFILIATED UTILITIES COMPANY[1]

## 8g    Avoid Euphemisms.

A **euphemism** is a squeamishly "nice" expression standing in the place of a more direct one. Some words that began as euphemisms, such as *senior citizen* and *funeral director,* have passed into common usage, but you should try to avoid terms that still sound like ways of covering up a meaning instead of conveying it. Euphemisms often conceal a devious political or commercial motive. If you want to be regarded as candid and trustworthy, do not write *discomfort* for *pain, memory garden* for *cemetery, pass away* for *die, relocation center* for *concentration camp, adult* for *pornographic,* and so forth.

mean
8g

DON'T:

x  The Governor is concerned about *human resources development.*

DO:

• The Governor is concerned about *unemployment.*

DON'T:

x  The candidate issued a press release *declaring* that her earlier remarks about her opponent were now to be considered *inoperative.*

DO:

• The candidate issued a press release *admitting* that her earlier remarks about her opponent were *untrue.*

DON'T:

x  We are recalling all late models because the bearings *at variance with production code specifications* may *adversely affect vehicle control.*

DO:

• We are recalling all late models because the *defective* bearings may cause drivers to *lose control of the steering.*

---

**EXERCISES**

9. Submit revised versions of the following sentences, substituting direct language for any euphemisms that you find:

A. The departed one is now receiving visitors in the adjacent slumber chamber, prior to journeying to his final resting place in the memory garden.

B. Repair of defective underground wastewater conveyance devices constituted her mode of employment.

C. The chairman of the board declared that certain facilities, along with their attendant personnel, would be granted an indefinite furlough from utilization in view of demand slackness throughout the consumer sector.

D. The Raiders have been known to get physical near the end of a hopelessly disadvantageous contest, provoking incidents of a questionably sportsmanlike nature.

E. In the absence of an affirmative sign of compliance with our repeated solicitations for appropriate reimbursement, we have no alternative to the regrettable option of terminating the dispensation of utilities to your residential fixtures.

level
8h

10. The following classic paragraph by George Orwell deals with euphemism in political language. Write a paragraph of your own about this passage, showing how it embodies or exemplifies its author's belief in the need for vivid diction.

> In our time, political speech and writing are largely the defence of the indefensible. Things like the continuance of British rule in India, the Russian purges and deportations, the dropping of the atom bomb on Japan can indeed be defended, but only by arguments which are too brutal for most people to face, and which do not square with the professed aims of political parties. Thus political language has to consist largely of euphemism, question-begging, and sheer cloudy vagueness. Defenceless villages are bombarded from the air, the inhabitants driven out into the countryside, the cattle machine-gunned, the huts set on fire with incendiary bullets: this is called *pacification*. Millions of peasants are robbed of their farms and sent trudging along the roads with no more than they can carry: this is called *transfer of population* or *rectification of frontiers*. People are imprisoned for years without trial, or shot in the back of the neck or sent to die of scurvy in Arctic lumber camps: this is called *elimination of unreliable elements*. Such phraseology is needed if one wants to name things without calling up mental pictures of them.[2]

# LIVELINESS

## 8h    Prefer Middle Diction in Most Contexts.

Different situations call for different levels of diction (word choice), from the slang that may be appropriate in a letter to a friend, to the formal language expected in a legal document, to the technical terms demanded by a scientific report. But whenever you are writing outside such special contexts, you should aim for *middle diction*—language that is neither too casual to convey serious concern nor too stiff to express feeling.

The best way to recognize levels of diction is to be an observant reader of different kinds of prose and a close listener to conversations. But if you have studied Latin or a "Latinate" modern language such as Spanish, French, or Italian, you have a head start toward spotting formal English diction. All the words in the right-hand column below are both formal and Latinate:

| SLANG | MIDDLE DICTION | FORMAL DICTION |
|---|---|---|
| mug | **face** | visage |
| kicks | **pleasure** | gratification |
| threads | **clothes** | attire |
| specs | **glasses** | spectacles |
| rip off | **steal** | expropriate |
| big-mouthed | **talkative** | voluble |

**EXERCISES**

11. Use your dictionary, if necessary, to help you decide which level of diction (formal, middle, or informal) is illustrated by each of the following words. Whenever you label a word as formal or informal, provide a middle-level equivalent:

    A. irritate
    B. hyperbole
    C. birdbrain
    D. zonked
    E. fluoridate
    F. refractory (*adjective*)
    G. indemnify
    H. gal
    I. oafish
    J. resist

12. For each of the following middle-level words, give one formal and one informal equivalent:

    A. friend
    B. understand
    C. smell (*noun*)

D. clothes
E. rob
F. see
G. idea
H. change (*verb*)
I. leave (*verb*)
J. good

13. Return to the "airline food" passage on page 85 and examine its language. Submit a paragraph or two explaining how the writer has achieved her effect in part by controlling levels of diction. Be specific in citing her words.

livel
8i

## 8i    Be Concise.

Your reader's attention will depend in large part on the ratio between information and language in your prose. Wordiness, or the use of more words than are necessary to convey a point, is one of the most common and easily corrected flaws of style. The fewer words you can use without harm to your meaning, the better.

| WORDY | CONCISE |
|---|---|
| among all the problems that exist today | among all current problems |
| an investment in the form of stocks and bonds | an investment in stocks and bonds |
| at the present time | now |
| due to the fact that | because |
| during the course of | during |
| for the purpose of getting rich | to get rich |
| for the simple reason that | because |
| in a very real sense | truly |
| in spite of the fact that | although |
| in the not too distant future | soon |
| in view of the fact that | since |
| it serves no particular purpose | it serves no purpose |
| majoring in the field of astronomy | majoring in astronomy |
| my personal preference | my preference |

| WORDY | CONCISE |
|---|---|
| on the part of | by |
| owing to the fact that | because |
| proceeded to walk | walked |
| rarely ever | rarely |
| seldom ever | seldom |
| the present incumbent | the incumbent |
| to the effect that | that |

**livel
8i**

## Avoiding Redundancy

A **redundancy** is an expression that conveys the same meaning more than once—for example, *circle around,* which says "go around around." The difference between writing *She circled the globe* and x *She circled around the globe* is that in the second version the word *around* delivers no new information and thus strains the reader's patience.

Examine your drafts to see if they contain redundancies, and be uncompromising in pruning them. The following examples are typical.

| REDUNDANT | CONCISE |
|---|---|
| adequate enough | adequate |
| advance planning | planning |
| both together | both |
| but yet | but |
| contributing factor | factor |
| deliberate lie | lie |
| equally as far | as far |
| exact same symptoms | same symptoms |
| few in number | few |
| final outcome | outcome |
| free gift | gift |
| join together | join |
| large in size | large |
| past experience | experience |

| REDUNDANT | CONCISE |
|---|---|
| past history | history |
| refer back | refer |
| set of twins | twins |
| share in common | share |
| shuttle back and forth | shuttle |
| two different reasons | two reasons |

## Avoiding Circumlocution

All redundancies fall into the broader category of **circumlocutions**—that is, roundabout forms of expression. But some circumlocutions, instead of saying the same thing twice, take several words to say almost nothing. Formulas like *in a manner of speaking* or *to make a long story short,* for example, are simply ways of making a short story long. Watch especially for cumbersome verb phrases like *give rise to, make contact with,* and *render inoperative;* prefer *arouse, meet, destroy.* And if you mean *because,* do not reach for *due to the fact that.* When five words do the work of one, all five are anemic.

| CIRCUMLOCUTION | CONCISE EXPRESSION |
|---|---|
| He was of a kindly nature. | He was kind. |
| It was of an unusual character. | It was unusual. |
| My father and I have differences about dating. | My father and I differ about dating. |
| At this point in time . . . | Now . . . |
| I finally made contact with my supervisor. | I finally met my supervisor. |
| The copy that is pink in color is for yourself. | Keep the pink copy. |
| She suspected she would be in an unemployment-type kind of situation when the overflow of customers due to the Christmas shopping circumstances was no longer in effect. | She suspected she would be laid off after the Christmas rush. |

livel
8i

## Pruning Intensifiers

In conversation most of us use **intensifiers**—"fortifying" words like *absolutely, basically, certainly, definitely, incredibly, intensely, just, of course, perfectly, positively, quite, really, simply,* and *very*—without pausing to worry about their meaning. And in telling stories or expressing opinions we veer toward the extremes of *fantastic, terrific, sensational, fabulous,* and *awful, horrible, terrible, dreadful.* Our listeners know how to allow for such exaggeration. Most written prose, however, aims at a more measured tone. Look through your drafts for intensifiers, and see how many of them you can eliminate without subtracting from your meaning. Your revised work will not only be more concise and therefore less taxing to read, it will also sound more assured. Readers sense that intensifiers are morale-building words meaning *maybe* or *I hope*; doing without such terms is a sign of your confidence that you are making a sound case for your ideas.

**level
8i**

### WITH INTENSIFIERS:

x It was another *very* routine start to a two-week vacation. I *definitely* had no fixed plans other than *simply* flying to Denver. I knew Colorado was a *fantastic* state, and *basically* that is all I thought about as I settled into my assigned seat. As the aircraft door was about to be closed, a man walked in and occupied the vacant seat next to me. He mumbled something to me in an *absolutely* foreign accent. The departure was *very* uneventful. All we *really* did was try to kill time, but the book he was reading *just* attracted my interest: *Cave Exploring in the USA.* I *certainly* was curious and asked him if cave exploring interested him. That was when he explained—*incredibly*—that in France he was a professional cave explorer. After the dinner service ended we talked, and his stories of days underground were *positively* fascinating. Finally, he invited me to join him, and I *quite* happily accepted.

### WITHOUT INTENSIFIERS:

• It was another routine start to a two-week vacation. I had no fixed plans other than flying to Denver. I knew Colorado was an exceptional state, and that is all I thought about as I settled into my assigned seat. As the aircraft door was about to be closed, a man walked in and occupied the vacant seat next to me. He mumbled something in a foreign accent. The departure was uneventful. All we did was try to kill time, but the book he was reading attracted my interest: *Cave Exploring in the USA.* I was curious and asked him if cave exploring interested him. That was when he explained that in France he was a professional cave explorer. After the dinner service ended we talked; his stories of days underground were fascinating. Finally, he invited me to join him, and I happily accepted.

## Putting Statements in Positive Form

Negative ideas are just as legitimate as positive ones; you may have to point out that something failed to occur or that an argument leaves you unconvinced. But the negative modifiers *no* and *not* sometimes make for wordiness and a slight loss of readability. If you write *We are not in agreement,* you are asking your reader to go through two steps, first to conceive of agreement and then to negate it. But if you simply write *We disagree,* you have saved three words and simplified the mental operation. The gain is small, but good writing results from a sum of small gains.

Of course you need not be mortified by every use of *no* or *not.* Observe, however, that negatively worded sentences tend to be slightly less emphatic than positive ones.

livel<br>8j

| NEGATIVE | POSITIVE |
|---|---|
| She did not do well on the test. | She did poorly on the test. |
| He was not convicted. | He was acquitted. |
| They have no respect for rationing. | They despise rationing. |
| It was not an insignificant amount. | It was a significant amount. |

### EXERCISES

14. Look through your own prose—earlier exercises, papers, or drafts—until you have found five sentences that seem deficient in conciseness. Submit the five sentences along with five adequately concise revisions.

15. Write a paragraph in which you deliberately use an abundance of wordy expressions, redundancies, circumlocutions, intensifiers, and negative modifiers. Submit it along with a suitably improved version.

## 8j   Avoid Clichés.

A **cliché** is a trite, stereotyped, overused expression such as *throw money around* or *bring the house down.* Clichés are **dead metaphors**—that is, they are figures of speech that no longer sound figurative. When someone writes *off the wall* or *the bottom line,* no reader sees a wall or a line. On the other hand, a writer could blunder into causing people to see real bricks by saying *On the first day that June worked in the construction* *crew, Steve fell for her like a ton of bricks.* (For such accidentally revived clichés, see 8l, p. 230.) But the usual effect of clichés is not unintended comedy but simple boredom. The reader feels that the writer is settling for prepackaged language instead of finding the exact words to convey a particular thought. And matters are not improved by the apologetic addition of *so to speak* or *as the saying goes.* When you need to apologize for any expression, change it.

The worst thing about cliché-ridden prose is its predictability. As soon as we register one element of the cliché, the rest of it leaps to mind like an advertising jingle:

**livel 8j**

pleasingly . . . plump

lines of . . . communication

the foreseeable . . . future

the pieces . . . of the puzzle . . . fall into place

The resultant prose—*to be brutally frank*—is a *far cry* from being a *sure winner* in the *hearts and minds* of readers *from every walk of life.*

Three lists of clichés follow. List A includes examples of gross clichés, which you can spot fairly easily and eradicate as you revise. List B includes less obvious clichés, pairs of seemingly inseparable adjectives and nouns, clusters that choke out your originality as a writer. List C consists of pat expressions that say too little in a wordy and predictable manner.

---

**LIST A: GROSS CLICHÉS**

| | |
|---|---|
| a needle in a haystack | old as the hills |
| a pig in a poke | on cloud nine |
| blind as a bat | quiet as a mouse |
| carve a niche for oneself | rule with an iron fist |
| drive one to distraction | sly as a fox |
| happy as a lark | smart as a whip |
| high as a kite | sow one's wild oats |
| live like a king | the top of the heap |
| look a gift horse in the mouth | tough as nails |
| make a beeline for | up the creek |

| LIST B: "INSEPARABLE" PAIRS | |
|---|---|
| bounce back | nuclear holocaust |
| flawless complexion | supreme moment |
| grave danger | unforeseen obstacles |
| high spirits | vicious circle |
| integral part | vital role |

| LIST C: PAT EXPRESSIONS | |
|---|---|
| after all is said and done | in the final [last] analysis |
| at this point in time | it goes without saying |
| far be it from me | it stands to reason |
| in a very real sense | once and for all |

livel
8k

**EXERCISES**

16. With classmates or friends, draw up a list of clichés supplementing those mentioned above. Then submit five sentences in which you call attention to the clichés by treating them literally.
    Examples:

    - She will *string him along* until he agrees to *tie the knot.*

    - Never trust ventriloquists; they *talk out of both sides of their mouth.*

17. Look through your own prose—earlier exercises, papers, or drafts—until you have found five clichés. Copy and submit the sentences in which they occur, adding revised versions in each case. If your own prose doesn't yield five instances, make up the quota from any published source.

## 8k   Be Concrete.

**Concrete** words name observable things or properties like *classroom* and *smoky*; **abstract** words convey ideas like *education* and *pollution*— nonphysical things that we can grasp only with our minds, not with our senses. Of course there are gradations between the extremes: a *university* is more concrete than *education* but less so than a *classroom,* a distinct physical place. The more concrete the term, the more vivid it will be to a reader.

Whenever you are describing something or telling a story, you can hardly go wrong by making your successive drafts more concrete. Suppose you are trying to characterize your new typewriter, which you have praised in your first draft as *extremely modern.* That is an abstract judgment that could mean anything to anyone. What precisely is modern about the machine? In revising, think about *the daisy wheel printing unit, the automatic return, the automatic correction, the sixteen-character memory, the programmable margin settings,* and so forth. Get the concrete details into your essay, convincing your reader that your general statements rest on observations.

Even in papers of analysis and argument, where the thesis is necessarily an abstract idea, concrete language will help you provide supporting details and retain your reader's interest. Here, for example, are two versions of a student paragraph. In drafting the first, the writer was evidently thinking of himself as a social-science major. When asked to revise for an essay audience, he looked for ways of turning abstract statements into concrete ones:

A. Lasting trauma from early stress is probably causally related to two factors: heritability of susceptibility and the age at which the stress occurs. In infant rhesus monkeys, certain members of the experimental population prove more susceptible to permanent disturbance than others; heritability is thus an indicated factor. Furthermore, the entire population yields a finding of greater vulnerability when administration of stress occurs between the precise ages of two and seven months. Such a finding suggests that among humans, too, a period of maximum vulnerability may obtain.

B. A recent study of rhesus monkeys may offer us some clues to the way people react—and sometimes don't react—to early stress. Baby monkeys who have been put into solitary cages tend to become feisty and to stay that way. We might have expected as much. But some monkeys, oddly, act normal again almost as soon as they have rejoined their fellows; it seems that they have inherited a resistance to trauma. Furthermore, the most aggressive monkeys turn out to be those who were isolated within a precise period, between the ages of two and seven months. If these findings carry over to humans, we can see why it is risky to generalize about the effects of *all* early stress. What matters may not be whether you suffered in infancy, but who your parents were and exactly when your ordeal occurred.

Neither of these paragraphs abounds in concrete language, but the relative concreteness of passage B helps to explain why it is easier to grasp and more pleasurable to read. Note that weighty, awkward abstractions like *heritability of susceptibility* have disappeared and that we now see *Baby monkeys . . . in solitary cages,* not a *population* that has undergone *administration of stress.*

---

18. Make the following sentences more vivid by substituting concrete language where it is appropriate:

    A. She attended scheduled sessions at the institution of higher learning with unfailing regularity.
    B. Daytime serial dramatic programs had his undivided concentration.
    C. The small rodents are of lasting interest to cats, who would never willingly forgo an opportunity for the pursuit and seizure of same.
    D. In northern regions, conspicuous display of emotions on the part of members of the populace is rather the exception than the rule.
    E. Loss of control of one's sense of reality has come to be recognized by courts of law as a factor tending to favor the acquittal of a defendant who was afflicted in that manner.

19. Professor X describes himself as follows in a classified advertisement:

    Sophisticated, debonair college prof., 35, recently divorced, with liberal values and classical tastes, seeks broadminded female companion for travel and cultural pursuits. Knowledge of vintage wines and modern verse desirable. Send photo. Box 307, NYR.

    What do you think Professor X is really like? Write a paragraph describing him vividly, and then underline all the concrete diction you have used.

---

## 8l   Sharpen Your Figurative Language.

If you think about an essay topic imaginatively as well as rationally, you will find yourself likening the material before you to other things. Such resemblances can lead you to choose a comparison-and-contrast framework for the whole essay or, on a smaller scale, to use an occasional *analogy* (2i, p. 46) to make a point more vivid. But even on the level of single words and phrases you can heighten interest and clarity by stating one thing in terms of another. The nonliteral diction that expresses imaginative comparison is called **figurative language**.

## Simile and Metaphor

Two closely related figures of speech allow you to draw imaginative likenesses. A **simile**, by including the word *like* or *as,* explicitly acknowledges that a comparison is being made.

SIMILE:

- *Like* a patio rotisserie, George's mind always keeps turning at the same slow rate, no matter what is impaled on it.

    George's mind is explicitly compared to a rotisserie.

A **metaphor** omits *like* or *as.*

METAPHOR:

- George's hedgeclipper mind gives a suburban sameness to everything it touches.

    George's mind is compared to hedgeclippers, but without either of the explicit terms of comparison, *like* or *as.*

In theory a metaphor is a more radical figure of speech than a simile, for it asserts an identity, not just a likeness, between two things (George's mind "is" a gardening tool). But in practice one kind of figure can be as striking as the other. What counts is not the choice between simile and metaphor but the suitability of the *image,* or word picture, to your intended meaning. The two images about George, for example, call to mind not only his conformism but also his specifically suburban background (the carefully tended hedge, the patio rotisserie).

Again:

SIMILE:

- The old judge's fingers were tapping absently like the keys of a player piano.

    A player piano, like the old judge, evokes another era. Just as that instrument played without anyone's touching the keys, so the judge presumably allows his mind to wander while his fingers stay active.

METAPHOR:

- In her eyes Rodney was a peacock, so obsessed with his own courtship display that he never noticed who she really was.

The peacock and Rodney, different in every other regard, are both showy suitors absorbed in their supposed magnificence.

## The Extended Figure of Speech

If you do have a suitable image, you may find that it is not altogether self-explanatory. Without running the image into the ground, you can sometimes add a sentence or two that clarifies its implications. Thus a student writer *extended* her simile:

- For me, the idea of going on for an advanced degree is like that of rowing across the ocean. Perhaps I could do it and perhaps I couldn't. But what, I wonder, is waiting for me on the other side, and isn't there some faster and safer way of getting there? Until I know the answers to these questions, I intend to keep my feet planted on familiar soil.

level
81

So, too, a professional author added a clarifying sentence of elaboration to a striking simile:

- This generation thinks — and this is its thought of thoughts — that nothing faithful, vulnerable, fragile can be durable or have any true power. Death waits for these things as a cement floor waits for a dropping light bulb. The brittle shell of glass loses its tiny vacuum with a burst, and that is that.[3]

In either of these passages one further sentence might have produced tedium. Both images are pursued just long enough to give us the full thought lying behind them.

Once in a while, you may find a figure of speech so rich in implication that it does merit fuller development. Note, for example, how one writer uses the image of a bird to tie together her memories of the great dancer Anna Pavlova:

As her little bird body revealed itself on the scene, either immobile in trembling mystery or tense in the incredible arc which was her lift, her instep stretched ahead in an arch never before seen, the tiny bones of her hands in ceaseless vibration, her face radiant, diamonds glittering under her dark hair, her little waist encased in silk, the great tutu balancing, quickening and flashing over her beating, flashing, quivering legs, every man and women sat forward, every pulse quickened. She never appeared to rest static, some part of her trembled, vibrated, beat like a heart. Before our dazzled eyes, she flashed with the sudden sweetness of a hummingbird in action too quick for understanding by our gross utilitarian standards, in action sensed rather than seen.

The movie cameras of her day could not record her allegro. Her feet and hands photographed as a blur.

Bright little bird bones, delicate bird sinews! She was all fire and steel wire. There was not an ounce of spare flesh on her skeleton, and the life force used and used her body until she died of the fever of moving, gasping for breath, much too young.[4]

## Avoiding Mixed Metaphor

If you remain aware that you are using figurative language and if you check to see that each image is carried through consistently, you will avoid the embarrassment of **mixed metaphor** — the clashing of one image with another.

livel
8l

**MIXED METAPHOR:**

x Although some analysts feel that the Presidential primary system is the wrong game plan for choosing the best nominee, they forget that primaries are an important mirror and proving ground of our democracy. To be sure, candidates can get burned out on the hustings. But by diving into the very heart of state and county politics, the survivors of this pressure cooker can acquire a hands-on feeling for the people they hope to govern.

This passage begins with a sports metaphor, *game plan,* but before the first sentence is over we have been taken through two more incompatible images, a *mirror* and a *proving ground.* The next sentence tells us that candidates can get *burned out on the hustings* (literally, speaking platforms) — a mixed metaphor that unintentionally suggests a public execution. And finally, those candidates who survive the *pressure cooker* are said to be *diving into a heart* where they can get a *hands-on feeling.* Emergency surgery in the kitchen? Clearly, this writer likes to reach for the handiest figurative language without taking responsibility for its implications.

**EFFECTIVE METAPHOR:**

• A tiger in the jungle of politics, he was a pussycat around the house.[5]

The images of *tiger* and *pussycat* are closely related, and the writer (characterizing his father-in-law, Harry Truman) fully controls the different implications of the two terms.

Perhaps you feel that you can avoid mixed metaphors by shunning figurative language altogether. But insofar as you do, your prose will be flat and colorless. Besides, it is not really possible to be completely unfigurative. Many ordinary terms and nearly all clichés (8j, p. 223) are **dead metaphors** — that is, they contain the faint implication of an image which we are not supposed to notice as such (the *leg* of a table, a *blade* of grass). When clichés are used in close succession, they mischievously come back to life as mixed metaphors:

x *Climbing to the heights* of oratory, the candidate *tackled* the issue.

x Either we *get a handle* on these problems or we are all *going down the drain.*

x You can't *sit on your hands* if a recession is developing, because *you don't know where the bottom is.*

x They thought it would be a *dynamite* movie, but it *bombed.*

livel
8l

Figurative language, then, can be tricky. When you intend an abstract meaning, you have to make sure that your dead metaphors stay good and dead. But when you do wish to be figurative, see whether your image is vivid, fresh, and consistent. Literal statement may be safe, but a striking figure carried through consistently can unify and intensify your sentences. For further insight into the uses of figurative language, see 1d, p. 16.

---

**EXERCISES**

20. List all the figures of speech you find in the following passage, and briefly discuss the relation of each image to the one preceding it. Do you find any problems of mixed metaphor? If so, explain.

> Academics, it has been said before, are very much like people who drive their cars by looking through their rear-view mirrors. Looking backward does offer certain satisfactions and provides splendid intellectual vistas, but it hardly brings into focus the best view of the road ahead. Academics may seem to bemoan the fact that the federals now hold the cards, and that they must do their bidding, however reluctantly. But the facts would appear to be otherwise: it is the federals who are at least trying to game-plan an extremely delicate future, while most academics remain on the sidelines, seized by fits of moral indignation about the felt deprivation of their intellectual autonomy. It would rarely occur to them that the federal planners would like nothing better than a showing of academia's own imaginative initiatives and social vision, if only they would gird themselves for that sort of resolve.[6]

21. Look through your own prose — earlier papers or drafts — until you find five examples of figurative language. Copy the complete sentence in each

instance, and submit it with a brief comment on the appropriateness or inappropriateness of the image you chose. If you now think a different image would have served better, present and justify that image. If your own writing doesn't yield five examples, make up the difference from any published source.

## 8m    Watch for Sound Patterns.

Knowing that repeated sounds draw attention, you can sometimes use them deliberately, as Mark Twain did in referring to

- the *calm confidence* of a *Christian* with four aces,

or as Thomas Paine did in writing

- These are the *times* that *try* men's souls,

or as Theodore Roosevelt did in advising his countrymen to

- *Speak softly* and carry a big *stick*.

In these examples the "poetic" quality goes along with the effort to make a concisely emphatic statement.

Unless you are after some such effect, however, beware of making your reader conscious of rhymes (*the side of the hide*) or alliteration (*pursuing particular purposes*) or repeated syllables (*apart from the apartment*). These snatches of "poetry" usually result from an unconscious attraction that words already chosen exert on subsequent choices. Having written *the degradation*, you write *of the nation* because the *-ation* sound is in your head. You may have to read your first draft aloud, attending to its sound and not its sense, in order to find where you have lapsed into jingling.

Abstract Latinate words—the ones that usually end in *-al, -ity, -ation*, or *-otion*—are especially apt to make a repetitive sound pattern. It is worth the pains to rewrite, for example, if you find bunched words like *functional, essential, occupational*, and *institutional* or *equality, opportunity, parity*, and *mobility*.

Finally, watch for clusters of prepositions that stand out annoyingly:

x A lot *of* journalists *of* different points *of* view were there.

x They learned a lesson *from* her conclusions *from* the incident.

Compare:

- Many journalists holding different points of view were there.
- Her conclusions from the incident taught them a lesson.

---

**EXERCISE**

22. Submit five sentences in which patterns of repeated sound cause an unwelcome distraction. Be original in your choice of words. Circle the words that cause the problem of bothersome "poetry." Then add five revised sentences that eliminate the problem.

---

## NOTES

[1] William Zinsser, "Frankly, Miss Dodds," *Atlantic* Apr. 1973: 94.

[2] George Orwell, "Politics and the English Language," *A Collection of Essays* (Garden City, N.Y.: Anchor, 1954) 172–73.

[3] Saul Bellow, *Herzog* (1964; New York: Viking, 1967) 290.

[4] Agnes De Mille, *Dance to the Piper* (New York: Da Capo, 1980) 43.

[5] Clifton Daniel, "Presidents I Have Known," *New York Times* 3 June 1984, sec. 6: 84.

[6] G[eorge] W. B[onham], "The Decline of Initiative," *Change* Apr. 1973: 16.

# IV

## USAGE

9. Complete Sentences

10. Subject-Verb Relations

11. Modifiers

12. Cases of Nouns and Pronouns

13. Pronoun Reference

14. Parallelism

15. Relations between Tenses

## USAGE

Whatever you have to say in your writing, you will want to say it within the rules of **standard written English**—the "good English" that readers generally expect to find in papers, reports, articles, and books. Fortunately, you already follow most of those rules without having to think about them. In fact, if you did think about them while composing, you would have trouble concentrating on your ideas. The time to worry about correctness is after you have finished at least one draft. Then you can begin making certain that your points will come across without such distractions as incomplete sentences, spelling errors, and subjects and verbs that are incorrectly related.

Problems with standard written English are usually divided into those of **usage** and those of **punctuation**—that is, between rules for the choice and order of words (usage) and rules for the insertion of marks to bring out a sentence's meaning (punctuation). But usage and punctuation work together toward the same end of making sentences coherent, or fitting together in an easily understood way. Certain classic "usage" problems, such as the sentence fragment and the run-on sentence, are punctuation problems as well. Therefore, though we review the punctuation marks and their functions separately (Chapters 16–20), we also deal with punctuation in the present set of chapters. For example, if you are having trouble with modifiers or parallel constructions, you will find those topics treated as whole units, without artificial postponement of the relevant comma rules.

# 9

## Complete Sentences

Since the sentence is the basic unit of written discourse, you must be able to recognize complete and incomplete sentences in your drafts. An incomplete sentence—a sentence fragment (9c, p. 244)—will annoy and possibly confuse your readers unless it creates an intended emphatic effect (9d, p. 247).

You know, of course, that a sentence begins with a capital letter and ends with a period, question mark, or exclamation point. But unacceptable (unintentional) sentence fragments show these same features. You need to know, then, that a grammatically complete **sentence** normally requires a verb and its subject within an independent clause.

## 9a   Recognize the Essential Sentence Elements.

### Verb

A **verb** is a word or group of words telling the state of its subject or an action that the subject performs. The verb either

1. transmits the action of the subject to a **direct object** (**transitive verb**):

- The doctor *solved* the *problem*.
  (V) (D OBJ)

- The technician *took* an *x-ray*.
  (V) (D OBJ)

2. in itself expresses the whole action (**intransitive verb**):

- The patient *recovered*.
  (V)

- Dr. McGill *lectures* often.
  (V)

or

3. connects the subject to a **complement**, an element that helps to identify or describe the subject (**linking verb**):

- Her training *has been scientific*.
  (V) (COMPL)

- She *is* a recognized *professional*.
  (V) (COMPL)

**frag
9a**

The verb plus all the words belonging with it make up the **predicate**.

### Verb Position

In normal word order for statements, the verb follows its subject:

- The *committee is meeting*.
  (S) (V)

- The *lawyers argued*.
  (S) (V)

- The *law will remain* on the books.
  (S) (V)

But in some questions the verb comes before the subject:

- *Are you* sure?
  (V) (S)

And in most questions the verb has two parts that surround the subject:

- *Is* the guitarist *playing* tonight?
  (V) (S)

- When *does* Claude *speak* Japanese?

- *Have* scientists *been consulted*?

### *Change of Verb Form*

Verbs show **inflection**, or changes of form, to indicate tense or time. Note the following examples.

| PRESENT TENSE | PAST TENSE | FUTURE TENSE |
|---|---|---|
| They *iron* their jeans. | They *ironed* their jeans. | They *will iron* their jeans. |
| He *fights* hard. | He *fought* hard. | He *will fight* hard. |

frag
9a

### *Verb versus Verbal*

Certain words resemble verbs and can even change their form to show different times. Yet these **verbals**—namely, **infinitives**, **participles**, and **gerunds**—function like nouns or modifiers instead of like verbs. Thus they do *not* always supply a key element for sentence completeness. Compare the fragments and sentences below.

| FRAGMENT | COMPLETE SENTENCE |
|---|---|
| INF (=NOUN)<br>*To break* our record. | V<br>We *will break* our record. |
| PART (=MOD)<br>*Laughing* out loud. | V<br>Eve *was laughing* out loud. |
| GER (=NOUN)<br>*Winning* the championship. | V<br>*Are* they *winning* the championship? |

Note how you can tell that the three verbals in the left-hand column are not functioning as verbs:

1. One kind of verbal, an infinitive, is often preceded by *to* (*to break*). A true verb in a sentence stands alone.

2. A verbal ending in *-ing* is one word. When a true verb ends in *-ing*, it is always preceded by a word or words that count as part of the verb (*was laughing, have been winning*).

You can write complete sentences that include verbals, but only by supplying true subject-verb combinations:

- *To break our record will be* difficult.

- Laughing out loud, *Eve ran* a victory lap.

- *Winning the championship is* not easy.

## Subject

A **subject** is the person, thing, or idea about which something is said or asked. Locating a subject therefore involves locating its accompanying verb.

Most subjects are **nouns**—words like *car, philosophy,* and *Herbert.* Some subjects are **pronouns**, such as *she* or *they* or *someone.* And others, which we will call **nounlike elements**, are whole groups of words that function together as single nouns: *to run fast, winning the championship,* etc. Thus you cannot spot a subject simply by its form. You must find the verb and then ask who or what performs the action of that verb or is in the state expressed by it:

- My car
  Whatever you see } *is* for sale.

  What is for sale? *My car, Whatever you see.*
  These two elements are the subjects.

- That law *affects* all drivers.

  What affects all drivers? *That law.*
  The subject is *That law.*

- *Does* anyone *speak* Japanese?

  Does who speak Japanese? The subject is *anyone.*

*Implied Subject*

You cannot write a grammatically complete sentence without a verb, but in commands the subject *you* typically disappears:

- [You] Watch out!

This example would not be considered a fragment, since the implied subject *You* is regarded as part of the sentence.

---

EXERCISES

1. Copy out the following sentences, and mark every subject (S), verb (V), direct object (DO), and complement (C) that you find.

   A. Biff grabs the opposing quarterback's face mask.
   B. A sore loser like Biff is not a credit to the game.
   C. The fans have become thoroughly disgusted.
   D. Why did Biff resent the quarterback's remark about his intelligence?
   E. The ape, after all, possesses many admirable traits.

2. Indicate which of the following items do not constitute complete sentences. In each faulty case, briefly explain the problem and offer an adequately revised version.

   A. Norbert has decided to become a guru.
   B. Giving advice even when it is not requested.
   C. Having completed years of strenuous self-discipline, and without encouragement from anyone.
   D. Take note of Norbert's progress.
   E. A noble achievement, to have earned the title "Norbert the Purified One of Daly City."

frag
**9b**

---

## 9b   Distinguish an Independent Clause from a Subordinate One.

A **clause** is a cluster of words containing a subject and a **predicate** — that is, something written about (the subject) and the verb plus all the words that go with it (the predicate):

- $\overset{\text{S}}{Mike}\ \overset{\text{PRED}}{sells\ chickens.}$

- Although $\overset{\text{S}}{Mike}\ \overset{\text{PRED}}{sells\ chickens,}\ \ldots$

As you can see, there is an important difference between these two examples. The first clause is **independent**; it can stand alone as a sentence. The second is **subordinate** (or dependent); other elements must accompany it to make a complete sentence. Again:

| INDEPENDENT CLAUSES | SUBORDINATE CLAUSES |
| --- | --- |
| The poster was badly printed. | Although the poster was badly printed, . . . |
| Dogs were running wild. | Because dogs were running wild, . . . |
| It rained on Tuesday. | After it rained on Tuesday, . . . |

Subordinate clauses serve important functions, but by themselves they are sentence fragments. You can learn to recognize most of them by the way they begin. A subordinate clause is usually introduced by either

**frag**
**9b**

1. a **subordinating conjunction**, a word like *although, as, because,* or *when,* which subordinates (makes dependent) the following subject and predicate,

or

2. a **relative pronoun**, a word like *who, which,* or *that,* which begins a relative clause.

A **relative clause** is a subordinate clause that relates its statement to an earlier, or **antecedent**, part of the sentence.

ANT      REL CLAUSE
- George, *who was glad to have a working wife,* had never missed an episode of *General Hospital.*

Sometimes you will find that an independent clause, like many subordinate ones, follows a conjunction. But that word must always be one of the seven **coordinating conjunctions**. If you keep those seven words distinct in your mind from subordinating conjunctions and relative pronouns, you will have a head start toward distinguishing between independent and subordinate clauses.

| COORDINATING CONJUNCTIONS (may precede independent clauses) | | | |
| --- | --- | --- | --- |
| and | for | or | yet |
| but | nor | so | |

| SUBORDINATING CONJUNCTIONS (begin some subordinate clauses) | | | |
| --- | --- | --- | --- |
| after | because | than | whenever |
| although | before | that | where |
| as | if | though | wherever |
| as if | in order that | till | while |
| as long as | provided (that) | unless | why |
| as soon as | since | until | |
| as though | so (that) | when | |

| RELATIVE PRONOUNS (begin relative subordinate clauses) | | | |
| --- | --- | --- | --- |
| who | whom | which | that |

frag
**9b**

Remember, then, that each of your sentences should normally contain at least one independent clause—a construction which, like *Mike sells chickens,* contains a subject and predicate but is not introduced by a subordinating conjunction or relative pronoun:

IND CLAUSE
- Acting on a hunch, *I removed the book from the shelf.*

IND CLAUSE
- As I opened the book, *twenty-dollar bills fluttered to the carpet.*

IND CLAUSE        IND CLAUSE
- *I stared intently,* and *my palms began to sweat.*

IND CLAUSE
- Although I am tempted to keep it, *this money will have to be turned over to the police.*

Note that there is nothing wrong with beginning a sentence with a coordinating conjunction such as *and* or *but,* provided you want the effect to be informal or conversational.

ACCEPTABLE:

- I said farewell to my friends in high school. *And in September I began a completely new life.*

---

EXERCISE

3. Submit five original sentences, each of which contains at least one subordinate clause. Use a different subordinating conjunction or relative pronoun to introduce each new subordinate clause. (Include at least two relative clauses.) In each sentence, underline the independent clause(s).

---

## 9c  Eliminate an Unacceptable Sentence Fragment.

A **sentence fragment** is a word or set of words beginning with a capital letter and punctuated as a sentence but lacking an independent clause (9b). Typically, a fragment is either a subordinate clause (9b) or a **phrase**—a cluster of words lacking a subject-predicate combination.

frag
9c

SUBORDINATE CLAUSES:

x Because milk and eggs are still a bargain.

x Unless winning at chess is important to you.

x Which makes my uncle nervous.

PHRASES:

x Such as milk and eggs.

x Winning at chess.

x My uncle being nervous.

Most unacceptable fragments are detached parts of a preceding sentence. They may be difficult to spot, for your mind supplies connections that are hidden from your reader. The handiest way to correct most fragments is to add them to that earlier sentence.

UNACCEPTABLE FRAGMENTS (italicized):

- Local agencies will become overcrowded and ineffective. x *Unless the number of mental health services is increased.*

- Alex and Dolores played tennis in the park. x *Instead of at school.*

- They stood back and watched the crows. x *Wheeling and cawing over the splattered melon.*

- It is still productive. x *The tobacco farm which has been in use since the Civil War.*

**COMPLETE SENTENCES:**

- Unless the number of mental health services is increased, local agencies will become overcrowded and ineffective.

- Alex and Dolores played tennis in the park instead of at school.

- They stood back and watched the crows wheeling and cawing over the splattered melon.

- The tobacco farm, which has been in use since the Civil War, is still productive.

frag
9c

## How to Spot a Fragment

You can recognize many fragments by the words that introduce them—subordinating terms such as *although, because, especially, even, except, for example, including, instead of, so that, such as, that, which, who,* and *when.* Some fragments lack such tipoff words, but when you see a draft "sentence" beginning with one of those terms, check to see if you have included a full independent clause (9b, p. 241).

**DRAFT (fragments italicized):**

I always helped my brother. *Especially with his car.* I assisted him in many chores. *Such as washing the car and vacuuming the interior.* He let me do whatever I wanted. *Except start the engine.* Now I drive my own car. *Which is a 1974 Chevy.* I am thinking of possible jobs to help pay the cost of upkeep. *Including driving a cab. Because maintaining a car these days can be expensive.*

**REVISED:**

I always helped my brother, especially with his car. I assisted him in many chores, such as washing the car and vacuuming the interior. He let me do whatever I wanted except start the engine. Now I drive my own car, a 1974 Chevy. I am thinking of possible jobs, including driving a cab, to help pay the cost of upkeep. Maintaining a car these days can be expensive.

Learn to recognize the following five types of fragments.

1. A subordinate clause posing as a whole sentence.

**DRAFT:**

Living in the city is more dangerous than ever. *Especially if you are wearing a gold chain.* During the past several weeks gold snatchers have been on a crime spree. *Although the police have tried to track down the thieves.* Nobody with a chain is safe. *Because the victims range from drivers stalled in traffic jams to students in gym classes.*

**REVISED:**

Living in the city is more dangerous than ever, especially if you are wearing a gold chain. Although the police have tried to track down the thieves, during the past several weeks gold snatchers have been on a crime spree. Nobody with a chain is safe; the victims range from drivers stalled in traffic jams to students in gym classes.

**frag
9c**

2. A verbal (9a, p. 239) unaccompanied by an independent clause.

**DRAFT:**

He found himself unable to proceed to Vancouver. *Having forgotten his raincoat.*

**REVISED:**

Having forgotten his raincoat, he found himself unable to proceed to Vancouver.

3. An appositive (11k, p. 288) standing alone.

**DRAFT:**

I love to read about the Roaring Twenties. *A decade that had its own personality.* For a while at least, people seemed to forget about the terrors of the twentieth century. *War, economic collapse, widespread hunger.*

**REVISED:**

I love to read about the Roaring Twenties, a decade that had its own personality. For a while at least, people seemed to forget about the terrors of the twentieth century—war, economic collapse, widespread hunger.

4. A disconnected second verb governed by a subject in the sentence before.

DRAFT:

The speech for my radio course took a long time to prepare. *And then turned out poorly.* I needed a live audience. *But didn't have one for the test.*

REVISED:

The speech for my radio course took a long time to prepare and then turned out poorly. I needed a live audience but didn't have one for the test.

5. A "sentence" lacking a main verb.

DRAFT:

*If there are no more malpractice suits, the hospital to win its license renewal.* But no one can be sure. *Because patients these days are very quick to go to court.*

REVISED:

If there are no more malpractice suits, the hospital will win its license renewal. But no one can be sure, because patients these days are very quick to go to court.

frag
9d

---

EXERCISE

4. Using each of the five categories listed above, submit five unacceptable fragments followed by revisions that eliminate the problem. In each revision, underline the independent clause that makes for an adequately complete sentence.

---

## 9d    Note the Uses of the Intentional Sentence Fragment.

Some composition instructors advise against any use of fragments in submitted work. They feel, understandably, that students ought to eliminate habitual mistakes before trying flourishes of style. But you should know that practiced writers do resort to an occasional **intentional fragment** when they want to reply to a question in the previous sentence or make a point concisely and emphatically. When you are sure you have the unacceptable fragment under control, you may want to try your hand at the intentional one.

ACCEPTABLE:

- He sets him up with jabs, he works to the body, he corners him on the

    INTENTIONAL FRAG

    ropes. *Then the finish, a left hook to the jaw that brings him down.*

- Many secretaries were outraged by the shift to a later working day.

    INTENTIONAL FRAG

    *But not quite all of them.*

    INTENTIONAL FRAG

- And now for the dessert. *Pecan pie and ice cream!*

You will see from your reading of published authors that intentional fragments usually possess a certain "shock value." Whereas an unacceptable fragment looks like a missing part of a neighboring sentence, an intentional fragment is a condensed means of lending punch to the previous sentence or, in some instances, the following one. For example:

**frag
9d**

A mounted steer's head. A 10-foot artificial tree with bird's nest. A life-sized stuffed pony. A 6-foot fluorescent sign. A slot machine. A 500-pound computer. Two tricycles with children still riding them. A leaded glass window. A piano bench. A robot. A car door. The drive shaft of a BMW automobile.

These were among the items that enterprising airline passengers recently hauled as carry-on baggage on their flights, according to a survey reported yesterday by the Association of Flight Attendants.[1]

---

**EXERCISE**

5. All of the following items contain sentence fragments. Even though they lack the usual makings of a sentence, some of the fragments are of the intentional variety that readers generally accept. Others would be perceived as unacceptable or unintentional. Write a brief evaluation of each fragment, explaining what prompts you to regard each one as either intentional or unacceptable. Revise the unacceptable ones to form complete sentences.

    A. This stock is selling at a price below its book value. What a bargain!
    B. Its price-earnings ratio is 1:0. Which is hard to beat.
    C. The market for laser death rays is expected to become firmer in the 1990s. Unless the peaceniks get control of the White House again.
    D. Why do you suppose it is listed as an under-the-counter stock? To attract the small investor, perhaps?
    E. Many people would kill for a chance to buy some shares. If they don't get killed first.

F.  Although he happens to be in jail at the moment. The chairman of the board has high hopes for General Catastrophe.

## 9e    Avoid a Run-on Sentence.

### How to Join Independent Clauses

There are two usual ways of joining independent clauses (9b, p. 241) within a single sentence. The first way is to put a comma after the first independent clause and to follow the comma with a coordinating conjunction: *and, but, for, nor, or, so, yet.*

run-on 9e

| IND CLAUSE | COORD CONJ | IND CLAUSE |

* George was lonely at first, *but* after a while he came to like having

the whole apartment to himself.

| IND CLAUSE | COORD CONJ | IND CLAUSE |

* He ate constantly, *but* he still couldn't get enough food to satisfy

his cravings.

If your independent clauses are closely related in meaning or make a pointed contrast, you can join them with a semicolon alone:

IND CLAUSE

* George's reliance on prepared foods was now total; Susan had gath-

IND CLAUSE

ered up her cookbooks before slamming the door for the last time.

IND CLAUSE         IND CLAUSE

* George's health soon improved; his diet had become rich in pre-

servatives.

If you remember how to join independent clauses, you will be able to spot and correct a **run-on sentence** — that is, a sentence in which two or more independent clauses are joined with no punctuation or with only a comma between them. The two usual types of run-on sentence are the comma splice and the fused sentence.

## Comma Splice

A run-on sentence in which a comma alone joins two independent clauses is known as a **comma splice**. Such a construction does not seriously garble the statement being made, but it fails to indicate how its two clauses are related in meaning.

DON'T:

|FIRST IND CLAUSE| |SECOND IND CLAUSE|
x Faulkner's novel is psychologically deep, they wanted to explore it further.

|FIRST IND CLAUSE| |SECOND IND CLAUSE|
x They discussed Faulkner's novel, the class hour ended all too soon.

If you find a comma splice in one of your drafts, you can revise it in a number of ways, including the subordinating of one element to another.

run-on 9e

COMMA AND COORDINATING CONJUNCTION:

* Faulkner's novel is psychologically deep, *and* they wanted to explore it further.

SEMICOLON:

* Faulkner's novel is psychologically deep; they wanted to explore it further.

SUBORDINATE CLAUSE (9b, p. 241):

* *Although they discussed Faulkner's novel,* the class ended all too soon.

PHRASE (9c, p. 244):

* The class hour came to an end, *leaving them unable to finish their discussion of Faulkner's novel.*

## Fused Sentence

A run-on sentence in which independent clauses are merged with no sign of their separateness — neither a comma nor a coordinating conjunction — is called a **fused sentence**.

DON'T:

|            IND CLAUSE            |        IND CLAUSE       |
| --- | --- |

x Some people can hide their nervous habits I envy them.

|                      IND CLAUSE                      |        IND CLAUSE       |
| --- | --- |

x Sometimes I have to stand up in front of other students it makes me sick.

Revise by choosing from the same options given above for correcting a comma splice.

### COMMA AND COORDINATING CONJUNCTION:

* Some people can hide their nervous habits, *and* I envy them.

### SEMICOLON:

* Some people can hide their nervous habits; I envy them.

### SUBORDINATE CLAUSE:

* I feel sick *whenever I have to stand up in front of other students.*

### PHRASE:

* I feel sick *standing up in front of other students.*

## False "Conjunctions"

Look through the following terms, which often lead a writer to commit a comma splice.

| SENTENCE ADVERBS | | |
| --- | --- | --- |
| again | hence | nonetheless |
| also | however | otherwise |
| besides | indeed | similarly |
| consequently | likewise | then |
| further | moreover | therefore |
| furthermore | nevertheless | thus (*etc.*) |

**run-on**
**9e**

| TRANSITIONAL PHRASES | | |
|---|---|---|
| after all | for example | in reality |
| as a result | in addition | in truth |
| at the same time | in fact | on the contrary |
| even so | in other words | on the other hand (*etc.*) |

A **sentence adverb** (also called a *conjunctive adverb*) is a word that modifies a whole previous statement. Note how such a term differs from an ordinary adverb.

### ORDINARY ADVERB:

- She applied for the job *again* in March.

- *Then* she made arrangements to have her furniture stored.

### SENTENCE ADVERB:

- *Again,* there is still another reason to delay a decision.

- We see, *then,* that precautions are in order.

An ordinary adverb modifies part of the statement in which it appears: she applied *again*; she stored her furniture *then*. But a sentence adverb modifies the whole statement by showing its logical relation to the preceding statement: after the already stated reason to delay, here (*again*) is another one; because of the preceding statement, we therefore (*then*) see that precautions are in order. A **transitional phrase** is a multiword expression that functions like a sentence adverb.

What makes these modifiers tricky is that they "feel like" conjunctions such as *and, but, although, so,* and *yet.* If you treat a sentence adverb or transitional phrase as if it were a conjunction, the result will be a comma splice.

DON'T:

SENT ADV
x George turned the oven dial to the "Clean" position, *however* the dishes seemed dirtier than ever when he took them out.

SENT ADV
x Severe rains washed away our seeds, *furthermore,* a late freeze occurred in April.

run-on
9e

x Our garden was a disappointment, *in fact* it was a disaster.
TRANS PHRASE

x We had no vegetables of our own, *as a result* we had to rely on the grocery store.
TRANS PHRASE

You can revise such sentences in any of the ways previously discussed, either by properly joining the independent clauses or by changing the whole construction.

DO:

* George turned the oven dial to the "Clean" position; however, the dishes seemed dirtier than ever when he took them out.

* Severe rains washed away our seeds; furthermore, a late freeze occurred in April.

* Our garden was not just a disappointment but a disaster.

* We had no vegetables of our own, and as a result we had to rely on the grocery store.

run-on
9e

If you are not sure whether a certain word is a sentence adverb, test to see whether it could be moved without loss of meaning. A conjunction must stay put, but a sentence adverb can always be moved to at least one other position:

* We planted a garden; *however,* nothing grew.
* We planted a garden; nothing, *however,* grew.
* We planted a garden; nothing grew, *however.*

For the punctuation of sentence adverbs and transitional phrases, see 111, page 289. Look ahead to that discussion before undertaking Exercise 7 below.

## Acceptable "Comma Splices"

### Tag Accompanying Quotation

A tag such as *she thought* or *he said* can be joined to a quotation by a comma alone, even if the quotation is another independent clause.

IND CLAUSE                    IND CLAUSE

* "That is a matter of opinion," Emily replied.

### Optional Conjunctions in Series of Independent Clauses

When you are presenting several brief, tightly related independent clauses in a series (14j, p. 325), you can gain a dramatic effect by doing without a coordinating conjunction:

- He saw the train, he fell to the tracks, he covered his head with his arms.

  By omitting *and* before the last clause, the writer brings out the rapidity and urgency of the three actions. This is a rare case of an acceptable comma splice.

### Reversal of Negative Emphasis

If a second independent clause reverses the negative emphasis of the first, consider joining them only with a comma:

run-on
9e

- That summer Thoreau did not read books, he hoed beans.

  The *not* clause leaves us anticipating a second clause that will say what Thoreau did do. The absence of a conjunction brings out the tight, necessary relation between the two statements.

Compare:

x Thoreau hoed beans all summer, he did not read books.

  Lacking a "reversal of negative emphasis," this sentence shows a classic *unacceptable* comma splice.

---

#### EXERCISES

6. Submit five complete sentences, each of which contains two independent clauses. In the first three sentences, join the independent clauses with a comma or a coordinating conjunction. In the other two, use a semicolon. Make sure that the two parts of each sentence are properly related in meaning.

7. Correct any comma splices and fused sentences that you find here:

   A. Henry James was fond of Italy, in fact, he wrote a whole book about its civilized pleasures.

B. This surprised Biff he had thought that Henry James had spent all his time playing the trumpet.

C. This book is not illustrated, however its text is very clear.

D. Dr. Dollar understands the rising concern for physical fitness, he also knows that many office workers cannot set aside time for an exercise period.

E. Many potential readers are just now changing their habits, therefore many of them ought to buy *The Complete Book of Hopping to Your Place of Business.*

---

## NOTE

[1] Ralph Blumenthal, "Unfriendly Baggage in the Friendly Skies," *New York Times* 17 July 1986, national ed.: 13.

run-
on
9e

# 10

## Subject-Verb Relations

### 10a   Avoid a Mixed Construction.

If your subjects and verbs (9a, p. 237) are to work efficiently together, you cannot leave your reader wondering which part of a sentence is the subject. Do not begin a sentence with one subject and then change your mind.

DON'T:

      S?         S?
x *Elderly people, they* should watch their step in the bathtub.

> The reader supposes at first that *Elderly people* will be the subject of *should watch*. But after the comma the writer serves up a new subject, *they,* leaving *Elderly people* grammatically stranded.

DO:
- Elderly people should watch their step in the bathtub.

The first "elderly people" sentence illustrates **mixed construction**, whereby a sentence sprouts a new element that violates its apparent structure.

DON'T:

x In doing the workbook problems was extremely useful.

> The sentence begins with a prepositional phrase (p. 597) that can only serve as a modifier (11a, p. 274) — as it would, for example, in this sentence: *In doing the workbook problems I had trouble with quadratic equations.* But the writer has tried unsuccessfully to turn *In doing the workbook problems* into a subject.

When you suspect that a draft sentence suffers from mixed construction, first isolate the predicate (9a, p. 241); then ask yourself what *one* thing makes that predicate meaningful. Thus, *what* was extremely useful? *Doing the workbook problems.* That phrase should become the subject.

DO:

● Doing the workbook problems was extremely useful.

The problem of mixed construction can extend beyond subjects and verbs to other sentence elements as well.

**mixed**
**10a**

DON'T:

      D OBJ?                  D OBJ?
x They gave *it* to her for Christmas *what* she had been asking for.

> Here *it* and *what* are competing to be the direct object (9a, p. 237) of the verb *gave.* The solution is to choose one or the other and make a consistent pattern.

DO:

● For Christmas they gave her what she had been asking for.

---

**EXERCISE**

1. If your instructor has found no instances of mixed construction in your submitted work, skip this exercise. Otherwise, copy up to five noted examples of the problem. For each sentence containing a mixed construction, provide an adequate revision. Mark the subject (S) and verb (V) in each revised construction.

## 10b    Make a Verb Agree with Its Subject in Number and Person.

In standard written English the ending of a verb often shows the *number* of the subject — that is, whether the subject is *singular* (one item) or *plural* (more than one item). A singular subject requires a singular verb; a plural subject requires a plural verb.

        S     V
- The *river flows* south.

> Here the *-s* ending on the verb *flows* indicates that the verb is in the third person, is singular, and is in the present tense.

In grammar we refer to three **persons**:

|  | EXAMPLE | IDENTITY |
|---|---|---|
| **First Person** | I pull | the speaker or writer |
|  | we pull | the speakers or writers |
| **Second Person** | you pull | the person or persons addressed |
| **Third Person** | he, she, it pulls<br>the mother speaks<br>the signal changes | the person or thing spoken or written about |
|  | they pull<br>the mothers speak<br>the signals change | the persons or things spoken or written about |

We also refer to the *time* of a verb as its **tense** — present, past, future, and so on.

The grammatical correspondence of subjects and verbs is called **agreement**. In *The river flows south* the verb *flows* is said to agree with its singular, third-person subject *river*. Note that the singular subject usually has no *-s* ending but that a singular, third-person verb in the present tense does have an *-s* ending: *flows*. Compare:

        S    V
- The *rivers flow* south.

> The lack of an *-s* ending on the verb *flow* indicates that the verb is plural, in agreement with its plural subject *rivers*.

agr
10b

Many native speakers of English use the same forms for both the singular and plural of certain verbs in the present tense: *she don't, they don't*; *he is, we is.* In standard written English, however, it is important to observe the difference: *she does not, she doesn't, they do not, they don't*; *he is, we are.*

DON'T:

x They *is* having a party.

x He *don't* expect to rent a car.

DO:

• They *are* having a party.

• He *does not* expect to rent a car.

• He *doesn't* expect to rent a car.

For further verb forms in various tenses, see 21b and 21c, pages 393, 400.

agr
10c

---

**EXERCISE**

2. If your instructor has found no instances of subject-verb disagreement in your submitted work, skip this exercise. Otherwise, copy out as many as five noted examples of the problem, and indicate how you would now recast either the subject or the verb to bring them into agreement.

---

## 10c   Be Sure You Have Found the True Subject.

The rule of subject-verb agreement (10b) is clear enough, but applying it can prove surprisingly hard. Among other difficulties, writers sometimes choose the wrong number for a verb because they have failed to identify its real subject. Here are the main sources of this confusion.

### Intervening Clause or Phrase

It is easy to lose track of your subject if it is followed by a phrase or clause instead of by the verb. The last word of the phrase or clause can get mistaken for the subject, and the result is subject-verb disagreement.

DON'T:

S                 INTERVENING CLAUSE               V

x The *highway* that runs through these isolated mountain towns *are* steep and narrow.

S     INTERVENING PHRASE    V

x The *pleasures* of a motorcyclist *includes* repairing the bike.

DO:

S        V
• The *highway* . . . *is* steep and narrow.

S        V
• The *pleasures* . . . *include* repairing the bike.

Learn to locate the true subject by asking who or what performs the action of the verb or is in the state indicated by the verb. Test for singular or plural by these steps:

1. Locate the verb and its subject.

2. Put the phrase between them into imaginary parentheses:

The pleasures (of a motorcyclist) $\frac{\text{include}}{\text{includes}}$ . . . .

3. Then say aloud:

"The pleasures include"

    and

"The pleasures includes."

The form of the verb that is correct without the element "in parentheses" is also correct with it: *The pleasures of a motorcyclist include. . . .*

## Additive Phrase

An **additive phrase** is an expression that begins with a term like *accompanied by, along with, as well as, in addition to, including,* or *together with.* Though it is typically set off by commas, it can deceptively "feel like" part of the subject. For example, if you say *Joan, together with her* *friends,* you certainly have more than one person in mind. But grammatically, additive phrases do *not* add anything to the subject. Disregard the additive phrase, just as you would any other intervening element. If the subject apart from the additive phrase is singular, make the verb singular as well.

DON'T:

          S                         ADDITIVE PHRASE

x *Practical knowledge,* in addition to statistics and market theory,

  V

*enter* into the training of an economist.

                      S               ADDITIVE PHRASE

x Stanley's *pamphlet printer,* along with his bullhorn and spray paint,

  V

*give* him a sense of comradeship with working people everywhere.

DO:

- Practical knowledge, in addition to statistics and market theory, *enters* into the training of an economist.

- Stanley's pamphlet printer, along with his bullhorn and spray paint, *gives* him a sense of comradeship with working people everywhere.

**agr 10c**

## Subject Following Verb

When a subject follows its verb, beware of allowing an earlier noun to govern the number of the verb.

DON'T:

x Immediately after the light rains of early November have dampened

              V      S

the woods *come* the *time* when Melody can be found gathering certain prized mushrooms.

> The writer has mistaken *woods,* the direct object of *have dampened,* for the subject of *come.* The verb must be *comes,* in agreement with the singular subject *time.*

DO:

- Immediately after the light rains of early November have dampened the woods *comes* the time. . . .

### Expressions Like <u>There Is</u>, <u>Here Comes</u>

Watch especially for agreement problems when the subject is delayed by an expression like *There is* or *Here comes*. By the time such a sentence is finished it may have acquired a plural subject.

DON'T:

        V                        S

x There *is* pay-as-you-write *typewriters* in the library.

        V              S

x Here *comes a clown and three elephants.*

DO:

- There *are* pay-as-you-write typewriters in the library.

- Here *come* a clown and three elephants.

Or, since this example sounds strained:

- Here *comes* a clown leading three elephants.

---

**EXERCISE**

3. For each sentence, identify the subject of the disputed verb, and choose the verb form that makes for subject-verb agreement.

    A. Above the wealthiest section of Rio *(stands, stand)* some of the world's most miserable slums.

    B. Baseball, along with all other sports, *(strikes, strike)* Priscilla as utterly meaningless.

    C. There *(is, are)* four candidates in this election.

    D. Any idea for improving the company's profits *(is, are)* welcome.

    E. Early darkness, together with cold weather and the usual miseries of flu, *(makes, make)* winter a difficult season to endure.

---

## 10d    Watch for Special Agreement Problems.

Even if you have correctly located a verb's subject, you may not always know whether that subject ought to be considered singular or plural. The following pages explain the tricky cases.

## Phrase or Clause as Subject

A phrase or clause acting as a subject takes a singular verb, even if it contains plural items. Do not be misled by a plural word at the end of the phrase or clause. The following sentences are correct:

- *Having the numbers of several bail bondsmen is* useful in an emergency.

  PHRASE AS S ... V

- *That none of his customers wanted to buy a matching fleet of De Sotos was* a disagreeable surprise for Henry.

  CLAUSE AS S ... V

## Collective Noun as Subject

A **collective noun** is one having a singular form but referring to a group of members: *administration, army, audience, class, crowd, orchestra, team,* and so forth. This conflict between form and meaning can lead to agreement problems. But in general you should think of a collective noun as singular and thus make the verb singular, too:

- The orchestra *is playing* better now that the conductor is sober.

- A strong, united faculty *is needed* to stand firm against the erosion of parking privileges.

- In Priscilla's opinion the middle class *is* altogether too middle-class.

## Numerical Word or Plural Term of Quantity as Subject

Numerical words (*majority, minority, number, plurality,* etc.) and plural terms of quantity (*three dollars, fifty years,* etc.) can take either a singular or a plural verb. If you have in mind the *totality* of items, make the verb singular.

- The Democratic *majority favors* the bill.

  S ... V

But if you mean the separate items that make up that totality, make the verb plural:

- *The majority of Democrats* on the North Shore *are opposed* to building a bridge.

  S ... V

### The Word <u>Number</u>

When the word *number* is preceded by *the,* it is always singular:

S                    V

- The *number* of unhappy voters *is growing.*

But when *number* is preceded by *a,* you must look to see whether it refers to the total unit (singular) or to individual parts (plural):

**TOTAL UNIT (SINGULAR):**

S                V

- A *number* like ten billion *is* hard to comprehend.

**INDIVIDUAL PARTS (PLURAL):**

S         V

- *A number of voters have arrived* at their choice.

> Note that although *of voters* looks like a modifier of the subject *number,* we read *a number of* as if it said *many.*

When your subject contains an actual number, decide once again whether you mean the total unit or the individual parts.

**TOTAL UNIT (SINGULAR):**

S        V

- *Twenty-six miles is* the length of the race.

**INDIVIDUAL PARTS (PLURAL):**

S        V

- *Twenty-six difficult miles lie* ahead of her.

### Compound Subject

A compound subject, such as *a clown and a bear,* is made up of more than one unit. Such a subject usually calls for a plural verb:

S        V

- *A teller and a guard operate* the drive-in window at the bank.

S                                    V        COMPL
* *A bouquet and a box of candy are* no substitute for a fair wage.

> Note that *substitute* is singular even though the subject and verb are plural. Agreement does not extend to complements (9a, p. 238) — words in the predicate that identify or modify the subject.

## *Or; Either . . . Or; Neither . . . Nor*

Compound subjects joined by *or, either . . . or,* or *neither . . . nor* are called **disjunctive**. They ask the reader to choose between two or more parts. Consequently, the verb should agree with only one of those parts — the one nearest the verb.

ADEQUATE:
* Neither apple pie nor her faded cat posters nor her neglected
  LAST ITEM IN S    V
  *guppy collection holds* the slightest interest for Priscilla any more.

Such is the schoolbook rule. In practice, however, most good writers will recast a sentence to avoid conflicts of number in disjunctive subjects.

BETTER:
* By now Priscilla cannot muster the slightest interest in either apple pie or her faded cat posters or her neglected guppy collection.

Some disjunctive subjects "feel plural" even though each item within them is singular, for the writer is thinking about two or more things. But so long as the individual disjunctive items are singular, the verb must be singular, too.

DON'T:
  DISJUNCTIVE S            V
x *Neither WNCN nor WQXR carry* the country-Western sing-off.

DO:
  NEAREST PART OF
  DISJUNCTIVE S    V
* Neither WNCN nor *WQXR carries* the country-Western sing-off.

## *Each or Every before Compound Subject*

*Each* or *every,* if it comes before the subject, guarantees that the subject will be singular even if it contains multiple parts:

agr
**10d**

$$\overset{S}{\overline{\hspace{4cm}}} \quad \overset{V}{\overline{\hspace{1.5cm}}}$$

- *Every linebacker and tackle in the league was pleased* with the settlement.

$$\overset{S}{\overline{\hspace{4cm}}} \quad V$$

- Before being put away for the summer, *each coat and sweater has* to be mothproofed.

But note that when *each* comes *after* a subject it has no effect on the number of the verb:

$$\overset{S}{} \quad \overset{V}{}$$

- *They* each *have* their own reasons for protesting.

### Subject That Is Compound in Form Only

Even when the parts of a compound subject are joined by *and,* common sense will sometimes tell you that only one thing or person is being discussed. Make the verb singular in such a case:

**agr
10d**

- My best friend and severest critic has moved to Atlanta.

  One person is both friend and critic. By changing the verb to *have* the writer would be saying that two people, not one, have moved to Atlanta. Both sentences could be correct, but their meanings differ.

### "Borderline" Indefinite Pronoun as Subject

An **indefinite pronoun** leaves unspecified the person or thing it refers to.

| INDEFINITE PRONOUNS | | |
|---|---|---|
| all | everybody | no one |
| another | everyone | nothing |
| any | everything | one |
| anybody | few | others |
| anyone | many | several |
| anything | most | some |
| both | much | somebody |
| each | neither | someone |
| each one | nobody | something |
| either | none | such |

Some of these words serve other functions, too; they are indefinite pronouns only when they stand alone without modifying another term.

**ADJECTIVE:**

- *All* leopards are fast.

**INDEFINITE PRONOUN:**

- *All* have spots.

Some indefinite pronouns, such as *another,* are obviously singular, and some others, such as *several,* are obviously plural. But there is also a "borderline" class: *each, each one, either, everybody, everyone, everything, neither, nobody, none, no one.* These terms have a singular form, yet they call to mind plural things or persons. According to convention you should generally treat them as singular:

- *Everyone seems* to be late tonight.
  - S — V

- *Neither has brought* the music for the duet.
  - S — V

Keep to a singular verb even when the indefinite pronoun is followed by a plural construction such as *of them*:

- *Neither* of them *has* the music for the duet.
  - S — V

- *Each* of those cordless phones *has* a touch-tone dial.
  - S — V

### *None*

*None* is usually treated as singular:

- *None* among us *is* likely to agree with Stanley's proposal to smash racism by blowing up Kentucky Fried Chicken.
  - S — V

But if you mean *all are not,* you can use a plural verb:

- *None* of us *are* enthusiastic about Operation Fingerlicker.
  - S — V

In doubtful cases you would do well to stick to the singular verb, preferred by purists.

## Subject with Plural Form but Singular Meaning

Some nouns have an *-s* ending but take a singular verb: *economics, mathematics, mumps, news, physics,* and so forth:

- *Physics* has made enormous strides in this century.

Some other nouns ending in *-s* can be singular in one meaning and plural in another. When they refer to a body of knowledge, they are singular.

AS BODY OF KNOWLEDGE:

- *Politics is* an important study for many historians.
  S    V

- *Acoustics requires* an understanding of mathematics.
  S          V

But when the same words are used in a more particular sense — not politics as a field but somebody's politics — they are considered plural.

IN PARTICULAR SENSE:

- Stanley's *politics are* somewhat to the left of center.
  S    V

- How *are* the *acoustics* in the new auditorium?
  V          S

## Title of a Work as Subject

Titles of works are generally treated as singular even when they have a plural form, because only one work is being discussed:

- Joyce's *Dubliners has justified* the author's faith in its importance.
  S          V

- Camus's *Lyrical and Critical Essays was* required reading in Comparative Literature 102 last term.
  S                    V

  The plural verb *were* would misleadingly refer to the individual essays rather than the whole book.

## Stating a Mathematical Operation

### *Adding or Multiplying*

When adding or multiplying, you can choose either a singular or a plural verb:

- One and one *is* two.
- One and one *are* two.
- Eleven times three *is* thirty-three.
- Eleven times three *are* thirty-three.

### *Subtracting or Dividing*

When subtracting or dividing, keep to the singular:

- Sixty minus forty *is* twenty.
- Sixty minus forty *leaves* twenty.
- Eight divided by two *is* four.

agr
**10d**

---

**EXERCISE**

4. For each sentence, choose the verb form that makes for subject-verb agreement.

    A. Neither of them *(remembers, remember)* who ran for President against Harry Truman.

    B. A number of people *(dislikes, dislike)* mushroom pizza.

    C. Each of them *(is, are)* equally certain of being right.

    D. A majority of votes *(is, are)* all you need to be elected.

    E. Neither age nor illness *(prevents, prevent)* her from laughing at the world's follies.

    F. *The Counterfeiters (was, were)* one of the strangest books I have ever read.

    G. Thirty less five *(leaves, leave)* twenty-five.

    H. The economics of that redevelopment project *(looks, look)* very faulty.

    I. An honest politician and a caring woman *(has, have)* finally been elected as our Governor.

    J. Every child throughout all the countries of Africa *(is, are)* facing an uncertain future.

## 10e  Make a Verb in a Relative Clause Agree with the Antecedent of the Relative Pronoun.

Consider the following correctly formed sentence:

REL CLAUSE
- The telephone bills *that are overdue* include a charge for a lengthy call to Paris.

Here *that are overdue* is a **relative clause** – a subordinate clause (9b, p. 241) that relates its statement to an earlier, or **antecedent**, part of the sentence. A relative clause usually begins with a word like *who, whom, whose, that,* or *which.* In this case the antecedent is *telephone bills.*

Relative clauses can make for tricky agreement problems. You will avoid trouble, however, if you remember that the verb in a relative clause agrees in number with its antecedent. Thus, in the example above, *are* agrees with the plural antecedent *telephone bills.* Again:

agr<br>10e

　　　　　　　　　　　　　　　　ANT　　V
- There have been complaints about *service* that *is* painfully slow.

Note, however, that you cannot automatically assume that the antecedent is the last term before the relative clause:

　　　　　　　　　ANT　　　　　　　　　　V
- There have been *complaints* about service that *were* entirely justified.

　　　　ANT　　　　　　　　　　　　V
- The *oceans* of the world, which *have become* a dumping ground, may never be completely unpolluted again.

Ask yourself what the verb in the relative clause refers to:

What is painfully slow? Service.

What was entirely justified? Complaints.

What has become a dumping ground? Oceans.

Once you have an answer, a singular or plural term, you also have the right number for the verb in your relative clause.

### Singular Complement in Relative Clause

Look at the following mistaken but typical sentence.

DON'T:

> PLURAL ANT            V         SING COMPL
> x *Math problems,* which *is* her *specialty,* cause her no concern.

A singular complement (9a, p. 238) in a *who, which,* or *that* clause can trick you into making the verb in that clause singular when the antecedent is actually plural. Here the complement *specialty* has wrongly influenced the number of the verb *is.* That verb, like any other verb in a relative clause, must agree with its antecedent.

DO:

- Math problems, which are her specialty, cause her no concern.

### *One of Those Who*

Consider the following sentences, both of which are correct:

> ANT            V
> - Joe is one of those *chemists* who *believe* that science is an art.

> ANT                        V
> - Joe is the only *one* of those chemists who *believes* that science is an art.

agr
10e

The expression *one of those who* contains both a singular and a plural term—*one* and *those.* To avoid confusion, be careful to decide which of the two is the antecedent. In most cases it will be the plural *those* (or *those chemists,* etc.), but to be sure you must isolate the relative clause and ask yourself what it modifies.

### *It Is* and Plural Subject as Antecedent

Consider this imperfect sentence:

> x It is the vegetables that makes Max feel queasy.

Here the writer has felt required to make the second verb agree with a singular antecedent, *It.* But *It* in this sentence is an **expletive** (p. 589), not a pronoun. Its function is simply to anticipate the true subject, *vegetables.* And since *vegetables* is also the antecedent of the relative pronoun *that,* the plural *vegetables* should govern the number of the verb in the relative clause: *make.*

---

**EXERCISE**

5. For each sentence, choose the verb form that makes for subject-verb agreement.

   A. It is their own secret vices that (*allows, allow*) people to tolerate the vices of others.
   B. Death threats, which (*is, are*) a rarity in most people's lives, (*is, are*) all too familiar to famous athletes.
   C. Problems with a rebellious class that (*pays, pay*) no attention (*occurs, occur*) all too frequently these days.
   D. Max is one of those tourists who (*expects, expect*) all the natives to be wearing peasant costumes.
   E. There are difficulties with substandard care that (*requires, require*) immediate attention.

---

## 10f Do Not Put an Unnecessary Comma between a Subject and Its Verb.

agr
10f

An element that comes between a subject and its verb may need to be set off by commas, as in the sentence *Teenage suicide, which has become common in recent years, is a matter of urgent public concern* (11j, p. 286). But beware of inserting commas simply to draw a breath, for the demands of grammar and of easy breathing do not always match up. You want to show your reader that a subject is connected to its verb. If the modifier following a subject is not a *grammatical* interruption, do not set it off with commas.

DON'T:

    S            V
x  *Ishi alone, remained* to tell the story of his tribe.

DO:

• Ishi alone remained to tell the story of his tribe.

Even when you have a lengthy subject, itself made up of parts separated by commas, you should try to connect it to its verb without interruption.

DON'T:

                    S                       V
x  *A pair of scissors, a pot of glue, and a stapler, are* still essential to a writer who does not use a word processor.

DO:

* A pair of scissors, a pot of glue, and a stapler are still essential to a writer who does not use a word processor.

DON'T:

x *Those construction workers who had collected unemployment checks in the slump of December through March, were delighted that spring* had finally arrived.

DO:

* Those construction workers who had collected unemployment checks in the slump of December through March were delighted that spring had finally arrived.

---

**EXERCISE**

6. Indicate which of the following sentences are incorrectly punctuated, and why.

    A. Animals, vegetables, and minerals, all get involved in the exciting game of "Twenty Questions."

    B. One good reason for moving to San Antonio is that it is the cleanest city in the United States.

    C. Every person, no matter how incompetent at everything else is the world's foremost expert at deciphering his or her own handwriting.

    D. A woman who has so little tact as to keep her old boyfriend's picture in her wallet is surely courting trouble with her husband.

    E. Power as an end in itself, never brings true satisfaction.

agr
**10f**

# 11
## Modifiers

### 11a  Recognize Modifiers and Their Functions.

A **modifier** is an expression that limits or describes another element:

- *tall* boy
- the tall boy *with blond hair*
- the tall boy *with blond hair who is locking his bicycle*
- The tall boy *with blond hair who is locking his bicycle* is *from Finland.*

A modifier can consist of a single word, a phrase, or a subordinate clause.

1. a single word:

- The *tall* boy is from Finland.
- A *new* star appeared in the *darkening* sky.
- They did it *gladly.*
- *That* proposal, *however,* was *soundly* defeated.

2. a **phrase**, or cluster of words lacking a subject-verb combination (9c, p. 244):

- The boy *with blond hair* is *from Finland.*
- *At ten o'clock* she gave up hope.
- *In view of the foul weather,* they remained *at home.*

3. a **subordinate clause**, or cluster of words that does contain a subject-verb combination but does not form an independent statement (9b, p. 241):

- The boy *who is locking his bicycle* is from Finland.
- The largest telephone company, *which once enjoyed a near monopoly on phone appliances,* is now being challenged in the open marketplace.
- My old friends from the block always play a game of stickball *when they come home for the holidays.*

A single-word modifier is usually either an adjective or an adverb. An **adjective** modifies a noun, pronoun, or other element that functions as a noun. An **adverb** can modify not only a verb but also an adjective, another adverb, a preposition, an infinitive, a participle, a phrase, a clause, or a whole sentence.

mod
11b

All modifiers are subordinate, or grammatically dependent on another element. But there is nothing minor about the benefit that a careful and imaginative use of modifiers can bring to your style. Some modifiers lend vividness and precision to descriptions, stories, and ideas, while others establish logical relationships, allowing a sentence to convey more shadings of thought and complexity of structure.

For the comparison of adjectives and adverbs, see Chapter 23, pages 416–418.

## CHOOSING AND PLACING MODIFIERS

### 11b  Place a Modifier Where It Will Bring Out Your Meaning.

#### Adjective and Adverb

The position you assign a modifier can significantly affect the meaning of your sentence. Most adjectives and adverbs occupy a position just before the modified term.

- It was a ADJ *beautiful* moon.

- We ADV *hastily* adjusted the telescope.

A **predicate adjective**, however, follows the verb:

- The moon was PRED ADJ *beautiful.*

Adverbs such as *only, just,* and *merely* often control the way an entire statement is interpreted. In order to avoid ambiguity, or double meaning, you should place them just before the modified element. Compare:

- *Only* I can understand your argument. [No one else can.]

- I can *only* understand your argument. [I cannot agree with it.]

- I can understand *only* your argument. [But not your motives; *or* The arguments of others mystify me.]

- She had *just* eaten the sandwich. [A moment before.]

- She had eaten *just* the sandwich. [Not the rest of the food.]

**mod
11b**

### Sentence Adverb

Unlike other adverbs, a **sentence adverb** (9e, p. 251) such as *however, nevertheless,* or *furthermore* puts a whole statement into logical relation to the preceding statement:

- Much of the world is threatened with famine in the next twenty years. *Nevertheless,* the populations of the most threatened areas continue to increase at a reckless pace.

The placement of a sentence adverb is especially flexible, but different positions suggest different emphases. In general, a sentence adverb puts stress on the word that precedes it:

- I, *however,* refuse to comply. [I contrast myself with others.]

- I refuse, *however,* to comply. [My refusal is absolute.]

In the first and last positions of a sentence, where a sentence adverb cannot be set off on both sides by commas, it makes a less pointed effect:

- *However,* I refuse to comply. ⎱ No single element within the main
- I refuse to comply, *however.* ⎰ statement is highlighted.

The final position is the weakest—the one that gets least stress from the logical force of the sentence adverb. In some sentences, however, this may be just the effect you are seeking.

### Transitional Phrase

The same principles of emphatic placement apply to **transitional phrases** like *in fact, on the contrary,* and *as a result,* which are really multiword sentence adverbs. Note how meaning as well as emphasis can sometimes be affected by different placement of the same transitional phrase:

- *In fact,* Marie was overjoyed. [Marie was not unhappy. No, indeed. . . .]

- Marie, *in fact,* was overjoyed. [Others were happy, but one person— singled out here—was more so.]

For fuller lists of sentence adverbs and transitional phrases, see 9e, p. 251.

mod
**11c**

---

**EXERCISE**

1. Submit a sentence of your own in which the transitional phrase *to be sure* occurs in some position other than first or last. Add a brief explanation of the effect you have created by choosing that position as opposed to other feasible ones.

---

## 11c  Avoid a Dangling Modifier.

When you use a modifier, it is not enough for you to know what thing or idea you are modifying; you must openly supply that modified term within your sentence. Otherwise you have written a **dangling modifier**— one that either modifies nothing at all or that wrongly appears to modify a nearby term.

### Missing Modified Term

DON'T:

DANGL MOD
x *Pinning one mugger to the ground,* the other escaped.

The person doing the pinning is left unmentioned. Readers will go through a two-step process of frustration. First they will take *the other* to be the modified term. Then, realizing their mistake, they will become annoyed with the writer for having given them a false lead.

DO:

MOD                                                    MODIFIED
                                                        TERM
• *Pinning one mugger to the ground,* the *victim* helplessly watched the other escape.

DON'T:

DANGL MOD
x *Once considered a culturally backward country,* Australian film-makers have surprised the world's most demanding audiences.

The writer, criticized for a dangling modifier, might protest, "Can't you see I was referring to Australia in the first phrase?" But where is *Australia* in the sentence? Since *Australian filmmakers* can hardly be called a *country,* the modifier does dangle.

**mod**
**11c**

DO:

MOD                                                    MODIFIED
                                                        TERM
• *Once considered a culturally backward country, Australia* has surprised the world's most demanding audiences with its excellent filmmakers.

DON'T:

DANGL MOD
x *To win in court,* an attorney's witnesses must convince the jury.

Precisely because it makes perfect grammatical sense, this is a dangerously misleading sentence. Readers must do a double take to realize that it is the attorney, not the witnesses, who wants to win in court.

DON'T:

MOD
x *Embracing the astonished Priscilla,* a rash erupted behind Philo's left knee.

The possessive form *Philo's* cannot serve as the modified term; its function is adjectival, and one adjectival element cannot modify another.

DO:

MOD          MODIFIED
                                      TERM
- *Embracing the astonished Priscilla, Philo* felt a rash erupting behind his left knee.

DON'T:

MOD

x *Anticipating every taste,* it was decided to advertise the car as "an oversexed, pulse-quickening respecter of environmental quality."

Nobody is doing the anticipating here.

DO:

MOD          MODIFIED
                                  TERM
- *Anticipating every taste, the agency* decided. . . .

### Mistaken Modified Term

Merely including the modified term is not enough; you must also place it where a reader will immediately identify it as such. Any noun or nounlike element just preceding or following a modifier will look like the modified term. When it is not, chaos or comedy results.

DON'T:

DANGL MOD                        APPARENT
                                      MODIFIED TERM
x *Stolen out of the garage the night before, my grandmother* spotted
MODIFIED TERM
*my station wagon* on Jefferson Street.

The reader must reassess the sentence to get over the impression that it was the grandmother who was stolen from the garage.

DO:

MOD
                                      MODIFIED TERM
- *Stolen out of the garage the night before, my station wagon* was on Jefferson Street when my grandmother spotted it.

DON'T:

MOD

x *Thinking that a Snoopy sweatshirt would win Priscilla over,* it only
MODIFIED TERM
remained for *Philo* to choose an appropriate greeting card.

Here the anticipatory pronoun *it* stands where the modified term ought to be.

DO:

> MOD                                    MODIFIED TERM

- *Thinking that a Snoopy sweatshirt would win Priscilla over, Philo* turned his attention to the choice of an appropriate greeting card.

## 11d   Avoid a Squinting Modifier.

You may find that in a draft sentence you have surrounded a modifier with two elements, either of which might be the modified term. Such a modifier is called **squinting** because it does not "look directly at" the real modified term.

DON'T:

> SQ MOD

x How Harry silenced the transmission *completely* amazed me.

> Did Harry do a complete job of silencing, or was the writer completely amazed? Readers should never be left with such puzzles to solve.

DO:

> MOD   MODIFIED TERM

- How Harry *completely silenced* the transmission amazed me.

or

> MOD   MODIFIED TERM

- I was *completely amazed* by the way Harry silenced the transmission.

DON'T:

> SQ MOD

x They were sure *by August* they would be freed.

> Were they sure by August, or would they be freed by August?

DO:

> MODIFIED TERM   MOD

- They were *sure by August* that they would be freed.

or

- They were sure that <sup>MOD</sup> by *August* they <sup>MODIFIED TERM</sup> *would be freed.*

Notice how the insertion of *that* either before or after the modifier clarifies the writer's meaning.

## 11e   Avoid a Split Infinitive If You Can Do So without Awkwardness.

Some readers object to every **split infinitive**, a modifier placed between *to* and the base verb form: *to thoroughly understand.* To avoid offending such readers you would do well to eliminate most split infinitives.

DON'T:

x It is important *to* <sup>SPLIT INF</sup> *clearly see* the problem.

DO:

- It is important *to see* <sup>INF</sup> the problem *clearly.* <sup>ADV</sup>

> mod
> 11e

But when you correct a split infinitive, beware of creating an awkward construction that announces in effect, "Here is the result of my struggle not to split an infinitive."

DON'T:

x It is important *clearly to see* the problem.

The writer has avoided a split infinitive but has created a pretzel. The "split" version, *It is important to clearly see the problem,* would be preferable. But *It is important to see the problem clearly* would satisfy everyone.

Even readers who do not mind an inconspicuous, natural-sounding split infinitive are bothered by *lengthy* modifiers in the split-infinitive position.

DON'T:

x We are going *to* <sup>SPLIT INF</sup> *soberly and patiently analyze* the problem.

DO:

- We are going to analyze the problem soberly and patiently.

or

- We are going to make a sober and patient analysis of the problem.

---

**EXERCISE (11c–11e)**

2. Some or all of the following sentences contain dangling modifiers or split infinitives. Submit a corrected version of each sentence that you find faulty, and explain why you are leaving other sentences (if any) unrevised.

    A. She realized in a calmer moment everything would be all right.

    B. Before going to bed, the false teeth should be removed for maximum comfort.

    C. If you want to quickly, safely, and pleasantly make your way through the dense jungle at Disneyland, a native guide is necessary.

    D. His coach, though he was still very inexperienced, believed he detected some athletic promise in the eight-foot Elbows Lodgepole.

    E. He paid the penalty for his crimes in prison.

---

mod<br>11f

## 11f   Do Not Hesitate to Make Use of an Absolute Phrase.

Fear of the dangling modifier (11c, p. 277) leads some writers to shun the **absolute phrase**, a group of words that acts as a modifier to the whole statement. (Compare *transitional phrase,* 9e, p. 252.) But a well-managed absolute phrase can be an effective resource.

DO:

                                            **ABS PHRASE**

- He rose from the negotiating table, *his stooped shoulders a sign of discouragement.*

Far from causing a usage problem, such added phrases enable you to write a graceful **cumulative sentence** (7v, p. 198) — one that sharpens or elaborates an initial main statement.

    A classic absolute phrase differs from a dangling modifier by containing its own "subject," such as *his stooped shoulders* in the example above. Again:

      "SUBJECT"

- *All struggle over,* the troops lay down their arms.

      **ABS PHRASE**

- The quarterback called three plays in one huddle, *the clock* having stopped after the incomplete pass.

"SUBJECT"
ABS PHRASE

Some other absolute phrases do look exactly like dangling modifiers, but they are accepted as *idioms*—that is, as "rule-breaking" expressions that everyone considers normal:

ABS PHRASE
- *Generally speaking,* Melody's memory is rather smoky.

ABS PHRASE
- *To summarize,* most of her energy has leaked into the cosmos at large.

## 11g   Avoid a Double Negative.

In written English the modifier *not* does all the work of denial that a negative statement needs. A **double negative**, though common in some people's speech, is considered a mistake rather than an especially strong negation.

mod
11g

DON'T:

x She *didn't* say *nothing.*

DO:

- She *didn't* say *anything.*

or

- She said *nothing.*

### Cumbersome Negative Formulas

Avoid certain negative constructions which are roundabout or confusing:

1. negatives following *shouldn't wonder, wouldn't be surprised,* and so on.

DON'T:

x I shouldn't wonder if it *didn't* rain.

DO:

- I shouldn't wonder if it *rained.*

2. *cannot help but*

DON'T:

x They *cannot help but* think sadly about the *Challenger* Seven.

DO:

• They *cannot help thinking* sadly about the *Challenger* Seven.

3. *can't hardly, can't scarcely,* and so on.

DON'T:

x We *can't hardly* wait to visit Montreal.

DO:

• We *can hardly* wait to visit Montreal.

4. *no doubt but what, no doubt but that*

DON'T:

x She does not *doubt but what* dreams foretell the future.

x There is *no doubt but that* writing assists the memory.

DO:

• She *does not doubt that* dreams foretell the future.

• There *is no doubt that* writing assists the memory.

mod<br>**11h**

---

**EXERCISE**

3. If your instructor has found no double negatives in your submitted work, skip this exercise. Otherwise, submit up to five examples of the problem. In each case, supply the single-negative expression that would have been preferable.

---

## PUNCTUATING MODIFIERS

### 11h    Include a Comma after an Initial Modifier That Is More than a Few Words Long.

If a modifier preceding your main clause takes up more than a few words, automatically follow it with a comma:

SUBSTANTIAL SUB CLAUSE
- *After Susan had walked out on him,* George spent a few evenings reading Dr. Lincoln Dollar's helpful book of advice, *The Aerobic Kama Sutra.*

SUBSTANTIAL PHRASE
- *In the memorable words of Dr. Dollar,* "No modern home should be without a queen-sized trampoline."

## 11i   Consider a Comma Optional after a Brief Initial Modifier.

If a modifier preceding your main clause is no more than a few words long, you can choose whether or not to end it with a comma. A comma marks a more formal separation between the modifier and the main clause.

mod
11i

ACCEPTABLE:

BRIEF SUB CL
- *When Susan came back* she found George sitting in the lotus posture and eating a Ho-Ho.

BRIEF PHRASE
- *Until that moment* she hadn't appreciated the spiritual side of his nature.

   Commas after *back* and *moment* would also be correct. When in doubt, supply the comma, especially if the opening element is a clause.

### Avoiding Ambiguity

Note that you *must* include the comma if your sentence would be ambiguous—double in meaning—without it.

- *Although Susan begged,* George said that she could go live with Julia Child for all he cared.

   Without the comma, we might think at first that the sentence says *Although Susan begged George. . . .*

## 11j  Master the Punctuation of Restrictive and Nonrestrictive Modifiers.

To punctuate modifiers in every position except the initial one (11h, 11i), you must recognize a sometimes tricky distinction between two kinds of modifiers—restrictive and nonrestrictive.

| RESTRICTIVE | NONRESTRICTIVE |
|---|---|
| This is the lamp *we bought yesterday.* | This lamp, *which we bought yesterday,* is defective. |
| Suzanne is a woman *who minds her own business.* | Suzanne, *who minds her own business,* is a strong woman. |
| The coffee *that comes from Brazilian mountainsides* is the best. | The best coffee, *which comes from Brazilian mountainsides,* is also the most expensive. |

mod
11j

### Restrictive Modifier

A **restrictive modifier** is essential to the identification of the term it modifies. It restricts or narrows down the scope of that term, identifying precisely *which* lamp, woman, or coffee the writer has in mind. Study the two columns above and you will see that only the left-hand sentences contain modifiers of this kind. In the right-hand sentences the lamp, woman, and coffee under discussion do not need to be identified by restrictive modifiers; presumably the reader already knows which person or thing the writer intends.

Note also how the absence or use of commas marks the difference of function. A restrictive modifier can do its job of narrowing only if it is *not* isolated by commas.

DON'T:

x Women, *who are over thirty-five,* tend to show reduced fertility.

Here the commas, which isolate the italicized element from the (misleading) statement *Women tend to show reduced fertility,* keep that element from properly restricting the subject to women over thirty-five. The commas absurdly suggest that all women are over thirty-five.

DO:

RESTR MOD
- Women *who are over thirty-five* tend to show reduced fertility.

  With the commas gone, the sentence says what the writer originally wanted to say; the restrictive modifier is free to do its narrowing work.

DON'T:

x A chocolate-covered apple a day was all Betsy allowed herself, *until
  the diet was completed.*

  The modifying clause limits the time of the action described in
  the main clause. Because it affects the meaning of that main
  clause, we want to read it without a break.

DO:

- A chocolate-covered apple a day was all Betsy allowed herself *until
  the diet was completed.*

mod
11j

DON'T:

x I had a dream, *in which I finally got to the end of the tightrope.*

  The comma after *dream* wrongly tells a reader that the main statement ends there. The writer wanted the restrictive element to
  identify a *particular* dream.

DO:

RESTR MOD
- I had a dream *in which I finally got to the end of the tightrope.*

DON'T:

RESTR MOD
x The discipline, *that George had recently adopted,* was called Transcendental Weight-watching.

  Here a restrictive clause, serving to specify which discipline
  the writer has in mind, is wrongly punctuated as if it were
  nonrestrictive.

DO:

- The discipline *that George had recently adopted* was called Transcendental Weight-watching.

The importance of setting off nonrestrictive modifiers at both ends may be brought home by this sentence from a newspaper:

x Noteworthy here are a painted settee and two armchairs, decorated with scrollwork and female figures that belonged to President Monroe.[1]

> *Female figures that belonged to President Monroe?* A comma after *figures* is needed to head off wild ideas about the Chief Executive's leisure pursuits.

## 11k    In Punctuating an Appositive, Observe the Restrictive/Nonrestrictive Rule.

An **appositive** is a word or phrase that identifies or restates an immediately preceding noun or noun substitute:

- Teresa, *an old friend of mine,* has scarcely changed through the years.

  > APP

- What they saw, *a black bear approaching the baby's cradle,* riveted them with fear.

  > APP

- The horn gave three blasts, *signals that we had to say our final good-byes.*

  > APP

Most appositives, like those above, are set off by commas, but you should not automatically make that choice. Instead, ask whether the appositive narrows down ("restricts") the term it follows or merely restates that term. To see why some appositives should appear without commas, compare these sentences:

- My sister, *Diane,* studied Portuguese in the Navy.

  > NONR APP

- My brother *Bert* played baseball in college, but my brother *Jack* was not athletic at all.

  > RESTR APP                                            RESTR APP

The commas in the first sentence tell us that the writer has only one sister —namely, Diane. The appositive does not restrict our understanding of *sister*; it merely supplies the sister's name. In contrast, the absence of commas in the second example reflects the fact that the writer has at least two brothers. *Bert* and *Jack* are restrictive appositives, since each name tells us *which* brother is meant.

The distinction here is a fine one, and few readers would object if the commas were dropped from the "Diane" example. But whenever you use an appositive to narrow the meaning of a term (which brother, which friend, etc.), you should omit the commas.

## 11l    Set Off a Sentence Adverb or a Transitional Phrase with Commas.

Sentence adverbs and transitional phrases (9e, p. 251) can never be restrictive (11j). Instead of narrowing the meaning of one element in a statement, they show a relationship between the whole statement and the one before it. To bring out this function, be sure your sentence adverbs and transitional phrases are "stopped" at both ends, either by two commas, by a semicolon and a comma, or by a comma and the beginning or end of the sentence:

> SENT ADV
- A circus, *furthermore,* lifts the spirits of young and old alike.

> SENT ADV
- Laughter is good for the soul; *moreover,* it reduces bodily tension.

> TRANS PHRASE
- *On the contrary,* she intends to stay where she is.

> TRANS PHRASE
- The deficit has continued to grow, *as a matter of fact.*

### Exception: Some Brief Sentence Adverbs

Even though they are nonrestrictive, certain brief sentence adverbs such as *thus* and *hence* are often seen without commas:

- We can *thus* discount the immediate threat of war.

- *Hence* there is no need to call up the reserves.

mod
11l

## 11m    Set Off an Interrupting Element at Both Ends.

Study the following sentences:

- INT EL
  A diet, *Betsy believed,* called for strong discipline during the sleeping hours.

- INT EL
  Reindeer droppings on the roof, *to be sure,* count as strong evidence for Santa's existence.

- INT EL
  You, *George,* have been chosen by the computer to be Betsy's mate.

- INT EL
  The computer, *an antique Univac,* is badly in need of repair.

**mod
11m**

In each instance the italicized words are an **interrupting element** (also known as a *parenthetical element*). An interrupting element can be a phrase, a clause, a sentence adverb like *however,* a transitional phrase like *in fact,* an appositive (11k), a name in direct address (*George,* in the example above), or an inserted question or exclamation. Since an interrupting element comes between parts of the sentence that belong together in meaning, you must set it off by punctuation at both ends. Note the commas in all four examples above.

The main risk in punctuating an interrupting element is that you may forget to close it off before resuming the main statement. The risk increases if the last words of the interrupting element happen to fit grammatically with the words that follow.

DON'T:
  x The Mayor's televised plea, which is rebroadcast every evening on the 6 o'clock news reaches everyone in town.

You can expect to come across such "unstopped" interrupting elements in your first drafts. When in doubt as to whether the element is truly an interruption, reread the sentence without it: *The Mayor's televised plea reaches everyone in town.* Since that statement makes complete sense, you know that the omitted part *is* interruptive and must be set off at both ends.

### Testing for an Interrupting Element

To be considered interrupting, a sentence element must meet two conditions: it must be nonrestrictive in meaning (11j, p. 286) and it must come *between* essential parts of a statement. Consider this sentence:

NONRESTR BUT NOT INTERRUPTING
- But *without hesitating for a moment,* Betsy enrolled in the biofeedback course.

The italicized phrase is nonrestrictive, but it comes completely *before* the clause that it modifies (*Betsy enrolled in the biofeedback course*). Thus the phrase cannot be considered interrupting, and the absence of a comma after *But* is well advised. (The comma after *moment* is prudent; see 11h, p. 284.)

### Other Punctuation

Commas are the most usual but not the only means of setting off an interrupting element. Extreme breaks such as whole statements, questions, or exclamations are often better served by parentheses or dashes:

mod
**11n**

INT EL
- The sky in New Mexico *(have you ever been there?)* is the most dramatic I have seen.

INT EL
- Our recent weather—*what snowstorms we have had!*—makes me long to be back in California.

When you need to interrupt quoted material to insert words of your own, enclose your insertion in brackets (20p, p. 387).

## 11n    Use Commas with Coordinate Modifiers.

If a draft sentence contains two or more modifiers in a row, should you put commas between them? The answer depends on whether the modifiers all modify the same term. Usually they do; such modifiers are **coordinate**, or serving the same grammatical function. You should separate coordinate modifiers from each other by commas:

- MOD          MOD
- George fixed himself a *delicious, nutritious* dinner of Gatorade and Chun King Chop Suey.

    Here *delicious* and *nutritious* are coordinate, for they both modify the same noun, *dinner.*

But note that some paired modifiers are not coordinate:

    MOD          MOD
- He wolfed down his *typical American* meal.

    Here *American* modifies *meal,* but *typical* does not; it modifies *American meal.* A comma after *typical* would wrongly imply that *typical* and *American* modify the same word.

To determine whether you have a coordinate series, try shifting the order of the terms. Truly coordinate items can be reversed without affecting their meaning: *a nutritious, delicious dinner.* Noncoordinate items look all wrong when reversed: x *an American typical meal.*

### Sandwiched Modifier

When a modifier is inserted ("sandwiched") between two parts of the modified term, you can set it off by commas on *both* sides:

        MOD
- His final, *unusually tedious,* lecture was poorly received.

The extra comma after *tedious* tells us that *final* and *unusually tedious* are not coordinate modifiers of *lecture.* Rather, the modified term is *final lecture*; the sentence is an alternative version of *His unusually tedious final lecture was poorly received.* Note the absence of commas in this simpler version.

## 11o   Do Not Place a Comma between the Final (or Only) Modifier and the Modified Term.

When a modifier comes just before the modified term, no punctuation should separate them. Thus, however many coordinate modifiers you supply, be sure to omit a comma after the final one.

DON'T:

FINAL MOD
x  O'Keeffe produced an intense, starkly simple, *radiantly glowing,*
MODIFIED
TERM
*painting* of a flower.

> The comma after *glowing* must be removed so that the whole set of coordinate modifiers — *intense, starkly simple, radiantly glowing* — can stand in proper relation to the modified term, *painting.*

For an exception to this rule, keep reading.

## 11p    Consider Enclosing a "Contrary" Modifier in Commas.

In some sentences one modifier opposes another:

CONTRARY MOD                MODIFIED
MOD                                          TERM
• She told a *fascinating but not altogether believable story.*

You can, if you choose, emphasize the opposition by enclosing the contrary modifier in commas.

ACCEPTABLE:
• She told a fascinating, but not altogether believable, story.

If you set off the contrary modifier at one end, be sure to supply a second comma at the other end.

DON'T:
x  She told a fascinating, but not altogether believable story.

---

EXERCISES (11h–11p)

4. Some or all of the following sentences show faulty use (or absence) of commas. Write a brief comment about each sentence, explaining *where* and *why* you would make changes, if any.

   A. Some judges have begun experimenting with a new concept, known as "house arrest."
   B. A convicted criminal, who is not considered dangerous, may be spared a prison sentence.

C. The criminal, however, is not allowed to go completely free.

D. Instead, he or she is required to stay within a restricted area venturing from home only to work and shop.

E. This policy spares nonviolent offenders, the degrading and unnecessary experience of being locked away for years.

5. Most or all of the following sentences show faulty use (or absence) of commas. When you find an adequately punctuated sentence, note that it is correct. For all the others, indicate what changes should be made.

A. Airline passengers seem to prefer a safe trip with armed guards, to an unsafe trip without them.

B. They won't lower the taxes, merely because people complain.

C. Most tightrope walkers it seems, suffer from aching feet.

D. Short-order cooks agree that soyburgers are the best, low-cost, high-protein, food to serve these days.

E. A porcupine has approximately 30,000 quills for your information.

F. As the press had expected the President announced on Friday that the price of steak, not gold, would henceforth define the value of the dollar.

G. In a house work is more tedious than in an office.

H. You Gertie are a woman of taste and sensitivity.

I. The one mystery, that Biff couldn't explain, was why his smiling teammate was trying to inhale the twenty-yard line.

mod
11p

---

NOTE

[1] David Maxfield, "What Nancy Reagan Has Done to the White House," *San Francisco Chronicle* 23 Dec. 1981: 16.

# 12

# Cases of Nouns and Pronouns

## 12a Recognize the Case Forms and Their Functions.

Nouns and pronouns change their form to show certain grammatical relations to other words within a sentence. These forms are called **cases**. They show whether a term is a subject of discussion or performer of action (**subjective case**), a receiver of action or an object of a preposition (**objective case**), or a "possessor" of another term (**possessive case**):

1. subjective case: *I, we, they, who, Bill, cars,* etc.

2. objective case: *me, us, them, whom,* etc.

3. possessive case: *my, mine; our, ours; their, theirs; whose, Bill's, cars',* etc.

Most personal pronouns (*I, she,* etc.) show changes of form for all three cases, and so does the relative pronoun *who.* Nouns, however, do not change for the objective case.

|  | SUBJECTIVE | OBJECTIVE | POSSESSIVE |
|---|---|---|---|
| **Personal Pronouns** | I | me | my, mine |
|  | you | you | your, yours |
|  | he | him | his |
|  | she | her | her, hers |
|  | it | it | its |
|  | we | us | our, ours |
|  | they | them | their, theirs |
| ***Who*** | who | whom | whose |
| **Nouns** | car | car | car's |
|  | mountains | mountains | mountains' |
|  | Janice | Janice | Janice's |
|  | Soviet Union | Soviet Union | Soviet Union's |

case
12a

A change in form helps to show which sentence function a word is performing. For example:

**SUBJECTIVE CASE**

1. Subject of verb:
   - *He* went home.
   - *They* went home.
   - The one *who* went home was disappointed.

2. Complement:
   - It was *she* who was guilty.
   - The victims are *we* ourselves.

**OBJECTIVE CASE**

1. Direct object of verb:
   - They praised *him.*
   - We fed the child *whom* the agency had entrusted to us.

2. Indirect object of verb:
   - They taught *him* a lesson.
   - The fine cost *them* a pretty penny.

3. Object of preposition:
   - She told it to *us.*
   - For *whom* did you work last year?

4. Subject of infinitive:
   - They wanted *her* to stay.
   - She expected *them* to give her a raise.

**POSSESSIVE CASE**

1. With nouns:
   - *Our* hats were all squashed.
   - *Jim's* case was the worst of all.
   - The *Beatles'* music still keeps its freshness.
   - *Whose* pen is this?

2. With gerunds (9a, p. 239):
   - *His* departing left us sad.
   - *Their* training every day made them too tired for fun.
   - *Jane's* humming all day drove everyone wild.

case
**12b**

In general, case forms must match sentence functions: subjective case for subjects of clauses, objective case for objects of several kinds, and possessive case for a possessing relation to the governed term.

We will see that in practice the choice of case can become tricky. Note at the outset that the "subject" of an infinitive takes the objective case and that the "subject" of a gerund usually takes the possessive case. The names are unfortunate, but most writers intuitively choose case by function, not by name.

## 12b   Keep the Subject of a Clause in the Subjective Case.

Standard usage requires that you avoid using objective-case pronouns for subjects of clauses.

DON'T:

x *Him* and *me* were good friends.

DO:

- *He* and *I* were good friends.

See 12g, p. 301, for a pronoun subject in a subordinate clause.

## 12c  Avoid an Awkwardly "Correct" Subjective Pronoun Complement.

Note the following sentences:

DON'T:

COMPL
x  The one I had in mind is *him*.

AVOID:

COMPL
x  The one I had in mind is *he*.

**case
12d**

The first example violates standard written English; pronoun complements (9a, p. 238) should not appear in the objective case. Yet the "correction" to *he* sounds pompous and awkward. Try, then, to avoid sentences that call for prissy "good English" at the expense of naturalness. Think of a new way of conveying the same point.

PREFER:

S
- *He* is the one I had in mind.

Shifted from a complement to a subject, *he* now sounds unstrained.

## 12d  Keep a Pronoun Object in the Objective Case.

The rule for pronoun objects of all kinds is simple: put them in the objective case.

### DIRECT OBJECT OF VERB:

- Many differences separate *us*.

### INDIRECT OBJECT OF VERB:

- She gave *me* cause for worry.

**OBJECT OF PREPOSITION:**

* Toward *whom* is your anger directed?

**SUBJECT OF INFINITIVE:**

* They asked *her* to serve a second term.

Choice of a correct objective form becomes harder when the object is **compound**, or made up of more than one term. Knowing that it is wrong to write *Him and me were good friends,* some writers "overcorrect" and put the subjective forms where they do not belong.

DON'T:

$$\overset{\text{V}}{} \qquad \overset{\text{D OBJS}}{}$$
x  They appointed *she* and *I* to a subcommittee.

$$\overset{\text{OBJS OF}}{}$$
$$\overset{\text{PREP}}{} \quad \overset{\text{PREP}}{}$$
x  That will be a dilemma for *you* and *I.*

DO:

* They appointed *her* and *me* to a subcommittee.

* That will be a dilemma for you and *me.*

When in doubt, test for case by disregarding one of the two objects. Since you would never write x *They appointed she* or x *That will be a dilemma for I,* you know that both of the objects must be objective in case.

The danger of choosing the wrong case seems to increase when a noun and a pronoun are paired as objects.

DON'T:

$$\overset{\text{OBJS OF}}{}$$
$$\overset{\text{PREP}}{} \quad \overset{\text{PREP}}{}$$
x  As for *Jack* and *I,* we will take the bus.

Would you write *As for I?* No; therefore keep to the objective case.

DO:

* As for Jack and *me,* we will take the bus.

## *Who* versus *Whom*

In informal speech and writing, *whom* has become a rare form even where grammar strictly requires it. When the pronoun appears first in a clause, the subjective *who* automatically comes to mind.

COLLOQUIAL:

- *Who* did he marry?

- *Who* will you play against?

In standard written English, however, the question of *who* versus *whom* is still determined by grammatical function, not by speech habits. Note the reason for choosing *whom* in each of the following revisions.

DO:

D OBJ ⌒V⌒
- *Whom* did he marry?

    *Whom* is the direct object of the verb *did marry.*

OBJ OF
PREP                                    PREP
- *Whom* will you play against?

or

**case
12e**

PREP    OBJ OF
PREP
- Against *whom* will you play?

    *Whom* is the object of the preposition *against.*

For more on *who* versus *whom,* see 12g, p. 301.


## 12e   Avoid an Awkward Choice of Pronoun Case after *Than* or *As.*

Many writers agonize over the case of a pronoun following *than* or *as.* Should one write *Alex is taller than I* or *Alex is taller than me*? Technically, both versions are correct. In the first instance *than* serves as a subordinating conjunction: *Alex is taller than I [am].* In the second, *than* has become a preposition with the object *me.*

In other sentences, however, one choice is clearly incorrect. Consider:

- The cows chased Margaret farther than $\left\{ \begin{array}{c} \text{I} \\ \text{me} \end{array} \right\}$ .

Here *I* would indicate that Margaret was chased by both the cows and the writer: *The cows chased Margaret farther than I did.* Since that is unlikely to be the intended meaning, the right choice is *me.*

When in doubt, consider your intended meaning and mentally supply any missing part of the clause:

- The cows chased Margaret farther than {they chased} me.

The added words will tell you which case to use for the pronoun.

Wherever both choices sound awkward, as in the "Alex" example above, look for an alternative construction:

SUB CLAUSE
- Alex is taller *than I am.*

> By supplying the whole subordinate clause, you can avoid any hesitation between *I* and *me.*

## 12f  Ignore the Influence of a Following Appositive on Pronoun Case.

When an appositive (11k, p. 288) follows a pronoun, many writers automatically put the pronoun in the subjective case. As often as not the result is a usage error.

DON'T:

OBJ OF
PREP    APP
x Parking is a tragic dilemma for *we* professors.

> Test the prepositional phrase without the appositive. Since *for we* is obviously wrong, so is *for we professors.* Ignore the appositive and give the pronoun its proper case.

DO:
- Parking is a tragic dilemma for *us* professors.

## 12g  Choose a Pronoun's Case by Its Function within Its Own Clause.

One of the hardest choices of case involves a pronoun that seems to have rival functions in two clauses.

DON'T:
x Wratto will read his poems to *whomever* will listen.

The writer has made *whomever* objective because it looks like the object of the preposition *to: to whomever.* But the real object of *to* is the whole subordinate clause that follows it.

DO:

$$\text{Wratto will read his poems to } \underbrace{\overset{\text{S}}{whoever} \overset{\text{V}}{\underset{\text{SUB CLAUSE}}{will\ listen.}}}$$

The subject of the subordinate clause *whoever will listen* belongs in the subjective case.

Whenever a subordinate clause is embedded within a larger structure, you can settle problems of case by mentally eliminating everything but the subordinate clause.

DON'T:

x Stanley had no doubt about *whom* would write the manifesto entitled "Smash Violence Now or Else."

The test for case shows that *whom would write the manifesto* is ungrammatical. The object of *about* is the whole subordinate clause, which requires a subject in the subjective case.

DO:

• Stanley had no doubt about *who* would write. . . .

When a choice of pronoun case is difficult, the air of difficulty may remain even after you have chosen correctly. Your reader may be distracted by the same doubt that you have just resolved. It is therefore a good idea to dodge the whole problem.

DO:

• Wratto will read his poems to *anyone* who will listen.

• Stanley was sure that *he* would be the author. . . .

## 12h    Use the Possessive Case for Most Subjects of Gerunds.

A **gerund** is a verbal (9a, p. 239) that functions as a noun. Most gerunds end in *-ing,* but there is also a two-word past form.

PRES GER
- There is less *swooning* in Hollywood movies than there used to be.

PAST GER
- *Having swum* across the lake made him generally less fearful.

A gerund can be preceded not only by a word like *a, the,* or *this,* but also by a governing noun or pronoun known as the **subject of the gerund**: *Wilson's achieving unity, his having achieved unity.* (A gerund can also take an object; see p. 595.) The name *subject* is misleading, for most subjects of gerunds, just like words that "possess" nouns, belong in the possessive case.

| POSSESSION OF NOUN | POSSESSION OF GERUND |
|---|---|
| his achievement | his achieving |
| our departure | our departing |
| Marian's reliance | Marian's relying |
| Edgar's loss | Edgar's having lost |

case
12h

In general, then, put subjects of gerunds into the possessive case.

DON'T:
S OF
GER      GER
x *Esther* commuting to Boston ended with her graduation.

DO:
- *Esther's* commuting to Boston ended with her graduation.

If the subject of a gerund feels like an object, you should nevertheless keep to the possessive form.

DON'T:
S OF
GER   GER
x Biff didn't know why everyone laughed at *him saying* he would like to be an astronaut and see all those steroids going by.

Here the writer has made *him* objective because it "feels like" the object of the preposition *at.* In fact, the object of that preposition is the whole gerund phrase that runs to the end of the sentence.

DO:
- Biff didn't know why everyone laughed at *his* saying. . . .

Note how the possessive *his* directs a reader's attention to the next word, *saying.* It is the activity, not the person, that inspired laughter.

### Exceptions

When the subject of a gerund is an abstract or inanimate noun — one like *physics* or *chaos* — it can appear in a nonpossessive form.

ACCEPTABLE:

S OF
GER        GER
- We cannot ignore the danger of *catastrophe striking* again.

But *catastrophe's* would also be acceptable here. Rather than choose, however, why not recast the sentence?

PREFERABLE:
- We cannot ignore the danger that catastrophe will strike again.

When a gerund's subject is separated from the gerund by other words, the gerund tends to change into a modifier — specifically, a *participle* (9a, p. 239). In such a sentence the possessive form is not used:

- People were surprised at him, a veteran speaker on many campuses,
PART
*having* no ready reply when Stanley seized the microphone and called him an irrelevant murderer.

> Without the intervening appositive (11k, p. 288), *a veteran speaker on many campuses,* we would consider *him* to be a gerund and change the pronoun case accordingly: *People were surprised at his having.* . . . But in the sentence as it stands, *him* is a direct object modified by the whole participial phrase from *having no ready reply* through *irrelevant murderer.*

## 12i   Use a Double Possessive When It Is Needed for Clarity.

The possessive relation for nouns is usually indicated either by an *-'s* or *-s'* (*Henry's, the three cats'*) or by an *of* construction (*of Henry, of the three cats*). But sometimes you can combine the two forms to avoid confusion. Compare:

- Priscilla remained unmoved by any thought of *Philo.*

- Priscilla remained unmoved by any thought of *Philo's.*

Both sentences are grammatical, but their meanings differ. The first sentence deals with any thought *about* Philo, the second with any thought *proposed by* Philo.

Some writers worry that the double possessive, like the double negative (11g, p. 283), is a usage error. But everyone uses the double possessive with pronouns: a *peculiarity of hers; that nasty habit of his,* and so forth. Feel free to treat nouns in exactly the same way: a *bookkeeping trick of Harry's; that sawed-off shotgun of Bobo's,* and so on.

---

**EXERCISE (12a–12i)**

1. Some or all of the following sentences show a mistaken or awkward choice of case. Indicate which, if any, sentences are problem-free, and explain why you would make changes in the others.

case **12i**

   A. It is hard for we Americans to realize how rapidly the balance of power is shifting.
   B. Whom could you trust with the keys to a BMW these days?
   C. For success in business, much depends on who you know.
   D. The customs officers gave her and we to understand that we would be thoroughly searched.
   E. Stanley is a man whom you could expect to lead a demonstration against Mother's Day.
   F. The person who we all want to serve as director is she.
   G. Bill hunting for an apartment for Sally and I proved exhausting.
   H. Biff can kick the ball twenty yards farther than me.
   I. A saying of Shakespeare's would appear to be applicable here.
   J. They admired her, a Canadian, enduring the heat of a Somali summer.

---

# 13

# Pronoun Reference

Pronouns offer you relief from the monotony of needlessly repeating a term or name when your reader already knows what or whom you mean. But precisely because many pronouns are substitutes for other words, they raise a variety of usage problems, including subject-verb agreement (Chapter 10) and choice of the correct case (Chapter 12). Here we consider **pronoun reference** – that is, the relation between a pronoun and its **antecedent**, the term it refers to. Those pronouns that require antecedents are the personal pronouns (*I, they,* etc.), the relative pronouns (*who, which,* etc.), and the demonstrative pronouns (*this, that, these, those*).

For the choice of a governing pronoun for a whole piece of writing, see 4a, p. 86.

## 13a   Avoid an Abrupt Pronoun Shift.

Your choice of a noun or pronoun in one sentence or part of a sentence establishes a certain person and number.

|  | SINGULAR NUMBER | PLURAL NUMBER |  |
|---|---|---|---|
| **First Person** | I | we | |
| **Second Person** | you | you | |
| **Third Person** | he, she, one, it | they | |
| | this | these | |
| | that | those | |
| and all other singular nouns { | car  Jones  Canadian | cars  Joneses  Canadians } | and all other plural nouns |

When you refer again to the same individual(s) or thing(s), do not shift unexpectedly between persons and numbers—for example, from the singular *someone* to the plural *they,* from the third-person *students* or *they* to the second-person *you,* or from the third-person plural *people* to the second-person singular *you.* Keep to one person and number.

ref
**13a**

DON'T:

            THIRD        SECOND
           PERSON     PERSON
x  A good song stays with *someone,* making *you* feel less alone.

Having committed the sentence to a third-person pronoun, the writer jars us by switching to the second-person *you.*

DO:

         PLURAL      PLURAL
          ANT        PRO
•  A good song stays with *people,* making *them* feel less alone.

Or, more informally:

          SAME PRO
•  A good song stays with *you,* making *you* feel less alone.

Still another solution is grammatically correct but offensive to many readers.

DON'T:

x  A good song stays with a *person,* making *him* feel less alone.

Both *person* and *him* are third-person singular; the sentence is not guilty of a pronoun shift. But it implies that all the "real" representatives of the human race are male. You would do well to avoid such constructions, which are widely considered to be sexist language (8e, p. 210).

## 13b   Supply an Explicit Antecedent.

In informal conversation, pronouns often go without antecedents, since both parties know who or what is being discussed: *He wants me to phone home at least once a week.* In writing, however, you want your antecedents to be explicitly (openly) stated.

DON'T:

x *They* say we are in for another cold winter.

Who is *They*?

x *It* explains here that the access road will be closed for repairs.

If the previous sentence offers no antecedent for *It,* revision is called for.

DO:

ANT                                PRO
• The *weather forecasters* have more bad news for us. *They* say we are in for another cold winter.

ANT                              PRO
• *This bulletin* tells why the backpacking trip was postponed. *It* explains that the access road will be closed for repairs.

Of course you can also do without the pronoun altogether: *The weather forecasters say. . . . This bulletin explains. . . .*

## 13c   Eliminate Competition for the Role of Antecedent.

If you allow a pronoun and its antecedent to stand too far apart, another element in your sentence may look like the real antecedent. This confusion is usually temporary, but you should work to avoid confusing your reader even momentarily.

ref
13c

DON'T:

ANT?                    ANT? PRO
x Keats sat under a huge *tree* to write his *ode. It* was dense and kept
him from the Hampstead mist.

The nearness of *ode* to *It* makes *ode* a likely candidate for antecedent, especially since an ode might be described as dense. With
a little extra thought the reader can identify *tree* as the real antecedent — but a good revision can make that fact immediately clear.

DO:

ANT    PRO
• Keats wrote his ode while sitting under a huge *tree, which* was dense
and kept him from the Hampstead mist.

or

ANT    PRO
• Keats wrote his ode while sitting under a huge *tree, whose* dense
foliage kept him from the Hampstead mist.

ref
13c

DON'T:

ANT?                              ANT?
x Before I sold *cosmetics,* I used to walk by all the *clerks* in the cos-
PRO
metics department, amazed by *their* variety.

What was various, the cosmetics or the clerks?

DO:

• Before I sold cosmetics, I used to walk by all the clerks in the cosmetics department, amazed by the variety of makeup on display.

DON'T:

ANT?              ANT?            PRO
x Because Biff now loved *Suzie* better than *Alice,* he made *her* return
his souvenir face mask.

After some reflection, a reader might see that *Alice* must be the
intended antecedent. But why not make the meaning clear at
once? Try *he made Alice return . . . ,* or rewrite the sentence:

DO:

• Because he had decided to split up with Alice, Biff made her return
his souvenir face mask.

## 13d    Make Sure the Antecedent Is a Whole Term, Not Part of One.

The antecedent of a pronoun should not be a modifier or a piece of a larger term.

DON'T:

                                ANT            PRO
x Alexander waited at the *train* station until *it* came.

> Here the word *train* is part of a larger noun, *train station*. The sentence contains no reference to a train, and thus *it* has no distinct antecedent. The pronoun "dangles" like a dangling modifier (11c, p. 277).

DO:

                                       ANT        PRO
• Alexander waited at the station for the *train* until *it* came.

ref
13d

DON'T:

                                                               PRO
x The peanut jar was empty, but Bobo was tired of nibbling *them* anyway.

> There are no *peanuts* here to serve as the antecedent of *them*.

DO:

         ANT                                                       PRO
• The jar of *peanuts* was empty, but Bobo was tired of nibbling *them* anyway.

DON'T:

x He was opposed to gun control because he felt that every citizen
                    PRO
should have *one* in case the cops staged a surprise raid.

> The word *gun* appears in the sentence, but only as an attributive (adjectival) noun.

DO:

                                          ANT
• He was opposed to the control of *guns* because he felt that every
          PRO
citizen should have *one* in case the cops staged a surprise raid.

## 13e    Beware of Vagueness in Using *This* and *That.*

Study the following unclear passage.

DON'T:

x The town board voted to eliminate school crossing guards, even
though a serious accident had recently occurred at the corner of
Jefferson and Truman. *This* brought the parents out in protest.

> Does *This* refer to the elimination of the crossing guards, to the
> accident, or to the whole preceding statement?

When *this, that, these,* or *those* is used alone, without modifying
another word, it is known as a **demonstrative pronoun.** Inexperienced
writers sometimes use the singular forms *this* and *that* imprecisely, hoping
to refer to a whole previous idea rather than to a specific antecedent. The
problem is that nearby terms may also look like antecedents. While all
writers use an occasional demonstrative pronoun, you should check each
*this* or *that* to make sure its antecedent is clear. The remedy for vagueness
is to make *this* or *that* modify another term or to rephrase the statement.

ref
13e

DO:

• The town board voted to eliminate school crossing guards, even
though a serious accident had recently occurred at the corner of
Jefferson and Truman. *This dangerous economy* brought the parents
out in protest.
MOD    MODIFIED TERM

> The writer has gone from *This* to *This dangerous economy,* turn-
> ing a vague demonstrative pronoun (*this*) into a precise modifier
> — a **demonstrative adjective.**

DON'T:

x The cat shed great quantities of fur on the chair. *That* made Mary
Ann extremely anxious.

> Though the antecedent of *that* (the whole previous sentence) is
> reasonably clear, the second sentence is not very informative.
> What was Mary Ann anxious about, the cat's health or the condi-
> tion of the chair?

DO:

• The cat shed great quantities of fur on the chair. Mary Ann worried
that when her mother saw the chair, the cat would be banished from
the house.

or

- The cat shed great quantities of fur on the chair. The possibility that he was ill made Mary Ann extremely anxious.

## 13f    Beware of Vagueness in Using *Which.*

When you find a clause beginning with the relative pronoun *which,* check to see whether that word refers to a single preceding term or to a whole statement. If the antecedent is a whole statement, you risk unclarity.

DON'T:

x In the subfreezing weather we could not start the car, *which* interfered with our plans.

> Although a reader can see on a "double take" that the antecedent of *which* is not *car* but the whole preceding statement, writers should not put readers to such pains.

DO:

- The subfreezing weather interfered with our plans, especially when the car would not start.

or

- Since the car would not start in the subfreezing weather, we had to change our plans.

DON'T:

x We skate on the frozen pond, *which* I enjoy.

> What is enjoyed, the activity or the pond?

DO:

- I enjoy skating on the frozen pond.

DON'T:

x The improving weather allowed her to fly home, *which* is what she had been hoping for.

> Had she been hoping that the weather would improve or that she could fly home? Even though the two facts are connected, a reader needs to know which one is meant.

DO:

- The improving weather allowed her to fly home, as she had hoped to do.

or

- The improving weather, which she had been hoping for, allowed her to fly home.

## 13g   Avoid Using Rival Senses of *It* within a Sentence.

*It* can serve as both a personal pronoun (*It is mine*) and an indefinite indicator (*It is raining*), but your reader will be momentarily baffled if you combine those two uses within a sentence.

DON'T:

    INDEFINITE                    PERSONAL
    INDICATOR                    PRO
x Although *it* is a ten-minute walk to the bus, *it* comes frequently.

DO:

- Although it is a ten-minute walk to the bus stop, *buses* come frequently.

ref
13g

---

EXERCISE (13a–13g)

1. Some or all of the pronouns in the following sentences show either an inadvisable shift of person or a faulty reference. For each sentence, submit an explanation of why the handling of the sentence strikes you as correct or incorrect, and indicate whatever changes you would recommend.

   A. If a person gets upset easily, you shouldn't play golf.
   B. I want to drum some statistics into your heads which are concrete.
   C. His father always told him what to do, but sometimes he wasn't familiar enough with the facts.
   D. Although she was worried at first, it diminished after a while.
   E. A woman who turns in their friend to the police isn't going to be very popular.
   F. If your goldfish won't eat its food, feed it to the canary.
   G. The weather is fine today, but they say a storm is going to arrive tomorrow.
   H. That storm will be a dangerous one, which is why I intend to stay indoors.
   I. She favored paper recycling because it could be used again for many purposes.
   J. The tide is too high now, but it is certain that it will be low enough three hours from now.

# 14
# Parallelism

When two or more parts of a sentence are governed by a single grammatical device, or *matched*, they are said to be structurally **parallel**.

| PATTERN | EXAMPLE |
|---|---|
| either *x* or *y* | either *boxing* or *wrestling* |
| neither *x* nor *y* | neither *tennis* nor *racquetball* |
| not only *x* but also *y* | He not only *sleeps soundly* but also *snores loudly.* |
| Let me *x* and *y.* | Let me *smile with the wise,* and *feed with the rich.* (Samuel Johnson) |
| It matters not *x* but *y.* | It matters not *how a man dies,* but *how he lives.* (Samuel Johnson) |
| The *x*'s are wiser than the *y*'s. | *The tigers of wrath* are wiser than *the horses of instruction.* (William Blake) |
| It is more blessed to *x* than *y.* | It is more blessed *to give* than *to receive.* |
| Do you promise to *x*, *y*, and *z*? | Do you promise to *love, honor,* and *cherish*? |
| I write entirely to find out *w*, *x*, *y*, and *z*. | I write entirely to find out *what I'm thinking, what I'm looking at, what I see,* and *what it means.* (Joan Didion) |

Note from these examples that parallelism can include both **comparisons** (more $x$ than $y$) and **series**, or the alignment of three or more elements (to $x$, $y$, and $z$). In general, parallelism entails matching the grammar, punctuation, and logic of two or more elements in a sentence.

As sections 7n–7q show in detail, the matching of parallel elements can lend your prose clarity, conciseness, and emphasis. But under the pressure of composing a draft, it is sometimes hard to keep track of all the parts of a parallel construction. In this chapter we will focus on the typical problems of faulty parallelism you should look for when revising.

## 14a    Use Like Elements within a Parallel Construction.

However many terms you are making parallel, the first of them establishes what kind of element the others must be. If the first term is a verb, the others must be verbs as well. Align a noun with other nouns or nounlike elements, a participle (9a, p. 239) with other participles, a whole clause (9b, p. 241) with other clauses, and so forth.

//
14a

DON'T:

x Melody was both habitually *late*$^x$ to work and a sound *sleeper*$^y$ on the job.

> The sentence awkwardly matches an adjective and a noun. Grammatically like elements — *late* and *sleepy,* or *latecomer* and *sleeper* — are needed for adequate alignment.

DO:

• Melody was both a habitual latecomer and a sound sleeper on the job.

DON'T:

x He enjoyed *rocking his torso*$^x$ and *to flail his arms.*$^y$

> The $x$ element is a gerund phrase (p. 597), requiring the $y$ element to be a gerund or gerund phrase as well. The infinitive phrase (p. 597) *to flail his arms* breaks the parallelism.

DO:

• He enjoyed *rocking his torso*$^x$ and *flailing his arms.*$^y$

DON'T:

$$\overset{x}{\overbrace{\text{She likes to } \textit{wear designer clothes,}}} \quad \overset{y}{\overbrace{\textit{listen to classical music,}}} \text{ and}$$

$$\overset{z}{\overbrace{\textit{gourmet food is essential.}}}$$

The series begins with the completion of an infinitive: *to wear.* At this point the writer has two good options: either to keep repeating the *to* or to supply further verb forms governed by the original *to.*

DO:

- $\overset{x}{\overbrace{\text{She likes } \textit{to wear designer clothes,}}} \quad \overset{y}{\overbrace{\textit{to listen to classical music,}}} \text{ and}$

$$\overset{z}{\overbrace{\textit{to eat gourmet food.}}}$$

**// 14a**   or

- $\overset{x}{\overbrace{\text{She likes to } \textit{wear designer clothes,}}} \quad \overset{y}{\overbrace{\textit{listen to classical music,}}} \text{ and}$

$$\overset{z}{\overbrace{\textit{eat gourmet food.}}}$$

Either version adequately corrects the earlier one, in which a whole clause, *gourmet food is essential,* was forced into parallelism with two infinitive constructions. A further option, one that keeps the emphasis of the original statement, is to end the parallelism early.

DO:

- $\overset{x}{\overbrace{\text{She likes to } \textit{wear designer clothes}}} \text{ and } \overset{y}{\overbrace{\textit{listen to classical music,}}} \text{ and}$
she finds gourmet food essential.

## Comparing Comparable Things

The problem of mismatched parallel elements arises most frequently in comparisons. The writer knows what is being compared with what, but the words on the page say something else.

DON'T:

x *The office in Boston* was better equipped than *New York.*

> The sentence appears to compare an office to a city. The writer must add *the one in* to show that one office is being compared to another.

DO:

• *The office in Boston* was better equipped than *the one in New York.*

DON'T:

x The twins swore that *their lives* would be different from *their parents.*

> The writer means to compare one set of lives to another, but the actual wording compares lives to people.

DO:

• The twins swore that *their lives* would be different from *those of their parents'.*

> The apostrophe after *parents* makes that word possessive (221, p. 409), allowing us to understand that the parents' *lives* are being compared with the twins' lives.

DON'T:

x *Solar heating for a large office building* is technically different from *a single-family home.*

> The writer is trying to compare one kind of solar heating to another, but the sentence actually compares one kind of solar heating to a single-family home.

DO:

• *Solar heating for a large office building* is technically different from *that for a single-family home.*

**//**
**14a**

## 14b    Make the Second Half of a Parallel Construction As Grammatically Complete As the First.

When you are aligning two elements $x$ and $y$, be careful not to omit parts of your $y$ element that are necessary to make it grammatically parallel with your $x$ element. The problem tends to arise when the parallelism comes at the beginning of the sentence, especially if the formula being used is *not only x but also y.*

DON'T:

> x  Not only *did Mendel study the color of the peas,* but also *the shapes*
>
> *of the seeds.*

> Some good writers would find this sentence adequate; after all, its meaning is clear. But other writers would want to make a better match between $x$ and $y$. Since the $x$ element contains a subject (*Mendel*) and a verb (*did study*), the $y$ element should follow suit.

IMPROVED:

> • Not only *did Mendel study* the color of the peas, but *he* also *studied* the shapes of the seeds.

> But this revision is wordy. Such a construction can be made more concise by shifting the *not only* to a later position.

PREFER:

> • Mendel studied not only *the color of the peas* but also *the shapes*
>
> *of the seeds.*

> For more about *not only . . . but also,* see 14h, page 323.

## 14c    Be Sure to Complete the Expected Parts of an Anticipatory Pattern.

Many parallel constructions are governed by **anticipatory patterns** (7o, p. 188)—formulas that demand to be completed in a certain predictable way. If you begin the formula but then change or abandon it, your sentence falls out of parallelism.

### Neither . . . Nor

A *neither* demands a *nor,* not an *or.*

DON'T:

x Banging his fist on the table, he insisted that he had *neither* a drinking problem *or* a problem with his temper.

Change *or* to *nor.*

### More Like x Than y

Do not sabotage this formula by adding the word *rather.*

DON'T:

x He seemed *more like* a Marine sergeant *rather than* a social worker.

Delete *rather.*

**//**
**14c**

### No Sooner x Than y

Here the common error is to change *than* to *when.*

DON'T:

x *No sooner* had I left *when* my typewriter was stolen.

*When* must be changed to *than* if the anticipatory formula is to complete its work.

### Not So Much x As y

Be sure that the necessary *as* is not replaced by an unwelcome *but rather.*

DON'T:

x She was *not so much* selfish, *but rather* impulsive.

DO:

• She was *not so much* selfish *as* impulsive.

or

- She was *not so much* selfish *as she was* impulsive.

  Note the absence of a comma in the two satisfactory versions (14i, p. 324).

## 14d In a *Not . . . Neither* Construction, Make Sure the First Negation Does Not Warp the Meaning of the Second One.

DON'T:

x The Marquis de Sade was *not an agreeable man,* and *neither are his novels.*

  The complement *man* in the *x* element makes the sentence appear to say that the novels were not an agreeable man.

DO:

- The Marquis de Sade was *not agreeable,* and *neither are his novels.*

## 14e Beware of a Suspended Verb or a Suspended Comparison.

### Suspended Verb

Watch out for a parallel construction involving a **suspended verb** — the use of two forms of the same delayed verb, governed by the same subject (*The project can, and in all likelihood will, succeed*). Sometimes the delayed verb is appropriate to only one of the two **auxiliary** forms.

DON'T:

x Melody *can,* and indeed *has been, hitchhiking* in both directions at once.

The way to check such sentences is to read them without the interruption: *Melody can hitchhiking,* etc. To save the present form of the sentence, you could write *Melody can hitchhike, and indeed has been hitchhiking, in both directions at once.* But that sounds clumsy. A better solution would be to get rid of the double construction.

DO:

- Melody has been hitchhiking in both directions at once.

## Suspended Comparison

Like those with a suspended verb, parallel constructions involving a **suspended** (delayed) **comparison** sometimes end in a tangle.

DON'T:

x Melody likes total strangers *as much,* if not *more than,* her closest friends.

The problem here, as in many suspended comparisons, is that the last part of the comparison fits with only one of the two elements that lead to it. *More than her closest friends* makes sense, but *as much her closest friends* does not. To be technically right, the suspended comparison would have to say *as much as, if not more than, her closest friends.* But why not do away with the clumsy suspended formula altogether?

DO:

• Melody likes total strangers at least as much as she does her closest friends.

**//**
**14e**

---

EXERCISE (14a–14e)

1. Some or all of the following sentences show a faulty handling of parallel structure. Submit correct versions wherever necessary.

   A. He is not an outstanding swimmer, and neither is his running.
   B. Her passion was to climb mountains and camping in the snow.
   C. Not only is abortion a hotly contested issue these days, but also surrogate motherhood.
   D. No sooner do I turn my back when you start going through my private papers.
   E. They can, and furthermore they have been, making progress on the case.

---

## 14f If You Begin a Parallelism with a *That* Clause, Be Sure to Repeat *That* in Introducing Other Clauses in the Parallelism.

It is all too easy, when you want to make whole clauses parallel, to allow the parallel effect to lapse after the first clause. The danger is greatest when the *x* element is a *that* clause.

DON'T:

$$\overbrace{\hphantom{that she hated her job,}}^{x} \qquad \overbrace{\hphantom{she was glad to be working.}}^{y}$$

x Sue wrote *that she hated her job,* but *she was glad to be working.*

As worded, this sentence allows the y element to become a direct statement about how Sue felt. But the writer's intention was to reveal two things that Sue *wrote.* A second *that* brings out that meaning.

DO:

* Sue wrote *that* she hated her job but *that* she was glad to be working.

    Some good writers would not have removed the comma after *job.* The case for doing so is stated at 14i, p. 324.

## 14g  Do Not Introduce *And Who, And Which, But Who,* or *But Which* without a Prior *Who* or *Which.*

DON'T:

x She is a woman of action, *and who* cares about the public good.

DO:

* She is a woman *who* takes strong action *and who* cares about the public good.

    Alternatively, you can rewrite the sentence without the *and: She is a woman of action who cares about the public good.*

DON'T:

x That is a questionable idea, *and which* has been opposed for many years.

DO:

* That is a questionable idea which has been opposed for many years.

or

* That is a questionable idea, and one which has been opposed for many years.

## 14h    Once You Have Begun a Parallel Construction, Do Not Repeat a Term that Came before the First Element.

Remember that elements already in place before a parallelism begins should not be repeated *inside* it.

### *Either . . . Or, Neither . . . Nor*

A parallelism involving one of these formulas may be grammatically dependent on an immediately preceding word or sentence element (*he wants either sausage or bacon*). Be sure to keep the preceding expression from reappearing inside the parallel construction itself.

DON'T:

x They serve *as* either guidance counselors or *as* soccer coaches.

> To check for a problem, isolate the whole parallelism—*either guidance counselors or as soccer coaches*—and then see if it repeats the word that came just before it. Yes: the second *as* must go.

DO:

• They serve as either guidance counselors or soccer coaches.

or

• They serve either as guidance counselors or as soccer coaches.

> Here *as* is repeated *within* the parallelism in order to make the *x* and *y* elements, *guidance counselors* and *soccer coaches,* fully parallel. Note how the two allowable versions differ from the faulty one:

either *x* or as *y*        wrongly repeats an earlier element, *as*
either *x* or *y*           fully parallel
either as *x* or as *y*     fully parallel

### *Not Only x But Also y*

This formula, useful when it works, can be easily misaligned. Once again you must see where the parallelism begins and avoid repeating an earlier element.

//
14h

DON'T:

x She remembered not only *her maps* but *she also remembered her tire repair kit.*

The first *remembered* comes just before the parallel construction and governs both of its parts. The second *remembered* thus breaks the parallel effect.

DO:

• She remembered not only *her maps* but also *her tire repair kit.*

Now *x* and *y* are parallel; they are the two things that were remembered. The sentence lines up like this:

She remembered { *not only* her maps
{ *but also* her tire repair kit.
(not only *x* but also *y*)

For more about *not only . . . but also,* see 14b, p. 318.

**||**
**14i**

EXERCISE (14f–14h)

2. Some or all of the following sentences show faulty handling of parallel structure. Submit correct versions wherever necessary.

A. Harry told his angry customer that the car was indeed loaded with options, just as he had claimed, and one option was whether or not to start on cold mornings.

B. She is an award-winning musician, but who never feels satisfied with her current level of achievement.

C. You are either acting very hostile tonight or I am covered with bedbugs.

D. He disliked not only colonial rule, but he also distrusted the whole idea of parliamentary government.

E. She will neither commit herself to marriage, nor will she break off the relationship.

## 14i    Join Most Paired Elements without an Intervening Comma.

To show that two elements are meant to be parallel, omit a comma after the first one.

DON'T:

x
_____
x Last night's storm blew out *my electric blanket,* and *my clock radio.*

The comma implies that the only direct object (9a, p. 237) of *blew out* has already been given and that the main statement is over. By removing the comma the writer can show that the *x* and *y* elements are parallel objects.

DON'T:

x                                                    y
_____                    _____
x Aspirin has been called *a blessing by some,* and *a dangerous drug*

*by others.*

Aspirin has been called *x* and *y*; remove the comma to show that *x* and *y* are tightly related.

### Pairing Independent Clauses

The no-comma rule above need not apply when the *x* element is an independent clause (9b, p. 241), as in *Not only did they adjust the fan belt, but they also adjusted the brakes.* But in *either . . . or* constructions you should omit the comma to keep the *y* statement from escaping the controlling effect of the parallelism.

DON'T:

x
_____
x Either *you are wrong about the guitar strings,* or *I have forgotten*

y
_____
*everything I knew.*

Remove the comma and notice how the two statements then fit more tightly together.

## 14j    As a Rule, Use Commas and a Coordinating Conjunction to Separate Items in a Series.

The normal way to present a **series** (three or more parallel items) is to separate the items with commas, adding a coordinating conjunction such as *and* or *or* before the last one:

- I used to sprinkle my writing with *commas,*[x] *semicolons,*[y] and *periods*[z] as though they were salt and pepper.

## Optional Final Comma

Many writers, especially journalists, omit the final comma in a series. So can you if you are consistent about it throughout a given piece of writing.

ACCEPTABLE:
- When George felt lonely in the kitchen, he drowned out the silence by turning on *the blender,*[x] *the food processor*[y] and *the garbage disposal.*[z]

Note, however, that the *x, y and z* formula may not always allow your meaning to come through clearly.

AMBIGUOUS:

x The returning knight had countless tales to tell of *adventure,*[x] *conquest of hideous monsters*[y] and *helpless damsels in distress.*[z]

Did he conquer the damsels as well as the monsters? A comma after *monsters* would remove all doubt. If you keep to the traditional *x, y, and (or) z* method, such problems will not arise.

## Conjunctions without Commas

If all the members of a series are connected by conjunctions, no commas are needed:

- In his new frame of mind, George began to understand that every man must learn to live alone with *his cable television*[x] and *his quadriphonic CD tape deck*[y] and *his video recorder.*[z]

## Emphatic Sequence of Clauses

You can sometimes omit a coordinating conjunction when presenting several brief, tightly related independent clauses in a sequence:

● George saw the frozen tamale pie, he yearned for it, he stuffed it eagerly into the shopping cart.

Here the lack of a conjunction before the third clause helps to bring out the rapidity and compulsiveness of the activities described.

## 14k    Carry Through with Any Repeated Modifier in a Series.

If you begin repeating any modifier within a series, be sure to keep doing so for all the remaining items.

DON'T:

x    He can never find *his textbooks, his tapes, calculator,* and *homework.*

The modifier *his* in the *x* element commits the writer to using the word again in *y* and *z*. Note the options for revision.

DO:

● He can never find *his textbooks, his tapes, his calculator,* and *his homework.*

or

● He can never find his *textbooks, tapes, calculator,* and *homework.*

## 14l    If an Item in a Series Contains a Comma, Use Semicolons to Show Where the Items End.

Once you have begun a series, you may find yourself using commas for two quite different purposes: to separate the *x, y,* and *z* elements and to punctuate *within* one or more of those elements. If so, your reader may have trouble seeing where each item ends. To show the important breaks between the main parallel items, separate *x, y,* and *z* with semicolons:

- Wratto's poem said that lack of energy could keep people out of a lot of trouble; that moving around and doing things, burning calories unnecessarily, makes people forget about important things, such as supporting poetry; and that by sitting perfectly still, just letting the universe run down all by itself, you can actually get *with* entropy and make it beautiful.

The semicolons help to show where each of the three items ends; otherwise the commas would be too confusing. Note that the items in a series punctuated by semicolons do not have to constitute independent clauses.

For other advice about the formation of effective series, see 7q, page 191.

---

**EXERCISE (14i–14l)**

//
**14l**

3. Some or all of the following sentences show inadvisable formation and/or punctuation of parallel constructions. Briefly comment on each, indicating where, why, and how you would make necessary changes.

  A. Whether the earthquake was caused by fault slippage, or by excessive drilling, could not be determined.

  B. Statisticians, who are slavishly admired by some people, and criticized as frivolous by others, have discovered that the taste for dill pickles declines after age sixty-five.

  C. George couldn't remember whether Susan used to stock up on low-fat milk, condensed milk, defatted, reconstituted, or evaporated milk.

  D. Stanley writes leaflets, makes underground broadcasts, tape recordings, and paints warnings on police station walls.

  E. The Director of Food Services said that during the renovation the students would have priority in the dining halls; that faculty members should plan to cook at home, eat elsewhere, or bring bag lunches to their offices; and that the college's neighbors, including several retired professors living nearby, would be barred from the student halls until the work had been completed.

---

# 15

## Relations between Tenses

Every time you use a verb, you are expressing a **tense** or time frame. (For tense forms see 21b–21c, pp. 392–400.) Some tenses are obviously appropriate to certain functions – the present for statements of opinion, the past for storytelling, the future for prediction. But choice of tense becomes trickier when you need to combine two or more time frames within a sentence. (*He said he would have been ready if the plane had not been late*; *She will have finished by the day we get home*; etc.) When revising your work, check to see that your combinations of tenses observe the following rules.

## 15a   Choose One Governing Tense for a Piece of Writing.

### Stating Facts and Ideas

The normal way to state facts or offer your ideas about any general or current topic is to use the present tense. For example:

- Water boils at 100° Celsius.

- Does the new divorce law protect the rights of children?

Note how the following passage establishes a present time frame, departing from it only to narrate events that occurred previously:

- The great debate *continues* [PRES] between heredity and environment. Some observers *believe* [PRES] that accidents of our circumstances *act* [PRES] upon us and *make* [PRES] us who we are. Others *believe* [PRES] that our genes *seal* [PRES] our destiny.

    Both sides have strong arguments, but I *am convinced* [PRES] that technology *adjusts* [PRES] our fate. My grandfather, for example, *was* [PAST] dead at thirty-six from diabetes, a disease that my father *has lived* [PRES PERF] with for sixty years, thanks to this century's advances in medical research.

If you are stating ideas about the past, many of your verbs will be in the past tense. Even so, the present is appropriate for conveying your current reflections about past events:

tense
15a

- I *believe* [PRES] we *can prove* [PRES] that the Etruscans *had* [PAST] much more influence on Roman civilization than most people *realize* [PRES].

### Narrating Events

The usual tense for narrating events is the past:

- She *arrived* [PAST] home in a fury, and she *was* [PAST] still upset when the phone *rang* [PAST].

- The solution *was allowed* [PAST] to stand for three minutes, after which 200 cc of nitrogen *were added* [PAST].

    In this second example the past verbs are in the passive voice (21c, p. 399).

Sometimes, to get a special effect of immediacy, you may even want to use the present for narration:

- When he *phones*<sup>PRES</sup> her, she *tells*<sup>PRES</sup> him to leave her alone.

But note that once you adopt this present-tense convention for storytelling, you have committed yourself to it throughout the piece of writing. Do not try to switch back to the more usual past.

DON'T:

x  When he *phones* her, she *tells* him to leave her alone. But he *acted* as if he *hadn't understood* her point.

> For consistency the verbs in the second sentence should be *acts* and *hasn't* (or *has not*) *understood*.

## 15b   Relate Your Other Tenses to the Governing Tense.

Once you have established a controlling time frame, or **governing tense**, shift into other tenses as logic requires.

**tense**
**15b**

### Present Time Frame

A present frame, established by a present governing tense, allows you to use a variety of other tenses to indicate the times of actions or states. Suppose, for example, you are writing a sentence that begins *Norbert meditates every day, and . . .* The following are ways of completing that sentence.

Norbert meditates every day, and . . .

| COMPLETION OF SENTENCE | TENSE |
| --- | --- |
| he *is meditating* right now. | present progressive (action ongoing in the present) |
| he *has meditated* five thousand times. | present perfect (past action completed thus far) |
| he *has been meditating* since dawn. | present perfect progressive (action begun in the past and continuing in the present) |
| he *meditated* again yesterday. | past (completed action) |

| COMPLETION OF SENTENCE | TENSE |
|---|---|
| he *was meditating* before I was born. | past progressive (action that was ongoing in a previous time) |
| he *had meditated* for years before hearing about the popularity of meditation. | past perfect (action completed before another past time) |
| he *had been meditating* for three hours before the interview. | past perfect progressive (ongoing action completed before another past time) |
| he *will meditate* tomorrow. | future (action to occur later) |
| he *will be meditating* for the rest of his life. | future progressive (ongoing action to occur later) |
| he *will have meditated* for more hours than anyone ever has. | future perfect (action regarded as completed at a later time) |
| he *will have been meditating* for ten years by the time he is thirty. | future perfect progressive (ongoing action regarded as having begun before a later time) |

**tense**
**15b**

### Past Time Frame

If your time frame is the past and you want to mention an action completed at a still earlier time, put the verb expressing that earlier action not in the past but the past perfect tense.

DON'T:

       PAST                                     PAST

x There *were* rumors around school that the Dean *was* a sergeant in the Army in the Korean War.

DO:

       PAST                                    PAST PERF

• There *were* rumors around school that the Dean *had been* a sergeant in the Army in the Korean War.

DON'T:

       PAST           PAST

x She *asked* us if we *saw* the Stanley Cup finals.

DO:

PAST          PAST PERF
- She *asked* us if we *had seen* the Stanley Cup finals.

But if the "still earlier" action was a continuing one, use the past perfect progressive.

DON'T:

PAST PROGR                              PAST
x We *were driving* for quite some time when we *came* to a diner.

DO:

PAST PERF PROGR                         PAST
- We *had been driving* for quite some time when we *came* to a diner.

If your time frame is the past and you want to look forward from that time to a subsequent one, use the auxiliary *would* plus the base (infinitive) form of the verb.

DON'T:

PAST            FUTURE
x I *knew* that I *will remember* this trip for a long time.

DO:

PAST          WOULD + BASE V
- I *knew* that I *would remember* this trip for a long time.

DON'T:

PAST       FUTURE
x The officer *said* that he *will lift* the motorcycle into the back of the paddy wagon.

DO:

PAST         WOULD + BASE V
- The officer *said* that he *would lift* the motorcycle into the back of the paddy wagon.

### Hypothetical Condition

Certain sentences containing *if* clauses set forth **hypothetical conditions**. That is, they tell what would be true or would have been true in certain imagined circumstances. Note that such sentences differ in both form and meaning from sentences proposing likely conditions.

**LIKELY CONDITION:**

- I *will dance* if you *clear* a space on the floor.
- If she *studies* now, she *will pass.*

**HYPOTHETICAL CONDITION:**

- I *would dance* if you *cleared* a space on the floor.
- If she *studied* now, she *would pass.*

The "likely condition" sentences anticipate that the condition may be met, but the "hypothetical condition" sentences are sheer speculation: what would happen if . . . ? These require use of the **subjunctive mood** (21d, p. 402) in the *if* clause. And in the "consequence" clause they require a *conditional* form, either present or past:

<table>
<tr><td colspan="3">CONDITIONAL FORMS</td></tr>
<tr><td>Present</td><td>would }<br>could } + base verb</td><td>would go<br>could go</td></tr>
<tr><td>Past</td><td>would }<br>could } + have + past participle</td><td>would have gone<br>could have gone</td></tr>
</table>

tense
15b

Thus:

| IF CLAUSE | CONSEQUENCE CLAUSE |
|---|---|
| PRES SUBJN<br>If you *worked* overtime, | PRES CONDL<br>you *would have* more spending money. |
| PAST SUBJN<br>If she *had concentrated,* | PAST CONDL<br>she *could have written* a perfect translation. |
| PRES SUBJN<br>If they *won* a million dollars, | PRES CONDL<br>what *would* they *do* with the money? |
| PAST SUBJN<br>If you *had been* old enough, | PAST CONDL<br>*would* you *have married* Barbara? |

Sometimes the consequence clause precedes the *if* clause:

| CONSEQUENCE CLAUSE | IF CLAUSE |
|---|---|
| You would have more spending money | if you worked overtime. |
| She could have written a perfect translation | if she had concentrated. |
| What would they do with the money | if they won a million dollars? |
| Would you have married Barbara | if you had been old enough? |

The most common mistake in combining tenses is to use *would* in both parts of a conditional statement. Remember that *would* goes only in the consequence clause, not in the *if* clause.

DON'T:

x If they *would* try harder, they would succeed.

x If they *would have* tried harder, they would have succeeded.

DO:

• If they *tried* harder, they would succeed.

• If they *had tried* harder, they would have succeeded.

## 15c  Change the Tense of a Verbal to Show a Different Relation to the Indicated Time of Action.

When you use a **verbal** (9a, p. 239) — an infinitive, a participle, or a gerund — ask yourself how it relates in time to the rest of your statement. Verbals change their form only if they characterize an *earlier* action or state than the main one.

### Same or Later Time: Present Form

Use the present form of a verbal if it conveys an action or state no earlier than the time established in the rest of the sentence.

SAME TIME:

    PRES    PRES INF
• We *try to snowboard* every day.

- PAST    PRES INF
- We *tried to snowboard* every day.

- PAST    PRES GER
- We *tried snowboarding* every day.

- PRES PART                                  PAST
- *Snowboarding* every day, we greatly *improved* our technique.

**LATER TIME:**

- PRES    PRES INF
- We *intend to snowboard* every day next winter.

- PRES                     PRES GER
- We *anticipate* months of *snowboarding*.

- PRES                     PRES PART
- We *hope* to become stronger, *snowboarding* every day.

## Earlier Time: Past Form

**tense 15c**

In the rare case when your verbal is placed into relation with a later time, put it into a past form:

- PAST INF
- We expect *to have improved* our snowboarding by next season.

- PAST INF
- We wanted *to have made* a breakthrough before the new season began.

- PAST INF
- Our goal will be *to have made* a breakthrough by then.

- PAST PART
- *Having improved* so much the year before, we had good reason to feel hopeful.

---

**EXERCISE (15a–15c)**

1. Some or all of the following sentences show a faulty choice of tense. Indicate which, if any, sentences you find correct, and explain how and why you would change the others.

    A. He knew she stopped smoking five years before.

    B. She had wanted to have quit even earlier.

    C. If I would have known Marilyn Monroe, I would have treated her respectfully.

D. She had always wanted to be named Mother of the Year, but she was not altogether pleased when the quintuplets had been born.
E. He was suffering quietly for years before his illness became public knowledge.

## 15d    Learn How Tenses Differ between Quotation and Indirect Discourse.

In the following chart, notice what happens to tenses when writers shift from what was actually said (quotation) to **indirect discourse**, or a report of what was said.

| | QUOTATION | INDIRECT DISCOURSE |
|---|---|---|
| present verb in quotation | "I find it difficult to remember your name," she said. | She said that she *found* it difficult to remember his name. |
| past verb in quotation | "Your interest in bowling gave cause for alarm," she revealed. | She revealed that his interest in bowling *had given* cause for alarm. |
| present perfect verb in quotation | She protested, "I have never encouraged your crude advances." | She protested that she *had never encouraged* his crude advances. |
| past perfect verb in quotation | "Until then," she reflected, "I had never known how barbarous a male could be." | She reflected that until then she *had* never *known* how barbarous a male could be. |
| future verb in quotation | She added, "You will do better to bestow your 'date,' as you choose to call it, for the 'demolition derby' on some companion more keenly appreciative of such cultural gatherings than myself." | She added that he *would do* better to bestow his so-called "date" etc. |

To summarize these changes of tense, indirect discourse:

|  | QUOTATION | INDIRECT DISCOURSE |
|---|---|---|
| makes a present verb past | want ⟶ | wanted |
| makes a past or present perfect verb past perfect | wanted ⎫ have wanted ⎭ ⟶ | had wanted |
| leaves a past perfect verb past perfect | had wanted ⟶ | had wanted |
| turns a future verb into *would* + a base (infinitive) form | will want ⟶ | would want |

You can deduce other tense changes in indirect discourse from these basic ones: *will have wanted* becomes *would have wanted, has been wanting* becomes *had been wanting,* and so on.

## 15e    Do Not Shift between Quotation and Indirect Discourse within a Sentence.

Once you have begun to quote someone's speech or writing, do not suddenly move into indirect discourse (15d). Similarly, do not leap from indirect discourse to quotation.

DON'T:

QUOTATION

x She said, *"I love science fiction movies,"* and *had I seen the one*
INDIRECT DISCOURSE

*about the teenage Martians on a rampage?*

DO:

QUOTATION

• She said, *"I love science fiction movies,"* and asked me, *"Have you*
QUOTATION

*seen the one about the teenage Martians on a rampage?"*

DON'T:

INDIRECT DISCOURSE          QUOTATION

x My boss said *the key was missing* and *are you the one who took it?*

DO:

|  | INDIRECT DISCOURSE | | INDIRECT DISCOURSE |
|---|---|---|---|

● My boss said *the key was missing* and asked *if I was the one who had taken it.*

---

**EXERCISE (15d–15e)**

2. Some or all of the following sentences show a faulty use of tense in quotation and/or indirect discourse. Indicate which, if any, sentences you find correct, and explain how and why you would change the others.

   A. He protested that he never wanted to join the armed forces.
   B. He said that he will look into a career in photography instead.
   C. "It is still snowing," she remarked, and shouldn't we stay inside the cabin?
   D. She reminded him that until then, "you have a consistent record of getting lost in snowstorms."
   E. He replied, however, that this time will be different.

---

tense
15f

## 15f   Learn the Uses of the Literary Present Tense.

### Discussing Actions within a Plot

Unlike a real event, a scene within a work of art does not happen once and for all. It is always ready to be experienced afresh by a new reader, viewer, or listener. Consequently, the time frame for discussing such a scene is the present. Though you should use the past tense to write about the historical creating of the art work, you should use the present tense to convey what the work "says to us." This function of the present tense is called the **literary present**.

**HISTORICAL PAST:**

● Shakespeare *was* probably familiar with the plays of Kyd and Marlowe when he *wrote* his great tragedies. He *expressed* his deepest feelings in those plays.

**LITERARY PRESENT:**

● Shakespeare *reveals* Hamlet's mind through soliloquy.

● Hamlet's unrelenting psychological dilemma *drives* him toward catastrophe.

- The Misfit, in Flannery O'Connor's story "A Good Man Is Hard to Find," *murders* an entire family.
- In the 1949 film version of *Oliver Twist,* Alec Guinness *plays* Fagin.

  If the verb in this last example were *played,* the sentence would be making a statement not about the movie but about an event in Alec Guinness's acting career.

### Discussing Ideas within a Work

No matter how long ago a book or other work was completed, use the literary present tense to characterize the ideas it expresses:

- In *The Republic* Plato *maintains* that artists are a menace to the ideal state.
- Thoreau *says* in *Walden* that we can find peace by staying exactly where we are.
- The *Rambo* and *Rocky* movies express an American infatuation with violence.
- The Parthenon speaks to us of the Greek love of proportion.

If, on the other hand, you want to refer to a noncontemporary author's ideas without reference to a particular work, use the past:

- Plato *believed* that artists were a menace to the ideal republic.
- Thoreau *was convinced* that people could find peace by staying exactly where they were.

## 15g  In Discussing a Plot, Relate Other Tenses to the Literary Present.

When an event in a plot follows certain developments or anticipates others that you want to mention, use the literary present (15f) for the action being immediately discussed and the past or future (and related tenses) for the earlier or later actions:

- When Hamlet's suspicions *were* [PAST] confirmed by the ghost, he *vowed* [PAST] revenge. But by Act Two he *fears* [PRES] that his self-doubts *have dulled* [PRES PERF]

tense
15g

PRES

his purpose. He *engages* a troupe of players to reenact the murder

PRES                    FUTURE

and *swears* that the play *will "catch* the conscience of the King. . . ."

Notice how the writer has chosen a point of focus in Act Two of *Hamlet.* The use of the literary present for that time determines which tenses are appropriate for the other described actions.

## 15h    Do Not Allow the Past Form of a Quoted Verb to Influence Your Own Choice of Tense.

It is hard to keep to the literary present (15f) when you have just quoted a passage containing verbs in the past tense. The tendency is to allow your own verbs to slip into the past. Keep to the rule, however: use the present tense for actions or states under immediate discussion.

DON'T:

tense
15h

PAST

x D. H. Lawrence *describes* Cecilia as "a big dark-complexioned,

PAST

pug-faced young woman who very rarely *spoke.* . . ." When she

PAST            PAST

*did speak,* however, her words *were* sharp enough to kill her aunt Pauline.

Here *did speak* and *were,* influenced by the quoted verb *spoke,* wrongly depart from the literary present.

DO:

* D. H. Lawrence *describes* Cecilia as "a big dark-complexioned, pug-faced young woman who very rarely spoke. . . ." When she *does speak,* however, her words *are* sharp enough to kill her aunt Pauline.

---

EXERCISE (15f–15h)

3. Some or all of the following sentences show a faulty use of tense with regard to works of art. Indicate which, if any, sentences you find correct, and explain how and why you would change the others.

    A. Forster publishes *A Passage to India* in 1924.

B. At the beginning of the novel, Aziz has no idea that he will be the defendant in a notorious trial.

C. "I warned you before," said the hero of the novel, "and now you are going to be sorry."

D. Two chapters earlier, Dimmesdale was sure he would be fleeing with Hester to England, but when he enters the pulpit to deliver his final sermon, he already knows that he will stay and confess his guilt.

E. A specialist in UFO research worked as a consultant to *Close Encounters of the Third Kind*, a film in which alien creatures really did visit our planet.

tense
15h

# V

## PUNCTUATION

16. Period, Question Mark, Exclamation Point

17. Comma

18. Semicolon and Colon

19. Dash and Parentheses

20. Quoting

## PUNCTUATION

Marks of punctuation are essential for clear meaning in written prose. Beyond showing where pauses or stops would occur in speech, they indicate logical relations that would otherwise be hard for a reader to make out. For example, parentheses, brackets, dashes, and commas all signal a pause, but they suggest different relations between main and subordinate material. The only way to be sure that your punctuation marks are working with your meaning, not against it, is to master the rules.

Part IV above, "Usage," covers a good many punctuation rules for handling such grammatical features as independent clauses, modifying elements, and parallel constructions. This part repeats those rules (giving cross references to the fuller discussions), adds other rules, and shows how you can choose between punctuation marks that are closely related in function. Whenever a rule is repeated, the relevant exercises will be found with the earlier treatment.

Note that standard practices of quotation are handled in Chapter 20 and that problems with apostrophes and hyphens are treated under spelling, Chapter 24. To see how punctuation marks are formed and spaced on the page, consult Chapter 27.

# 16

# Period,
# Question Mark,
# Exclamation Point

## PERIOD

**16a  Place a Period at the End of a Sentence
Making a Statement, a Polite Command,
or a Mild Exclamation.**

STATEMENT:

- I think the Olympic Games have become too politicized.
- Art historians are showing new respect for nineteenth-century narrative painting.

POLITE COMMAND:

- Tell me why you think the Olympic Games have become too politicized.
- Consider the new respect that art historians are showing toward nineteenth-century narrative painting.

MILD EXCLAMATION:

* What a pity that the Olympic Games have become so politicized.

* How remarkable it is to see the art historians reversing their former scorn for nineteenth-century narrative painting.

    Exclamation points at the end of these two sentences would have made them more emphatic; see 16j, p. 349.

## 16b    End an Indirect Question with a Period.

An **indirect question**, instead of taking a question form, reports that a question is or was asked. Thus an indirect question is a **declarative sentence** — one that makes a statement. As such, it should be completed by a period, not a question mark.

DON'T:

x Ted asked me whether I was good at boardsailing?

DO:

* Ted asked me whether I was good at boardsailing.

**16c**

## 16c    Consider a Period Optional after a Courtesy Question.

Some questions in business letters (Chapter 32) are really requests or mild commands. You can end such a sentence with either a period or a question mark.

DO:

* Would you be kind enough to reply within thirty days.

or

* Would you be kind enough to reply within thirty days?

The period makes a more impersonal and routine effect. If you want to express actual courtesy toward a reader you know, keep to the question mark.

## 16d    Eliminate an Unacceptable Sentence Fragment [9c, p. 244].

DON'T:

$\overbrace{\qquad\qquad\qquad}^{\text{FRAG}}$

x They stood back and watched the crows. *Wheeling and cawing over the splattered melon.*

DO:

* They stood back and watched the crows wheeling and cawing over the splattered melon.

For the intentional sentence fragment, see 9d, p. 247.

## 16e    If a Sentence Ends with an Abbreviation, Do Not Add a Second Period.

DON'T:

x Send the money directly to Lincoln Dollar, M.D..

DO:

* Send the money directly to Lincoln Dollar, M.D.

## QUESTION MARK

## 16f    Place a Question Mark after a Direct Question.

Most questions are complete sentences, but now and then you may want to add a question to a statement or insert a question within a statement. In every instance, put a question mark immediately after the question:

* Can a camel pass through the eye of a needle?
* I know that many strange things are possible, but can a camel really pass through the eye of a needle?
* It was just fifteen years ago today—remember?—that the camel got stuck in the eye of the needle.
* "Can a needle," asked the surrealist film director when he met the Arab veterinary surgeon, "pass through the eye of a camel?"

But if your sentence poses a question that is then modified by other language, place the question mark at the end:

- How could he treat me like that, after all the consideration I showed him?

## 16g   Use a Question Mark within Parentheses to Express Doubt.

- Saint Thomas Aquinas, 1225(?)–1274, considered faith more important than reason.

  If the dates here were in parentheses, the question mark would go inside brackets: *(1225[?]–1274).*

### Sarcastic Question Mark

No grammatical rule prevents you from getting a sarcastic effect from the "doubting" question mark. But if you are determined to be sarcastic, quotation marks will do a better job of conveying your attitude.

AVOID:
x The President expects to make four nonpolitical (?) speeches in the month before the election.

PREFER:
- The President expects to make four "nonpolitical" speeches in the month before the election.

## 16h   If a Sentence Asking a Question Contains a Question at the End, Use Only One Question Mark.

- Why didn't Melody stop to ask herself, "Isn't it strange that I'm the only person in this whole zoo who is trying to feed peanuts to the elephant train?"

## 16i   As a General Practice, Do Not Use a Comma or a Period after a Question Mark.

DON'T:
x Now I know the answer to the question, "Why study?".

DO:
- Now I know the answer to the question, "Why study?"

DON'T:
x "Where is my journal?", she asked.

DO:
- "Where is my journal?" she asked.

An exception is made for material inserted within parentheses. See 19i, p. 372.

---

## EXCLAMATION POINT

### 16j     Use Exclamation Points Sparingly to Show Intensity.

When you quote an outburst or want to express extremely strong feeling, end the sentence or intentional sentence fragment (9d, p. 247) with an exclamation point.

- "My geodesic dome! My organic greenhouse! My Tolkien collection! When will I ever see them again?"

- Standing in the bread line, he had a moment of revelation. So *this* was what his economics professor had meant by structural unemployment!

Frequent use of exclamation points, however, dulls their effect. And though an exclamation point, like a question mark, can be inserted parenthetically to convey sarcasm (16g), the effect is usually weak.

AVOID:
x Warren thought that a black-and-white photocopy (!) of the Rembrandt painting would give him everything he needed to write his art history paper.

---

EXERCISE (16a–16j)

1. Submit corrections for any inadvisable handling of periods, question marks, or exclamation points in the following sentences.

A. Aunt Sophia was disoriented by the family reunion. Never having played frisbee with thirty-five people before.

B. He wondered if I would like to shoot the rapids with his novelist friend?

C. I am not sure—will you correct me if I'm wrong—that porpoises are more intelligent than raccoons.

D. She wanted her psychiatrist to tell her whether it was possible to get seasick in Iowa?

E. His fellow workers at the car wash did not seem very impressed (!) by his Ph.D..

!
16j

# 17
## Comma

### 17a Join Two Independent Clauses Either with a Comma and a Coordinating Conjunction or with a Semicolon.

For discussion of this point, see 9e, p. 249.

- Many students enrolled in the course, *but* few have kept pace with the heavy workload.

- Many students enrolled in the course; few have kept pace with the heavy workload.

### 17b Avoid a Run-on Sentence [9e, p. 249].

DON'T:

x They discussed Faulkner's novel, the class hour ended all too soon. [comma splice]

x I hate having a brainy sister it makes me feel stupid. [fused sentence]

DO:
- They discussed Faulkner's novel, *but* the class hour ended before they could get very far.

- I hate having a brainy sister, *since* it makes me feel stupid.

351

**DON'T:**

x Some people know how to hide their nervous habits, I do not.

x I get nervous in front of the class I start to stutter.

**DO:**

• Some people know how to hide their nervous habits, *but* I do not.

• I get nervous in front of the class; I start to stutter.

## 17c  Do Not Put a Comma between Sentence Elements That Belong Together.

**Subject and Verb (9a, p. 237)**

**DON'T:**

     S     V
x Only *Betsy, had* trouble chanting through the dinner hour.

**DO:**

• Only Betsy had trouble chanting through the dinner hour.

**Verb and Direct Object (9a, p. 237)**

**DON'T:**

    V                                  D OBJ
x She *saw* in her mind's eye, the chocolate-covered *apple* that was sitting in the refrigerator.

**DO:**

• She saw in her mind's eye the chocolate-covered apple that was sitting in the refrigerator.

**Verb and Complement (9a, p. 238)**

**DON'T:**

            V                             COMPL
x Alpha waves *were* to an alarming degree, *deficient* in essential sugars.

**DO:**

• Alpha waves were to an alarming degree deficient in essential sugars.

or

,
17c

- Alpha waves were, to an alarming degree, deficient in essential sugars.

  (See 11m, page 240, for the need to set off an interrupting element on *both* sides.)

## Subordinating Conjunction and the Rest of Its Clause (9b, p. 242)

DON'T:

<u>SUBORD CONJ</u>   <u>REST OF SUBORD CLAUSE</u>

x Another problem with biofeedback was *that, the name reminded her of getting fed.*

DO:

- Another problem with biofeedback was that the name reminded her of getting fed.

## Preposition and Its Object (p. 595)

DON'T:

<u>PREP</u>   <u>OBJ OF PREP</u>

x Her thoughts kept returning *to, dripping cakes, aromatic pies, and quarts of non-diet soda.*

DO:

- Her thoughts kept returning to dripping cakes, aromatic pies, and quarts of non-diet soda.

  No matter how long the object of a preposition may be, no comma should follow the preposition itself.

## Exceptions: Comma Allowed

When a direct object precedes the subject and verb, you can follow it with a comma to indicate that it is not the subject:

<u>D OBJ</u>   S <u>V</u>

- *That we are here on earth merely to pass along our DNA, I cannot believe.*

The same rule applies to an initial **objective complement** – that is, a complement of a direct object:

$$\overbrace{\text{OBJ COMPL}}$$   S   V   D OBJ
* *What she calls happiness, I call slavery.*

---

**EXERCISE (17c; for 17a–17b, see p. 254)**

1. Some or all of the following sentences show a faulty handling of commas. Indicate where and why you would recommend changes of punctuation.

   A. Did you know that, the first baseball game played under electric lights occurred in 1883?

   B. The nutrition expert voiced some doubts about the health of American children raised on, "Crazy Cow, Baron Von Redberry, Sir Grapefellow, Count Chocula, and Franken-Berry."

   C. What Shaw called the most licentious of institutions, other people call holy matrimony.

   D. The old woodshed on the back lot, made a perfect clubhouse for the children.

   E. As his weight-training program drew to a close, Biff found himself admiring, new curves in the most surprising places.

---

**, 17e**

**17d    Include a Comma after an Initial Modifier That Is More than a Few Words Long [11h, p. 284].**

* Instead of having the chocolate mousse, Walter ordered an apple for dessert.

* Since we ate lunch after three o'clock, we are not interested in dinner now.

**17e    Consider a Comma Optional after a Brief Initial Modifier [11i, p. 285].**

* Until this week, I had kept up with my assignments.

* In 1912, the *Titanic* sank in icy waters off the coast of Newfoundland.

or

* Until this week I had kept up with my assignments.

* In 1912 the *Titanic* sank in icy waters off the coast of Newfoundland.

## 17f    Master the Punctuation of Restrictive and Nonrestrictive Modifiers [11j, p. 286].

RESTRICTIVE:

          RESTR MOD
* Women *who are over thirty-five* tend to show reduced fertility.

                   RESTR MOD
* Some women *who have taken up running in their thirties and forties* have proved to be world-class marathoners.

NONRESTRICTIVE:

                   NONRESTR MOD
* Women, *who have rarely been treated equally in the job market,* still tend to be relatively underpaid.

               NONRESTR MOD
* Women, *whose adaptability to long-distance running was not appreciated until recently,* seem better able to manage fatigue than their male counterparts.

## 17g    In Punctuating an Appositive, Observe the Restrictive/ Nonrestrictive Rule [11k, p. 288].

RESTRICTIVE APPOSITIVE:

        RESTR APP                        RESTR APP
* My brother *Bert* played baseball in college, but my brother *Jack* was not athletic at all.

    *Bert* and *Jack* are restrictive appositives, telling in each case which brother is meant.

NONRESTRICTIVE APPOSITIVE:

        NONRESTR APP
* My sister, *Diane,* studied Portuguese in the Navy.

    The commas tell us that the writer has only one sister, Diane. Thus the appositive does not restrict the meaning of the preceding term, *sister.*

RESTRICTIVE APPOSITIVE:

             NONRESTR APP
* In her poem *"The bustle in a house,"* Emily Dickinson uses ordinary domestic images to express the emotional aftermath of a death in the family.

,
17g

Dickinson wrote many poems; the lack of a comma before the appositive shows that it is restrictive, narrowing the reference to just one of those poems.

NONRESTRICTIVE APPOSITIVE:

NONRESTR APP
- In writing his play, *Otho the Great*, Keats collaborated with Charles Brown.

*Otho the Great* is the only play Keats is known to have written. The first comma indicates this fact; the nonrestrictive appositive names the play but does not single it out from others.

## 17h   Set Off a Sentence Adverb or a Transitional Phrase with Commas [11l, p. 289].

SENT ADV
- A circus, *furthermore*, lifts the spirits of young and old alike.

TRANS PHRASE
- The deficit has continued to grow, *as a matter of fact*.

For exceptions, see p. 289.

## 17i   Set Off an Interrupting Element at Both Ends [11m, p. 290].

INT EL
- Our leading advocate of clean streets, *you understand*, is the Mayor.

INT EL
- Every morning at nine, certain students *—always the wrong ones—* hear Professor Fry's advice about habits of punctuality.

## 17j   Use Commas with Coordinate Modifiers [11n, p. 291].

COORDINATE MODIFIERS:

- I arrived at my new school on a *sunlit, windy* day.
- The show included the work of a *small, innovative* group of local artists.

The group is both small and innovative; the two coordinate adjectives modify the same term, as the comma shows.

**NONCOORDINATE MODIFIERS:**

- She never forgave them for the way they insulted her on that *infamous first* day of school.

- A *small support* group of battered wives meets at the high school on Wednesday evenings.

  What is *small* is not a group but a *support group*; thus *small* and *support* are not coordinate, and no comma is called for.

## 17k   Do Not Place a Comma between the Final (or Only) Modifier and the Modified Term [11o, p. 292].

- FINAL MOD
  O'Keeffe produced an intense, starkly simple, *radiantly glowing*
  MODIFIED TERM
  *painting* of a flower.

- Flemish artists of the seventeenth century painted merry, sensual,
  FINAL  MODIFIED
  MOD    TERM
  *ironic scenes* of peasant life.

## 17l   Consider Enclosing a "Contrary" Modifier in Commas [11p, p. 293].

**ACCEPTABLE:**

- She told a fascinating, but not altogether believable, story.

- The Senator's speech was a bitter, though carefully worded, reply to his opponents.

or

- She told a fascinating but not altogether believable story.

- The Senator's speech was a bitter though carefully worded reply to his opponents.

## 17m   Join Most Paired Elements without an Intervening Comma [14i, p. 324].

- Last night's storm blew out *my electric blanket* and *my clock radio*.

- A graduating senior should know how to write *an effective business letter* and *a confident résumé*.

## 17n    As a Rule, Use Commas and a Coordinating Conjunction to Separate Items in a Series [14j, p. 325].

- I used to sprinkle my writing with *commas*, *semicolons*, and *periods* as though they were salt and pepper.
- Now I use punctuation for *clarity*, *emphasis*, *logic*, and *variety*.

## 17o    Learn the Uses of the Comma in Numbers, Dates, Addresses, Titles, and Degrees.

### Number of More Than Four Digits

Commas should separate every three digits (counting from the right) of a number consisting of more than four digits: *109,358,452*. In four-digit numbers the comma is optional: *6083* and *6,083* are both correct.

No commas separate the digits of years (*2001*), telephone numbers, ZIP codes, serial numbers, and other figures meant to identify an item or place. Such figures are sometimes divided into segments by hyphens, as are Social Security numbers: *053-26-3537*.

### Date

A comma should separate the day of the month and the year if the month is given first: *July 4, 1934*. If the sentence continues after the date, then the year, too, should be followed by a comma:

- July 4, 1934, was the date of her birth.

When the day is given first, no punctuation is necessary:

- She was born on 4 July 1934 in Peralta Hospital.

When only the month and the year are stated, commas before and after the year are optional. You can write either *July 1934 was the month of her birth* or *July, 1934, was the month of her birth*.

### Address

- New York, New York
- 7713 Radnor Road, Bethesda, MD 20034

- Department of Economics, Simon Fraser University, Burnaby, B.C. V5A 1S6, Canada

Within a sentence, put commas both before and after the name of a state or province that identifies a specific town or geographic feature.

- Laramie, Wyoming, celebrates its Jubilee Days every July.

- Mount McKinley, Alaska, is the highest peak in North America.

### Title or Degree Following Name

As a rule, titles or degrees have been set off by commas on both sides:

- Herbert Moroni, Ph.D., was present.

- Herbert Moroni, Jr., began studying for his college entrance exams in eighth grade.

But when the abbreviation following a name is numerical, omit the commas:

- Adlai Stevenson III served on the committee.

For the use of a comma to introduce a quotation, see 20j and 20k, page 383.

,
17o

---

EXERCISE (17o; for 17d–17n, see pp. 293, 328)

2. Some or all of the following sentences show a faulty use (or absence) of commas. Indicate where and why you would recommend changes of punctuation.
    A. September 1939 was a bad time to be in Europe.
    B. The issue of 16 October, 1975 contained some of the finest prose he had ever read.
    C. New York, New York is a wonderful town.
    D. Sammy Davis Jr. was a founding member of Hollywood's Rat Pack.
    E. Last year the police reported 2571 more felonies than the year before.

# 18

# Semicolon
# and Colon

## SEMICOLON

### 18a  If Two Statements Are Closely Related in Meaning, Join Them with a Semicolon.

The punctuation mark that comes nearest in function to the semicolon is the period. But whereas a period keeps two statements apart as separate sentences, a semicolon shows that two statements within one sentence are intimately related. When one statement is a consequence of another or contrasts sharply with it, you can bring out that tight connection by joining them with a semicolon instead of with a comma and a coordinating conjunction (9e, p. 249):

- The University conducts art history classes in Europe; the accessibility of great museums and monuments gives students a firsthand sense of the subject.

- Some of those painters influenced Cézanne; others were influenced by him.

360

Note that when a semicolon is used, the second statement often contains a sentence adverb or transitional phrase (111, p. 289) pointing out the logical relation between the two clauses:

- Misunderstanding is often the root of injustice; perfect understand-
  SENT ADV
  ing, *however,* is impossible to attain.

  TRANS PHRASE
- Some parents weigh every word they speak; others, *in contrast,* do not think twice about their harsh language.

## 18b    Do Not Follow a Semicolon with a Sentence Fragment.

An unacceptable sentence fragment (9c, p. 244) is just as faulty when it follows a semicolon as when it stands alone.

DON'T:

FRAG

x  I used to be afraid to talk to people; *even to ask the time of day.* I

FRAG

always let my brother speak for me; *because he was everyone's buddy.*

DO:
- I used to be afraid to talk to people; even asking the time of day was an ordeal. I always let my brother speak for me; he was everyone's buddy.

or:

- I used to be afraid to talk to people—even to ask the time of day. I always let my brother speak for me, because he was everyone's buddy.

## 18c    In Appropriate Circumstances, Feel Free to Follow a Semicolon with a Coordinating Conjunction.

There is nothing wrong with following a semicolon with a conjunction, so long as the second statement is an independent clause (9b, p. 241). Do so if you want to make explicit the logical connection between the statements coming before and after the semicolon:

CONJ
- All day long we loaded the van with our worldly goods; *but* when we were all ready to leave the next morning, full of eagerness for the trip, we saw that the van had a flat tire.

A comma after *goods* would also be appropriate, but the semicolon recommends itself because the second statement already contains two commas. Thus the semicolon helps to show the main separation in the sentence.

### 18d  If an Item in a Series Contains a Comma, Use Semicolons to Show Where the Items End [14l, p. 327].

- Student dining halls include the Servery, which is located on the ground floor of the Student Union; the Cafeteria, temporarily relocated in Jim Thorpe Gymnasium; and the Rathskeller, now in the basement of Anne Bradstreet Hall.

## COLON

### 18e  Use a Colon to Show an Equivalence between the Items on Either Side.

:
18e

A colon introduces a restatement, a formal listing, or a quotation. Use a colon if you can plausibly insert *namely* after it:

- Dinner arrives: [*namely*] a tuna fish sandwich and a cup of tea.
- The bill is unbelievable: [*namely*] $8.50 for the sandwich and $1.95 for the tea.
- Samuel Johnson offered the following wise advice: [*namely*] "If you would have a faithful servant, and one that you like, serve yourself."

The *namely* test can help you avoid putting semicolons where colons belong and vice versa.

DON'T:
x The results of the poll were surprising; 7 percent in favor, 11 percent opposed, and 82 percent no opinion.

*Namely* would be appropriate here; therefore the semicolon should be a colon.

x We slaved for years: we remained as poor as ever.

*Namely* is inappropriate, since the second clause makes a new point. The colon should be a semicolon.

## 18f  Make Sure You Have a Complete Statement before a Colon.

Like a semicolon, a colon must be preceded by a complete statement.

DON'T:

FRAG
x *Occupations that interest me:* beekeeper, horse groomer, dog trainer, veterinarian.

DO:

COMPLETE STATEMENT
• *Occupations involving animals interest me:* beekeeper, horse groomer, dog trainer, veterinarian.

But remember that unlike a semicolon, a colon need not be *followed* by a whole statement (compare 18b, p. 361).

## 18g  Do Not Allow a Colon to Separate Elements That Belong Together.

DON'T:

V                     D OBJ
x Before buying my Cavalier, I *tested: a Toyota Corolla, a Ford Escort, and a Nissan Sentra.*

The colon separates a verb from its three-part direct object. Note that this practice would still be wrong if the direct object had any number of parts and extended for many lines.

V                     COMPL
x Her favorite holidays *are: Christmas, Halloween, and the Fourth of July.*

The colon separates a verb from its three-part complement (9a, p. 238).

x The exhibit contained work by many famous photographers, *such as:*
<sup>PREP</sup>
*Avedon, Adams, Weston, and Lange.*
<sub>OBJ OF PREP</sub>

The colon separates a preposition from its four-part object.

x The Renaissance naval adventurers set out *to: sack enemy cities,*
COMPLETION OF INF PHRASES
*find precious metals, and claim colonial territory.*

The colon separates the infinitive marker *to* from the completion of three infinitive phrases (p. 597). Even if you had a long series of such phrases, the colon would be wrong.

In each of the four examples above, you need only drop the colon to make the sentence acceptable.

## 18h   Use No More than One Colon in a Sentence.

Once you have supplied a colon, your reader expects the sentence to end with the item or items announced by the colon. A second colon makes a confusing effect.

DON'T:

x She needed three things: a new hat, warmer gloves, and boots that would be serviceable in all kinds of bad conditions: snow, slush, mud, and rain.

DO:

• She needed three things: a new hat, warmer gloves, and boots that would be serviceable in snow, slush, mud, and rain.

## 18i   Use a Colon to Separate Hours and Minutes, to End the Salutation of a Business Letter, and to Introduce a Subtitle.

HOURS AND MINUTES:

• The train should arrive at 10:15 P.M.

SALUTATION:

• Dear Mr. Green:

**SUBTITLE:**

* *Virginia Woolf: A Biography*

For the use of a colon to introduce a quotation, see 20k, p. 383.

---

**EXERCISE (18a–18c, 18e–18i; for 18d, see p. 328)**

1. Correct any errors in the use of colons and semicolons:

   A. A penny saved is a penny earned: but rich people, I have noticed, tend to put their pennies into shrewd investments.
   B. The planning commissioner said that in his judgment the new skyscraper had: "all the earmarks of an eyesore."
   C. Rescuers found that the ferry had capsized too quickly for very many people to escape at once from the enclosed lower hall; that others, in desperation, had smashed windows and taken their chances in the 37-degree water; and that still others, whether through fear or calculation, had stayed put, counting on possible air pockets to save them from drowning.
   D. The robber asked for only two things; her money and her life.
   E. Biff told his teammates to watch out on the next play for one of the following: a quarterback sneak; a statue of liberty play; or a drop-kick field goal.

---

:

**18i**

# 19

## Dash
## and
## Parentheses

Both dashes and parentheses, as well as commas, can be used to set off interrupting elements (11m, p. 290). The difference is that dashes call attention to the interrupting material, whereas parentheses suggest that it is truly subordinate in meaning.

| **Dash** | — | most emphatic | The monsoon season—with incessant driving rain and flooding—causes much hardship. |
| **Comma** | , | neutral | The monsoon season, with incessant driving rain and flooding, causes much hardship. |
| **Parentheses** | ( ) | least emphatic | The monsoon season (with incessant driving rain and flooding) causes much hardship. |

# DASH

## 19a  Learn the Principal Functions of the Dash.

EMPHATIC EXPLANATION:

* Narcissus was the most modern of mythological lovers — he fell in love with himself.

FRAMING OF A STRIKING INSERTION:

* Narcissus — the most modern of mythological lovers — fell in love with himself.

ABRUPT INTRODUCTION OF A LIST:

* At least Betsy had accumulated some souvenirs — a black eye from Encounter, bruised ribs from Rolfing, and a whiplash from Aikido.

INTERRUPTION OF DIALOGUE:

* "Run, Jane, run!" yelled Dick. "I see the principal and he's coming toward us with — "
      "It's too late, Dick, it's too late! The curriculum enrichment consultants have blocked the gate and — "
      "Oh, Jane, oh, Jane, whatever will become of us?"

If a character's speech "trails off" instead of being interrupted, an ellipsis (20m, p. 384) is more appropriate than a dash: *"Well, it beats me. . . ."* Note that you should begin a new paragraph for each change of speaker.

ISOLATION OF AN INTRODUCTORY ELEMENT:

* Depression, compulsion, phobia, hallucination — these disorders often require quick and emphatic treatment.

In a sentence that makes a "false start" for rhetorical effect (7t, p. 197), you want to give a signal that the opening element is an appositive (11k, p. 288) rather than the subject of the verb. A dash serves the purpose.

19a

## 19b    If Your Main Sentence Resumes after an Interruption, Use a Second Dash.

When you begin an interruption with one dash, you must end it with another.

DON'T:

ˣ Narcissus looked into a lake—so the story goes, and fell in love with his own reflection.

ˣ Although Betsy took up massage—somebody had told her it would increase her human potential, she soon discovered that she was too ticklish.

DO:

• Narcissus looked into a lake—so the story goes—and fell in love with his own reflection.

• Although Betsy took up massage—somebody had told her it would increase her human potential—she soon discovered that she was too ticklish.

## 19c    Make Sure Your Sentence Would Be Coherent If the Part within Dashes Were Omitted.

The elements of your sentence before and after the dashes must fit together grammatically.

DON'T:

ˣ *Because* he paid no attention to her—he was riveted to his cable sports channel day and night—*so* she finally lost her temper.

Ask yourself if the sentence makes sense without the material between dashes: ˣ *Because he paid no attention to her so she finally lost her temper.* Recognizing that this shortened sentence is grammatically askew, you can then correct the original.

DO:

• Because he paid no attention to her—he was riveted to his cable sports channel day and night—she finally lost her temper.

## 19d    Do Not Use More than One Dash or Pair of Dashes in a Sentence.

Dashes work best when used sparingly. Within a single sentence, one interruption marked by dashes should be the maximum.

DON'T:

x We cannot expect a tax reform bill—or indeed any major legislation —to be considered on its merits in an election year—a time when the voters' feelings—not the country's interests—are uppermost in the minds of lawmakers.

DO:

• We cannot expect a tax reform bill, or indeed any major legislation, to be considered on its merits in an election year—a time when the voters' feelings, not the country's interests, are uppermost in the minds of lawmakers.

## 19e    Do Not Combine a Dash with a Comma or a Period.

A comma and a dash together are redundant; a period and a dash are contradictory.

DON'T:

x The people who knew Betsy most intimately,—her doctor, her pharmacist, and her lawyer—were eager to know what she would try next.

x She did find one organization that suited her temperament—the Cult of the Month Club—.

DO:

• The people who knew Betsy most intimately—her doctor, her pharmacist, and her lawyer—were eager to know what she would try next.

• She did find one organization that suited her temperament—the Cult of the Month Club.

**19e**

---

### EXERCISE (19a–19e)

1. Some or all of the following sentences show an inadvisable handling of dashes. Indicate where and why you would recommend changes of punctuation.

A. He didn't want to accuse her of being forward with other suitors—after all, women were supposed to be more independent nowadays, but he couldn't help wondering why she had a toll-free telephone number.

B. It is simply untrue,—and nothing you can say will convince me—that trees make wind by waggling their branches.

C. Western clothes, rock and roll, student demonstrations for greater democracy—the Chinese government decided that things had gotten out of hand.

D. Somehow my aunt sensed the danger—perhaps she realized that my uncle should have been home by then—and she phoned me to come over—the sooner the better—to wait with her.

E. Since my calendar is so blank—hardly anyone has realized that I am back in town—so you can pick any date you like.

---

# PARENTHESES

## 19f   Use Parentheses to Enclose and Subordinate an Incidental Element or to Provide Reference Information.

Parentheses are appropriate for sealing off and subordinating an incidental illustration, explanation, comment, number, date, or citation.

ILLUSTRATION:

- Some tropical reptiles (the Galápagos tortoise, for example) sleep in puddles of water to cool themselves.

EXPLANATION:

- Julia Moore (revered in her lifetime as "the Sweet Singer of Michigan") offered the memorable observation that "Literary is a work very difficult to do."

PASSING COMMENT:

- The Ouse (a rather pretty, harmless-looking river) is known to literary people as the body of water in which Virginia Woolf drowned herself.

NUMBER:

- The furniture will be repossessed in thirty (30) days.

DATE:

- The article on outcomes of psychotherapy appears in *The Behavioral and Brain Sciences* 6 (1983), pages 275–310.

CITATION:

- Guevara first began studying Marxism in Guatemala in 1954 (Liss 256–57).

## 19g Learn When to Supply End Punctuation for a Parenthetical Sentence within Another Sentence.

If your whole sentence-within-a-sentence is a statement, do not end it with a period:

- Shyness *(mine was extreme)* can be overcome with time.

But if you are asking a question or making an exclamation, do supply the end punctuation:

- Today I am outspoken *(who would have predicted it?)* and sometimes even eloquent.
- To be able to give a talk without panic *(what a relief at last!)* is a great advantage in the business world.

Notice that the parenthetical sentence-within-a-sentence does not begin with a capital letter.

**( )
19h**

## 19h When Placing a Parenthetical Sentence between Complete Sentences, Punctuate It as a Complete Sentence.

A whole sentence within parentheses, if it is not part of another sentence, must begin with a capital letter and contain end punctuation of its own, *within* the close-parenthesis mark:

- Shyness can be a crippling affliction. *(The clinical literature is full of tragic cases.)* Yet some victims suddenly reach a point where they decide they have been bullied long enough.

## 19i Do Not Allow Parentheses to Affect Other Punctuation.

Remember these two rules:

1. No mark of punctuation comes just before an open-parenthesis.
2. The rest of the sentence must keep to its own punctuation, as if the parenthetical portion were not there.

Thus, to decide whether a close-parenthesis mark should be followed by a comma, mentally disregard the interruption:

- After she had tried Primal Jogging and I'm-O.K.-You're-Not-O.K. (she still hadn't met any interesting men), Betsy resolved to become a Hatha Backpacker.

  If you cross out the entire parenthesis, you can tell that the comma is needed (see 11h, p. 284).

- Betsy discovered (though not with true surprise) that swarms of mosquitoes were no remedy for loneliness.

  Discounting the parenthesis, you can see that a comma would wrongly separate a verb from its direct object: x *Betsy discovered, that swarms of mosquitoes were no remedy for loneliness.* See 17c, p. 352.

## 19j Do Not Use Parentheses to Interrupt a Quotation.

Brackets (20p, p. 387), not parentheses, are required when you want to insert information or commentary into quoted material.

DON'T:
x "Joan (Benoit) has to be the favorite in this race," Nancy said.

DO:
- "Joan [Benoit] has to be the favorite in this race," Nancy said.

---

EXERCISE (19f–19j)

2. Some or all of the following sentences show faulty handling of parentheses. Indicate where and why you would recommend changes of punctuation.

A. "We'd better double-team Ralph (Sampson)," the coach advised.
B. Although some people suspect that the cocaine wave has been exaggerated by the media, most police chiefs (knowing the association between "crack" and violent crime), disagree.
C. Student unrest reached a peak in the late 1960s. (Those were the years of strongest protest against the Vietnam War).
D. Melody told the campers in her tent to be careful with matches, (she remembered her own early troubles) especially if they hadn't learned how to roll paper properly.
E. A modem (a device for connecting a computer terminal to a central source of data), could easily be mistaken for an ordinary telephone.

( )
19i

# 20

## Quoting

Handling quoted material is more than a matter of following the procedures covered in this chapter. You want to quote only where the quoted language is important to your point; you want to avoid letting quotations crowd out your own reasoning; and you want to quote accurately and give proper acknowledgment of the source (29a, p. 501). Yet it is also good to know the small details of managing a quotation—introducing the words smoothly, showing just where the quotation begins and ends, and signaling where you have made an omission or inserted an explanatory word or phrase.

### 20a Recognize the Punctuation Marks Used with Quotations.

The marks used in handling quotations are double and single **quotation marks**, the **slash**, the **ellipsis**, and **brackets**.

| NAME | FORM | FUNCTION |
|------|------|----------|
| double quotation marks (20b) | " " | to mark the beginning and end of a quotation |
| single quotation marks (20c) | ' ' | to mark a quotation within a quotation |

| NAME | FORM | FUNCTION |
|------|------|----------|
| slash (20g) | / | to mark a line break in a brief quotation of poetry |
| ellipsis (20m) | . . . | to mark an omission from a quotation |
| brackets (20p) | [ ] | to mark an explanatory insertion within a quotation |

Note that these marks have other functions as well.

| MARK | OTHER FUNCTION | EXAMPLE |
|------|----------------|---------|
| quotation marks | to show distance from a dubious or offensive expression | Hitler's "final solution" destroyed six million Jews. |
| slash | to indicate alternatives | Try writing an invoice and/or a purchase order. |
| | to mean "per" in measurements | 60 ft./sec. (feet per second) |
| | to indicate overlapping times | the Winter/Spring issue of the journal |
| ellipsis | to show that a statement contains further implications | And thus he came to feel that he had triumphed over the government. How little he knew about the workings of bureaucracy. . . . |
| | to show that dialogue "trails off " | "What I am trying to tell you is . . . is . . ." |
| brackets | to supply identifying information within a citation | *Star-Ledger* [Newark, NJ], 3 Jan. 1988: 2. |
| | to insert material into a passage that is already within parentheses | (See, however, D. L. Rosenhan in *Science* 179 [1973]: 250–58.) |

quot
**20a**

---

## SETTING OFF A QUOTATION

### 20b    Use Double Quotation Marks to Set Off Quoted Material That You Have Incorporated into Your Own Prose.

If you are representing someone's speech or quoting a fairly brief passage of written work—no more than five typed lines of prose or no more than two or three lines of poetry—you should **incorporate** the quotation. That is, you should make it continuous with your own text instead of **extracting** it by skipping lines and indenting it (20h, p. 380). Be sure to enclose an incorporated quotation in quotation marks. In North American (as opposed to British) English, those marks should be double (" "):

- Betsy yelled, "You get away from those chocolate chips right now, you nasty old bear!"

- "Take a loftier view of your blisters," writes Dr. Dollar. "Regard them as so many lucky opportunities to expose the real inner you."

### 20c    Use Single Quotation Marks for a Quotation within a Quotation.

quot
20c

If the passage you are incorporating already contains quotation marks, change them to single marks (' '):

- E. F. Carpenter, writing in *Contemporary Dramatists,* says of Butterfield: "The playwright knows where his best work originated. 'Everything that touches an audience,' he told me, 'comes from memories of the period when I was down and out.' "

Similarly, if a title that belongs in quotation marks (26a, p. 451) is contained within other quotation marks, make those "inside" marks single:

- "The concluding lines of Wratto's 'Ode to Amerika,' " observes Pieper in *The Defenestrated Imagination,* "rest on an ingenious paradox."

### Double Quotation within a Quotation

Try to avoid quoting a passage that already contains single quotation marks; the effect will be confusing. But if you find no alternative, change those single marks to double ones. Then check carefully to see that your *three* sets of marks are kept straight (" ' " ' "):

- Orwell's friend Richard Rees informs us that "when Socialists told him that under Socialism there would be no such feeling of being at the mercy of unpredictable and irresponsible powers, he remarked: 'I notice people always say "*under* Socialism." They look forward to being on top—with all the others underneath, being told what is good for them.' "[1]

   Here the main quotation is from Rees. Since Rees quotes Orwell, Orwell's words appear within single marks. But when those words themselves contain a quotation, that phrase ("*under* Socialism") is set off with double marks.

## 20d  When Quoting Dialogue, Indent for a New Paragraph with Each Change of Speaker.

After you have completed a quotation of speech, you can comment on it without starting a new paragraph. You can also resume quoting the speaker's words after your own. But do indent for a new paragraph as soon as you get to someone else's speech.

   "I can't understand," I said, "how you can win world-class distance races without having been coached in high school or college."

   "Oh, but sir," he protested with a polite smile, "I have been running since I was a little child. In Kenya this is how we get from village to village."

   "Yes, yes, but where did you get your training?" This man seemed to defy everything I knew about the making of a great runner.

   "Oh, my *training!*" He threw his head back and laughed. "Mister reporter, *you* run every day, year after year, at 8,000 feet, carrying boxes and fuel and whatnot. Then please come back and tell me if you think you need some training!"

## 20e  When Quoting Speech of More than One Paragraph, Put Quotation Marks at the Beginning of Each New Paragraph but at the End of Only the Final Paragraph.

In general, quotation marks come in pairs: for every mark that opens a quotation there must be another to close it. But there is one exception. To show that someone's quoted speech continues in a new paragraph, put quotation marks at the beginning of that paragraph, and keep doing so until the passage ends:

> "I have two things to bring up with you," she said. "In the first place, which of us is going to be keeping the stereo? I'd like to have it, but it's no big deal to me.
>     "Second, what about the dog? I'm the one who brought her home as a puppy, and I intend to keep her!"

## 20f    Learn How to Combine Quotation Marks with Other Marks of Punctuation.

1. Always place commas and periods inside the close-quotation marks. You do not have to consider whether the comma or period is part of the quotation or whether the quotation is short or long. Just routinely put the comma or period first:

* Benjamin Franklin wrote, "Fish and visitors stink after three days."

* "They don't stifle enough of them," remarked Flannery O'Connor when asked whether courses in creative writing stifle aspiring authors.

2. Always place colons and semicolons outside the close-quotation marks:

* "A village explainer": that is what Gertrude Stein called Ezra Pound.

* Stein called him "a village explainer"; others have been much less charitable toward Pound's eccentric and inflammatory views.

3. Place question marks, exclamation points, and dashes either inside or outside the close-quotation marks, depending on their function. If they are punctuating the quoted material itself, place them inside:

* "Do you think it will snow?" she asked.

* "Of course it will!" he replied.

But put the same marks *outside* the close-quotation marks if they are not part of the question or exclamation:

* Was Stephanie a sophomore when she said, "I am going to have a job lined up long before I graduate"?

* I have told you for the last time to stop calling me your "little sweetie"!

4. When the quotation must end with a question mark or exclamation point and your own sentence calls for a closing period, drop the period:

- Grandpa listens to Dan Rather every evening and constantly screams, "Horsefeathers!"

5. In all other situations, the end punctuation of the quotation makes way for your own punctuation. For example, if the quoted passage ends with a period but your own sentence does not stop there, drop the period and substitute your own punctuation, if any:

- "I wonder why they don't impeach newscasters," said Grandpa.

  The quoted passage would normally end with a period, but the main sentence calls for a comma at that point.

6. When a quotation is accompanied by a footnote number, that number comes after all other punctuation except a dash that resumes your own part of the sentence:

- According to Kenneth Lynn, "Hadley outdid all the men by catching six trout in less than half an hour out of a pool beneath a waterfall."[6]

- Lynn reports that "Hadley outdid all the men"[6]—but in *The Sun Also Rises* Hemingway awards the fishing prowess to his own counterpart, Jake Barnes.

7. When a quotation is incorporated into your text (without indention) and is followed by a parenthetical citation (29d, p. 519; 29e, p. 523), the parenthesis comes after the final quotation marks but before a comma or period—even if the comma or period occurs in the quoted passage:

- John Keegan begins his book about famous battles by confessing, "I have not been in a battle; nor near one, nor heard one from afar, nor seen the aftermath" (*The Face of Battle* 15).

8. But if the incorporated quotation ends with a question mark or exclamation point, include it before the close-quotation marks and add your own punctuation after the parenthesis:

- He raises the question, "How would *I* behave in a battle?" (Keegan 18).

9. If you extract a quotation (indent it and set it apart from your text), and if you then supply a parenthetical citation, place that citation after all punctuation on a separate line.

quot
20f

- I'm just sittin here washing television
  washin telvsn
  wshn t.v.
  (yeah!)
  wshn *tee veeee.*
      ("Ode to Amerika," lines 13–17)

## 20g When Incorporating More than One Line of Poetry, Use a Slash to Show Where a Line Ends.

You can incorporate as many as three lines of poetry instead of extracting them (20h). But if your passage runs beyond a line ending, you should indicate that ending with a slash preceded and followed by a space:

- Wratto tells us, "Ain't got my food stamps yet this month, & wonder if / Maybe this is fascism at last."

## 20h Extract a Longer Quotation from the Main Body of Your Text.

quot
20h

If your prose quotation extends beyond five typed lines, or if you are quoting more than two or three lines of poetry, you should extract the passage. In the examples below, the red numbers are keyed to rules given on pages 381–382.

EXTRACTED PROSE:

```
Margot Slade points to the bond between siblings that

is like no other connection between human beings: ————— 1
          5                                     ————————— 2
         ⎧  Welcome to the sibling bond, that twilight
         ⎪  zone of relationships between brothers and
         ⎪  sisters, and any combination thereof, where
         ⎪  parents must walk but often fear to tread.
         ⎪  With good reason.  As one well-seasoned
   3, 4 ⎨  father put it: "Under most circumstances, it
         ⎪  can be suicide to interfere." —————————————→ 6
         ⎪ 7——Siblings generally constitute an exclu-
         ⎪  sive state--exclusive, that is, of parents.
         ⎪  They are the keepers of each other's secrets
         ⎩  and the supporters of each other's goals.
```

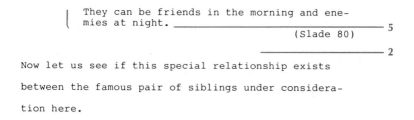

```
    They can be friends in the morning and ene-
    mies at night. _____
                         (Slade 80)            5

                      _____ 2

Now let us see if this special relationship exists

between the famous pair of siblings under considera-

tion here.
```

The writer is quoting from Margot Slade's article, "Siblings: War and Peace." For proper citation form see 29d, p. 519.

**EXTRACTED POETRY:**

```
In "Crossing Brooklyn Ferry" Whitman calls out to his

fellow citizens of the future as well as the present: ___ 1
    5
     \                                      _____ 2
    /  I am with you, you men and women of a generation,
   |      or ever so many generations hence,
3,4{ 8 — Just as you feel when you look on the river and
   |      sky, so I felt,
   |   Just as any of you is one of a living crowd,
    \     I was one of a crowd, . . .  _____ 5

                                       _____ 2

By creating a bond with unborn Americans, Whitman

prophesies the coming greatness of his country.
```

1. In most cases, introduce the passage with a colon.

2. Separate the passage from your main text by skipping an extra line above and below.

3. Indent the whole passage ten spaces from your left margin, or somewhat less if the quoted lines of poetry are very long.

4. If you are submitting a paper for a course, use single or double spacing according to your instructor's advice. But if you are writing for publication, double-space the passage, treating it just like your main text.

5. Omit the quotation marks you would have used to surround an incorporated quotation.

6. Copy exactly any quotation marks you find in the quoted passage itself.

7. In extracting prose, indent all lines equally if the passage consists of one paragraph or less. When you extract more than one paragraph of prose, indent the first line of each full paragraph by three additional spaces. If the first sentence in that extracted quotation does not begin a paragraph in the original, do not indent it any further than the passage as a whole.

8. In extracting poetry, follow the spacing (beginnings and endings of lines) found in the original passage.

---

**EXERCISE (20a–20h)**

1. Correct any errors in the use of quotation marks:

    A. "They don't call him "Doctor K" for nothing," said the commentator after Gooden's fifteenth strikeout.

    B. Is it true that the witness said, "I refuse to answer on the grounds that my answer might tend to incinerate me?"

    C. The poet tells us a good deal about his life when he writes,

> "Counted up Fri. and saw I still got
> Four lids and two caps,
> One lovin' spoonful,
> Three buttons from Southatheborder,
> Some coke but no Pepsi,
> And a bottle of reds.
> O Amerika we can still be friends fer a few more weeks."

    D. The secretary had never met anyone who *demanded* a MacArthur Fellowship before. "But Mr. Wratto," she protested, "That just isn't how we handle the selection process." "It is now, Toots," replied the poet. "Just write out the check for 350 grand and I promise you won't see me in here no more."

    E. That brazen young man with the tattoos and the buckskin shirt had the nerve to address me as "Toots!"

**quot**
**20i**

---

# INTRODUCING A QUOTATION

## 20i    If a Quotation Fits into One of Your Own Clauses or Phrases, Introduce It without Punctuation.

The way to decide which punctuation, if any, to use in introducing a quotation is to read the quoted matter as part of your own sentence. Use introductory punctuation only if it would have been called for anyway, with or without the quotation marks:

- Macbeth expresses the depth of his despair when he characterizes life as "a tale told by an idiot."

  Since the quotation serves as an object of the writer's preposition *as*, a preceding comma would be wrong here (see 17c, p. 352). Note how smoothly the quoted passage completes the writer's sentence.

## 20j   Follow an Introductory Tag with a Comma.

Even if you do not feel that a pause is called for, put a comma after an introductory clause such as *She said* or *He replied*:

- He said, "I'd like to comment on that."
- She replied, "Yes, you are always making comments, aren't you?"

If the tag follows or interrupts the quoted speech, it must still be set apart:

- "I'd like to comment on that," he said.
- "Yes," she replied, "you are always making comments, aren't you?"

## 20k   Use Either a Comma or a Colon to Introduce an Incorporated Quotation That Does Not Fit into Your Own Clause or Phrase.

You can choose between a comma and a colon to introduce a quotation that makes a new statement apart from your own language. The comma is more usual and less formal in effect.

- Gandhi, when asked what he thought of Western civilization, smiled and replied, "I think it would be a very good idea."

  A colon would be equally correct here, but it would mark a more formal pause.

- Surrounded by surging reporters and photographers, the accused chairman tried to hold them all at bay with one repeated sentence: "I will have no statement to make before tomorrow."

The colon is especially appropriate here because it matches *one repeated sentence* with the actual words of that sentence.

## 20l  As a Rule, Use a Colon before an Extracted Passage.

Since an extracted quotation (20h, p. 380) appears on the page as an interruption of your prose, you should usually introduce it with a colon, implying a formal stop.

- Here is Macbeth's gloomiest pronouncement about life:

> it is a tale
> Told by an idiot, full of sound and fury,
> Signifying nothing.

But if the quoted passage begins with a fragment that completes your own sentence, follow rule 20i (p. 382) and omit any special introductory punctuation:

- Macbeth considers life to be

> a tale
> Told by an idiot, full of sound and fury,
> Signifying nothing.

A colon would be wrong here, since it would separate an infinitive (*to be*) from its complement (*a tale* . . .). Note that a comma would be unacceptable for the same reason.

---

## OMITTING MATERIAL FROM A QUOTATION

## 20m  Use an Ellipsis Mark to Show That Something Has Been Omitted from a Quotation.

If you want to omit unneeded words or sentences from a quoted passage, accuracy requires that you show where you are doing so.

### WHOLE PASSAGE:

- As I have repeatedly stated, those claims, which irresponsible promoters of tax shelter schemes continue to represent as valid, have been disallowed every time they have come before the IRS.

quot
20m

PARTIAL QUOTATION:

* Gomez reports that "those claims . . . have been disallowed every time they have come before the IRS."

## 20n   Distinguish between Three Kinds of Ellipsis.

### Three Dots

If an omission is followed by material from the same sentence being quoted, type the ellipsis mark as three spaced periods preceded and followed by a space:

* President Clearance declared that he had "nothing . . . to hide," and that "secrecy in University affairs is . . . contrary to all my principles."

If the sentence preceding your ellipsis ends with a question mark or exclamation point, keep that mark and add three spaced dots:

* "Is Shaw," she asked, "really the equal of Shakespeare? . . . That seems extremely dubious."
* The champion shouted, "I am the greatest! . . . Nobody can mess up my pretty face."

quot
20n

### Four Dots

Use four dots—a normal period followed by three spaced dots—if you are omitting (1) the last part of the quoted sentence, (2) the beginning of the next sentence, (3) a complete sentence or more, or (4) one or two complete paragraphs.

* Clearance was lavish in his praise for the University: "Everything is fine. . . . We've tooled up to turn out a real classy product."
* "I resent the implication that nerve gas is being developed. . . . Besides, every safety precaution has been taken."

A four-dot ellipsis is appropriate whenever your quotation skips material and then goes on to a new sentence, whether or not you are omitting material *within* a sentence. But note that you should always have grammatically complete statements on both sides of a four-dot ellipsis.

DON'T:

x She wrote, "I am always bored. . . . nothing here to keep me occupied."

Here the four-dot ellipsis is wrongly followed by a fragment.

## Row of Dots

Mark the omission of a whole line or more of poetry by a complete line of spaced periods.

Wratto continues:

> What have U done fer yr poets O Amerika?
> I'm sitting here waiting fer a call from the Nash
> Ional Endowment fer the Arts and Humanities.
> Is it arty to keep me waiting Amerika?
> Is this yr crummy idea of a humanity?
> . . . . . . . . . . . . . . . . . . . . . .
> How much longer must I borrow & steal?
> O Amerika I hold U responsible fer this hole in the seat of my Levis!

Notice that the line of spaced periods is about the same length as the preceding line of poetry. For nearly all omissions of prose, however, four dots should serve.

**quot**
**20o**

## 20o    Avoid Beginning a Quotation with an Ellipsis.

If you make a quoted clause or phrase fit in with your own sentence structure (20i, p. 382), you should not use an ellipsis mark to show that you have left something out.

DON'T:

x The signers of the Declaration of Independence characterized George III as ". . . unfit to be the ruler of a free people."

DO:

• The signers of the Declaration of Independence characterized George III as "unfit to be the ruler of a free people."

## INSERTING MATERIAL INTO A QUOTATION

### 20p   Use Brackets to Insert Your Own Words into a Quotation.

To show that you are interrupting a quotation rather than quoting a parenthetical remark, be sure to enclose your interruption in brackets, not parentheses (19j, p. 372):

* "None of us who saw Martina [Navratilova] play will ever forget her," he declared.

   Note that parentheses in place of brackets would imply a parenthetical remark by the speaker, not by the writer. Brackets are necessary to indicate that the quotation is being interrupted.

[*sic*]

The bracketed and usually italicized Latin word *sic* (meaning "thus") signifies that a peculiarity—for example, a misspelling—occurs in the quoted material:

* "Beachcombbing [*sic*] no longer appeals to me," Melody wired. "Send money."

   Do not abuse the legitimate function of [*sic*] by applying it sarcastically to claims that you find dubious.

DON'T:

   x Are we supposed to believe the "humane" [*sic*] pretensions of the National Rifle Association?

   The quotation marks are already sarcastic enough without [*sic*] to redouble the effect. But why not eliminate both devices and let the language of the sentence do its own work?

DO:

* Are we supposed to believe the humane pretensions of the National Rifle Association?

quot
20p

---

## EXERCISE (20i–20p)

2. Correct any errors in the handling of quoted material:

   A. "Since I want to try a mountain gig anyway," wrote Melody on her application form, "I might as well pick up some bread being a counciler (sic)."
   B. Is Wratto referring to his high vocation when he writes that he is ". . . waiting fer a call"?
   C. In a snowstorm, says the noted Japanese poet Bashō

   > "Even a horse
   > Is a spectacle."

   D. Melody answered sharply "Just get off my cloud, will you"?
   E. Wordsworth writes: "O'er rough and smooth she trips along, / And never looks behind; / And sings a solitary song / That whistles in the wind."

---

### NOTE

[1] Richard Rees, *George Orwell: Fugitive from the Camp of Victory* (London: Secker, 1961) 153.

quot
**20p**

# VI

## CONVENTIONS

21. Verb Forms

22. Plurals and Possessives

23. Comparing Adjectives and Adverbs

24. Spelling

25. Capitals

26. Italics, Abbreviations, Numbers

27. Forming and Spacing Punctuation Marks

## CONVENTIONS

*In this section we consider rules affecting the form a word or punctuation mark can take. These are small matters—if you get them right. If you do not, you will be handicapped in communicating your ideas. It is essential, then, to spell correctly and to be accurate in showing different forms of verbs, nouns and pronouns, and modifiers. And it is useful, if less urgent, to know where such conventions as italics, abbreviations, and written-out numbers are considered appropriate in a piece of writing. Once the conventions have become second nature, both you and your reader can put them out of mind and concentrate on larger issues.*

# 21

# Verb
# Forms

## 21a   Note How Verbs Change Their Form to Show Person and Number in the Present Tense.

Within most **tenses**, or times of action (21b), English verbs show no differences of form for person and number. That is, the verb remains the same whether its subject is the speaker, someone spoken to, or someone (or something) spoken about, and whether that subject is one person or thing or more than one. The past-tense forms of *move,* for example, look like this:

|               | SINGULAR          | PLURAL    |
|---------------|-------------------|-----------|
| **First Person**  | I moved           | we moved  |
| **Second Person** | you moved         | you moved |
| **Third Person**  | he, she, it moved | they moved |

But in the most common tense, the present, the third-person singular verb is **inflected** — that is, it changes its form without becoming a different word.

|              | SINGULAR          | PLURAL    |
|--------------|-------------------|-----------|
| **First Person**  | I move            | we move   |
| **Second Person** | you move          | you move  |
| **Third Person**  | he, she, it **moves** | they move |

The third-person singular form of a present-tense verb ends in -*s*. If the base form of the verb ends in -*ch*, -*s*, -*sh*, -*x*, or -*z*, the addition is -*es*.

| BASE FORM | THIRD-PERSON SINGULAR PRESENT |
|-----------|-------------------------------|
| lurch     | he lurches                    |
| pass      | she passes                    |
| wash      | Harry washes                  |
| fix       | Betty fixes                   |
| buzz      | it buzzes                     |

In some spoken dialects of English, this third-person -*s* or -*es* does not occur. Standard written English, however, requires that you observe it. You may have to check your final drafts to be sure that your -*s* or -*es* endings are in place.

DON'T:

x When Meg *get* a new idea, she always *say* something worth hearing.

DO:

• When Meg *gets* a new idea, she always *says* something worth hearing.

**verb
21b**

## 21b    Note How the Verb Tenses Are Formed in the Active Voice.

The various tenses are shown by changed forms of the base verb (*try*— *tried*; *go*—*went*) and through forms of *be* and *have* in combination with base (*try*) and participial (*trying*) forms (*will try, was trying, had tried, will have tried*). Here, in the active voice only (see 21c for the passive), are the most commonly recognized tenses, shown in the third-person singular only.

| TENSE | VERB FORM |
|---|---|
| **present** (action happening now) | laughs<br>does |
| **present progressive** (action ongoing in the present) | is laughing<br>is doing |
| **present perfect** (past action completed thus far) | has laughed<br>has done |
| **present perfect progressive** (action begun in the past and continuing in the present) | has been laughing<br>has been doing |
| **past** (completed action) | laughed<br>did |
| **past progressive** (action that was ongoing in a previous time) | was laughing<br>was doing |
| **past perfect** (action completed before another past time) | had laughed<br>had done |
| **past perfect progressive** (ongoing action completed before another past time) | had been laughing<br>had been doing |
| **future** (action to occur later) | will laugh<br>will do |
| **future progressive** (ongoing action to occur later) | will be laughing<br>will be doing |
| **future perfect** (action regarded as completed at a later time) | will have laughed<br>will have done |
| **future perfect progressive** (ongoing action regarded as having begun before a later time) | will have been laughing<br>will have been doing |

**verb
21b**

Here are all the active-voice forms—first, second, and third person, singular and plural—for a verb, *walk,* in eight commonly used tenses.

| ACTIVE VOICE | | |
|---|---|---|
| **Present:** | | |
| I | he, she, it | we, you (sing./pl.), they |
| walk | walks | walk |
| **Present Progressive:** | | |
| I | he, she, it | we, you (sing./pl.), they |
| am walking | is walking | are walking |

| ACTIVE VOICE | | |
|---|---|---|
| **Present Perfect:** | | |
| I | he, she, it | we, you (sing./pl.), they |
| have walked | has walked | have walked |
| **Past:** | | |
| I | he, she, it | we, you (sing./pl.), they |
| walked | walked | walked |
| **Past Progressive:** | | |
| I | he, she, it | we, you (sing./pl.), they |
| was walking | was walking | were walking |
| **Past Perfect:** | | |
| I | he, she, it | we, you (sing./pl.), they |
| had walked | had walked | had walked |
| **Future:** | | |
| I | he, she, it | we, you (sing./pl.), they |
| will walk | will walk | will walk |
| **Future Perfect:** | | |
| I | he, she, it | we, you (sing./pl.), they |
| will have walked | will have walked | will have walked |

In the future tense, *I* and *we* can be accompanied by *shall* instead of *will*. *Shall* is normal in questions about plans:

- *Shall* we go to the movies?

**verb
21b**

In addition, some writers still keep to the once common use of *shall* for all first-person statements (*I shall go to the movies*) and for taking a commanding tone ( *you shall go to the movies!* ). But *will* is now usual in these functions. Keep to *will* unless you want to make an unusually formal effect.

### Principal Parts of Irregular Verbs

All verbs have three **principal parts** used in tense formation: the infinitive or base form (*lift*), the past tense (*lifted*), and the past participle (*lifted*). You must be careful to get the right past participles of irregular verbs — that is, verbs that do not simply add -*d* or -*ed* to form both the past tense and the past participle (*drive, drove, driven*). The past participle is used with forms of *have* and with auxiliaries (*could, would,* etc.) to form various other past tenses (*had tried, would have tried,* etc.).

**Regular verbs** form their principal parts simply by adding -*d* or -*ed* to the base, but **irregular verbs** change more radically.

|  | BASE | PAST TENSE | PAST PARTICIPLE |
|---|---|---|---|
| **Regular** | bake | baked | baked |
|  | adopt | adopted | adopted |
|  | compute | computed | computed |
| **Irregular** | choose | chose | chosen |
|  | eat | ate | eaten |
|  | write | wrote | written |

To avoid errors in tense formation, you can consult the principal parts of irregular verbs given below.

| BASE | PAST TENSE | PAST PARTICIPLE |
|---|---|---|
| awake | awaked, awoke | awaked, awoke, awoken |
| be | was, were | been |
| beat | beat | beaten, beat |
| become | became | become |
| begin | began | begun |
| bend | bent | bent |
| bite | bit | bit, bitten |
| bleed | bled | bled |
| blow | blew | blown |
| break | broke | broken |
| bring | brought | brought |
| build | built | built |
| burst | burst | burst |
| buy | bought | bought |
| catch | caught | caught |
| choose | chose | chosen |
| come | came | come |

**verb**
**21b**

| BASE | PAST TENSE | PAST PARTICIPLE |
|------|-----------|-----------------|
| cost | cost | cost |
| cut | cut | cut |
| deal | dealt | dealt |
| dig | dug | dug |
| dive | dived, dove | dived |
| do | did | done |
| draw | drew | drawn |
| dream | dreamed, dreamt | dreamed, dreamt |
| drink | drank | drunk |
| drive | drove | driven |
| eat | ate | eaten |
| fall | fell | fallen |
| feed | fed | fed |
| feel | felt | felt |
| fight | fought | fought |
| find | found | found |
| fit | fitted, fit | fitted, fit |
| fly | flew | flown |
| forget | forgot | forgotten, forgot |
| freeze | froze | frozen |
| get | got | gotten, got |
| give | gave | given |
| go | went | gone |
| grow | grew | grown |
| hang (an object) | hung | hung |
| hang (a person) | hanged | hanged |
| hear | heard | heard |
| hide | hid | hidden, hid |
| hit | hit | hit |
| hold | held | held |
| hurt | hurt | hurt |
| keep | kept | kept |
| kneel | knelt, kneeled | knelt, kneeled |

verb
21b

| BASE | PAST TENSE | PAST PARTICIPLE |
|------|------------|-----------------|
| knit | knit, knitted | knit, knitted |
| know | knew | known |
| lay (put) | laid | laid |
| lead | led | led |
| lean | leaned, leant | leaned, leant |
| leave | left | left |
| lend | lent | lent |
| let | let | let |
| lie (recline) | lay | lain |
| light | lighted, lit | lighted, lit |
| lose | lost | lost |
| make | made | made |
| mean | meant | meant |
| meet | met | met |
| pay | paid | paid |
| prove | proved | proved, proven |
| put | put | put |
| quit | quit, quitted | quit, quitted |
| read | read | read |
| rid | rid, ridded | rid, ridded |
| ride | rode | ridden |
| ring | rang | rung |
| run | ran | run |
| say | said | said |
| see | saw | seen |
| sell | sold | sold |
| send | sent | sent |
| set | set | set |
| shake | shook | shaken |
| shine | shone, shined | shone, shined (transitive) |
| shoot | shot | shot |
| show | showed | showed, shown |

**verb
21b**

| BASE | PAST TENSE | PAST PARTICIPLE |
|------|-----------|-----------------|
| shrink | shrank | shrunk |
| shut | shut | shut |
| sing | sang, sung | sung |
| sink | sank | sunk |
| sit | sat | sat |
| sleep | slept | slept |
| slide | slid | slid, slidden |
| speak | spoke | spoken |
| speed | sped, speeded | sped, speeded |
| spend | spent | spent |
| spin | spun | spun |
| spring | sprang, sprung | sprung |
| stand | stood | stood |
| steal | stole | stolen |
| stick | stuck | stuck |
| sting | stung | stung |
| strike | struck | struck, stricken |
| swear | swore | sworn |
| swim | swam | swum |
| swing | swung | swung |
| take | took | taken |
| teach | taught | taught |
| tear | tore | torn |
| tell | told | told |
| think | thought | thought |
| throw | threw | thrown |
| wake | waked, woke | waked, woke, woken |
| wear | wore | worn |
| win | won | won |
| wring | wrung | wrung |
| write | wrote | written |

**verb
21b**

For the tense forms of verbals — infinitives, participles, and gerunds —
see 15c, p. 335.

### Past Participle versus Past Tense

It is not enough to know the correct forms for the past participles of irregular verbs. You must also recall that past participles can form tenses only when they are combined with other words (*have gone, would have paid*). Do not use an irregular past participle where the past tense is required.

DON'T:

x She *begun* her singing lessons last Tuesday.

x They *seen* him put on the wrong jacket.

x We *swum* across the pool.

DO:

• She *began* her singing lessons last Tuesday.

• They *saw* him put on the wrong jacket.

• We *swam* across the pool.

## 21c  Learn the Tense Forms in the Passive Voice.

The **voice** of a verb shows whether its grammatical subject performs or receives the action it expresses. A verb is **active** when the subject performs the action (*Frankie shot Johnny*) but **passive** when the subject is acted upon by the verb (*Johnny was shot by Frankie*).

ACTIVE VOICE:

• The paramedics *took* the old man to the hospital.

> Note that the performers of the action (the paramedics) are also the grammatical subject.

PASSIVE VOICE:

• The old man *was taken* to the hospital by the paramedics.

> Note that the performers of the action (the paramedics) are not the grammatical subject of the passive verb *was taken*.

One peculiarity of the passive voice is that you need not mention the performer of action at all: *Johnny was shot; The old man was taken to the hospital.*

verb
21c

Here are the passive-voice forms for the tenses whose functions are explained at 21b, page 392. (A few active-voice tenses are omitted because their passive forms are too ungainly to be used with good effect.)

---

**PASSIVE VOICE**

**Present:**

| I | he, she, it | we, you (sing./pl.), they |
|---|---|---|
| am shown | is shown | are shown |

**Present Progressive:**

| I | he, she, it | we, you (sing./pl.), they |
|---|---|---|
| am being shown | is being shown | are being shown |

**Present Perfect:**

| I | he, she, it | we, you (sing./pl.), they |
|---|---|---|
| have been shown | has been shown | have been shown |

**Past:**

| I | he, she, it | we, you (sing./pl.), they |
|---|---|---|
| was shown | was shown | were shown |

**Past Progressive:**

| I | he, she, it | we, you (sing./pl.), they |
|---|---|---|
| was being shown | was being shown | were being shown |

**Past Perfect:**

| I | he, she, it | we, you (sing./pl.), they |
|---|---|---|
| had been shown | had been shown | had been shown |

**Future:**

| I | he, she, it | we, you (sing./pl.), they |
|---|---|---|
| will be shown | will be shown | will be shown |

**Future Perfect:**

| I | he, she, it | we, you (sing./pl.), they |
|---|---|---|
| will have been shown | will have been shown | will have been shown |

---

**verb
21c**

For the use of *shall* as an alternative to *will,* see 21b, page 394.

For the stylistic uses and limitations of the passive voice, see 7g, page 173.

## 21d   Learn the Forms and Uses of the Indicative, Imperative, and Subjunctive Moods.

Verbs show certain other changes of form to convey the **mood** or manner of their action.

### Indicative

Use the **indicative** mood if your clause is a statement or a question:

- The Secretary of State *advises* the President.
- *Does* the Secretary of State *advise* the President?

The forms of the indicative mood are those already given for normal tense formation (21b, p. 392; 21c, p. 399).

### Imperative

Use the **imperative** mood for giving commands or directions, with or without an explicit subject:

- *Call* the police at once.
- You *stay* out of this!

The imperative mood uses the second-person form of the present tense.

### Subjunctive

For a variety of less common purposes, use the **subjunctive** mood.

verb<br>**21d**

1. Expressions of a wish in which *may* is understood:
   - long *live* the Queen [not *lives*]
   - *be* it known [not *is*]
   - so *be* it [not *is*]
   - *suffice* it to say [not *suffices*]

2. Hypothetical conditions:
   - He is, as it *were*, a termite gnawing at the foundations of our business.

     *As it were* is a fixed expression indicating that the writer is using a figure of speech (81, p. 227) instead of making a literal statement.

- If I *were* on the moon now, I would tidy up the junk that has been left there. [not *was*]

- I wish I *were* in Haiti now. [not *was*]

3. *That* clauses expressing requirements or recommendations:

- The IRS requires that everyone *submit* a return by April 15. [not *submits*]

- It is important that all new students *be* tested immediately. [not *are*]

For nearly all verbs, the subjunctive differs from the indicative only in that the third-person singular verb loses its -*s* or -*es*: *come what may*, not *comes what may*. The verb *to be* uses *be* for "requirement" clauses (*I demand that she be here early*) and *were* for conditions contrary to fact (*if he were an emperor*).

See 15b, p. 333, for conditional sentences that express the imagined consequences of hypothetical conditions, as in *If he had taken that plane, he would be dead today.*

---

EXERCISES (21a–21d)

1. Consider the following one-word sentence: *Choose!*
   A. Name the person, tense, voice, and mood of that verb.
   B. Write a brief sentence using the same verb in a different person, tense, voice, and mood.
   C. Identify the person, tense, voice, and mood of the verb in your sentence.

**verb 21d**

2. Look through the list of principal parts for irregular verbs (pp. 395–398), and find three verbs whose past tense and/or past participle strike you as especially tricky. For each of the three verbs, submit four sample sentences, showing:

   (a) the past tense, active voice;
   (b) the past participle, active voice;
   (c) the past tense, passive voice; and
   (d) the past participle, passive voice.

3. Submit five original sentences illustrating different uses of the subjunctive voice.

# 22

# Plurals and Possessives

## PLURALS

**22a    Form the Plural of Most Nouns by Adding -s or -es to the Singular.**

| | |
|---|---|
| class | classes |
| house | houses |
| shoe | shoes |
| summons | summonses |
| waltz | waltzes |

**22b    Note the Differences in Plural Form among Nouns Ending in -o.**

Most nouns ending in a vowel plus -o become plural by adding -s:

| | |
|---|---|
| patio | patios |
| studio | studios |

Nouns ending in a consonant plus -*o* become plural by adding -*es*:

| | |
|---|---|
| potato | potatoes |
| veto | vetoes |

But some plurals disobey the rule:

| | |
|---|---|
| piano | pianos |
| solo | solos |
| soprano | sopranos |

And some words have alternative, equally correct forms:

| | |
|---|---|
| zero | zeros/zeroes |
| cargo | cargos/cargoes |

Where your dictionary lists two forms, always adopt the first, which is more commonly used.

## 22c  To Form the Plural of a Noun Ending in a Consonant plus -*y*, Change the -*y* to -*i* and Add -*es*.

| | |
|---|---|
| army | armies |
| candy | candies |
| duty | duties |
| penny | pennies |
| warranty | warranties |

**pl
22d**

## 22d  To Make a Name Plural, Add -*s* or -*es* without an Apostrophe.

Add -*s* to most nouns:

| | |
|---|---|
| Smith | the Smiths |
| Kennedy | the Kennedys |
| Helen | both Helens |
| Goodman | the Goodmans |
| Carolina | two Carolinas |

When a name ends in *-ch, -s, -sh, -x,* or *-z,* add *-es.* The extra syllable that results should be pronounced:

| | |
|---|---|
| Burch | the Burches |
| Weiss | the Weisses |
| Cash | the Cashes |
| Fox | the Foxes |
| Perez | the Perezes |

## 22e    Form the Plural of a Noun Ending in *-ful* by Adding *-s* to the End.

| | |
|---|---|
| cupful | cupfuls |
| shovelful | shovelfuls |
| spoonful | spoonfuls |

Beware of the "genteel" but incorrect *cupsful, shovelsful,* etc.

## 22f    Follow Common Practice in Forming the Plural of a Noun Derived from Another Language.

A number of words taken from foreign languages, especially Greek and Latin, keep their foreign plural forms. But some foreign-based words have also acquired English plural forms. The rule for deciding which plural to use is this: look it up!

Even so, the dictionary cannot settle your doubts in all cases. It may not tell you, for example, that the plural of *appendix* is *appendixes* if you are referring to the organ but either *appendixes* or *appendices* if you mean supplementary sections at the ends of books. Similarly, your dictionary may not reveal that while an insect has *antennae,* television sets have *antennas.* The way to get such information is to note the practice of other speakers and writers.

When in doubt, prefer the English plural.

pl
22f

| SINGULAR | PREFER | NOT |
|---|---|---|
| cherub | cherubs | cherubim |
| crocus | crocuses | croci |
| curriculum | curriculums | curricula |

| SINGULAR | PREFER | NOT |
|----------|--------|-----|
| sanatorium | sanatoriums | sanatoria |
| stadium | stadiums | stadia |

But note that certain foreign plurals are still preferred.

| SINGULAR | PLURAL |
|----------|--------|
| criterion | criteria |
| datum | data |
| phenomenon | phenomena |
| vertebra | vertebrae |

Confusions between the singular and plural forms of these four terms are common. Indeed, *data* as a singular is now widely accepted. Many careful writers, however, while avoiding the rare *datum,* use *data* only when its sense is clearly plural: *these data,* not *this data.*

Note that Greek derivatives ending in -*is* regularly change to -*es* in the plural.

| SINGULAR | PLURAL |
|----------|--------|
| analysis | analyses |
| crisis | crises |
| parenthesis | parentheses |
| thesis | theses |

pl
22g

## 22g   To Form the Plural of a Word Presented *as* a Word, Add -'s.

Add an apostrophe and an -*s* to show the plural of a word you are discussing as a word, not as the thing it signifies:

- The editor changed all the *he*'s in Chapter 4 to *she*'s.

    Note how the writer's meaning is made clearer by the italicizing of each isolated word but not of the -'s that follows it.

**22h    Add -s, without an Apostrophe, to Form the Plural of Most Hyphenated Nouns, Capital Letters, Capitalized Abbreviations without Periods, Written-out Numbers, and Figures.**

- two stand-ins
- the three Rs
- four RSVPs
- counting by fives and tens
- temperature in the nineties
- counting by 5s and 10s
- temperature in the 90s
- the 1980s

**Exceptions**

Some good writers prefer apostrophes with plural capitals and figures: *the three R's, the 1980's.* Even if you keep to the majority practice, use *-'s* wherever it is needed to avoid confusion.

DON'T:

x She received four *As* in her first semester.

Here the plural of *A* looks confusingly like the preposition *as.*

DO:

- She received four *A's* in her first semester.

pl
22i

**22i    Add -'s to Form the Plural of an Uncapitalized Letter, an Abbreviation Ending with a Period, or a Lower-Case Abbreviation.**

- *a's, b's,* and *c's*
- the two *i's* in *iris*
- too many *etc.'s* in your paper
- a shortage of M.D.'s
- thousands of rpm's

EXERCISE (22a–22i)

1. Write the plural forms of the following words:

A. ox
B. ax
C. phylum
D. radio
E. wish
F. woman

G. alloy
H. ferry
I. Murphy
J. tomato
K. wrong turn
L. chairman-elect

M. forkful
N. phenomenon
O. analysis
P. 14
Q. Ph.D.

## POSSESSIVES

A possessive form implies either actual ownership (*my neighbor's willow, Alice's computer*) or some other close relation (a *stone's throw, the Governor's enemies*). Nouns and some pronouns form the possessive either by adding an apostrophe with or without an -*s* or by preceding the "possessed" element with *of: my husband's first wife, her parents' car, the wings of the canary.*

### 22j    Add -'s to Form the Possessive of a Singular Noun.

- farm's

- Bill's

poss
22j

- Hayakawa's

Follow the rule even if the singular noun ends with an -*s* sound:

- horse's

- bus's

- quiz's

- Les's

- Jones's

- Keats's

### Exception for Certain Names

In names of more than one syllable, the -s after the apostrophe is optional when it might not be pronounced.

| PRONOUNCED -S | UNPRONOUNCED -S |
| --- | --- |
| Dickens's | Dickens' |
| Berlioz's | Berlioz' |
| Demosthenes's | Demosthenes' |

Whichever of these practices you follow, make sure you keep to it throughout a given piece of writing.

## 22k  Watch for Certain Unusual Singular Possessives.

Where an added -s would make for three closely bunched -s sounds, use the apostrophe alone:

* Moses'

* Ulysses'

* Jesus'

   Note also that in certain fixed expressions (*for* _____ *sake*) the possessive -s is missing: *for goodness' sake, for conscience' sake, for righteousness' sake.* Some writers even drop the apostrophe from such phrases.

poss
22l

## 22l  Make Most Plural Nouns Possessive by Adding an Apostrophe Alone.

* several *days'* work
* the *Americans'* views
* the *dictionaries'* definitions
* the *Stuarts'* reigns
* the *Beatles'* influence

**22m    If a Plural Noun Does Not End in -s, Make It Possessive in the Same Way You Would a Singular Noun.**

- the *children's* room
- those *deer's* habitat
- the *mice's* tracks
- the *alumni's* representative

**22n    Keep the Apostrophe in a Plural Possessive of Time.**

In expressions like *two years' parole,* many writers now drop the apostrophe: *two years parole.* But since that practice is widely regarded as wrong, you would do well to keep the rule:

- in two days' time
- a three months' increase in prices
- five years' worth of wasted effort

**22o    In Compound Possessives Showing "Joint Ownership," Give the Possessive Form Only to the Final Name.**

When two or more words are "joint possessors," make only the last one possessive:

- Laurel and *Hardy's* comedies
- John, Paul, George, and *Ringo's* movie
- Sally and *Vic's* restaurant

But give the possessive form to each party if different things are "owned":

- *John's, Paul's, George's,* and *Ringo's* personal attorneys once met to see if the Beatles could be kept from splitting up.

**22p    To Make a Hyphenated Term Possessive, Add -'s to the Last Element.**

- the mayor-*elect's* assistant
- my daughter-in-*law's* career

poss
22p

## 22q  Do Not Add an Apostrophe to a Pronoun That Is Already Possessive in Meaning.

| DON'T | DO |
|---|---|
| his' | his |
| her's, hers' | hers |
| our's, ours' | ours |
| your's, yours' | yours |
| their's, theirs' | theirs |
| who'se | whose |

Note also that the possessive pronoun *its* (like *his*) has no apostrophe. *It's* is the correct form for the contraction of *it is* but a blunder for the possessive *its*. Similarly, *who's* is the correct contraction for *who is* but a blunder for the possessive *whose*.

DON'T:

x  This album is *her's*.

x  Why don't you drive *our's* and we drive *your's*?

x  The dog seems to have lost *it's* collar.

x  This is the man *who's* computer broke down.

DO:

• This album is *hers*.

• Why don't you drive *ours* and we drive *yours*?

• The dog seems to have lost *its* collar.

• This is the man *whose* computer broke down.

DON'T:

x  The college canceled *it's* Saturday night film series.

x  *Its* a baby girl!

x  *Its'* a baby girl!

x  *Whose* going to make the announcement?

poss
22q

DO:

* The college canceled *its* Saturday night film series.
* *It's* a baby girl!
* *Who's* going to make the announcement?

## 22r   Do Not Confuse Plural and Possessive Forms.

In going over your drafts, watch for any confusion between plural and possessive forms. Note these differences.

| SINGULAR | PLURAL | SINGULAR POSSESSIVE | PLURAL POSSESSIVE |
|---|---|---|---|
| temple | temples | temple's | temples' |
| pass | passes | pass's | passes' |
| squash | squashes | squash's | squashes' |
| annex | annexes | annex's | annexes' |
| Ford | Fords | Ford's | Fords' |

DON'T:

x The two *priest's* made many *contribution's* to the parish.

x The *Kennedy's* have been stalked by tragedy.

x In many *place's* the *oceans* depth is unknown.

x The *clocks* hands stopped all across the city.

DO:

* The two *priests* made many *contributions* to the parish.
* The *Kennedys* have been stalked by tragedy.
* In many *places* the *ocean's* depth is unknown.
* The *clocks'* hands stopped all across the city.

poss
22s

## 22s   To Avoid an Awkward Possessive, Make Use of the *of* Construction.

Wherever an *-s* possessive sounds awkward, consider shifting to the *of* form. Suppose, for example, your "possessing" term or your "possessed" one is preceded by several modifiers. You can get rid of the bunched effect by resorting to *of*.

DON'T:

x  the revised and expanded edition's index

DO:

●  the index of the revised and expanded edition

A possessive form following a term in quotation marks may sound all right but look awkward on the page. Again, prefer the *of* construction.

DON'T:

x  "Eleanor Rigby" 's melody

DO:

●  the melody of "Eleanor Rigby"

Watch, too, for an unnatural separation of the -'s from the word it belongs with.

DON'T:

x  the house on the corner's roof

DO:

●  the roof of the house on the corner

Finally, nouns for inanimate (nonliving) things often make awkward possessives.

DON'T:

x  the page's bottom

x  social chaos's outcome

DO:

●  the bottom of the page

●  the outcome of social chaos

poss
22t

## 22t   Notice Which Indefinite Pronouns Cannot Form the Possessive with -'s.

Some indefinite pronouns (10d, p. 266) form the possessive in the same manner as nouns: *another's, nobody's, one's*. But others can be made possessive only with *of*:

|   |   | all | few | several |
|---|---|-----|-----|---------|
| of | { | any | many | some |
|   |   | both | most | such |
|   |   | each | much |   |

DON'T:

x  I have two friends in Seattle, and I can give you *each's* address.

DO:

• I have two friends in Seattle, and I can give you the address of each.

## 22u   Master the Other Uses of the Apostrophe.

### Contractions

Use an apostrophe to join two words in a contraction:

| did not | didn't |
|---------|--------|
| have not | haven't |
| can not, cannot | can't |
| she will | she'll |
| we will | we'll |
| they are | they're |
| he is | he's |
| he has | he's |
| you have | you've |

Beware of placing the apostrophe at the end of the first word instead of at the point where the omission occurs.

DON'T:

x  He *did'nt* have a chance.

x  They *have'nt* done a thing to deserve such punishment.

DO:

• He *didn't* have a chance.

• They *haven't* done a thing to deserve such punishment.

## Omission of Digits

Use an apostrophe to mark the omission of one or more digits of a number, particularly of a year: *the summer of '88.* In dates expressing a span of time, however, drop the apostrophe: *1847–63.* And omit the apostrophe when you are shortening page numbers: *pp. 267–91.*

## Certain Past Tense Forms and Past Participles

Use an apostrophe to form the past tense or past participle of a verb derived from an abbreviation or a name:

- Pellini was *K.O.'d* in the twelfth round.

- They *Disney'd* the old amusement park beyond recognition.

---

**EXERCISES (22j–22u)**

2. Write the alternative possessive form for each of the following:
   - A. of the victor
   - B. of the bystanders
   - C. for the sake of goodness
   - D. of a Pisces
   - E. of the children
   - F. of the louse
   - G. a journey of four days
   - H. the wives of the Yankee pitchers
   - I. the partnership of Manny, Moe, and Jack
   - J. the fault of somebody

poss
**22u**

3. In the following sentences, correct any inadvisable use (or absence) of apostrophes.
   - A. The battered, barnacle'd, leaky ship's prow was a sorry sight.
   - B. Melody was'nt altogether sure why she found herself on the ferry to Marthas Vineyard.
   - C. In Advance'd Placement English we were Shakespeared to the point of crying, "Hold, enough!"
   - D. In the spring of 87 she traded in her rusty Mazda '626.
   - E. Its no simple matter to follow *One Hundred Years of Solitude's* plot.

---

# 23

# Comparing Adjectives and Adverbs

## 23a Recognize the Forms Showing Degrees of Adjectives.

Most adjectives can be *compared,* or changed to show three **degrees** of coverage.

| POSITIVE DEGREE | COMPARATIVE DEGREE | SUPERLATIVE DEGREE |
| --- | --- | --- |
| wide | wider | widest |
| dry | drier | driest |
| lazy | lazier | laziest |
| relaxed | more relaxed | most relaxed |
| agreeable | more agreeable | most agreeable |
| wide | less wide | least wide |
| dry | less dry | least dry |
| lazy | less lazy | least lazy |
| relaxed | less relaxed | least relaxed |
| agreeable | less agreeable | least agreeable |

The base form of an adjective is in the *positive* degree: *thin.* The *comparative* degree puts the modified word beyond one or more items: *thinner* (than he is; than everybody). And the *superlative* degree unmistakably puts the modified word beyond all rivals within its group: *thinnest* (of all). The comparative and superlative degrees of adjectives are formed in several ways.

1. For one-syllable adjectives: *wide, wider, widest* (but *less wide, least wide*).

2. For one- or two-syllable adjectives ending in *-y,* change the *-y* to *-i* and add *-er* and *-est*: *dry, drier, driest; lazy, lazier, laziest* (but *less lazy, least lazy*).

3. For all other adjectives of two or more syllables, put *more* or *most* (or *less* or *least*) before the positive form: *relaxed, more relaxed, most relaxed* (*less relaxed, least relaxed*).

4. For certain "irregular" adjectives, supply the forms shown in your dictionary. Here are some common examples.

| POSITIVE DEGREE | COMPARATIVE DEGREE | SUPERLATIVE DEGREE |
|---|---|---|
| bad | worse | worst |
| good | better | best |
| far | farther, further | farthest, furthest |
| little | littler, less, lesser | littlest, least |
| many, some, much | more | most |

ad
**23b**

## 23b Recognize the Forms Showing Degrees of Adverbs.

Like adjectives, adverbs can be compared: *quickly, more quickly, most quickly; less quickly, least quickly.* Note that *-ly* adverbs—that is, nearly all adverbs—can be compared only by being preceded by words like *more* and *least.* But some one-syllable adverbs do change their form: *hard/harder/hardest, fast/faster/fastest,* and so on.

## 23c   Avoid Redundancy in Comparing Adjectives and Adverbs.

Be careful not to "double" the comparison of an adjective or adverb.

DON'T:

x more funnier

x most warmest

x less darker

x least brightest

DO:

• funnier

• warmest

• less dark

• least bright

DON'T:

x more quicklier

x more closelier

x more sooner

DO:

• more quickly

• more closely

• sooner

**ad
23c**

---

EXERCISE (23a–23c)

1. If your instructor, in reading your submitted work, has found no faulty comparison of adjectives or adverbs, skip this exercise. Otherwise, submit up to five original sentences, making correct use of the forms that gave you trouble.

---

# 24

# Spelling

If spelling causes you trouble, do not label yourself a poor speller and leave it at that; work to eliminate the wrong choices. You can attack the problem on two fronts, memorizing the right spellings of single words and learning rules that apply to whole classes of words. We will cover both of these strategies below.

If there is one key to better spelling, it is the habit of consulting your college dictionary whenever you are in doubt (8a, p. 202). You need not pick up the dictionary until you have completed a draft, but you should check your final copy carefully for both habitual misspellings and typing errors.

## TROUBLESOME WORDS

### 24a  Keep a Spelling List.

Keep an ongoing spelling list, including not only the words you have already misspelled in your essays but also words whose spelling in published sources looks odd to you.

The most serious misspellings are not those that would eliminate you from the finals of a spelling contest but slips with ordinary words. If you regularly make such slips, you may not be able to cure them simply by noting the correct versions. You will need to jog your memory with a special reminder. Try a three-column spelling list, using the middle column to show how the real word differs from the misspelling.

| MISSPELLING | REMEMBER | CORRECT SPELLING |
|---|---|---|
| (seperate) | not like *desperate* | sep*a*rate |
| (alot) | one word is not *a lot* | a lot |
| (hypocracy) | not like *democracy* | hypocr*isy* |
| (heighth) | get the *h* out of here! | height |
| (concieve) | *i* before *e* except after *c* | conc*ei*ve |
| (mispell) | don't *miss* this one! | mi*s*spell |
| (fiting) | doesn't sound like *fighting* | fi*tt*ing |
| (beautyful) | *y* misspell it? | beaut*i*ful |
| (wierd) | a *weird* exception to *i* before *e* | w*ei*rd |
| (goverment) | *govern* + *ment* | gover*n*ment |
| (complection) | *x* marks the spots | comple*x*ion |

## 24b  Note How Spelling Differs among English-Speaking Countries.

Many words that are correctly spelled in British English are considered wrong in American English. Canadian English resembles British in most but not all features. Study the following differences, which are typical.

| AMERICAN | CANADIAN | BRITISH |
|---|---|---|
| cent*er* | cent*re* | cent*re* |
| flav*or* | flav*our* | flav*our* |
| preten*se* | preten*ce* | preten*ce* |
| real*ize* | real*ize* | real*ise* |
| trave*l*er | trave*ll*er | trave*ll*er |

## 24c    Beware of Words That Sound or Look Alike.

Note these differences:

accept (*receive*), except (*exclude, excluding*)

adapt (*change for a purpose*), adopt (*take possession*)

advice (noun), advise (verb)

affect (verb: *influence;* noun: *feeling*), effect (verb: *bring about;* noun: *result*)

all ready (*all prepared*), already (*so early*)

all together (*everyone assembled*), altogether (*entirely*)

allusion (*passing reference*), illusion (*deceiving appearance*)

altar (of a church), alter (*change*)

ante- (*before*), anti- (*against*)

bare (adjective: *naked;* verb: *expose*), bear (*carry, endure*)

beside (*at the side of*), besides (*in addition to*)

bias (noun: *prejudice*), biased (adjective: *prejudiced*)

born (*brought into the world*), borne (*carried*)

breadth (*width*), breath (noun: *respiration*), breathe (verb: *take breath*)

business (*job*), busyness (*being busy*)

by (preposition), buy (*purchase*)

capital (*governmental city, funds*), capitol (*statehouse*)

chord (*tones*), cord (*rope*)

cite (*mention*), sight (*view*), site (*locale*)

climactic (*of a climax*), climatic (*of a climate*)

coarse (*rough*), course (*direction, academic offering*)

complement (noun: *accompaniment;* verb: *complete*), compliment (*praise*)

comptroller (*financial officer*), controller (*regulator*)

council (*committee*), counsel (*advice, attorney*)

descent (*lowering*), dissent (*disagreement*)

desert (*barren area, abandon*), dessert (*last course in meal*)

device (noun: *instrument*), devise (verb: *fashion*)

die (*expire*), dying (*expiring*); dye (*color*), dyeing (*coloring*)

sp
24c

discreet (*prudent*), discrete (*separate*)

dual (*double*), duel (*fight*)

elicit (*draw forth*), illicit (*unlawful*)

eminent (*prominent*), imminent (*about to happen*)

envelop (*surround*), envelope (for mailing)

every day (*each day*), everyday (*normal*)

every one (*each one* of specified items), everyone (*everybody*)

fair (*just*), fare (*charge*)

faze (*daunt*), phase (*period*)

forbear (*refrain*), forebear (*ancestor*)

foreword (*preface*), forward (*ahead*)

hangar (for airplanes), hanger (for coats)

it's (*it is*), its (*of it*)

lead (noun: *metal*; verb: *direct*; adjective: *head*), led (past tense of verb *lead*)

lessen (*reduce*), lesson (*teaching*)

lightening (*getting lighter*), lightning (*flash*)

loath (*reluctant*), loathe (*despise*), loathsome (*disgusting*)

loose (*slack*), lose (*mislay*), losing (*mislaying*)

material (*pertaining to matter*), materiel (*military supplies*)

miner (*digger*), minor (*lesser, under legal age*)

mislead (present), misled (past)

moral (*ethical*), morale (*confidence*)

naval (*nautical*), navel (*bellybutton*)

passed (*went by*), past (*previous*)

peace (*tranquillity*), piece (*part*)

persecute (*single out for mistreatment*), prosecute (*bring to trial*)

personal (*individual*), personnel (*employees*)

pray (*implore*), prey (*victim*)

precede (*go ahead of*), proceed (*go forward*)

predominant (adjective), predominate (verb)

prejudice (noun), prejudiced (past participle, adjective)

principal (adjective, noun: *chief*), principle (noun: *rule*) prophecy (*prediction*), prophecies (*predictions*), prophesy (*predict*), prophesies (*predicts*)

prostate (*gland*), prostrate (*prone*)

rack (*framework*), wrack (*ruin*)

rain (*precipitation*), rein (*restrain*), reign (*rule*)

some time (*span of time*), sometime (*at an unspecified time*), sometimes (*now and then*)

stationary (*still*), stationery (*paper*)

suppose (verb), supposed (past participle)

tack (*course*), tact (*discretion*)

than (for comparison), then (*at that time*)

their (*belonging to them*), there (*that place*), they're (*they are*)

to (*toward*, infinitive marker), too (*also, excessively*), two (*one plus one*)

track (*path*), tract (*area, treatise*)

waive (*relinquish*), wave (verb: *move to and fro;* noun: *spreading movement*)

weather (*state of the atmosphere*), whether (*if* )

who's (*who is*), whose (*of whom*)

wreak (*inflict*), wreck (*ruin*)

your (*of you*), you're ( *you are*)

## 24d   Check the Spelling of Words with Unusual Pronunciation.

sp<br>24d

### Words Having Silent Letters

| | |
|---|---|
| column | Wednesday |
| mortgage | withdrawal |
| sword | |

### Words Having Letters Unpronounced by Some Speakers

| | |
|---|---|
| environment | recognize |
| government | strength |
| pumpkin | |

## Words Frequently Mispronounced

1. Added or erroneous sound:

| | |
|---|---|
| athlete | (not ath<u>a</u>lete) |
| escape | (not e<u>x</u>cape) |
| height | (not heigh<u>th</u>) |
| memento | (not m<u>o</u>mento) |
| pejorative | (not pe<u>r</u>jorative) |
| wintry | (not wint<u>e</u>ry) |

2. Sound sometimes left unpronounced:

| | |
|---|---|
| ar<u>c</u>tic | su<u>r</u>prise |
| can<u>d</u>idate | temper<u>a</u>ment |
| proba<u>b</u>ly | temper<u>a</u>ture |
| quan<u>ti</u>ty | vet<u>e</u>ran |
| soph<u>o</u>more | |

3. Sounds sometimes wrongly reversed:

| | |
|---|---|
| modern | (not mod<u>re</u>n) |
| nuclear | (not nuc<u>u</u>lar) |
| perform | (not p<u>re</u>form) |
| professor | (not p<u>er</u>fessor) |
| realtor | (not real<u>a</u>tor) |
| perspiration | (not p<u>re</u>spiration) |

sp
24e

## 24e    Review Other Commonly Misspelled Words.

A good way to begin your private spelling list (24a, p. 419) is to look through the following commonly misspelled words, along with those already mentioned above, and pick out the ones that trouble you. (The letters *C/B* indicate Canadian and British forms wherever they differ from American.)

| | |
|---|---|
| absence | across |
| accidentally | actually |
| accommodate | address |
| acknowledgment | adolescence, adolescent |

aggravate, aggravated, aggravating
aggress, aggressive, aggression
aging
allege
all right
altogether
always
analysis, analyses (plural)
analyze
anesthesia
annihilate
apparent
appearance
appreciate, appreciation
aquatic
argument
assassin, assassination
assistant, assistance
attendance
bachelor
balloon
beggar
benefit, benefited, *C/B:* benefitted
besiege
bigoted
bureau
bureaucracy, bureaucratic
burglar
bus
cafeteria
calendar
camouflage
category

ceiling
cemetery
changeable
commit, commitment
committee
competent
concomitant
conscience
conscious
consensus
consistent, consistency
consummate
control, controlled, controlling
controversy
convenience, convenient
coolly
corollary
correlate
correspondence
corroborate
counterfeit
criticism, criticize
deceive
defendant
defense, *C/B:* defence
definite, definitely
deity
dependent
desirable
despair
desperate, desperation
destroy
develop, development

sp
24e

dilapidated
dilemma
disastrous
discipline
dispensable
divide
divine
drunkenness
duly
ecstasy
eighth
emanate
embarrass, embarrassed,
    embarrassing
equip, equipped, equipment
evenness
exaggerate
exceed
excellent, excellence
exercise
exhilarate
existence
exorbitant
expel
extraordinary
fallacy
familiar
fascinate
fascist
February
fiend
fiery
finally

forehead
foresee, foreseeable
forfeit
forgo
forty
fourth
friend
fulfill
fulsome
futilely
gases
gauge
glamour, glamorous
grammar, grammatically
greenness
grievance, grievous
gruesome
guarantee
guard
handkerchief
harangue
harass
heroes
hindrance
hoping
idiosyncrasy
imagery
immediate
impel
inadvertent
incidentally
incredible
independent, independence

indestructible
indispensable
infinitely
innuendo
inoculate
interrupt
irrelevant
irreparable, irreparably
irreplaceable, irreplaceably
irresistible, irresistibly
jeopardy
jewelry, *C/B:* jewellery
judgment, *C/B:* judgement
knowledge, knowledgeably
laboratory
legitimate
leisure
length
library
license, *C/B:* licence
loneliness
lying
maintenance
maneuver
manual
marriage
marshal (verb and noun),
    marshaled, marshaling
mathematics
medicine
millennium, millennial
mimic, mimicked
mischief, mischievous

missile
more so
naïve, naïveté
necessary
nickel
niece
noncommittal
noticeable, noticing
occasion
occur, occurred, occurring,
    occurrence
omit, omitted, omitting, omission
opportunity
optimist, optimistic
paid
pajamas
parallel, paralleled
paralysis
parliament
pastime
perceive
perennial
perfectible, perfectibility
permanent
permissible
phony
physical
physician
picnic, picnicked, picnicking
playwright
pleasant
pleasurable
possess, possession

sp
24e

practically
practice, *C/B:* practice, noun;
    practise, verb
prairie
privilege
probably
pronunciation
propaganda
propagate
psychiatry
psychology
pursue, pursuit
putrefy
quizzes
rarefied
realize
receipt
receive
recipe
recognizable
recommend
refer, referred, referring
regretted, regretting
relevant, relevance
relieve
remembrance
reminisce, reminiscence
repellent
repentance
repetition
resistance
restaurant
rhythm

ridiculous
roommate
sacrilegious
said
schedule
secretary
seize
sergeant
sheriff
shining
shriek
siege
significance
similar
smooth (adjective and verb)
software
solely
soliloquy
sovereign, sovereignty
specimen
sponsor
stupefy
subtlety, subtly
succeed, success
succumb
suffrage
superintendent
supersede
suppress
surprise
symmetry
sympathize
tariff

tendency
terrific
than
therefore
thinness
thorough
threshold
through
traffic, trafficked, trafficking
tranquil, tranquillity
transcendent, transcendental
transfer, transferred, transferring
tries, tried
truly
unconscious
unmistakable, unmistakably
unnecessary

unshakable
unwieldy
vacillate
vacuum
vegetable
vengeance
venomous
vice
vilify, vilification
villain
wield
withhold
woeful
worldly
worshiped, worshiping, *C/B:* worshipped, worshipping
writing
yield

## SPELLING RULES

### 24f   Notice How Words Change When They Add Suffixes.

**sp**
**24f**

A **suffix** is one or more letters that can be added at the end of a word to make a new word (*-ship, -ness,* etc.) or a new form of the same word (*-ed, -ing,* etc.). Since many spelling mistakes are caused by uncertainty over whether and how the root word changes when the suffix is tacked on, you should go over the following rules. (If a rule is hard to follow, you can get the point by studying the sample words that follow it.)

1. Change a final *-y* preceded by a consonant to *-i* when making formations other than the plural.

    beauty        beautiful
    easy          easily

| | |
|---|---|
| happy | happier, happiest |
| hurry | hurries |
| imply | implies |
| ordinary | ordinarily |
| salty | saltier |
| tyranny | tyrannical |
| ugly | ugliness |

2. Do not drop the final -*y* of a word adding -*ing*.

| | |
|---|---|
| embody | embodying |
| gratify | gratifying |
| hurry | hurrying |
| study | studying |

3. When adding a suffix that begins with a vowel, usually drop a final -*e*.

| | |
|---|---|
| desire | desirable |
| drive | driving |
| future | futuristic |
| hope | hoping |
| impulse | impulsive |
| mate | mating |
| sincere | sincerity |
| suicide | suicidal |

Exceptions: In words ending in -*ce* or -*ge,* retain the "s" or "j" pronunciation by keeping the -*e* before a suffix that begins with *a* or *o*.

| | |
|---|---|
| notice | noticeable |
| peace | peaceable |
| courage | courageous |
| manage | manageable |

And note two further exceptions:

| | |
|---|---|
| acre | acreage |
| mile | mileage |

4. Usually keep the final -e of a word when adding a suffix that begins with a consonant.

advance          advancement
precise          precisely
safe             safely
tame             tameness

Exceptions: Look out for a few words that drop the -e before adding a suffix beginning with a consonant.

argue            argument
judge            judgment (in American English)
nine             ninth
true             truly

5. In a one-syllable word having a final consonant that is preceded by a single vowel, double the consonant before adding a suffix beginning with a vowel.

beg              begging
chop             chopper
clip             clipped
fun              funny
thin             thinnest

6. In a word of more than one syllable having a final consonant that is preceded by a single vowel, follow these suffix rules.

a. If the word is accented on its last syllable, double the consonant before adding a suffix that begins with a vowel.

begín            beginning
detér            deterrent
contról          controlled
occúr            occurrence
prefér           preferring
regrét           regrettable

b. If the accent does not fall on the last syllable, do not double the final consonant.

sp
24f

| bárgain | bargained |
|---------|-----------|
| díffer | difference |
| ópen | opener |
| stámmer | stammering |
| trável | traveler (in American English) |

c. If, in adding the suffix, the accent shifts to an earlier syllable, do not double the final consonant.

| infér | ínference |
|-------|-----------|
| prefér | préference |
| refér | réference |

## 24g  Remember the Old Jingle for *ie/ei*.

| *i* before *e* | (achieve, believe, friend, grieve) |
|---|---|
| except after *c* | (deceive, ceiling, receive) |
| or when sounded like *a* | |
| as in *neighbor* and *weigh* | (freight, neighbor, vein, weigh) |

Exceptions:

| ancient | efficient | leisure | seize |
|---------|-----------|---------|-------|
| conscience | foreign | science | weird |

## 24h  Overcome the Confusion between *-sede, -ceed,* and *-cede.*

sp
24h

supersede        This is the only English word that ends in *-sede.*

exceed
proceed    }    Only three words end in *-ceed.*
succeed

accede
concede
intercede
precede    }    Several words end in *-cede.*
recede
secede

---

**EXERCISE (24a–24h)**

1. Go through all the previously graded papers (for this and other courses) that you have on hand, noting all the words that were marked as misspelled. Then carefully review the list on pages 424–429, checking the words you think you might misspell. From these two sources, begin a spelling list such as the one shown on page 420. Submit ten entries from your list, using the three-column format ("Misspelling," "Remember," "Correct Spelling").

---

## HYPHENATION RULES

Another source of uncertainty in spelling is doubt as to whether a word contains a hyphen. Short of looking up every questionable word, you can observe certain rules. For the sake of keeping together the whole discussion of hyphens, we begin with conventions for dividing words at the end of a line.

### 24i    Observe the Conventions for Dividing Words at Line Endings.

In a manuscript or typescript, where right-hand margins are normally uneven, avoid breaking words at line endings. Just finish each line with the last word you can complete. When you must hyphenate, observe the following conventions:

1. Divide words at syllable breaks as marked in your dictionary. Spaces or heavy dots between parts of a word indicate such breaks: *en•cy•clo•pe•di•a.*

2. Never divide a one-syllable word, even if you might manage to pronounce it as two syllables (*rhythm, schism*).

3. Do not leave one letter stranded at the end of a line (*o-ver, i-dea*), and do not leave a solitary letter for the beginning of the next line (*Ontari-o, seed-y*).

4. If possible, avoid hyphenating the last word on a page.

5. If a word is already hyphenated, divide it only at the fixed hyphen. Avoid x *self-con-scious, ex-Pre-mier.*

hyph
**24i**

6. You can anticipate what your dictionary will say about word division by remembering that:

   a. Double consonants are usually separated: *ar-rogant, sup-ply.*

   b. When a word has acquired a double consonant through the adding of a suffix, the second consonant belongs to the suffix: *bet-ting, fad-dish.*

   c. When the root of a word with a suffix has a double consonant, the break follows both consonants: *stall-ing, kiss-able.*

## 24j   Use a Hyphen to Separate Certain Prefixes from the Root Words to Which They Are Attached.

A **prefix** is a letter or group of letters that can be placed *before* a root word to make a new word. (Compare **suffix**, 24f, p. 429.) Dictionaries do not always agree with each other about hyphenation after a prefix, but the following guidelines will enable you to be consistent in your practice.

*All-, ex-, self-*

Words beginning with *all-, ex-,* and *self-,* when these are prefixes, are hyphenated after the prefix:

- all-powerful
- ex-minister
- self-motivated

**hyph
24j**

Note that in words like *selfhood, selfish, selfless,* and *selfsame,* the accented syllable *self* is not a true prefix; no hyphen is called for.

### Prefixes with Names

Prefixes before a name are always hyphenated:

- pre-Whitman
- un-American
- anti-Soviet

### Words Like *Anti-Intellectual* and *Preempt*

Prefixes ending with a vowel usually take a hyphen if that same vowel comes next, or if a different following letter would make for an awkward or misleading combination:

- anti-intellectual
- semi-independent
- pro-organic
- co-worker

But prefixed terms that are very common are less likely to be misconstrued, and many double vowels remain unhyphenated:

- cooperate
- coordinate
- preempt
- reentry

Some dictionaries recommend a dieresis mark over the second vowel to show that it is separately pronounced: *reëntry.* In contemporary prose, however, you will not come across many instances of the dieresis.

### Constructions Like *Post-Heart Surgery*

When a prefix applies to two or more words, attach it to the first one with a hyphen:

hyph
24j

- a pre-aurora borealis phenomenon
- the anti-status quo faction

### Constructions Like *Pre-* and *Postwar*

When a modifier contains compound prefixes, the first prefix usually stands alone with a hyphen, whether or not it would take a hyphen when joined directly to the root word:

- There was quite a difference between *pre-* and postwar prices.
- *Pro-* and antifascist students battled openly in the streets of Rome.

## 24k  Follow Your Dictionary in Hyphenating a Compound Noun or Verb.

Many compound words (formed from more than one word) are hyphenated in most dictionaries: *bull's-eye, secretary-treasurer, spring-cleaning, water-ski* (verb only), and so on. Many others, however, are usually written as separate words (*fire fighter, head start, ice cream, oil spill,* etc.) or as single unhyphenated words (*earring, scofflaw, scoutmaster, skydive,* etc.). To make matters more confusing, practice is always in flux; as compound terms become more familiar, they tend to lose their hyphens. All you can do, then, is be alert to the compound words you see in print and consult an up-to-date dictionary whenever you are in doubt.

## 24l  Study the Guidelines for Hyphenating Compound Modifiers.

**Before Modified Term**

A **compound modifier** (containing more than one word) is usually hyphenated if it meets two conditions:

1. it comes before the term it modifies, and

2. its first element is a modifier.

These two conditions are met in the following examples:

- a *well-trained* philosopher
  
  MOD

- a *short-tempered* umpire
  
  MOD

- some *deep-ocean* drilling
  
  MOD

- *nineteenth-century* art
  
  MOD

- an *out-of-work* barber
  
  MOD

In such phrases the hyphens sometimes prevent confusion. Consider what would happen, for example, if you wrote:

x  a short tempered umpire

x  some deep ocean drilling

Is the umpire short in stature but tempered in judgment? Is it the drilling rather than the ocean that is deep? When hyphens are added, a reader can see at once that *short* is part of the compound modifier *short-tempered* and that *deep* is part of the compound modifier *deep-ocean*. In such a case the hyphen tells us not to take the next word to be the modified term.

If the first word in a compound modifier is a noun, as in *school program administrator,* do not put a hyphen after it. A noun generally runs a low risk of being mistaken for a modifier of the next word. The following phrases are correct:

- the *ocean salinity* level

  MOD

- a *barbecue sauce* cookbook

  MOD

- a *mercury vapor* lamp

  MOD

But do use a hyphen if the initial noun is followed by a modifier:

- a *picture-perfect* landing

  MOD

- that *time-honored* principle

  MOD

> Here the hyphens are needed to show that the initial noun does not stand alone; it is part of a compound modifier.

Even when the first part of a compound modifier is itself a modifier, leave it unhyphenated if it forms a familiar pair with the following word and if there is no danger of confusion:

- the *Modern Language* Association

  MOD

- an *electric typewriter* store

  MOD

- the *happy birthday* card

  MOD

hyph
24I

As you can see, compound modifiers pose especially sensitive problems of hyphenation. Call on your good judgment: use a hyphen where it is needed to prevent ambiguity, but leave it out if you think your reader can get along without it.

### After Modified Term: *Well Trained*

When a compound modifier *follows* the modified term, the hyphen usually disappears:

- The philosopher was *well trained*.

- A barber *out of work* resents people who cut their own hair.

### Modifiers Like *Barely Suppressed*

When a compound modifier contains an adverb in the *-ly* form, it does not have to be hyphenated in any position. There is no danger of ambiguity, since the adverb, clearly identifiable *as* an adverb, can only modify the next word:

- a *barely suppressed* gasp

- an *openly polygamous* chieftain

- a *hypocritically worded* note of protest

### Modifiers Like *Fast-Developing*

Adverbs lacking the *-ly* form do run the risk of ambiguity. Whether they come before or after the modified term, you should always hyphenate them:

- a *fast-developing* crisis

- a *close-cropped* head of hair

- The traffic was *slow-moving*.

hyph
24l

### Modifiers with Fixed Hyphens

If you find that a modifier is hyphenated in the dictionary, keep it hyphenated wherever it occurs:

- She was an *even-tempered* instructor.

- She was *even-tempered*.

## 24m    Study the Guidelines for Hyphenating Numbers.

### Numbers *Twenty-one* to *Ninety-nine*

Always hyphenate these numbers, even when they form part of a larger number:

- Two hundred *seventy-five* years ago, religious toleration was almost unknown.

### Number as Part of a Modifier

If the number and the term it modifies work together as a modifier, place a hyphen after the number:

- A *twelve-yard* pool is hardly long enough for swimming.

### Noun Formed from Hyphenated Number

Hyphenate a noun formed from an already hyphenated number:

- The seats were reserved for *sixty-five-year-olds.*

### Fractions with and without Hyphens

Hyphenate a fraction only if you are using it as a modifier.

**AS MODIFIER:**

- The luggage compartment was *five-eighths* full.

**NOT AS MODIFIER:**

- *Five eighths* of the space had already been taken.

    In the first sentence, *five-eighths* modifies the adjective *full.* In the second, *five eighths* is the subject of the verb.

Some good writers, however, overlook this distinction. In your reading you will find that the more common fractions such as *one quarter* and *two thirds* are sometimes left unhyphenated even when they serve as modifiers. When in doubt, you would still do well to follow the rule.

hyph
24m

## 24n   Use a Hyphen to Connect Numbers Expressing a Range.

- pages 37–49
- September 11–October 4
- 1979–1988

---

**EXERCISES (24l–24n)**

2. If it were necessary to hyphenate these words at the end of a line, where would breaks be appropriate? Indicate possible breaks by vertical lines.

    A. overripe
    B. ex-Republican
    C. passionate
    D. butted
    E. penning

3. Correct any errors of hyphenation in the following items:

    A. selfsufficient
    B. antiAmerican
    C. semi-incapacitated
    D. redesign
    E. pre and postinflationary
    F. suicide leap
    G. father-in-law
    H. an ill schooled student
    I. The doctor was poorly prepared.
    J. Teachers are under-paid.
    K. a bad looking thunderhead
    L. a finely-tuned violin
    M. sixty-five days
    N. a hundred-thirty-one times
    O. a three sixteenths opening
    P. four-elevenths of those people
    Q. forty-three eighty-ninths
    R. a delay of between 8–10 hours
    S. between pages 45–50
    T. a completely unsettling experience

**hyph**
**24n**

# 25

# Capitals

## 25a Capitalize the First Letter of Every Sentence or Intentional Sentence Fragment.

- *Are* you a Pisces? *Certainly* not! *Too* bad.

### Whole Sentence within a Sentence

If a sentence within a sentence is a quotation or a representation of some-one's thoughts, begin it with a capital letter:

- Max asked Bessie: *"Why* don't we skip the tourist spots and just hang around American Express today?"
- I wondered, *How* am I ever going to finish this book?

But once in a while, words that might be construed as sentence openers are left uncapitalized:

- Max was curious. Who had invented that awful French coffee? *when? and* why?

    By leaving *when* and *and* in lower case, the writer emphasizes that Max was asking a three-part question, not three distinct questions. Capitals would have been equally correct and more usual.

Note that indirect questions (16b, p. 346) are not capitalized:

• I wondered *how* I was ever going to finish that book.

## 25b    If You Are Not Quoting Speech or Representing Someone's Thoughts, Do Not Capitalize the First Letter after a Colon.

• Home was never like this: *twenty-four* roommates and a day starting at 5:00 A.M.

• I finally understood how the Air Force makes a pilot of you: *after* the crowded barracks, every cadet yearns for the solitude of flight.

## 25c    Capitalize the First Word of a Sentence in Parentheses Only If the Parenthetic Sentence Stands between Complete Sentences.

### CAPITALIZED:

• Max and Bessie had a fine time in Moscow. (*They* especially liked shopping for used blue jeans and drinking Pepsi with Herb and Gladys.) But in Bulgaria Max missed the whole World Series because no one would lend him a shortwave radio.

### UNCAPITALIZED:

• Dr. Dollar's best seller, *Be Fat and Forget It* (*the* publisher decided on the title after a brainstorming session with his advertising staff), has freed millions of Americans from needless anxiety.

**cap**
**25d**

## 25d    Learn When to Capitalize within a Quotation.

Capitalize the first letter of a quotation only if (1) it is capitalized in the original, (2) it represents the beginning of a speaker's sentence, or (3) it begins your own sentence.

### CAPITALIZED IN THE ORIGINAL:

• Ben Jonson believed that "*Talking* and eloquence are not the same: to speak, and to speak well, are two things."

BEGINNING OF A SPEAKER'S SENTENCE:

- Bessie told Max, "*There's* nothing like a good American cup of freeze-dried coffee."

BEGINNING OF THE WRITER'S OWN SENTENCE:

- "*Citizen's* band radio" was the phrase Max kept muttering to himself as he walked through Sofia, wondering how a civilization could have survived so long without the bare necessities of technology.

When a quotation does not meet any of these three tests for capitalization, leave its first letter in lower case:

- Bessie said that she didn't mind the coffee's tasting like lentil soup, "*if* only they would make it hot."

    The quotation is a subordinate clause (9b, p. 241), not Bessie's full statement.

## 25e   Capitalize the First, the Last, and All Other Important Words in a Title or Subtitle.

If an article, a coordinating conjunction, or a preposition does not occur in the first or last position, leave it in lower case:

- *The House of the Seven Gables*
- *The Mismeasure of Man*
- *Dr. Dollar Raps with the Newborn*

Do capitalize the first letter of a subtitle:

- *Peasants into Frenchmen: The Modernization of Rural France, 1870–1914*
- "Male Gymnasts: The Olympic Heights"
- "Working within the System: A Guide to Sewer Repair"

## 25f   Capitalize Both Parts of Most Hyphenated Terms in a Title.

The Modern Language Association recommends that you capitalize both parts of a hyphenated term in a title:

cap
25f

- *Fail-Safe*
- *Through the Looking-Glass*
- *Self-Consuming Artifacts*

When an obviously minor element is included in a hyphenated term, however, leave it uncapitalized:

- "A Guide to Over-*the*-Counter Medications"

## 25g    Capitalize the Name of a Person, Place, Business, or Organization.

- Joyce Carol Oates
- Western Hemisphere
- New Canaan, Connecticut
- Lifeboat Associates
- Canadian Broadcasting Corporation
- Marvelous Max's Junktiques

## 25h    Capitalize an Adjective Derived from a Name.

- Shakespearean
- Malthusian
- the French language
- Roman numerals

But note the lower-case *roman type, italic type.*

## 25i    Capitalize a Family Relation If It Is a Name or Part of a Name, but Not If It Merely Identifies the Relationship.

NAME OR PART OF NAME (CAPITALIZED):

- Everyone has seen posters of *Uncle* Sam.
- Oh, *Mother,* you're so old-fashioned!

NOT PART OF NAME (UNCAPITALIZED):

* My *uncle* Sam wasn't the same man after the Dodgers moved to Los Angeles.
* You are the only *mother* on this block who objects to pierced noses.

## 25j Capitalize a Rank or Title Only When It Is Joined to a Name or When It Stands for a Specific Person.

CAPITALIZED:

* General Dwight D. Eisenhower
* The Colonel was promoted in 1983.

UNCAPITALIZED:

* Two *generals* and a *colonel* were reprimanded for mislaying the B-52s.

## 25k Capitalize Certain High Offices Even When No Particular Occupant Is Being Discussed.

* the Queen of England
* the President of the United States
* the Secretary of Defense
* the Chief Justice of the United States

    (There is no such office as *Chief Justice of the Supreme Court.*)

cap
25l

## 25l Capitalize the Name of a Specific Institution or Its Formal Subdivision, but Not of an Unspecified Institution.

When you are designating a particular school or museum, or one of its departments, use capitals:

* Museum of Modern Art
* University of Chicago

- the Department of Business Administration
- Franklin High School

Subsequent, shortened references to the institution or department are sometimes left uncapitalized:

- She retired from the *university* last year.

  But *University* would also be correct here.

Do not capitalize a name that identifies only the *type* of institution you have in mind:

- a strife-torn *museum*
- Every *university* must rely on contributions.
- She attends *high school* in the daytime and *ballet school* after dinner.

### 25m Capitalize a Specific Course of Study, but Not a General Branch of Learning.

**CAPITALIZED:**

- Physics 1A
- Computer Science 142B

**UNCAPITALIZED:**

- He never learned the rudiments of *physics*.
- Her training in *computer science* gained her a job as a programmer.

If a branch of learning is a language, however, capitalize it: *German, English, Japanese.*

### 25n Capitalize a Sacred Name, but Not a Word Derived from It.

Whether or not you are a believer, use capitals for the names of deities, revered figures, and holy books:

cap
25n

- the Bible
- the Gospels
- God
- the Lord
- He, Him, His [referring to the Judeo-Christian deity]
- the Virgin Mary
- the Koran

But in general, do not capitalize a word derived from a sacred name:

- biblical
- godlike
- scriptural
- the gospel of getting ahead

## 25o  Capitalize the Name of a Specific Historical Event, Movement, or Period.

- the Eighties
- the Bronze Age
- the Civil War
- the Romantic poets
- the Depression

cap
25p

## 25p  Capitalize a Day, a Month, or a Holiday, but Not a Season or the Numerical Part of a Date.

**CAPITALIZED:**

- next Tuesday
- May 1988
- Christmas
- Passover
- Columbus Day

**UNCAPITALIZED:**

- next fall

- a winter storm

- July twenty-first

- the third of August

**25q    Capitalize the Name of a Group or Nationality, but Not of a Looser Grouping.**

**CAPITALIZED:**

- Moslem

- Hungarian

- Friends of the Earth

**UNCAPITALIZED:**

- the upper class

- the underprivileged

- environmentalists

**25r    Capitalize a Geographic Direction Only If It Is Part of a Place Name or a Widely Recognized Section of a Country.**

cap
25r

**CAPITALIZED:**

- Northwest Passage

- Southeast Asia

- The South and the Midwest will be crucial in the election.

**UNCAPITALIZED:**

- northwest of here

- Go west for two miles and then turn south.

## 25s Reproduce a Foreign Word or Title As You Find It in the Original Language.

- *Weltanschauung* (Ger.: world view)
- *una cubana* (Sp.: a Cuban woman)
- *La terre* (title of a French novel: *The Earth*)

## 25t Notice That a Word May Have Different Meanings in Its Capitalized and Uncapitalized Forms.

- The Pope is a *Catholic.* [He belongs to the Church.]
- George has *catholic* tastes. [His tastes are wide-ranging.]
- He became a *Democrat* after the President declared a national day of prayer for the Redskins. [He joined the Party.]
- Tocqueville saw every American farmer as a *democrat.* [He believed that they all supported the idea of equality.]

---

**EXERCISE (25a–25t)**

1. Correct any errors of capitalization:

   A. Our most musical president was Harry Truman, who, after reading a review of one of his Daughter Margaret's concerts, threatened to beat up the critic.
   B. Each year the Pelicans fly south to build their nests near the outfall pipe.
   C. Realizing that her marriage was in trouble, Susan went straight to the lingerie department and asked if she could try on a Freudian slip.
   D. She wondered Whether it was really necessary for the management to frisk people who lingered near the meat counter.
   E. Stanley believed that the People, guided by himself and a few trusted friends, knew more about their true interests than any politician did.
   F. Max and Bessie spent the whole summer in Ireland, where they hoped to trace the ancestry of the Boston celtics.
   G. Dr. Dollar's Gospel was to worship the Almighty Goddess Success.
   H. A University lacking an Art School is hardly worthy of the name.
   I. Bob and Ray believe that the prince of Wales ought to be a civil service position.
   J. In a parisian cafe Bessie told Max, "you won't believe this, but some jerk in the kitchen must have accidentally dropped some stale bread into this Onion Soup."

cap
**25t**

# 26
## Italics, Abbreviations, Numbers

## ITALICS

Ordinary typeface is known as *roman,* and the thin, slightly slanted type-face that contrasts with it is *italic* — as in *these three words.* In manuscript or typescript, "italics" are indicated by underlining.

**MANUSCRIPT:**

• *The Great Gatsby*

**TYPESCRIPT:**

• The Great Gatsby

**PRINT:**

• *The Great Gatsby*

## 26a    Learn Which Kinds of Titles Belong in Italics.

ITALICS:

| | |
|---|---|
| *One Hundred Years of Solitude* | [a novel] |
| *Paradise Lost* | [a long poem published as a whole volume] |
| *Waiting for Godot* | [a play] |
| *Casablanca* | [a film] |
| *New York Times* | [a newspaper] |
| *Popular Mechanics* | [a magazine] |
| *The Firebird* | [a long musical work] |
| *The Smithsonian Collection of Classic Jazz* | [a record album] |
| *All Things Considered* | [a radio series] |
| *Family Ties* | [a television series] |

QUOTATION MARKS:

| | |
|---|---|
| "Araby" | [a short story] |
| "To Autumn" | [a poem] |
| "The Political Economy of Milk" | [a magazine article] |
| "Magic and Paraphysics" | [a chapter of a book] |
| "Eleanor Rigby" | [a song] |

Note the following special conditions.

1. In the name of a newspaper, include the place of publication in the italicized title:

• She read it in the *Philadelphia Inquirer.*

   The article preceding the place name is usually not italicized (or capitalized).

2. The title of a poem, story, or chapter may also be the title of the whole volume in which that smaller unit is found. Use italics only when you mean to designate the whole volume:

ital
26a

- "The Magic Barrel" [Bernard Malamud's short story]
- *The Magic Barrel* [the book in which Malamud's story was eventually republished]

3. Some publications, especially newspapers, use italics sparingly or not at all. If you are writing for a specific publication, follow its style. If not, observe the rules given here.

4. Do not italicize or use quotation marks around the Bible and its divisions.

DO:

- the Bible
- the New Testament
- Leviticus

5. When one title contains another title that would normally be italicized, make the embedded title roman. That is, you should not underline it.

- She was reading *The Senses of* Walden to get ideas for her paper.

## 26b    Italicize a Foreign Word That Has Not Yet Been Adopted as a Common English Expression.

STILL "FOREIGN" (ITALICIZE):

- *la dolce vita*
- *sine qua non*
- *La Belle Époque*
- *Schadenfreude*

FAMILIAR IN ENGLISH (DO NOT ITALICIZE):

- ad hoc
- blitzkrieg
- cliché
- de facto
- guru
- junta
- sushi

ital
26b

## Latin Abbreviations

Latin abbreviations are often italicized, but the tendency is now to leave them in roman. For example, according to the general practice these may be left in roman:

| | | | |
|---|---|---|---|
| cf. | et al. | i.e. | viz. |
| e.g. | f., ff. | q.v. | vs. |

See 26g, p. 455, for the meanings of these and other abbreviations used in documentation.

### Translating a Foreign Term

When translating into English, put the foreign term in italics and the English one in quotation marks:

- The Italian term for "the book" is *il libro*; the French is *le livre.*

The Modern Language Association also allows a translation to be placed within single quotation marks without intervening punctuation:

- *ein wenig* 'a little'
- They called the Fiat 500 *Topolino* 'little mouse.'

## 26c    Italicize the Name of a Ship.

- *Queen Elizabeth II*
- *Cristoforo Colombo*

But do not italicize abbreviations such as *SS* or *HMS* preceding a ship's name:

- SS *Enterprise*

ital
26d

## 26d    Use Italics or Quotation Marks to Show That You Are Treating a Word *as* a Word.

- When Frank and Edith visited the rebuilt neighborhoods of their childhood, they understood the meaning of the word *gentrified.*

    It would be equally correct to keep *gentrified* in roman type and enclose it in quotation marks: "gentrified."

## 26e   To Add Emphasis to a Quoted Expression, Italicize the Key Element.

If you want to emphasize one part of a quotation, put that expression in italics. And to show that the italics are your own rather than the author's, follow the quotation with a parenthetical acknowledgment such as *emphasis added*:

- The author writes mysteriously of a "*rival* system of waste management" (emphasis added).

## 26f   Use Italics Sparingly to Emphasize a Key Expression in Your Own Prose.

To distinguish one term from another or to lend a point rhetorical emphasis, you can italicize (underline) some of your own language:

- No doubt she can explain where she was in the month of June. *But what about July?* This is the unresolved question.

Beware, however, of relying on emphatic italics to do the work that should be done by effective sentence structure and diction. Prose that is riddled with italics makes a frenzied effect.

DON'T:
x   The hazard from *immediate* radiation is one issue—and a *very important* one. But the *long-term* effects from *improper waste storage* are *even more crucial,* and *practically nobody* within the industry seems to take it seriously.

This passage would inspire more confidence if it lacked italics altogether.

---

# ABBREVIATIONS

## 26g   Use Abbreviations in Parenthetical Citations, Notes, Reference Lists, and Bibliographies.

For purposes of documentation (Chapter 29), you can use the following abbreviations.

| ABBREVIATION | MEANING |
| --- | --- |
| anon. | anonymous |
| b. | born |
| bibliog. | bibliography |
| © | copyright |
| c. or ca. | about (with dates only) |
| cf. | compare (not *see*) |
| ch., chs. | chapter(s) |
| d. | died |
| diss. | dissertation |
| ed., eds. | editor(s), edition(s), edited by |
| e.g. | for example (not *that is*) |
| esp. | especially |
| et al. | and others (people only) |
| etc. | and so forth (not interchangeable with *et al.*) |
| f., ff. | and the following (page or pages) |
| ibid. | the same (title as the one mentioned in the previous note) |
| i.e. | that is (not *for example*) |
| introd. | introduction |
| l., ll. | line(s) |
| ms., mss. | manuscript(s) |
| n., nn. | note(s) |
| N.B. | mark well, take notice |
| n.d. | no date (in a book's imprint) |
| no., nos. | number(s) |
| p., pp. | page(s) |
| pl., pls. | plate(s) |
| pref. | preface |
| pt., pts. | part(s) |
| q.v. | see elsewhere in this text (literally *which see*) |
| rpt. | reprint |
| rev. | revised, revision; review, reviewed by (beware of ambiguity between meanings; if necessary, write out instead of abbreviating) |
| sc. | scene |
| sec., secs., sect., sects. | section(s) |
| ser. | series |
| st., sts. | stanza(s) |
| tr., trans. | translator, translation, translated by |
| v. | versus (legal citations) |
| viz. | namely |
| vol., vols. | volume(s) |
| vs. | versus |

abbr
26g

Note that *passim,* meaning "throughout," and *sic,* meaning "thus," are not to be followed by a period; they are complete Latin words. For the function of *sic,* see 20p, p. 387.

## 26h    Learn Which Abbreviations Are Allowable in Your Main Text.

### Allowed in Main Text

Some abbreviations are considered standard in any piece of writing, including the main body of an essay:

1. *Mr., Ms., Mrs., Dr., Messrs., Mme., Mlle., St.,* and so forth, when used before names. Some publications now refer to all women as *Ms.,* and this title has rapidly gained favor as a means of avoiding designation of marital status.

2. *Jr., Sr., Esq., M.D., D.D., D.D.S., M.A., Ph.D., LL.D.,* etc., when used after names.

3. abbreviations of, and acronymns (words formed from the initial letters in a multiword name) for, organizations that are widely known by the shorter name: *CIA, FBI, ROTC, NOW, NATO, UNESCO,* etc. Note that very familiar designations such as these are usually written without periods between the letters.

4. B.C., A.D., A.M., P.M., *mph.* These abbreviations should never be used apart from numbers (x in the P.M.). B.C. always follows the year, but A.D. usually precedes it: *252* B.C., but A.D. *147.*

5. places commonly known by their abbreviations: *U.S., D.C., USSR,* etc.

### Inappropriate in Main Text

|  | DON'T | DO |
|---|---|---|
| 1. titles | the Rev., the Hon., Sen., Pres., Gen. | the Reverend, the Honorable, Senator, President, General |
| 2. given names | Geo., Eliz., Robt. | George, Elizabeth, Robert |

|  | DON'T | DO |
|---|---|---|
| 3. months, days of the week, and holidays | Oct., Mon., Vets. Day | October, Monday, Veterans Day |
| 4. localities, cities, counties, states, provinces, and countries | Pt. Reyes Natl. Seashore, Phila., Sta. Clara, N.M., Ont., N.Z. | Point Reyes National Seashore, Philadelphia, Santa Clara, New Mexico, Ontario, New Zealand |
| 5. roadways | St., La., Ave., Blvd. | Street, Lane, Avenue, Boulevard |
| 6. courses of instruction | Bot., PE | Botany, Physical Education |
| 7. units of measurement | ft., kg, lbs., qt., hrs., mos., yrs. | feet, kilogram, pounds, quart, hours, months, years |

### Technical versus Nontechnical Prose

In general, you can do more abbreviating in technical than in nontechnical writing. See the following examples.

| TECHNICAL WRITING | OTHER PROSE |
|---|---|
| km | kilometer(s) |
| mg | milligram(s) |
| sq. | square |

abbr
26h

Even in general-interest prose, however, abbreviation of a much-used term can be a convenience. Give one full reference before relying on the abbreviation:

- Among its many services, the Harvard Student Agency (HSA) sponsors the *Let's Go* series of travel books for students. HSA also functions as a custodial agency, rents photographic equipment and linens, acts as an employment clearinghouse, and caters parties.

## 26i    Be Consistent in Capitalizing or Not Capitalizing Abbreviations Following Times.

Authorities disagree over A.M. and P.M. versus *a.m.* and *p.m.* Either form will do, but do not mix them.

DON'T:

x She was scheduled to arrive at 11 a.m., but we had to wait for her until 2 P.M.

DO:

• She was scheduled to arrive at 11 a.m., but we had to wait for her until 2 p.m.

or

• She was scheduled to arrive at 11 A.M., but we had to wait for her until 2 P.M.

## 26j    Learn Which Kinds of Abbreviations Can Be Written without Periods.

Good writers differ in their preference for periods or no periods within an abbreviation. Practice is shifting toward omission of periods. With some exceptions (notably *U.S.*), you can feel safe in omitting periods from abbreviations written in capital letters:

• JFK

• USSR

**abbr
26j**

• IOU

• NJ

Note that *N.J.*, with periods, is an option for abbreviating *New Jersey* but not for supplying a mail code before a ZIP number: *NJ 08540*.

But most abbreviations that end in a lower-case letter still require periods:

• Ont.

• Chi.

• Inc.

• i.e.

Note that there are commonly recognized exceptions: *mph, rpm,* etc. Also, abbreviations for metric measures are usually written without periods: *ml, kg,* and so forth.

## 26k    Leave Spaces between the Initials of a Name, but Close Up Other Abbreviations and Acronyms.

SPACED:

- T. S. Eliot
- E. F. Hutton
- A. J. P. Taylor

UNSPACED:

- e.g.
- A.M. (or a.m.)
- Ph.D.
- CIA

## NUMBERS AND FIGURES

## 26l    Know Which Circumstances Call for Written-out Numbers.

### Technical versus Nontechnical Prose

In scientific and technical writing, figures *(67)* are preferred to written-out numbers *(sixty-seven),* though very large multiples such as *million, billion,* and *trillion* are written out. Newspapers customarily spell out only numbers *one* through *nine* and such round numbers as *two hundred* and *five million.* In your nontechnical prose, prefer written-out numbers for the whole numbers *one* through *ninety-nine* and for any of those numbers followed by *hundred, billion,* and so forth.

| TECHNICAL PROSE | NONTECHNICAL PROSE |
| --- | --- |
| 3/5 | three fifths |
| 4 | four |
| 93 | ninety-three |
| 202 | 202 |
| 1500 (or 1,500) | fifteen hundred |
| 10,000 | ten thousand |
| 38 million | thirty-eight million |
| 101 million | 101 million |
| 54 billion | fifty-four billion |
| 205 billion | 205 billion |

## Special Uses for Written-out Numbers

1. In nontechnical prose, write out a concise number between one thousand and ten thousand that you can express in hundreds: not *1600* but *sixteen hundred*. This rule does not apply to dates.

2. Write out round (approximate) numbers that are even hundred thousands:

• Over six hundred thousand refugees arrived here last year.

3. Always write out a number that begins a sentence.

• *Eighty-four* students scored above grade level.

   But if the number would not ordinarily be written out, it is usually better to recast the sentence.

• The results were less encouraging for *213* other takers of the test.

   It would have been awkward to begin the sentence with *Two hundred thirteen*.

4. Write out a whole hour, unmodified by minutes, if it appears before *o'clock, noon,* or *midnight: one o'clock, twelve noon, twelve midnight*. Do not write *twelve thirty o'clock* or *12:30 o'clock*.

## Special Uses for Figures

1. Use figures with abbreviated units of measure:

• 7 lbs.

- 11 g
- 88 mm

2. If you have several numbers bunched together, use figures regardless of the amounts:

- Harvey skipped his birthday celebrations at ages 21, 35, and 40.

3. When two or more related amounts call for different styles of representation, use figures for all of them:

- The injured people included 101 women and 9 children.

4. Use figures for all of the following:

   a. apartment numbers, street numbers, and ZIP codes:

- Apt. 17C, 544 Lowell Ave., Palo Alto, CA 94301.

   b. tables of statistics.

   c. numbers containing decimals: *7.456, $5.58, 52.1 percent.*

   d. dates (except in extremely formal communications such as wedding announcements): *October 5, 1988; 5 October 1988; October 5th.*

   e. times, when they precede *A.M.* or *P.M.* (*a.m.* or *p.m.*): *8 A.M., 6 P.M., 2:47 P.M.*

   f. page numbers: *p. 47, pp. 341–53.*

   g. volumes (*vol.* 2), books of the Bible (*2 Corinthians*), and acts, scenes, and lines of plays (*Macbeth I.iii.89–104*).

## 26m    Use Roman Numerals Only Where Convention Requires Them.

In general, **Roman numerals** (*XI, LVIII*) have been falling into disuse as **Arabic numerals** (*11, 58*) have taken over their function. But note the following exceptions.

1. In some citation styles, upper- and lower-case Roman numerals are still used in combination with Arabic numerals to show sets of numbers in combination. Thus *Hamlet III.ii.47* refers to line 47 in the second scene of the play's third act.

2. Use Roman numerals for the main divisions of an outline (4e, p. 93).

3. Use lower-case Roman numerals to cite pages at the beginning of a book that are so numbered:

- (Preface v)

- (Introduction xvi–xvii)

4. Use Roman numerals as you find them in the names of monarchs, popes, same-named sons in the third generation, racing boats, etc.:

- Elizabeth II

- Leo IV

- Orville F. Schell III

- *Kookaburra II*

The following list will remind you how Roman numerals are formed.

| | | | | | | | |
|---|---|---|---|---|---|---|---|
| 1 | I | 10 | X | 50 | L | 200 | CC |
| 2 | II | 11 | XI | 60 | LX | 400 | CD |
| 3 | III | 15 | XV | 70 | LXX | 499 | CDXCIX |
| 4 | IV | 19 | XIX | 80 | LXXX | 500 | D |
| 5 | V | 20 | XX | 90 | XC | 900 | CM |
| 6 | VI | 21 | XXI | 99 | XCIX | 999 | CMXCIX |
| 7 | VII | 29 | XXIX | 100 | C | 1000 | M |
| 8 | VIII | 30 | XXX | 110 | CX | 1500 | MD |
| 9 | IX | 40 | XL | 199 | CXCIX | 3000 | MMM |

**num**
**26n**

## 26n  Distinguish between the Uses of Cardinal and Ordinal Numbers.

Numbers like *one, two,* and *three* (*1, 2, 3*) are called **cardinal numbers**; those like *first, second,* and *third* (*1st, 2d, 3d*; note the shortened spelling) are called **ordinal numbers**. The choice between cardinal and ordinal numbers is usually automatic, but there are several differences between spoken and written convention:

| SPEECH | WRITING |
|--------|---------|
| Louis the Fourteenth | Louis XIV |
| July seventh, 1988 | July 7, 1988 *or* 7 July 1988 |
| *But:* | |
| July seventh [no year] | July 7th *or* July seventh |

Note that the rules of choice between written-out numbers and figures are the same for cardinal as for ordinal numbers (26l, p. 459).

### Adverbial Ordinal Numbers

The word *firstly* is now rarely seen; *first* can serve as an adverb as well as an adjective.

ADJECTIVE:

- The *first* item on the agenda is the budget.

ADVERB:

- There are several items on the agenda. *First, . . .*

When you begin a list with *first,* you have the option of continuing either with *second, third,* or with *secondly, thirdly.* For consistency of effect, drop all the *-ly* forms.

- Let me say, *first,* that the crisis has passed. *Second,* I want to thank all of our employees for their extraordinary sacrifices. And *third, . . .*

But as soon as you write *secondly,* you have committed yourself to *thirdly, fourthly,* and so forth.

Finally, beware of mixing cardinal and ordinal forms.

DON'T:

x  *One,* a career as a writer presents financial hardship. *Second,* I am not sure I have enough emotional stamina to face rejection. *Third, . . .*

For consistency, change *One* to *First.*

num
26n

**EXERCISES (26a–26n)**

1. Correct any errors in the use of italics, abbreviations, and numbers:

 A. Most drunk drivers would find it difficult to count backward from 135 to twenty-one by threes.

 B. He had only one reason for not wanting to ride — e.g., he was afraid of horses.

 C. 40 dollars will buy an adequate dinner for 1 at that restaurant.

 D. Four six'es are twenty-four.

 E. The attack was planned for precisely 7:42 o'clock.

 F. "Gone with the Wind" was the film that introduced profane language to the Hollywood screen.

 G. Alimony was never an issue for the ex-wives of King Henry the VIIIth.

 H. *The Falmouth Enterprise* is a typical small-town newspaper.

 I. You can still get a sporty sedan, fully equipped with roll bars, seat belts, impact-absorbing bumpers, and collision insurance, for nine thousand eight hundred forty-four dollars.

 J. Melody thought that *A Midsummer Night's Dream* was the most realistic play she had ever seen.

 K. She made an appointment with Dr. Calvin Gold, D.D.S.

 L. The Titanic at its launching was the world's largest, and soon thereafter the world's wettest, ocean liner.

 M. Over the loudspeaker came an urgent and repeated request for a dr.

 N. Criminals are treated leniently in Rome if they committed their offenses during lo scirocco, the hot, dry wind that supposedly makes people behave irrationally.

 O. He won the primary election on June 8th, 1976.

 P. Since he hoped to become a dog trainer when his football career was over, Biff was especially eager to read the article in "National Geographic" called *Sikkim*.

**num**
**26n**

2. The following paragraph contains errors in the use or absence of italics, abbreviations, and numbers. Find the errors and make a list of your corrections.

No piece of criticism has ever been harsher or funnier than Mark Twain's essay, *Fenimore Cooper's Literary Offenses,* which can be found in a vol. called "Selected Shorter Writings of Mark Twain." Twain asserts that Cooper, in novels such as *The Deerslayer, The Last of the Mohicans,* et al., has committed one hundred fourteen offenses against literary art out of a possible 115. "It breaks the record," says Twain. He proves that Cooper's Natty Bumppo, the indian Chingachgook, etc., perform physically impossible deeds and speak wildly different kinds of English from 1 page to the next. The attack is hilarious, but on a 2nd reading it can also be taken as seriously indicating Twain's allegiance to the literary realism of the later XIXth century.

# 27

# Forming and Spacing Punctuation Marks

To see how punctuation marks are normally handled by typewriter, examine the typescript essays beginning on pages 130 and 532. In addition, note the following advice about forming marks and leaving or omitting spaces around them.

## 27a  Learn the Three Ways of Forming a Dash.

Dashes come in three lengths, depending on their function.

1.  A dash separating numbers is typed as a hyphen:

- pages 32_39

- October 8_14

- Social Security Number 203_64_7853

2.  As a sign of a break in thought—its most usual function—a dash is typed as two hyphens with no space between:

- `Try it--if you dare.`
- `They promise--but do not always come through with--`
  `overnight delivery.`

3. Use four unspaced hyphens for a dash that stands in the place of an omitted word:

- `He refused to disclose the name of Ms. ----.`

This is the only kind of dash that is preceded by a space; see 27g, page 468, for the general rule.

## 27b   Learn How to Form Brackets.

If your typewriter lacks keys for brackets, you can improvise them by either

1. typing slashes (/) and completing the sides with underlinings:

   `/⁻_7`

2. typing slashes and adding the horizontal lines later in ink:

   `[ ]`

3. leaving blank spaces and later writing the brackets entirely in ink:

   `[ ]`

## 27c   Learn How to Form the Three Kinds of Ellipses.

1. An ellipsis (20n, p. 385) is formed with three spaced dots if it signifies the omission of material within a quoted sentence. Note that a space is left before and after the whole ellipsis as well as after each dot:

`"The government," she said, "appears to be abandoning`

`its . . . efforts to prevent nuclear proliferation."`

2. A four-dot ellipsis, signifying the omission of quoted material that covers at least one mark of end punctuation, begins with that *unspaced* mark:

```
"The government," she said, "appears to be abandoning its

formerly urgent efforts to prevent nuclear prolifera-

tion. . . . There may be a terrible price to pay for this

negligence."
```

3. Leave spaces between all the dots of an ellipsis that covers a whole row, signifying the omission of one or more lines of poetry.

```
The river glideth at its own sweet will:

. . . . . . . . . . . . . . . . . .

And all that mighty heart is lying still!
```

## 27d  Learn the Two Ways of Spacing a Slash.

1. When a slash separates two quoted lines of poetry that you are incorporating into your text (20g, p. 380), leave a space before and after the slash:

```
Shakespeare writes, "Shall I compare thee to a summer's

day? / Thou art more lovely and more temperate."
```

2. But if your slash indicates alternatives or a span of time, leave no space before or after the slanted line:

```
We are not dealing with an either/or situation here.

Biff had his greatest season in 1987/88, when he endorsed

a mouthwash, an athlete's foot ointment, and a home

permanent kit.
```

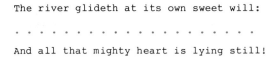

p/
form
27e

## 27e  Leave Two Spaces after a Period, a Question Mark, an Exclamation Point, or a Four-Dot Ellipsis.

```
The Chinese leaders appear to be ready for a new dialogue

with the United States.  Should we let this opportunity slip
```

away? Certainly not! Remember the words of the Foreign Min-
ister: "If we do not take steps to ensure peace, we may find
ourselves drifting into war. . . . Our two nations can
work together without agreeing about everything."

## 27f   Leave One Space after a Comma, a Colon, a Semicolon, a Closing Quotation Mark, a Closing Parenthesis, or a Closing Bracket.

Here is the real story, we believe, of last week's disturbance: it was not a riot but a legitimate demonstration.  The
city police chief thinks otherwise; but his description of
the "riot" is grossly inaccurate.  The chief (a foe of all
progressive causes) erred in more than his spelling when he
wrote of a "Comunist [sic] uprising."

## 27g   Leave No Space before or after a Dash, a Hyphen, or an Apostrophe within a Word.

Wilbur--a first-rate judge of toothpaste flavors--prefers
Carter's Sparklefoam for its gum-tickling goodness.

## 27h   When an Apostrophe Ends a Word, Leave No Space before Any Following Punctuation of That Word.

This ranch, the Johnsons', has been in the family for
generations.

## 27i   When Two Marks Punctuate the Same Word, Put Them Together without a Space.

Here is the true story of the "riot."

When I heard the truth about the riot (as the police chief
called it), I was outraged.

```
The protest, which the police chief called the work of "Com-
munists" [sic], was actually organized by members of the
business community.
```

## 27j    Do Not Begin a Line with Any Mark That Punctuates the Last Word of the Preceding Line.

DON'T:

```
X Here is why Josephine refuses to sign the petition
  : she objects to the dangerously vague language about
  waterfront development.
```

DO:

```
● Here is why Josephine refuses to sign the petition:
  she objects to the dangerously vague language about
  waterfront development.
```

## 27k    Do Not Carry an Ellipsis from One Line to the Next.

DON'T:

```
X Josephine objected to the petition because of "the . .
  . language about waterfront development."
```

DO:

```
● Josephine objected to the petition because of "the . . .
  language about waterfront development."
```

p/
form
**27k**

For combining quotation marks with other punctuation marks, see 20f, p. 378. For the spacing of periods within an abbreviation, see 26k, p. 459.

---

EXERCISE (27a–27k)

1. If your instructor, in reading your submitted work, has found no incorrectly formed or spaced punctuation marks, skip this exercise. Otherwise, submit up to five sentences illustrating the accepted form that you now recognize.

---

# VII

# THE RESEARCH ESSAY

28. Finding and Mastering Sources

29. Documenting Sources

30. A Sample Research Essay

## THE RESEARCH ESSAY

When assigned a research essay to write, some students feel they must set aside everything they have learned about effective rhetoric and concentrate instead on showing how much library reading they can do. The result may be a paper crammed with references but lacking a clear point or any concern for the reader's patience. A research essay is above all an essay—one that happens to be based in part on library materials (Chapter 28), duly documented (Chapter 29). You should never allow those features to usurp your main task of winning sympathy for a central idea.

The following chapters should thus be regarded not as a self-sufficient unit but as a supplement to Chapters 3–5. A brief review of those chapters is advisable before you begin work on your research essay.

# 28

# Finding and Mastering Sources

A college library is in essence an information retrieval system. As with a computer, the knack of using it successfully consists in knowing the right questions to present it with. Searching through the stacks without any questions at all would be as senseless as trying to browse in the computer's memory bank; you have to be looking for something from the outset. And the more specific your question, the more shortcuts you can take. Experienced researchers do not run through all the ways of seeking information described in this chapter. Rather, they find a few key works as early as possible and then allow those works—especially those containing a *bibliography*, or list of further books and articles on the topic—to suggest how to proceed.

## 28a Get Acquainted with the Parts of Your Library.

Perhaps your college library strikes you as mysterious or even vaguely threatening. If so, bear in mind that you do not have to understand the whole system—just some procedures for retrieving the books and articles you need. Watch for free library tours and information packets, and do not hesitate to ask a *reference librarian* for help in getting an efficient start on your project.

Although no two libraries are quite alike, your college library may contain as many as seven places to serve essential functions:

1. *Stacks.* These are shelves on which most books and bound periodicals are stored. In the "open stack" system, all users can enter the stacks, find materials, and take them to a check-out desk. If your library has "closed stacks," access to the stacks is limited by status; see the next item.

2. *Circulation desk.* You can check out a book or bound periodical by submitting a *call slip*—a card identifying what you need—to the *circulation desk,* to which a clerk will return either with the book or with an explanation that it is on reserve (see item 4), out to another borrower, or missing. If it is out to another borrower, you can "put a hold" on it—that is, indicate that you want to be notified as soon as the book has been returned. Since you may have to wait as long as two weeks for some items, it is important to begin your research early.

3. *Catalog.* Near the circulation desk you will find cabinets full of alphabetically filed cards, listing all the library's printed holdings (books, periodicals, pamphlets, and items on microfilm, but no manuscripts, records, or tapes). This is the *card catalog.* Its listings are by author, title, and subject. In some libraries the card catalog has been supplemented or replaced by a *microfiche catalog,* consisting of miniaturized photographic entries on plastic cards that can be read when placed in a microfiche reader, available nearby. Your library may even have an *on-line catalog*—that is, a continually updated computer file. If so, you will see computer terminals, accompanied by appropriate instructions, near the circulation desk. Whatever its form, the catalog is your master key to the stacks, for it gives you call numbers enabling you or a clerk to locate the books you need.

4. *Reference room.* In the *reference room* (or behind the reference desk) are stored sets of encyclopedias, indexes, dictionaries, bibliographies, and similar multipurpose research tools. You cannot check out reference volumes, but you can consult them long enough to get the names of promising-looking books and articles that you *will* be able to get from the main collection. The reference room usually doubles as a *reading room,* enabling you to do much of your reading near other sources of information.

5. *Reserve desk.* Behind the *reserve desk* (or in the reserve book room) are kept multiple copies of books that are essential to current courses. The distinctive feature of reserved books is that they must be returned quickly,

usually within either an hour or a day or a week. When you learn that a book is "on reserve," even for a course other than your own, you can be reasonably sure of finding an available copy.

6. *Periodical room.* In the *periodical room* you can find magazines and journals too recent to have been bound as books. Thus, if you do research on a topic of current interest, you are certain to find yourself applying to the periodical room for up-to-date articles.

7. *Newspaper room.* Take your call slips to this room to get a look at newspaper articles and editorials. Most newspapers are stored on *microfilm,* which can be read only with a microfilm reader. Ask a clerk to show you how the machine works.

Thus your research is likely to take you back and forth between various sites:

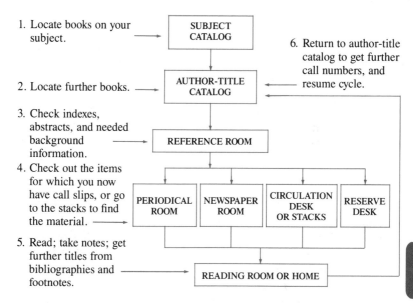

1. Locate books on your subject. → SUBJECT CATALOG

6. Return to author-title catalog to get further call numbers, and resume cycle.

2. Locate further books. → AUTHOR-TITLE CATALOG

3. Check indexes, abstracts, and needed background information. → REFERENCE ROOM

4. Check out the items for which you now have call slips, or go to the stacks to find the material. → PERIODICAL ROOM | NEWSPAPER ROOM | CIRCULATION DESK OR STACKS | RESERVE DESK

5. Read; take notes; get further titles from bibliographies and footnotes. → READING ROOM OR HOME

libr
28a

At some point, obviously, this cycle has to be interrupted; the first draft beckons. But even as you write successive drafts, you may find yourself dipping back into library sources to check new leads and follow up ideas that now look more fruitful than they did at first.

## EXERCISES

1. Find out—if necessary by asking a reference librarian—what catalogs your main campus library has, where they are located, and whether they are equally up-to-date. Submit a paragraph that supplies these pieces of information.

2. If your library offers guided tours, take one. If not, check the various rooms and functions on your own. (Never mind about branch libraries or special collections; look for the rooms discussed above.) Submit a brief report of what you have learned, including any questions that remain unresolved for you.

## 28b   Learn the Most Efficient Ways to Search for Books.

### Subject Catalogs

If you are searching for a topic within a general subject area, the first thing you want to do is check your library's holdings within that area. You can do so by consulting the *subject catalog,* which is arranged not by authors and titles of books but by fields of knowledge, problems, movements, schools of thought, and so forth. Once you locate an array of relevant titles, you should fill out call slips for the most recent appropriate-looking works. If you get hold of just one recent book that has a *bibliography*—a list of consulted works—in the back, you may discover that you already have the names of all the further books and articles you will need.

### Guide to Subject Headings

But how do you know which headings your subject catalog uses to classify the entries you will want to review? You can try your luck, sampling a number of alternative phrases, or you can take a more systematic and reliable approach. Your subject catalog follows the headings adopted by the Library of Congress in Washington, D.C. Ask your reference librarian where a book called *Library of Congress Subject Headings* is to be found. That book is heavily *cross-indexed*; in other words, if you look up a plausible-sounding phrase, you will not only learn whether it constitutes a Library of Congress subject heading, you will also be directed to other phrases that do serve as headings.

Thus the student who wanted to investigate computer crime for his research paper (pp. 532–540) began by going to the *Library of Congress*

*Subject Headings* pages referring to *Computers*. There he found the following valuable listing:

**Computer crimes** *(Indirect)* *(HV6773)* ——————————— 1
2 ———————————— *sa* Computers – Access control
Electronic data processing departments
– Security measures
Privacy, Right of
3 ———————————— *x* Computer fraud
Computers and crime
4 ———————————— *xx* Computers – Access control
Crime and criminals
Privacy, Right of
White collar crimes

Observe in this typical entry:

1. The Library of Congress call number of a key book on the subject—
   one that proved to be an authoritative government study containing
   a bibliography.

2. The symbol *sa* ("see also") introduces three related headings that
   can be consulted to locate titles that may not be covered under the
   main heading *Computer crimes*.

3. The symbol *x* tells the reader not to bother looking up *Computer
   fraud* or *Computers and crime*; since these are not Library of Congress headings, they will not be headings in the campus library
   catalog either.

4. The symbol *xx* introduces four *broader* headings that will cover
   some works on computer crime. By checking these phrases in the
   subject catalog, the reader can see the chosen problem in several
   wider perspectives.

## Shelf List

**libr
28b**

Armed with this much information, the student researcher was able to
make use of the subject catalog without a single wasted step. And already
possessing a key call number, he could also inspect the related cards in his
library's *shelf list*—still another catalog, this one arranged in order of call
numbers. Since his library followed the Library of Congress system of
numbering, and since call numbers in any library are ordered by subject,
he could be sure of finding relevant material near card HV6773.

### On-Line Catalog

The student was aware, however, that his library had recently begun to compile an *on-line* (computer) catalog which would eventually replace the card catalog. Though this catalog was still fragmentary, he knew it would be more up-to-date than any of the others. Following the instructions listed beside a terminal, he told the computer to retrieve all titles about *Computer crimes* listed in the on-line catalog. Here is what he read on the display and copied out:

> Your search for: subject words COMPUTER CRIMES retrieved: 9 books.
>
> 1. Bequai, August. COMPUTER CRIME. 1978
> 2. Deighton, Suzan. THE NEW CRIMINALS: A BIBLIOGRAPHY OF COMPUTER . . . 1978
> 3. Leibholz, Stephen W. USERS' GUIDE TO COMPUTER CRIME: ITS . . . 1974
> 4. Lin, Joseph C. COMPUTER CRIME, SECURITY, AND PRIVACY: A SELECTED . . . 1979
> 5. McKnight, Gerald. COMPUTER CRIME. 1973
> 6. McKnight, Gerald. COMPUTER CRIME. 1974
> 7. McNeil, John. THE CONSULTANT: A NOVEL OF COMPUTER CRIME. 1978
> 8. THE NEW CRIMINALS: A BIBLIOGRAPHY OF COMPUTER RELATED CRIME . . . 1979
> 9. Parker, Donn B. CRIME BY COMPUTER. 1976

Like most examples of computer retrieval, this list contained some obviously false leads. Items 6 and 8 were simply reprints of items 5 and 2, respectively, and item 7 was a work of fiction. But items 1, 2, and 9 turned out to be centrally important.

libr
28b

### Author-Title Catalog

If you know that your essay will deal with a certain author, you can bypass the various subject catalogs and go directly to the *author-title catalog,* which lists works alphabetically by both author and title and includes subject cards as well (see below). The last entries in your author's listing, after his or her own works, may be useful books of biography, criticism, and commentary. Thus the author-title catalog is itself a kind of subject catalog, with prominent authors as the subjects. Even if you are writing about a general problem, you can pick up likely references by browsing in the author-title catalog under possible key terms (*Computer, Crime,* etc.).

The most important piece of information on any catalog card is the *call number* in the upper left corner; it tells exactly where the book or bound journal is shelved. But you can also get several other kinds of information from a card. Consider, for example, an author card actually encountered by the writer of the computer crime paper on pages 532–540:

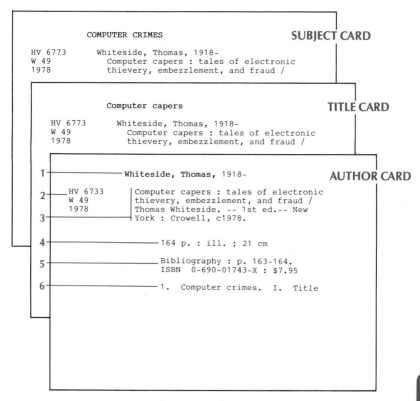

In addition to some coded information chiefly of interest to librarians, this author card contains six potentially useful kinds of knowledge:

1. The author's name.

2. The call number, enabling someone to apply for the book at the circulation desk or to locate it in the stacks.

3. The title of the book, the author's name as it appears on the title page, the fact that this is a first edition, the place of publication, the publisher, and the date of copyright. A researcher would want to get all this information (except "1st edition") recorded on a bibliography card (28e, p. 494).

4. Physical features of the book. It contains 164 pages, is illustrated, and is 21 centimeters in height. The key point here is the length; this book will be more worth looking into than, say, a forty-page pamphlet would be.

5. Notes on the contents of the book. In this case we are promised a bibliography—that is, a list of other related materials—which could prove extremely helpful for a research paper.

6. A list of all the headings under which this book is filed in the library's catalogs. By going to "Computer crimes" in the subject catalog, a researcher might find several items of related interest.

Once in a while you may come across a reference to an apparently indispensable book that is unlisted in your library's catalog. Since there are some sixty thousand new volumes published each year in English alone, no library but the Library of Congress itself could acquire more than a minority of them. You can get essential information about the book's author, title, publisher, and date from the *National Union Catalog,* which reproduces the Library of Congress Catalog and includes titles from other libraries as well. If you cannot visit a library that has the book, you can probably borrow it through *interlibrary loan.* The same holds for journals as well. By consulting the *Union List of Serials in Libraries of the United States and Canada,* you can discover which libraries own sets of hard-to-find journals.

---

EXERCISES

libr
28b

3. Choose a sample research project—preferably one that you hope to carry out in the weeks ahead. Go to the *Library of Congress Subject Headings* and find what appears to be the main heading for your topic. Copy out a passage beginning from that heading (as on page 477) and submit it along with an explanation of the symbols accompanying the entries.

4. The passage you have copied for Exercise 3, like the example on page 477, contains further headings that may be relevant to your topic. Using one or more of those categories, consult your library's subject catalog, its

author-title catalog, and its shelf list (if any), looking for key books on your subject. Submit a paragraph or two explaining the steps of your search and the relative usefulness of the catalogs you examined.

5. List what you take to be the three most important books to consult for the sample research project you undertook for Exercise 3. For each book, explain which information on the entry card (or in the microfiche or on-line entry) made you eager to see that book.

6. Check out the three books you discussed in Exercise 5. When you have been able to scan two of those books, submit a paragraph about each of them, explaining how acquaintance with that book could influence the direction of your sample research project. Are you closer than before to having a precisely focused topic? What sources would you want to investigate next?

## 28c   Learn How to Find Recent Articles and Reviews.

If you have chosen a topic of current interest—the spread and control of a new disease, say, or the changing American family structure—you will want to review the latest available information. You cannot find it in even the most recently published books, which will necessarily be a year or two behind the times. Newspaper articles will be best for following events as they occur. Magazine articles, such as those in *Harper's* or *The Atlantic,* will give you a general perspective that may be just right for the audience and level you have in mind. And in professional journals—specialized scholarly periodicals such as the *New England Journal of Medicine* or the *Bulletin of the Atomic Scientists*—you will get access to detailed knowledge and theory that may not yet have appeared in hard cover. You may also want to check expert reviews of books you hope to use. Digests of reviews (p. 483) can show you how much trust you should place in a given book.

### Indexes and Abstracts

libr
28c

Obviously, you would be wasting your time poring over the handiest newspapers, magazines, and journals in the hope of finding relevant items. The efficient thing is to consult indexes and abstracts, which you will find shelved together in your library's reference room. *Indexes* are books, usually with a new volume each year, containing alphabetically ordered references to articles on given subjects. And *abstracts* are summaries of articles, allowing you to tell whether or not a certain article is important enough to your project to be worth tracking down. It is the reference room, then—not the newspaper room or the periodical room—that holds the key to your search for pertinent articles and reviews.

1. *To Newspapers.* The only newspaper index you may ever need to consult is the *New York Times Index* (1913–   ), which covers a vast array of news and commentary having national or international importance. Since it is issued every two weeks before being bound into annual volumes, you can be sure of staying current with developments in your subject. For coverage of newspapers in Chicago, Los Angeles, New Orleans, and Washington, D.C., try the *Newspaper Index* (1972–   ). And for international and especially British coverage, consult the *Index to the* [London] *Times* (1906–   ).

2. *To Magazines.* If you want to find an article in a general-interest magazine, go to the *Reader's Guide to Periodical Literature* (1900–   ), which covers about 160 magazines on a twice-monthly basis. Indeed, the *Reader's Guide* is so useful for the typical research essay that many students begin their investigation there, saving the subject catalog until they have seen whether their topic has engaged the public lately. Browsing through the headings in the *Reader's Guide* may help you focus your topic better. If you draw a blank from the *Reader's Guide,* ask yourself whether your topic is too broad, too narrow, too specialized, or too outdated to merit pursuing.

A typical segment of a column in the *Reader's Guide* looks like this:

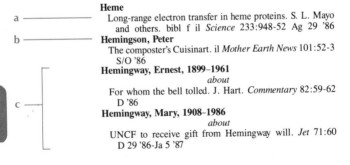

Here you see:

a. *An entry listed by subject.* The article about heme proteins appeared in the journal *Science,* volume 233, August 29, 1986, on pages

948 through 952, and it contained a bibliography, footnotes, and illustrations.

   b. *An entry listed by the author's name.*

   c. *Two entries listed by the individuals who are discussed.*

3. *To Journals.* While the *Reader's Guide* gives you good access to such popular magazines as *Time* and *Psychology Today,* it does not cover journals such as *Science* and *Modern Language Quarterly.* Journals are issued less often than magazines and are far more technical in nature. Although you probably want to keep a general-interest focus in your paper, an important piece of information may be accessible to you only in a journal. The key indexes for access to journal articles are the *Humanities Index* (1974–   ) and the *Social Sciences Index* (1974–   ). The *Humanities Index* should be your first choice for post-1973 articles in archaeology, area studies, classics, folklore, history, language and literature, literary criticism, performing arts, philosophy, religion, and theology. Use the *Social Sciences Index* for post-1973 articles in anthropology, economics, environmental science, geography, law and criminology, medicine, political science, psychology, public administration, and sociology. For years before 1973, consult the *International Index* (1907–1965) and the *Social Sciences and Humanities Index* (1965–1974); the latter was the parent of the now separate *Humanities Index* and *Social Sciences Index.*

4. *To Book Reviews.* If you want to know how reliable a certain book is, you can quickly learn what some of the book's original reviewers had to say by consulting *Book Review Digest* (1905–   ). Thus, for example, the writer of the research paper on pages 532–540 needed to decide how much trust to place in Thomas Whiteside's 1978 book *Computer Capers: Tales of Electronic Thievery, Embezzlement, and Fraud.* By looking in *Book Review Digest* in the period following publication, he was able not only to find citations of reviews but also to get a sense of the book's strengths and limitations:

**libr 28c**

**WHITESIDE, THOMAS.** Computer capers; tales of electronic thievery, embezzlement, and fraud. 164; $7.95 '78 Crowell

364.1 Computers. Crime
ISBN 0-690-01743-X    LC 77-25184

"The capabilities of computers to greatly expand the criminal's reach are explored in this . . . . book, much of which originally appeared in the New Yorker. (Library J) Bibliography.

"In addition to money, industrial secrets, client lists, personal data, and even computer time are vulnerable to theft via computer. No prior knowledge of computer science is expected of the reader: where needed, readable and precise technical explanations are provided. Whiteside has succeeded both in avoiding the oversimplifications that so often accompany books on technical subjects for the general reader and in retaining the essentials of good storytelling. For those desiring a more complete and authoritative discussion of computer crime, Donn B. Parker's Crime by Computer [BRD 1976] is the classic treatment." N. L. Bloom
**Library J** 103:736 Ap 1 '78 110w

"On one level, Thomas Whiteside's book . . . is an entertaining account of computer-involved larcenies. Computers can be raided for valuable information, manipulated to skim accounts, used to issue fraudulent checks, to destroy or rewrite important records, or to purloin expensive equipment, all of which have been done frequently and with remarkable ease, to the tune of many millions of dollars each year. On another level [this] is a cautionary tale, for our society has become utterly dependent on computers. The records, transactions and plans of business and government, including classified defense material, are heavily computerized, as are the data of our private lives; and the computer has not yet been designed that cannot be penetrated or sabotaged. The abuses have been rampant; the disasters, as Mr. Whiteside demonstrates, may be waiting to happen." Andrew Bergman
**N Y Times Bk R** p59 Ap 30 '78 260w

"Most Americans relish the benefits that the computer age provides in consumer and governmental services, but they worry too (as new opinion surveys clearly show) about the increasing vulnerabilities of automated life. Whiteside's book provides a nice introduction to one facet of this growing dilemma. It also pays tribute to man's ability to maintain his larcenous drives in each new stage of civilization and to run a sting even on IBM's best." A. F. Westin
**Sat R** 5:35 My '78 900w

**libr**
**28c**

These positive reviews inspired confidence in Whiteside's reporting, especially in view of the revelation that his book had first appeared in *The New Yorker,* a magazine famous for its fact checking. At the same time, the reference to "a more complete and authoritative discussion" alerted the student to the value of Donn B. Parker's *Crime by Computer,* a book that turned out to be important to the eventual research essay.

For other guides to book reviews, see *Book Review Index* (1965–   ),

*Current Book Review Citations* (1976–   ), and *The New York Times Book Review Index* (1896–1970).

Here is a list of useful indexes and abstracts:

*Abstracts in Anthropology* (1970–   )
*Abstracts of Health Care Management Studies* (1978–   )
*Accountant's Index* (1944–   )
*America: History and Life: A Guide to Periodical Literature* (1964–   )
*American Statistics Index* (1973–   )
*Applied Science and Technology Index* (1913–   )
*Art Index* (1947–   )
*Arts and Humanities Citation Index* (1978–   )
*Astronomy and Astrophysics Abstracts* (1969–   )
*Bibliographic Index* (1933–   )
*Biography Index* (1947–   )
*Biological Abstracts* (1926–   )
*Biological and Agricultural Index* (1964–   )
*Bioresearch Index* (1967–   )
*British Humanities Index* (1962–   )
*Business Periodicals Index* (1958–   )
*Chemical Abstracts* (1907–   )
*Child Development Abstracts and Bibliography* (1927–   )
*Computer and Control Abstracts* (1967–   )
*Congressional Digest* (1921–   )
*Current Index to Journals in Education* (1969–   )
*Dissertation Abstracts International* (1938–   )
*Education Abstracts* (1936–   )
*Education Index* (1929–   )
*Engineering Index* (1920–   )
*Environment Abstracts* (1971–   )
*Essay and General Literature Index* (1934–   )
*Film Literature Index* (1973–   )
*General Science Index* (1978–   )
*Geo Abstracts* (1972–   )
*Historical Abstracts* (1955–   )
*Index Medicus* (1961–   )
*Index to Legal Periodicals* (1908–   )
*MLA Abstracts of Articles in Scholarly Journals* (1971–   )
*MLA International Bibliography* (1921–   )
*Monthly Catalog of United States Government Publications* (1895–   )
*Music Index* (1949–   )
*Philosopher's Index* (1967–   )
*Physics Abstracts* (1895–   )

*Psychological Abstracts* (1927–  )
*Public Affairs Information Service Bulletin* (1915–  )
*Religious and Theological Abstracts* (1958–  )
*RILA Abstracts (International Repertory of Art Literature)* (1975–  )
*RILM Abstracts (International Repertory of Music Literature)* (1967–  )
*Science Abstracts* (1898–  )
*Science Citation Index* (1961–  )
*Social Sciences Citation Index* (1973–  )
*Sociological Abstracts* (1977–  )
*Urban Affairs Abstracts* (1971–  )
*Women's Studies Abstracts* (1972–  )

## On-Line Searching

In increasing numbers, printed indexes, abstracts, reports, conference proceedings, and government documents are being gathered in the alternative form of *databases*—that is, computer files that can be instantly scanned. If your library has an on-line catalog (28b, p. 478), then that catalog is itself a database. But that is just the beginning. If your library subscribes to such databases as, say, *Pharmaceutical News Index, Population Bibliography,* and *Pollution Abstracts,* you can instruct the computer to retrieve every relevant article from one or more of those sources.

Such *on-line searching* can save time, unearth very recent references, and ferret out specific topics that do not constitute subject headings in the index itself. Suppose, for example, you are interested in the connection between child abuse and alcoholism. Instead of asking for all items within each of those large subjects, you can tell the computer to display only those items whose titles refer to *both* problems. The outcome will be a relatively short but highly efficient list, fairly free of "dumb mistakes" on the computer's part.

On-line searching can produce dramatic results if you have a well-defined topic in mind. But there are serious disadvantages as well:

1. You will be charged a fee—possibly a steep one—for the search.

2. You will need the assistance of a trained technician.

3. It is hard to "browse" in computer files; if your chosen keywords do not appear in the title of a relevant article, the computer will probably overlook it.

On the whole, then, for the purposes of a college essay it is better to do your searching in printed sources. But remember that on-line searching

**libr**
**28c**

is available if you should need it. A reference librarian can tell you whether your project is one that lends itself readily to a computer search.

---

**EXERCISES**

7. Resume the sample research project you began for Exercise 3, or begin a new one. Using the *New York Times Index,* locate two relevant articles or editorials in the *Times.* Find those items (probably on microfilm) in your library's newspaper room, and take notes on their content. Submit a paragraph or two in which you give precise references to those items, and summarize what you learned from them.

8. Repeat Exercise 7, this time using magazine articles traced through the *Reader's Guide.* One of your two articles should be so recent that it can be found in an unbound copy of a magazine; the other should be at least two years old.

9. Repeat Exercise 7, this time using journal articles traced through one or more of the indexes and abstracts listed above. As in Exercise 8, retrieve one of your two items from an unbound issue of a journal.

10. Use *Book Review Digest* to find summaries of the reviews of any one book that looks promising for your sample research project. Submit a paragraph or two referring specifically to some of the reviews and explaining how they have affected your assessment of the book.

---

## 28d   Consult Background Sources as Necessary.

The steps we have already covered should be enough to give you all the information you need for a typical research essay. Sometimes, however, you may want an out-of-the-way bit of knowledge or a broad introduction to the field you are going to treat. Where should you turn? Most of the works mentioned below can be found in the reference room.

If you know an author's name but not the title of the book, if you have the title but not the author, or if you want to know when a certain book appeared, try consulting *Books in Print* (1948–   ), *Cumulative Book Index* (1898–   ), *Paperbound Books in Print* (1955–   ), or *Subject Guide to Books in Print* (1957–   ). The last of these volumes can give you a quick idea of what you could hope to find under a given subject heading of your card catalog. If you see an essential item in the *Subject Guide* that is missing from your catalog, you may be able to send for it through inter-library loan.

Reference works—books that survey a field and tell you how to find materials within that field—are now so numerous that you may need to consult an even more general book that lists reference works and explains their scope. Try especially Eugene P. Sheehy, *Guide to Reference Books* (1976, with later supplements), which can lead you to the most appropriate bibliographies and indexes to articles.

For a college research paper, however, you will probably need at the most one survey of your field and one guide to sources. Here is a representative sample of titles to consult:

## Art and Music

*Britannica Encyclopedia of American Art* (1976)
*Encyclopedia of Painting*, ed. Bernard S. Myers (1979)
*Encyclopedia of World Art* (1959–83)
*The McGraw-Hill Dictionary of Art*, ed. Bernard S. Myers (1969)
*The New College Encyclopedia of Music*, by Jack A. Westrup and
    F. L. Harrison (1976)
*The New Grove Dictionary of Music and Musicians*, ed. Stanley Sadie
    (1980)
*The New Harvard Dictionary of Music*, ed. Don Randel (1986)
*The New Oxford Companion to Music*, ed. Dennis Arnold (1983)
*The New Oxford History of Music*, by J. A. Westrup et al. (1986–   )
*The Oxford Companion to Art*, ed. Harold Osborne (1970)
*The Oxford Dictionary of Music*, by Michael Kennedy (1985)
*Phaidon Dictionary of Twentieth-Century Art* (1977)
*The Praeger Encyclopedia of Art* (1971)

## Business and Economics

*Dictionary of Economics and Business*, ed. Erwin E. Nemmers (1978)
*Encyclopedia of Banking and Finance*, ed. Glen G. Munn (1983)
*The Encyclopedia of Management*, ed. Carl Heyel (1982)
*The McGraw-Hill Dictionary of Modern Economics*, ed. Douglas Greenwald
    (1984)

## Drama and Film

*International Encyclopedia of the Film* (1972)
*McGraw-Hill Encyclopedia of World Drama*, ed. Stanley Hochman (1984)
*Modern World Drama: An Encyclopedia*, by Myron Matlaw (1972)
*The New York Times Directory of the Theater* (1973)
*New York Times Film Reviews, 1913–1974*

*The Oxford Companion to American Theatre*, by Gerald Bordman (1984)
*The Oxford Companion to the Theatre*, ed. Phyllis Hartnoll (1983)
*The World Encyclopedia of the Film*, ed. Tim Cawkwell and John Milton
    Smith (1972)

## Education

*A Dictionary of Education*, by Derek Rowntree (1982)
*The Encyclopedia of Education*, ed. Lee C. Deighton (1971)
*International Encyclopedia of Higher Education*, ed. Asa K. Knowles (1977)
*Second Handbook of Research on Teaching*, ed. R. M. W. Travers (1973)
*The Teacher's Handbook*, ed. Dwight W. Allen and Eli Seifman (1971)

## Folklore and Mythology

*The Encyclopedia of Classical Mythology*, by A. Van Aken (1965)
*Funk & Wagnalls Standard Dictionary of Folk-lore, Mythology and Legend*
    (1949–50)
*Larousse World Mythology* (1965)
*Motif-Index of Folk-Literature*, by Stith Thompson (1966)
*The Study of American Folklore*, by Jan Harold Brunvand (1987)

## History

*Dictionary of American History*, ed. James Truslow Adams (1976–78)
*Encyclopedia of American History*, by Richard B. Morris and Jeffrey B.
    Morris (1982)
*An Encyclopedia of World History*, ed. William L. Langer (1972)
*Harper Encyclopedia of the Modern World*, ed. Richard B. Morris and
    Graham W. Irwin (1970)
*Harvard Guide to American History*, ed. Frank Freidel and Richard K.
    Showman (1974)
*Larousse Encyclopedia of Ancient and Medieval History* (1963)
*Larousse Encyclopedia of Modern History*, ed. Marcel Dunan (1972)
*The Oxford Companion to American History*, by Thomas H. Johnson (1966)
*The Oxford History of the Classical World*, ed. John Boardman et al. (1986)

**libr
28d**

## Literature

*Black American Literature*, by Roger Whitlow (1976)
*The Cambridge Guide to English Literature*, by Michael Stapleton (1983)
*Cassell's Encyclopedia of World Literature*, ed. John Buchanan-Brown (1973)

*Columbia Dictionary of Modern European Literature*, ed. Jean-Albert Bede
and William Edgerton (1980)
*A Handbook to Literature*, by C. Hugh Holman (1986)
*Harvard Guide to Contemporary American Writing*, ed. Daniel Hoffman
(1979)
*A Literary History of England*, by Albert C. Baugh (1967)
*Literary History of the United States*, by Robert E. Spiller et al. (1974)
*Macmillan Guide to World Literature*, by Martin Seymour-Smith (1985)
*The Oxford Companion to American Literature*, by James D. Hart (1983)
*The Oxford Companion to Canadian Literature*, by William Toye (1983)
*The Oxford Companion to Classical Literature*, by Paul Harvey (1937)
*The Oxford Companion to English Literature*, by Margaret Drabble (1985)

## Philosophy and Religion

*The Catholic Encyclopedia*, ed. Robert Broderick (1976)
*Dictionary of Non-Christian Religions*, by Geoffrey Parrinder (1981)
*Dictionary of the Bible*, by John L. McKenzie (1965)
*Encyclopedia Judaica* (1972)
*The Encyclopedia of Philosophy*, ed. Paul Edwards (1972–   )
*Handbook of Denominations in the United States*, by Frank S. Mead (1980)
*A History of Philosophy*, by Frederick C. Copleston (1947–75)
*The Oxford Dictionary of the Christian Church*, by F. L. Cross and
Elizabeth A. Livingstone (1983)
*Philosophy of Religion*, by John Hick (1983)
*A Reader's Guide to the Great Religions*, by Charles J. Adams (1977)

## Science and Technology

*Cambridge Encyclopedia of Astronomy* (1977)
*Challinor's Dictionary of Geology*, ed. Antony Wyatt (1986)
*Dictionary of Electronics*, by S. W. Amos (1982)
*The Encyclopedia of Chemistry*, ed. Clifford A. Hampel and Gessner G.
Hawley (1973)
*Encyclopedia of Computers and Data Processing* (1978–   )
*Encyclopedia of Environmental Science and Engineering* (1983)
*Encyclopedia of Physics*, ed. Robert M. Besancon (1985)
*The Encyclopedia of the Biological Sciences*, ed. Peter Gray (1981)
*Grzimek's Animal Life Encyclopedia*, ed. Bernhard Grzimek (1972–75)
*Grzimek's Encyclopedia of Ecology*, ed. Bernhard Grzimek (1976)
*McGraw-Hill Encyclopedia of Science and Technology* (1982)
*The Universal Encyclopedia of Mathematics* (1964)
*Van Nostrand's Scientific Encyclopedia*, ed. Douglas M. Considine (1976)

## Social and Political Science

*Dictionary of American Politics*, ed. Edward C. Smith and Arnold J. Zurcher (1968)

*The Dictionary of Political Analysis*, by Jack C. Plano et al. (1982)

*Dictionary of Psychology and Related Fields*, by Hugo G. Beigel (1971)

*A Dictionary of the Social Sciences*, by Hugo F. Reading (1977)

*Encyclopedia of American Foreign Policy*, ed. Alex DeConde (1978)

*Encyclopedia of Black America*, ed. W. Augustus Low and Virgil A. Clift (1986)

*The Encyclopedia of Human Behavior*, ed. Robert M. Goldenson (1970)

*Encyclopedia of Psychology*, ed. Raymond J. Corsini (1984)

*The Encyclopedia of Sociology* (1981)

*Encyclopedia of the Third World*, by George Thomas Kurian (1982)

*Handbook of International Data on Women*, by Elise Boulding et al. (1976)

*International Encyclopedia of the Social Sciences*, ed. David L. Sills (1977–79)

*Reference Encyclopedia of the American Indian*, ed. Barry T. Klein (1978)

*Worldmark Encyclopedia of the Nations* (1984)

When you need to chase down a particular fact—the population of a country, an event in someone's life, the origin of an important term, the source of a quotation, and so forth—you can go to one of the following sources.

## General Encyclopedias

An up-to-date edition of a general encyclopedia can provide initial orientation to a field or problem and a limited amount of bibliographic guidance. See especially:

*Encyclopaedia Britannica* (1985)

*Encyclopedia Americana* (revised annually)

*The New Columbia Encyclopedia* (1975)

*The Random House Encyclopedia* (1977)

libr
**28d**

## Almanacs, Yearbooks, and Compilations of Facts

These volumes can be consulted for miscellaneous facts and statistics:

*The Americana Annual* (1923–   )

*Britannica Book of the Year* (1938–   )

*CBS News Almanac* (1976–   )

*Facts on File* (1940–  )
*Information Please Almanac* (1947–  )
*The Statesman's Year-Book* (1864–  )
*Statistical Abstract of the United States* (1878–  )
*The World Almanac and Book of Facts* (1868–  )
*Year Book of World Affairs* (1947–  )

## Atlases

You can locate geographical knowledge in:

*The National Atlas of the United States of America,* ed. Arch C. Gerlach
(1970)
*National Geographic Atlas of the World* (1981)
*The New Atlas of the Universe,* by Patrick Moore (1984)
*The Times Atlas of the World* (1985)
*Webster's New Geographical Dictionary* (1980)

## Specialized Dictionaries

Dictionaries for everyday reference are discussed in 8a, p. 202. For research into the origins and changing meaning of words, see:

*A Comprehensive Etymological Dictionary of the English Language,* by
Ernest Klein (1971)
*A Dictionary of Slang and Unconventional English,* by Eric Partridge (1984)
*New Dictionary of American Slang,* ed. Robert L. Chapman (1986)
*A New English Dictionary on Historical Principles* (more commonly known
as *The Oxford English Dictionary*) (1888–1985)
*Webster's New Dictionary of Synonyms* (1978)
*Webster's Third New International Dictionary of the English Language* (1976)

## Biography

Names can be identified and lives studied in the following:

**libr
28d**

*Chambers Biographical Dictionary* (1986)
*Contemporary Authors* (1962–  )
*Current Biography* (1940–  )
*Dictionary of American Biography* (1918–  )
*Dictionary of Literary Biography* (1978–  )
*Dictionary of National Biography* [British], ed. Leslie Stephen and Sidney
Lee (1885–1963)

*Dictionary of Scientific Biography*, ed. Charles Coulston Gillispie (1970–80)
*The McGraw-Hill Encyclopedia of World Biography* (1973)
*Notable American Women, 1607–1950*, ed. Edward T. James and Janet Wilson James (1971–  )
*Notable American Women: The Modern Period*, ed. Barbara Sicherman et al. (1980)
*Webster's Biographical Dictionary* (1980)
*Who's Who* [British] (1849–  )
*Who's Who in America* (1889–  )
*Who's Who in the World* (1976–  )

## Quotations

Your best hope of tracking down an unattributed quotation lies with one of these sourcebooks:

*Dictionary of Quotations*, by Bergen Evans (1968)
*Familiar Quotations*, by John Bartlett and E. M. Beck (1980)
*The Home Book of American Quotations*, by Bruce Bohle (1967)
*The Oxford Dictionary of Quotations* (1979)

---

### EXERCISES

11. For each of the following proposed topics, list two or three sources (a dictionary, the subject catalog, etc.) that you would *begin* by consulting:

    A. The reception of Saul Bellow's 1987 novel *More Die of Heartbreak*.
    B. Should abortions be automatically granted on demand?
    C. Pickett's Charge.
    D. The wave of terrorism in France in 1986.
    E. Recent advances in semiconductor memory systems for computers.
    F. The development of logical positivism as a philosophical school.
    G. Beethoven's reputation today.
    H. Beethoven's childhood.
    I. The origin and evolving meaning of the word *wit* in English.
    J. Who wrote the line "The proper study of mankind is man"?

    **libr**
    **28d**

12. Which of the following books are still in print? Which ones are available in paperbound editions? (See p. 487.)

    A. Milan Kundera, *The Book of Laughter and Forgetting*
    B. Oliver Perry Medsger, *Edible Wild Plants*
    C. James Herndon, *Sorrowless Times: A Narrative*

D. Maria Lemnis and Henryk Vitry, *Old Polish Traditions in the Kitchen and at the Table*

E. Flannery O'Connor, *The Habit of Being*

13. Read one article in a general encyclopedia (p. 491) encompassing the problem treated in your sample research project (Exercise 3 and/or Exercise 7), and look up the same problem in any two of the reference sources listed on pages 488–491. Submit two or three paragraphs identifying the three sources you used and indicating what you have learned from them.

14. Check several biographical sources (pp. 492–493) for information about any one prominent figure in the field of knowledge that includes your sample research project. Submit a paragraph or two identifying the sources you checked and comparing their usefulness in this one instance.

## 28e   Take Full and Careful Notes from Your Reading.

A typical library book or journal will be available to you for a few hours or days or weeks, depending on its importance to other borrowers. When you try to get it again, you may find that it is on loan to someone else, or has been sent to the bindery or even misplaced or stolen. Thus you have to be sure to get everything you need from the work on your first try, and your notes must be clear and full enough to be your direct source when you write. Although it is always a good idea to keep the work before you and recheck it for accurate quotation and fair summary, you should assume that this will not be possible. Your notes should contain all the information necessary for full citations (Chapter 29), and you should make sure your notes are error-free before you let the book or article out of your hands.

**libr 28e**

### Bibliography Cards versus Content Cards

The notes you take from your reading will serve two distinct purposes: to keep an accurate list of the works you have consulted and to record key information you have found in them. Sooner or later most researchers understand that these purposes demand different kinds of notecards. To compile a *bibliography* or list of works consulted, one card per entry is ideal; but *content* (or informational) notes may run through many cards.

To avoid confusion use $3'' \times 5''$ bibliography cards to identify the works you have consulted, and larger (usually $4'' \times 6''$) content cards for quotations, summaries, and miscellaneous comments. Or, if you prefer, use cards of different colors.

You may prefer to jot down ideas on sheets of paper rather than on cards (3d, p. 65). For quoting and summarizing published statements, however, cards are easier to keep track of and to rearrange as the organization of your essay takes shape.

Observe the following sample cards. (Note that once a separate bibliography card has been prepared, the researcher can give the briefest of references on a content card: *Kolata, p. 1216.*

**BIBLIOGRAPHY CARD:**

AQ 53
Ser 2
V. 215

Kolata, Gina
"Students Discover Computer
Threat." Science 215 (1982):
1216-17.
(Tells how Berkeley undergrads
broke into university computer
system, using a "simple but
powerful" masquerading device.
Points to general vulnerability
of user entry codes.)

**CONTENT CARD:**

Kolata, p. 1216                          helplessness
                                          of authorities

" 'We always wondered what
would happen if someone found
a way to compromise large systems
of computers. Now someone has
and we don't know what to do
about it,' says Donn Parker of
SRI."
       Reminder: read Parker's book!

## Form of Notecards

The more systematic you are about note taking, the less likely you will be
to misquote, summarize unfairly, or supply inaccurate references. Here
are some tips about form:

1. Use cards of one uniform size or color for all your bibliography
   notes, and cards or sheets of another uniform size or color for all
   your content notes. This will make for easy filing and reshuffling.

2. Write in ink. Penciled notes smudge when pressed against other
   notes.

3. Never put entries from different sources on one card or page, and
   never write on the reverse side. Otherwise you will probably lose
   track of some of your work.

4. Include the call number of any book or magazine you have found
   in the library. You never know when you may want to retrieve it
   for another look.

5. Quote exactly, including the punctuation marks in the original, and check each quotation as soon as you have copied it.

6. Use quotation marks only when you are actually quoting verbatim, and check to see that the marks begin and end exactly where they should. Use the dots known as ellipses (20m, p. 384) to indicate where you have skipped some material within a quotation.

7. Be attentive to oddities of spelling and punctuation in quoted material. If, for instance, the original text omits a comma that you would have included, you can place a bracketed [*sic*], meaning *this is the way I found it,* at the questionable point in your notes; this will remind you not to improve the quotation illegitimately when reproducing it in your essay. But do not retain the [*sic*] in your paper unless it refers to an obvious blunder.

8. Supply page references for all quotations, paraphrases, and summaries.

9. Do not allow any ambiguities in your system of abbreviations. If two of your symbols mean the same thing, change one of them.

10. Distinguish between your own comments and those of the text you are summarizing. Slashes, brackets, or your initials can be used as signals that the following remarks are yours, not those of the author.

11. When copying a passage that runs from one page to another, mark where the first page ends: *"One other point might be noted, in view of the White / House concern over the military implications of lasers."* If you finally quote only a portion of the excerpt in your paper, you will want to know where it ended in the original.

12. Use a portion of the card or page to evaluate the material and to remind yourself of possibilities for further study. You might say, for example, *This looks useless—but reconsider chapter 13 if discussing astrology.*

13. Leave some space in the margin or at the top for an indexing symbol, so that you can easily keep related items together.

*With a Word Processor:* If a note contains a long quotation, you may find it worthwhile to store the note as a document, first carefully checking for accuracy of wording, punctuation, and citation. Without retyping, you can transfer the quotation directly into your first draft— and so on indefinitely until you have arrived at your final copy. This procedure will save labor and, more important, ensure that you won't introduce errors in the process of retranscribing the passage several times.

---

EXERCISE

15. Using any books or articles you have handy, submit two sample bibliography cards and two content notes. One of your notes should quote a passage; the other should summarize that same passage. Be sure your two bibliography cards give full and exact citations.

---

## 28f  Summarize or Paraphrase Pertinent Material That You Are Not Quoting.

The most accurate way of noting what you have read is to quote it exactly (Chapter 20) or to photocopy it. But in your notes you can only quote a fraction of the important material you have seen, and once you have photocopied many pages, you still face the task of drawing from them what is essential to your own purpose. Here is where *summary,* or brief restatement, and *paraphrase,* or more ample restatement, can come to your aid.

A **summary** of a text concisely presents the author's key ideas, omitting examples and descriptive detail. Insofar as possible you should use your own language, though some repetition of the author's terms may be inevitable. The knack of efficient summary is to strip away everything but the essential content.

### ORIGINAL TEXT:

The modern world began on 29 May 1919 when photographs of a solar eclipse, taken on the island of Principe off West Africa and at Sobral in Brazil, confirmed the truth of a new theory of the universe. It had been apparent for half a century that the Newtonian cosmology, based upon the straight lines of Euclidean geometry and Galileo's notions of absolute time, was in need of serious modification. It had stood for more than two hundred years. It was the framework within which the European Enlightenment, the Industrial Revolution, and the vast expansion of human knowledge, freedom and prosperity which characterized the nineteenth century, had taken place. But increasingly powerful telescopes were revealing anomalies. In particular, the motions of the planet Mercury deviated by forty-three seconds of arc a century from its predictable behaviour under Newtonian laws of physics. Why?

In 1905, a twenty-six-year-old German Jew, Albert Einstein, then working in the Swiss patent office in Berne, had published a paper, "On the electrodynamics of moving bodies," which became known as the Special Theory of Relativity. Einstein's observations on the way in which, in certain circumstances, lengths appeared to contract and clocks to slow down, are analogous to the effects of perspective in painting. In fact the discovery that space and

time are relative rather than absolute is comparable, in its effect on our perception of the world, to the first use of perspective in art, which occurred in
Greece in the two decades c. 500–480 B.C.

The originality of Einstein, amounting to a form of genius, and the curious elegance of his lines of argument, which colleagues compared to a kind of
art, aroused growing, world-wide interest. In 1907 he published a demonstration that all mass has energy, encapsulated in the equation $E=mc^2$, which a
later age saw as the starting point in the race for the A-bomb. Not even the
onset of the European war prevented scientists from following his quest for an
all-embracing General Theory of Relativity which would cover gravitational
fields and provide a comprehensive revision of Newtonian physics. In 1915
news reached London that he had done it. The following spring, as the British
were preparing their vast and catastrophic offensive on the Somme, the key
paper was smuggled through the Netherlands and reached Cambridge, where
it was received by Arthur Eddington, Professor of Astronomy and Secretary of
the Royal Astronomical Society.[1]

## SUMMARY:

Johnson dates "the modern world" from the solar eclipse observations of 29 May 1919, confirming Albert Einstein's General Theory of Relativity.  The world had already shown great
interest in Einstein after his 1905 publication of the Special Theory of Relativity, indicating that space and time are
relative categories, and his 1907 demonstration that mass
possesses energy ($E=mc^2$).  The General Theory, embracing
gravitational fields, completed the overthrow of Newtonian
physics, based in its turn on Euclid's geometry and Galileo's
absolute time.  The Einsteinian revolution affected our perception of the world as radically as the ancient Greek discovery of perspective in art.

A **paraphrase** is a running restatement of the original passage in your
own words. You should follow the order of the text and include important
detail. Since a paraphrase is closer to the original than a summary, you
must be careful not to repeat the author's wording without quotation marks;
that practice could lead you into accidental **plagiarism** (29a, p. 501), or
the presentation of someone else's words (or ideas) as your own.

**libr
28f**

## PARAPHRASE:

Johnson dates "the modern world" from the 29 May 1919 observations of a solar eclipse, taken in Africa and Brazil, confirming Einsteinian cosmology.  For fifty years the existing
Newtonian conception, based on Euclid's geometry and Galileo's absolute time, had been in trouble.  It had been the
set of assumptions behind the Enlightenment, the Industrial
Revolution, and nineteenth-century progress in learning,

democracy, and wealth, but it had been placed in doubt by
unaccountable telescopic data such as the deviated motion of
Mercury.

The new universe began to take shape with Albert Einstein's
1905 paper, "On the electrodynamics of moving bodies" (the
Special Theory of Relativity), showing how in some conditions
time and space are variable.  This discovery affected our way
of seeing the world as profoundly as did the Greeks' use of
artistic perspective in the fifth century B.C.

In 1907 Einstein proposed that all mass has energy ($E=mc^2$),
an idea later seen as having begun the race to develop the
atomic bomb.  Not even the outbreak of World War I could stop
scientists from participating in his search for a General
Theory of Relativity that would include gravitational fields.
Word of Einstein's having completed that theory arrived in
London in 1915, and in 1916, at the height of the awful war,
the key paper reached Arthur Eddington, Secretary of the
Royal Astronomical Society, in Cambridge.

---

## EXERCISE

16. Photocopy and submit a paragraph from a book or article that you expect
to be using in your research project. (If you have not yet settled on a project, choose any handy source.) Also submit (a) a summary, and (b) a
paraphrase, of that same paragraph.

---

## NOTE

[1] Paul Johnson, *Modern Times: The World from the Twenties to the
Eighties* (New York: Harper, 1983) 1–2.

# 29

# Documenting
# Sources

## 29a Learn Where Documentation Is Called For.

If you have done research for a paper, there are several reasons why you should cite your sources, using a standard form of documentation. You want credit for your efforts, and your documentation will help to show a reader that your ideas are consistent with facts and expert judgments that have already appeared in print. In some cases you may even want to pose a challenge to received views, showing that you know what those views are and where they can be found. And documentation is also a courtesy to your readers, who ought to be able to check your sources either to see if you have used them responsibly or to pursue an interest in your topic.

### Avoiding Plagiarism

A further reason for providing documentation is to avoid **plagiarism** — the serious ethical violation of presenting other people's words or ideas as your own. Plagiarism does tempt some student writers who feel too rushed or insecure to arrive at their own conclusions. Yet systematic dishonesty is only part of the problem. For every student who buys a term paper or copies a whole article without acknowledgment, there are dozens who indulge in "little" ethical lapses through thoughtlessness, haste, or a momentary sense of opportunity. Though nearly all of their work is original, they too are plagiarists – just as someone who robs a bank of $2.39 is a bank robber.

Unlike the robber, however, some plagiarists fail to realize what they have done wrong. Students who once copied encyclopedia articles to satisfy school assignments may never have learned the necessity of using quotation marks and citing sources. Others may think that by *paraphrasing* a quotation or *summarizing* an idea (28f, p. 498) – that is, by putting it into their own words – they have turned it into public property. Others acknowledge the source of their idea but fail to indicate that they have borrowed words as well as thoughts. And others plagiarize through sloppy note taking (28e, p. 494). Since their notes do not distinguish adequately between personal observations and the content of a consulted book or article, their papers repeat the oversight. And finally, some students blunder into plagiarism by failing to recognize the difference between fact and opinion. They may think, for example, that a famous critic's opinion about a piece of literature is so authoritative that it belongs to the realm of common facts – and so they paraphrase it without acknowledgment. All these errors are understandable, but none of them constitutes a good excuse for plagiarism.

## What to Acknowledge

Consider the following source and three ways that a student might be tempted to make use of it.

### SOURCE:

The joker in the European pack was Italy. For a time hopes were entertained of her as a force against Germany, but these disappeared under Mussolini. In 1935 Italy made a belated attempt to participate in the scramble for Africa by invading Ethiopia. It was clearly a breach of the covenant of the League of Nations for one of its members to attack another. France and Great Britain, as great powers, Mediterranean powers, and African colonial powers, were bound to take the lead against Italy at the league. But they did so feebly and half-heartedly because they did not want to alienate a possible ally against Germany. The result was the worst possible: the league failed to check aggression, Ethiopia lost her independence, and Italy was alienated after all.[1]

doc
29a

**VERSION A:**

```
Italy, one might say, was the joker in the European deck.
When she invaded Ethiopia, it was clearly a breach of the
covenant of the League of Nations; yet the efforts of England
and France to take the lead against her were feeble and half-
hearted.  It appears that those great powers had no wish to
alienate a possible ally against Hitler's rearmed Germany.
```

*Comment:* Clearly plagiarism. Though the facts cited are public knowledge, the stolen phrases are not. Note that the writer's interweaving of his
own words with the source does *not* make him innocent of plagiarism.

**VERSION B:**

```
Italy was the joker in the European deck.  Under Mussolini in
1935, she made a belated attempt to participate in the scram-
ble for Africa by invading Ethiopia.  As J. M. Roberts points
out, this violated the covenant of the League of Nations
(Roberts 845).  But France and Britain, not wanting to
alienate a possible ally against Germany, put up only feeble
and half-hearted opposition to the Ethiopian adventure.  The
outcome, as Roberts observes, was "the worst possible: the
league failed to check aggression, Ethiopia lost her inde-
pendence, and Italy was eliminated after all" (Roberts 845).
```

*Comment:* Still plagiarism. The two correct citations of Roberts serve as a
kind of alibi for the appropriating of other, unacknowledged phrases.

**VERSION C:**

```
Much has been written about German rearmament and militarism
in the period 1933-1939.  But Germany's dominance in Europe
was by no means a foregone conclusion.  The fact is that the
balance of power might have been tipped against Hitler if one
or two things had turned out differently.  Take Italy's grav-
itation toward an alliance with Germany, for example.  That
alliance seemed so very far from inevitable that Britain and
France actually muted their criticism of the Ethiopian inva-
sion in the hope of remaining friends with Italy.  They
opposed the Italians in the League of Nations, as J. M. Rob-
erts observes, "feebly and half-heartedly because they did
not want to alienate a possible ally against Germany" (Rob-
erts 845).  Suppose Italy, France, and Britain had retained
a certain common interest.  Would Hitler have been able to
get away with his remarkable bluffing and bullying in the
later Thirties?
```

doc
**29a**

*Comment:* No plagiarism. The writer has been influenced by the public facts mentioned by Roberts, but he has not tried to pass off Roberts' conclusions as his own. The one clear borrowing is properly acknowledged.

There *is* room for disagreement about what to acknowledge; but precisely because this is so, you ought to make your documentation relatively ample. Provide citations for all direct quotations and paraphrases, borrowed ideas, and facts that do not belong to general knowledge.

Ask yourself, in doubtful cases, whether the point you are borrowing is an opinion or a fact. Opinions are by definition ideas that are not yet taken for granted; document them. As for facts, do not bother to document those that could be found in any commonly used source—for example, the fact that World War II ended in 1945. But give references for less accessible facts, such as the numbers of operational submarines that Nazi Germany still possessed at the end of the war. The harder it would be for readers to come across your fact through their own efforts, the more surely you need to document it.

If you are quoting, paraphrasing, or making an **allusion** to statements or literary passages that are not generally familiar, cite the source. A phrase from Lincoln's Gettysburg Address could get by without a citation, but a remark made in a presidential news conference could not.

| DO NOT DOCUMENT | DOCUMENT |
|---|---|
| the population of China | the Chinese balance of payments in 1987 |
| the existence of a disease syndrome called AIDS | a possible connection between AIDS and the virus that carries cat leukemia |
| the fact that Dickens visited America | the supposed effect of Dickens's American visit on his subsequently written novels |
| the fact that huge sums are wagered illegally on professional football games | an alleged "fix" of a certain football game |
| a line from a nursery rhyme | a line from a poem by Elizabeth Bishop |

doc
29a

## EXERCISE

1. If you intended to make the following statements in college papers, which ones would require documentation? What kind of documentation,

if any, would be appropriate in each case? Briefly explain each of your decisions.

   A. The "black hole" hypothesis, once generally dismissed, has been steadily gaining favor among astronomers in recent years.
   B. To be or not to be: that is indeed the central question for anyone who experiences suicidal feelings.
   C. There can be no denying the fact that industrialization and lung disease are inseparable twins; where you find the first, you are bound to find his grim brother.
   D. The oppressed people of the world must often feel like those who cried out, "How long, O Lord, holy and true, dost thou not judge and avenge our blood . . . ?"
   E. The first direct act of atomic warfare occurred at Hiroshima in August 1945.

## 29b   Observe the Differences between Reference List Form and Footnote/Endnote Form.

In your reading you will encounter many documentation styles, but every version will belong to one of two general forms. In **reference list** form, parenthetical citations in the main text are keyed to a list of "Works Cited" or "References" appearing at the end of the article, chapter, or book. In **footnote/endnote** form, raised numbers in the main text—usually at the ends of sentences—are keyed to notes appearing either at the foot of the page or after the end of the main text. Both forms allow for **supplementary notes** that make comments or mention further sources.

| REFERENCE LIST FORM | FOOTNOTE/ENDNOTE FORM |
| --- | --- |
| No note numbers are used (except for supplementary notes). | Raised numbers appear in text. |
| No notes are used to cite works. | Notes appearing at foot of page or at end of text give citations corresponding to note numbers in text. |
| All references are made through parenthetical citations within text. | Parenthetical citations within text are used only for "subsequent references" to frequently cited works. |

doc
**29b**

| REFERENCE LIST FORM | FOOTNOTE/ENDNOTE FORM |
|---|---|
| Supplementary notes, if any, appear after main text but before reference list. | Supplementary notes, if any, are integrated into footnotes or endnotes. |
| A reference list, identifying only works cited or consulted, appears at the end. The listed works match the parenthetical citations in the text. | A bibliography, identifying both works cited and works consulted, may appear after all the notes. |

Until recently, reference list form was generally prevalent in the sciences and footnote/endnote form in the humanities. Today, however, reference list form is gaining ground in the humanities as well. It is better suited to handling a large number of citations without distracting a reader from the main text. But since we remain in a transitional period and since some of your college instructors may prefer footnote/endnote form, you should know how both systems work. (Footnote/endnote form is discussed at 29e, p. 523.)

In some disciplines—for example, mathematics, chemistry, physics, biology, and engineering—the textual citations in reference list form are Arabic numerals that correspond to numbered items in the reference list. A numbered item may mention any number of works.

SENTENCE IN TEXT:

It appears that female choice is frequently involved in the evolution of the conspicuous acoustic signals that precede mating (2, 3).

ITEMS IN REFERENCE LIST:

doc
29b

2. L. Fairchild, *Science 212,* 950 (1981); R. D. Howard, *Evolution 32,* 850 (1978); M. J. Ryan, *Science 209,* 523 (1980).

3. R. D. Alexander, in *Insects, Science, and Society,* D. Pimentel, Ed. (Academic Press, New York, 1975), p. 35; P. D. Bell, *Can. J. Zool. 58,* 1861 (1980); W. Cade, *Science 190,* 1312 (1975); in *Sexual Selection and Reproductive Competition in Insects,* M. S. Blum and N. A. Blum, Eds. (Academic Press, New York, 1979); D. J. Campbell and E. Shipp, *Z. Tierpsychol. 51,* 260 (1979); A. V. Popov and V. F. Shuvalov, *J. Comp. Physiol. 119,* 111 (1977); S. M. Ulagaraj and T. J. Walker, *Science 182,* 1278 (1973).[2]

In other disciplines—for example, botany, geology, zoology, economics, psychology, and sociology—the parenthetical citations include the author(s) and date of publication (*Comstock & Fisher, 1975*), and the reference list is ordered alphabetically.

If you are writing for publication in any field, look at a relevant journal and adopt its conventions. You can also consult one of the following style manuals if it corresponds to your subject matter.

**BIOLOGY:**

Council of Biology Editors. Style Manual Committee. *Council of Biology Editors Style Manual: A Guide for Authors, Editors, and Publishers in the Biological Sciences.* 5th ed. Bethesda: Council of Biology Editors, 1983.

**CHEMISTRY:**

American Chemical Society. *Handbook for Authors of Papers in American Chemical Society Publications.* Washington: American Chemical Soc., 1978.

**GEOLOGY:**

United States Geological Survey. *Suggestions to Authors of the Reports of the United States Geological Survey.* 6th ed. Washington: GPO, 1978.

**LAW:**

Harvard Law Review Association. *A Uniform System of Citation.* Cambridge: Harvard UP.

**LINGUISTICS:**

Linguistic Society of America. *L.S.A. Bulletin,* Dec. issue, annually.

**MATHEMATICS:**

American Mathematical Society. *A Manual for Authors of Mathematical Papers.* 7th ed. Providence: American Mathematical Soc., 1980.

doc
**29b**

**MEDICINE:**

International Steering Committee of Medical Editors, "Uniform Requirements for Manuscripts Submitted to Biomedical Journals." *Annals of Internal Medicine* 90 (Jan. 1979): 95–99.

PHYSICS:

American Institute of Physics. Publication Board. *Style Manual for Guidance in the Preparation of Papers.* 3rd ed. New York: American Inst. of Physics, 1978.

## 29c    Learn How to Present a Reference List According to MLA or APA Style.

Traditionally, research papers written for composition courses have followed the footnote/endnote style of the Modern Language Association (29e, p. 523). The MLA, however, now endorses a reference list style, spelled out in Joseph Gibaldi and Walter S. Achtert, *MLA Handbook for Writers of Research Papers* (2nd ed., 1984). A similar approach has long prevailed in the social sciences, as typified by the specifications of the *Publication Manual of the American Psychological Association* (3rd ed., 1983). Your instructor may ask you to follow either MLA or APA style.

For an extended illustration of the MLA style, see the sample research paper on pages 532–540 below. To get a quick idea of the differences between MLA and APA reference lists, compare the MLA "Works Cited" on pages 539–540 with the APA "References" on pages 541–542.

Place your "Works Cited" or "References" after your main text and any supplementary notes (29f, p. 529). Start on a new page, consecutively numbered with the foregoing ones. Space your list like the relevant sample below (either p. 539 or p. 541).

### Order of Entries

Order your reference list alphabetically by authors' last names or, when no author appears, by the first significant word of the title (omitting *A, An,* and *The*). If the author is an institution—for example, SRI International— list it by the first letter in the corporate name's first significant word (in this case *S*).

If you are citing more than one work by a given author, note that:

1. In MLA style, follow the alphabetical order of that author's *titles.* In APA style, follow the order of that author's *dates of publication* (earliest first).

doc
29c

2. If a cited author is also the co-author of another cited work, put the single-author work first.

3. If a cited author has different co-authors for two cited works, place the works according to the alphabetical order of the co-authors' last names.

4. In APA style, if you are citing two works showing the same author(s) and date, follow the alphabetical order of the titles and add lower-case letters to the dates:

> Mauldin, C., & Valle, R. (1988a). Apple-Growing . . .
> Mauldin, C., & Valle, R. (1988b). Bee-Keeping . . .

### Order within Entries

In MLA style, present information (where relevant) within each entry in the following order:

| BOOKS | ARTICLES |
|---|---|
| 1. Author's name      APA | 1. Author's name      APA |
| 2. Title of part of book | 2. Title of article |
| 3. Title of book | 3. Name of periodical |
| 4. Name of editor, translator, or compiler | 4. Series number or name |
| 5. Edition used | 5. Volume number |
| 6. Number of volumes | 6. Date of publication |
| 7. Name of series | 7. Page numbers |
| 8. Place of publication, shortened name of publisher, date of publication | |
| 9. Page numbers | |

doc
29c

In APA style, modify this order as indicated by the arrows.

Here are sample entries covering typical kinds of works that might appear in your reference list.

## Books

### A BOOK BY A SINGLE AUTHOR:

**MLA**    Langbaum, Robert. The Modern Spirit: Essays on the
Continuity of Nineteenth- and Twentieth-Century
Literature. New York: Oxford UP, 1970.

**APA**    Langbaum, R. (1970). The modern spirit: Essays on the
continuity of nineteenth- and twentieth-century
literature. New York: Oxford University Press.

> Note the different conventions for capitalization of titles.
> Observe also that APA leaves one space, not two, after
> a period.

### TWO OR MORE BOOKS BY THE SAME AUTHOR:

**MLA**    Michaels, Leonard. I Would Have Saved Them If I
Could. New York: Farrar, 1975.
---. The Men's Club. New York: Farrar, 1981.

**APA**    Michaels, L. (1975). I would have saved them if I
could. New York: Farrar, Straus & Giroux.
Michaels, L. (1981). The men's club. New York: Farrar,
Straus & Giroux.

### A BOOK BY TWO AUTHORS:

**MLA**    Liehm, Mira, and Antonin J. Liehm. The Most Important
Art: Soviet and Eastern European Film after 1945.
Berkeley: U of California P, 1977.

**APA**    Liehm, M., & Liehm, A. J. (1977). The most important
art: Soviet and eastern European film after 1945.
Berkeley: University of California Press.

## A BOOK BY THREE AUTHORS:

**MLA**    Burns, James MacGregor, J. W. Peltason, and Thomas E.

Cronin. Government by the People. 12th ed.

Englewood Cliffs: Prentice-Hall, 1984.

**APA**    Burns, J. M., Peltason, J. W., & Cronin, T. E. (1984).

Government by the people. (12th ed.). Englewood

Cliffs, NJ: Prentice-Hall.

## A BOOK BY MORE THAN THREE AUTHORS:

**MLA**    Lauer, Janice, M., et al. Four Worlds of Writing.

2nd ed. New York: Harper, 1985.

**APA**    Lauer, J. M., Montague, G., Lunsford, A., & Emig, J.

(1985). Four worlds of writing. (2nd ed.). New

York: Harper & Row.

> Observe that APA requires that all authors, no matter how many, be named. Compare the MLA's preference for *et al.* (Latin 'and others').

## A BOOK BY A CORPORATE AUTHOR:

**MLA**    American Society of Hospital Pharmacists. Consumer

Drug Digest. New York: Facts on File, 1982.

**APA**    American Society of Hospital Pharmacists. (1982). Con-

sumer drug digest. New York: Facts on File.

## AN ANONYMOUS BOOK:

**MLA**    Chicago Manual of Style. 13th ed. Chicago: U of Chi-

cago P, 1982.

**APA**    Chicago manual of style. (1982). (13th ed.). Chicago:

University of Chicago Press.

doc
**29c**

## A WORK IN AN ANTHOLOGY:

**MLA**    Herbert, George. "The Pulley." The Bedford Introduc-

tion to Literature. Ed. Michael Meyer. New

York: St. Martin's, 1987: 790-91.

**APA**    Herbert, G. (1987). The pulley. In M. Meyer (Ed.), The

Bedford introduction to literature (pp. 790-791).

New York: St. Martin's.

If you are citing more than one work from an anthology, provide an entry for the anthology itself, and cite it along with the references to the separate works, as follows.

### THE ANTHOLOGY ITSELF:

**MLA**    Meyer, Michael, ed. The Bedford Introduction to Lit-

erature. New York: St. Martin's, 1987.

**APA**    Meyer, M. (Ed.). (1987). The Bedford introduction to

literature. New York: St. Martin's.

### A WORK FROM A COLLECTION BY ONE AUTHOR:

**MLA**    Mill, John Stuart. On Liberty. Three Essays: On Lib-

erty, Representative Government, The Subjection

of Women. New York: Oxford UP, 1975. 1-141.

**APA**    Mill, J. S. (1975). On liberty. In Three essays: On

liberty, Representative government, The subjection

of women (pp. 1-141). New York: Oxford University

Press. (Original work published 1859)

### THE EDITED WORK OF AN AUTHOR:

**MLA**    Plato. The Collected Dialogues of Plato: Including

the Letters. Ed. Edith Hamilton and Huntington

Cairns. Princeton: Princeton UP, 1961.

APA Plato. (1961). <u>The collected dialogues of Plato: In-</u>
<u>cluding the letters</u>. (E. Hamilton & H. Cairns,
Eds.). Princeton: Princeton University Press.

## A BOOK EDITED BY TWO OR THREE PEOPLE:

MLA White, George Abbott, and Charles Newman, eds. <u>Lit-</u>
<u>erature in Revolution</u>. New York: Holt, 1972.

APA White, G. A., & Newman, C. (Eds.). (1972). <u>Literature</u>
<u>in revolution</u>. New York: Holt.

## A BOOK EDITED BY MORE THAN THREE PEOPLE:

MLA Kermode, Frank, et al., eds. <u>The Oxford Anthology of</u>
<u>English Literature</u>. 2 vols. New York: Oxford
UP, 1973.

APA Kermode, F., Hollander, J., Bloom, H., Price, M.,
Trapp, J. B., & Trilling, L. (Eds.). 1973. <u>The</u>
<u>Oxford anthology of English literature</u>. (Vols.
1-2). New York: Oxford University Press.

## A TRANSLATION:

MLA Kundera, Milan. <u>The Book of Laughter and Forgetting</u>.
Trans. Michael Henry Heim. New York: Knopf,
1981.

APA Kundera, M. (1981). <u>The book of laughter and forget-</u>
<u>ting</u>. (M. H. Heim, Trans.). New York: Knopf.
(Original work published 1978)

## A REPUBLISHED BOOK:

MLA Conroy, Frank. <u>Stop-time</u>. 1967. New York: Penguin,
1977.

APA Conroy, F. (1977). <u>Stop-time</u>. New York: Penguin.
(Original work published 1967)

doc
29c

## Articles in Journals, Magazines, and Newspapers

### AN ARTICLE IN A JOURNAL WITH CONTINUOUS PAGINATION:

**MLA**    Cooper, Arnold M. "Psychoanalysis at One Hundred: Beginnings of Maturity." Journal of the American
Psychoanalytic Association 32 (1984): 245-67.

**APA**    Cooper, A. M. (1984). Psychoanalysis at one hundred:
Beginnings of maturity. Journal of the American
Psychoanalytic Association, 32, 245-267.

### AN ARTICLE IN A JOURNAL THAT DOES NOT IDENTIFY THE EXACT DATE OF EACH ISSUE:

**MLA**    Wheeler, Richard P. "Poetry and Fantasy in Shakespeare's Sonnets 88-96." Literature and Psychology 22.3 (1972): 151-62.

**APA**    Wheeler, R. P. (1972). Poetry and fantasy in Shakespeare's sonnets 88-96. Literature and Psychology,
22 (3), 151-162.

### AN ARTICLE IN A MAGAZINE WITH SEPARATE PAGINATION FOR EACH ISSUE:

**MLA**    Begiebing, Robert. "Twelfth Round: An Interview with
Norman Mailer." Harvard Magazine Mar.-Apr. 1983:
40-50.

**APA**    Begiebing, R. (1983, March-April). Twelfth round: An
interview with Norman Mailer. Harvard Magazine, pp.
40-50.

### A REVIEW

**MLA**    Schwendener, Peter. Rev. of Red and Hot: The Fate of
Jazz in the Soviet Union, 1917-1980, by S. Frederick Starr. American Scholar 53 (1984): 429-30.

**doc
29c**

**APA**    Schwendener, P. (1984). [Review of Red and hot: The

fate of jazz in the Soviet Union]. American

Scholar, 53, 429-430.

### AN UNSIGNED MAGAZINE ARTICLE:

**MLA**    "Drugs That Don't Work." New Republic 29 Jan. 1972:

12-13.

**APA**    Drugs that don't work. (1972, January 29). New

Republic, pp. 12-13.

### A SIGNED NEWSPAPER ARTICLE:

**MLA**    Nelson, Jack, and Michael Wines.    "North Reportedly

Shredded Papers." San Francisco Chronicle

27 Nov. 1986, five-star ed.: 1+.

**APA**    Nelson, J., & Wines, M. (1986, November 27). North

reportedly shredded papers. San Francisco Chroni-

cle, pp. 1, 28.

### AN UNSIGNED NEWSPAPER ARTICLE OR EDITORIAL:

**MLA**    "Insider Trading: A Matter of Trust." New York Times

23 Nov. 1986, national ed.: E5.

**APA**    Insider trading: A matter of trust. (1986, Novem-

ber 23). New York Times, sec. E, p. 5.

## Other Written Works

### AN ENCYCLOPEDIA ENTRY:

**MLA**    L[ustig], L[awrence] K.    "Alluvial Fans." Encyclo-

paedia Britannica: Macropaedia. 1985.

> The author's initials appear at the end of the entry;
> they are identified elsewhere. Note that volume and
> page numbers are unnecessary when items appear in

**doc
29c**

alphabetical order. But since the *Britannica* from 1974 onward has three sets of contents, the note should indicate which one is intended—in this case the "Macropaedia."

**APA**    L[ustig], L. K. (1985). Alluvial fans. Encyclopaedia
           Britannica: Macropaedia.

### A PAMPHLET OR MANUAL:

**MLA**    Kater, David A.  Epson FX-80 Printer User's Manual.
           Torrance, CA: Epson, 1983.

**APA**    Kater, D. A. (1983). Epson FX-80 printer user's man-
           ual. Torrance, CA: Epson.

### A DISSERTATION:

**MLA**    Boudin, Henry Morton.  "The Ripple Effect in Classroom
           Management."  Diss.  U of Michigan, 1970.

**APA**    Boudin, H. M. (1970). The ripple effect in classroom
           management. Unpublished doctoral dissertation,
           University of Michigan, Ann Arbor.

### A PUBLIC DOCUMENT:

**MLA**    United States Dept. of Agriculture.  "Shipments and
           Unloads of Certain Fruits and Vegetables, 1918-
           1923."  Statistical Bulletin 7 (Apr. 1925).

**APA**    United States Dept. of Agriculture. (1925, April).
           Shipments and unloads of certain fruits and vege-
           tables, 1918-1923. Statistical Bulletin, 7.

### A PUBLISHED LETTER:

**MLA**    Allen, Steve.  Letter.  Popular Photography June 1978:
           4.

**doc 29c**

**APA**   Allen, S. (1978, June). [Letter to the editor]. <u>Popu-</u>
<u>lar Photography</u>, p. 4.

### AN UNPUBLISHED LETTER:

**MLA**   Graff, Gerald. Letter to the author. 18 Aug. 1984.

**APA**   Graff, G. (1984, August 18). [Letter to the author].

## Nonwritten Works

### A THEATRICAL PERFORMANCE:

**MLA**   <u>A Moon for the Misbegotten</u>. By Eugene O'Neill.   Dir.
David Leveaux.   With Kate Nelligan, Ian Bannen,
and Jerome Kilty.   Cort Theatre, New York.
23 June 1984.

**APA**   Leveaux, D. (Director). (1984, June 23). <u>A moon for</u>
<u>the misbegotten</u> [Play]. Cort Theatre, New York
City.

### A FILM:

**MLA**   <u>The Color of Money</u>.   Dir. Martin Scorsese.   With Paul
Newman and Tom Cruise.   Touchstone/Silver Screen,
1986.

**APA**   Scorsese, M. (Director). (1986). <u>The color of money</u>.
Touchstone/Silver Screen.

### A RADIO OR TELEVISION PROGRAM:

doc
**29c**

**MLA**   <u>The World's Worst Air Crash</u>.   Narr. Bill Moyers.   PBS,
Los Angeles.   27 July 1979.

**APA**   Moyers, B. (1979, July 27). <u>The world's worst air</u>
<u>crash</u>. Los Angeles: PBS.

## A RECORDING:

**MLA**    Beethoven, Ludwig van. Symphony no. 8 in F, op. 93.

Cond. Pierre Monteux. Vienna Philharmonic Orch.

Decca, STS 15238, 1964.

> MLA requires that names of musical works be underlined except when (as here) the work is identified by its form, number, and key rather than by a title.

**APA**    [No form specified]

## A LECTURE:

**MLA**    Hirsch, E. D., Jr. "Frontiers of Critical Theory."

Wyoming Conference on Freshman and Sophomore English, U of Wyoming. Laramie, 9 July 1979.

**APA**    Hirsch, E. D., Jr. (1979, July). Frontiers of critical

theory. Paper presented at the Wyoming Conference

on Freshman and Sophomore English, University of

Wyoming, Laramie.

> Note that APA omits the precise day of a lecture.

## AN INTERVIEW:

**MLA**    Collier, Peter, and David Horowitz. Personal interview. 5 Nov. 1987.

**APA**    Collier, P., & Horowitz, D. (1987, November 5).
[Interview with the author].

**doc 29c**

## COMPUTER SOFTWARE:

**MLA**    The Benchmark. Computer Software. Metasoft, 1984.
IBM DOS, Version 4.0, disk.

**APA**    The benchmark. (1984). [Computer program]. Metasoft,
IBM DOS, Version 4.0.

2. Submit a sample list of "Works Cited" or "References" containing five items, preferably from your actual research project. Choose a different kind of source (edited book, translation, journal article, etc.) for each entry. Make use of either MLA or APA style, according to your instructor's preference.

## 29d  Learn How to Present Parenthetical Citations according to either MLA or APA Style.

The idea behind all parenthetical citations is to give the minimum of information that will send a reader to the correct item in the reference list (29c) and, where applicable, to the cited portion of the work. As you might expect, MLA citations rely on authors' *names* and, if necessary for clarity, the *titles* of their works, whereas APA citations rely on *names* and *dates*.

### MLA Parenthetical Citations

If you are referring to a whole work and if the author's name appears in your sentence, MLA does not require you to supply any further information:

- Cooper's presidential address struck a gloomy note.

But the same sentence would require a parenthetical page reference — without repeating the author's name — if you had in mind only part of the item:

- Cooper's presidential address struck a gloomy note (249–52).

Where the author's name does not appear in your sentence, supply it in the citation:

- One prominent spokesman has expressed serious doubt about the current health of the profession (Cooper 249–52).

doc
**29d**

For an extracted quotation (20h, p. 380), place your end-punctuation before rather than after the parenthesis.

The following sample MLA citations cover a variety of features in the cited works:

## A MULTIVOLUME WORK:

- Sidney shows a healthy distrust of what he calls, in "An Apology for Poetry," "that honey-flowing matron Eloquence" (Abrams et al. 1:503).

## A WORK LISTED BY TITLE:

- The name of our planet is usually capitalized only when other bodies in the Solar System are also named (*Chicago Manual* 7.113).

   Note the shortened title; compare page 511. No edition number is needed, since the reference list contains only one entry under this name. Note, too, the citing of a section rather than a page of a reference work thus ordered.

## A WORK BY A CORPORATE AUTHOR:

- The American Society of Hospital Pharmacists considers methicillin "particularly useful" in treating hospital-acquired infections (89).

   "Corporate" names are usually too long to be inserted into a parenthetical citation without distracting the reader. Make an effort to get the name into the main part of your sentence. Here the remark about methicillin is attributed to page 89 of the book in the reference list named under *American Society of Hospital Pharmacists.*

## TWO OR MORE WORKS BY THE SAME AUTHOR:

- "I feel you're feeling anger," says Kramer after his wife has clobbered him with an iron pot (Michaels, *Men's Club* 172).

   The title of the work is included in the citation when two or more works by the same author appear in the reference list (p. 510).

doc
29d

## AN INDIRECT SOURCE:

- Writing in *Temps Modernes* in 1957, Woroszylski expressed surprise at "how much political nonsense we allowed ourselves to be talked into" (qtd. in Liehm and Liehm 116).

   If you have no access to the original text, use *qtd. in* to show that your source for the quotation is another work.

A CLASSIC VERSE PLAY OR POEM:

- "I prithee, daughter," begs Lear, "do not make me mad" (II.iv.212).

  Cite acts, scenes, and lines instead of pages. The capital and lower-case Roman numerals here help to distinguish the act and scene from the line number; however, *2.4.212* would also be acceptable.

MORE THAN ONE WORK IN A CITATION:

- The standard view of "scientific method" has come under concentrated attack in recent years (Kuhn; Lakatos; Laudan).

  But if your parenthetical citation becomes too cumbersome, consider replacing it with a substantive note (29f, p. 529).

## APA Parenthetical Citations

In a first APA citation, include the date of publication:

- Cooper (1984) struck a gloomy note in his address.

Observe that in APA style the parenthetical date comes immediately after the author's name. In this example the whole work is being cited. If, on the other hand, you wanted to cite a specific passage, you would put the page numbers into a separate, later, parenthesis:

- Bercovitch (1986) mentions a growing sense among critics that race, class, and gender are essential categories of textual analysis (p. viii).

  The following examples show further APA rules in action:

- "I feel you're feeling anger," says Kramer after his wife has clobbered him with an iron pot (Michaels, 1981, p. 172).

  Even though the reference list may contain more than one work by Michaels, the date alone suffices to show which one is meant.

- Karsh (1987b) has proposed a rival explanation.

  The date-plus-letter shows which work is meant among two or more by the same author in the same year.

- Preston and Martini (1967) examined the backgrounds of 234 schizophrenic patients.

  If there are two authors, always mention both.

doc
29d

- A study of 234 patients produced no support for the idea that schizophrenia is caused by unusual family tensions (Preston & Martini, 1967).

  Note the use of the ampersand ("&") within the parenthetical citation but not in the main sentence (previous example).

- Lauer, Montague, Lunsford, and Emig (1985) emphasize that writers must make their evaluative standards known to their readers (p. 200).

- Writers must make their evaluative standards known to their readers (Lauer, Montague, Lunsford, & Emig, 1985, p. 200).

  In a first citation, APA requires that all co-authors, no matter how many, be mentioned.

- Lauer et al. (1985) acknowledge their debt to Kinneavy (1971) for key rhetorical terms.

- The authors acknowledge their debt to Kinneavy (1971) for key rhetorical terms (Lauer et al., 1985, p. 21).

  Both of these sentences illustrate a "subsequent citation"; that is, the four co-authors have already been named. Consequently, the *et al.* ("and others") formula can now be used to save space. Note also how each of these sentences efficiently cites *two* items from the reference list.

- According to Nietzsche, Greek tragedy arose "out of the spirit of music" (cited in Merquior, p. 83).

  This sentence shows how to cite a quotation from an indirect source.

**doc
29d**

EXERCISE

3. Using either MLA or APA style according to your instructor's preference, submit five sentences containing references to the works you used in Exercise 2 (p. 519). Make each citation illustrate a different kind of circumstance (single author, two authors, two works by the same author, etc.).

## 29e   Observe the Features of the "Alternative MLA" Footnote/Endnote Style.

If your instructor prefers the "alternative MLA" style of citation, you will use either **footnotes** or **endnotes** instead of parenthetical citations and a reference list. A footnote appears at the bottom of the page on which its corresponding number appears within the text. Endnotes, by contrast, appear in sequence at the end of the paper, article, chapter, or book. Except for their single-spacing, the endnotes ("Notes") to chapters in this book follow MLA specifications.

Wherever you decide to put your notes, you should follow these rules for handling the note numbers within your text:

1. Number all the notes consecutively (1, 2, 3, . . . .).

2. Elevate the note numbers slightly, as here.$^8$

3. Place the numbers after, not before, the quotations or other information being cited: not x As Rosenhan says,$^{11}$ "the evidence is simply not compelling," but As Rosenhan says, "the evidence is simply not compelling."$^{11}$

4. Place the numbers after all punctuation except a dash; even parentheses, colons, and semicolons should precede note numbers.

### Endnotes versus Footnotes

Type endnotes on a new page after your main text, but before a bibliography if you are supplying one. Here is the standard form.

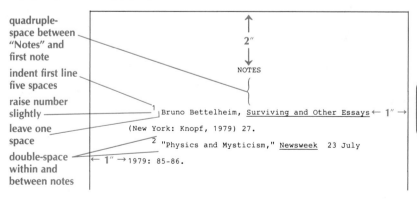

quadruple-space between "Notes" and first note

indent first line five spaces

raise number slightly

leave one space

double-space within and between notes

```
                              2"
                            NOTES

        1 Bruno Bettelheim, Surviving and Other Essays  ← 1" →
        (New York: Knopf, 1979) 27.
        2 "Physics and Mysticism," Newsweek  23 July
 ← 1" → 1979: 85-86.
```

doc
29e

when only 1" remains at the bottom of the page, continue notes on a following page

Handle footnotes just like endnotes except for these differences:

1. On each page where you will have notes, stop your main text high enough to leave room for the notes.

2. Quadruple-space between the end of the text and the first note on a page.

3. Single-space within the notes, but double-space between them.

4. If you have to carry a note over to the next page, type a solid line a full line below the last line of text on that new page, quadruple-space, and continue the note. Then continue any new notes.

Thus, footnotes at the bottom of a page look like this.

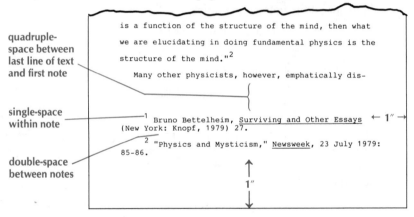

And here is a footnote carried over from a preceding page.

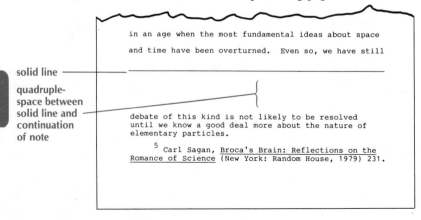

doc
29e

## First Notes

To see how notes differ from reference list entries, compare the following sample notes with the corresponding entries on pages 510–518. Notes 1–18 include references to specific parts of the cited works.

[1] Robert Langbaum, The Modern Spirit: Essays on the Continuity of Nineteenth- and Twentieth-Century Literature (New York: Oxford UP, 1970) 64.

[2] Mira Liehm and Antonin J. Liehm, The Most Important Art: Soviet and Eastern European Film after 1945 (Berkeley: U of California P, 1977) 234-45.

[3] American Society of Hospital Pharmacists, Consumer Drug Digest (New York: Facts on File, 1982) 107.

[4] Chicago Manual of Style, 13th ed. (Chicago: U of Chicago P, 1982) 8.14.

[5] George Herbert, "The Pulley," The Bedford Introduction to Literature, ed. Michael Meyer (New York: St. Martin's, 1987) 790-91.

[6] Plato, The Collected Dialogues of Plato: Including the Letters, ed. Edith Hamilton and Huntington Cairns (Princeton: Princeton UP, 1961) 327.

[7] Frank Kermode et al., eds., The Oxford Anthology of English Literature, 2 vols. (New York: Oxford UP, 1973) 1:209-11.

[8] Milan Kundera, The Book of Laughter and Forgetting, trans. Michael Henry Heim (New York: Knopf, 1981) 54-61.

[9] Frank Conroy, Stop-time (1967; New York: Penguin, 1977) 8.

[10] Arnold M. Cooper, "Psychoanalysis at One Hundred: Beginnings of Maturity," Journal of the American Psychoanalytic Association 32 (1984): 250.

doc
29e

[11] Richard P. Wheeler, "Poetry and Fantasy in Shakespeare's Sonnets 88-96," Literature and Psychology 22.3 (1972): 159.

[12] Peter Schwendener, rev. of Red and Hot: The Fate of Jazz in the Soviet Union, 1917-1980, by S. Frederick Starr, American Scholar 53 (1984): 429.

[13] "Drugs That Don't Work," New Republic 29 Jan. 1972: 13.

[14] Jack Nelson and Michael Wines, "North Reportedly Shredded Papers," San Francisco Chronicle 27 Nov. 1986, five-star ed.: 1+.

[15] L[awrence] K. L[ustig], "Alluvial Fans," Encyclopaedia Britannica, 1985, Macropaedia.

[16] Henry Morton Boudin, "The Ripple Effect in Classroom Management," diss., U of Michigan, 1970, 78-93.

[17] United States, Dept. of Agriculture, "Shipments and Unloads of Certain Fruits and Vegetables, 1918-1923," Statistical Bulletin 7 (Apr. 1925): 208.

[18] Steve Allen, letter, Popular Photography June 1978: 4.

[19] Eugene O'Neill, A Moon for the Misbegotten, dir. David Leveaux, with Kate Nelligan, Ian Bannen, and Jerome Kilty, Cort Theatre, New York, 23 June 1984.

[20] The Color of Money, dir. Martin Scorsese, with Paul Newman and Tom Cruise, Touchstone/Silver Screen, 1986.

[21] The World's Worst Air Crash, narr. Bill Moyers, PBS, Los Angeles, 27 July 1979.

[22] Ludwig van Beethoven, Symphony no. 8 in F, op. 93, cond. Pierre Monteux, Vienna Philharmonic Orch., Decca, STS 15238, 1964.

[23] Peter Collier and David Horowitz, personal interview, 5 Nov. 1987.

## Subsequent References

After you have provided one full endnote or footnote, you can be brief in
citing the same work again:

    24 Langbaum 197.

If you refer to more than one work by the same author, add a shortened title:

    25 Michaels, Men's Club 45.

    26 Michaels, I Would Have Saved Them 89-91.

If you cite the same work a third time, do not use the obsolete abbreviations *ibid.* or *op cit.*; repeat the identifying information given in your
first shortened reference. If the title of the whole work is cumbersome,
abbreviate it.

FIRST NOTE:

    27 The McGraw-Hill Encyclopedia of World Biography.

12 vols. (New York: McGraw-Hill, 1973) 6: 563; hereafter

cited as MEWB.

SUBSEQUENT NOTE:

    28 MEWB 8: 354.

If the same work comes up repeatedly in your notes, provide one full reference and then shift to parenthetical citations.

FIRST NOTE:

    29 William Shakespeare, The Merchant of Venice, ed.

Louis B. Wright and Virginia LaMar (New York: Washington

Square, 1957) II.iii.43.

SUBSEQUENT PARENTHETICAL REFERENCE:

- Portia tells Nerissa that she will do anything "ere I will be married to
  a sponge" (I.ii.90–91).

doc
29e

## Bibliography

A bibliography is a list of works that you have consulted or that you recommend to your readers for further reference. Research papers, dissertations, and scholarly books that do not follow a reference list style of documentation (29b–29d) typically contain bibliographies at the end. If you are supplying endnotes or footnotes, you can decide whether or not to include a bibliography by asking whether your notes have given a sufficient idea of your sources.

For bibliographical form, follow the conventions specified for an MLA reference list of "Works Cited" (29c, p. 508). In practice, the only differences between a bibliography and a reference list are that (a) parenthetical citations are not keyed directly to a bibliography, and (b) a bibliography may include some works that were consulted but are not actually cited in the text.

---

### EXERCISES

4. Write sample first endnotes (double-spaced) giving the usual amount of information about the following sources:

   A. A quotation from page 228 of this present book.
   B. A book by Herman Ermolaev called *Soviet Literary Theories 1917–1934: The Genesis of Socialist Realism.* The book was published in 1963 by the University of California Press, whose offices are in Berkeley and Los Angeles, California.
   C. A 1940 pamphlet issued by the United States Department of the Interior, Bureau of Indian Affairs, called *Navajo Native Dyes: Their Preparation and Use.* The pamphlet was published by the U.S. Government Printing Office in Washington, D.C.
   D. A story by Philip Roth called "On the Air," published in Number 10 of *New American Review,* on pages 7 through 49. This magazine did not carry dates, and its pagination began anew with each issue.
   E. A two-volume book called *American Literary Masters,* edited by Charles R. Anderson and seven other people. The work was published in 1965 by Holt, Rinehart and Winston, whose places of publication are listed on the back of the title page as New York, Chicago, San Francisco, and Toronto.

5. If you are now working on a research project, supply first endnotes (double-spaced) to five items you have examined, including at least one article in a magazine or newspaper. In addition, supply a subsequent note or parenthetical reference for each item, using the MLA style shown above.

doc
29e

## 29f    Learn the Uses of Supplementary Notes.

If you are using a reference list form of documentation (29b–29d), you will not be routinely supplying footnotes or endnotes. But you may nevertheless want to include some notes—usually endnotes, placed between the final paragraph of your main text and the beginning of your reference list —to make substantive comments (**substantive notes**) and to supply more references than you could gracefully fit into one set of parentheses (**bibliographic notes**). Although APA generally discourages use of supplementary notes, MLA does not.

### SUBSTANTIVE NOTE:

[1] According to Jalby, the peasants of Languedoc dressed lightly on the whole, but on feastdays, regardless of the heat, they wore their best winter clothes over their best summer ones to demonstrate their sense of luxury (194).

### BIBLIOGRAPHIC NOTE:

[2] See also E. R. Dodds, The Greeks and the Irrational (Berkeley: U of California P, 1951) 145-62; Richard Stillwell, "The Siting of Classical Greek Temples," Journal of the Society of Architectural Historians 13 (1954): 5; and Robert Scranton, "Group Design in Greek Architecture," Art Bulletin 31 (1949): 251.

If the works cited in this note appeared in the reference list, the note could be briefer:

[2] See also Dodds 145-62; Stillwell 5; Scranton 251.

doc
29f

If you have been following a footnote/endnote form, your "supplementary" notes should be integrated with the others. But whichever form you use, beware of demoting important points from your main text to your notes. Remember that readers would be annoyed by having to lurch back and forth between text and notes in order to follow your reasoning.

---

**EXERCISE**

6. Using either MLA or APA style, submit a bibliographic note that mentions all five of the items you included in Exercise 5 (p. 528).

---

## NOTES

[1] J. M. Roberts, *History of the World* (New York: Knopf, 1976) 845.

[2] The example is taken from Christine R. B. Boake and Robert R. Capranica, "Aggressive Signal in 'Courtship' Chirps of a Gregarious Cricket," *Science* 218 (1982): 580–82.

doc
29f

# 30

# A Sample
# Research Essay

To illustrate the fruits of library research, here is an analytic paper about computer crime. The documentation illustrates MLA reference list style (29c–29d, pp. 508–522). See page 541 for the same reference list in APA style.

Information about this writer's research procedures can be found in Chapter 28, pages 476–478, and 483–484.

## 30a   Note the Features of a Typical Research Essay.

Barry Lewis

English 101

Mr. Swenson

13 May 1983

Computer Theft: Crime Wave of the Future?

It is hardly a secret these days that computers are quickly becoming an indispensable feature of our lives. The Internal Revenue Service, the Census Bureau, Social Security, banks, insurance companies, corporations, universities, hospitals, small businesses, farmers, families, and students all use computers to maintain files, solve problems, and perform many other vital operations. Our checking accounts, taxes, bills, school registration, and grades are all routinely handled by computer. With personal computer sales for 1982 estimated at 2.8 million units as compared with 724,000 in 1980 ("The Computer Moves In" 14), the age of universal data processing is at hand. It is little wonder that <u>Time</u>'s "Man of the Year" for 1982 was no man at all but a machine, the computer ("The Computer Moves In" 14).

But if our number one hit is now the computer, its flip side is bound to be computer crime. In the new cybernetic world, just how safe from theft and misuse will our records and money be? How well can

The parenthetical citations are keyed to the "Works Cited" list on p. 8.

The writer narrows to his topic, computer crime.

2

access to sensitive data be controlled? Will computer
fraud become, as The Futurist magazine predicted back
in 1976, "the dominant mode of criminal conduct"
in America ("Crime in a Cashless Society" 132)?

The problem of computer crime is such a novelty
that we must still consult experts to learn just what
the phenomenon is. We must go, for example, to the
U.S. Department of Justice's publication Computer
Crime: Criminal Justice Resource Manual, which divides
the field into the introduction of fraudulent records
or data into a computer system; unauthorized use of
computer-related facilities; the altering or destroying of information or files; and the stealing of
money, financial instruments, property, services, or
valuable data (SRI 5). And if that sounds too
abstract, the manual also gets down to specific
capers, including "data diddling," "salami techniques"
(such as rounding down on accounts and depositing the
fractions of a cent in a favored account), and "scav-
enging" to obtain procedures, codes, and proprietary
secrets (SRI 9-29).

Though computer crime is in its infancy, outlaws
have already disabled computers, held them for ransom,
destroyed essential files, stolen equipment, pirated
programs, created huge insurance frauds, and "borrowed" company time to develop gambling systems

*The writer surveys the various types of computer crime.*

*Examples of current and potential crimes make the topic more concrete.*

3

**Several items from the "Works Cited" list are combined in one citation.**

(Bartimo; Gomes; Parker; Whiteside). Nevertheless, bigger game may lie ahead. Recent articles have speculated about the advent of electronic terrorism and war, whereby extremists or enemy powers may create riots by crippling the computers that process welfare checks or black out the air traffic control computers across the country. Donn Parker, a Stanford Research Institute computer security expert and the author of Crime by Computer, has outlined several possible battle plans that might cause national or even international computer failures.

Whether or not such scenarios are exaggerated, there is no doubt that computer theft is already lucrative, relatively easy, and on the rise. Donn Parker believes that wrongdoers will find the computer

**To indicate the widening scope of the problem, the writer calls on authorities and numerical data.**

a more and more attractive target. The average computer bank robbery, he points out, nets $500,000 as opposed to $2500 for the conventional version. Estimated annual losses from computer crime already range from $300 million to $5 billion (Ball 21). Everyone knows, furthermore, that those figures are unrealistically low. "Much chicanery goes undetected, and even when culprits are caught, the victimized company often tries to hush up the scandal and absorb its losses rather than admit to having poor computer security" (Alexander 60).

4

It is a mistake, furthermore, to think that only a handful of evil geniuses are capable of computer fraud. The robbers, according to one expert's profile,

> tend to be relatively honest and in a position of trust; few would do anything to harm another human, and most do not consider their crime to be truly dishonest. . . . Between the ages of 18 and 30, they are usually bright, eager, highly motivated, adventuresome, and willing to accept technical challenges. Actually, they sound like the type of person managers would like to employ. (Ball 23)

For a prose quotation of more than four typed lines, the writer uses the extracted form, indenting by ten spaces and omitting quotation marks.

One typical, if spectacular, case can illustrate how the odds on computer theft presently favor the criminal. On October 25, 1978, Stanley Mark Rifkin, a 32-year-old computer consultant who still phoned his mother every day, managed to steal $10.2 million from Security National Bank in Los Angeles--with three telephone calls and a computer code number. The theft went unnoticed for eight days and was discovered then only because Rifkin's lawyer had revealed it to an unsuspecting agent of the FBI's white-collar crime unit in Los Angeles. Nor did Rifkin have to draw on much of his expertise to carry out the plan. The bank's passwords were reportedly posted on a bulletin board, and Rifkin obtained the code for transferring funds simply by posing as a Federal Reserve Bank consultant (Henderson and Young 38).

One case dramatically illustrates lax computer security.

Form for citing coauthors of a single article.

5

The Rifkin story makes it clear that we are still in the horse-and-buggy stage of computer security.[1] Such conventional safeguards as identification cards, keys, badges, code numbers, and passwords would cause little trouble for an alert, strategically placed thief. Moreover, there is a natural tendency for bright, inquisitive people to test their wits against a computer's "electronic fences"--and for the winning secret to be passed around.

**A second long example reinforces the writer's point.**

In 1981, for example, undergraduates at the University of California at Berkeley found an astonishingly simple way to invade other users' programs within the university's computer network. Luckily, the students had no criminal intent; they planted anonymous messages within the computer explaining its vulnerability (Petit 6). Not so luckily, the January 11, 1982, issue of InfoWorld, a computer trade newsletter, divulged the incident. Appalled officers of the Stanford Research Institute, the Computer and Business Equipment Manufacturers Association, and

**Substantive footnotes can be combined with reference list documentation.**

[1] "Most managers," observes Herman MacDaniel, president of Management Resources International, "have the misconception that the technology is so sophisticated that it doesn't need to be protected. But most of the frauds have been [committed] by people who were not technically [sophisticated]" ("Locking the Electronic File Cabinet" 123).

6

the National Security Agency only managed to spread the tantalizing news to potential thieves (Kolata 1217).

Needless to say, the would-be computer crook will face tougher obstacles in the future. New programs are being developed to trace internal transactions (Levin 6). Transactions outside banks are now increasingly protected by "encryption," a mathematical scrambling procedure (Meinel 73). Furthermore, fingerprint identification devices, retina scanners, and "signature dynamics" machines may soon be used to control access to data and equipment (Yulsman 28).

**Having sketched the present situation, the writer turns to recent developments that could make computer crime difficult.**

Even with better management and technology, however, the forces of crime prevention will be handicapped until the law itself is brought up to date. As of now, specific legal deterrents to computer fraud exist only at the state level--and in only eleven states (Frenkel 28). As Alan G. Merten, professor of computer and information systems at the University of Michigan, acknowledges, "There just aren't laws out there yet" ("Locking the Electronic File Cabinet" 124). And though the FBI has established a school to train special agents in investigating computer crime, under current standards of evidence conviction is difficult and sentencing light. "Our legal system," says

**But in one important area— the law—reform has scarcely begun.**

7

August Bequai in <u>White-Collar Crime: A Twentieth-Century Crisis</u>, "has fallen behind our technology" (109).

**The writer concludes by hazarding a general prediction about the future of computer crime.**

It seems safe to predict that in the longer run, neither side will permanently gain the upper hand. This struggle, like the nuclear arms race, will be one of moves and countermoves based on inside knowledge of the other party's latest advances. How can we be sure that the government, the banks, and the corporations will not find a way to make their systems absolutely crimeproof? The answer is that the security devices will be invented, of course, by computer experts--experts "just like Stan Rifkin" (Henderson and Young 47). As one analyst has concluded with a sigh, "the only completely secure computer would be one that <u>nobody</u> could use" (Coniff 94).

**The writer has saved two striking quotations for the end of his paper.**

8

Works Cited

Alexander, Charles. "Crackdown on Computer Capers."
    Time 8 Feb. 1982: 60-61.

Ball, Leslie D. "Computer Crime." Technology Review
    Apr. 1982: 21-27+.

Bartimo, Jim. "Three WP Typists at Ford Named in Bet-
    ting Operation." Computerworld 10 Jan. 1983: 11.

Bequai, August. White-Collar Crime: A Twentieth-
    Century Crisis. Lexington, Mass.: Lexington,
    1978.

"The Computer Moves In." Time 3 Jan. 1983: 14-24.

Conniff, Richard. "Computer War." Science Digest
    Jan. 1982: 14-15+.

"Crime in a Cashless Society." The Futurist June
    1976: 132.

Frenkel, Karen A. "Computers in Court." Technology
    Review Apr. 1982: 28-29.

Gomes, Lee. "Secrets of the Software Pirates."
    Esquire Jan. 1982: 58-65.

Henderson, Bruce, and Jeffrey Young. "The Heist."
    Esquire May 1981: 36-40+.

Kolata, Gina. "Students Discover Computer Threat."
    Science 215 (1982): 1216-17.

Levin, Stephen E. "Security Possible in Communica-

9

tions Networks." Computerworld 31 Jan. 1983:
5-10.

"Locking the Electronic File Cabinet." Business Week
18 Oct. 1982: 123-24.

Meinel, Carolyn. "Encryption: Can Spies and Thieves
Break It?" Technology Review Nov.-Dec. 1982:
72-74.

Parker, Donn B. Crime by Computer. New York: Scribner's, 1976.

Petit, Charles. "UC Students' Computer Trick Worries
Experts." San Francisco Chronicle, 2 Mar.
1982: 6.

SRI International. Computer Crime: Criminal Justice
Resource Manual. Washington: US Dept. of Justice, 1977.

Whiteside, Thomas. Computer Capers: Tales of Electronic Thievery, Embezzlement, and Fraud. New
York: Crowell, 1978.

Yulsman, Tom. "Amazing Laser Locks." Science Digest
June 1982: 26+.

## The Same References in APA Style

### References

Alexander, C. (1982, February 8). Crackdown on computer
  capers. Time, pp. 60-61.

Ball, L. D. (1982, April). Computer crime. Technology
  Review, pp. 21-27, 30.

Bartimo, J. (1983, January 10). Three WP typists at Ford
  named in betting operation. Computerworld, p. 11.

Bequai, A. (1978). White-collar crime: A twentieth-century
  crisis. Lexington, MA: Lexington Books.

The computer moves in. (1983, January 3). Time, pp. 14-24.

Conniff, R. (1982, January). Computer war. Science Digest,
  pp. 14-15, 26, 28, 94.

Crime in a cashless society. (1976, June). The Futurist,
  p. 132.

Frenkel, K. A. (1982, April). Computers in court. Technology
  Review, pp. 28-29.

Gomes, L. (1982, January). Secrets of the software pirates.
  Esquire, pp. 58-65.

Henderson, B., & Young, J. (1981, May). The heist. Esquire,
  pp. 36-47.

Kolata, G. (1982). Students discover computer threat. Science, 215, 1216-1217.

Levin, S. E. (1983, January 31). Security possible in communications networks. Computerworld, pp. 5-10.

Locking the electronic file cabinet. (1982, October 18).
  Business Week, pp. 123-124.

Meinel, C. (1982, November/December). Encryption: Can spies and thieves break it? Technology Review, pp. 72-74.

Parker, 'D. B. (1976). Crime by computer. New York: Scribner's.

Petit, C. (1982, March 2). UC students' computer trick worries experts. San Francisco Chronicle, p. 6.

SRI International. (1977). Computer crime: Criminal justice resource manual. Washington, DC: U.S. Department of Justice.

Whiteside, T. (1978). Computer capers: Tales of electronic thievery, embezzlement, and fraud. New York: Crowell.

Yulsman, T. (1982, June). Amazing laser locks. Science Digest, pp. 26, 28.

## EXERCISES

1. Why did the writer begin with remarks about the growing importance of computers in our society? Would the paper have been more, or less, effective without that opening paragraph? Think of possible reasons for either answer.

2. The writer's first idea was to write about a much narrower topic: the breaking of long-distance telephone codes. Was he well-advised to tackle the whole field of computer crime instead? What aspect of that field makes his choice look more sensible than it otherwise would?

res
30a

# VIII

## APPLIED WRITING

31. Examination Answers and In-Class Essays

32. Business Letters

33. Résumés

## APPLIED WRITING

*Several of the skills that go into a successful college essay will help you in other writing situations as well. This section begins by showing how you can simplify the composing process to produce cogent prose "on demand" within the classroom (Chapter 31). We then look beyond college to means of presenting yourself to potential employers, customers, and others who may want your services or your patronage. Chapter 32 takes you through the standard ways of writing a business letter, and Chapter 33 gives you a model for the résumé—a summary of your background that will show your accomplishments to best advantage when you are applying for a job.*

# 31

## Examination Answers and In-Class Essays

### 31a Be Prepared for the Special Conditions of an Examination.

Most of the skills you are developing for the writing of essays will serve you well in answering essay questions on exams. At the same time, it is vital to understand the ways in which the exam situation limits your options and calls for a more direct and emphatic style of writing. Here are eleven points of advice, the first of which you can put into operation weeks before the exam.

1. *Try to anticipate questions.* Listen and take notes throughout the term. Attend especially to topics and theories that keep coming up week after week, so that you arrive at the exam with ideas that tie together the assigned material.

2. *Read through all instructions and questions before beginning any answer.* Determine whether you must answer all the questions. If you have a choice, decide which questions you can answer best. Responding

to more than the required number may take time from your strong area to answer an unnecessary question in a weaker area, and the grader will usually be under no obligation to count "extra credit" answers.

3. *Gauge your available time.* Translate the point value of a question into a time value. A 30-point question in a 50-minute, 100-point exam should not take much more of your time than 15 minutes (30 percent of 50). If you find yourself running over, stop and leave some blank space while you get something written on *all* other questions.

4. *Note the key instruction in each question.* Always pause and study the wording of each question. Be aware that most questions begin with a key word that tells you what to do: *compare, contrast, discuss, analyze, classify, list, define, explain, summarize, describe, justify, outline.* Let that word guide the writing of your answer. If you are asked to *describe* how lasers are used to unblock obstructed arteries, do not waste time *explaining* possible causes of the obstruction. And do not be tempted into writing prepared answers to questions that were not asked. If you are to contrast *X* with *Y,* be sure you are not setting out to give 90 percent of your emphasis to *X.* If you are to state the relationship between *A* and *B,* do not throw in *C* for good measure. And if the question tells you to analyze the content and style of a quoted passage, do not suppose that a double effort on content alone will gain you full credit. Break the question into its parts and attend to all of them.

5. *Plan your answer.* For longer answers, draw up a scratch outline (4e, p. 93), and check the outline against the question to make sure it covers the required ground.

6. *Do not waste time restating the question.* A grader can only be annoyed by a hollow introductory paragraph that merely announces your willingness to address the question. Your grader will already be looking for ideas.

7. *Begin with a clear statement of your thesis in the opening paragraph.* Use your first paragraph to announce your main point and to establish the structure of everything that will follow. Do not fear that your strategy will be made too obvious. There is no such thing as being too obvious about your thesis in an examination answer. The danger, on the contrary, is that a harried grader will miss it.

8. *Highlight your main points.* Remember that your grader will be reading rapidly and will appreciate signals that make the structure of your answer clear. Consider enumerating key points, either with actual numbers (*1, 2, 3*) or with words (*First, Second, Third*); you can even underline the most essential statements to ensure that they will come to the grader's notice.

9. *Support your generalizations with specific references.* Most essay questions are broad enough to allow for a variety of "right" answers. Give your grader evidence that you have done the reading and have thought about it carefully. Your own ideas, backed by examples drawn from the assigned reading, will be much more impressive than unsupported statements taken directly from lectures and textbooks.

10. *Keep to the point.* In an examination answer you have no time for digressions—passages that stray from the case being made. You should not, for example, try to befriend your grader with humorous asides or pleas for sympathy.

11. *Read through your completed answer.* Try to leave time to go over your answer. Read it as if you were the grader, and try to catch inconsistencies, incoherent sentences, illegible scribbles, and unfulfilled predictions about what follows. Do not hesitate to cross out whole paragraphs if necessary or to send your grader, through an inserted arrow and a boldly printed note, to an extra page in the back of the blue book.

## A Sample Answer

For a further idea of the way an examination answer typically goes straight to the point and reveals its structure, read this answer to a question on an American history final.

*Question:*
Summarize and explain the importance of Jefferson's reforms in the Virginia Legislature after 1776.

*Answer:*

**Thesis first** → Jefferson's purpose in revising the laws of Virginia was to get rid of all traces of aristocracy and to lay the foundations for a democratic government. There were four key reforms—governing inheritance, education, and religion—that helped to change Virginia from a royal colony to a republican state.

**Preview of supporting points** →

> First, the abolition of primogeniture. This ancient practice meant that the first-born son inherited all the father's wealth. The importance of the reform was that wealth could now be distributed among several surviving offspring, thereby breaking down the holdings of large landowners and distributing ownership to a wider number of Virginians.
>
> Second, the repeal of the laws of entail. These laws provided that a landowner who had inherited an entailed estate

exam
**31a**

had to leave it whole to a fixed line of heirs. Jefferson's reform allowed an owner to divide up his property and leave it to whomever he liked. The importance, again, was that the repeal broke the power of a landed aristocracy, a sure threat to a young democracy.

**Each numbered point receives a paragraph of its own. Each paragraph both summarizes and explains the importance of its point.**

Third, the establishment of a system of general education. Jefferson felt it was the duty of the state to provide education and libraries for the poor. He felt that free education was the only guarantee against tyranny—that only educated people could become useful citizens by participating in the drafting of sound laws, thereby insuring the well-being and happiness of all citizens.

And fourth, the disestablishment of the state church and the guarantee of freedom of conscience. A deist himself, Jefferson supported the ethical teachings of religion but rejected a church/state alliance, which he felt unavoidably led to favoritism and tyranny. He proposed that Virginians be free of statutory taxation in support of a state church. Jefferson's legislation went beyond mere tolerance to guarantee freedom of religion for all by law.

**A brief concluding paragraph emphasizes that the terms of the question have been met.**

→    These four reforms broke down a landed aristocracy, educated a democratic citizenry to participate in government, and guaranteed for all a separation of church and state, thereby eradicating all traces of hereditary rank and privilege in Virginia.

## 31b    Modify Your Composing Method to Suit the Conditions of the In-Class Essay.

Nearly all the advice in this book applies to the writing of in-class as well as at-home essays. But an in-class essay resembles an examination (31a) in requiring you to make the "first draft" fully adequate. As in an exam, you must carefully gauge your available time, be absolutely sure you are meeting the terms of the question, and foreshorten your planning and revision.

If you are given an hour to produce an essay, do not feel that you have been directed to write for exactly sixty minutes. Take out about ten minutes for planning, and try to finish in time to read through the whole essay and make emergency corrections. The key period is the beginning: you must not start writing until you have a clear idea of your thesis. If you search for ideas as you go along, your essay will probably show a meandering structure or even a self-contradictory one.

To guide your writing, make a scratch outline (4e, p. 93) indicating the anticipated order of your points. Steer clear of elaborate or highly unusual structures that could turn out to be unworkable. Get your thesis into the first or second paragraph, and then concentrate on backing it with important points of evidence.

Your instructor will make allowances for the time constraint when judging your essay. Remember as you write, however, that it *is* an essay—one that should show such virtues as clear statement, coherent paragraph development, and variety of sentence structure. Do not, then, write like someone who has crammed for a test and who must now hastily spill out page after page of sheer information. The length of your in-class essay will be less crucial than the way it hangs together as a purposeful structure controlled by a thesis.

In your remaining time, check first to see that you have adequately developed your thesis, and insert any needed additions as neatly as you can (see 31a, point 11, p. 547). Then check for legibility and correctness of usage, punctuation, spelling, and diction, making needed changes as you go. Your instructor will not object to a marked-up manuscript if it remains reasonably easy to read.

exam
31b

# 32

# Business Letters

To write an effective business letter, you must come across as "all business." You can expect a good reception only if your letter shows neatness, accuracy, consistency, courtesy, efficiently concise and unpretentious statement, and adherence to standard form.

## 32a  Master the Standard Features of the Business Letter.

### Customary Elements

Examine the business letter on the following page. Here you see:

1. *The heading.* It contains your address and the date of writing. Notice the absence of end punctuation.

2. *The inside address.* Place this address high (or low) enough so that the body of the letter will appear centered on the page. Include the name of the addressee, that person's title or office, the name of the company or institution, and the full address:

```
Joan Lacey, M.D.             Mr. Kenneth Herbert
Pioneer Medical Group        Director of Personnel
45 Arrow Avenue              Cordial Fruit Cooperative
Omaha, NE 68104             636 Plumeria Boulevard
                             Honolulu, HI 96815
```

**[MODIFIED BLOCK FORMAT]**

2264 N. Cruger Avenue ——— 1. heading
Milwaukee, WI 53211
February 22, 1988

Mr. Robert F. Stone
Customer Relations
Kaiser Appliances, Inc. ————————————————— 2. inside address
834 La Salle Street
Chicago, IL 60632

Dear Mr. Stone: ————————————————————— 3. salutation

The Kitchen-Aid dishwasher I purchased in your
store on February 14 was installed yesterday. Unfortunately, the installation was complete before
the plumber and I noticed a large chip on the edge
of the white front panel. Since the panel was
still in its carton when the plumber arrived, it
was probably defective upon delivery. The serial
number of the dishwasher is T53278004; I enclose a
copy of the bill, already paid.

In my phone conversation with you yesterday, I
agreed to put this complaint in writing. I would
like you to send a representative here to replace
the damaged panel. To fix a time, please call me
at home after 5:30 P.M. at (414) 565-9776.

Thank you for your prompt attention to this
matter.

4. body

Sincerely, ——— 5. complimentary close

*Kevin Oppenheimer* ——— 7. signature

Kevin Oppenheimer ——— 6. typed name

KO: sms ——————————————————————— 8. special notations
enc.

3. *The salutation.* This formal greeting appears two lines lower than the inside address:

```
Dear Dr. Lacey:           Dear Ms. Diaz:

Dear Mr. Herbert:         Dear Reverend Melville:
```

*Ms.* is now the preferred form for addressing a woman who has no title such as *Dr.* or *Professor.* Use *Miss* or *Mrs.* only if your correspondent has put that title before her own typed name in a letter to you: *(Mrs.) Estelle Kohut.* And unless you see otherwise, you should assume that a woman wishes to be known by her own first name, not her husband's.

When writing to an institution or a business, you can avoid the possibly offensive *Dear Sir* or *Dear Sirs* by choosing a neutral salutation:

```
Dear Personnel Manager:   Dear Editor:

Dear Sir or Madam:        Dear Macy's:

Dear Bursar:              To Whom It May Concern:
```

Note that business salutations end with a colon. Only if the addressee happens to be a friend should you strike a more informal note: *Dear Estelle, Dear Andy, . . .*

4. *The body.* Use the body of your letter to explain the situation and to make your request or response in a straightforward, concise way. You can write briefer paragraphs than you would use in an essay. Prefer middle-level diction, avoiding both slang and legalese: not x *You really put one over on me* or x *The undersigned was heretofore not apprised of the circumstances cited hereabove* but *I was not aware of the problem.*

Single-space the paragraphs of your letter but leave a double space between one paragraph and the next.

5. *The complimentary close.* Type the complimentary close two lines below the last line of the body. The most common formulas are:

```
Sincerely,                Yours sincerely,

Sincerely yours,          Very truly yours,

Yours truly,              Cordially,
```

Of these tags, *Cordially* is the only one that hints at actual feeling.

6. *Your typed name.* Leave four lines between the complimentary close and your typed name as you intend to sign it. If you have a professional title or role that is relevant to the purpose of the letter, add it directly below your name:

```
Nicole Pinsky              Jackson Marley
Assistant Manager          Lecturer
```

In general, such titles are appropriate when you are using letterhead stationery.

7. *Your signature.* Always use blue or black ink. Match your signature and your typed name; a briefer signature is a sign of impatience.

8. *Special notations.* Lowest on the page, always flush left, come notations to indicate the following circumstances if they are applicable:

| NOTATION | MEANING |
|---|---|
| cc: A. Pitts<br>F. Adler | "Carbon copies" (probably photocopies) are being simultaneously sent to interested parties Pitts and Adler. |
| encl. | The mailing contains an enclosure (always mentioned in the body of the letter). |
| att. | A document has been attached to the letter. |
| BR:clc *or*<br>BR/clc | The writer (initials *BR*) has used the services of a typist (initials *CLC*). |

### Alternative Formats

There are three recognized ways of handling the arrangement of a business letter's elements on the page. You can choose any of the three, but they make somewhat different impressions. For extreme impersonality, *block format* works best. A middle style, very commonly used, is *modified block format.* And if you want your business letter to have some of the flavor of a personal letter, *indented format* is available.

Here are the three formats in a nutshell:

**bus
32a**

|  | BLOCK FORMAT | MODIFIED BLOCK FORMAT | INDENTED FORMAT |
|---|---|---|---|
| **Heading** | Flush left | Toward right margin | Toward right margin |
| **Inside Address** | Flush left | Flush left | Flush left |
| **First Lines of Paragraphs** | Flush left | Flush left | Indented 5–10 spaces |
| **Complimentary Close, Name, and Signature** | Flush left | Toward right margin | Toward right margin |
| **Special Notations** | Flush left | Flush left | Flush left |

("Flush left" means that the lines begin at the left margin. "Toward right margin" means that the lines should end at or near the right margin.)

These differences may sound complicated, but they are easy to see in examples:

BLOCK FORMAT: p. 556
MODIFIED BLOCK FORMAT: pp. 551, 557
INDENTED FORMAT: p. 558

Note that indented format is simply modified block format plus indentions for the first lines of paragraphs.

### Form of Envelope

Make the address on your envelope identical to the inside address. In the upper left corner, type your own address as it appears in the heading:

```
Kevin Oppenheimer
2264 N. Cruger Avenue
Milwaukee, WI 53211




                    Mr. Robert F. Stone
                    Customer Relations
                    Kaiser Appliances, Inc.
                    834 La Salle Street
                    Chicago, IL 60632
```

## 32b    Recognize the Main Purposes of the Business Letter.

### Asking for Information

Make your inquiry brief, and limit your request to information that can be sent in an available brochure or a brief reply. Be specific, so that there can be no doubt about which facts you need.

### Ordering Merchandise

Begin by stating which items you are ordering, using both product names and stock or page numbers. Tell how many units of each item you are ordering, the price per item, and the total price. If you want to receive the shipment at a different address, say so. Mention that you are enclosing payment, ask to be billed, or provide a credit card name and number and expiration date.

### Stating a Claim

Take a courteous but firm tone, setting forth the facts so fully and clearly that your reader will be able to act on your letter without having to ask for more information. If you are complaining about a purchase, supply the date of purchase, the model and serial number, and a brief description. If you have been mistakenly billed twice for the same service or product, state what that service or product is, the date of your payment, and the check number if you paid by check. If possible, enclose a photocopy of the canceled check (both sides). In a second paragraph, calmly and fairly state what adjustment you think you are entitled to. (See page 551 for a sample claim letter.)

### Making an Application

Tailor your letter to the particular job, grant, or program of study you are applying for. Name the opening precisely. If you are asking to be considered for a job, explain how you heard about it. If a person in authority recommended that you apply, say who it was. Tell how you can be reached, and express your willingness to be interviewed.

When applying for a job, include your **résumé** (Chapter 33, pp. 559–561) and mention that you have included it. Emphasize those elements in the résumé that qualify you for *this* position. Avoid boasting and false modesty alike. The idea to get across is that the facts of your record make such a strong case for your application that no special pleading is necessary.

**[BLOCK FORMAT]**

36 Hawthorne Hall
University of the North
Bridgewater, CT 06413
January 15, 1988


NF Systems, Ltd.
P. O. Box 76363
Atlanta, GA 30358

Dear NF Systems:

Please send me the following software items for use on
the IBM Personal Computer, as described on page 40 in
the December 1987 issue of <u>Softalk</u> magazine:

|   |   |   |
|---|---|---|
| 1 | "Household Aids," a group of six programs, total package, | $49.95 |
| 1 | "Check Register," includes 40 ledger/ budget headings, | 39.95 |

Kindly ship this merchandise to the address shown
above. I enclose my check #186 for $89.90. Since your
advertisement does not specify shipping costs, please
bill me for them separately if they are not included
in the prices.

Sincerely yours,

*Lily Marks*

Lily Marks

The following letters illustrate how an applicant can state qualifications in different ways for different opportunities. Both letters pertain to the résumé appearing on page 561. Notice how each letter brings out "job-related" elements in the writer's background.

---

### [MODIFIED BLOCK FORMAT]

137-20 Crescent Street
Flushing, NY 11367
August 17, 1987

F 1384
New York Times
New York, NY 10018

Dear Personnel Manager:

I am applying for the position of "Accounting Aide to CPA firm," which was advertised in yesterday's Times. I have completed my second year at Queens College as an Accounting major and plan to take a year off to supplement my education with relevant work.

From my enclosed résumé, you can see that I have been working in the business offices of Gristede's Food Stores, where I have assisted the bookkeeper in auditing procedures, including applications to computerized systems. My work requires strong mathematics skills and some familiarity with the Lotus 1-2-3 spreadsheet.

As a prospective accountant, I am especially interested in spending next year with a CPA firm. I can send you the names of references both at Queens College and at Gristede's and would be grateful for the chance to be interviewed. Please write to me at the above address or call me at (718) 317-1964 after 5:30 P.M.

Sincerely yours,

*Janet Madden*

Janet Madden

encl.

---

**[INDENTED FORMAT]**

137-20 Crescent Street
Flushing, NY 11367
August 17, 1987

Ms. Charlotte DeVico
Rock of Ages Health Related
    Facility
7481 Parsons Boulevard
Flushing, NY 11367

Dear Ms. DeVico:

   Mr. Gene Connelly of the Flushing YMCA has suggested I write to you about working as a recreation
assistant or bookkeeper in your facility beginning
this fall. I am an Accounting major with a minor in
Communications, and I plan to take a year off from
school to supplement my education with relevant work.

   From my enclosed résumé you can see that, in
addition to a business background, I have experience
in working with people. At the Flushing "Y" I have
helped stage the annual talent show, held informal
"chat" sessions, and presented films. I enjoy this
work and find the elderly full of ideas and a willingness to make themselves happy.

   Mr. Connelly has offered to write you about my
work at the "Y," and I can also send you the name of
my supervisor at Gristede's. I would be grateful for
the chance to be interviewed. Please write to me at
the above address or call me at (718) 975-1122 between
9:00 A.M. and 4:30 P.M.

                              Sincerely yours,

                              *Janet Madden*

                              Janet Madden

encl

# 33

# Résumés

## 33a    Recognize the Standard Features of the Résumé.

Your résumé is a brief (usually one-page) record of your career and qualifications. Along with your letter of application (32b, p. 555), it can land
you a job interview. To that end it should be clear, easy on the eye, and
totally favorable in emphasis. Have your résumé typed by a professional if
your typewriter cannot create a polished, near-printed look.

Divide your résumé into the following sections:

1. *Personal information.* Provide only what is necessary: name, present
address, permanent address, phone numbers. Add your age, marital status, and condition of health only if you know they are relevant to the job
you want.

2. *Career objective.* Include a statement of your career goals. Avoid being
so specific that you exclude reasonable opportunities or so broad as to be
uninformative. Cite two goals if necessary, and mention any geographical
limitations.

3. *Education.* Begin with the college you currently attend or have attended
most recently, and work backward to high school. (If you have already
graduated from college, omit high school.) Give dates of attendance,
degrees attained, major and minor areas of study, and memberships in

special societies. Briefly explain any outstanding projects or courses. Include your grade-point average only if it happens to be high.

4. *Work experience.* Begin with your current or most recent employment, and list all relevant jobs since high schol. Try not to leave suspicious-looking gaps of time. Give the name and address of each employer, the dates of employment, and a brief description of your duties. Include part-time or volunteer work that may be relevant. Remember that you can mention relevant skills learned on a job that seems unrelated. If you are seeking a teaching position, consider beginning this part of your résumé with a section called *Teaching Experience* and following it with another called *Other Work Experience.*

5. *Special skills, activities, and honors.* Include special competencies that make you a desirable candidate, such as proficiency in a foreign language, ability to operate equipment, or skill in unusual procedures or techniques. Mention any honors, travel, or community service.

6. *References.* Supply the address of your college placement office, which will send out your dossier (dáhss-ee-ay) upon request. The dossier is a complete file of your credentials, including all letters of recommendation and transcripts. You may wish to give the names, positions, and addresses of three people you can trust to write strong letters in your behalf. Be sure you have their permission, however.

Further advice:

1. *Keep the format clear and the text concise.* Single-space within each section, and double-space between sections. Try to keep your résumé to one page; do not exceed two pages.

2. *Do not mention the salary you want.* You will be considered for more openings if you stay flexible on this point.

3. *Update your résumé periodically.* Do not hesitate to ask for new letters of recommendation.

4. *Rewrite your résumé for a particular job opening.* Rewriting allows you to highlight those elements of your background and goals that will suit the job you are aiming for.

JANET MADDEN

**Current Address:**
137-20 Crescent Street
Flushing, NY 11367
(718) 317-1964

**Permanent Address:**
28 Pasteur Drive
Glen Cove, NY 11542
(516) 676-0620

CAREER
OBJECTIVE:    Position as accountant or assistant
accountant in an accounting firm.
(Temporary position as a recreation
assistant or bookkeeper in a recre-
ational facility.)

EDUCATION:    Queens College (CUNY)
B.A. expected June 1990
Majoring in Accounting
Minoring in Communications

Pratt High School, Glen Cove, New
York
Received Regents Diploma, June 1985

EXPERIENCE:

Summer 1987    Assistant bookkeeper, Gristede
Brothers Food Stores, Bronx, New
York

Summers
1985-86    Dramatics Counselor, Robin Hill Day
Camp, Glen Cove, New York

1985-87    Volunteer, Flushing YMCA. Worked
with elderly. Assistant director,
annual "Y" talent show.

SKILLS:    Type 65 wpm.
Use Lotus 1-2-3 spreadsheet.

REFERENCES:    Placement Office
Queens College
Flushing, NY 11367

# An Index of Usage

The Index of Usage does not dwell on differences between dialect expressions, slang, and informal usage. It simply labels *colloq.* ("colloquial") any terms that are inadvisable for use in college essays and papers.
The following abbreviations appear in the Index of Usage.

| | |
|---|---|
| adj. | adjective, adjectival |
| adv. | adverb, adverbial |
| ambig. | ambiguous, having more than one possible meaning |
| awk. | awkward |
| colloq. | colloquial, to be avoided in standard written English |
| compl. | complement |
| conj. | conjunction |
| coord. | coordinating |
| e.g. | for example |
| i.e. | that is |
| inf. | infinitive |
| intrans. | intransitive: the verb takes no object |
| jarg. | jargon |
| n. | noun |
| neg. | negative |
| obj. | direct object |
| part. | present participle |

| plu. | plural |
|------|--------|
| p.p. | past participle |
| prep. | preposition, prepositional |
| pro. | pronoun |
| redt. | redundant, conveying the same meaning twice |
| S.E. | standard written English |
| sing. | singular |
| subj. | subject of a verb |
| subord. | subordinating |
| syn. | synonym, a word having the same meaning as another |
| trans. | transitive: the verb takes an object |
| v. | verb |
| x | marks an illustration of a typical mistake or awkward construction |

**above** (n., adj.) Stuffy in phrases like x *in view of the above* and x *for the above reasons.* Wherever possible, substitute *therefore, for these reasons,* etc.

**A.D.** Should precede the date: *A.D. 1185.* Note that it is redt. to write x *in the year A.D. 1185,* since *A.D.* already says "in the year of our Lord" (Latin *anno Domini*).

**affect, effect** As a v., *affect* means to *influence: Rain affected the final score. Affect* may also be used as a n. meaning *feeling* or *emotion.* The v. *effect* means to *bring about* or *cause: She effected a stunning reversal.* When *effect* is a n., it means *result: The effect of the treatment was slight.*

**afraid** See *frightened.*

**again, back** Redt. after *re*-prefixed words that already contain the sense of *again* or *back: rebound, reconsider, refer, regain, reply, resume, revert,* etc. Do not write x *refer back.*

**ain't** Colloq. for *is not, are not.*

**all, all of** Use either *all* or *all of* when separable items are involved: *All of the skillets were sold.* When there are no items to be counted, use *all* without *of: All her enthusiasm vanished; He was a hermit all his life.*

**all that** Colloq. in sentences like x *I didn't like her all that much.*

**allusion, illusion, delusion** An *allusion* is a *glancing reference: an allusion to Shakespeare.* An *illusion* is a *deceptive impression: Shakespeare created the illusion of enormous battlefields.* A *delusion* is a *mistaken belief,* usually with pathological implications: *He suffered from the delusion of thinking that he was Shakespeare.*

**also**  Do not use as a coord. conj.: x *She owned two cars, also a stereo.* Try *Along with her two cars, she also owned a stereo.* Here *also* serves its proper function as an adv.

**alternate, alternative** (adjs.)  Very different. *Alternate* means *by turns: on alternate Fridays. Alternative* means *substitutive: One alternative plan might work if this one fails.*

**A.M., P.M.**  These abbreviations, which most writers now capitalize, should not be used as nouns: x *at six in the A.M.* And do not accompany *A.M.* or *P.M.* with *o'clock,* which is already implied. Write *six A.M.* or *six o'clock* but not x *six A.M. o'clock.*

**among, between**  *Among* is appropriate when there are at least three separable items: *among his friends; among all who were there.*

*Between* can be used for any plu. number of items, though some writers reserve it for two items (also see *between*). The more widely recognized difference is that *among* is vaguer and more collective than *between,* which draws attention to each of the items:

- They hoped to find one good person *among* the fifty applicants.

- The mediator saw a basis for agreement *between* management and the union.

**amount, number**  For undivided quantities, use *amount of: a small amount of food.* For countable items, use *number of: a small number of meals.* The common error is to use *amount* for *number,* as in x *The amount of people in the hall was extraordinary.*

**analyzation**  A mistake for *analysis.*

**angry**  See *mad.*

**anybody, any body; nobody, no body; somebody, some body**  The first member of each pair is an indefinite pro.: *Anybody can see. . . .* The others are adj.-n. pairs: *Any body can be dissected.*

**anyway, any way, anyways**  *Anyway* is an adv.: *There is no hope, anyway. Any way* is an adj.-n. pair: *I have not found any way to do it. Anyways* is colloq.

**anywheres**  Colloq. for *anywhere.*

**apt, liable, likely**  Close in meaning. But some writers reserve *liable* to mean *exposed* or *responsible* in an undesirable sense: *liable to be misunderstood; liable for damages. Likely* means *probably destined: She is likely to succeed. Apt* is best used to indicate habitual disposition: *They are apt to complain when you tell them to work faster.*

**argue, quarrel**  These can be syns., but *argue* also has a special meaning of *make a case,* without overtones of quarrelsomeness.

**around**  If you mean *about,* it is better to write *about: about five months,* not x *around five months.*

**as** (conj., prep.)  The subord. conj. *as* in the sense of *because* is often ambig.: x *As she said it, I obeyed.* Does *as* here mean *because* or *while*? Use *because* if you mean *because.*

Do not use *as* to mean *whether* or *that:* x *I cannot say as I do.*

**as, like**  *As* is usually a conj. introducing an adv. clause, and *like* is usually a prep. introducing a prep. phrase.

CONJUNCTION:

- *As* the forecaster predicted, it rained all day.

PREPOSITION:

- *Like* anyone else, she has made her share of mistakes.

In speech, many people use *like* as a conj.: x *Like he said, . . .* This is inadvisable written usage.

Note that when *as* is a prep., it differs in meaning from *like*:

- He runs *like* a deer.

- He is running *as* the vegetarian candidate.

**as, such as**  Not syns. Do not write x *The burglar's bag contained many items, as masks, screwdrivers, and skeleton keys. Such as* would be appropriate.

**as far as . . .**  Be sure to complete this formula with *is/are concerned.* Do not write x *As far as money, I have no complaints.* Try *As far as money is concerned, I have no complaints,* or *As for money, I have no complaints,* or, better, *I have no complaints about money.*

**as good as, as much as**  Colloq. when used for *practically:* x *He as good as promised me the job.*

**aspect**  Literally, an *aspect* is a *view from a particular vantage.* Moving around an object, you see various *aspects* of it. Instead of using *aspect* as a syn. for *feature* (x *The problem has five aspects*), try to use the term with at least a hint of concreteness: *When the issue is regarded from this perspective, it shows a wholly new aspect.*

**author** (v.)  Widely used, but also widely condemned as substandard: x *He has authored four novels.* Use *has written,* and keep *author* as a n.

**back of** Colloq. for *behind*: x *You can find it back of the stove. Behind* is also preferable to *in back of.*

**bad** Do not use as an adv. meaning *badly* or *severely*: x *It hurt him bad.*

**before, ago** When referring to the past from a present perspective, use *ago*: *I told you to get ready two hours ago, and you still aren't even dressed.* When focusing on a past time and referring to an even more distant past, use *before*: *She had told him to get ready two hours before, but he still wasn't even dressed.*

**being** (part.) Often redt.: x *The city is divided into three districts, with the poorest being isolated from the others by the highway.* Either *with* or *being* should be dropped.

**bemused** Means *bewildered*, not *amused.*

**better than** Colloq. as a syn. of *more than*: x *Better than half an hour remained.*

**between** Can be used for more than two items (see *among, between*), but it does require at least two. Do not write either x *Hamlet's conflict is between his own mind* or x *The poems were written between 1983–84.* In the second sentence *1983–84* is one item, a period of time. Try *The poems were written between 1983 and 1984.*

   *Between* always requires a following *and*, not *or*. Avoid x *The choice is between anarchy or civilization.* See also *among, between.*

**between each, between every** Because *between* implies at least two items, it should not be joined to sing. adjs. like *each* and *every*: x *He took a rest between each inning.* Try *He rested after every inning* or *He rested between innings.*

**between you and I** A "genteel" mistake for *between you and me.* As twin objs. of the prep. *between*, both pros. must be objective in case.

**bored** Should be followed by *by* or *with*, not *of.* Avoid x *He was bored of skiing.*

**broke** (adj.) Colloq. both in the sense of *having no money* and as the p.p. of *break*: x *The faucet was broke.* Prefer *broken* for this meaning.

**bunch, crowd** (n.) A *bunch* is a dense collection of *things*; a *crowd*, of *people* or *animals.* Avoid x *a bunch of my friends.*

**but that, but what** These are awk. equivalents of *that* in clauses following an expression of doubt: x *I do not doubt but that you intend to remain loyal.*

**calculate** See *figure.*

**calculated** See *designed.*

**can, may** Both are now acceptable to indicate permission. *May* has a more polite and formal air: *May I leave?*

**can not, cannot**  Unless you want to underline *not,* always prefer *cannot,* which makes the negative meaning immediately clear.

**cause, reason**  Not syns. A *cause* is what produces an effect: *The earthquake was the cause of the tidal wave.* A *reason* is someone's *professed motive or justification: He cited a conflict of interest as his reason for not accepting the post.* Note that the actual *cause* of his refusal could have been something quite different.

**cause is due to**  Redt. Write *The cause was poverty,* not x *The cause was due to poverty.*

**censor, censure**  (n.) A *censor* is an official who judges whether a publication or performance will be allowed. *Censure* is vehement criticism. *The censor heaped censure on the play.*

**center around**  Since a center is a point, *center around* is imprecise. *Center on* or *center upon* would be better: *The investigation centered on tax evasion.*

**character**  Often redt. x *He was of a studious character* means, and should be, *He was studious.*

(v.) *Classify* is preferable. Avoid x *He classed the documents under three headings.*

**commence**  Usually pompous for *begin, start.*

**compare, contrast**  *Compare* means either *make a comparison* or *liken.* To compare something *with* something else is to make a comparison between them; the comparison may show either a resemblance or a difference. To compare something *to* something else is to assert a likeness between them.

To *contrast* is to emphasize *differences: She contrasted the gentle Athenians with the warlike Spartans.* As a v., *contrast* should be followed by *with.*

**comprise, compose, constitute**  *Comprise* means *embrace, include: The curriculum comprises every field of knowledge. Compose* and *constitute* mean *make up: All those fields together compose* [or *constitute*] *the curriculum.* The most common mistake is to use *comprise* as if it meant *compose:* x *The parts comprise the whole. Is comprised of* is not an adequate solution: x *The whole is comprised of the parts.* Try *The whole comprises the parts* or *The parts compose the whole.*

**concept, conception, idea**  The broadest of these terms is *idea,* and you should prefer it unless you are sure you mean one of the others. A *concept* is an abstract notion characterizing a class of particulars: *the concept of civil rights.* A *conception* is a stab at an idea, possibly erroneous: *She had an odd conception of my motives.* Note that *idea* would have been suitable even in these examples.

**concur in, concur with** You *concur in* an action or decision: *He concurred in her seeking a new career.* But you *concur with* a person or group: *He concurred with her in her decision.*

**conscious, aware** Almost syns., but you can observe a difference. People are *conscious* of their own perceptions but *aware* of events or circumstances.

**consensus** Avoid this n. unless you mean something very close to unanimity. And beware of the redt. x *consensus of opinion* and x *general consensus. Opinion* and *general* are already contained in the meaning of *consensus.*

**considerable** Colloq. in the sense of *many* (items): x *Considerable dignitaries were there.* Use the word to mean *weighty, important: The costs were considerable; The Secretary-General is a considerable figure.*

**consist of, consist in** Something *consists of* its components: *The decathlon consists of ten events. Consist in* means *exist in* or *inhere in: Discretion consists in knowing when to remain silent.*

**contemptible, contemptuous** Very different. *Contemptible* means *deserving contempt. Contemptuous* means *feeling or showing contempt. They felt contemptuous of such a contemptible performance.*

**continual, continuous** *Continual* means *recurring at intervals. Continuous* means *uninterrupted.* A river flows *continuously* but may overflow its banks *continually* through the years.

**contrary to** Since *contrary* is an adj., avoid constructions in which *contrary to* serves as an adv. modifier: x *Contrary to Baldwin, Orwell is not directly concerned with race.* This sentence makes it appear that Orwell is "contrary to Baldwin," whereas the writer means to compare the two authors' *concerns.* Try *Orwell, unlike Baldwin, is not directly concerned with race.* Save *contrary to* for sentences like *The order to surrender was contrary to everything they had been taught.*

**convey** Do not follow with a *that* clause: x *They conveyed that they were happy.* Choose a n. as obj.: *They conveyed the impression that they were happy.*

**convince, persuade** Often treated as syns., but you can preserve a valuable distinction by keeping *convince* for *win agreement* and *persuade* for *move to action.* If I *convince* you that I am right, I may *persuade* you to join my cause. Avoid x *He convinced his father to lend him the car.*

**could of** Always a mistake for *could have.*

**couple, pair** *Couple* refers to two items that are united. It is colloq. when the items are only casually linked: x *I have a couple of points I want to raise with you.* When you do use *couple of,* be sure not to drop the *of:* x *a couple reasons.*

*Pair* refers to two things that are inseparably joined in function or feeling: *The Joneses are a couple, but they are not much of a pair.*

Prefer *pairs* to *pair* for the plu.: *four pairs of shoes,* not x *four pair of shoes.*

Verbs governed by *couple* or *pair* are generally plu., although a sing. v. could be appropriate in a rare case: *A couple becomes a trio when the first child is born.*

criteria  Always plu.: *these criteria.* The sing. is *criterion.*

data  Opinion is divided over the number of *data,* which is technically the plu. form of *datum.* The safe course is to continue treating *data* as plu.: *The data have recently become available.* Even so, the sing. *data* is by now very common.

deduce, deduct  Both form the same n., *deduction,* but *deduce* means *derive* or *infer* and *deduct* means *take away* or *detract. He deduced that the IRS would not allow him to deduct the cost of his hair dryer.*

depend  Do not omit *on* or *upon,* as in x *It depends whether the rain stops in time.* And avoid *it depends* without a following reason: x *It all depends* is incomplete.

designed, calculated  Misused in passive constructions where no designing agent is envisioned: x *The long summer days are designed to expose your skin to too much ultraviolet light.* Try *The long summer days are likely to expose your skin to too much ultraviolet light.* Again, do not write x *This medicine is perfectly calculated to turn you into an addict.* Try *This medicine is likely to turn you into an addict.*

differ from, differ with  To *differ from* people is to *be different from* them; to *differ with* them is to *express disagreement with* them: *The Sioux differed from their neighbors in their religious practices; they differed with their neighbors over hunting rights.*

different from, different than  Some readers regard *different than* as an error wherever it occurs. But most readers would not object to *different than* when it helps to save words. *The outcome was different than I expected* is more concise than *The outcome was different from what I expected.*

disinterested, uninterested  Many writers use both to mean *not interested,* but in doing so they lose the unique meaning of *disinterested* as *impartial: What we need here is a disinterested observer.* Reserve *disinterested* for such uses. Avoid x *She was completely disinterested in dancing.*

doubtless(ly)  Since *doubtless* is already an adv., the *-ly* is excessive: *She will doubtless be ready at eight.*

**drastic** Once meant *violent,* and still retains a sense of harshness and grim urgency. Avoid x *a drastic improvement.*

**dubious, doubtful** An outcome or a statement may be *dubious,* but the person who calls it into question is *doubtful* about it. Though some writers overlook the distinction, you would do well to keep *doubtful* for the mental state of harboring doubts.

**due to** Do not use adverbially, as in x *Due to her absence, the team lost the game.* In such a sentence use *because of* or *owing to,* and save *due to* for sentences like *The loss was due to her absence.*

**effect** See *affect.*

**e.g., i.e.** Often confused. The abbreviation *e.g.* means *for example*; it can be used only when you are *not* citing all the relevant items. The abbreviation *i.e.* means *that is*; it can be used only when you are giving the *equivalent* of the preceding term. In the main text of an essay or paper, it is best to write out *for example* and *that is.*

Once you have written *e.g.,* do not add *etc.,* as in x *See, e.g., Chapters 4, 7, 11, etc.* The idea of unlisted further examples is already present in *e.g.*

**enhance** Does not mean *increase,* as in x *I want to enhance my bank account.* It means *increase the value or attractiveness of,* as in *He enhanced his good reputation by performing further generous acts.* In order to be enhanced, something must be already valued.

Note that the quality, not the person, gets enhanced. Avoid x *She was enhanced by receiving favorable reviews.*

**enormity, enormousness** Not syns. *Enormity* means *atrocious wickedness.* Do not write x *the enormity of his feet.*

**enthuse** Looks like a plausible substitute for *show enthusiasm,* but it has not won full acceptance. Be safe and prefer the longer expression.

**escape** (v.) When used with an obj., it should mean *elude,* as in *They escaped punishment.* Avoid x *They escaped the jail.* Make *escaped* intrans. here: *They escaped from the jail.*

**especially, specially, special** *Especially* means *outstandingly*: *an especially interesting idea. Specially* means *for a particular purpose, specifically*: *This racket was specially chosen by the champion.*

Watch for meaningless uses of *special*: x *There are two special reasons why I came here.* This would make sense only if there had been many reasons, only two of which were special ones. Just delete *special.*

**et al.** Means *and other people,* not *and other things.* It belongs in citations, not in your main text.

**etc.** Means *and other things,* not *and other people. Et al.* serves that rival meaning. In formal prose, use a substitute expression such as *and so forth.*

Do not use *etc.* after *for example* or *such as:* x *America is composed of many ethnic groups, such as Germans, Poles, Italians, etc.*

**eventhough** A mistake for *even though.*

**everywheres** A mistake for *everywhere.*

**exceeding(ly), excessive(ly)** *Exceeding* means *very much; excessive* means *too much.* It is not shameful to be *exceedingly rich,* but to be *excessively rich* is a demerit.

**except** Do not use as a conj., as in x *She told him to leave, except he preferred to stay.* Keep *except* as a prep. meaning *excluding: He remembered everything except his toothbrush.*

**expect** Mildly colloq. in the sense of *suppose, believe:* x *I expect it will snow tomorrow.*

**facet** A *facet* is one of the surfaces of a gem; thus it comes into view as the gem is turned. When you use *facet,* try to keep some sense of this shift in perspective: *An unexpected facet of the problem appears when we adopt the migrant workers' point of view.* Simply as a syn. of part, *facet* is stale: x *Let us address three facets of the issue.*

**factor** A *factor* is an *element helping to produce a given result,* as in *They overlooked several factors in seeking the causes of the riot.* Do not use *factor* simply as a syn. of *item* or *point.* Note that *contributing factor* is always redt.

**feel, feeling** Many careful writers prefer to keep *feel* a v. and *feeling* a n. Thus they would avoid x *She has a sensitive feel for the piano.*

**few, little** *Few* refers to things or persons that can be counted; *little* refers to things that can be measured or estimated but not itemized. *Few people were on hand, and there was little enthusiasm for the speaker.*

**fewer, less, lesser, least** *Fewer* refers to numbers, *less* to amounts: *fewer members, less revenue.* Beware of advertising jarg.: x *This drink contains less calories.* Since the calories are countable, only *fewer* would be correct here.

*Lesser* is an adj. meaning *minor* or *inferior: The lesser emissaries were excluded from the summit meeting. Least* is the superlative of *little.* As an adj. it should be used only when more than two items are involved: *That was the least of her many worries.*

Note that *fewer in number* is redt.

**figure, calculate** Colloq. as syns. of *think, suppose,* or *believe:* x *They figured she would be too frightened to complain.*

**flaunt, flout** Widely confused. To *flaunt* is to *display arrogantly: They flaunted their superior wisdom.* To *flout* is to *defy contemptuously:*

usage

*They flouted every rule of proper behavior.* The common error is to use flout for *flaunt*: x *The pitcher flouted his unbeaten record.*

**flunk** Colloq. for *fail*, as in x *He flunked Biology 23.*

**for example** See *e.g.*

**fortuitous** Means *by chance*, whether or not an advantage is implied. Do not allow *fortuitous* to mean simply *favorable, auspicious*, or *lucky*: x *How fortuitous it was that fate drew us together!*

**free, freely** *Free* can serve as both an adj. and an adv., meaning, among other things, *without cost*. If you write *I give it to you freely*, you are conveying something else: *I give it to you without mental reservation.* Do not be afraid to write *I give it to you free* if you mean *without charging you.*

**frightened, scared, afraid** You are *frightened* or, more informally, *scared* by an immediate cause of alarm; you are *afraid* of a more persistent danger or worry: *He was frightened [scared] by noises in the middle of the night; he was afraid he would have to buy a watchdog.*

**fulsome** Does not mean *abundant*; it means *offensively insincere.* Thus it would be wrong to write: x *I love the fulsome scents of early spring.*

**fun** Colloq. as an adj., as in x *a fun party.*

**good, well** *You look good tonight* means that you are attractive. *You look well tonight* means that you do not look sick.

**guess** Colloq. as a syn. of *suppose:* x *I guess I should give up trying.*

**had better** Do not shorten to *better*, as in x *You better pay attention.*

**half a** Do not precede with a redt. *a*, as in x *He was there for a half a day.*

**hanged, hung** The regular p.p. of *hang* is *hung*, but you should use *hanged* when referring to capital punishment: *He was hanged for his crimes; his lifeless body hung from the noose.*

**hard, hardly** Both can be advs. Fear of using *hard* as an adv. can lead to ambiguity: x *She was hardly pressed for time.* This could mean either *She was rushed* or, more probably, *She was scarcely rushed.* There is nothing wrong with writing *She was hard-pressed for time.* Note the hyphen, however.

**high, highly** *High* can be an adv. as well as an adj. Prefer it to *highly* in expressions like *he jumped high, a high-flying pilot.* An antique vase may be *highly prized* and therefore *high-priced* at an auction.

**hopefully** Many readers accept this word in the sense of *it is hoped*, but others feel strongly that *hopefully* can mean only *in a hopeful manner.* Keep to this latter meaning if you want to give no offense. Write *He prayed hopefully* but not x *Hopefully, his pains will subside.*

**how**  Avoid in the sense of *that,* as in x *I told her how I wouldn't stand for her sarcasm any more.*

**how ever, however**  Distinct terms. *How ever are you going to untie that knot? You, however, know more about it than I do.*

  *However* is correct in the sense of *in whatever manner: However you consider it, the situation looks desperate.*

**i.e.**  Means *that is;* see *e.g.*

**if not**  Potentially ambig., as in x *There were good reasons, if not excellent ones, for taking that step.* Does this mean that the reasons decidedly were not excellent or that they may indeed have been excellent? Try *but not excellent ones* or *indeed, excellent ones,* depending on the intended sense.

**ignorant, stupid**  Often confused. To be *ignorant* of something is simply not to know it: *Newton was ignorant of relativity.* An *ignorant* person is one who has been taught very little. A *stupid* person is mentally unable to learn: *The main cause of his ignorance was his stupidity.*

**implicit, explicit, tacit**  *Implicit* can be ambig., for it means both *implied* (left unstated) and *not giving cause for investigation.* Consider, e.g., x *My trust in her was implicit.* Was the trust left unstated, beyond question, or both? Try *My trust in her was left implicit* or *My trust in her was absolute.*

  *Explicit* is the opposite of *implicit* in the sense of *implied: In his will he spelled out the explicit provisions that had previously been left implicit. Tacit* is close to this sense of *implicit,* but it means *silent, unspoken;* its reference is to speech, not to expression in general.

**imply, infer**  Widely confused. To *imply* is to *leave an implication;* to *infer* is to *take an implication. She implied that she was ready to leave the company, but the boss inferred that she was bluffing.* The common error is to use *infer* for *imply.*

**in back of**  See *back of.*

**in case**  Can usually be improved to *if: If* [not *In case*] *you do not like this model, we will refund your money.* Save *in case* for *in the event: This sprinkler is provided in case of fire.*

**in connection with**  See *in terms of.*

**in terms of, along the lines of, in connection with**  Vague and wordy. Instead of writing x *In terms of prowess, Tarzan was unconquerable,* just write *Tarzan was unconquerable.* Similarly, x *He was pursuing his studies along the lines of sociology* should be simply *He was studying sociology.*

**include**  Do not use loosely to mean *are,* as in x *The Marx Brothers included Groucho, Harpo, Chico, and Zeppo.* Only when at least one member is unnamed should you use *include*: *The Marx Brothers included Harpo and Zeppo.*

Note also that *include* is inappropriate after you have already indicated a limitation: x *Two of my reasons include my drive for success and my wish to please my mother.*

**individual** (n.) Often pompous for *person:* x *He was a kind-hearted individual.* Use *individual* where you want to draw attention to the single person as contrasted with the collectivity, as in *Our laws respect the individual.*

**inside of** Widely regarded as colloq.; can always be shortened to *inside.*

**inspite of** A mistake for *in spite of.*

**is because** See *reason is because.*

**is when, is where** Often involved in faulty predication: x *A war is when opposing countries take up arms*; x *Massage is where you lie on a table and . . .* Match *when* only with times, *where* only with places: *When she was ready, she went where she pleased.* Most predication problems can be solved by changing the v.: *A war occurs when . . .*

**kind of, sort of, type of** When used at all, these expressions should be followed by the sing.: *this kind of woman.* But *such a woman is* preferable.

*Sort of* and *kind of* are awk. in the sense of *somewhat,* and they are sometimes followed by an unnecessary *a*: x *He was an odd sort of a king.* Do not use *sort of* or *kind of* unless your sentence needs them to make sense: *This kind of bike has been on the market for only three months.*

**leave, let** Have different senses in clauses like *leave him alone* and *let him alone.* The first means *get out of his presence*; the second means *don't bother him* (even if you remain in his presence). Don't write x *leave him go in peace.*

**level** (n.) Overworked in the vague, colorless sense illustrated by x *at the public level*; x *on the wholesale level.* Use only when the idea of degree or ranking is present: *He was a competent amateur, but when he turned professional he found himself beyond his level.*

**lie, lay** If you mean *repose,* use the intrans. *lie*: *lie down.* The trans. *lay* means, among other things, *set* or *put*: *lay it here.*

All forms of these verbs are troublesome. The following sentences use three common tenses correctly:

| PRESENT | PAST | PRESENT PERFECT |
| --- | --- | --- |
| I lie in bed. | I lay in bed. | I have lain in bed. |
| I lay down my cards. | I laid down my cards. | I have laid down my cards. |

**like**  See *as, like.*

**likely**  Weak as an unmodified adv.: x *He likely had no idea what he was saying.* Some readers would also object to x *Very likely, he had no idea what he was saying.* Try *probably,* and reserve *likely* for adj. uses: a *likely story.* See also *apt, liable, likely.*

**likewise**  An adv., not a conj. You can write *Likewise, Myrtle failed the quiz,* but not x *Jan failed the quiz, likewise Myrtle.*

**literally**  Means *precisely as stated, without a figurative sense.* If you write x *I literally died laughing,* you must be writing from beyond the grave. Do not use *literally* to mean *definitely* or *almost.* It is properly used in a sentence like *The poet writes literally about flowers, but her real subject is forgiveness.*

**lot, lots**  Somewhat colloq. in the sense of *many*: x *I could give you lots of reasons. A lot* and *lots* make distinctly colloq. advs., too: x *She pleases me lots.* Try *very much.* Note also the common misspelling x *alot.*

**mad, angry**  *Mad* means *insane.* It is colloq. in the sense of *angry*: x *They were mad at me.*

**majority**  Do not use unless you mean to contrast it with *minority*: *The majority of the members voted to disband the club.* In x *the majority of the time,* the term is out of place because *time* does not contain members that could be counted as a majority and a minority.

**many, much**  *Many* refers to countable items, *much* to a total amount that cannot be divided into items (see *amount, number*): *Many problems make for much difficulty.* Do not write x *There were too much people in the line.*

**media**  Increasingly used as a sing. term, but since it is the plu. of *medium,* you would still do well to keep it plu. Write *The media are to blame.*

**militate, mitigate**  Often confused. To *militate* is to *have an adverse effect.* It is followed by *against,* as in *His poor eyesight militated against his becoming a pilot. Mitigate* means *reduce* (an unpleasant effect). It always takes an obj., as in *The doctor's cheerful manner mitigated the pain.*

  The common error is to use *mitigate* for *militate,* as in x *Their stubborn attitude mitigated against their chances of success.*

**mix, mixture**  Many careful writers prefer to keep *mix* a v. and *mixture* a n. Thus they would avoid x *There was a fascinating mix of interests around the table.*

**most**  Colloq. as an adv. meaning *almost*: x *We were most dead by the time we got there.*

**much less**  Avoid x *Skiing is difficult, much less surfing.* The *much less* construction requires an initial negation, as in *He has not even appeared, much less begun his work.*

**muchly** A mistake for *much.*

**myself** Do not use this intensive pro. merely as a substitute for *I* or *me*: x *My friends and myself are all old-timers now*; x *She gave the book to Steve and myself.* Save *myself* for emphatic or reflexive uses: *I myself intend to do it; I have forgiven myself.*

**not too, not that** Colloq. when used to mean *not very*: x *She was not too sure about that*; x *They are not that interested in sailing.*

**nothing like, nowhere near** Do not use in place of *not nearly,* as in x *I am nothing like* [or *nowhere near*] *as spry as I used to be.*

**nowheres** A mistake for *nowhere.*

**numerous** Properly an adj. You can write *He still had numerous debts,* but avoid x *Numerous of his debts remained unpaid.*

**occur, take place** The narrower term is *take place,* which should be used only with scheduled events. Avoid x *The storm took place last Tuesday.*

**off of** Should be either *off* or *from*: *She jumped off the bridge* or *She jumped from the bridge.* Avoid x *She jumped off of the bridge.*

**oftentimes** Colloq. for *often.*

**old-fashion** Colloq. for *old-fashioned.*

**on, upon, up on** *On* and *upon* mean the same thing, but you should save *upon* for formal effects: *She swore upon her word of honor.* Note that *up on* is not the same as *upon: He climbed up on the ladder.*

**on account of** Never preferable to *because of.*

**only** Do not use as a conj.: x *He tries to be good, only his friends lead him astray.* Keep *only* as an adj. or adv.: *That is his only problem; He only needs some better advice.*

**oral, verbal** *Oral* means *by mouth*; *verbal* means *in words,* whether or not the words are spoken. Write a *verbal presentation* only if you have in mind a contrast with some form of communication that bypasses words.

**other than that** Considered awk.: x *Other than that, I can follow your reasoning.* Try a more definite expression: *except for one point, apart from this objection,* etc.

**other times** Do not use as an adv., as in x *Other times she felt depressed.* Use the complete prep. phrase *at other times.*

**otherwise** Allowable as an adv. meaning *in other respects* or *differently*: *Otherwise, I feel healthy; She decided otherwise.* But do not use *otherwise* to replace the adj. *other*: x *He loved old buildings, Victorian and otherwise.*

**ourself** Should be *ourselves.*

**outside of** Should be *outside*. And in figurative uses you should prefer *except for*: not x *outside of these reasons* but *except for these reasons*.

**part, portion** A *part* is a *fraction of a whole*; a *portion* is a *part allotted to some person or use*. Thus you should avoid x *A large portion of the ocean is polluted.*

**phenomena** Not a sing. word, but the plu. of *phenomenon*.

**place** Some readers regard terms like *anyplace, no place,* and *someplace* as colloq. It is safer to write *anywhere, nowhere, somewhere.* Note, in any event, the two-word spelling of *no place.*

**plan** The v. is best followed by *to*, not *on*: *He plans to run,* not x *He plans on running.* Note that since *plan* implies a future action, expressions like x *plan ahead* and x *future plans* are redt.

**plus** Not a coord. conj.: x *He was sleepy, plus he had not studied.* Nor is it a sentence adv.: x *She enjoyed her work; plus, the hours were good.* Keep *plus* as a prep. with numbers: *Two plus two is four.* Look for a syn. when you are not dealing in numbers: x *Her challenging work plus her long vacations made her happy.* Try *and* or *along with.*

**poorly** Colloq. in the sense of *ill* or *sick*: x *I feel poorly today.* Keep as an adv.: *I performed poorly on the exam.*

**popular** Implies favor with large numbers of people. Avoid when you have something smaller in mind: x *The hermit was popular with his three visitors*; x *That idea is not very popular with me.*

**possible** Do not use as an adv.: x *a possible missing airliner.* Try *possibly.*

**pressure** Has not gained full acceptance as a v.: x *He pressured us to agree.* Try *pressed.*

**quote** (n.) Widely considered colloq. when used to mean *quotation,* as in x *this quote,* or when written in the plu. to mean quotation marks, as in x *She put quotes around it.* In formal writing, take the trouble to use the full terms *quotation* and *quotation marks.*

**raise, rise** As a v., *raise* is trans.: *raise your arm. Rise* is intrans.: *rise and shine.* Do not confuse these words.

As a n., *raise* is by now fully accepted: *a raise in pay.*

**real** Colloq. as an adv., as in x *I am real committed.* Prefer *really.*

**reason is because** A classic predication error. You can write either *She stayed home because of her health* or *The reason was her health,* but it is redt. to write x *The reason she stayed home was because of her health.*

**rebut, refute** To *rebut* an argument is to *speak or write against* it; to *refute* an argument is to *disprove* it. The common error is to use *refute* for *rebut*: x *You may be right, but I will refute what you said.*

**reckon** Colloq. for *suppose, think*: x *I reckon I can handle that.* Use in the sense of *count* or *consider*: *She is reckoned an indispensable member of the board.*

**relation, relationship** These overlap in meaning, and some writers use *relationship* in all contexts. But *relation* is preferable when you mean an abstract connection: *the relation of wages to prices.* Save *relationship* for mutuality: *the President's relationship with the press.*

**relevant** Requires a following prep. phrase: x *The course was extremely relevant.* To what?

**replace** See *substitute.*

**reticent** Does not mean *reluctant,* as in x *They were reticent to comply.* It means *disposed to be silent,* as in *Reticent people sometimes become talkative late at night.*

**scared** See *frightened, scared, afraid.*

**similar** Means *resembling,* not *same.* Avoid x *Ted died in 1979, and Alice suffered a similar fate two years later.* Try *the same fate.*

  Do not use *similar* as an adv. meaning *like:* x *This steak smells similar to the one I ate yesterday.* Try *like the one.*

**since** An indispensable word, but watch for ambiguity: x *Since she left, he has been doing all the housework.* Here *since* could mean either *because* or *ever since.* Prefer one of these terms.

**sit, set** With few exceptions, *sit* is intrans.: *She sat down. Set* is usually trans.: *They set the banquet table.* You can of course write *She sat her baby in the high chair* and *The sun set,* but avoid x *I set there sleeping* or x *I want to sit these weary bones to rest.*

**some** Do not use as an adv. meaning *somewhat,* as in x *He worried some about his health.* Try *He was somewhat worried about his health.*

**something** Avoid as an adv. meaning *somewhat,* as in x *He is something over six feet tall.* Note also that x *He smells something awful* is both ambig. and colloq. in the intended sense of *He smells bad.*

**somewheres** A mistake for *somewhere.*

**sort of** See *kind of.*

**special, specially** See *especially.*

**substitute, replace** *Substitute* takes as its obj. the new item that is supplanting the old one: *He substituted margarine for butter. Replace* takes as its obj. the item being abandoned: *She replaced the butter with margarine.* Note that these sentences are recounting the same act.

**such as** See *etc.*

**suppose to** A mistake for *supposed to,* as in x *We are suppose to watch our manners.*

**sure** Colloq. as an adv.: x *She sure likes muffins.* Since *surely* would sound awk., try *certainly.*

**sympathy for, sympathy with, sympathize with** To feel *sympathy for* someone is to experience compassion: *She has sympathy for the people of Bangladesh.* *Sympathy with* is a feeling of kinship or identity: *Her sympathy with Gloria Steinem made her a feminist.* To *sympathize with,* however, is once again to experience compassion: *She sympathized with the poor.*

**that** Beware of using *that* as an unexplained demonstrative adj.: x *He didn't have that much to say.* How much is *that* much?

In restrictive clauses (11j, p. 286), prefer *that* to *which*: *Alberta is the province that fascinates me.*

**theirself, theirselves** Mistakes for *themselves.*

**those kind, type,** etc. Should be *that kind, type,* etc. But prefer *such,* which is more concise: not x *that kind of person* but *such people.*

**thusly** A mistake for *thus.*

**till, until, til, 'til, 'till** *Till* and *until* are interchangeable. The other three forms are inappropriate.

**too** Avoid as a syn. of *very*: x *It was too good of you to help.*

**try and** Should be *try to*: not x *Try and do better* but *Try to do better.*

**type** Colloq. in place of *type of*: x *You are a headstrong type person.* But *type of* is itself objectionably wordy; try *You are headstrong.*

**usage, use** Widely confused. Save *usage* for contexts implying convention or custom: *English usage; the usages of our sect.* Avoid x *They discouraged the usage of cocaine* or x *Excessive usage of the car results in high repair bills.* Substitute *use* in both sentences.

Even *use of* often proves wordy: x *By his use of symbolism Ibsen establishes himself as a modern playwright.* Why not just *By his symbolism Ibsen establishes himself as a modern playwright?*

**use** (v.), **utilize; use** (n.), **utilization** *Utilize* and *utilization* are almost always jarg. for *use.* To *utilize* is properly to *put to use* or to *turn a profit on,* and it makes sense when coupled with an abstraction: *to utilize resources.* But the word has a dehumanizing air; prefer *use* in ordinary contexts. Note that *utilization* is almost four times as long as *use,* which can always stand in its place.

**use to** In an affirmative past construction, be sure to write *used to,* not *use to*: x *They use to think so*; x *They are not use to the cold.* In addition, certain past neg. constructions with *use* always sound awk.: x *Didn't she use to take the bus?* Try *She used to take the bus, didn't she?*

**verbal, oral** See *oral.*

**violently** Not a syn. of *strongly,* as in x *I violently oppose your program.* Only thugs and terrorists oppose programs *violently,* causing actual physical damage.

**ways**  Avoid in the sense of *distance*: x *It was only a short ways.* The right form is *way.*

**what ever, whatever**  Distinct terms. *What ever will we do about the heating bills? Whatever we do, it will not solve the problem.*

**where**  Do not use in place of *whereby,* as in x *Tai-chi is an exercise regimen where one slowly activates every muscle group. Whereby,* the right word here, means *by means of which.* Save *where* for actual places: *That storefront studio is where we study Tai-chi.*

**where . . . at**  Redt. and colloq., as in x *She had no idea where he was at.* Always delete the *at.*

**-wise**  Acceptable when it means *in the manner of,* as in *clockwise* and *lengthwise,* and when it means *having wisdom: penny-wise and pound-foolish; a ring-wise boxer.* Note the hyphens in this second set of examples.

Avoid *-wise* in the sense of *with respect to*: x *taxwise, agriculturewise, conflict resolutionwise.* Such terms do save space, but many readers find them ugly. Look for concise alternatives: not x *the situation taxwise* but *the tax situation*; not x *America's superiority agriculturewise* but *America's superiority in agriculture.*

**with**  See *being.*

**would like for**  Colloq. in sentences like x *They would like for me to quit.* Try *They would like me to quit.*

# Glossary of Terms

The Glossary offers simple definitions of terms used in this book. Words appearing in **boldface** have separate entries which you can consult if the term is unfamiliar. The abbreviation *cf.* means "compare"—that is, note the difference between the term being defined and another. And *e.g.* means "for example."

**abbreviation** (26g) A shortened word, with the addition of a period to indicate the omission (*Dr.*).

**absolute phrase** (11f) A **phrase** that, instead of modifying a particular word, acts like an **adverb** to the rest of the **sentence** in which it appears:

> ABS PHRASE
> • *All struggle over,* the troops laid down their arms.

Absolute phrases are not considered mistakes of usage. Cf. **dangling modifier**.

**abstract language** (8k) Words that make no appeal to the senses: *agree, aspect, comprehensible, enthusiasm, virtuously,* etc. Cf. **concrete language**.

**active voice** See **voice**.

**additive phrase** (10c) An expression beginning with a term like *accompanied by* or *as well as*. It is not strictly a part of a subject, and thus it should not affect the number of a verb.

*ad hominem* **reasoning** (3n) A **fallacy** whereby someone tries to discredit a position by attacking the person, party, or interest that supports that position.

**adjectival clause** See **clause**.

**adjective** (11a) A **modifier** of a **noun**, **pronoun**, or other **nounlike element** — e.g., *strong* in *a strong contender.* Most adjectives can be compared: *strong, stronger, strongest.* See **degree**. See also **interrogative adjective**.

**adverb** (11a) A word modifying either a **verb**, an **adjective**, another adverb, a **preposition**, an **infinitive**, a **participle**, a **phrase**, a **clause**, or a whole **sentence**: *now, clearly, moreover,* etc. Any one-word modifier that is not an adjective or an **article** is sure to be an adverb.

**adverbial clause** See **clause**.

**agreement** (10b) In grammar, the correspondence of a **verb** with its **subject** in **number** and **person**. In *I stumble,* e.g., the verb *stumble* "agrees with" the subject *I*; both are singular and first-person in form. Cf. **pronoun reference**.

**allusion** (29a) A passing reference to a work or idea, either by directly mentioning it or by borrowing its well-known language. Thus, someone who writes *She took arms against a sea of troubles* is alluding to, but not mentioning, Hamlet's most famous speech. The sentence *He did it with Shakespearean flair* alludes directly to Shakespeare. Quotation through allusion differs from **plagiarism** in that readers are expected to notice the reference.

**analogy** (2i) In general, a similarity of features or pattern between two things: *The nearest analogy to human speech may be the songs of whales.*

In **rhetoric**, an analogy is an extended likeness purporting to show that the rule or principle behind one thing also holds for the different thing being discussed. Thus, someone who disapproves of people leaving their home towns might devise this analogy: *People, like trees, must find their nourishment in the place where they grow up; to seek it elsewhere is as fatal as removing a tree from its roots.* Like most analogies, this one starts with an obvious resemblance and proceeds to a more debatable one.

**analysis** (p. 28) In a narrow sense, the breaking of something into its parts or functions and showing how those smaller units go to make up the whole. More broadly, analysis is the application of explanatory strategies to a given problem. In this book, analysis (or *exposition*) is treated as a rhetorical **mode**, along with **description**, **narration**, and **argument**.

**antecedent** (10e) The word for which a **pronoun** stands:

     ANT                      PRO
- *Jane* was here yesterday, but today *she* is at school.

**anticipation** (1h)  The narrative device of gaining dramatic effect by beginning with a later scene and then doubling back in time.

**anticipatory pattern** (7o)  A structure, such as *both x and y* or *not x but y,* which gives an early signal of the way it will be completed.

**APA style** (29c)  The **reference list** documentation style of the American Psychological Association.

**aphorism** (7p)  A memorably concise sentence conveying a very general assertion: *If wishes were horses, beggars would ride.* Many aphorisms show **balance** in their structure.

**appositive** (11k)  A word or group of words whose only function is to identify or restate an immediately preceding **noun, pronoun,** or **noun-like element**:

APP
- Mike *the butcher* is quite a clown.

**Arabic numeral** (26m)  A figure such as *3, 47,* or *106,* as opposed to a **Roman numeral** such as *III, XLVII,* or *CVI.*

**argument** (p. 28)  The **mode** of writing in which a writer tries to convince the reader that a certain position on an issue is well-founded. Cf. **description, analysis, narration.**

**article**  An indicator or determiner immediately preceding a **noun** or **modifier.** Articles themselves may be considered modifiers, along with **adjectives** and **adverbs.** The *definite article* is *the*; the *indefinite articles* are *a* and *an.*

**attributive noun** (8c)  A **noun** serving as an **adjective:** *beach* in *beach shoes,* or *Massachusetts* in *the Massachusetts way of doing things.*

**auxiliary** (21b)  A **verb** form, usually lacking **inflection,** that combines with other verbs to express possibility, likelihood, necessity, obligation, etc.: *She can succeed*; *He could become jealous.* The commonly recognized auxiliaries are *can, could, dare, do, may, might, must, need, ought, should,* and *would. Is, have,* and their related forms act like auxiliaries in the formation of **tenses:** *He is coming*; *They have gone.*

**baited opener** (5d)  An introductory **paragraph** which, by presenting its early sentences "out of context," teases its reader into taking further interest.

**balance** (7p)  The effect created when a whole **sentence** is controlled by the **matching** of grammatically like elements, as in *He taught us the intricate ways of the city; we taught him the simple ways of nature.* A balanced sentence typically repeats a grammatical pattern and certain words in order to highlight important differences.

gl

**base form of verb** (21a) An **infinitive** without *to*: *see, think,* etc. Base forms appear with **auxiliaries** (*should see*) and in the formation of present and future **tenses** (*I see, I will see*).

**begging the question** (3k) The **fallacy** of treating a debatable idea as if it had already been proved. If, in a paper favoring national health insurance, you assert that only the greedy medical lobby could oppose such an obviously needed program, you are begging the question by assuming the rightness of your position instead of establishing it with **evidence**.

**bibliographic note** (29f) A **supplementary note** directing the reader to further sources of information than the origin of a specific cited passage. Cf. **substantive note**.

**bibliography** (29e) A list of consulted works presented at the end of a book, article, or **essay**. Also, a whole book devoted to listing works within a certain **subject area**.

**block quotation** See **extracted quotation**.

**bound element** (7k) A modifying word, **phrase**, or subordinate **clause** which, because it is **restrictive**, is not set off by commas. Cf. **core element**, **free element**.

**brainstorming** (3f) The process of entertaining many suggestions for a topic without regard for links between them.

**cardinal number** (26n) A number like *four* (*4*) or *twenty-seven* (*27*), as opposed to an **ordinal number** like *fourth* (*4th*) or *twenty-seventh* (*27th*).

**case** (12a) The **inflectional** form of **nouns** and **pronouns** indicating whether they designate actors (*subjective* case: *I, we, they*), receivers of action (*objective* case: *me, us, them*), or "possessors" of the thing or quality modified (*possessive* case: *his* Toyota, *their* indecision, *Geraldine's* influence). *Personal pronouns* also have "second possessive" forms: *mine, theirs,* etc. Cf. **double possessive**.

**choppiness** (7r) The undesirable effect produced by a sequence of brief sentences lacking **significant pauses**.

**circular thesis** (3j) A faulty **thesis** that doubles back on itself, self-evidently saying only what is already implied by some of its own language: x *If we had more good weather in this part of the country, the climate would be much improved.*

**circumlocution** (8i) Roundabout expression, or one such expression— e.g., *when all is said and done* in place of *finally.*

**clause** (9b) A cluster of words containing a **subject** and a **predicate**. All clauses are either *subordinate* (dependent) or *independent*. A subordinate clause cannot stand alone: x *When he was hiding in the closet.* An

independent clause, which is considered grammatically complete, can stand alone: *He was hiding in the closet.*
There are three kinds of subordinate clauses:

1. An *adjectival* clause serves the function of an **adjective**:

> ADJ CLAUSE
> • Marty, *who was extremely frightened,* did not want to make a sound.

The adjectival clause modifies the **noun** *Marty.*

2. An *adverbial* clause serves the function of an **adverb**:

> ADV CLAUSE
> • Marty held his breath for forty seconds *when he was hiding in the closet.*

The adverbial clause modifies the **verb** *held.*

3. And a *noun* clause serves the function of a **noun**:

> NOUN CLAUSE
> • *That an intruder might slip through his bedroom window* had never occurred to him.

The noun clause serves as the **subject** of the **verb** *had occurred.*

cliché (8j) A trite, stereotyped, overused expression: *an open and shut case*; *a miss is as good as a mile.* Most clichés contain **figurative language** that has lost its vividness: *a heart of gold, bring the house down,* etc. When two clichés occur together, the effect is usually **mixed metaphor**.

collective noun (10d) A **noun** that, though singular in form, designates a group of members: *band, family,* etc.

comma splice (9e) A **run-on sentence** in which two independent clauses are joined by a comma alone, without the necessary coordinating conjunction: x *It is raining today, I left my umbrella home.* Cf. **fused sentence**.

common gender (8e) The intended sexual neutrality of **pronouns** used to indicate an indefinite party. Traditionally, indefinite (*one*) and masculine personal pronouns (*he*) were used, but the masculine ones are now widely regarded as **sexist language**.

comparative degree See **degree**.

comparison and contrast (2e) The analytic strategy of exploring the resemblances and differences between two or more things.

complement (9a) Usually, an element in a **predicate** that identifies or describes the **subject**. A single-word complement is either a *predicate noun* or a *predicate adjective*:

PRED N
- He is a *musician*.

PRED ADJ
- His skill is *unbelievable*.

In addition, a **direct object** can have a complement, known as an *objective complement*:

D OBJ          OBJ COMPL
- They consider *the location desirable*.

**Infinitives**, too, can have complements:

INF          COMPL INF
- They beg him *to be* more *cooperative*.

See also **objective complement**.

compound, adj. (10d) Consisting of more than one word, as in a compound verb (They *rode* and *drove*), a compound noun (*ice cream*), a compound preposition (*in spite of*), a compound subject (*He and she* were there), or a compound modifier (*far-gone*).

concession (2h) In **rhetoric**, the granting of an opposing point, usually to show that it does not overturn one's own **thesis**.

conciseness (8i) Economy of expression. Not to be confused with simplicity; conciseness enables a maximum of meaning to be communicated in a minimum of words.

concrete language (8k) Words describing a thing or quality appealing to the senses: *purple, car, buzz, dusty,* etc. Cf. **abstract language**.

conjunction (9e) An un**inflected** word that connects other words, **phrases**, or **clauses**: *and, although,* etc.

A *coordinating* conjunction—*and, but, for, nor, or, so, yet*—joins grammatically similar elements without turning one into a **modifier** of the other: *You are sad, but I am cheerful.*

A *subordinating* conjunction joins grammatically dissimilar elements, turning one of them into a modifier and specifying its logical relation to the other—e.g., *Although* in *Although you are sad, I am cheerful.*

*Correlative* conjunctions are matched pairs with a coordinating or a disjunctive purpose: *either/or, neither/nor,* etc.

**connotation** (8d)  An association that a word calls up, as opposed to its **denotation**, or dictionary meaning. Thus, the word *exile* denotes enforced separation from one's home or country, but it connotes loneliness, homesickness, and any number of other, more private, thoughts and images.

**continuity** (6b)  The felt linkage between sentences or whole paragraphs, achieved in part by keeping related sentences together and in part by using **signals of relation** to indicate how sentences tie in with the ones they follow.

**contraction** (22u)  The condensing of two words to one, with an apostrophe added to replace the omitted letter or letters: *isn't, don't,* etc. Contractions are used primarily in speech and informal writing.

**"contrary" modifier** (11p)  A **modifier** that opposes the emphasis of a preceding one:

> "CONTRARY" MOD
> • an attractive, *but finally unworkable,* solution.

The commas surrounding such a modifier are optional.

**coordinating conjunction**  See **conjunction**.

**coordination** (9e)  The giving of equal grammatical value to two or more parts of a **sentence**. Those parts are usually joined by a *coordinating conjunction: He tried, but he failed*; *The lifeguard reached for her megaphone and her whistle.* Cf. **subordination**.

**core element** (7a)  The heart of the statement, question, or exclamation in a **sentence**, usually consisting of an independent **clause** and any **bound elements** accompanying it. Expressions falling outside the core element (namely, **free elements**) are set off by punctuation, usually commas. In the sentence *She tried, although not as hard as she might have, to find a job that would satisfy her,* the core element is *She tried to find a job that would satisfy her.*

**correlative conjunction**  See **conjunction**.

**cumulative sentence** (7v)  A **sentence** that continues to develop after its main idea has been stated, adding **clauses** or **phrases** that **modify** or explain that assertion: *She crumpled the letter in her fist, trembling with rage, wondering whether she should answer the accusations or simply say good riddance to the whole affair.* Cf. **suspended sentence**.

**dangling modifier** (11c)  The **modifier** of a term that has been misplaced or wrongly omitted from the sentence:

> DANGL MOD
> x *Not wishing to be bothered,* the telephone was left off the hook.

The person who did not wish to be bothered goes unmentioned and is thus absurdly replaced by the telephone.

**dead metaphor** (8l) A **metaphor** that has become so common that it usually does not call to mind an **image**: *a devil of a time, rock-bottom prices,* etc. When overworked, a dead metaphor becomes a **cliché**.

**declarative sentence** (16b) A **sentence** that presents a statement rather than a question or an **exclamation**: *Lambs are woolly.*

**degree** (23a) The form of an **adjective** or **adverb** showing its quality, quantity, or intensity. The ordinary, uncompared form of an adjective or adverb is its *positive* degree: *quick, quickly.* The *comparative* degree is intermediate, indicating that the modified term surpasses at least one other member of its group: *quicker, more quickly.* And an adjective or adverb in the *superlative* degree indicates that the modified term surpasses all other members of its group: *quickest, most quickly.*

**demonstrative adjective** (13e) A *demonstrative pronoun* form serving as a **modifier**, e.g., *those* in *those laws.*

**demonstrative pronoun** See **pronoun**.

**denotation** (8a) The primary, "dictionary," meanings of a word. Cf. **connotation**.

**dependent clause** See **clause**.

**description** (1a) The **mode** of writing in which a writer tries to acquaint the reader with a place, object, character, or group. Cf. **argument**, **analysis**, **narration**.

**dialogue** (20d) The direct representation of speech between two or more persons. Cf. **indirect discourse**.

**diction** (8h) The choice of words. Diction is commonly divided into three levels: formal (*deranged*), middle (*crazy*), and slang (*nuts*).

**digression** (6a) A temporary change of topic within a **sentence, paragraph**, or whole discourse. In an **essay**, an *apparent digression*—one that later turns out to have been pertinent after all—may sometimes serve a good purpose. In general, however, digressions are to be avoided.

**direct discourse** (15d) The use of quotation as opposed to summary of a speaker or writer's words (**indirect discourse**).

**direct object** (9a) A word naming the item directly acted upon by a **subject** through the activity of a **verb**:

    S   V      D OBJ
- She hit the *jackpot.*

Cf. **indirect object, object of preposition**.

**direct paragraph** (6f) A **paragraph** in which the **main sentence** comes at or near the beginning and the remaining sentences support it, sometimes after a **limiting sentence** or two.

**disjunctive subject** (10d) A **subject** containing elements that are alternative to one another, as in *Either you or I must back down.*

**distinct expression** (7a) The forming of **sentences** in the clearest manner, without causing a reader to guess at the meaning or the relations between elements. Distinct expression is enhanced by effective punctuation, **subordination**, and **conciseness** of phrasing.

**division** (2b) The analytic strategy of spelling out the parts or stages that make up some whole.

**double negative** (11g) The nonstandard practice of conveying the same negative meaning twice: x *They don't want no potatoes.*

**double possessive** (12i) A possessive form using both *of* and -*'s*: *an idea of Linda's.* Double possessives do not constitute faulty usage.

**either-or reasoning** (3l) The depicting of one's own position as the better of an artificially limited and "loaded" pair of alternatives—e.g., x *If we do not raise taxes this year, a worldwide depression is inevitable.*

**ellipsis** (20m) The three or four spaced dots used to indicate material omitted from a quotation: *"about the . . . story."* A whole row of dots indicates omission of much more material, usually verse.

**emotionalism** (5c) The condition of someone who is too upset to think clearly. Strong emotion can be a valuable aid to writing; emotionalism is always a handicap.

**endnote** (29e) A note placed in a consecutive series with others at the end of an **essay**, article, chapter, or book.

**essay** (p. 4) A fairly brief (usually between two and twenty-five typed pages) piece of nonfiction that tries to make a point in an interesting way. For the essay **modes** see **analysis**, **argument**, **description**, **narration**.

**euphemism** (8g) A vague or "nice" expression inadvisedly used in place of a more direct one; e.g., *rehabilitation facility* for *prison,* or *disincentive* for *threat.*

**evidence** (3o) Facts, reasons, and testimony tending to support a **thesis**. One statement can be used as evidence for another only if there is a high likelihood that readers will accept it as true.

**exclamation** (16j) An extremely emphatic statement or outburst: *Get out of here! What a scandal!* Cf. **interjection**.

**expletive** The word *it* or *there* when used only to postpone a **subject** coming after the verb:

EXPL   V
- *There* are many reasons to doubt his story.

**exposition** See **analysis**.

**extracted quotation** (20h) A quoted passage set apart from the writer's own text. Prose quotations of more than four typed lines and verse quotations of more than two or three lines are customarily extracted. Such passages are **indented** by ten spaces, and quotation marks at the beginning and end are dropped. Also called *block quotation*. Cf. **incorporated quotation**.

**fallacy** (2g) A formal error or illegitimate shortcut in reasoning. See *ad hominem* **reasoning, circular thesis, begging the question, either-or reasoning, faulty generalization,** *post hoc* **explanation**, and **straw man**.

**false start** (7t) A device whereby a **sentence** appears to present its grammatical **subject** first but then breaks off and begins again, thus turning the opening element into an **appositive**: *Elephants, gorillas, pandas — the list of endangered species grows longer every year*. A false start can be a good means of seizing a reader's attention. Cf. **mixed construction**.

**faulty generalization** (3i) The **fallacy** of drawing a general conclusion from insufficient **evidence** — e.g., concluding from one year's drought that the world's climate has entered a long period of change.

**figurative language** (8l) Language that heightens expressiveness by suggesting an imaginative, not a **literal**, comparison to the thing described — e.g., *a man so emaciated that he looked more like an x-ray than a person*. See **metaphor, simile**. Cf. **literal language**.

**footnote** (29e) A *note* at the bottom of a page. Cf. **endnote**.

**fragment** See **sentence fragment**.

**free element** (7k) A **modifying** word, **phrase**, or subordinate **clause** that deserves to be set off by commas. Most but not all free elements are **nonrestrictive**; some **restrictive modifiers** at the beginnings of sentences can be treated as free — that is, with a following comma. Cf. **bound element, core element**.

**freewriting** (3f) The practice of writing continuously for a fixed period without concern for logic or correctness. In *focused freewriting* the writer begins with a specific **topic**.

**funnel opener** (5d) An introductory **paragraph** beginning with a broad assertion and gradually narrowing to a specific **topic**.

**fused sentence** (9e) A **run-on sentence** in which two independent **clauses** are joined without either a comma or a coordinating **conjunction**: x *He is a dapper newscaster I love his slightly Canadian accent.*

gender (8e) The grammatical concept of sexual classification determining the forms of masculine (*he*), feminine (*she*), and neuter (*it*) *personal pronouns* and the feminine forms of certain nouns (*actress*). Cf. **common gender, sexist language**.

gerund (12h) A form derived from a **verb** but functioning as a **noun** — e.g., *Skiing* in *Skiing is dangerous*. Gerunds take exactly the same form as **participles**, and they are capable of having **subjects** (usually possessive in **case**) as well as **objects**:

S OF GER     GER        OBJ GER
• *Elizabeth's winning* the *pentathalon* was unexpected.

Cf. **participle**.

governing pronoun (4a) The prevailing **pronoun** in a piece of writing, helping to establish the writer's point of view.

governing tense (15a) The prevailing verb **tense** in a piece of writing, establishing a time frame for reported events.

image (8l) An expression that appeals to the senses. More narrowly, an example of **figurative language**. In both senses, the use of images is called *imagery*.

imperative mood See **mood**.

implied subject (9a) A **subject** not actually present in a **clause** but nevertheless understood: [*You*] *Watch out!* The customary implied subject, as here, is *you*.

incorporated quotation (20b) A quotation placed within quotation marks and not set off from the writer's own prose. Cf. **extracted quotation**.

indefinite pronoun See **pronoun**.

indention (20h) The setting of the first word of a line to the right of the left margin, as in a new paragraph (5 spaces) or an **extracted quotation** (usually 10 spaces).

independent clause See **clause**.

index (28c) A book, usually with a new volume each year, containing alphabetically ordered references to articles (and sometimes books) in a given field. Also, an alphabetical list of subjects and the page numbers where they are treated in a nonfiction book, as on pages 607–629 below.

indicative mood See **mood**.

indirect discourse (15d) Reporting what was said, as opposed to directly quoting it. Not *She said, "I am tired,"* but *She said she was tired*. Also called *indirect statement*. Cf. **indirect question**.

indirect object (12a) A word designating the person or thing for whom or which, or to whom or which, the action of a **verb** is performed. An indirect object never appears without a **direct object** occurring in the same clause:

IND OBJ                    D OBJ
- She sent *Fernando* a discouraging *letter.*

**indirect question** (16b) The reporting of a question without use of the question form—not *She asked, "Where should I turn?"* but *She asked where she should turn.* Cf. **indirect discourse.**

**infinitive** (9a) The **base form of a verb**, usually but not always preceded by *to*: *to win; prove; to prove.*

**inflection** (9a) A change in the ending or whole form of a word to show a change in function without creating a new word. Thus *he* can be inflected to *his, George* to *George's, go* to *went,* etc.

**intensifier** (8i) A "fortifying" expression like *absolutely, definitely,* or *very.* Habitual use of intensifiers weakens the force of assertion.

**intensive pronoun** See **pronoun.**

**interjection** A word that stands apart from other constructions in order to command attention or show strong feeling: *aha, hey, wow,* etc. Cf. **exclamation.**

**interpretation** (2j) The making of judgments about the meaning or coherence of a piece of writing, a work of art, or an event or movement.

**interrogative adjective** An interrogative **pronoun** form that combines with a **noun** to introduce a question—e.g., *Whose* in *Whose socks are these?*

**interrogative pronoun** See **pronoun.**

**interrupting element** (11m) A word or group of words that interrupts the main flow of a sentence:

INT EL
- You, *I regret to say,* are not the one.

Interrupting elements (also called *parenthetical elements*) should be set off at both ends by punctuation, usually by commas.

**intransitive verb** (9a) A **verb** expressing an action or state without connection to a **direct object** or a **complement**—e.g., *complained* in *They complained.* Cf. **linking verb, transitive verb.**

**introductory tag** (20j) A **clause**, such as *He said* or *Agnes asked,* introducing a quotation. A tag may also interrupt or follow a quotation.

**inverted syntax** (7u) The reversal of the expected order among sentence elements, usually for rhetorical effect: *After many bitter hours came the dawn.*

**irony** (4c) A sharply incongruous or "poetically just" effect—created, for example, when the Secretary of the Treasury has to borrow a coin to make a phone call.

In **rhetoric**, irony is the saying of one thing in order to convey a different or even opposite meaning: *Brutus is an honorable man* [he really isn't]. Irony can be *broad* (obvious) or *subtle*, depending on the writer's purpose. Cf. **sarcasm**.

**irregular verb** (21b) A **verb** that forms its past **tense** and its past **participle** in some way other than simply adding *-d* or *-ed*: *go* (*went*, *gone*), *swim* (*swam*, *swum*), etc.

**jargon** (8f) Technical language used in inappropriate, nontechnical contexts — e.g., *upwardly mobile* for *ambitious, positive reinforcement* for *praise, paranoid* for *upset*.

**leading idea** (6a) The "point" of a **paragraph**, to which all other ideas in that paragraph should relate. Cf. **main sentence**.

**limiting sentence** (6g) A **sentence** that addresses a possible limitation, or contrary consideration, to the **leading idea** of a paragraph.

**linking verb** (9a) A **verb** connecting its **subject** to an identifying or modifying **complement**. Typical linking verbs are *be, seem, appear, become, feel, sense, grow, taste, look, sound*:

       S   LV    COMPL
- They *were* Mormons.

       S   LV    COMPL
- She *became* calmer.

Cf. **intransitive verb, transitive verb**.

**literal language** (8l) Words that factually represent what they describe, without poetic embellishment. Cf. **figurative language**.

**literary present tense** (15f) The present **tense** form of a verb when it is used to express the ongoing action or meaning of an art work or other text: *Willie Loman tries to hide from reality; The play addresses some of our deepest anxieties.*

**main clause** See **clause**.

**main sentence** (6a) The sentence in a paragraph that conveys its **leading idea**. Often called *topic sentence*.

**matching** (7n) The placing into related or identical grammatical structures of elements that are related in meaning: *not only eggs but also bacon; days of struggle and nights of terror.* Matching is an act of **coordination**, creating an effect of **parallelism**.

**metaphor** (8l) An implied comparison whereby the thing at hand is figuratively asserted to be something else: *His fists were a hurricane of ceaseless assault.* Cf. **simile**.

**mixed construction** (10a) The use of two clashing structures within a **sentence**, as in x *Even a friendly interviewer, it is hard to keep from being nervous.*

**mixed metaphor** (8l) A **metaphor** whose elements clash in their implications: *Let's back off for a closer look*; *He is a straight arrow who shoots from the hip.*

**MLA style** (29c) The **reference list** style of documentation adopted by the Modern Language Association in 1984. For "alternative MLA" (**footnote/endnote**) style, see 29e.

**mode** A type of writing characterized by its **rhetorical** purpose. The modes recognized in this book are **analysis, argument, description,** and **narration.** One essay can make use of several modes.

**modifier** (11a) A word, **phrase**, or **clause** that limits or describes another element:

- MOD
  the *gentle* soul

- MOD                                                MOD
  *When leaving,* turn out the lights *on the porch.*

- MOD
  *Before you explain,* I have something to tell you.

**mood** (21d) The manner or attitude that a speaker or writer intends a **verb** to convey, as shown in certain changes of form. Ordinary statements and questions are cast in the *indicative* mood: *Is he ill? He is.* The *imperative* mood is for commands: *Stop! Get out of the way!* And the *subjunctive* mood is used for certain formulas (*as it were*), unlikely or impossible conditions (*had she gone*), *that* clauses expressing requirements or recommendations (*They ask that she comply*), and *lest* clauses (*lest he forget*).

**narration** (1f) The **mode** of writing in which a writer recounts something that has happened. Cf. **analysis, argument, description.**

**nonrestrictive modifier** (11j) A **modifier**, often a **phrase** or **clause**, that does not serve to identify ("restrict") the modified term and is therefore set off by punctuation:

- NONRESTR MOD
  That woman, *whom I met only yesterday,* already understands my problems.

Cf. **restrictive modifier.**

**noun** (9a) A word like *house, Jack, Pennsylvania,* or *assessment,* usually denoting a person, place, thing, or idea, capable of being **inflected** for both plural and possessive forms (*houses, house's, houses'*) and of serving a variety of sentence functions.

**noun clause** See **clause**.

**nounlike element** (9a) A word or group of words having the same function as a **noun** or **pronoun**, but not the same **inflectional** features — e.g., *what you mean* in *He knows what you mean.* Also called *nominal* or *substantive*.

**number** (10b) In grammar, the distinction between *singular* and *plural* form. The distinction applies to **verbs** (she *drives*, they *drive*), **nouns** (*boat, boats*), and personal **pronouns** (*I, we*).

**numeral** (26l) A number expressed as a figure (*6, 19*) or a group of letters (*VI, XIX*) instead of being written out (*six, nineteen*).

**object** (9a) A **noun, pronoun,** or **nounlike element** representing a receiver of an action or relation. See **direct object, indirect object,** and **object of preposition.** In addition, **infinitives, participles,** and **gerunds** can take objects:

OBJ OF INF
- to chair the *convention*

OBJ OF PART
- Chairing the *convention* impartially, she allowed no disorder.

OBJ OF GER
- Chairing a turbulent *convention* is a thankless task.

**object of preposition** (12a) A **noun, pronoun,** or **nounlike element** following a **preposition** and completing the prepositional **phrase** — e.g., *November* in *throughout November,* or *siesta* in *during a long siesta.*

**objective case** See **case**.

**objective complement** (17c) A **complement** of a **direct object**:

OBJ OF COMPL            D OBJ
- *What she calls happiness,* I call *slavery.*

**ordinal number** (26n) A number like *fourth* (*4th*) or *twenty-seventh* (*27th*), as opposed to a **cardinal number** like *four* (*4*) or *twenty-seven* (*27*).

**outline** (4e) A schematic plan showing the organization of a piece of writing. A *scratch outline* merely lists points to be made, whereas a *subordinated outline* shows, through indention and more than one set of numbers, which points are the most important ones. A further distinction is made between the *topic outline,* whose headings are concise **phrases**, and the *sentence outline,* which calls for complete **sentences**.

**paragraph** (p. 139) A unit of prose, usually consisting of several **sentences**, marked by **indention** of the first line (or sometimes by an extra blank line, as on p. 557). A well-wrought paragraph of **analysis** or **argument** is expected to provide support for one **leading idea**.

**paragraph block** (5e) A group of paragraphs addressing the same part of a **topic**, with strong continuity from one paragraph to the next.

**parallelism** (14a) The structure or the effect that results from **matching** two or more parts of a **sentence**—e.g., the words *Utica, Albany,* and *Rye* in the sentence *He went to Utica, Albany, and Rye,* or the three equally weighted **clauses** that begin this sentence: *That he wanted to leave, that permission was denied, and that he then tried to escape—these facts only became known after months of official secrecy.* Cf. **balance, coordination, matching**.

**paraphrase** (28f) Sentence-by-sentence restatement, in different words, of the meaning of a passage. Cf. **summary**.

**parenthetical citation** (29d) A reference to a work, given not in a **footnote** or **endnote** but in parentheses within a main text—e.g., *(Meyers 241–75)*.

**parenthetical element** See **interrupting element**.

**participle** (9a) An **adjectival** form derived from a **verb**—e.g., *Showing* in *Showing fear, he began to sweat.* Participles can be present (*showing*) or past (*having shown*) and active or passive (*having been shown*). Like other **verbals**, they can have **objects** (*fear* in the sentence above), but unlike other verbals, they do not have **subjects**. Cf. **gerund**.

**part of speech** Any of the major classes into which words are customarily divided, depending on their dictionary meaning and their syntactic functions in **sentences**. Since many words belong to more than one part of speech, you must analyze the sentence at hand to see which part of speech a given word is occupying. The commonly recognized parts of speech are:

| | |
|---|---|
| **Verb** | try, adopts, were allowing |
| **Noun** | Cynthia, paper, Manitoba |
| **Pronoun** | she, himself, each other, nothing, these, who |
| **Preposition** | to, among, according to |
| **Conjunction** | and, yet, because, although, if |
| **Adjective** | wide, lazier, more fortunate |
| **Adverb** | agreeably, seldom, ahead, together, however |

| **Interjection** | oh, ouch, gosh |
| **Article** | a, an, the |
| **Expletive** | it [is], there [were] |

passive voice See **voice**.

past participle See **participle**.

person (10b) In grammar, a characteristic of **pronouns** and **verbs** indicating whether someone is speaking (*first* person: *I go, we go*), being spoken to (*second* person: *you go*), or being spoken about (*third* person: *he, she, it goes; they go*).

personal pronoun See **pronoun**.

phrase (9c) A cluster of words functioning as a single **part of speech** and lacking a **subject-predicate** combination. Cf. **clause**.

A **noun** and its **modifiers** are sometimes called a *noun phrase* (*the faulty billiard balls*), and a **verb** form consisting of more than one word is sometimes called a *verb phrase* (*had been trying*). But the types of phrases most commonly recognized are *prepositional, infinitive, participial, gerund,* and **absolute**.

A *prepositional phrase* consists of a **preposition** and its **object**, along with any **modifiers** of those words:

PREP  MOD    MOD      MOD  OBJ PREP
• among her numerous painful regrets
PREP PHRASE

An *infinitive phrase* consists of an **infinitive** and its **object** and/or **modifiers**:

S INF   INF  MOD  MOD      MOD OBJ INF
• They asked *John to hit the almost invisible target.*
INF PHRASE

A *participial phrase* consists of a **participle** and its **object** and/or **modifiers**:

MOD        PART   MOD  MOD     OBJ PART
• *Quickly reaching the correct decision,* he rang the bell.
PART PHRASE

A *gerund phrase* consists of a **gerund** and its **object** and/or **modifiers**, and it may also include a *subject of the gerund*:

S GER      GER     OBJ GER   MOD
• *Their sending Matthew away* was a bad mistake.
GER PHRASE

gl

An **absolute phrase** (see entry) may contain an **infinitive** or a **participle**, but it always modifies an entire statement.

**pivoting paragraph** (6g) A paragraph that begins with one or more **limiting sentences** but then makes a sharp turn to its **main sentence**, which may or may not be followed by **supporting sentences**.

**plagiarism** (29a) The taking of others' thoughts or words without due acknowledgment. Cf. **allusion**.

**point of view** (1b) Literally, a place of observation—a vantage on a scene. More broadly, an attitude or mental perspective, a way of seeing things. An essay ought to imply a consistent point of view in this second sense.

**positive degree** See **degree**.

**possessive case** See **case**.

*post hoc, ergo propter hoc* (3m) A **fallacy** whereby the fact that one event followed another is wrongly taken to prove that the first event caused the later one. (In Latin, *post hoc, ergo propter hoc* means "after this, therefore because of it.")

**predicate** (9a) In a **clause**, the **verb** plus all the words belonging with it:

PRED

• He *had a serious heart attack.*

Cf. **subject**.

**predicate adjective** See **complement**.

**predicate noun** See **complement**.

**predication** (7c) The selection of a **predicate** for a given **subject**. The problem of *faulty predication* appears when subjects and predicates are mismatched in meaning: x *The purpose of the film wants to change your beliefs.* **Mixed construction** is a more radical form of faulty predication.

**prefix** (24j) One or more letters that can be attached before the root or base form of a word to make a new word: *pre-, with-,* etc., forming *prearranged, withstand,* etc. Cf. **suffix**.

**preposition** (12a) A function word that introduces a prepositional **phrase** —e.g., *to* in *to the lighthouse.* Cf. **conjunction**. A preposition consisting of more than one word is **compound**: *along with, apart from,* etc. See also **object**.

**present participle** See **participle**.

**principal parts** (21b) The **base** or simple **infinitive** form of a **verb**, its past **tense** form, and its past **participle**: *walk, walked, walked*; *grow, grew, grown.*

**process analysis** (2f) The **analysis** of a series of steps constituting a complete activity (cooking a stew, making a candle, testing a product, etc.).

**pronoun** (12a) One of a small class of words mostly used in place of **nouns** for a variety of purposes:

1. A *demonstrative* pronoun (*this, that, these, those*) singles out what it refers to: *This is what we want.*

2. An *indefinite* pronoun (*anybody, each, whoever,* etc.) leaves unspecified the person or things it refers to: *Anyone can see that you are right.*

3. An *intensive* pronoun (*myself, yourself, itself, ourselves,* etc.) emphasizes a preceding noun or pronoun: *She herself is a vegetarian.*

4. An *interrogative* pronoun (*who, whom, whose, which, what*) introduces a question: *Who will win the election?*

5. A *personal* pronoun (*I, you, he, she, it, we, they*) stands for one or more persons or things and is used in the tense formation of verbs: *They are willing to compromise.* Personal pronouns also have objective (*him, them*) and possessive (*his, their*) forms: *We asked her to recognize our rights.*

6. A *reciprocal* pronoun (*each other, each other's, one another, one another's*) expresses mutual relation: *We recognized each other's differences of outlook.*

7. A *reflexive* pronoun (*myself, yourself, itself, ourselves,* etc.) differs from an intensive pronoun in serving as a **direct** or **indirect object**. The reflexive pronoun shows that the **subject** of the **clause** is the same person or thing acted upon by the **verb**: *He hurt himself on the track.*

8. A *relative* pronoun (*who, whom, that, which*) introduces a relative or adjectival clause: *My uncle, who lives next door, slept through the earthquake.* Some grammarians also recognize an "indefinite relative pronoun" (one lacking an antecedent): *She knows what you mean.* See also **relative clause**.

**pronoun reference** (13b) The correspondence of **pronouns** with their **antecedents**, with which they should correspond in **number**, **person**, and **gender**. Thus, in the sentence *When they saw Bill, they gave him a cool welcome,* the pronoun *him* properly refers to the singular, third-person, masculine antecedent *Bill.* Cf. **agreement.**

**punctuation marks** (chapters 16–20) Marks used to bring out the meaning of written **sentences**. They are:

gl

| | |
|---|---|
| period  . | parentheses  ( ) |
| question mark  ? | brackets  [ ] |
| comma  , | apostrophe  ' |
| semicolon  ; | hyphen  - |
| colon  : | quotation marks  " " |
| dash  — | slash  / |

**racist language** (8e) **Diction** that can give offense by using a derogatory name for an ethnic group or by perpetuating a demeaning stereotype: *greaser, dumb Pole,* etc.

**rebuttal** (2h) An opposing **argument**, intended to overturn an argument already made. Rebuttals do not always succeed; cf. **refutation**.

**reciprocal pronoun** See **pronoun**.

**redundancy** (8i) The defect of unnecessarily conveying the same meaning more than once. Also, an expression that does so—e.g., *retreat back, ascend up.*

**reference list** (29b) A list of "Works Cited" or "References," supplied at the end of an **essay**, paper, article, or book, and showing where and when the cited or consulted materials appeared. The **parenthetical citations** within the text refer to items in the reference list.

**reflexive pronoun** See **pronoun**.

**refutation** (2h) The disproving of a point. By definition, all refutations are successful; cf. **rebuttal**.

**regular verb** (21b) A **verb** that forms both its past **tense** and its **past participle** by adding -*d*: *hike (hiked, hiked )*, etc. Cf. **irregular verb**.

**relative clause** (9b) In this book, any adjectival **clause**.

**relative pronoun** See **pronoun**.

**restrictive modifier** (11j) A **modifier**, often a **phrase** or **clause**, that "restricts" (establishes the identity of) the modified term. Unless it comes first in the sentence, a restrictive modifier is not set off by commas:

RESTR MOD
- The woman *whom I met* has disappeared.

RESTR MOD
- The man *in the black suit* is following you.

RESTR MOD
- *On long ocean voyages,* seasickness is common.

Because it is brief, the restrictive modifier that begins the last example could also appear without a following comma. Cf. **nonrestrictive**

**rhetoric** (p. 4) The strategic placement of ideas and choice of language, as in *His rhetoric was effective* or *His ideas were sound but his rhetoric was addressed to the wrong audience.* Note that *rhetoric* need not mean deception or manipulation.

**rhetorical question** (7s)  A question posed for effect, without expectation of a reply: *How often have we seen this same pattern of betrayal?*

**Roman numeral** (26m)  A figure such as *III, XLVII,* or *CVI,* as opposed to an **Arabic numeral** such as *3, 47,* or *106.*

**run-on sentence** (9e)  A **sentence** in which two or more independent **clauses** are improperly joined. One type of run-on sentence is the **comma splice**: x *She likes candy, she eats it every day.* The other type is the **fused sentence**: x *She likes candy she eats it every day.* Run-ons are typically corrected either with a semicolon (*She likes candy; she eats it every day*) or with a comma and a coordinating **conjunction** (*She likes candy, and she eats it every day*).

**sarcasm** (16g)  Abusive ridicule of a person, group, or idea, as in *What pretty phrases these killers speak!* Cf. **irony**.

**scratch outline**  See **outline**.

**sentence** (9a)  A grammatically complete unit of expression, usually containing at least one independent **clause**, beginning with a capital letter and ending with a period, question mark, or exclamation point. See also **sentence fragment**.

**sentence adverb** (9e)  An **adverb** that serves to indicate a logical connection between the modified **clause** or whole **sentence** and a previous statement — e.g., *therefore* in *She took the job; therefore, she had to find child care.* Also called *conjunctive adverb*.

**sentence fragment** (9c)  A set of words punctuated as a **sentence** but lacking one or more of the elements usually considered necessary to a sentence: x *When they last saw her.*

In general, sentence fragments are regarded as blunders. But an *intentional sentence fragment* — one whose context shows that it is a shortened sentence rather than a dislocated piece of a neighboring sentence — can sometimes be effective:

INT FRAG
- How much longer can we resist the enemy? *As long as necessary!*

**sentence outline**  See **outline**.

**series** (14j)  A set of more than two **parallel** items within a **sentence**:

SERIES
- They were upset about *pollution, unemployment, and poverty.*

**sexist language** (8e)  Expressions that can give offense by implying that one sex (almost always male) is superior or of primary importance or that the other sex is restricted to certain traditional roles: *lady doctor; a man-sized job; Every American pursues his own happiness,* etc.

**signal of relation** (6c) A word or phrase, such as *therefore* or *subsequently* or *on the contrary,* that indicates how a sentence relates to the preceding one. Such signals contribute vitally to **continuity** between sentences and between whole paragraphs. A repeated word or a pronoun can also serve as a signal of relation.

**significant pause** (7r) A pause, marked by punctuation, that serves to combat **choppiness** in a sequence of **sentences**. The pauses between items in a **series** are not significant, but a pause between **clauses** or **phrases** is: *When she inquired, no one could tell her anything*; *He tried, along with his weight training, to run at least five miles a day.*

**simile** (8l) An explicit or open comparison, whereby the object at hand is **figuratively** asserted to be like something else: *His eyes that morning were like an elephant's.* Cf. **metaphor.** Both similes and metaphors are called *metaphorical* or **figurative language.** See also **analogy, image.**

**slash** (20g) The punctuation mark /. A slash is used to separate alternatives (*either/or*) and to indicate line endings in **incorporated quotation** of verse. Sometimes called *virgule.*

**split infinitive** (11e) An **infinitive** interrupted by at least one **adverb**: *to firmly stand.* Some readers consider every split infinitive an error; others object only to conspicuously awkward ones such as x *Jane wanted to thoroughly and finally settle the matter.*

**squinting modifier** (11d) A **modifier** awkwardly trapped between sentence elements, either of which might be regarded as the modified term:

SQ MOD
x Why he collapsed *altogether* puzzles me.

Did he collapse altogether, or is the writer altogether puzzled?

**stance** (4b) The **rhetorical** posture a writer adopts toward an audience, establishing a consistent **point of view.** This book recognizes two stances, *forthright* and *ironical.* A forthright stance implies that the writer's statements are to be taken "straight"; an ironical stance implies that the reader is to "read between the lines" and uncover a different or even opposite meaning.

**straw man** (3n) The **fallacy** of misrepresenting an opponent's position so that it will appear weaker than it actually is. The writer "knocks over a straw man" by attacking and dismissing an irrelevant point.

subject (9a) The part of a **clause** about which something is **predicated**:

SUBJ
* *Ernest* shot the tiger.

The subject alone is called the *simple subject*. With its **modifiers** included it is called the *complete subject* – e.g., *The only thing to do* in *The only thing to do is compromise.*

Not only **verbs** but also **infinitives**, **gerunds**, and **absolute phrases** can have "subjects":

S OF INF    INF
* They wanted *Alexander* to be king.

S OF GER    GER
* *Alexander's* refusing upset them.

S OF ABS PHRASE
* *The summit conference having ended,* the diplomats went home.
  ABS PHRASE

subject area (3a) A wide range of related concerns within which the **topic** of an **essay** or paper may be found. Cf. **thesis, topic**.

subjective case See **case**.

subjunctive mood See **mood**.

subordinate clause See **clause**.

subordinated outline See **outline**.

subordinating conjunction See **conjunction**.

subordination (9b) In general, the giving of minor emphasis to minor elements or ideas. In syntax, subordination entails making one element grammatically dependent on another, so that the subordinate element becomes a **modifier** of the other element, limiting or explaining it. Thus, in *They were relieved when it was over,* the subordinate **clause** *when it was over* limits the time to which the **verb** *were relieved* applies.

substantive note (29f) A **supplementary note** which, instead of merely giving a reference for a cited passage or idea, makes further comments. Cf. **bibliographic note**.

suffix (24f) One or more letters that can be added at the end of a word's root or base to make a new word or form: *-ed, -ing, -ship, -ness,* etc., as in *walked, singing, membership, weakness*. Cf. **prefix**.

summary (28f) A concise recapitulation of a passage. Cf. **paraphrase**.

supplementary note (29f) A **footnote** or **endnote** which, instead of merely giving a reference for a specific passage or idea, adds further commentary or reference information. See **bibliographic note, substantive note**.

**supporting sentence** (6f) A **sentence** that restates, elaborates, or provides **evidence** or context for some aspect of a paragraph's **leading idea**.

**suspended comparison** (14e) A comparison proposing two possible relations between the compared items, in which the second item is stated only at the end of the construction: *Taco Bell is as good as, if not better than, Pizza Hut.*

**suspended paragraph** (6h) A paragraph that builds, without a decisive shift of direction, toward a **main sentence** at or near the end. Cf. **direct paragraph, pivoting paragraph**.

**suspended sentence** (7w) A **sentence** that significantly delays completing the statement of its main idea while **clauses** and/or **phrases** intervene: *The important thing is not to study all night before the exam, nor to try reading the instructor's mind, nor to butter up the TA, but to keep up with the assignments throughout the term.* Also called *periodic sentence*.

**suspended verb** (14e) A construction in which one subject governs two forms of the same delayed **verb**: *She can, and assuredly will, comply with the law.* Note how the verb *can comply* is "suspended" by the intervening element.

**syllogism** (2g) A chain of deduction from premises to a conclusion:

| | |
|---|---|
| Premise: | All massive die-offs of fish in Lake Erie are caused by pollution. |
| Premise: | Last year there was a massive die-off of fish in Lake Erie. |
| Conclusion: | Last year's massive die-off of fish in Lake Erie was caused by pollution. |

**tense** (21b) The time a **verb** expresses: present (*see*), future (*will see*), etc.

**thesis** (3a) The point, or one central idea, of an **essay**, paper, article, book, etc. Cf. **subject area, topic**.

**thesis statement** (3o) A one-**sentence** statement of the **thesis** or central idea of an **essay** or paper. In this book a thesis statement is considered to be full only if it is complex enough to give organizing guidance.

**tone** (5c) The quality of feeling conveyed by something. Words like *factual, sober, fanciful, urgent, tongue-in-cheek, restrained, stern, pleading,* and *exuberant* may begin to suggest the range of tones found in **essays**. Cf. **stance, voice**.

**topic** (3a) The specific subject of an **essay** or paper; the ground to be covered or the question to be answered. Cf. **subject area, thesis**.

**topic outline**  See **outline**.

**topic sentence** Replaced in this book by the term **main sentence**, since the key sentence in a paragraph is the one stating the **leading idea**, not the one announcing a "topic."

**transitional paragraph** (5e) A whole paragraph devoted to announcing a major shift in focus.

**transitional phrase** (9e) A **phrase** having the same function as a **sentence adverb**, modifying a whole **clause** or **sentence** while showing its logical connection to a previous statement:

TRANS PHRASE
- She says she simply can't bear to be late for anything; *in other words,* she expects the rest of us to show up on time.

**transitive verb** (9a) A **verb** transmitting an action to a **direct object**:

TR V
- They *cast* the dice.

Cf. **intransitive verb, linking verb**.

**trial thesis** (3h) A possible **thesis**, or central idea, considered before a final thesis has been chosen.

**trial topic** (3g) A tentative **topic** that requires further evaluation before being judged suitable for an essay.

**understatement** (4c) A device of **rhetoric**, often used for **irony**, whereby the writer conveys the importance of something by appearing to take it lightly: *Living near the edge of a runway for jumbo jets is not altogether relaxing.*

**verb** (9a) A word or words like *goes, saw,* or *was leaving,* serving to convey the action performed by a **subject**, to express the state of that subject, or to connect the subject to a **complement**.

**verbal** (9a) A form derived from, but different in function from, a **verb**. Verbals are either **infinitives, participles,** or **gerunds**. When mistakenly used as verbs, they cause **sentence fragments**:

VERBAL
x George *going* to the movies tonight.

**voice** (4a, 21b) The form of a **verb** indicating whether the **subject** performs the action (*active* voice: *we strike*) or receives the action (*passive* voice: *we are struck*). Also, the "self" projected by a given piece of writing. In the latter sense, this book recognizes two voices, the *personal* and *impersonal*.

**weaseling thesis** (3j) A **thesis** that fails to take any definite stand: x *People can be found who oppose gun control*; x *Abortion is quite a controversial topic.*

# Index

NOTE: Main entries in **boldface** are defined in the Glossary of Terms (pp. 581–605). Page numbers in *italics* indicate the main discussion of a topic; go to those pages first.

abbreviation, 454–59; appropriateness in main text, 456–57; capitalization of, 458; of course of instruction, 457; of day, 457; in documentation, 454–56; of given name, 456, 459; in Index of Usage, 562–63; initials as, 458–59; italics vs. roman in, 453; Latin, 453; listed, 455; of months, days, and holidays, 457; past tense or participle derived from, 415; with or without periods, 458–59; of place name, 457–58; plural of, 407; punctuation of, 347, 458–59; of roadway, 457; sentence ending in, 347; spacing of, 459; of state, 458; in technical prose, 457; after time, 456, 458; of title with name, 456; of unit of measure, 457, 459, 460–61; before ZIP code, 458
*above*, 563
**absolute phrase**, 282–83; subject of, 603
**abstract language**, 10–12, *225–27*
abstracts, in library, 481–86
*accept* vs. *except*, 421
acknowledgement of sources. *See* documentation
acronym: punctuation of, 456; spacing of, 459
action: best conveyed by verb, 172; as means of description, 15–16, 18
active voice, 392–99; and sentence strength, 172–73
A.D., 456, *563*
*adapt* vs. *adopt*, 421
**additive phrase**, and verb agreement, 260–61

address: in business letter, 551–52, 554; comma in, 358–59; direct, 290
*ad hominem* **reasoning**, 79
**adjective**, 275; attributive noun as, 208; capitalization of, 444, 447; degree of, 416–18; demonstrative, 147, 311, *588*; derived from name, 444, 447; indefinite pronoun vs., 267; irregular, 417; placement of, 275–76
**adverb**, 275; degree of, 417–18; irregular, 417; ordinal number as, 463; placement of, 275–77, 280–81. *See also* sentence adverb
*advice* vs. *advise*, 421
*affect* vs. *effect*, 421, 563
*afraid* vs. *frightened, scared*, 572
*again, back*, may be redundant, 563
*ago* vs. *before*, 566
agreement. *See* pronoun reference; subject-verb agreement
*ain't*, disapproved use of, 563
*all ready* vs. *already*, 421
*all together* vs. *altogether*, 421
*all* vs. *all of*, 563
alliteration, 232
*all that*, disapproved use of, 563
**allusion**, 504; vs. *illusion*, 421
*allusion* vs. *illusion, delusion*, 563–64
almanacs, 491–92
*alot*, as misspelling, 575
*also*, 564
*altar* vs. *alter*, 421
*alternate* vs. *alternative*, 564
"alternative MLA" documentation style, 523–28
*although* clause, in thesis statement, 82

A.M., 456, 458, 461, *564*

ambiguity: and hyphenation, 436–38; with *if not*, 573; in modification, 280–81, 285; in pronoun reference, 308–13; in punctuation of series, 326; with *since*, 578

American Psychological Association, documentation style of, 508–22, 541–42

*among* vs. *between*, 564

*amount* vs. *number*, 564

analogy, 46–47

analysis, 8, *28–55*, 58; analogy as, 46–47; cause and effect, 33–35; comparison and contrast, 35–38; to develop topic, 70–71; definition as, 29–30; division as, 31–32; evidence in, 40–43; illustration as, 32–33; literary, 48–55; process, 38–40

*analyzation*, no such word, 564

*and who, and which*, and parallelism, 322

*angry* vs. *mad*, 575

*ante-* vs. *anti-*, 421

antecedent of pronoun, 116, 242, 306; and reference problems, 308–13; and verb agreement, 207–71. *See also* pronoun reference

anticipation: of exam question, 545; in matching sentence elements, 188–90; in narration, 22–23; of objection to thesis, 44–45

anticipatory pattern, 188–90; and parallelism, 318–20

antonym, 204–5

*anybody* vs. *any body*, 564

*anyway* vs. *any way, anyways*, 564

*anywheres*, disapproved, 564

*APA Publication Manual*, 508

APA style, *508–22, 541–42*

aphorism, 190

apology, undesirable: for cliché, 224; in closing paragraph, 105

apostrophe, 408–15; in contraction, 414; with hyphenated term, 410; with name showing joint ownership, 410; in number, 415; omitted from plural of name, 404–5; omitted from possessive pronoun, 413–14; in past tense

or participle derived from name, 415; in plural of word presented *as* word, 406; in plural of possessive of time, 410; in possessive, 408–14; spacing with, 468

application, letter of, 555

appositive: and case of preceding pronoun, 301; introductory, 367; punctuation of, *288–89*, 367; as fragment, 246

*apt* vs. *liable, likely*, 564

Arabic numeral, 461–62

*argue* vs. *quarrel*, 565

argument, 8, *28–55*, 58; *ad hominem*, 79

*around*, weak as *about*, 565

article (part of speech), capitalization of, in title, 443

article, published: cited in note, 523–27; cited in reference list, 508–9, *514–16*; how to locate, 481–87

art reference books, 488

*as*: case of pronoun after, 300–1; *like* vs., 565; *such as* vs., 565; in vague subordination, 185, *565*

*as far as*, vague, *185–86*, 565

*as good as, as much as*, 565

*aspect*, 565

*as to*, in vague subordination, 185

atlases, 492

attributive noun, 208

audience, classmates or instructor as, 2–4

author card, in library, 479

authority, appeal to. 43

author-title catalog, 478–80

auxiliary, 19–20

*aware* vs. *conscious*, 568

*back, again*, may be redundant, 563

*back of*, colloquial for *behind*, 566

*bad*, disapproved as adverb, 566

baited opener, *107*, 127

balance, 190–91

*bare* vs. *bear*, 421

base form of verb, 392

B.C., 456

*be*: overuse of, 170–71; subjunctive of, 402

*because* clause, in thesis statement, 81–82

*before* vs. *ago,* 566

**begging the question,** *76–77,* 210

*being,* as redundant participle, 566

*being as,* in vague subordination, 184–85

*bemused* vs. *amused,* 566

*beside* vs. *besides,* 421

*better than,* colloquial as *more than,* 566

*between:* vs. *among,* 564; and number of items, 566

*between each, between every,* 566

*between you and I,* as case error, 566

*bias* vs. *biased,* 421

Bible: capitalization of, 446–47; figures for books of, 461; italics or quotation marks not used for, 452

**bibliographic note,** 529

**bibliography:** and bibliography card, 494–95; as research source, 473; spacing of, 122

bibliography card, 494–95

biography, dictionaries of, 492–93

biology documentation style, 506–7

bloated paragraph, 160–61

block format, for business letter, 554, 556; modified, 551, 557

block quotation. *See* extracted quotation

book, cited: in note, 523–27; in reference list, 508–13

book reviews, location and use of, 483–85

"borderline" plural pronoun, 266–68

*bored,* preposition following, 566

*born* vs. *borne,* 421

botany documentation style, 507

**bound element,** 180–82

brackets: formation of, 466; functions of, 375; for insertion in quotation, 372, *387;* within parentheses, 375; parentheses vs., 372; *sic* in, 387; spacing with, 468

**brainstorming,** 68

branch of learning, uncapitalized, 446

*breadth* vs. *breath, breathe,* 421

British spelling, 420, 424–29

*broke,* as colloquial adjective, 566

*bunch* vs. *crowd,* 566

business letter, 550–58; courtesy question in, 346; elements of, 550–53; envelope for, 554; formats for, 551, 553–54, 556–58; notations in, 553; punctuation of, 346, 364, *550–53;* purposes of, 555–58

business name, capitalization of, 444

business reference books, 488

*business* vs. *busyness,* 421

*but: however* vs., 252–53; in pivoting paragraph, 154–55

*but that, but what,* as awkward redundancy, 566

*by* vs. *buy,* 421

*calculate,* as colloquial verb, 571

*calculated,* requires an agent, 569

call number, in library, 477, *479*

*can* vs. *may,* 566

Canadian spelling, 420, 424–29

*can not* vs. *cannot,* 567

capitalization, 441–49; of abbreviation, 458; of adjective derived from name, 444; of Bible, 446–47; of branch of learning, 446; of business name, 444; after colon, 442; of course of study, 446; of date, 447–48; of day, 447; of family relation, 444–45; of first letter in sentence, 441–42; of foreign word or title, 449; of geographic direction, 448; of high office, 445; of historical event, movement, or period, 447; of holiday, 447; of hyphenated term in title, 443–44; of indirect question, 442; of institution or department, 445–46; of intentional fragment, 441; meaning changed by, 449; of month, 447–48; of name, 444–45; of nationality or group, 448; of parenthetic sentence, 442; of place name, 444, 448; within a quotation, 442–43; of rank or title, 445; of represented thought, 441; of sacred name, 446–47; of season, 447–48; of sentence within sentence, 441; with time, 458; of title or subtitle, *443–44,* 449

capital letter, plural of, 407

*capital* vs. *capitol,* 421

card catalog, in library, 474
**cardinal number**, 462–63
**case**: forms of, 295–97; usage problems with, 297–305
catalogs, in library, 474, *476–80*
cause and effect reasoning, *33–35*, 71, 125
*cause is due to*, redundancy of, 567
*cause* vs. *reason*, 567
*censor* vs. *censure*, 567
*center around*, imprecision of, 567
*character*, redundant use of, 567
Checklist for Revision, 120–21, inside front cover
chemistry documentation style, 506–7
**choppiness**: in paragraph, *159–60*, 187; in sentence, 116, *193–95*
*chord* vs. *cord*, 421
**circular thesis**, 75
circulation desk, in library, 474
**circumlocution**, 221
citation. *See* documentation; parenthetical citation
*cite* vs. *sight, site*, 421
*class* vs. *classify*, 567
classification: in definition, 29; in division, 31–32
classmates, as audience, 3
**clause**, 241–46; emphatic sequence of, 326–27; as fragment, 244–47; independent vs. subordinate, 241–44; intervening, and number of verb, 259–60; as modifier, 274–75; relative, *242–43*, 270–71; as subject, 263; *that* or *what*, unnecessary, 175–76. *See also* independent clause; subordinate clause
**cliché**, *223–25*, 231
*climactic* vs. *climatic*, 421
climax, in series, 191–93
clinching statement, in closing paragraph, 112–13
closing paragraph, 111–13; clinching statement saved for, 112–13; deadly, 111; looking beyond thesis in, 112; omitting formal conclusion, 113; opening paragraph recalled in, 113; and suspended pattern, 157–58

closing sentence of paragraph, 142–43; and suspended structure, 157
*coarse* vs. *course*, 421
**collective noun**, verb agreement with, 263
college dictionary, *202–5*, 419
colloquial diction, 116, 205, *218*
colon, 362–65; capital after, 442; complete statement before, 363; equivalence shown by, 362–63; with hours and minutes, 364; incorrect use of, 363–64; to introduce list or restatement, 362; to introduce quotation, 362, *383–84*; to introduce subtitle, 364–65; and *namely* test, 362–63; note number after, 379, 523; and quotation marks, 378; after salutation of letter, 364; semicolon vs., 362–63; spacing with, 468–69; in times, 364
comic effect, 33; with irony, 88–90
comma, 351–59; in address, 358–59; and ambiguity, 285; with appositive, 288–89; not combined with dash, 369; not combined with question mark, 348–49; with "contrary" modifier, 293; with coordinate modifiers, 291–92; in date, 358; with degree, 359; with free element, 180–84; to introduce incorporated quotation, 383–84; between independent clauses, 249–54; after initial direct object, 353; after initial modifier, 284–85; with interrupting element, *290–91*, 366; after introductory tag, 253, *383;* with modifier, 284–93; in number, 358; omitted after final or only modifier, 292–93; with paired elements, 324–25; with parentheses, 372; after question mark, not used, 348–49; with quotation marks, 378–79; with restrictive vs. nonrestrictive modifier, 286–88; and run-on sentence, 249–54; with sentence adverb, 289; sentence elements wrongly separated by, 352–53; to separate items in series, 325–27; significant pause marked by, 193–95; spacing with, 468–69; splice, 250–54; between subject and verb,

comma *(continued)*
272–73; with title after name, 359; with transitional phrase, 289; unnecessary, 272–73, 285–89, 324–26, 352–53, 369, 372, 382–83. *See also* comma splice
**comma splice**, 250–54; acceptable, 253–54
command: imperative mood for, 401; implied subject in, 241; punctuation of, 345–46, 349
*commence,* as pompous verb, 567
**common gender**, 211–13
comparative degree, 416–18
*compare* vs. *contrast,* 567
comparison: of adjective or adverb, 416–18; parallelism in, 315–17, 319–321; suspended, 321
**comparison and contrast**, 35–38; to develop topic, 71; emphatic order of, 37–38; and pivoting paragraph, 155–56
**complement**, 166; objective, 354, 595; pronoun, 298; vs. *compliment,* 421; wrongly isolated by comma, 352–53
complete sentence, usage problems with, 244–54
complete subject, 603
*compose* vs. *comprise, constitue,* 567
composing, 62–134; analytic strategies in, 70–71; asking reporter's questions in, 70; for an audience, 2–4; brainstorming in, 68; course work used in, 66; diagrams of, 62–63; of exam essay, 545–48; experienced used in, 65–66; flexibility of, *62–63,* 92, 97–98; freewriting in, 67–68, 69–70; of in-class essay, 548–49; journal used in, 66; narrowing subject area in, 63–64; notes used in, 65–66; outlining in, 93–96; and revision, 99–134; of sample essay, 124–29; thesis choice in, 59–61, *72–79;* thesis statement in, *80–82,* 91; topic choice in, 63–71; trial thesis in, 72; trial topic in, 69–71. *See also* essay
**compound**: modifier, hyphenation of, 436–38; noun, hyphenation of, 436; object, 299; possessive, 410; prefix,

435; subject, and verb agreement, 264–66; verb, hyphenation of, 436
*comprise* vs. *compose, constitute,* 567
*comptroller* vs. *controller,* 421
computer: jargon, 214–15; with library database, 486–87; with on-line catalog, 474, *478;* software, cited in reference list, 518. *See also* word processor
*concept* vs. *conception, idea,* 567
**concession**, *44–45,* 82
**conciseness**: in diction, 115, 128–29, *219–23;* in linking paragraphs, 110
conclusion: in syllogism, *42,* 604. *See also* closing paragraph
**concrete language**, 10–12, *225–27*
*concur in* vs. *concur with,* 568
condition, hypothetical: and verb form, 333–35, 401–2
conditional form of verb, 334–35
**conjunction**: coordinating, *242–43,* 249–54, 325–27, 361–62; in matching, 187–88; optional in series of independent clauses, 254; after semicolon, 361–62; sentence adverb vs., 251–53; subordinating, *242–46,* 353; transitional phrase vs., 252–53
conjunctive adverb. *See* sentence adverb
**connotation**, 209–10
*conscious* vs. *aware,* 568
*consensus,* imprecise use of, 568
*considerable,* colloquial use of, 568
consistency: in paragraph, 141–43; in series, 191–93
*consist of* vs. *consist in,* 568
*constitute* vs. *comprise, compose,* 567
*contemptible* vs. *contemptuous,* 568
context, for essay, 2–3
*continual* vs. *continuous,* 568
**continuity**. *See* paragraph continuity
**contraction**, 414
contradiction, within paragraph, 141
**"contrary" modifier**, 293
*contrary to,* not adverbial, 568
*contrast* vs. *compare,* 567
conversational effect: by cumulative sentence, 198–99; by sentence beginning with coordinating conjunction, 243

*convey,* no *that* clause after, 568
*convince* vs. *persuade,* 568
coordinate modifiers, commas with, 291–92
coordinating conjunction, 586; and items in series, 325–27; to join independent clauses, *242–43,* 249–54, 325–27; listed, 243; omitted for emphasis, 326–27; after semicolon, 361–62; sentence beginning with, 243–44; in title, capitalization of, 443
**coordination.** *See* coordinating conjunction; matching; parallelism
**core element,** in sentence: *163–65,* 167; and choppiness, 194; and free element, 180–84; subordination to highlight, 170, *178–79*
correction, on final copy, 122–23
correlation, in cause and effect reasoning, 34–35
correlative conjunction, 586
*could of,* always wrong, 568
*council* vs. *counsel,* 421
*couple* vs. *pair,* 568–69
courtesy question, punctuation of, 346
*criteria,* always plural, 569
*crowd* vs. *bunch,* 566
**cumulative sentence,** *198–99,* 282

**dangling modifier,** 116, *277–80*
dash, 366–69; in dialogue, 367; formation and spacing of, 465–66, 468; functions of, 367; with interrupting element, 366–69; to isolate introductory element, 367; kinds of, 465–66; note number before, 523; other punctuation with, 369, 378; overuse of, 369; sentence coherence before and after, 368; and sentence variety, 197
*data,* number of, 406, *569*
database, for research, 486–87
date: A.D. and B.C. with, 456, 563; capitalization of, 447–48; comma in, 358; figures vs. numbers in, 461; as span of time, 467
day: abbreviation for, 457; capitalization of, 447
**dead metaphor,** *231*
deadly conclusion, 111

deadly opener, *104–5,* 127
**declarative sentence,** 196; indirect question as, 346
*deduce* vs. *deduct,* 569
deduction, in reasoning, 42
definition: as analytic strategy, *29–30,* 71; to develop topic, 71; in dictionary, 202–5; by example, 30; as weak opener, 29–30, *105*
**degree:** of adjective or adverb, 416–18; after name, punctuation of, 359
deity, capitalization of, 446–47
delayed subject, and verb agreement, 261–262
delaying formula, 174–75
*delusion* vs. *illusion, allusion,* 563–64
**demonstrative adjective:** as cure for vagueness, 311; as relational signal, 147
demonstrative pronoun, 311–12, 599
**denotation,** 202–8
department, capitalized name of, 445–46
*depend,* requires *on* or *upon,* 569
derivation (etymology), *204,* 492
*descent* vs. *dissent,* 421
**description,** 8–19; abstract vs. concrete language in, 10–12; figurative language in, 16–18; pictorial, 10–12; revealing action in, 15–16; vividness in, 9–12; ways of ordering, 18–19
*desert* vs. *dessert,* 421
*designed,* requires an agent, 569
detail: in closing paragraph, 113; concrete, 10–12, 225–27; in thesis statement, 80–81
*device* vs. *devise,* 421
dialect, 392
**dialogue:** indention of, 377–78; vs. indirect discourse, 21–22; with introductory tag, 383; interruption of, 367; paragraph break in, 382; paragraph length in, 159; punctuation of, 367, 377–79
**diction,** 201–33; abstract, 10–12; in business letter, 552; circumlocution in, 221; cliché in, 223–25; colloquial, 116, 205, *218*; concise vs. wordy, 219–23; concrete, 10–12,

**diction** *(continued)*
225-27; connotation of, 209-10; denotation of, 202-8; and dictionary, 202-5; established sense of, 207-8; euphemism in, 216; figurative, 227-31; formal vs. middle vs. informal, 217-18; general, 10; in Index of Usage, 562-80; intensifiers in, 222; jargon in, 213-15; key virtues of, 201; Latinate, 232; lively, 217-33; loaded, 210; metaphor in, 228-31; positive vs. negative, 223; racist, 210; redundant, 220-21; revision of, 114-17; sexist, 210-13; simile in, 228-29; sound in, 232-33; specific, 10-12; and tone, 86, 101-3, 222; vocabularly list for, 206-7

dictionary: and hyphenation, 203; college, 202-5; and foreign plural, 405; of quotations, 493; specialized, 492; stale quotation from, 105; thesaurus vs., 206

*die* vs. *dye, dyeing,* 421

*different from* vs. *different than,* 569

**digression**: in exam essay, 547; in paragraph, 142

direct address, name in, 290

**direct discourse,** 21

direction, capitalization of, 448

**direct object**: in distinct expression, 166-67; and pronoun case, 298-300; wrongly isolated by comma, 352

**direct paragraph,** 152-54; main sentence delayed in, 154

direct question, punctuation after, 347-48

discourse. *See* direct discourse; indirect discourse

*discreet* vs. *discrete,* 422

*disinterested* vs. *uninterested,* 569

**disjunctive subject,** 265

dissertation, cited: in note, 526; in reference list, 516

**distinct expression,** 164-76

**division**: as analytic strategy, 31-32; to develop topic, 71; mathematical, and verb agreement, 269

document, cited: in note, 526; in reference list, 516

documentation, 501-29; abbreviations used in, 455; "alternative MLA" style of, 523-28; first note in, 525-26; main forms contrasted, 505-8; MLA reference list style of, 508-22; parenthetical citation as, 519-22; and plagiarism, 501-4; reasons for, 501-2; in sample research essay, 539-42; scientific, 506-8; subsequent reference as, 527; supplementary note as, 505, *529;* what to acknowledge, 502-4. *See also* bibliography; endnote; footnote; footnote/endnote form; parenthetical citation; reference list form

dossier, submitted with résumé, 560

double comparison of modifier, 418

double meaning. *See* ambiguity

**double negative,** 283-84

**double possessive,** 304-5

doubt, expression of: by question mark in parentheses, 348; by quotation marks, 348, 375, 387; by *[sic],* 387. *See also* sarcasm

*doubtless(ly),* 569

draft: first, 84-98; seeking response to, 99-100; revision of, 99-134

drama reference books, 488-89

*drastic,* harsh sense only, 570

*dual* vs. *duel,* 422

*due to,* wrong adverbial use of, 570

*each,* and verb agreement, 265-66

*each one,* and verb agreement, 265-67

economics: as source of jargon, 213-14; documentation style, 507; reference books in, 488

editorial *we,* 86-87

education reference books, 489

*effect* vs. *affect,* 563

*e.g.* vs. *i.e.,* 570; roman type for, 453

*either,* and verb agreement, 266-67

*either . . . or*: and parallelism, 323; punctuation with, 325; and verb agreement, 265

**either-or reasoning,** 77

*elicit* vs. *illicit,* 422

**ellipsis**: at beginning of quotation, 386; formation and spacing of, 385–86, *466–69*; functions of, 375, *384–86*; kinds of, 385–86; row of dots as, 386

*eminent* vs. *imminent*, 422

**emotionalism**, 101–3

emphasis, 186–93; by active or passive voice, 172–73; by anticipatory pattern, 188–90; by balance, 190–91; and dashes, 197, 366–67; by delaying formula, 174–75; in exam essay, 546; by exclamation, 196; by false start, 197; by free subordination, 183–84; by independent clauses joined without conjunctions, 326–27; by intentional fragment, 247–48; by interruption, 197; by inverted syntax, 197–98; by italics, 454; by matching, 186–91; by paragraph structure, 152–58; personal, 86–87; and placement of modifiers, 275–77; by rhetorical question, 196; by series, 191–93

encyclopedia: cited in note, 526; cited in reference list, 515; in library, 491

**endnote**. *See* footnote; footnote/endnote form

engineering documentation style, 506

*enhance*, implies prior value, 570

*enormity* vs. *enormousness*, 570

*enthuse*, as disapproved verb, 570

enumeration of points, 109

*envelop* vs. *envelope*, 422

epigrammatic sentence, *107–8*, 190

*escape*, not transitive, 570

*especially* vs. *specially*, 570

**essay**, 1–6; audience for, 2–4; compared to sentence and paragraph, 139, 163; exam, 545–48; final copy of, 121–23; first draft of, 84–98; handwritten, 122–23; in-class, 548–49; logic in, *42–43*, 75–79; modes of, 8, 594; organizing, 90–96; research, 472–542; revision of, 99–134; sample, 24–26, 49–55, 130–34, 532–42; thesis of, 59–61; thesis statement for, 80–82; title of, 118–19; topic for, 59–71

established sense of diction, 207–8

*et al.*, 453, 455, *570*

*etc.*, 455, *570–71*

etymology (derivation), *204*, 492

**euphemism**, 216

*eventhough*, always wrong, 571

*every day* vs. *everyday*, 422

*every, everybody, everyone, everything*, and verb agreement, 265–67

*every one* vs. *everyone*, 422

*everywheres*, always wrong, 571

**evidence**, 40–43; appeal to authority as, 43; in exam essay, 547; facts and figures as, 41; in paragraph continuity, 149–50; reasoning as, 43; in thesis statement, 80–81

exaggeration: by intensifiers, 222; of opposing view, 76–79

examination essay, 545–48

*exceeding(ly)* vs. *excessive(ly)*, 571

*except*, disapproved as conjunction, 571

**exclamation**: as interrupting element, 291; parenthetical, 371; punctuation of, 345–46, 349; for sentence variety, 196

exclamation point: ellipsis after, 385; and quotation marks, 378–79; sarcastic, 349; to show intensity, 349; spacing with, 467–68

*expect*, colloquial use of, 571

experience: generalizing from, 74–75; and personal voice, 85–86; related to modes, 8; as topic source, 65–66

explanation. *See* analysis

**expletive**, *589–90*, 597

*explicit* vs. *implicit, tacit*, 573

exposition. *See* analysis

extended figure of speech, 229–30

**extracted** (indented) quotation, *380–82*, 535; colon before, 384; parenthetical citation for, 379–80

*facet*, and visual meaning, 571

fact vs. opinion: in acknowledgment, 502, 504; as evidence, 41

*factor*, imprecise use of, 571

facts, compilations of, 491–92

fad words, 207–8

fairness, in essay, 45, *76–79*, 101–3

*fair* vs. *fare*, 422

**fallacy**, 42–43; *ad hominem* reasoning, 79–80; begging the question, 76–77; circular thesis, 75; either-or reasoning, 77; faulty generalization, 73–74; *post hoc* explanation, 77–78; straw man, 78–79
**false start**, in sentence, deliberate, 197; dash after, 367
family relation, capitalization of, 444–45
**faulty generalization**, 73–74
faulty predication, 116, *168–69,* 256–57
*faze* vs. *phase,* 422
*feel* vs. *feeling,* 571
*few* vs. *little,* 571
*fewer* vs. *less, lesser, least,* 571
fiction, interpretation of, 48–52
**figurative language**, 227–31; in description, 16–18; extended, 229–30; mixed metaphor, 230–31; simile vs. metaphor, 228–29
*figure,* as colloquial verb, 571
figures, 459–61. *See also* numbers
film: italics for title of, 451; cited in note, 526; cited in reference list, 517; reference books on, 488–89
final copy of essay, 121–23
first draft of essay, 84–98
*first* vs. *firstly,* 463
fixed expression, possessive of, 409
*flaunt* vs. *flout,* 571–72
*flunk,* colloquial for *fail,* 572
focused freewriting, 69–70
folklore reference books, 489
**footnote**: continued from previous page, 524; endnote vs., 523–24; number for, 523; placement of, 523–24; with quotation marks, 379; typed form of, 523. *See also* footnote/endnote form
footnote/endnote form, 523–28; bibliographic note in, 529; and bibliography, 528; endnote vs. footnote, 523–24; number for, 523; parenthetical reference in, 527; reference list form vs., 505–8; sample first notes in, 525–26; subsequent reference in, 529; and supplementary note, 529
*forbear* vs. *forebear,* 422

foreign-based word, plural of, 405–6
foreign term: capitalization of, 449; italics for, 452–53; translation of, 453
*foreword* vs. *forward,* 422
form, for final copy, 121–23
formal diction, 218
*fortuitous,* does not mean *lucky,* 572
fraction, hyphenation of, 439
fragment. *See* sentence fragment
**free element**, 163, *180–84;* significant pause with, 193–95
*free* vs. *freely,* 572
**freewriting**, *67–68,* 124; brainstorming vs., 68; focused, 69–70
*frightened* vs. *scared, afraid,* 572
*fulsome,* does not mean *abundant,* 572
*fun,* colloquial as adjective, 208, 572
**funnel opener**, *106–7,* 127
**fused sentence**, 250–51

**gender**, and sexism, 211–13
generalization, faulty, 73–74
general language, 10
geographic direction, capitalization of, 448
geology documentation style, 507
**gerund**: in fragment, 239–40; object of, 595; phrase, 597; subject of, 297, *302–4,* 603; tense of, 335–36
gerund phrase, 597
*gift,* as colloquial verb, 208
Glossary of Terms, 581–605
*God,* capitalization of, 446–47
*good* vs. *well,* 572
**governing pronoun**, 86–87
**governing tense**, 329–36
grammar: aligned with meaning, *165–67,* 170, 188–90, 324–28. *See also* usage problems
Greek derivative, plural of, 405–6
group name, capitalization of, 448
*guess,* colloquial as *suppose,* 572
*Guide to Reference Books,* 488
guide to subject headings, 476–77

*had better,* both words necessary, 572
*half a,* no *a* preceding, 572
handwritten essay, form for, 122–23
*hangar* vs. *hanger,* 422

*hanged* vs. *hung,* 572
*hard* vs. *hardly,* 572
*here comes,* and verb agreement, 262
*high* vs. *highly,* 572
high office, capitalization of, 445
historical event, movement, or period,
    capitalization of, 447
historical past vs. literary present, 339–
    41
history reference books, 489
holiday: abbreviation of, 457; capitali-
    zation of, 447
holy book, capitalization of, 446–47
*hopefully,* not always accepted, 572
*how,* colloquial as *that,* 573
*however: but* vs., 252–53; *how ever* vs.,
    573; in pivoting paragraph, 154–56
humor, 33; with irony, 88–90
hyphen, 433–40; in compound modi-
    fier, 436–38; in compound noun or
    verb, 436; fixed, 438; in formation of
    dash, 465–66; in fraction, 439; at
    line ending, 433–34; meaning made
    clear with, 436–38; in number, 439–
    40; with prefix, 434–35; spacing
    with, 468. *See also* hyphenated terms
hyphenated terms: and capitalization in
    title, 443–44; plural of, 407; posses-
    sive of, 410; spelling of, 433–40
hypothetical condition, tense with, 333–
    35

*ibid.,* 527
*idea* vs. *concept, conception,* 567
idiom, 283
*i.e.,* 453, 455, *573*
*if* clause, and verb form, 333–35
*if not,* ambiguity of, 573
*ignorant* vs. *stupid,* 573
*illusion* vs. *allusion, delusion,* 563–64
illustration, as analytic strategy, 32–33;
    to develop topic, 71
**image,** 227–31
imperative mood, 401
impersonal vs. personal voice, 84–87
*implicit* vs. *explicit, tacit,* 573
implied point of story, 24–26
**implied subject,** 241

*imply* vs. *infer,* 573
improvising vs. planning, 97–98
inanimate thing, possessive of, 413
*in back of,* colloquial for *behind,* 566
*in case,* usually wordy, 573
in-class essay, 548–49
*include,* does not mean *are,* 573–74
*in connection with,* vague use of, 185
**incorporated quotation,** *376–80,* 382–
    87
indefinite pronoun, 599; adjective vs.,
    267; listed, 266; possessive of, 413–
    14; and verb agreement, 266–68
indented format, for business letter,
    553–54, 558
indented quotation. *See* extracted (in-
    dented) quotation
**indention:** in business letter, 553–54,
    558; of extracted quotation, 380–82;
    in outline, 94–96; of paragraph, *122,*
    140, 377–78, 382; in quoted dia-
    logue, 377–78. *See also* margin;
    spacing
independent clause, 241–47; and core
    element, 164–65; defined, 242;
    joined with another, 249–54, 326–27;
    and revision of fragment, 245–47;
    after semicolon, 361; in series, 254,
    326–27; subordinate clause vs., 241–
    44
**index:** in library, 481–86; of book, 591
Index of Usage, 562–80
indicative mood, 401
**indirect discourse:** quotation vs., *21–
    22,* 338–39; tense with, 337–38
**indirect object,** 298
**indirect question:** not capitalized, 442;
    period after, 346
*individual,* pompous for *person,* 574
*infer* vs. *imply,* 573
**infinitive:** in fragment, 239–40; object
    of, 595; phrase, 597; split, 281–82;
    subject of, 297, 299; tense of, 335–
    36
infinitive phrase, 597
**inflection:** in dictionary, 205; of verb,
    239, *391–92*
informal diction, 218
initial modifier, and comma, 284–85

initials: periods with, 458; spacing of, 459
insertion: brackets for, 372, 375, *387*; in final copy, 123; within already parenthetic material, 375
*inside of,* colloquial use of, 574
*inspite of,* as misspelling, 574
institutional name, capitalized, 445–46
instructor as audience, 3
**intensifiers**, overuse of, 222
intensive pronoun, 599
intentional sentence fragment, 151, *247–48*, 441
**interjection**, 592
interlibrary loan, 480
*in terms of,* vague, 184–85, 573
**interpretation**, literary, 48–55
**interrogative adjective**, 592
interrogative pronoun, 599
**interrupting element**: emphatic, 197; exclamation or question as, 291; placement of, 276–77; punctuation of, *290–91*, 366–68, 370–71
intervening clause or phrase, and number of verb, 259–60
*in the area of, in the framework of,* vague, 185
**intransitive verb**, 238
introductory paragraph. *See* opening paragraph
**introductory tag**, 253, *383*
**inverted syntax**, 197–98
*invite,* as disapproved noun, 208
**irony**, 88–90
irregular adjective or adverb, 417
**irregular verb**, 395; principal parts of, 395–98
*is because. See* reason is because
*is when, is where,* and predication, 574
*it*: as expletive, *589–90*, 597; as indefinite indicator, 313
italics, 450–54; for abbreviation, 453; for Bible citation, not used, 452; emphasis by, 454; for foreign word, 452–53; for name of ship, 453; for newspaper name, 451; overuse of, 454; in quotation, for emphasis, 454; quotation marks vs., 451–52; for title of work, 451–52; for title within title,

452; with translation, 453; underlining for, 450; for word presented *as* word, 453
*it is,* and verb agreement, 271
*it's* vs. *its,* 411–12, 422

**jargon**, 213–15
"joint ownership," possessive form, 410
journal: cited in note, 525–26; cited in reference list, 514; in library, 475, *481–83*; personal, 66

*kind of,* awkward use of, 574

Latin abbreviation, italics for, 453
Latinate diction, 232
law documentation style, 507
**leading idea**, in paragraph, 140–43
*lead* vs. *led,* 422
*leave* vs. *let,* 574
*lessen* vs. *lesson,* 422
*less* vs. *lesser, least, few,* 571
letter of alphabet, plural of, 407
letter writing. *See* business letter
*level,* as vague noun, 574
*liable* vs. *likely, apt,* 564
library, features of: abstracts, 481–86; almanacs, yearbooks, and compilations of facts, 491–92; articles and reviews, 481–87; atlases, 492; background sources, 487–93; biographies, 492–93; call number, 477, *479*; catalogs, 474, *476–80*; circulation desk, 474; computer terminals, 474, *478*, 486–87; dictionaries, 492; encyclopedias, 491; guide to subject headings, 476–77; guides to reference books, 488; indexes, 481–86; interlibrary loan, 480; journals, 475, *481–83*; magazines, 481–83; newspapers, 475, *482*; on-line catalog, 474, *478*; on-line databases, 486–87; order of research steps, 475; parts, 474–75; periodical room, 475; quotations, books of, 493; reference books, 487–91; reference librarian and room, 474; reserve desk, 474–75; shelf list, 477; stacks, 474
*lie* vs. *lay,* 574

*lightening* vs. *lightning*, 422
*like* vs. *as*, 565
*likely*: as weak adverb, 575; vs. *liable, apt*, 564
*likewise*, not a conjunction, 575
**limiting sentence**, in paragraph, 149, *152–56*
line ending: and hyphenation, 433–34; and continued punctuation, 469
linguistics documentation style, 507
linkage: between paragraphs, 108–10; within paragraph, 144–51
**linking verb**, 238
list: colon before, 362; dash before, 367; *firstly*, etc., 463
**literal language**, 227
*literally*, illegitimate use of, 575
literature: citation of, 504, 510, 512, 525; reference books in, 489–90; tense in discussion of, 339–41; writing about, 48–55
**literary present**, 339–41
"little me" apology, 105
*little* vs. *few*, 571
lively diction, 9–12, *217–33*
loaded language, 210
*loath* vs. *loathe, loathesome*, 422
logic, 42–43; fallacies in, 75–79
*loose* vs. *lose, losing*, 422
*lot, lots*, colloquial use of, 575

*mad* vs. *angry*, 575
magazine: cited in notes, 526; cited in reference list, 514–15; in library, 481–83
main idea of sentence, highlighted through subordination, 178–79
**main sentence**, of paragraph, 140–41; and patterns of development, 152–57
*majority*, needs countable items, 575
*mankind*, and sexism, 211
manuscript, form for, 121–23
*many* vs. *much*, 575
margin: in final copy, 122. *See also* indention; spacing
**matching** sentence elements, 186–93; anticipatory patterns in, 188–90; balance in, 190–91; pairing of, 186–88; in series, 191–93. *See also* parallelism

*material* vs. *materiel*, 422
mathematical operation, and verb agreement, 269
mathematics documentation style, 506–7
*may* vs. *can*, 566
meaning: aligned with grammar, *165–67*, 188–90; and appropriate diction, 202–16; changed by capitalization, 449; confusion of, 206–7, *421–23*; connotative, 209–10; denotative, 202–8; established, 207–8; figurative vs. literal, 227–31; and hyphenation, 436–38; literary, 48–55; and placement of modifier, 275–81; of words that sound or look alike, 421–23. *See also* ambiguity
measurement: abbreviations and figures for, 457, 459, 460–61; slash with, 375
*media*, preferably plural, 575
medicine documentation style, 507
**metaphor**, 16–18, *228–31*; dead, 223–24, *231*; mixed, 230–31; simile vs., 228–29
metaphorical language. *See* figurative language
microfiche catalog, 474
middle diction, 217–18
*miner* vs. *minor*, 422
*mislead* vs. *misled*, 422
misspelling: avoiding, 419–40; within quoted material, 387
*mitigate* vs. *militate*, 575
*mix* vs. *mixture*, 575
**mixed construction**, 168, *256–57*
**mixed metaphor**, 230–31
*MLA Handbook*, 508
**MLA style**, *508–22*, 532–40. *See also* "alternative MLA" documentation style; footnote/endnote form; reference list form
**mode** of writing, 8, 594. *See also* analysis; argument; description; narration
modified block format, for business letter, 551, 554, 557
**modifier**, 274–93; absolute phrase as, 282–83; adjective or adverb as, 275; ambiguous, 280–81, 285; appositive

**modifier** *(continued)*
as, 288–89; clause as, 274–75; compound, hyphenation of, 436–38; with compound prefix, 435; "contrary," 293; coordinate, 291–92; dangling, 277–80; defined, 274; double negative as, 283–84; final, no comma after, 292–93; hyphenation of, 436–38; initial, and comma, 284–85; interrupting element as, 290–91; missing modified term, 277–79; mistaken modified term, 279–81; in mixed construction, 257; optional comma after, 285; phrase as, 274–75; placement of, 275–82; predicate adjective as, 276; punctuation of, 284–93; repeated within series, 327; restrictive vs. nonrestrictive, 286–89; sandwiched, 292; sentence adverb as, 276–77, 289–90; split infinitive as, 281–82; squinting, 280–81; subordinate clause as, 275; transitional phrase as, 277, 289–90; types of, 274–77; usage problems with, 275–84
month: abbreviation of, 457; capitalization of, 447–48
**mood** of verb, 401–2
*moral* vs. *morale,* 422
*more like x than y,* 319
*most,* colloquial as *almost,* 575
*mph,* 456, 459
*Ms.,* 456, 552
*much less,* needs prior negation, 575–76
*muchly,* mistake for *much,* 576
multiplication, and verb agreement, 269
musical work: italics for, 451; reference books about, 488
*myself,* wrongly used for *I* or *me,* 576
mythology reference books, 489

name: abbreviation of, 456, 458–59; adjective derived from, 444, 447; capitalization of, 444–45; degree after, 359; in direct address, 290; of group or nationality, 448; initials in, 458–59; in "joint ownership," 410; of newspaper, 451; plural of, 404–5; possessive of, 408–10, 412; prefix before, 434; pronunciation of, 405, 409; rank with,

445; Roman numeral with, 462; sacred, 446–47; of ship, 453; title with, 359, 445, 456; verb derived from, 415; woman's, in letter, 552; of work, italics vs. quotation marks with, 451–52. *See also* place name
**narration,** 8, *19–26;* anticipatory, 22–23; direct vs. indirect discourse in, 21–22; implied point in, 24–26; reader participation in, 20; verb tense for, *19–20, 330–31*
*National Union Catalog,* 480
*naval* vs. *navel,* 422
negative: double, 283–84; emphasis, reversal of, and punctuation, 254; form of statement, weak, 223
*neither,* and verb agreement, 266–67
*neither . . . nor:* and parallelism, 323; and verb agreement, 265
newspaper: cited in note, 526; cited in reference list, 515; in library, 475, *482;* numbers vs. figures in, 459; paragraph length in, 158; place as part of name of, 451
*nobody: no body* vs., 564; and verb agreement, 266
*none,* and verb agreement, 267–68
**nonrestrictive modifier,** 180–82, *286–89*
*no one,* and verb agreement, 266
*no sooner x than y,* 319
note, for documentation. *See* endnote; footnote; footnote/endnote form
note number, and other punctuation, 379
notes from reading: bibliography card as, 494–95; to develop thoughts, 65; content, 494–96; for exam, 545; form of, 65, *496–97;* and plagiarism, 502; sample cards, 495–96
*nothing like,* weak use of, 576
*not . . . neither,* and parallelism, 320
*not only x but also y,* 323–24
*not so much x as y,* 319–20
*not that, not too,* weak use of, 576
**noun:** attributive, 208; clause, 585; collective, 263; colorless use of, 172; compound, 436, 586; hyphenated, plural of, 407; phrase, 597; plural of,

**noun** *(continued)*
*403-7,* 409-10; possessive of, 295,
297, 302-5, *408-16;* as subject, 240
noun clause, 585
**nounlike element**, 240
noun phrase, 597
*nowhere near,* colloquial use of, 576
*nowheres,* always wrong, 576
*number: amount* vs., 564; and verb
agreement, 263-64
**number**: of noun or pronoun, 258-59,
306-8; of verb, *258-71,* 391-92
numbers, 459-63; adverbial, 463; apostrophe in, 415; Arabic numeral, 461-
62; bunched, 461; cardinal vs. ordinal,
462-63; comma in, 358; in date, 461;
with decimal, 461; in documentation,
509-27; figures vs., 459-61; hyphenation of, 439-40; note, 379, *523;* in
outline, *94-96,* 462; of pages in submitted work, 122; in parentheses,
370; for play citation, 461, *521;* plural of, 407; prefatory, 462; punctuation of, 358; range between, 440;
Roman numeral, 461-62; sentence
beginning with, 460; in technical
prose, 459-61; and verb agreement,
263-64
**numeral**, Arabic vs. Roman, 461-62
numerical word, and verb agreement,
263-64
*numerous,* must remain an adjective,
576

**object**. *See* direct object; indirect object; object of gerund, infinitive, or
participle; object of preposition
objection, meeting: fairness in, 44-45,
*78-79;* and thesis revision, 100
objective case, 295-97; usage problems
with, 297-304
**objective complement**, 354, 595
object of gerund, infinitive, or participle, 595
**object of preposition**, 297, 299, 353
*occur* vs. *take place,* 576
*of* construction, possessive, 412-14
office, capitalization of, 445
*off of,* should be *off,* 576

*oftentimes,* awkward for *often,* 576
*old-fashion,* needs *-ed,* 576
*on* vs. *upon, up on,* 576
*on account of,* weak use of, 576
"one essay from start . . . ," 124-34
*one of those who,* number of, 271
on-line: catalog, 474, *478;* database,
486-87
*only,* not a conjunction, 576
opening paragraph, 104-8; baited, 107;
deadly, 104-5; delay in composing,
97; for exam essay, 546; first sentence
of, 107-8; funnel, 106-7; recalled at
end, 113; and suspended structure, 157
opening sentence, of essay, 107-8
opinion. *See* fact vs. opinion
*or,* and verb agreement, 265
*oral* vs. *verbal,* 576
**ordinal number**, 462-63
organization, for essay, 90-92; revision
of, 100-101. *See also* outline
*other than that,* colloquial, 576
*other times,* not an adverb, 576
*otherwise,* not an adjective, 576
*ourself,* mistake for *ourselves,* 576
**outline**, 93-96; after a draft, 93; for
exam essay, 546; form for, 122;
scratch, 93-94; sentence vs. topic,
95-96; subordinated, 94-96; and thesis statement, 93
*outside of* vs. *outside,* 577
overstuffed statement, 169-70

page numbers: in documentation, 508-
27; figures for, 461; prefatory, 462;
shortening of, 415; for submitted
essay, 122
*pair* vs. *couple,* 568-69
paired elements: and comma, 324-25.
*See also* matching sentence elements
**paragraph**, 104-13, *139-61;* baited
opener, 107; block, 109-10; bloated,
160-61; in business letter, 552;
choppy, *159-60,* 187; closing, *111-
13,* 157; compared to essay, *139,*
163; compared to sentence, 163; continuity in, 142, *144-51;* contradiction in, 141; deadly opener, 104-5;
development, 152-58; in dialogue,

**paragraph** *(continued)*
159, *377–78,* 382; digression in, 142; direct, 152–54; funnel opener, 106–7; indention of, *122,* 140, 382; last sentence of, 142–43, *156–58;* "last word" in, 142–43; leading idea in, 140–43; length of, 158–61; limiting sentence in, 149, 152–56; linkage between, 108–10; main features of, 139; main sentence in, 140–41, *152–57;* opening, 104–8, 157; pivoting, 154–56; related sentences kept together in, 149–50; repeated sentence structure in, 146–48, *150–51;* revision of, 104–13; signal of relation in, 145–48; supporting sentence in, 149, *152–55;* suspended, 156–58; transitional, 110; types of development, 152–58; unity in, 117–18, *140–43;* varied sentence structure in, 150–51. *See also* closing paragraph; opening paragraph

**paragraph block**, 109–10

paragraph continuity, 142, *144–51. See also* paragraph

paragraph development, 152–58. *See also* paragraph

paragraph length, 158–61

paragraph unity, 117–18, *140–43. See also* paragraph

**parallelism**, 186, *314–28;* with *and who* or *and which,* 322; and anticipatory pattern, 318–20; in comparison, 315–17, 319–21; completion of, 318–22; defined, 314; with *either . . . or,* 323; like elements in, 315–17; as matching, 186–93; with *more like x than y,* 319; with *neither . . . nor,* 323; with *no sooner x than y,* 319; with *not only x but also y,* 323–24; with *not so much x as y,* 319–20; paired elements within, 324–25; punctuation of, 324–28; between sentences in a paragraph, 150–51; with series, 315–16, 325–28; with suspended comparison, 321; with suspended verb, 320; with *that* clause, 321–22; wrongly repeating an earlier element, 323–24. *See also* matching sentence elements

**paraphrase**, 498–500; page reference for, 497; and plagiarism, 502

parentheses, 370–72; between complete sentences, 371; brackets vs., 372; brackets within, 375; and capitalization, 442; functions of, 370–71; for interrupting element, 291, 366; not used to interrupt quotation, 372; other punctuation with, 372, 379–80; for sentence within sentence, 371; spacing with, 468. *See also* parenthetical citation

**parenthetical citation**: abbreviations used in, 455–56; APA form for, 519, 521–22; with extracted quotation, 379–80; of indirect source, 520; MLA form for, 519–21; more than one work in, 521; punctuation of, 379; rival forms compared, 505–6; scientific, 506–7; of writer's added italics, 454

parenthetical element. *See* interrupting element

parenthetic question, 371

parenthetic sentence: capitalization of, 442; punctuation of, 371–72

**participle**: in fragment, 239–40; object of, 595; past, *394–99,* 596; past tense vs., 399; present, 239

**part of speech**, 203; listed, 596–97

*part* vs. *portion,* 577

*passed* vs. past, 422

passive voice, 399–400; and emphasis, 172–73; tenses shown in, 400

past participle, *394–99,* 596; apostrophe in, 415; past tense vs., 399

past tense, 393–400; derived from name, 415; literary present vs., 339–41; past participle vs., 399

pause, significant, 193–95

*peace* vs. *piece,* 422

peer editing, 99–100

period, 345–47; with abbreviation, 347, 458–59; and courtesy question, 346; with initial, 458; after indirect question, 346; after mild exclamation, 345–46; omitted after question mark, 348–49; after polite command, 345; with quotation marks, 378–79; semicolon vs., 360; after sentence, 345;

period *(continued)*
    after sentence ending in an abbreviation, 347; spacing with, 467–68
periodical room, in library, 475
periodic sentence. *See* suspended sentence
period of history, capitalization of, 447
*persecute* vs. *prosecute,* 422
**person**: of pronoun, 258, *306–8*; and verb agreement, 258–59
*-person,* and avoidance of sexism, 211
personal pronoun, 599; antecedent of, 116, 242, 306, *308–13*; case forms for, 296; case problems with, 297–305
personal vs. impersonal voice, 84–87
*personal* vs. *personnel,* 422
*persuade* vs. *convince, 568*
*pertaining to,* 185
*phenomena,* always plural, 577
philosophy reference books, 490
**phrase,** 244; additive, 260–61; as fragment, 244–46; intervening, and number of verb, 259–61; kinds of, 597–98; as modifier, 274–75; as subject, 263; transitional, *252–53,* 277, 290–91, 361
physics documentation style, 506, 508
picture, creating a, 10–12
**pivoting paragraph,** 154–56
*-place,* questionable forms of, 577
place name: abbreviation of, 457–58; capitalization of, 444, 448; in newspaper name, 451
**plagiarism,** 501–4
*plan,* best followed by *to,* 577
planning vs. improvising, 97–98
platitude, in opening paragraph, 105
play, citation of, 451, 461, 521
plot, tense for discussing, 239–41
plural, 403–7; of abbreviation, 407; of figure, 407; of foreign-based word, 405–6; of hyphenated noun, 407; of letter, 407; of name, 404–5; of noun ending in consonant plus *-y,* 404; of noun ending in *-ful,* 405; of noun ending in *-o,* 403–4; of number, 407; possessive vs., 412; and verb agreement, 258–71; of word presented *as* word, 406
*plus,* not a conjunction, 577
*P.M.,* 456, 458, 461, *564*
poetry: citation of, 512, 521, 525; interpretation of, 48–49, 53–55; omission from quotation of, 384, 386; quotation of, *380–82,* 384, 386, 467; slash with, 467
**point of view**: descriptive, 12–14; as mental perspective, 14
political science reference books, 491
*poorly,* colloquial as *ill,* 577
*popular,* implies large numbers, 577
*portion* vs. *part,* 577
positive degree, 416–18
positive form of statement, lively, 223
possessive, 408–18; awkward, 412–14; compound, 410; double, 304–5; formation of, 295–97, *408–14*; of hyphenated term, 410; of inanimate thing, 413; of indefinite pronoun, 413–14; in "joint ownership," 410; of name, 408–10, 412; *of* form of, 412–14; of plural noun, 409–10; plural vs., 412; of pronoun, *295–97, 302–5,* 411, 413–14; of singular noun, 295–97, *408–9*; for subject of gerund, 297, *302–4*; of time, 410; of title, 413; unpronounced, 408–9; usage problems with, 302–5
possessive pronoun, no apostrophe with, 413–14
*possible,* not an adverb, 577
***post hoc* explanation,** 77–78
*pray* vs. *prey,* 422
*precede* vs. *proceed,* 422
**predicate,** 238, *241,* 257; adjective, *276,* 586; noun, 586. *See also* predication
**predication,** 116, *168–69,* 256–57
*predominant* vs. *predominate,* 422
preface, page numbers for, 462
**prefix**: compound, 435; hyphen with, 434–35; before name, 434
prejudgment of issue, *76–77,* 210
*prejudice* vs. *prejudiced,* 422
premise, *42,* 604

**preposition**: object of, 297, 299; overuse of, 232–33; in title, capitalization of, 443–44; wrongly followed by comma, 353
prepositional phrase, 257, *597*
*pressure*, questionable as verb, 577
prewriting, 62–82. *See also* composing
**principal parts** of verb, 394–98
*principal* vs. *principle*, 422
**process analysis**, *38–40*, 71
pronoun: antecedent of, 242, 306, *308–13*; with appositive, 301; case of, 295–305; complement, 298; demonstrative, 147, 311, *599*; governing, 86–87; indefinite, 266–68, 413–14, *599*; intensive, *599*; interrogative, *599*; number of, 306–8; object, case of, 298–300; person of, 258, 306–8; personal, *295–305*, *599*; possessive, *295–97*, 302–5, 411, 413–14; reciprocal, *599*; reference of, 116, *308–13*; reflexive, *599*; as relational signal, 147; relative, 242, *599*; sexist, 211–13; shift, 306–8; after *than* or *as*, 300–301; *who* vs. *whom*, 299–302
pronoun complement, awkward, 298
pronoun as direct object, 298–300
pronoun reference, 308–13; explicit antecedent, 308; rival senses of *it*, 313; single antecedent, 308–9; vague *this* or *that*, 311–12; vague *which*, 312–13; whole term as antecedent, 310
pronoun shift, 306–8
pronunciation: in dictionary, 202–3; of certain plural names, 405; of certain possessive names, 408–9; and spelling, 408–9, 423–24, 430
proofreading, of final copy, 123
*prophecy, prophecies* vs. *prophesy, prophesies*, 423
*prostate* vs. *prostrate*, 423
psychological jargon, 213–15
psychology: documentation style, *508–22*, 541–42; reference books, 491
punctuation, 345–87; of abbreviation, 347, 458–59; of acronym, 456; of address, 358–59; apostrophe, 408–15; of appositive, 288–89, 367; brackets, 372, 375, 387, 466, 468; of business

letter, 550–53; with citation, 379, 523; colon, 362–65, 384; comma, 351–59, 383; of courtesy question, 346; dash, *366–69*, 465–66, 468; of dialogue, 377–79; of direct question, 347–48; ellipsis, 375, *384–86*, 466–69; exclamation point, *349*, 467–68; formation and spacing of, 465–69; and fragment, 244–48; of free element, 180–84; general function of, 344; hyphen, 433–40, 468; of indirect question, 346; of interrupting element, 290–91; of modifier, 284–93; of note number, 379, 523; of objective complement, 354; of page number, 122; of paired elements, 324–25; of parallelism, 324–28; parentheses, 370–72; of parenthetic sentence, 371–72; period, *345–47*, 467–68; question mark, *347–49*, 467–68; of quotation, 374–87; of restrictive and nonrestrictive modifiers, 286–88; semicolon, 327–28, *360–62*; of sentence adverb, 289; of sentence elements that belong together, 352–54; of series, 254, 325–28; slash, 375, 380, 467; of transitional phrase, 289
**punctuation marks**: listed, 599–600. *See also* punctuation

quantity term, and verb agreement, 263
*quarrel* vs. *argue*, 565
question: courtesy, 346; direct, 347–48; in exam, 545–47; indirect, 346, 442; as interrupting element, 291; parenthetic, 371; rhetorical, 196; for sentence variety, 196; *shall* vs. *will* in, 394. *See also* question mark
question mark: after direct question, 347–48; never double, 348; doubt expressed with, 348; ellipsis after, 385; within parentheses, 348; with other punctuation, 348–49; quotation marks with, 378–79; sarcastic, 348; spacing with, 467–68
quotation, 374–87; brackets within, 372, 387; capitalization within, 442–43; checking, 123; of dialogue, 21–22, 377–78; documentation for,

quotation *(continued)*
501–29; ellipsis in, 384–86; extracted, *380–82,* 384, 535; incorporated, *376–80,* 382–87; indention of, 380–82; indirect discourse vs., 21–22; insertion of material into, 387; introduction of, 382–84; italics for emphasis in, 454; marks used with, 374–75; misspelling in, 387; on notecard, 494–97; note number with, 379, 523; omission from, 384–86; parenthetical citation after, 379–80, 519–21; of poetry, 380–82, 384, 386; punctuation of, 376–88; within a quotation, 376–77; and writer's own tense, 341. *See also* quotation marks

quotation marks: for Bible, not used, 452; for dialogue, 21–22, 377–78; and extracted quotation, 380–82; for incorporated quotation, 376–80; italics vs., 451–52; with note number, 379, 523; with other punctuation marks, 378–80; sarcastic, 348, 387; to show psychological distance, 375; single, 374, *376–77;* spacing with, 468; for speech including paragraph break, 382; for title, 451–52; for translation, 453; for word presented *as* word, 453

quotations, dictionaries of, 493

*quote,* colloquial as noun, 577

**racist language,** 210

*rack* vs. *wrack,* 423

radio or television program: cited in note, 526; cited in reference list, 517; italicized title of, 451

*rain* vs. *rein, reign,* 423

*raise* vs. *rise,* 577

rank, capitalization of, 445

readability, *163–70,* 174–76, 180–82, 184–86

*Reader's Guide,* 482–83

*real,* not an adverb, 577

reasonable tone, 101–3

reasoning, 42–43; *ad hominem,* 79; cause and effect, 33–35, 71, 125; either-or, 77. *See also* fallacy

*reason is because,* redundant, 577

*reason* vs. *cause,* 567

*rebut* vs. *refute,* 577

**rebuttal,** 600

reciprocal pronoun, 599

*reckon,* colloquial for *suppose,* 577–78

recommendation, and subjunctive, 402

recording: cited in note, 526; cited in reference list, 518; italicized title of, 451

**redundancy:** avoiding, 220–21; in comparison of adjective or adverb, 418; in parallelism, 323–24; in restating exam question, 546; in sound, 232–33. *See also* repetition

reference books, 487–91

reference (citation). *See* documentation

reference librarian, 474

**reference list:** order of entries, 508–9; order within entries, 509; sample entries, 510–18

reference list form: abbreviations for, 454–56; footnote/endnote form vs., 505–8; parenthetical citation in, 518–22; reference list in, 508–18; in sample essay, 539–42. *See also* reference list

reference of pronoun. *See* pronoun reference

reference room, 474

reflexive pronoun, 599

**refutation,** *44–45,* 82

**regular verb,** principal parts of, 394

relation, signal of, 145–48

*relation* vs. *relationship,* 578

**relative clause,** 242–43; and verb agreement, 270–71

relative pronoun, 242, *599;* antecedent of, 116, 242, 306, *308–13;* listed, 243

*relevant,* needs *to,* 578

religion reference books, 490

repetition: and balance, 190–91; implied, 147; and paragraph continuity, 146–48, 150–51; of sound, 232–33. *See also* redundancy

*replace* vs. *substitute,* 578

reporter's questions, asking, 70

requirement, and subjunctive, 402

research. *See* library

research essay, 472–542; documentation for, 501–29; sample, 532–42; sources for, 473–500

reserve desk, in library, 474–75

restatement of question: in exam answer, 546; in opening paragraph of essay, 105

restrictive label, in dictionary, 205

**restrictive modifier**, 180–82, *286–89*

résumé, 559–61

*reticent* vs. *reluctant,* 578

reversal of negative emphasis, and "acceptable comma splice," 254

review of book. *See* book review

revision, 2, *99–134*; to arouse curiosity, 104–8; of bound element, 180–82; checklist for, 120–21, inside front cover; and composing process, 99–100; of conclusion, 111–13; conceptual, 100–101; for continuity, 108–10; of diction, 207–33; editorial, 114–18; of exam essay, 547; on final copy, 122–23; need for, 2, 99–100; organizational, 100–101; of paragraph, 104–13; for reasonable tone, 100–103; symbols for, inside back cover; of thesis, 72–79, 126; of thesis statement, 80–82; of title, *118–19, 129*

revision symbols, inside back cover

**rhetoric**, 4; modes of, *8, 594*

**rhetorical question**, 196

rhyme, 232

**Roman numeral**: formation of, 462; after name, 462; in outline, 94–96; for play citation, 461, 521; for prefatory pages, 462

roman type, 450

**run-on sentence**: avoidance of, 249–54; comma splice, 250–54; fused sentence, 250–51; and reversal of negative emphasis, 254


sacred name, capitalization of, 446–47

sample essays, 24–26, 49–55, 130–34, 532–42

sandwiched modifier, 292

**sarcasm**, shown by: exclamation point, 349; question mark, 348; quotation marks, 348, 387; *[sic],* 387

*scared* vs. *frightened, afraid,* 572

science: documentation styles for, 506–8; reference books, 490. *See also* technical writing

scratch outline, 93–94

season, not capitalized, 448–49

self-contradiction, in paragraph, 141

semicolon, 360–62; colon vs., 362–63; conjunction after, 361–62; no fragment after, 361; with independent clauses, 360–61; note number after, 379, 523; period vs., 360; with quotation marks, 378; in series, 327–28; spacing with, 468–69

**sentence**, 163–99; active voice in, 172–73; anticipatory pattern in, 188–90; aphorism in, 190; balance in, 190–91; beginning with a coordinating conjunction, 243–44; beginning with a number, 460; choppy, 193–95; compared to paragraph and essay, 163; complete, 237–54; concluding, in a paragraph, 142–43, *156–58*; core element in, 163–65, 167, 170, 178, 180–84; cumulative, *198–99, 282*; declarative, 196; delaying formula in, 174–75; distinct expression in, 164–76; emphasis in, 186–93; end punctuation of, 345–49; epigrammatic, 107–8, 190; essential elements of, 237–41; as exclamation, 196; "false start" in, 197; fragment, 244–48, 361; free element in, 163, *180–84*, 193–95; fused, 250–51; grammar aligned with meaning in, *165–67*, 170, 188–90, 314–28; interruption in, *197*, 291; inverted syntax in, 197–98; key ways to improve, 163–64; limiting, 149, *152–56*; main idea in, 178–79; major and minor elements of, 163; matching in, 186–93; mixed construction in, 168, *256–57*; overstuffed, 169–70; parenthetic, capitalization of, 442; parenthetic, punctuation of, 371–72; passive voice in, 172–73; predication in, *168–69,* 256–57; question in, 196; readability

**sentence** *(continued)*
of, *163-70,* 174-76, 180-82, 184-86; restrictive vs. nonrestrictive modifier in, 180-82, *286-89;* run-on, 249-54; series in, *191-93,* 315-16, 325-28; significant pause in, 193-95; subordination in, 178-86; supporting, 149-50, *152-55;* suspended, 199; unnecessary *that* or *what* clause in, 175-76; variety in, 150-51, *193-99;* verb *to be* overused in, 170-71; verb to convey action in, 172; within another sentence, capitalization of, 441

**sentence adverb:** conjunction vs., 251-53; as interrupting element, 290; list of, 251; logical relation shown by, 361; ordinary adverb vs., 252; placement of, 276-77; punctuation of, 289-90

sentence elements, essential, 237-41

**sentence fragment,** 244-48; appositive as, 246; intentional, 151, *247-48,* 441; phrase or clause as, 244-46; recognition of, 245-47; after semicolon, 361; verbal as, 246

sentence outline, 95

sentence pattern, 186-99. *See also* sentence

sentence within a sentence, 441

series: climax and consistency in, 191-93; of independent clauses, 254, 326-27; omission of conjunctions in, 192, 254; and parallelism, 315-16, 325-28; punctuation of, 254, *325-28;* repeated modifier in, 327

**sexist language,** *210-13,* 308

*shall* vs. *will,* 394

shelf list, in library, 477

shift: between cardinal and ordinal numbers, 463; of diction level, 217-18; from *firstly* to *second,* etc., 463; of pronoun, 86-87, 306-8; between quotation and indirect discourse, 338-39; of tense, 338-39

ship, italicized name of, 453

*[sic],* 160, 234, *387,* 464

**signal of relation,** 145-48

**significant pause,** 193-95

*similar,* does not mean *same,* 578

simile: extended, 229; metaphor vs., 228-29

simple subject, 603

*since,* possible ambiguity of, 578

single quotation marks: for quotation within quotation, 376-77; for translation, 453

*sit* vs. *set,* 578

slang, 116, 205, *218*

**slash** (virgule): for corrections on final copy, 122; functions of, 375; in notecard, 497; in quotation of poetry, *380,* 467; spacing with, 467

social science: reference books, 491. *See also* APA style

software. *See* computer; word processor

*some,* wrongly used for *somewhat,* 578

*somebody* vs. *some body,* 564

*something,* not an adverb, 578

*some time* vs. *sometime, sometimes,* 423

*somewheres,* always wrong, 578

*sort of,* awkward use of, 574

sound patterns, in sentence, 232-33

spacing: of abbreviation or acronym, 459; of business letter, 550-54; of essay lines, 122; of extracted quotation, 380-82; of notes, 122, *523-24;* of punctuation marks, 465-69; of reference list, 508-18. *See also* indention; margin

span of time, punctuation of, 440, 467

speaker, change of, in dialogue, 377

*special,* needless use of, 570

*specially* vs. *especially,* 570

speech. *See* dialogue

specific language, 10-12

spelling, 419-40; British and Canadian, 420, 424-29; common errors of, 421-29; of compound modifier, 436-38; of compound possessive, 410; in dictionary, 203; of foreign-based plural, 405-6; and hyphenation, 433-40; keeping list for, 419-20; of plural letter or figure, 407; of plural word, 403-7; of possessive, 408-14; and pronunciation, 408-9, 423-24, 430; rules for, 429-32; and suffixes,

spelling *(continued)*
429–32; of words that sound or look
alike, 421–23
**split infinitive**, 281–82
square brackets. *See* brackets
**squinting modifier**, 280–81
stacks, in library, 474
**stance**: analytic, 11; forthright, 87;
ironic, 88–90
standard written English, 236; dialect
vs., 392
state name, abbreviation of, 459
*stationary* vs. *stationery,* 423
stereotype, racial or sexual, 210–11
strategies, rhetorical. *See* analysis;
argument; description; narration
**straw man**, 78–79
*stupid* vs. *ignorant,* 573
**subject**: of absolute phrase, 603; and
choice of case, 297–98; complete,
603; compound, 264–66; disjunctive,
265; finding, *240–41, 259–62*; following verb, 261; of gerund, 297,
*302–4,* 603; implied, 241; of infinitive, 297, 299, 603; number of, 258–
71; numerical, 263; simple, 603; no
comma after, 272–73, 352; of verb,
166–67, *240–41*; and verb agreement, 258–71. *See also* subject area;
subject-verb agreement
**subject area**, 59–61; narrowing, 63–
64
subject card, in library, 479
subject catalog, in library, 474
subject of gerund, 297, *302–4,* 603
subject headings, guide to, 476–77
subjective case, 295–302
subject of infinitive, *297,* 299, 603
subject-verb agreement, problems with,
258–71; additive phrase, 260–61; collective noun as subject, 263; compound subject, 264–66; disjunctive
subject, 265; with *either . . . or, neither . . . nor,* 265; indefinite pronoun
as subject, 266–68; intervening clause
or phrase, 259–60; *it is,* and plural
subject, 271; mathematical operation,
269; mixed construction, 168, *256–*

*57; number* as subject, 263–64; numerical term as subject, 263–64; *one
of those who,* 271; phrase or clause as
subject, 263; subject after verb, 261–
62; subject with plural form but singular meaning, 268; *there is, here
comes,* etc., 262; title of work as subject, 268
subjunctive mood: for hypothetical condition, 333–35, 401–2; for requirement or recommendation, 402; of
verb *to be,* 402; for wish, 401; *would*
error with, 335
subordinate clause, 241–47; to correct
run-on, 251; in fragment, 244–46;
independent clause vs., 241–44; as
modifier, 275; and pronoun case,
301–2
subordinating conjunction, *242–46,*
586; listed, 243; no comma after, 353
**subordination**, 178–86; bound, 180–
82; and core element, 170, *178–79*;
free, 180–84; vague, 184–86. *See
also* subordinate clause
subsequent reference, 527
substantive. *See* nounlike element
**substantive note**, *529,* 536
*substitute* vs. *replace,* 578
subtitle: capitalization of, 443–44;
colon before, 364–65; with striking
title, 119
subtraction, and verb agreement, 269
*such as* vs. *as,* 565
**suffix**: *-cede, -ceed, -sede,* 432; and fad
words, 207; and hyphen, 434; and
plural, 405; and spelling, 429–32
**summary**, 498–99; page reference for,
497; and plagiarism, 502
summary paragraph, omitted, 92, *113*
superlative degree, 416–18
**supplementary note**, 529
support. *See* evidence
supporting sentence, in paragraph,
149–50, *152–55*
*suppose to,* missing a *-d,* 578
*suppose* vs. *supposed,* 423
*sure,* colloquial as adverb, 578
**suspended comparison**, faulty, 321

**suspended paragraph**, 156–58
**suspended sentence**, 199
**suspended verb**, and parallelism, 320
syllable division, 203, 433–34
**syllogism**, 42
symbols, revision, inside back cover
*sympathy for* vs. *sympathy with, sympathize with,* 579
synonym, *204,* 206
syntax: aligned with meaning, 165–67; inverted, 197–98

*tacit* vs. *implicit, explicit,* 573
*tack* vs. *tact,* 423
tag, with quotation, 253, *383*
*take place* vs. *occur,* 576
technical writing: abbreviations in, 455, 457; documentation styles for, 506–8; jargon from, 213–15; numbers in, 459–61; paragraph length in, 159; process analysis in, 39; reference books for, 490
technology reference books, 490
television program. *See* radio or television program
**tense,** 258, *391–400;* in active voice, 391–99; with condition, 333–35; in discussion of literature, 339–41; for facts and ideas, 329–30; governing, 329–36; in indirect discourse, 337–39; listed, 393; in narration, *19–20,* 330–31; in passive voice, 399–400; past, vs. past participle, 399; and person and number, 391–94; with quotation, 337–39; relations between, 329–41; of verbal, 335–36
textual analysis, literary, 48–55
*than,* case of pronoun after, 300–1; vs. *then,* 423
*that:* vague, 311–12; *which* vs., 579
*that* clause: parallel, 321–22; subjunctive with, 402; awkward, 175–76
*theirself, theirselves,* wrong, 579
*their* vs. *there, they're,* 423
*there is,* and verb agreement, *262*
thesaurus, 206
**thesis,** 4, 58, *59–61,* 62; circular, 75; and composing process, 62–63; developing a, 72–82; for exam essay, 546; fairness in, 78–79; fallacies in, 76–79; implied, 24–26; for in-class essay, 548–49; limiting scope of, 73–74; revealed too baldly, 105; revision of, *72–79,* 126; subject area and topic vs., 59–61; thesis statement vs., 80; trial, 72; weaseling, 75. *See also* thesis statement, full

**thesis statement,** full, *80–82,* 91; form for submitting, 122; as guide to draft, 91; main details in, 80–81; objections met in, 82; outline from, 93; reasons in, 81; trial, 126
*this,* vague use of, 311–12
*those kind, those type,* wrong, 579
thought, capitalized, 441
*thusly,* mistake for *thus,* 579
*till, until, 'til, 'till,* 579
time: abbreviation with, 456, 458; *A.D.,* 456, *563; A.M., P.M.,* 456, 458, 461, *564; B.C.,* 456; colon with, 364; event, movement, or period, 447; in exam, 546; figures vs. numbers with, 460; *o'clock* in, 460; plural possessive of, 410; slash with, 467; span of, 440, 467. *See also* date
title, of cited work: capitalization of, *443–44,* 449; colon in, 364–65; foreign, 449; hyphenated term in, 443–44; italics vs. quotation marks for, 451–52; in note, 523–39; in parenthetical citation, 520; possessive of, 413; in reference list, 508–18; in subsequent reference, 527; and verb agreement, 268; within another title, 452
title card, in library, 479
title of essay, choosing, *118–19,* 129
title page, of submitted essay, 122
title with name: abbreviation of, 456; in letter, 550, 552; capitalization of, 445; punctuation of, 359
*to be:* overuse of, 170–71; subjunctive of, 402
*to* vs. *too, two,* 423
**tone:** and audience, 2–4; and intensifiers, 222; reasonable, 100–103; and voice, 85–86

*too,* weak as *very,* 579
**topic:** choice of, 59–71; subject area and thesis vs., *59–61,* 73; trial, 69–71. *See also* composing
topic outline, 95–96
**topic sentence.** *See* main sentence
*track* vs. *tract,* 423
**transitional paragraph,** 110
**transitional phrase:** conjunction vs., 252–53; as interrupting element, 290; logical relation shown by, 361; partial list of, 252; placement of, 277; punctuation of, 252–53, *289–90*
**transitive verb,** 237–38
translation: abbreviation to indicate, 455; cited in note, 525; cited in reference list, 513; italics for, 453; single quotation marks for, 453
**trial thesis,** 72
**trial topic,** 69–71
*try and,* prefer *try to,* 579
*type:* in fad words, 207; wrongly used for *type of,* 579
*type of,* needs singular object, 574
typing: of final copy, 121–23; italics in, 450; of letter, 550–54; of notes, 523–27; of reference list, 508–18; of résumé, 559–61; of subsequent reference, 527; and word division, 433–34. *See also* spacing

underlining, for italics, 450
**understatement,** 103
*uninterested* vs. *disinterested,* 569
units of measurement. *See* measurement
unity. *See* paragraph unity
*until, till, til, 'til, 'till,* 579
*upon* vs. *up on, on,* 576
*usage* vs. *use,* 579
usage problems: with case, 297–305; with complete sentence, 244–54; with dangling modifier, 116, *277–80*; in dictionary, 205; Index of Usage, 562–80; with joining clauses, 249–51, 325–27; with mixed construction, 168, *256–57*; with modifier, 275–93; with parallelism, 186, *314–28*; with possessive, 302–5; with predication, 116, *168–69,* 256–57; with pronoun

reference, 116, *308–13*; with pronoun shift, 306–8; with subjective case, 297–304; with subject-verb relations, 256–71; with tense, 329–41
*use to,* lacking a *-d,* 579
*utilize* vs. *use, utilization,* 579

vagueness: in subordination, 184–86; with *this* or *that,* 311–12; with *which,* 312–13. *See also* ambiguity
variety, sentence, 150–51, *193–99*; by cumulative pattern, 198–99; by emphatic interruption, 197; by inversion, 197–98; by question or exclamation, 196; by significant pause, 193–95; by suspended pattern, 199
**verb,** 166–67, *237–41*; agreement with, 258–71; auxiliary in, 19–20; base form of, 392; before subject, 261; comma before, 272–73; and complement, 238; conditional, 334–35; derived from abbreviation or name, 415; direct object of, 237–38; inflection of, 239, *391–92*; intransitive, 238; irregular, 395; linking, 238; missing from fragment, 246–47; mood of, 401–2; number and person of, *258–59,* 391–92; phrase, 597; position of, 238–39; predicate of, 238, *241,* 257; preferred to noun for action, 172; principal parts of, 394–98; recognizing, 237–39; regular, 394; and sentence strength, 165–69; tense of, 258, 329, *391–400*; *to be, 170–71,* 402; transitive, 237–38; verbal vs., 239–40; voice of, 172–73, *391–400. See also* subject-verb agreement
**verbal:** gerund, 239, 302–4; infinitive, 239, 281–82; object of, 595; participle, 239, *394–99*; phrase, 597; and sentence completeness, *239–40,* 246; subject of, 603; tense of, 335–36; verb vs., 239–40
*verbal* vs. *oral,* 576
verb phrase, 597
*violently,* not same as *strongly,* 579
virgule. *See* slash (virgule)
vivid description, 9–12
vocabulary list, keeping, 206–7

**voice**: active, 172–73, 392–99; and governing pronoun, 86–87; and irony, 88–90; passive, 172–73, 399–400; personal vs. impersonal, 84–87; and tone, 85–86

*waive* vs. *wave*, 423
*ways*, colloquial as *distance*, 580
*we*, editorial, 86–87
**weaseling thesis**, 75
*weather* vs. *whether*, 423
*well* vs. *good*, 572
*what* clause, unnecessary, 175–76
*what ever* vs. *whatever*, 580
*where*, not same as *whereby*, 580
*where . . . at*, colloquial, 580
*which*: and parallelism, 322; *that* vs., 579; vague use of, 312–13
*who* vs. *whom*, 299–302
*who's* vs. *whose*, 411–12, 423
*will* vs. *shall*, 394
*-wise*, colloquial use of, 207, *580*
wish, subjunctive for, 401
*with*, vague use of, *185*, 566
*with regard to*, vague, 184–85

word choice. *See* diction
word as word: italics or quotation marks for, 453; plural of, 406
word processor, in composing: accurate quotation with, 497; in freewriting, 68; in linking paragraphs, 110; in outline, 96; in word mastery, 207
wordiness, 115, 128–29, *219–23*; circumlocution in, 221; intensifiers in, 222; negative statement in, 223; redundancy in, 220–21
works cited. *See* reference list
*would*, verb forms with, 333–35
*would like for*, colloquial, 580
*wreak* vs. *wreck*, 423
writing about literature, 48–55

yearbooks, in library, 491–92
*you*, and pronoun shift, 307
*your* vs. *you're*, 423

ZIP code: no comma in, 358; figures for, 461; mail code before, 458
zoology documentation style, 507

# About the Author

Frederick Crews, Professor of English at the University of California, Berkeley, received the Ph.D. from Princeton University. Throughout a distinguished career he has attained many honors, including a Guggenheim Fellowship, appointment as a Fulbright Lecturer in Italy, and recognition from the National Endowment for the Arts for his essay "Norman O. Brown: The World Dissolves." His writings include the widely used *Borzoi Handbook for Writers* (with Sandra Schor) as well as highly regarded books on Henry James, E. M. Forster, and Nathaniel Hawthorne, the best-selling satire *The Pooh Perplex,* and two volumes of his own essays entitled *Out of My System* and *Skeptical Engagements.* Professor Crews has published numerous articles in *Partisan Review, The New York Review of Books, Commentary, Tri-Quarterly,* and other important journals. He has twice been Chairman of Freshman Composition in the English Department at Berkeley.

# Symbols for Comment and Revision

When commenting on your written work, your instructor may use some of the following marks. If a mark calls for revision, consult the chapter or section of the *Handbook* printed in boldface type.

| | |
|---|---|
| ✓ | Excellent point; well said |
| ✓ arg | Effective argument |
| ✓ concr | Good use of concrete language |
| ✓ d | Effective diction |
| ✓ det | Effective supporting detail |
| ✓ dev | Effective development of the point |
| ✓ fig | Apt figure of speech |
| ✓ // | Effective parallelism |
| ✓ p | Effective choice of punctuation |
| ✓ trans | Good transition |

| | |
|---|---|
| abbr | Faulty abbreviation, **26g–k** |
| ad | Faulty comparison of adjective or adverb, **23** |
| agr | Faulty subject-verb agreement, **10b–f** |
| awk | Awkward expression |
| cap | Capitalize this letter, **25** |
| case | Wrong pronoun case, **12** |
| chop | Choppy sequence of sentences, **7r** |
| cl | Cliché, **8j** |
| coh | Coherence lacking, **7a–i** |
| colloq | Colloquial expression, **8h** |
| comp | Faulty comparison, **14a, 14e** |
| cs | Comma splice, **9e** |
| d | Inappropriate diction (word choice), **8, Index of Usage** |

| | |
|---|---|
| dm | Dangling modifier, **11c** |
| doc | Faulty documentation form, **29** |
| emp | Weak or inappropriate sentence emphasis, **7n–q** |
| exag | Exaggeration; overstated claim, **3i** |
| fig | Inappropriate figure of speech, **8l** |
| frag | Sentence fragment, **9a–d** |
| fs | Fused sentence, **9e** |
| gl | Look up this expression in the Glossary of Terms |
| hyph | Faulty hyphenation, **24i–n** |
| ital | Underline (italicize), **26a–f** |
| jarg | Jargon, **8f** |
| lc | Do not capitalize (leave in lower case), **25** |
| livel | Stale language; rewrite for liveliness, **8h–m** |
| log | Faulty logic, **3j–n** |
| mixed | Mixed construction, **10a** |
| ms | Faulty manuscript form, **5j** |
| no ¶ | Do not begin a new paragraph here, **6i** |
| num | Inappropriate form for a number, **26l–n** |
| p | Faulty punctuation, **16–20** |
| pass | Inappropriate use of passive voice, **7g** |
| p/form | Faulty form or spacing of punctuation mark, **27** |